SECOND EDITION

W9-DGN-387

EASTERN CIVILIZATIONS

G. Robina Quale
Albion College

PRENTICE-HALL, INC., ENGLEWOOD CLIFFS, NEW JERSEY

Library of Congress Cataloging in Publication Data
QUALE, GLADYS ROBINA
   Eastern civilizations.

   Includes bibliographies and index.
   1. Civilization, Oriental.   I. Title.
CB253.Q3 1975   915'.03   74–31062
ISBN 0–13–222976–5
ISBN 0–13–222992–7 (pbk)

© 1975, 1966 by PRENTICE-HALL, INC., Englewood Cliffs, New Jersey

All rights reserved. No part of this book may be
reproduced in any form or by any means
without permission in writing from the publisher.

PRINTED IN THE UNITED STATES OF AMERICA

10 9 8 7 6 5 4 3 2 1

PRENTICE-HALL INTERNATIONAL, INC., London
PRENTICE-HALL OF AUSTRALIA, PTY., LTD., Sydney
PRENTICE-HALL OF CANADA, LTD., Toronto
PRENTICE-HALL OF INDIA PRIVATE LIMITED, New Delhi
PRENTICE-HALL OF JAPAN, INC., Tokyo

To "the bank behind the book":
Mr. and Mrs. L. A. Quale

CONTENTS

v

PART TWO **SOUTH ASIA**

PART THREE **EAST ASIA**

PART FOUR **SOUTHEAST ASIA**

PART FIVE **CONCLUSION**

PREFACE TO
THE SECOND EDITION

Since the first edition of this book was published, many changes have taken place in South, East, and Southeast Asia and in the Middle East. Most of these changes have borne out the concern (expressed in chapter after chapter of both that edition and this) for the need to persuade dissatisfied groups that in the long run, their interests will be better served by working with others in a larger framework than by a separatist movement. The same need to persuade the dissatisfied has also become more evident both in the newest states of Africa and in states which come directly out of the European tradition.

In response to the requests of those who used the first edition, this edition includes more discussion of twentieth-century developments, longer lists of suggested readings, and some comparisons between Africans and the peoples of South, East, and Southeast Asia. It also gives less space to the Middle Eastern experience, treating that primarily as a background for understanding the interplay of Western and local forces in South, East, and Southeast Asia.

It has been a rewarding experience for me to receive the suggestions, comments, and criticisms of those who have used the first edition. I have appreciated reading and hearing them all, and have made careful use of them in preparing this edition. I also wish to thank Ms. Judi Markowitz of Appleton-Century-Crofts, Ms. Marian Moskowitz and Ms. Adrienne Neufeld of Prentice-Hall, and their staffs for their assistance in the preparation of this edition. Finally, I wish to express again my gratitude to my friends from other countries for the insights they have given me, to my professional colleagues for their support and suggestions, to my students for their comments, and to my mother for her stylistic criticism and continuing encouragement.

G. R. Q.

PREFACE TO
THE FIRST EDITION

Most of the world's people live in the geographic region from Morocco to Japan. This region, the Eastern world, contains the civilizations of the Islamic Middle East, the Indo-Pakistan subcontinent, the traditionally Chinese-dominated world of East Asia, and Southeast Asia, through which merchants and pilgrims from all the others have passed. Each of these civilizations has its own distinctive social, political, religious, philosophic, and literary traditions. Each one has also influenced the others. All of them have affected the life of the West, and all of them have been affected in return. Indeed, the transformations they have initiated in recent generations, under the influence of the West, are perhaps the most marked in their histories.

Like the people of the early modern West, the people of the East are now experiencing changes in centuries-old forms of economic, social, and political organization. The great majority of them still live in agricultural villages rather than industrial cities; but roads, radios, and schools are bringing the outside world to them, replacing a household-centered life with a nation-centered one. In order for us to understand the momentous changes taking place in Eastern civilizations and in the lives of these people, it is essential that we know something of their past. To comprehend a Mao Tse-tung today, it is necessary to know a Confucius of the sixth century B.C., a Karl Marx and a Tseng Kuo-fan of the nineteenth century A.D., and a Yuan Shih-k'ai of the early twentieth century.

The growth of the nation-state in western Europe is not an unexplainable accident. It has resulted from the interaction between the peoples of Europe and their neighbors in both West and East. Therefore, a brief outline of the history of western Europe is given as an introduction to the histories of the peoples of the East, who are now developing nation-states in much the same manner as did the West. This brief review is fol-

lowed by lengthier discussions of the histories of the Middle East, the
Indo-Pakistan subcontinent, East Asia, and Southeast Asia. To give a
sense of the historical continuity of each region's development, each is
treated as a separate unit. The patterns of economic, social, and political
organization and the philosophical and religious concepts which its people have evolved through the centuries are described. The experience of
its people with the West and their reactions to that experience are discussed. In the later sections, significant comparisons are drawn between
the concepts, organizational patterns, and experiences of the area under
discussion and the areas previously discussed. The last section is concerned with common problems which the peoples of all these regions face
today. Throughout, the unceasing interplay of environmental, economic,
social, political, intellectual, and religious factors is stressed.

The primary purpose of this book is to provide the reader with a
basic knowledge of the historical growth of the major Eastern civilizations. The book may be used in introductory college courses in world
history or world civilization as a supplement to texts which do not give
adequate coverage to the Eastern world. It may also be used as a basic
text in introductory college courses on Asian or non-Western civilizations. Or it may simply be read for profit and, I hope, for pleasure. I have
sought to transliterate names and terms consistently and simply, but when
other forms are already widely known, the popular usage has ordinarily
been followed. In compiling the lists of suggested readings, I have drawn
on the works used in preparing the book. Those books which are marked
with an asterisk are available in paperback. From the many stimulating
and informative books which might have been chosen, only a few have
been selected. No periodical literature has been included, although many
excellent articles are available.

The plan for this book was formulated as a result of my teaching
experience at Albion College. The generous grant of a Carnegie Foundation Faculty Internship in Asian Studies at the University of Michigan
and the patient assistance of the University's library staff enabled me to
put together the first draft in 1961–1962. Portions of that draft were
read by Professors John Bowditch, Albert Feuerwerker, Russell Fifield,
George Grassmuck, George Hourani, Charles Hucker, Louis Orlin, William Schorger, James Stewart-Robinson, and Sylvia Thrupp of the University of Michigan; Professors John Cady of Ohio University, Robert
Crane and Zafar Islam of Duke University, John Hall of Yale University,
Lennox Mills of the University of Minnesota, and Paul Wheatley of the
University of California; Dr. John Kelly, author of *Eastern Arabian
Frontiers* (New York: Praeger, 1964); Dr. Melville Kennedy, author of
The Chaitanya Movement: A Study of Vaishnavism in Bengal (Calcutta:
Association Press, 1925); and Dr. Robert Spaulding, Jr., of the University
of Michigan Center for Japanese Studies. Their comments, criticisms, and

suggestions were invaluable. However, I take full responsibility for all interpretations and selections of data. In addition, I am indebted to my many friends from the countries discussed for their numerous contributions to my better understanding of their homelands. I am grateful for the encouragement of Professor Coy H. James, Chairman of the Department of History at Albion College, and of my departmental colleagues. I have also appreciated the opportunity to test the effectiveness of this method of presentation with my students. Whatever readability these pages may possess they owe to my mother, Mrs. L.A. Quale, whose stylistic criticism was thorough and constructive, and who has given me unfailing encouragement and assistance since I first began to set words on paper.

G. R. Q.

MAPS

For other historical maps, the following atlases are suggested:

GENERAL

Palmer, Robert R., et al. *Atlas of World History.* Chicago: Rand McNally, 1965.
*Palmer, Robert R., et al. *Abridged Historical Atlas.* New York: Rand McNally, 1958.
Shepherd, William R. *Historical Atlas,* 8th ed. Pikesville, Md.: Colonial Offset Press; distributed by Barnes and Noble, 1956.

EUROPE

*Fox, Edward W. *Atlas of European History.* New York: Oxford University Press, 1957.

MIDDLE EAST

Hazard, Harry W. *Atlas of Islamic History,* 3rd ed. rev. and corr. Princeton: Princeton University Press, 1954.

SOUTH AND SOUTHEAST ASIA

Davies, Cuthbert C. *An Historical Atlas of the Indian Peninsula,* 2nd ed. New York: Oxford University Press, 1959.
Roolvink, Roelot. *Historical Atlas of the Muslim People.* Cambridge: Harvard University Press, 1957.

EAST AND SOUTHEAST ASIA

Herrmann, Albert. *An Historical Atlas of China,* new ed. Chicago: Aldine, 1966.
*Sellman, Roger Raymond. *An Outline Atlas of Eastern History.* New York: St. Martin's, 1970.

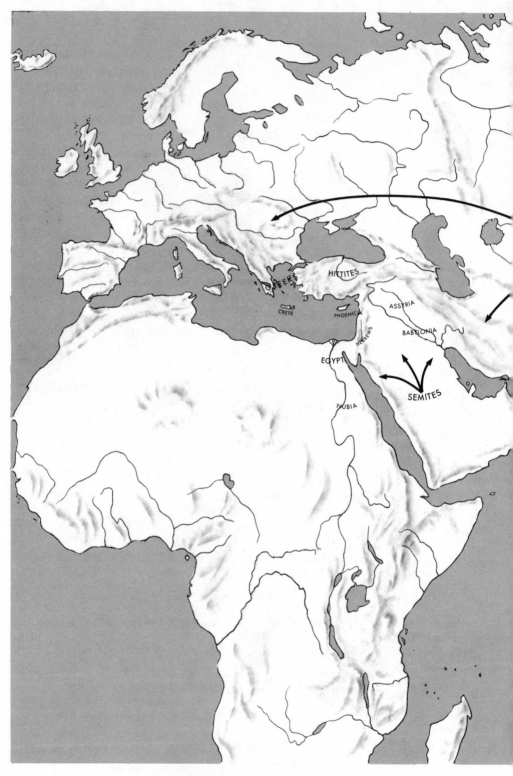

MAP I   1200 B.C.

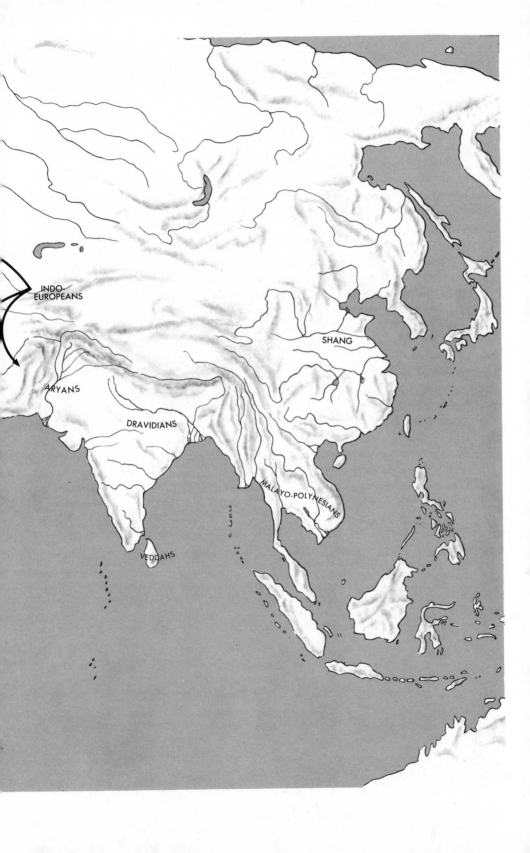

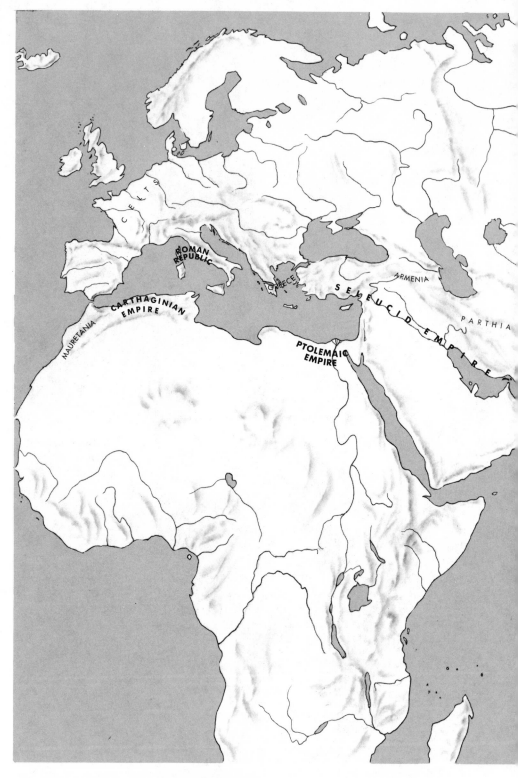

CELTS

ROMAN
REPUBLIC

GREECE

ARMENIA

SELEUCID EMPIRE

PARTHIA

CARTHAGINIAN
EMPIRE

MAURETANIA

PTOLEMAIC
EMPIRE

MAP II   200 B.C.

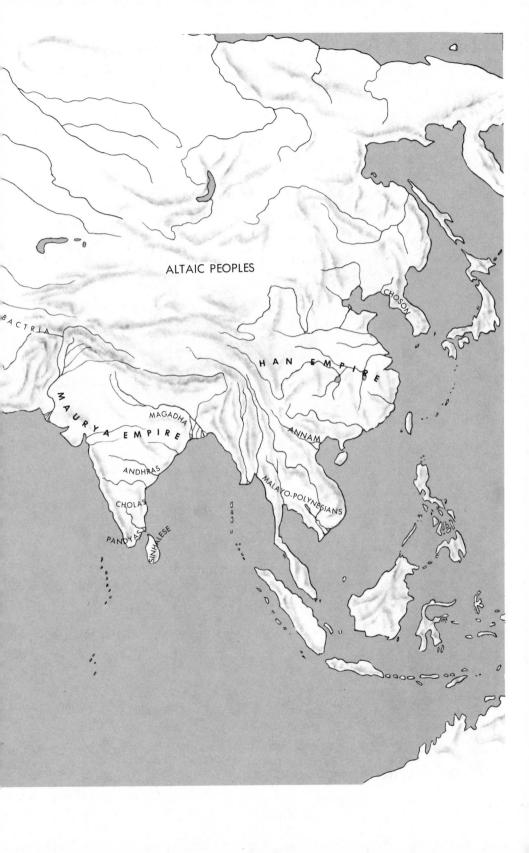

ALTAIC PEOPLES

BACTRIA

CHOSON

HAN EMPIRE

MAURYA EMPIRE

MAGADHA

ANNAM

ANDHRAS

CHOLAS

MALAYO-POLYNESIANS

PANDYAS

SINHALESE

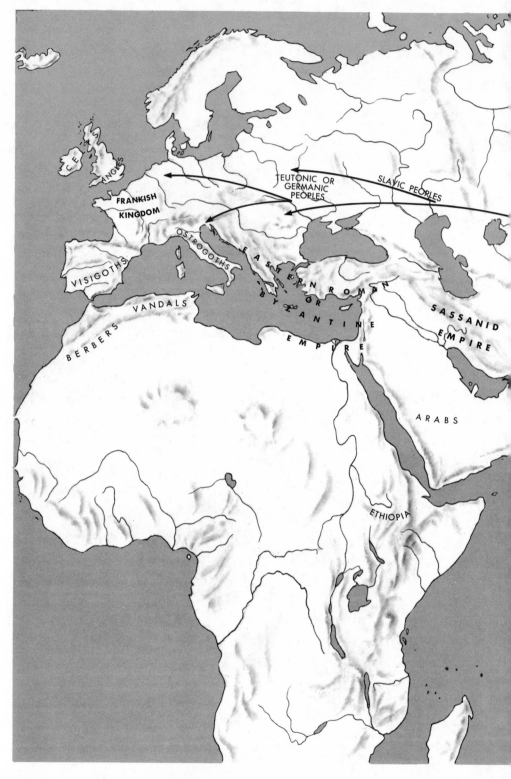

MAP III   A.D. 500

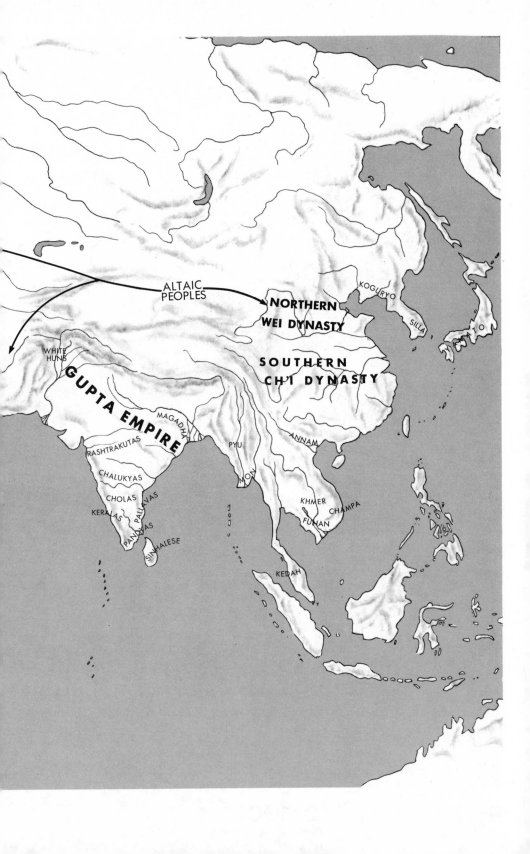

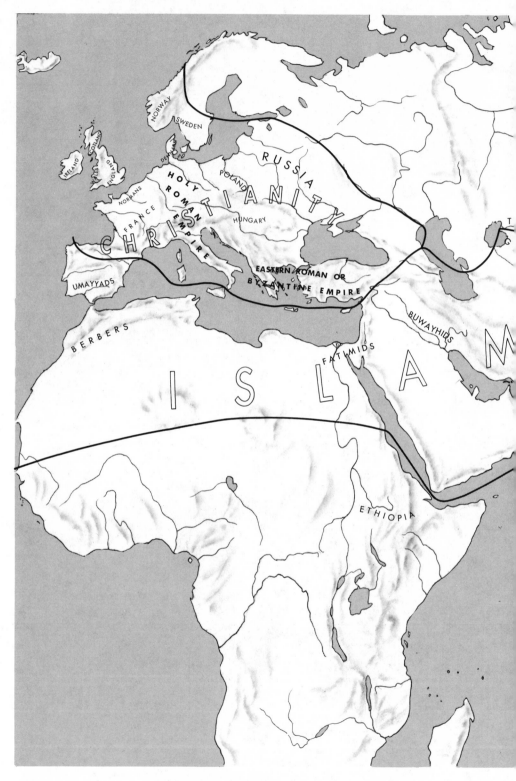

MAP IV   A.D. 1000

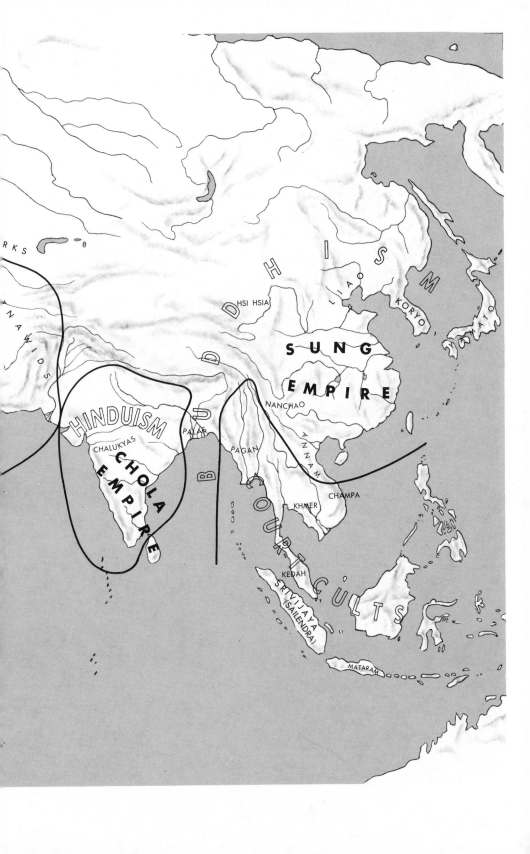

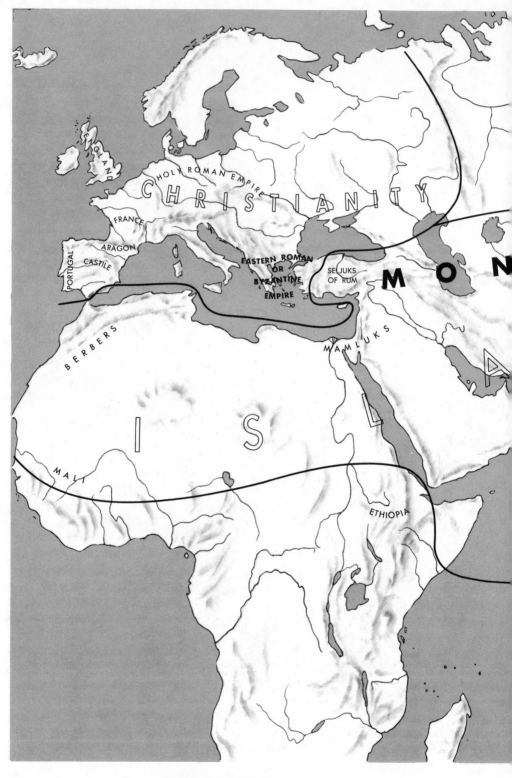

ENGLAND

HOLY ROMAN EMPIRE

C H R I S T I A N I T Y

FRANCE

ARAGON

PORTUGAL

CASTILE

EASTERN ROMAN
OR
BYZANTINE
EMPIRE

SELJUKS
OF RUM

M O N

BERBERS

MAMLUKS

I S L

MALI

ETHIOPIA

MAP V   A.D. 1300

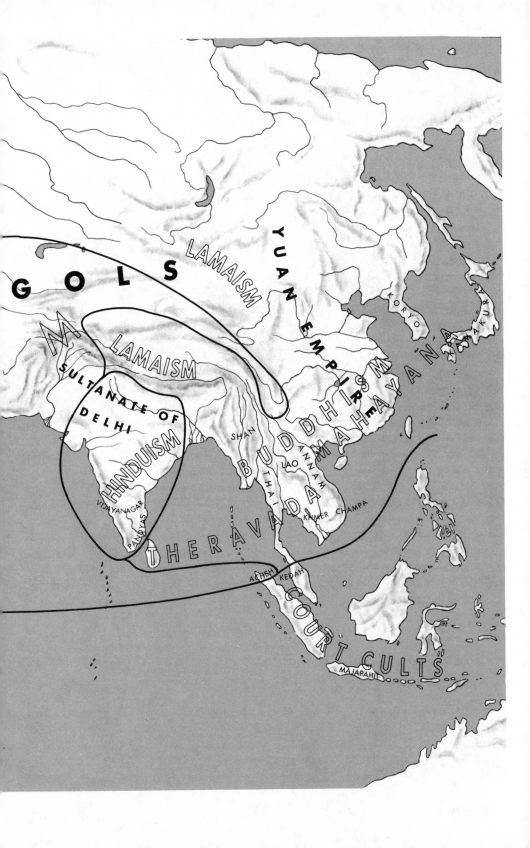

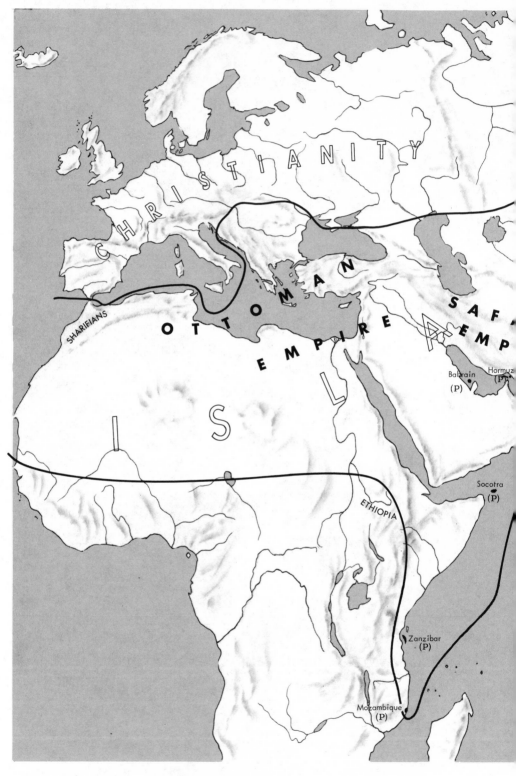

CHRISTIANITY

OTTOMAN

SAF

EMPIRE

EMP

ISLAM

SHARIFIANS

Bahrain
(P)

Hormuz
(P)

Socotra
(P)

ETHIOPIA

Zanzibar
(P)

Mozambique
(P)

MAP VI　　　A.D. 1600

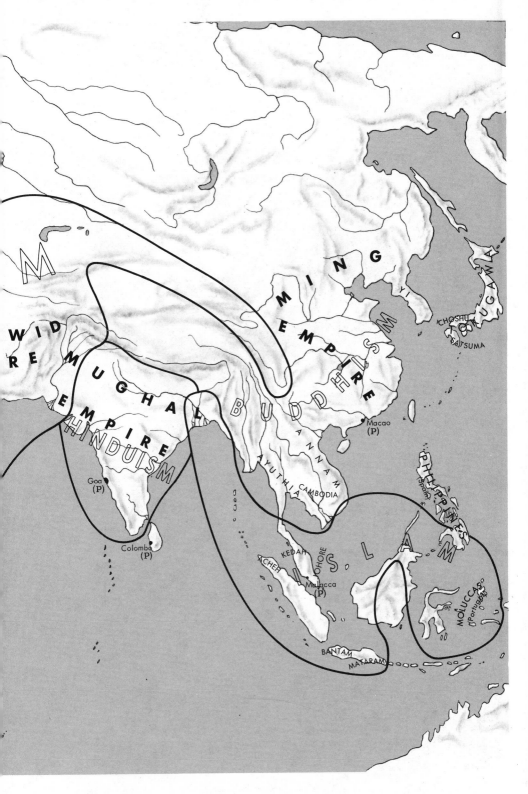

WID
RE

M

MUGHAL
EMPIRE
HINDUISM

Goa
(P)

Colombo
(P)

MING
EMPIRE

BUDDHISM

ANNAM

AYUTHIA
CAMBODIA

KEDAH

ACHEH

JOHORE

Malacca
(P)

I S L A M

BANTAM

MATARAM

Macao
(P)

YI

ICHOSHU
SATSUMA

TOKUGAWA

PHILIPPINES
(Spain)

MOLUCCAS
(Portugal)

(P) Strategic Localities Held by Portugal

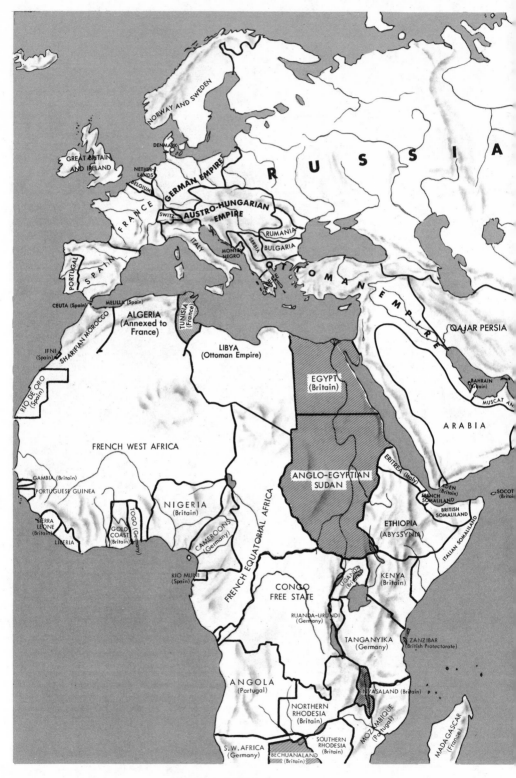

MAP VII   A.D. 1900

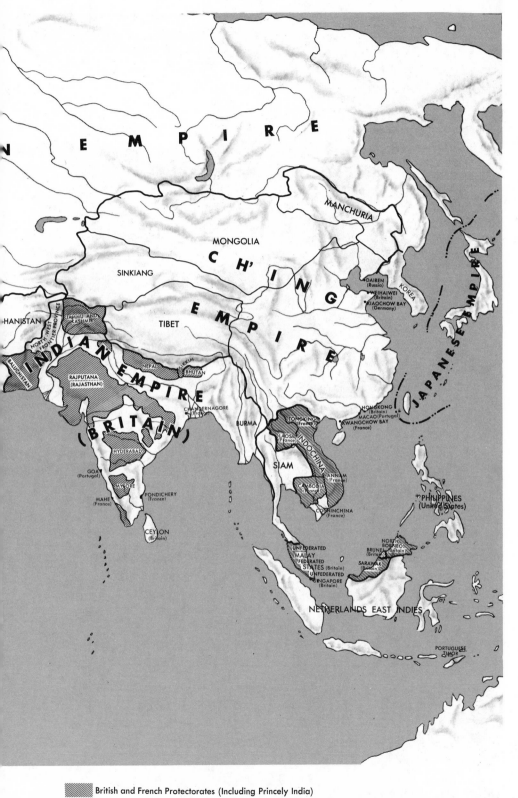

British and French Protectorates (Including Princely India)

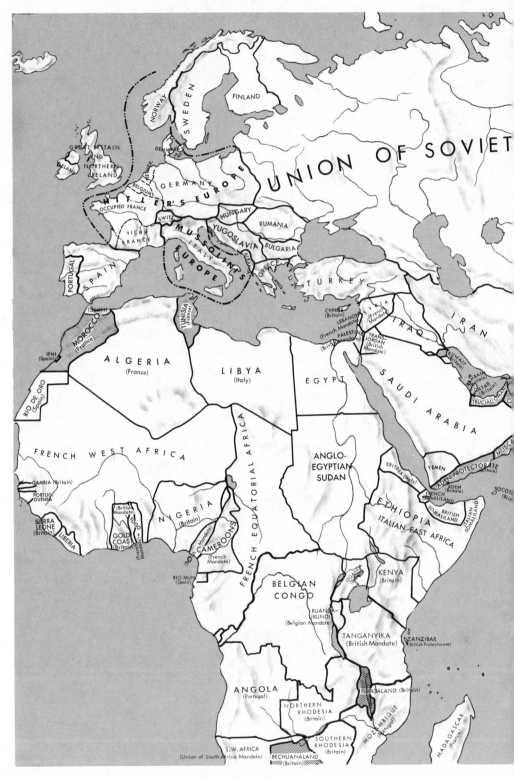

NORWAY

SWEDEN

FINLAND

UNION OF SOVIET

GREAT BRITAIN AND NORTHERN IRELAND

IRELAND

DENMARK

NETH.

BELGIUM

GERMANY

HITLER'S EUROPE

OCCUPIED FRANCE

VICHY FRANCE

SWITZ.

MUSSOLINI'S

HUNGARY

RUMANIA

YUGOSLAVIA

BULGARIA

ALBANIA

ITALY

EUROPE

GREECE

TURKEY

PORTUGAL

SPAIN

CYPRUS (Britain)

SYRIA (French Mandate)

IRAQ

IRAN

LEBANON (French Mandate)

PALESTINE (British Mandate)

TRANS-JORDAN (British Mandate)

KUWAIT (Britain)

MOROCCO (Spain)

MOROCCO (France)

IFNI (Spain)

TUNISIA (France)

ALGERIA (France)

LIBYA (Italy)

EGYPT

SAUDI ARABIA

BAHREIN (Britain)

QATAR (Britain)

TRUCIAL OMAN

RIO DE ORO (Spain)

FRENCH WEST AFRICA

ANGLO-EGYPTIAN SUDAN

MUSC

GAMBIA (Britain)

PORTUG. GUINEA

SIERRA LEONE (Britain)

LIBERIA

GOLD COAST (Britain)

TOGO (French Mandate)

NIGERIA (Britain)

(British Mandate)

RIO MUNI (Spain)

CAMEROONS (French Mandate)

FRENCH EQUATORIAL AFRICA

ERITREA (Italy)

YEMEN

ADEN PROTECTORATE (Britain)

ADEN (Britain)

FRENCH SOMALILAND

BRITISH SOMALILAND

ITALIAN SOMALILAND

SOCOTRA (Brit.)

ETHIOPIA

ITALIAN EAST AFRICA

BELGIAN CONGO

UGANDA

KENYA (Britain)

RUANDA-URUNDI (Belgian Mandate)

TANGANYIKA (British Mandate)

ZANZIBAR (British Protectorate)

ANGOLA (Portugal)

NORTHERN RHODESIA (Britain)

NYASALAND (Britain)

MOZAMBIQUE (Portugal)

MADAGASCAR (France)

S.W. AFRICA (Union of South Africa Mandate)

BECHUANALAND (Britain)

SOUTHERN RHODESIA (Britain)

MAP VIII

A.D. 1940

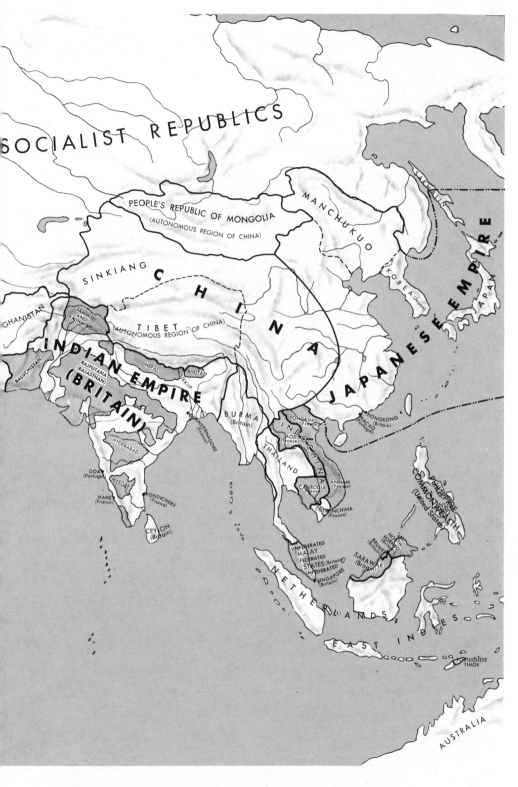

British and French Protectorates (Including Princely India)

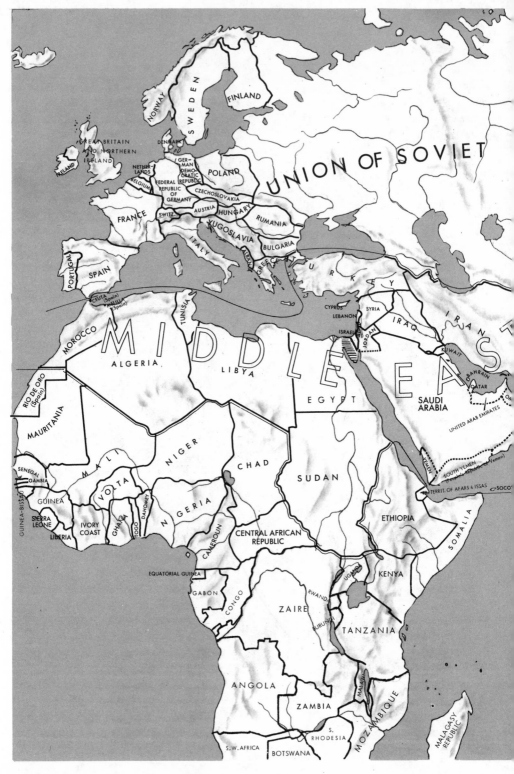

MAP IX A.D. 1974

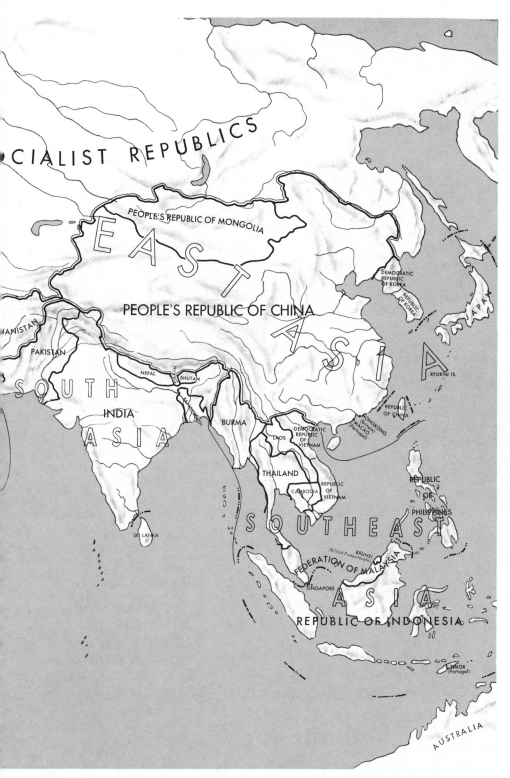

SOCIALIST REPUBLICS

EAST ASIA

PEOPLE'S REPUBLIC OF MONGOLIA

PEOPLE'S REPUBLIC OF CHINA

DEMOCRATIC
REPUBLIC
OF KOREA

REPUBLIC
OF KOREA

JAPAN

AFGHANISTAN

PAKISTAN

NEPAL

BHUTAN

SOUTH

ASIA

INDIA

BANGLADESH

BURMA

RYUKYU IS.

REPUBLIC
OF CHINA

HONGKONG
(Britain)
MACAO
(Portugal)

LAOS

DEMOCRATIC
REPUBLIC
OF VIETNAM

THAILAND

CAMBODIA

REPUBLIC
OF
VIETNAM

REPUBLIC
OF
PHILIPPINES

SRI LANKA

SOUTHEAST

ASIA

BRUNEI
(British Protectorate)

FEDERATION OF MALAYSIA

SINGAPORE

REPUBLIC OF INDONESIA

TIMOR
(Portugal)

AUSTRALIA

▦ Territory Occupied by Israel in 1967.
▪▪▪▪▪▪▪ Undemarcated Boundaries.

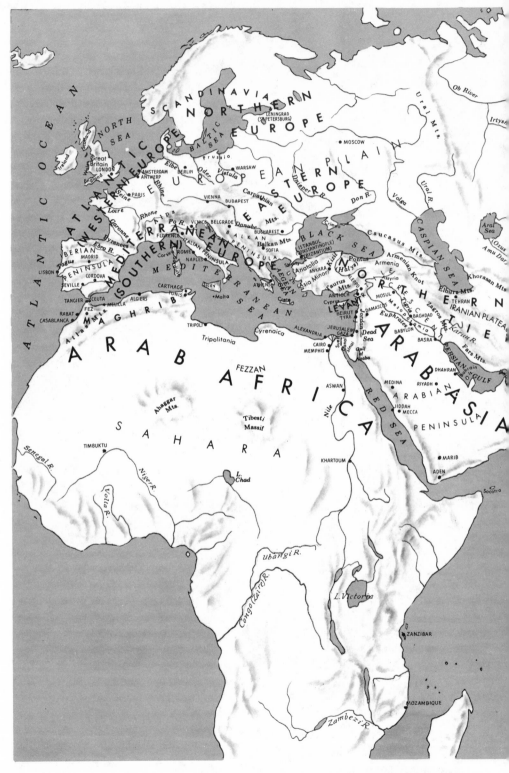

ATLANTIC OCEAN

NORTH SEA

SCANDINAVIA

NORTHERN EUROPE

BALTIC SEA

Ireland

Great Britain

England

LONDON

NORTH ATLANTIC EUROPE

WESTERN ATLANTIC EUROPE

AMSTERDAM

ANTWERP

Rhine

PARIS

Loire

Garonne

PYRENEES

Elbe

BERLIN

Oder

Vistula

Prussia

WARSAW

EASTERN PLAIN EUROPE

Danube R.

Carpathian Mts.

BUDAPEST

VIENNA

Rhone

Alps

Po R.

VENICE

BELGRADE

FLORENCE

ROME

ITALIAN PENINSULA

NAPLES

Corsica

Sardinia

BALKAN PENINSULA

SOFIA

Danube

BUCHAREST

Crimea

BLACK SEA

Caucasus Mts.

CASPIAN SEA

MEDITERRANEAN SOUTHERN EUROPE

Sicily

Malta

MEDITERRANEAN SEA

ATHENS

AEGEAN

Crete

ISTANBUL (CONSTANTINOPLE) (BYZANTIUM)

Anatolia (Asia Minor)

ANKARA

Halys

Pontus

Taurus Mts.

ANTIOCH

Cyprus

BEIRUT

TYRE

DAMASCUS

Armenian Knot

Armenia

Assyria

MOSUL

Tigris

Zagros Mts.

BAGHDAD

Euphrates

BABYLON

BASRA

IRANIAN PLATEAU

Elburz Mts.

TEHRAN

Khorasan Mts.

Aral Sea

Oxus

Amu Dar.

Ural R.

Volga

Don R.

Dnieper R.

MOSCOW

Ural Mts.

Ob River

Irtysh

NORTHERN TIER

ASIA

LEVANT

JERUSALEM

GAZA

Dead Sea

Sinai

Suez

Gulf of Aqaba

Fars Mts.

Karun R.

DHAHRAN

Bahrain

PERSIAN GULF

RIYADH

LENINGRAD (ST.PETERSBURG)

IBERIAN PENINSULA

Douro

MADRID

LISBON

Ebro R.

Tagus

SEVILLE

CORDOVA

TANGIER

CEUTA

RABAT

CASABLANCA

FEZ

MELILLA

ALGIERS

Atlas Mts.

MAGHRIB

CARTHAGE

TUNIS

TRIPOLI

Tripolitania

Cyrenaica

ALEXANDRIA

CAIRO

MEMPHIS

ARABA

AFRICA

FEZZAN

SAHARA

Ahaggar Mts.

Tibesti Massif

TIMBUKTU

Senegal R.

Niger R.

Volta R.

L. Chad

KHARTOUM

ASWAN

Nile

RED SEA

MEDINA

MECCA

JIDDAH

ARABIAN PENINSULA

ARABIA

MARIB

ADEN

Socotra

Ubangi R.

Congo (Zaire) R.

L. Victoria

ZANZIBAR

MOZAMBIQUE

Zambezi R.

MAP X

Geographical Features,

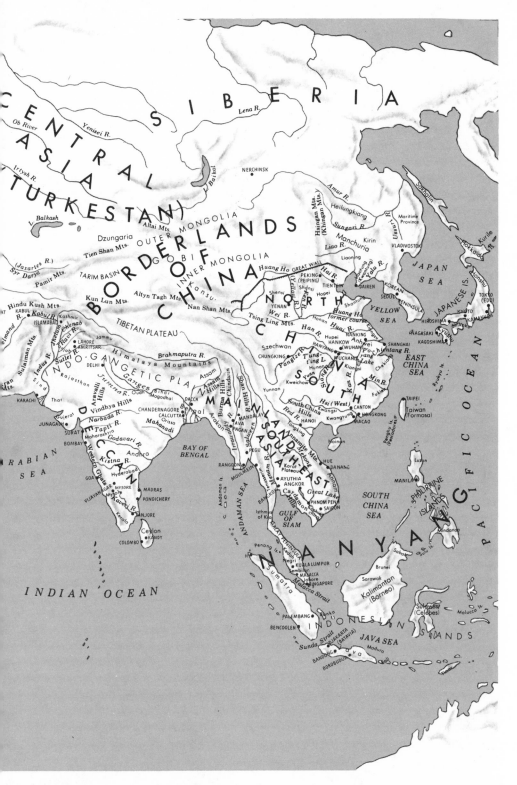

Regions, and Cities

PART ONE

INTRODUCTION

1

WESTERN EUROPEAN
BACKGROUND

Europe and Its Neighbors

The relationship between western Europe and its neighbors in Asia and Mediterranean Africa has altered radically in recent generations. Today western Europe is closely scrutinized, as others strive to profit from western European experience in building a new type of society which extends the benefits of modern forms of economic and political life from the few to the many. In the past, however, western Europeans studied the societies of Asia and Mediterranean Africa much more carefully than those societies studied western Europe.

Three thousand years ago, western Europeans depended on outsiders to bring goods, techniques, and ideas from the lands of the eastern Mediterranean and the still more distant regions of India and China. At that time the trade between Europe's Atlantic seaboard and more urbanized regions was monopolized by the Phoenicians, who lived along the part of the eastern Mediterranean coast known as the Levant and controlled a number of strategically located points on the other shores of the Meriterranean. Two thousand years ago, when the Romans constructed the first strong political bonds between western Europe and the Mediterranean world, a few western Europeans left their native region to serve in the Roman legions or the imperial court. Some returned home to regale their families and friends with tales of the wonders of the East; but for the most part, western Europeans continued to draw their knowledge of the world on the other side of the Mediterranean from outsiders such as the Levantine Jewish and Syrian traders of the cities. These traders became the chief link between western Eu-

3

rope and the East after the Roman imperial government lost its grip
on the lands north and west of Italy in the fifth and sixth centuries A.D.,
and they retained that position through the tenth century.

By the middle of the eighth century A.D., western Europeans became conscious of the rise of a new power along the shores of the Mediterranean, as the followers of the recently founded Islamic faith captured most of Spain and sent raiding parties into France and Italy. During the next few generations, western Europeans learned to think of
themselves as the defenders of Christendom against Islam. In the course
of the eleventh century, they burst forth in the first of the explosions of
energy which in the past thousand years have brought them into ever
closer relations with the peoples of the rest of the world. They made
headway against the forces of Islam in Spain, in Sicily, and in the Levant.
Soon the Italian traders who helped them to reach Syria and Palestine replaced the Levantines as leaders in Mediterranean commerce.
Two centuries later, the rise of the vast Mongol empire in the lands
from the Black Sea to the Pacific made it easier than ever before to travel from Europe to Persia, Central Asia, and China. By that time
European merchants were in full control of Europe's trade with the
Islamic world. They were eager to extend their commercial network
into India, China, and Southeast Asia, whose products they still had to
obtain from the traders of Egypt and the Levant. The discovery of the
all-water route to Asia at the close of the fifteenth century enabled the
European traders to achieve their desire at last. Thereafter their influence expanded rapidly in the lands that border the Atlantic, Indian, and
Pacific oceans.

Until long after the first European vessel entered the Indian Ocean,
western Europeans continued to regard the states and empires of the
southern Mediterranean world and Asia as wealthy, powerful, and highly
advanced in the arts of civilization. However, western Europe's own
economic, social, political, intellectual, and religious lives were then
undergoing far-reaching transformations. By the close of the eighteenth
century these transformations were evidenced both in growing wealth
and in changing attitudes. Western Europeans gradually lost the respect-
ful fear they had previously felt toward the older urban-centered societies.
They came to feel a combination of pity and disdain for the poverty of
the illiterate masses of the states of Asia and Africa, and for the inade-
quacies of their rulers. During the nineteenth century, demonstrations
of European power even convinced many in the Middle East, India, and
East and Southeast Asia that the pattern of life of western Europe was
superior to their own in some ways. Consequently, they themselves began
to modify long-standing patterns of thought and behavior in their socie-

ties, so as to be able to take advantage of the experience of the peoples of western Europe.

Europe's Geographic Foundations

TOPOGRAPHY AND DISTRIBUTION OF PEOPLES

The theory that climate and terrain are linked to national characteristics is at least as old as the Greek historian Herodotus of the fifth century B.C. Although the experience of western Europe can hardly be explained entirely by geographic factors, the development of western Europe and its differences from development elsewhere cannot be understood without some knowledge of European geography.

Europe is the westernmost extension of the Eurasian land mass, a peninsula divided into north and south by the mountains known as the Pyrenees, the Alps, and the Carpathians. It is also divided into south, northeast, and west by climatic variations which are largely explainable in terms of land forms and the influence of the warm waters of the Mediterranean and the Atlantic Gulf Stream. Its coasts have many natural harbors sheltered from gales by promontories or islands. Its rivers are generally navigable for some distance inland from the coast, and no portion of western or southern Europe lies more than five hundred miles from either the Atlantic, the Baltic, or the Mediterranean. Thus maritime transportation has been relatively easy and has been used for many centuries to carry the products of each of Europe's varying regions to those areas which lack them.

The mountain and river systems of Europe do not always encourage interregional trade. To the south of the mountain barrier, only eastern Spain, southeastern France, Italy, and Greece are linked to the Mediterranean by their river valleys. Portugal and the remainder of Spain look to the Atlantic, while Hungary, Yugoslavia, Bulgaria, and Rumania look toward the Black Sea. North of the mountain wall, the rivers flow to the Atlantic, the North Sea, the Baltic, or, in the extreme east, the Black Sea. Only the Rhone of eastern France flows from north of the mountains southward to the Mediterranean. Therefore movement between northern and southern Europe has been largely restricted to the mountain passes, the passage from the Rhine to the Rhone, the Hungarian plain, and the straits between the Black Sea and the Mediterranean. Once urban-centered patterns of life spread from southern Europe to the Atlantic by way of these routes, the peoples of western

Europe could continue to develop on their own. They brought into being a way of life related to that which had grown up earlier in the south yet unmistakably distinct from it. They continued to trade with the south through the mountain passes, but they also opened trade with the northeast across the great European plain that stretches from the Pyrenees into Asia. The interrelationship of the peoples around the relatively protected areas of the North Sea and the Baltic became particularly marked by the tenth century A.D.

During the centuries after 1500 B.C., Indo-European peoples of Greek, Italic, Celtic, Teutonic, and Slavic speech penetrated into every part of Europe. Sometimes they isolated earlier inhabitants like the Basques in almost inaccessible regions such as northwest Spain, but usually they absorbed the earlier peoples, modifying their own habits of language and behavior in consequence. The Greeks soon spilled out of the narrow confines of the Greek peninsula to settle along many parts of the Mediterranean coast, bringing the ways of Hellenic civilization with them. They were followed by the Romans, who extended their empire northward across largely Celtic areas to the Rhine and the Danube in an effort to protect the Mediterranean world from the expanding Teutonic or Germanic peoples. The Teutonic push into Celtic territories in turn reflected pressures from the Slavs still farther to the east and from the Altaic peoples of Central Asia. The combination of Greek settlement, Roman rule, and continued movements of Celts, Germans, and Slavs eventually resulted in the formation of the major cultural and linguistic groups of modern Europe, most of which have become embodied in national states in recent centuries.

The majority of existing European linguistic, cultural, and political boundaries have been deeply affected by the ease or difficulty of communications. Where there are hills, mountains, and seas, they have usually acted as effective barriers. In the plain to the north of the mountain wall between northern and southern Europe, the natural tendency to use river valleys for transport has been an important factor in the rise of distinctive groupings of peoples from the Gascons along the Garonne to the Poles along the Vistula. Nevertheless, the history of the Rhine valley shows that the interplay of geographic, economic, and political factors is far from simple. For centuries the Rhine valley has flourished economically because of its great diversity of resources and products, but that same diversity has tended to counteract any plans for unification. Furthermore, the recognition that any power which could unify the Rhine from source to mouth could then command the entire North Sea area has led the peoples of the North Sea coasts to oppose such unification lest it interfere with their independence of action.

CLIMATE AND NATURAL RESOURCES

Rain is one of nature's greatest gifts to western Europe. The region north of the mountain barrier is close to the sea, and the mountains force the winds from the Atlantic to yield their water vapor before reaching areas farther south and east. Therefore western Europe north of the Pyrenees receives an average of at least twenty to forty inches of precipitation annually, and it is distributed throughout the year. Although agriculture becomes impossible when the cold of winter turns the water vapor into snow rather than rain, western European cultivators are fortunate. They can rely on having enough rain every year to grow most of the usual crops without irrigation. If they do choose to irrigate some fields, they still benefit from the rain, for the number, size, and steady flow of the nearby lakes, streams, springs, or wells from which the water comes are dependent on the rains of summer and the melting snows of spring.

South of the mountains, cold and snow are rare; but so is rain, in the warm summer months which are best for growing crops. The northern and western slopes of the mountains have already caught most of the water vapor borne by the winds that blow from the Atlantic toward the summer-heated land mass of Asia. In dry regions like eastern Spain, irrigation must be used for most crops. The Mediterranean region's greatest rainfall comes in winter, when the winds from the Atlantic cross the Mediterranean toward the Indian Ocean, circling around the winter-frozen core of Asia. The water vapor they carry is then deposited as rain on the western slopes of the mountains that line the northern and eastern Mediterranean shores. Like the rain, the sources of irrigation tend to run driest in the warm months when they are most needed. Therefore complex means of irrigation—such as underground tunnels or systems of reservoirs and aqueducts—are required.

Because of heavier rains, the soils of the north are wetter and heavier than those of the south and require deep rather than shallow plowing. The rains also help to make the northern soils more fertile. The heavier vegetation of the wetter north provides the soil with more humus or organic matter. Furthermore, the summer rains help northern soils to retain their mineral salts by retarding the process of evaporation, thereby slowing down the process of leaching during which the minerals brought to the surface by evaporation are dissolved and washed far down into the soil by later rainstorms.

These differences in climate and soils between north and south are expressed in variations in the natural forest vegetation. They also help to explain why northern Europeans could successfully refine the practice of mixed farming—or the integration of livestock-raising with the growth of field crops—to make it unprecedentedly productive. In the great European plain, the availability of water and good soil has made it possible for the cultivator to use plants and animals as complements to each other in a cycle which has greatly expanded total agricultural output per worker since the pre-Christian era. In drier regions, however, livestock and crops have often had to compete with each other for water and nutrients, and a scarcity of wood has led to the use of animal excrement as fuel rather than as a rebuilder of soil fertility. Consequently, agricultural output per worker has not expanded as rapidly as in northern Europe.

Reliance on mixed farming is one reason that Europe has supported one-fifth of the world's population on one-thirtieth of the world's land area for the past few centuries, but there are other reasons as well. One of these is Europe's industrial and commercial growth. Another is Europe's large proportion of arable land. Over thirty percent of Europe is under cultivation, but less than ten percent of Asia is used for crops. Land forms, rainfall, temperature patterns, and soils all favor the European cultivator. The high productivity of European agriculture has been a significant factor in the growth of trade and manufacturing in recent centuries. It has meant that the farm-dweller has had a surplus to trade for goods and services, including the services of government. It has also meant that the town-dweller could rely on that surplus for food—a circumstance which has favored the growth of both old and new cities.

In terms of available resources, artisans and merchants in the towns of pre-modern western and southern Europe were as fortunate as farm-dwellers. There were ample woodlands to provide carpenters with materials for buildings and furnishings. Stonecutters, makers of brick and tile, and masons found usable stone and clay in many regions. Deposits of iron, lead, copper, tin, zinc, silver, and gold were also fairly numerous, widely spread, and easily worked. In fact, mining and metallurgy were important to Europe's economy long before the fifteenth-century voyages of exploration began. The availability of wood as fuel for smelting was as important to this early growth as the wide distribution of rich coal fields on the continent would be for the more rapid industrialization of later years. Water power was also used for processes such as the crushing of ore, as mine owners and metalworkers sought to expand production to meet increasing demand. Textile-makers had little difficulty obtaining flax, wool, and silk, although their markets and their supplies were limited in the pre-modern era by the fact that many rural people spun their own thread and wove their own cloth during the slack seasons of the agricultural year. Leatherworkers could obtain skins and hides from the numerous farm animals. The products of these various industries found markets widening as populations and agricultural productivity increased. As trade expanded, trade networks grew in scope until the entire continent was linked together by traveling merchants.

Pre-Modern European Social
and Political Organization

TRIBE, HOUSEHOLD, VILLAGE, CITY, AND GUILD

Natural resources and facilities for travel were not the only components of western Europe's development. Social and political factors also contributed to the expansion of European horizons.

In western Europe as in every part of the world, the oldest social unit was the kinship group. Originally it had been the basic unit of sustenance, protection, and continuity, or in other words, of economic, political, and social life. All of the individual's needs were met through it. The wandering Germanic tribe of thousands of years ago was an example of a kinship group. Its members maintained their unity through the generations by continued acknowledgment of a blood tie. They cooperated in the tending of their flocks and herds, settled disputes among themselves by agreed methods, and united to fight against outsiders. Since these tasks were carried on primarily by the men, it was the bonds of relationship between the men which held the tribe together. They remained closely knit throughout their lives, and the recognized line of descent was the patrilineal one from father to son. A woman ordinarily left her parents' household to become part of her husband's family at the time of marriage. Only by marriage or by adoption could anyone from outside the tribal lineage become part of the tribe. Within the tribe, the normal small unit was the household of father, sons, and possibly (although infrequently) grandsons, together with their wives and offspring, all of whom recognized the father as their leader.

A tribal grouping of related households was admirably suited to the nomadic herding life the Germans followed until the centuries immediately before the Christian era, when they began to cultivate the open portions of the western European plain. It was cohesive in time of need because of the recognition of a permanent bond, yet subdivided into many small units, each of which could take care of itself most of the time. However, the meaning of the kinship bond was modified when a tribe settled down and became attached to one particular plot of ground. The patrilineal household remained the fundamental unit, but attention turned from shared ancestry to shared land use as a basis of cooperation. Much intermarrying took place between those in the same locality, and there was a tendency to think of those who lived nearby as part of the same family. Yet relationships of residence gradually took their place beside relationships of blood as a means of defining the group within which disputes were to be settled peacefully.

The members of each farming household met as many of their needs as they could and relied on others as little as possible, but no household was completely self-sufficient. It was often advantageous for members of several households to work together on tasks like harvesting and house-building, which could be done more rapidly by many hands. It was also useful to have a few specialists such as carpenters, millers, bakers, and smiths; and it was always helpful to have an experienced midwife close at hand. Furthermore, the lone household was rarely strong enough to protect itself from attack by outsiders. For all these reasons, agricultural households tended to cluster into villages, much as nomadic households clustered into tribes.

The village had little to do with the outside world. Its people raised their own food, built their own houses, made their own clothing, settled their own disputes, and taught their children how to follow in their footsteps. They grew up, worked, married, raised their children, and died within a few miles of where they were born. They were unaccustomed to having strangers in their midst, and therefore tended either to distrust outsiders as agents of some authority which might interfere with the rhythm of their lives or, less frequently, to look on them as potential workers of miracles. Yet in order to continue their usual life, the villagers ordinarily needed some associations with others outside their village, for they required a small but steady supply of items such as salt and iron which they could not obtain from the field or the forest. If they lived in the mountains or on the seashore, they could procure iron or salt in the seasons when there was neither plowing, seeding, cultivating, nor harvesting to be done. If they lived elsewhere, they had to rely on someone to bring them these and other articles to trade for part of their crops. Therefore a few individuals became specialists in the exchange of goods, carrying salt to the interior and iron to the coast. Some of these traders were from the districts where the items were in demand; others, from the districts where they were produced.

In some of the villages through which the traders passed, the inhabitants began to make goods for exchange—fine pottery if there were good clay deposits in the vicinity, or cabinetwork if there were hardwood forests nearby. As the excellence of their products became known, they became able to exchange their handicrafts for the food raised in other villages. Gradually they turned from growing crops to producing their specialties. Such villages were becoming cities—settlements whose residents specialized in providing goods and services to such an extent that the residents of neighboring settlements looked to them for political, intellectual, and religious leadership as well as for material items. The relationship between a city and the people who used its services might be voluntary (as when villagers came to town on market day to trade their vegetables for household utensils), or it might be partly involuntary (as when a government official required the villagers to maintain the roads leading to the city); but the existence of such relationships was one of the major factors which distinguished the city from the village. Other familiar characteristics of the life of cities, such as the knowledge of how to smelt and alloy metals and the knowledge of how to write and keep records, were simply a part of the city's specialized goods and services. As the cities expanded in size and complexity, their inhabitants tended to group themselves along occupational lines: merchants in merchants' guilds, weavers in weavers' guilds. Yet each individual's first loyalty remained with the household, which continued to be the basic unit of production and consumption in the cities as it had been among the villagers from whom the city-dwellers had descended.

City and village were interdependent, each wanting the products of the other, but the city needed the villagers more than they needed the city. The people of the city could not live without a network of affiliated villages to provide them with food through trade, but the villagers could get along well enough with only the visits of itinerant merchants. Therefore leaders in every city usually sought to extend their control over as many villages as possible by attracting a sizable portion of the villagers' produce in exchange for goods and then using what was not consumed by artisans and merchants to feed other types of specialists whose services were valuable to the villagers. These specialists included students of the cosmos who kept track of the seasons and notified villagers when to expect heat, cold, flood, or drought. They also included the military, who could protect the crops from hungry bands of wanderers. The priests could draw on a superior knowledge of the universe to inspire the villagers with awe for the deities worshiped in the city, while the military could prevent the villagers from trading with other cities. Not only the villagers but the city-dwellers themselves came under the rule of the military and the priesthood, each of whom considered its own group primary and the other secondary. Soldiers and priests constantly sought to use each other to further their own goals, but within the city walls which protected them both, neither group ever completely dominated the other.

RULERS, NOBLES, AND CLERGY

Western Europe was only beginning to become organized around cities in the fashion just described when the process of urbanization was interrupted by the breakdown of the Roman empire and the era of invasions which followed it. Between the fifth and tenth centuries A.D., Huns, Ostrogoths, Visigoths, Vandals, Angles, Franks, Vikings, Saracens, and Magyars raided and overran western and southern Europe. As the last of these invaders either settled down or withdrew, the restoration of order enabled the population of western Europe to increase. Population growth in turn spurred on the expansion of agriculture, encouraging the merchant and artisan, and making city life both possible and profitable once more. However, by that time the functions of guardianship and leadership, previously performed by the inhabitants of Roman camps and cities, were firmly in the hands of castle-dwelling rulers and nobles or monastery-dwelling clergymen.

Rulers, nobles, and clergy depended for the necessities of life on the land they held and on the villagers who worked it in exchange for protection during the era of invasions. The rulers and nobles, many of whom were themselves descended from conquering tribes, followed the customary practice of stressing the importance of kinship ties. The clergy did not. Instead, the church hierarchy was organized in theory as a bureaucracy in which one advanced through merit which was measured in terms of ability, experience, and marks of divine favor. Anyone might enter this clerical bureaucracy. Anyone might advance to any position in it, although those whose family background had encouraged them to develop habits of leadership naturally stood a better chance than others. However, the ideal of advancement by merit could only be realized if rules against clerical marriage were enforced. Otherwise, in the family-organized society of the time, fathers would find ways of passing their positions to their sons regardless of the latters' qualifications. Even then, as rules against nepotism indicate, positions passed from uncle to nephew, as incumbents brought their brothers' sons into the clergy and groomed them as successors.

As the standard of living of the upper clergy rose with the increasing income of the church from endowments and donations, the church hierarchy became a much-sought refuge for younger sons of the nobility. Most noble families practiced primogeniture—inheritance by the eldest son—which was a convenient way to minimize disputes over inheritance and to prevent the division of the property which supported the prestige of the family. Consequently, younger sons generally had to resign themselves to poverty, parasitism, the risks of venturing into strange lands, or the restricted but secure life of the clergy. The resultant presence of large numbers of noblemen's sons in the upper clergy, coupled with the respect given the clergy as interpreters between the realm of God and the human realm, made the upper clergy equal or even superior to the nobility in the social pyramid in spite of the inclusion of individuals of every social and occupational background in the clerical bureaucracy. Together, nobility and higher clergy formed a tiny but powerful upper class which exchanged its services for the products of peasants and artisans.

The upper class held its position through a fivefold leadership: social, economic, political, intellectual, and religious. As long as prestige, wealth, power, and secular and sacred learning were concentrated in its members, they controlled the rest of society. They settled disputes and dealt with grievances in royal, baronial, and ecclesiastical courts. They defended the existing order from invaders and rebels by military prowess and the use of excommunication. They ensured the continuance of society by sanctioning the establishment of new households through marriage. They also recorded the experience of the past and interpreted it for the instruction of the future. So firmly entrenched were the clergy and nobility that they retained their positions of leadership long after the restoration of order in the tenth century facilitated increases in population, trade, and urbanization.

RULERS, TOWNSPEOPLE, AND NATIONAL MONARCHIES

The reappearance and rapid growth of towns and cities in western Europe from the eleventh century onward introduced a new element into the society which nobles and clergy had long been accustomed to control. The rising town-dwellers established municipal courts and occupational guilds to settle difficulties, and guardsmen and walls for defense, but they did not challenge the nobility and upper clergy to a direct test of strength. Instead they sought to infiltrate the upper class by forming close ties with the rulers, who had been recognized as the heads of human society by both clergy and nobility since the dissolution of the Roman empire in western Europe.

An important factor in the growth of an alliance between the monarchs of western Europe and its townspeople was the town-dwellers' realization that rulers had authority to give patents of nobility to commoners who ministered to their needs—and a ruler who sought to exercise any real control over the nobility and clergy always had needs. Every ruler wished to transform nominal headship of the state into actual mastery, but to do so, money was needed to pay soldiers and administrators. Otherwise the ruler would remain unable to deprive the nobles and prelates of their power to act independently of royal commands.

By the end of the fifteenth century the alliance between rulers and townspeople in western Europe had introduced the institution of the national monarchy in which the ruler was superior not only in prestige but also in power. No longer was the ruler merely one of a number of great nobles, each of whom paid the monarch homage and rendered a few services when called on but was otherwise largely free of royal control. Now the ruler appointed and paid the officials who governed every part of the realm, though it was usually many years before laws, taxes, coinages, and standards of weight and measure could be made the same throughout the provinces. In France this process was not completed until the era of the French Revolution.

In all the national monarchies, the dialect of the capital became the standard of language usage throughout the country as the administrators of the central government spread from one end of the realm to the other. This was truer for townspeople than for villagers, since villagers usually saw the administrators only when regular and special levies were being raised, while townspeople lived side by side with them. Nevertheless, the speech of all regions gradually tended to approach the pattern set at the center, even in border regions where local dialects might have once been closer to those of neighbors across the boundary than to the speech of the capital.

The young national monarchies of fifteenth-century western Europe continued to be dominated socially by the upper class. However, the rulers were delegating their newly gathered political power to their supporters among the wealthier townspeople who, in turn, were rapidly reaching an economic level which enabled them to rival the landholding upper class in leisure, luxury, and learning. In Germany and Italy, the Holy Roman Emperor and the Pope also used town-dwellers to attempt to weaken the nobility, thereby helping members of merchant families like the pawn-broking Medici of Florence to become not only patrons of the arts but even nobles, queens, and popes. Emperors and popes did not seek national consolidation, though. Instead they sought to master all rivals so that the unity enjoyed by Europe in Roman times might be revived in a consolidation of all western Christendom.

Patterns of language and of the exercise of political power were not all that was affected by the growth of centralized monarchies. The clergy were also swept along with the current. Once it became clear that popes and emperors were wearing each other out in their struggle for European supremacy, monarchs demanded and received the right to a voice in the promotion of the clergy in their realms. The rulers thereby weakened the international character of the church hierarchy and acquired effective control over its members. As for the merchants, the monarchs not only used them in government but spurred them to venture overseas so that taxes on trade might fill the royal treasuries. Monarchs also encouraged merchants to establish new enterprises at home.

Thus at the end of the fifteenth century most western Europeans were living and working in family households which were grouped according to their members' occupation—into villages in the countryside, artisans' and merchants' guilds in the towns, and the landholding nobility. Alongside and above them were the clergy and the newly established royal bureaucracy which was taking over the governing functions of the nobles. Yet the development of this increasingly urbanized society had not been smooth. The expansion of trade and city life became less rapid during the thirteenth century. Mines began to give out, while increased population required the development of less fertile fields than those carved out of the forests in the eleventh and twelfth centuries. In fact, expansion almost halted during the wars, famines, and pestilences of the fourteenth century. These disasters so alarmed guilds and governments that for a time they sought to forestall further decay by forbidding changes in wages, methods of production, prices, and habits of consumption. However, from the fifteenth century onward it was clear that as western Europe's economy began to recover, the forces of change would prove too strong to be denied.

Western European Thought-Patterns

CHRISTIAN, GREEK, ROMAN, AND GERMANIC ELEMENTS

Western Europe's intellectual and religious heritage was as significant in its development as were economic, social, and political factors. That heritage included a number of elements which were fused during the thousand years from the fall of Rome to the rise of national monarchies. Dominant among these elements were Christian doctrine, Greek philosophy, Roman law, and Germanic family and tribal loyalty.

As Christians, western Europeans believed that the universe was created and governed by God and that therefore it had a certain reality. As the sphere of human action, the created world could merit some of one's attention, but since the world was temporary, temporal, it should not engage all of one's thoughts. One should also contemplate the eternal God, the all-powerful Creator Who was transcendent, wholly other than the created world, and yet personal. God had taken a direct interest in the human beings who were fashioned in the divine image. He had sent them the prophets of the Old Testament and the Messiah of the New Testament, and had provided them with the sacraments of the Christian church as administered by the clergy. Men and women therefore ought to take their proper place in the realm of creation by availing themselves of the sacraments. They should obey the divine instructions to love and serve both God and human beings, and they should persuade others to join with them in the church.

The Christians of Europe were notably successful in carrying out the task of conversion. By 1000 A.D. the missionaries of Rome had taught Christianity to the peoples of western, northern, and central Europe, while the missionaries of Constantinople had brought most of eastern Europe into the Christian fold. The remaining pagan peoples of the Baltic were converted in the thirteenth and fourteenth centuries. In fifteenth-century western Europe only the Muslims of southeastern Spain and a handful of Jews in cities from Naples to Antwerp remained aloof from the church of Rome.

The Christian profession which bound western Europeans together had a noticeable effect on their treatment of other portions of their heritage. Like the Greeks, western Europeans came to look for orderliness in nature. They observed, made comparisons, and set up experiments to test the correctness of the conclusions they drew from their observations, but they did these things with the underlying Christian purpose of understanding God's creation better so that they might live in it more easily. They also refined the methods of logical argument developed by the Greeks, for they believed that the disciplined use of the human mind was in line with the divine plan. Like the Romans, western Europeans accepted the idea that there was a single natural law (the law of God, in Christian eyes) to which all human codes of law were approximations. They also agreed with the Romans that in the final analysis the law should be the same for all, although for the time being they were usually willing to wait for divine justice to punish a wrongdoer whose wealth or position led to lenient treatment in the courts. In fact, they had inherited from imperial Rome their whole system of using formally constituted courts to settle conflicts over marriages, inheritances, contracts, thefts, abductions, murders, and the whole calendar of disputes. In addition they accepted the principle that in any given case someone was guilty and someone else was innocent, so that the proper course of action was to discover who was at fault and then require that person to make amends in whatever way possible. Such a court system fit rather well with the Christian description of the Last Judgment at the end of the created world as a separation of those who were welcomed into the presence of God from those who were cast into outer darkness.

Christian belief in the equality of human beings in the eyes of God, Greek emphasis on the importance of actually studying things as they are rather than merely accepting the statements of others about them, Roman desire to find and apply to everyone the principles of natural law—all these gave strong support to the idea that one should be judged on one's merits, not on one's family ties. Nevertheless, for centuries these three forces were largely countermanded by the heritage from a long-distant tribal past. As recently as the eighteenth century, many Europeans still insisted that kinship relationships were so important that they should determine the nature of the opportunities open to the individual. They even believed that relationships such as guild membership, which were originally entered voluntarily, should become as permanent and binding as the ties of blood.

Most notable among the early modern western European adaptations of Germanic tribal institutions was the revitalization of monarchy.

The Romans of the early Christian era had emphasized the power wielded by the ruler; the Germanic tribes had emphasized the ruler's heroic descent and the ancestral links between ruler and people. These appeals to power and to ancestry became intertwined in the medieval concept of monarchy. In the sixteenth and seventeenth centuries, the national monarchs of western Europe made full use of both claims to leadership. They also sought alliance with the clergy, who had come to be regarded as valuable friends and dangerous foes because of the veneration which the laity gave them. The result was the elaboration of the theory advanced by rulers and their supporters that monarchs had a divinely granted right to rule. According to this theory, the ruler's ancestry showed that the monarch had been chosen by God to rule, while the ruler's power and authority showed that the monarch was responsible to God alone—not to those whom the monarch ruled, as stated by the upholders of the earlier parliamentary traditions that arose from the informal councils of the Germanic tribe.

Ae befitted those in such a commanding position, the monarchs of western Europe strove to ally themselves with the clergy on their own terms. One way of doing so was to use Roman law, which had been carefully studied during the revival of learning which accompanied the economic expansion of the twelfth century. This study had been intended as a preparation for the reunification of western Christendom under the inheritors of the leadership of Rome; but since emperors and popes could not agree on the identity of Rome's true heirs, it was the western European monarchs who profited from the study of Roman law. The monarchs revived the concept of law as territorial rather than personal, applying equally to all within the ruler's domains rather than varying with the individual's status or occupation. They then used the territorial concept of law to restrict the jurisdiction of church courts, which in turn set limits to the power of the clergy. In fact, as Henry VIII of England showed in the sixteenth century, rulers were quite capable of setting up their own national churches and throwing off allegiance to the papacy at Rome if they deemed such a step advisable.

FROM PASSIVE TO ACTIVE ATTITUDES

Despite the persistence of hereditary monarchy, the western Europeans of later medieval and early modern times were gradually turning away from the idea that some were born to lead and the rest to follow. In particular, town-dwellers were demonstrating that wealth, prestige, and power were not monopolized by the landholding upper class. Commoners could also gain these advantages through manufacturing and trade, as the great merchants clearly showed by their opulence, their representation in the parliaments and councils called by monarchs to discuss affairs of state, and their service as officials in the royal governments of western Europe.

As other commoners sought to follow in the footsteps of the great merchants, reliance on family ties as a means of advancement began to be replaced by reliance on the proven abilities of individuals. Family members left the parental roof to try their fortune elsewhere. Villagers sought jobs outside of agriculture. Guild members chafed at restrictions which prevented them from adopting new methods that would enable them to save time, energy, or raw material without sacrificing the quality of their work. The general ferment even affected government affairs. The principle of consulting representatives of every major group won such wide support that in the fourteenth and early fifteenth centuries it seemed that parliaments might soon relegate rulers to a purely ceremonial role. The monarchs postponed the victory of representative parliamentary democracy for a time by winning support from both the clergy and the townspeople against the nobility, but in later centuries, when the nobles were weakened, those who favored parliamentary rule again began to question the right of rulers to absolute power.

At the close of the fifteenth century the revival of the expansive and energetic spirit of the twelfth century was well under way, not only in political and economic life but also in scientific speculations. As early as the fourteenth century, physicists had begun to theorize that it was as natural for a moving object to keep on moving as it was for a stationary object to remain at rest, an idea which contrasted strongly with the previously accepted theory that rest was natural but motion was unnatural. Growing belief that the universe and its inhabitants were constantly undergoing change was followed by a vague recognition that an increase in material well-being for one part of society did not necessarily mean deprivation for another. People began to speculate that all of the members of society might improve their lot simultaneously if they increased their total output and enabled everyone to share in its distribution. In the early sixteenth century, both the rational English churchman Thomas More and the fanatical Millennialists of the towns of northern Europe grasped something of this new idea which was to become one of the driving forces behind the transformation of western Europe and eventually of the world.

The ideas which sprang from experience with an expanding economy, increasing social mobility, and experimental scientific study upset the traditional belief that the universe was dedicated to the perpetuation of the familiar round. Instead it came to be believed that one could take the initiative, cooperating with nature in an active rather than a passive way. Ordinary people could hope to improve their position by entering the fields for which their abilities were best suited, rather than going unquestioningly into the occupations of their forebears. In short, by 1500 an attitude of active optimism had widely replaced the older attitude of passive resignation. In the next few centuries, practical applications of that optimism altered western Europe almost beyond recognition and affected distant continents.

Modern European Social and Political Organization

SOCIAL, ECONOMIC, AND RELIGIOUS DEVELOPMENTS

The exploration of the continents and oceans which western Europeans undertook in earnest from the fifteenth century onward was itself a sign of their dynamic spirit of enterprise. Even before the discovery of the New World and the sea route to India, western Europeans had demonstrated their ingenuity through the development of movable type, the printing press, and new ways of utilizing the familiar forces of wind and water. By the time they invented the steam engine and applied it to purposes ranging from spinning to sea travel, the family was already ceasing to be the basic unit of production and consumption.

By the end of the eighteenth century, home workshops and small fields were giving way to factories and large commercial farms, and individuals had to turn from supplying their own wants to earning money so that they could purchase what they needed. They had to demonstrate their ability to an employer who was often a stranger, and pay still other strangers for their food, clothing, and shelter. The ties of kinship beyond the basic conjugal group of husband, wife, and children were stretched to the breaking point. Within the small conjugal family, parental control over household expenditures and vocational or marital choices disappeared, for sons and even daughters now made their own way in the world, outside rather than inside the family.

The breakdown of family ties was greatest for those who left the countryside for the city, as western Europeans had been doing since the revival of trade and towns in the eleventh century. Migration to urban centers accelerated rapidly, as large-scale farming and factory industry replaced older patterns of small-scale production. In 1815 not even Great Britain had thirty percent of its people in cities. By 1930 each western European state from Spain to Sweden classified at least thirty percent of its people as city-dwellers. In addition, many of the country residents were commuting to work in nearby towns, rather than farming. Those who still cultivated the soil grew their crops to sell for money. They no longer concentrated on producing for their own consumption, for commercial agriculture had replaced subsistence agriculture.

The changes in social and economic patterns smoothed the path for those who wished to enter occupations other than those of their parents. Occupational mobility was even greater in European settlements overseas in the Americas, in Australasia, and in smaller numbers in Africa and Asia. In fact, the opportunity to rise rapidly was one of the lures that drew seventy million people out of Europe between 1820 and 1939, a quarter of them from Great Britain alone. However, occupations continued to be ranked hierarchically in order of the amount of manual labor and grime they entailed. Only in the twentieth century did these distinctions begin to be blurred, more noticeably overseas than in western Europe itself. Manual laborers became increasingly able to afford the same food, clothes, housing, transportation, amusements, and schooling for their children as clerical workers; and clerical workers in turn began to approach the level of smaller-income business or professional people.

The social and economic changes which took place in early modern Europe also played their part in the virtual disappearance of the power formerly held by the upper class on the fivefold basis of honorable descent, land ownership, political control, religious leadership, and a monopoly of formal education. Family ancestry lessened in importance as a criterion for leadership when opportunities began to become available to individuals on the basis of ability. At the same time, land ownership was replaced by industrial, financial, and commercial activity as the major source of great wealth. Political control shifted from rulers and their courts to elected officials who paid less heed to pedigrees than to the number of votes a person could influence; and a variety of factors contributed to the loss of religious and intellectual prestige by the clergy and nobility.

From at least the sixteenth century onward, the social and political power of the clergy of western Europe lessened, for the awe in which they had been held was lessening also. An important factor in this development was the increasing acceptance of the idea that one could commune directly with one's Creator without the mediation of a priest. This theory was advanced by the Protestant reformers of the sixteenth century and by eighteenth-century pietist or evangelical reformers among both Protestants and Roman Catholics. Another factor was the growth in numbers of those who could read the scriptures for themselves, as literacy and the printing press made their way across the face of Europe. Close and profitable associations between church officials and royal governments also lessened the willingness of many lay people to see clergy continue to be active in political life.

Church hierarchies began to be intertwined with governments even before the Reformation era of the sixteenth century, as rulers appointed educated and capable clergy to administrative posts. When the Reformation movement threatened to split the body politic of many western European states between Roman Catholics and Protestants, almost every monarchy eventually chose to support one branch of the now-divided church and persecute all others as traitors to both church and state. The clergy of the state-supported church thus became even more linked with the government, and remained so even after the possibility that heresy need not mean treason began to be accepted. The old distinction between spiritual and secular affairs (as having to do with inward belief and outward action, respectively) then ceased to seem useful, and was replaced by the assumption that "sacred" and "secular" referred to two different types of action-and-belief—one directed toward God and the other toward one's fellow men and women. This reinterpretation—which, in effect, relegated the task of the clergy to a part rather than the whole of life—also contributed to the weakening of the clergy's social and political authority.

Even more striking than the waning of the clergy's political role was the disappearance of the monopoly of the clergy and aristocracy over the fields of teaching and learning. This monopoly began to be challenged at least as early as the thirteenth century, when Emperor Frederick II established the University of Naples as a state institution in which commoners' sons might obtain the learning needed for service to the state. When printing with movable type was introduced, it made possible a wide and rapid interchange between literate commoners, clergy, and aristocracy which further weakened upper-class domination of intellectual life. During the nineteenth century, as one government after another accepted a responsibility for the instruction of the young, both the giving and the receiving of education ceased to be the prerogative of the few. The resulting universalization and secularization of education cut deeply into the power of the upper class to mold the thinking of the members of the society of which they were a part.

POLITICAL DEVELOPMENTS

The social, economic, intellectual, and religious changes which took place in the national monarchies of early modern western Europe required fundamental alterations in political structure and activity as well. In making these alterations, western Europeans drew on the experience of previous centuries.

Long before 1500 A.D., the national monarchs appointed talented individuals of many classes to positions in the administrative organs set up to oversee or even to replace the nobles. After 1200 A.D. rulers from Portugal to Sweden expanded their councils so as to include representatives of the newly affluent townspeople, as well as the nobility and higher clergy. Since the days of the Germanic tribe, the council had been the traditional mechanism by which ruler and nobles reached decisions on matters of state, such as the nature of the contribution which the nobles would make toward carrying out the monarch's policies. The contribution of the town-dwellers tended at first to be in terms of money rather than of time, energy, and talent; but gradually the capable merchant or financier was also drawn into the tasks of governing.

In order to enter the government, wealthy townsmen had to give up their livelihood in a way which the landholding nobles who lived on the products of the peasants' labor did not need to do. Consequently townsmen who came to spend part or all of their time in government also came to receive part or all of their income from the ruler's treasury, which made their relationship to the ruler different from that of the nobles. The nobles continued to receive an income whether or not the ruler's decrees were carried out, for the nobles' income was the revenue from their family lands. The government-paid officials had to obey the ruler or lose their income. The recognition of this difference between nobles and officials led rulers to use every available means to expand their income so that they could establish bureaucracies and standing armies, relegating the nobles to as small a role as possible.

Prior to the sixteenth century, England followed much the same pattern of political development as the monarchies of the continent. However, English rulers continued to use self-supporting members of the lesser gentry to administer rural districts. At first the gentry co-operated with the rulers against the greater nobles, but when the rulers began to try to weaken their position too, they combined forces with the townspeople. Together, town-dwellers and lesser gentry succeeded during the seventeenth century in expanding the prerogatives of the council of the realm to a degree unknown in England's continental neighbors. As a result, the law-making and the law-enforcing aspects of English government came to be embodied in two distinct organs—Parliament and the royal administration. At the same time, as the eighteenth-century French writer Montesquieu perceived, the courts served as a check on the way the law was applied. The introduction of a strong law-making body to limit what the ruler could do, and a strong independent judiciary to watch how it was done, proved to be highly effective in diminishing the autocratic power of the monarchs. All over Europe, the cause of representative parliamentary constitutional government was taken up as a means of combating the power of royal bureaucracies and standing armies. During the one hundred and forty years between the American and the Russian revolutions, the states of Europe and a number of their overseas extensions remodeled themselves along lines which approximated the English form of government, including the use of election as the means of selecting the members of at least one house of the legislature.

As the power of wholly or partly elected parliaments grew, it soon became evident that the parliament members paid progressively less attention to the head of the state and more to the voters who chose them at the polls. Political leadership ceased to depend on widespread but unvoiced acceptance of a small ruling group which perpetuated itself through marriage and inheritance, and came to depend on active support from a number of different groups as demonstrated in political parties, campaigns, and elections. Political parties, which began as factions within the legislature, became vote-seeking groups vying for the favor of the electorate. Party leaders in the parliaments soon extended the franchise from the propertied and educated few to the many who lacked either wealth or lengthy formal schooling. Sometimes they did so in hope of securing new supporters; sometimes, in fear of seeing the legislature overturned by popular rebellion. On the side of the voters, interest groups ranging from labor union to societies for prevention of cruelty to animals exerted pressure on the legislators in behalf of the measures they desired.

Both interest groups and political parties differed from older bodies like the guilds, for the ties which bound their members were recognized as ties of mutual interest in a limited set of problems rather than as lifelong bonds affecting every aspect of each member's activities. This change in the nature of human associations signified an elevation of the position of the individual in comparison to that of the group. Now both men and women were freer to do as they chose in forming—and, even more importantly, in dissolving—their bonds with those outside the family. This was only natural in an era when the individual was replacing the household as the basic unit in social and economic relationships, but it was also encouraged by significant elements in the western European heritage. For many generations the idea of the individual rather than the group as the ultimate maker of human decisions had been encouraged by the Christian belief than one was free to accept or to reject the opportunity of salvation, although this belief was tempered by the doctrine that God knew who would and who would not be saved. The importance of the individual was also upheld by the insistence of Roman law that no one should be punished for another's wrongdoing, and by the teaching of the ancient Greeks that one should strive to develop one's unique combination of talents to the fullest.

Some of the major problems with which political parties and interest groups concerned themselves were associated with the social and economic changes of the industrial era. As industrialization and the commercialization of agriculture increased the scale of economic activity, nations virtually replaced farms, villages, and towns as the most important economic units of society. Small groups like families and guilds found that they could no longer provide for most of their members' basic needs. Individuals began to find it necessary to look to larger groups for safeguards against personal calamities like accident, illness, and death. One answer lay in the development of private insurance companies which received small payments from thousands of policyholders, few of whom knew each other, and used the collected money to help those policyholders who experienced misfortune. Another answer lay in reliance on the state. This answer was highly attractive to those whose incomes hardly sufficed to keep themselves and their families alive. The poorer members of society used their newly received votes to exert pressure on governments to meet their needs out of the taxes which they and their richer fellow-citizens paid. Governments from the municipal to the national level were induced to add various types of social security measures to existing provisions for the relief of the destitute. To ensure the continuance of society, a major responsibility of any political system, governments undertook accident, sickness, unemployment, and retirement programs, as well as minimum-wage laws meant to ensure incomes above the bare subsistence level even for those in the lowest-paid jobs. Governments also undertook to underwrite the broad educational programs required in the new era.

The change from a local to a national scale in economic, social, and political life drastically revised the educational needs of ordinary men and women. They could no longer learn all they would need to know by observing those among whom they were raised, for now they were likely to move to a strange place, enter a different occupation from those followed by their parents and their friends, or mingle with people other than those among whom they had been reared. There were many risks involved in such ventures, but these risks could be lessened if one could learn about them beforehand by questioning someone who had experienced them—or if one could read about them. Literacy became the goal of the many instead of the privilege of the few, as the secrets of urban and urbane living were exposed in books of etiquette, in novels varying in style and quality from the stories of Horatio Alger to those of Henry James, and in a rash of publications on how to achieve success. Universal schooling became the corresponding responsibility of governments, but it was soon discovered that simple literacy was not enough. The knowledge which individuals needed grew increasingly complex as labor-saving devices, requiring men and women to use brain more than muscle, proliferated in offices, factories, farms, and homes. Consequently governments at various levels gradually extended their educational activities from elementary to secondary, college, and university education.

Nineteenth-Century European Attitudes toward Other Civilizations

As ordinary people joined those in positions of leadership in assuming that the most important unit of social, economic, and political life was the nation-state rather than the larger realm of Christendom or a smaller unit such as district, town, village, or family, the nation-states of western Europe and its overseas extensions became increasingly united or integrated politically, economically, and socially. During this process of national integration, almost everyone within each nation-state came to accept the same set of basic principles and loyalties as his or her fellow-nationals. At the same time, most of those who lived in such nation-states began to differentiate sharply between countries which shared the pattern of social, economic, and political life of post-1800 Europe and countries which did not. Given the evident differences between the two groups, this was hardly surprising.

The West (*Europe and its overseas extensions*)	*Elsewhere*
1. The individual increasingly regarded as the basic unit of society.	1. The family household still the fundamental unit.
2. Opportunity for the qualified individual in a wide range of positions.	2. Confinement of all but the most exceptional individuals to a narrow range of occupations in each segment of society.
3. Under law, individual held responsible only for his or her own deeds.	3. Often, individual held liable for the action of members of his or her family, village, or guild.
4. Sphere of religion gradually limited to the relationship between the human and divine (nonphysical) worlds; all other relationships treated as secular (nonreligious).	4. Few such distinctions drawn.
5. Growing assumption that changes in human activities and relationships were possible and beneficial.	5. Fear that change might lead to disaster.
6. Economic life increasingly urban and interdependent, stressing production for the market and for exchange of goods.	6. Emphasis on subsistence agriculture.
7. Political activities divided among numerous distinct organizations; most of the people involved in some aspect of national affairs.	7. Political activities the concern of small self-perpetuating groups; for the majority of people, a focus on local matters and no sense of participation in national affairs.

Some of the organizations and institutions among which political activities were divided in the West were directly connected with politics and government, while others were not. The desires of various sectors of the populace were expressed by a number of privately organized interest groups. Political parties combined these desires, modifying them somewhat so that the party program would be acceptable enough to win wide support and unobjectionable enough to meet little opposition. Legislatures turned the most widely supported measures into law; administrative organs carried out both new and old laws; judiciaries determined whether each law had been carried out properly. Mass media —newspapers, magazines, and pamphlets in the nineteenth century, joined by radio, motion pictures, and television in the twentieth—provided interest groups, parties, legislatures, administrations, and judiciaries with the flow of information and opinion they needed to keep in touch with what their compatriots were thinking and doing.

This brief list of differences indicates some of the reasons why the people of nineteenth-century western Europe were convinced that their way of life was the model for the world, since it was leading to growing opportunities for increasing numbers of people to acquire more goods, more leisure, and more knowledge, with less use of manual effort, than had ever before been possible. It also indicates why Westerners grew increasingly impatient with other societies. Few Westerners realized, for example, that cheap imported textiles did not seem a boon to poverty-stricken villagers in economies based on subsistence agriculture. Radical changes were needed in such economies before the average household could afford to give up the cloth its members wove in the slack season out of home-grown fibers in favor of the products of foreign mills. No matter how inexpensive the foreign cloth might be, villagers had to find means to pay for it. They rarely had much left after providing for their daily needs, and the little they did have was usually put aside for such social necessities as dowries, bride-gifts, feasts, and funerals. To the individualistic Westerner these seemed to be nonproductive expenditures, but to the family-minded villager in Egypt or China they seemed essential to the maintenance of the household—far more essential than the saving of labor involved in the substitution of cheap store-bought cloth for the homemade variety.

The combination of assurance and impatience made the newly industrializing states of the West more than willing to use their economic and political strength to win a measure of control over the affairs of others. Not only smaller peoples fell under Western rule, but even societies whose populations were larger than those of Western states. Some members of these societies reacted by completely rejecting all things Western. Others tried to maintain their traditional beliefs while adopting those Western practices which seemed desirable or necessary for self-preservation. Still others, usually those dissatisfied with their lot, rejected their own heritage and turned hyper-Western.

None of these approaches proved completely workable. Those who rejected the West failed to persuade their fellows that the West was entirely inferior; those who rejected their own past failed to persuade their compatriots that the West was entirely superior. Those who tried to preserve old beliefs by using new techniques made the mistake of acting as though behavior can be divorced from the principles on which it is based, only to find that those who were learning modern ways began to question such long-standing principles of social organization as the assignment of tasks on the basis of family connections.

Out of the mingling of these reactions, varying blends of ancient and modern ways of thought and action evolved. In each region, the characteristics of the mixture depended partly on the heritage of the past and partly on the specific circumstances under which the impact of the industrialized West was felt. Since both these factors varied considerably, the resulting patterns of life display some marked contrasts; yet there are also strong similarities, for the pre-modern societies did have important factors in common and the Western carriers of modernization who influenced them were inspired by broadly similar visions.

In preparation for looking at South, East, and Southeast Asia, the next chapter will sketch the experiences of the peoples of the Middle East. Their interactions with Europeans set patterns for Western behavior in the rest of Asia. Their responses to Europeans, conditioned by their Islamic beliefs, are also instructive for understanding the responses of Muslim Asians from Pakistan to Indonesia.

2

MIDDLE EASTERN
BEGINNINGS

Geographic Foundations and Social Organization

REGIONS, RESOURCES, AND PEOPLES

The Middle East is defined here as the broad region from Morocco to Afghanistan rather than the smaller area from Egypt to Iran. It can be divided into two distinct portions by a line from Antioch east to Mosul and southeast to Basra. South of this line, most of the country is level or rolling (except for the mountains of northwest Africa, the Levant, and southern Arabia) and the overwhelming majority of the people speak Arabic. North of the line lie the great mountain-ringed basins of the northern tier (Anatolia, Armenia, Iran, and Afghanistan) where Arabic is rarely used except for religious purposes. Yet the people of these two differing regions are linked by a common need to solve the problem of livelihood posed by a generally dry climate. They also share the precepts of the Arabic Quran, the sacred book of Islam, the religion of over ninety percent of all Middle Easterners.

On both sides of the Antioch-to-Basra line the mountains have served as barriers to travel and as refuges for their inhabitants. They are the source of the rivers which bring water to the basins and the plains, for they are high enough to catch rainfall from the winds which circle from the Atlantic to the Indian Ocean in the winter months, or which blow from the sea toward Yemen, Oman, and southeastern Afghanistan in the summer. The mountains are primary sources of iron, copper, chrome, silver, building stone, and clay, and also of wood, where long centuries of human use have not led to deforestation. The one major natural resource of the area that does not come from the mountains is petroleum, which is found in the dry lowlands from the Persian Gulf to the central Sahara.

Very few portions of the Middle East are as well-watered as western Europe. Even where annual rainfall averages twenty to forty inches, as in the coastal plains and mountains of northwest Africa, the Levant, Turkey, northern Iran, and Yemen, hot summers and mild winters lead to rapid evaporation. Therefore unirrigated agriculture is possible only in a few portions of northwest Africa, northern Turkey, and northern Iran. Yet only northwest Africa, the Levant, Yemen, Oman, Anatolia, Armenia, western and northern Iran, and northern and eastern Afghanistan receive at least the eight or more inches a year needed to support irrigation from local wells, springs, and streams. Most of the rest of northern Africa, Arabia, and central Iran receives less than four inches a year. In the driest areas a torrential downpour may be followed by ten years without a single shower. Settled agriculture is possible only along great mountain-fed rivers, like the Nile, the Euphrates, the Tigris, the Karun of Iran, and the Helmand of Afghanistan, or in the oases where springs and wells draw on seasonal streams which flow only during the rainy winter. Outside the oases and the river valleys, the inhabitants of the Saharan and Arabian deserts and the central Iranian basin must rely on animal husbandry, driving their flocks and herds from place to place as rainfall makes grass and water available.

Time and time again, certain regions figure in Middle Eastern political history. In northern Africa, there are the well-watered Atlas mountains of Roman Mauretania and Morocco which extend along the Algerian coast into Tunisia, ending west of ancient Carthage and modern Tunis; Tripolitania and Cyrenaica, separated rather than linked by a band of desert three hundred miles wide; and Egypt, the gift of the Nile. In southwestern Asia, there are the mountain districts of southern Arabia and the Levant; the rainfed foothills between the Levant and the Tigris-Euphrates valley of ancient Mesopotamia and modern Iraq; Meso-potamia-Iraq itself; the Arabian desert; and the mountain basins of Anatolia, Armenia, western and eastern Iran, and Afghanistan in the northern tier.

Middle Eastern linguistic groupings tend to reflect landforms. The Semitic languages like Arabic and Hebrew, with their three-consonant word roots into which other sounds are inserted to indicate shades of meaning (*s-l-m*, to submit; *Islam*, submission; *Muslim*, one who submits), have been used in the lowlands for thousands of years. Today, Arabic reigns almost unchallenged there, except for Hebrew in Israel and Ber-ber (not a Semitic tongue) in Morocco. The Indo-European languages like Persian, Kurdish, Armenian, and Pushto, which tend to use auxiliary words to convey gradations of meaning, have been used in various mountain basins and valleys from Armenia eastward since the Hittite invasions more than thirty-five centuries ago. The Altaic languages like Turkish and Mongol, which add prefixes and suffixes to an unchanging word root, came to Anatolia and other portions of the northern tier after the tenth century A.D. All three language families use syllabic scripts and alphabets, derived largely from the ancient Semitic scripts of Mesopotamia and Phoenicia. After the Muslim conquest of the seventh century A.D., the Arabic script was adopted throughout the region, but in the twentieth century the Turks discarded it in favor of the Latin alphabet used in western Europe.

Religious groupings may also reflect topographical divisions. The mountains and valleys of the Levant have sheltered religious dissidents since Phoenician times three thousand years ago. At present they are divided between Jews and at least seventeen varieties of Sunni (orthodox) and Shia (heterodox or nonorthodox) Muslims, Orthodox and Roman Catholic Christians, and others such as the Druzes, an offshoot of Shia Islam. In southern Arabia, the mountains of Yemen and Oman each shelter members of a different heterodox Islamic sect. The Iranian basin has become the chief center of Shia Islam. The hills of northern Iraq shield Sunni Muslims, some of whom speak Kurdish rather than Arabic, from their Shia neighbors in Iran and the southeastern Tigris-Euphrates plain.

As political, linguistic, and religious groupings have reflected landforms, population densities have reflected the availability of the water supplies essential to agriculture. When population outgrew the land available in the areas of greatest rainfall, like the southern Caspian shore, families moved elsewhere. In the foothills they constructed underground conduits, in the mountains they cut the trees and terraced the slopes, and in the rainless valleys of Egypt and Mesopotamia they built intricate networks of canals. These canal networks were usually basin-irrigation projects, leading the yearly flood directly to the fields, not permanent-irrigation projects in which river water was stored behind great dams for use throughout the year. Permanent irrigation was not introduced into the Nile valley until the nineteenth century A.D. Since then the fertilizing silt has been filling the reservoirs instead of enriching the fields.

ORGANIZATION OF VILLAGE LIFE

For at least six thousand years the rhythm of the agricultural village has been the pattern of life for most Middle Easterners. Like western European cultivators, they have usually practiced mixed farming, raising both field crops and animals. However, Middle Easterners have been forced by their cutting of the mountain forests to use the dung of their animals for fuel rather than fertilizer, even though their soils are usually light and short of humus. In addition, the dry Middle Eastern climate makes the cultivator unwilling to use fields to raise hay, for fields must either be irrigated or left unused every second or third year to store up rainwater. Consequently, both fields and animals are less productive than those of modern western Europe.

In most Middle Eastern villages, the patrilineal household of parents, sons, unmarried daughters, and the wives and children of married sons has been the basis of economic, social, and political organization. Only the men are lifelong members, for daughters leave to become other men's wives, and wives come in from other households. To resolve the possible conflicts of loyalty for a woman when she changes households, she has always been expected to obey her husband unquestioningly. The father is the head of the household and has usually been the only one to take part in making village decisions.

Although villagers have always been largely self-sufficient, they have also been accustomed to trading with the pastoral nomads and urban merchants who have come to them to purchase food. The city-dwellers and nomad tribes have usually needed more food from the villages than they could obtain for essentials like salt. Consequently, both cities and tribes have generally tried to control as many villages as possible, so as to exact additional food supplies by taxation. At times they have even competed with each other for control of certain villages, in a triangular city-village-tribe relationship whose outcome was always the control of the village by either the city or the tribe.

The villagers of the river valleys and the oases have been the most thoroughly controlled from outside. Scanty rainfall has forced them to stay near the canals and wells, while the level land and warm climate have enabled city-based soldiers and desert nomads to compel their obedience. Whether the village headman has been chosen by the villagers or by their overlords, he has always been the one responsible to the city governor or the tribal chieftain for the payment of taxes and the maintenance of order.

Most other villagers have also been controlled from outside, except in remote districts like the Atlas. In Berber villages, household heads are still accustomed to discussing issues in full council and reaching acceptable decisions by bargain and compromise, unlike Arab, Persian, Turk, and Kurd household heads who may take part in village discussion but may also be ignored if the headman thinks it either necessary or safe to do so. Yet the Berbers' unwillingness to let others be their representatives has made it as difficult for them to use modern parliamentary forms as it was for the citizens of classical Athens. Representative democratic government has been even harder to implement where villagers have had less experience with effective political participation.

ORGANIZATION OF CITY LIFE

Not all those born in villages have remained there. Many have gone to the cities, seeking work or new experiences. In former times, when people might become slaves either by capture or by the decision to sell themselves into bondage for the sake of a guaranteed livelihood, some followed their masters to the cities while others were sent to work in mines or on great landed estates.

Cities need an effective system of internal policing. The physical congestion of a city makes one's actions affect one's neighbors even more than in a village. Yet the fact that most city-dwellers are comparative strangers tends to make them feel free to behave with less regard for each other's reactions than most village people would dare to do. Until recently, most Middle Eastern city rulers followed a system of policing based on village experience. In the village, each household head was responsible for keeping the members of his household from disturbing the peace, while the village headman was responsible for the village as a whole. In the city, where they were too many household heads to be directly accountable to the authorities, subordinate groupings of households were established whose heads were made responsible to the city rulers. These heads might be chosen either by those they led or by the city authorities.

From earliest times, such subordinate groupings were based on occupation, like the merchants' and artisans' guilds, or on residence in one of the walled sections into which most cities were divided. Often, all who followed the same calling were encouraged to live in the same quarter. This simplified the supervision of the guilds, which were controlled by the city government, not participants in city government like the guilds of late medieval western Europe. Foreigners usually lived in a separate quarter, where they governed themselves while the authorities supervised their trade with the merchants and workers of the city.

In Alexander's time, a further subdivision of cities along religious lines was foreshadowed by his granting of special privileges to Jews, Greeks, and Hellenized non-Greeks who worshiped Greek deities. However, not until the Muslim era was the head of each formally recognized religious group given full authority over the private relationships of its members. Thereafter, each religious group tended to cluster in its own quarters and to enter a distinctive set of occupations. Despite this high correlation between religion, residence, and occupation, city-dwellers recognized a difference between the associations connected with each sphere more readily than did villagers, who ordinarily recognized only the single occupational-residential-religious unit of the village. City residents also dealt more often than did villagers with people who did not share their religion, their occupation, or their residential area.

Each occupational, residential, or religious subdivision largely policed itself, but to ensure the general peace there were also rules which took precedence in case of conflict between those of different religious, residential, or occupational groups. This all-encompassing fourth set of rules was developed and administered by two other self-governing and self-perpetuating bodies, the military specialists and those who could record and interpret precedents—the men of the sword and the pen, as the Muslims called them.

ORGANIZATION OF TRIBAL LIFE

DESERT TRIBES. From earliest times the cities of Egypt and Mesopotamia were linked to the outside world by the merchants of the Mediterranean and the Indian Ocean. However, not until shortly before 1000 B.C. did the domestication of the camel make it possible for them to treat the desert as a sea, trading directly across it rather than by the more circuitous routes along its grassy edges. Within a few centuries goods from India and Southeast Asia and even China were being unloaded in Yemen, to be carried by camel caravan through the Arabian peninsula to the lands from Egypt to Mesopotamia. After the domesticated camel was introduced into the Sahara in Roman times, a similar trans-Saharan trade in ivory, gold, slaves, salt, and grain sprang up between coastal northwest Africa and the grasslands from the upper Senegal to the middle Niger.

Once the camel came into use, city-based governments soon found they could not control the nomads who raised the camels. Since the introduction of the horse from the grassy steppes of central Asia shortly after 2000 B.C., governments had used cavalry to increase their soldiers' mobility; but cavalry could not chase camel nomads as they could those who lived by raising other animals. Yet city merchants and camel nomads depended on each other, for the merchants needed camels while the nomads wanted goods, to make their frugal life more bearable. Consequently close ties developed between camel nomads and merchants.

Camel nomads strove to define their relationships with others in terms of the tribal household, the only economic, social, and political unit they recognized. Oasis-dwellers and those who herded slower animals were treated as clients or dependents, entitled to protection but not to participation in the making of decisions. Slaves, traveling blacksmiths, and other artisans were treated as permanent servitors. Merchants, officials, pilgrims, and others who passed through nomad territory were ordinarily treated as guests, as long as they did not attack the nomads. However, such guests were expected to repay their hosts before leaving, if they were not associated with other tribal households from which the nomads in turn might seek hospitality in future.

Since the tribes recognized no law but their own, those who were neither clients, servitors, nor guests might be raided at will. All was peace within the tribal domain, except when intruders refused to behave as expected; but outside, all was war. Desire for independence and dislike of risk tended to keep the nomads from raiding the settlements which ringed the desert, except perhaps for momentary plunder. Yet at any time they might use their mobility to seize control of villages and cities, as the Arabs demonstrated in the seventh century A.D.

CONTRASTS BETWEEN DESERT TRIBES AND STEPPE AND MOUNTAIN TRIBES. The kinship group of the tribe was also the only governing unit willingly recognized by steppe and mountain nomads. In both hill and desert country, the basic unit within the tribe was the patrilineal household, which organized its relations with other households on the basis of nearness or distance in the line of kinship, calling on nearer ones for assistance in minor emergencies and on increasingly remote ones as more hands or brains were needed. However, there were significant differences in permanence of organization, linked to differences in the patterns of their lives.

Throughout the Middle East, nomad herders have usually lived where there was rain enough to grow some vegetation but not enough for crops. The resulting shortage of pasturage forced them to move periodically during the year. In the uplands, herd and keepers stayed together throughout the year in a straight-line pattern of seasonal migration upward in summer and downward in winter, necessitating a permanent form of organization. Therefore, the heads of the tribe and its subdivisions were usually selected for life and given distinctive titles, so that the head of a subdivision could not be confused with the head of the entire tribe. A similar pattern developed in the horse-raising steppes of central Asia, where each band had to remain together for fear that other bands might destroy its members if they were scattered.

In the desert lowlands, each herd and its keepers clustered around a few springs and wells in the dry season. Then the coming of the rains let them move out to the limits of the territory in which they were free to range, only to return to the wells when the rains ceased and the grass gave out. Where the tribe was scattered much of the year, leaders were not selected for life. A capable leader might retain power for years, or a different household head might be chosen as leader each time a subdivision or a tribe had to act as a unit. Therefore, the same title was given to all household heads in the desert regardless of their current position.

These differences in internal organization meant that Arab and Berber desert tribes were accustomed to acting as overlords, but not to the permanent hierarchy of steppe Turks or mountain Kurds. Such variations help to explain some of the differences between the empires founded by Arabs, Berbers, Turks, and Kurds when they used their maneuverability to overrun the river valleys and the coastal plains.

Historical Development: The Formation of States

PRE-ISLAMIC PERIOD (TO 7TH CENTURY A.D.)

From the appearance of the first city-states before 3000 B.C. until after the domestication of the camel nearly two thousand years later, Middle Eastern states and empires were ordinarily limited to one or at most two of the regions of Mesopotamia, Egypt, and the Fertile Crescent. After 1800 B.C. Indo-European invaders from the north, such as the Hittites, used their horses, chariots, and iron weapons to establish new dynasties. They were beaten back eventually by the Egyptians and by Semites, such as the Assyrians on the upper Tigris, the Phoenicians in the northern Levant, and the Hebrews in Palestine. Then, after 900 B.C., Assyria gradually mastered its neighbors to the east and west. In 672 B.C. it linked the lands from the lower Nile to the head of the Persian Gulf, in the first of the great empires to rely on camels as well as horses. However, the Egyptians drove out the Assyrians before they could try to move westward toward the Phoenician colony of Carthage.

The Assyrians failed to set up an empire with no competitors; but their example proved helpful to the Persians, who began their sweep westward to the Nile and eastward to the Indus in the later sixth century B.C. Not until the seventh century A.D. did the peoples of Egypt, Mesopotamia, and the Fertile Crescent break free of the rule of outsiders from the north. In the later fourth century B.C. the Persians fell to Alexander and his Hellenistic successors. Several generations later they succumbed in turn to the Romans in the west and the steppe-bred Parthians in the east (who were replaced by the Sassanids in the third century A.D.). Even after Teutonic incursions loosened the Roman grip on the former Carthaginian sphere of influence in northwest Africa, the eastern Roman capital of Constantinople held Egypt, the Levant, and Anatolia until the Muslims wrested them from its grasp.

All of the later empires drew to some extent on the methods of the Persians. Darius I (521–485 B.C.), who established the Persian administrative system, kept the area of the capital under his direct control. The rest of the empire was divided into provinces, each of whose governors he appointed and removed at will. The governors were responsible for maintaining public order and collecting and remitting tribute. To be sure they carried out these tasks faithfully, Darius himself also appointed the commanders of the provincial garrisons and the heads of the provincial financial administrations. All three sets of provincial officials were required to report directly and separately to the monarch, who could then check on each official by reading the reports of those who served in the same province. To guard against possible collusion among provincial governors, commanders, and financial administrators, a corps of traveling inspectors was established. This elaborate system of reports and inspections, which was largely based on Assyrian experience, was supported by the construction of roads along which both messengers and troops could move rapidly throughout the empire. The importance of a good road network to the maintenance of a large state was one of the chief lessons the Romans learned from Darius's successors.

The system of administration worked out by Darius functioned well as long as the ruler who received the reports remained clear in mind, firm in decision, and strong in will. However, as each dynasty progressed, its rulers were increasingly cut off from a knowledge of the world by the pomp and luxury of palace life. As a result, arbitrary caprice often replaced deserved (though sometimes excessive) punishments and rewards. Corruption and incompetence then replaced probity and efficiency.

The lessons of road-building and administration were more easily learned than that of the value of tolerance. Few of the Persians' successors remembered that they had weakened disloyal tendencies by recognizing the legitimacy of religious and cultural differences among their subjects. Alexander and his successors promoted Hellenization by granting special privileges to those who worshiped Greek deities. The Romans excused Jews from paying divine honors to the reigning emperor, but refused to excuse Christians until the fourth century A.D. Then, when their faith was elevated to the rank of state religion, Christians in turn persecuted those who rejected official interpretations of Christian doctrine. Even the Sassanids, who claimed descent from Darius, failed to practice tolerance. They countered Roman-sponsored Christianity with Sassanid-sponsored Zoroastrianism. However, the Muslim Arabs who came to power in the seventh century A.D. relied on toleration as a principle of government as much as on the threefold division of both provincial and central affairs into departments of state, war, and finance.

Long centuries of foreign dominance scarcely affected the daily lives of Middle Eastern villagers, who continued to think and act much as before. The establishment and maintenance of orderly imperial government had more effect on cities and on the merchants, sailors, and camel nomads involved in the internal and external trade of the Middle East. Indian Ocean trade enabled the people of Yemen to construct the high Marib dam that provided water for their fields for a thousand years, and enriched way-stations like Mecca on the route to the Fertile Crescent.

However, the volume of traffic across Arabia fell off in the sixth century A.D., when the introduction of the silkworm into the Byzantine or Eastern Roman empire lessened dependence on China for the silken fabrics desired by the wealthy. The loss of trade proved disastrous to Arabian merchants. During the same century the Marib dam collapsed, probably from lack of maintenance, disrupting the life of the peninsula still further as homeless villagers and townspeople from the south became herders and moved into the interior.

ARABS, PERSIANS, TURKS, AND MONGOLS
(7TH TO 14TH CENTURIES A.D.)

FORMATION AND EXPANSION OF THE ISLAMIC STATE: MUHAMMAD AND HIS SUCCESSORS (622–661). After 600 A.D. the cities of western Arabia were caught between warring Romans and Sassanids to the north, unsubservient camel nomads to the east, and a new Sassanid-dominated regime to the south. Only Mecca with its widely revered shrine of the Kaaba (then dedicated to the moon-god) still ruled itself; and its leading tribe, the Quraish, was split by cutthroat commercial competition. Then a member of the lesser Hashimite clan of the Quraish, Muhammad, began to call on Meccans to submit to God's commands and live in peaceful community with all others who accepted them. Few heeded him at first. The dominant Umayyad clan of the Quraish opposed him, for his doctrine of one God Whose true worship was right living could endanger their income from pilgrims to the Kaaba. After being invited to come to his mother's city of Medina to make peace between its quarreling inhabitants, he left Mecca in 622. His political acumen soon made him undisputed leader in Medina and its environs, while the reinterpretation of the Kaaba as a symbol of the oneness of God reconciled the Umayyads to him before his death in 632.

Confusion reigned for a time after Muhammad's death. In the end, however, the leading Muslims of Medina chose as *khalifa* (caliph), or successor, an early Quraish convert and close associate of Muhammad. He soon extended the community of the faithful to include all Arabia. As the precepts of Islam halted intertribal raiding (always important for supplementing income and relieving boredom), growing restiveness led to the capture of Roman Palestine, Syria, and Egypt and to the overthrow of the Sassanids of Iran and Mesopotamia under his successor. The soldiers of the third caliph, the Umayyad leader Uthman (644–656), expanded the Muslim domains into Tripolitania and Armenia, and raided as far as Tunisia and Afghanistan.

The first three caliphs were chosen in accustomed Arab fashion by the recognized leading men of the Islamic community. After a band of dissatisfied Arabs assassinated Uthman, however, the choice of the fourth caliph was affected by traditional respect for ties of blood and a widening acquaintance with Roman and Sassanid practice. At the insistence of Arab garrisons in Egypt and Iraq (as the Arabs called Mesopotamia), the mantle of the prophet was given to Ali, cousin to Muhammad, husband to his daughter Fatima, and father of his only descendants. Ali promptly moved the capital from Medina to Iraq, where he had been governor for years.

The selection of Ali was not universally accepted. Many suspected him of involvement in Uthman's death. Others resented his preferment of the Quraish to other Arabs. Some convinced themselves that he betrayed the principle of submission to God's will when he offered to accept human arbitration of a quarrel between himself and Muawiya, the Umayyad governor of Syria and a close relative of Uthman. A number of the resentful Arabs formed a party called the Kharijites, or Seceders. Their revolt in 659 failed, but one of them assassinated Ali two years later. Muawiya had already been proclaimed caliph in 660 by his supporters in Syria. Ali's elder son Hasan was accepted as caliph in Iraq, but Hasan was uninterested in government and readily accepted a pension from Muawiya. By the end of 661 there was again only one caliph in Islam.

CONSOLIDATION, EXPANSION, AND STRIFE: UMAYYADS, ABBASIDS, FATI-MIDS, AND TURKS (661–1090s). When Muawiya established Damascus as his capital, the elective caliphate ended and the first great hereditary Muslim dynasty began. True to the principles of the caliphate's Arab tribal background, no set rule like primogeniture was recognized either by the Umayyads or by most other Muslim dynasties. Instead, the ruler (who had to be male) usually designated a specific son or brother as his successor. If he failed to do so, or if something happened to the one selected, the eldest male among his sons or brothers usually succeeded; but there was much opportunity for palace intrigue to affect the succession.

The first four caliphs had simply left most of the previous Roman and Sassanid officials in their posts and put Arabs in the highest positions. Persecution almost disappeared as Muhammad's principle of toleration for all who lived by a scriptural revelation was put into practice, but the burden of taxation was placed entirely on the tolerated Christians, Jews, and Zoroastrians—the "People of a Book," *dhimmi* (protected) but subordinate and weaponless, like the oasis-dwelling clients of a desert tribe. Muawiya and his successors soon found that the simple distinction between tax-paying dhimmis and tax-free Muslims needed rethinking. Cultivated land was rapidly being removed from the tax rolls, as Arab Muslims acquired agricultural land and local non-Muslim landowners became converts to Islam. Eventually, all cultivated land was taxed, but the dhimmis were required to pay a head tax in addition to the land tax.

The early Umayyads also overhauled the legal system. New courts with Muslim judges were established throughout the empire, primarily to apply Muslim law to Muslims. The dhimmis were formally recognized as being under the jurisdiction of the leaders of their religious communities, coming into Muslim courts only when the case in question involved a Muslim. This system of separate courts for each religious group, like differential taxation and Muslim monopolization both of military force and of high administrative posts, continued to be a cornerstone of Islamic polity throughout the centuries which followed.

The Umayyads divided the empire into the capital district of Syria and five great viceroyalties: lower Iraq and Iran, upper Iraq and Armenia, Arabia, Egypt, and the Maghrib (as the Arabs called northern Africa west of the Nile valley). Each viceroyalty was divided into provinces whose governors and garrison commanders were made responsible to the viceroy. The caliph retained the authority to send into the provinces tax collectors who were directly responsible to him, not to a viceroy.

The reshaping of the administration was accompanied by shifts in language and religious affiliation. By 700, Arabic was replacing Greek and Persian for governmental communication. Arabic speech eventually prevailed from the Maghrib to Iraq. Only the Berbers, Armenians, Kurds, and Iranians continued to regard it as merely a second language, and only the Armenians, a scattering of other Christians in Egypt and the Levant, and the Jews refused to accept the Muslim faith of their rulers.

After 700, Muawiya's successors extended Umayyad rule to northwest Africa and Spain, Afghanistan, the steppes of Turkestan, and the Indus valley. This external expansion was accompanied by internal strife, as old tribal feuds resurfaced among the Arabs, while non-Arab converts rebelled against the client status in which the Arabs sought to keep them. Both Arabs and non-Arabs turned against the Umayyads, some as Kharijites striving to re-establish an elective caliphate, some as Shiites or Partisans supporting the claims of Muhammad's descendants through Ali. The Abbasids, descendants of Muhammad's uncle, took advantage of the spreading discontent to fan revolt in Iraq and Iran. In 750 the last Umayyad caliph was overthrown. The new Abbasid caliphate promptly moved the capital from Syria to Iraq, where the city of Baghdad was built shortly after 760.

The shift of the capital marked the growth of Iranian or Persian influence in the Muslim community. Court ceremonial increased, and slave officials drawn from the newly conquered and converted Turks began to exercise authority. However, no Abbasid caliph was ever recognized as ruler from the Pyrenees to the Indus. One of the vanquished Umayyads escaped to found an independent line of rulers in Spain, which lasted until the Christian reconquest of central Spain overwhelmed it in 1031. By 800 the Maghrib was turning Shiite and gravitating toward the Spanish Umayyads. In the mid-ninth century the newly converted peoples of the Indus valley, Afghanistan, and Turkestan went their separate ways, though the Turkish Ghaznawids reunited them briefly in the early eleventh century. Iran too was lost. From 945 to 1055 the Shiite Buwayhids of western Iran even controlled Baghdad, and with it the Abbasid caliph—an ironic position for the supposed leader of the orthodox Muslim community, for by then the Shiites gave such devotion to Ali and his descendants that they were distinct from the orthodox majority theologically as well as politically. During the Buwayhid era, in 969, the Abbasids lost Egypt to the Shiite dynasty of the self-proclaimed Fatimid caliphs, who continued to contest the claims of the Abbasids until they themselves were overthrown in 1171.

By the time the orthodox Seljuk Turks drove the Buwayhids from Baghdad in 1055, the Abbasid caliph was only a figurehead. The Seljuks quickly overran the lands from the Levant to Afghanistan and conquered much of Byzantine Anatolia, which had long been under Muslim attack. In the process they forced the Ghaznawids to concentrate on northwest India. However, the Seljuks soon fell to quarreling among themselves. This squabbling helped to enable crusading western Europeans to capture much of the Levant when the Byzantine emperor invited them to recover Anatolia from the Seljuks.

THE VICTORY OF ORTHODOX ISLAM: CRUSADERS, SHIITES, SUNNITES, AND MONGOLS (11TH to 14TH CENTURIES). The Crusaders of the 1090s were eager to carry the reconquest of formerly Christian lands to the eastern end of the Mediterranean. Western Europe had been greatly encouraged by the success of Christian campaigns in Spain in the 1030s, and by the recovery of Sicily in the 1070s after more than two centuries of Muslim rule. However, the Crusaders' successes in the Levant were short-lived. In the late twelfth century the orthodox Salah ad-Din (Saladin), a Kurd, became determined to root out heretic rule in the center of the Islamic world. To that end he overthrew decaying Fatimids in 1171, seized Jerusalem in 1187, and soon confined the Crusaders to a few coastal towns. His heirs were replaced in 1250 by their largely Turkish slaves the Mamluks (*mamluk* means "possessed"), who expelled the last Crusaders in 1291 and reigned until 1517 in a succession which was determined more by force and intrigue than by blood ties.

The defeat of the Fatimids and the Crusaders was not the only demonstration of orthodox strength. In northwest Africa, Shiites along the coast lost their grip on the interior during the eleventh century, as plundering Arab nomads expelled from Fatimid Egypt laid waste the settlements. Soon puritanical orthodox movements among the Berbers south of the Atlas overthrew the coastal rulers and destroyed the last remnants of Shiite influence. The victorious Berbers united northwest Africa with Muslim Spain in 1091, but resurgent Christian forces drove them back to the Maghrib in 1235. Shortly thereafter the few remaining Muslims of Spain were confined to the southeast corner of the peninsula, and in 1492 their last stronghold was overrun. However, the Muslim loss of Spain and Portugal was counterbalanced by the conversion of much of the region south of the Sahara to orthodox Islam after 1050. The victory of orthodoxy in the Maghrib was complete. Even when a descendant of Muhammad established the Sharifian dynasty of Morocco in the seventeenth century, it was not Shiite. Indeed, after the Fatimids fell in 1171 the only major strongholds left to the Shiites were Iran and lower Iraq, where Shia Islam had begun with the support given Muhammad's son-in-law Ali as the rightful heir to the caliphate.

Shia Iran and Iraq soon fell into the hands of the Mongols, who entered Turkestan in 1220 and Afghanistan in 1221 under their first great leader, Genghis Khan. His successors ravaged Iran, Armenia, and Iraq, decimating the population and destroying a number of the irrigation networks that had supported agricultural prosperity for thousands of years. They also put an end to the Abbasid caliphate when they entered Baghdad in 1258, and forced the Seljuks of Rum (Rome), as the Muslims called Anatolia, to acknowledge Mongol overlordship. Only the Mamluks stood firm, preventing the Mongols from establishing themselves on the Mediterranean. By the mid-fourteenth century the Mongols had declined in strength and fierceness, but they held onto Turkestan until the late fifteenth century and a few decades later moved from Turkestan to India as the Persianized Mughal dynasty. The collapse of Mongol rule left the field almost entirely to leaders of Turkish origin: the Mamluks of Egypt and the Levant; the Turkomans of western Iran, Armenia, and Iraq; and the deteriorating Seljuks of Rum, in whose western domains the new and dynamic Osmanli or Ottoman state was growing.

THE OTTOMAN ERA (14TH TO 18TH CENTURIES A.D.)

The bitter Seljuk-Byzantine warfare of the early thirteenth century and the decline of Seljuk authority in Mongol times led to the establishment of autonomous frontier warrior states along the Byzantine border, of which that of Osman or Othman (c. 1290–1326) proved most stable and enduring. As the closest warrior state to Constantinople, it attracted only the bravest of the warriors who flocked to Anatolia to escape disturbed conditions in Mongol-held regions. Osman's son facilitated the absorption of conquered areas by carefully maintaining the traditional toleration of Christians and Jews as long as they paid the required taxes, and encouraged artisans and merchants to come to his state and form guilds to serve its needs. By 1389 the Ottomans held most of the formerly Byzantine and Seljuk territory from the Danube to central Anatolia. Thereafter, they continued to hammer at the remnants of the Byzantine empire and finally captured Constantinople in 1453. They promptly re-named the city Istanbul and moved their capital there.

In the next few decades the Ottomans adopted the old Persian system of making the governor, military commander, and financial ad-ministrator of each province separately responsible to the ruler. To fill these and other posts, they expanded the century-old *yenicheri* (new troops) or Janissary system, under which part of the periodic tribute from non-Muslim provinces was taken in young boys who were taught the precepts of Islam and trained for the Ottoman army. In the new Janissary system, the boys were prepared for either a military or an ad-ministrative career, in accord with their capabilities, but they were still formally regarded as slaves of the head of the Ottoman state, the sultan. The Ottomans also established the *millet* or community system, under which the head of each non-Muslim religious group was formally granted jurisdiction over temporal as well as spiritual matters among his people. Among the Muslims of the empire, the Shaikh al-Islam, or head of the learned scholars of Islam, was chosen by the sultan to pronounce judg-ment on cases tried in Muslim courts and to issue advisory statements concerning actions of the Ottoman civil and military administration. Such cases as were not handled in the various religious courts were left to the civil administrators' courts.

Two thousand years before, a broadly similar system had prevailed in the Persian empire, even to the placing of the lives of officials at the disposal of the ruler. Like the Persian system, that of the Ottomans worked excellently as long as the head of the state paid close attention to governmental matters and was experienced enough in the arts of war and peace to judge the reliability of conflicting reports. However, after the sixteenth century, control fell largely into the hands of the court favorites who made and unmade sultans almost at will.

As the sixteenth century opened, the Ottomans were challenged by the militantly Shiite dynasty of the Safawids in Iran, who claimed descent from Ali. Fearing the possibility of a Mamluk-Safawid alliance, the Ottomans used their new artillery to seize the Mamluk territories in the Levant and Egypt in 1516 and 1517. They also conquered Iraq and brought Hungary into the sphere of Ottoman influence for a time. In addition, they began receiving tribute from the states of coastal north-west Africa, whose rulers shared their desire to harass the Mediterranean fleets of the European powers. Even western Arabia acknowledged Otto-man overlordship. However, by the seventeenth century Ottoman claims to authority in the Arab world were frequently disregarded, as local notables from Cairo to Lebanon and Baghdad wrested the substance of authority from Ottoman appointees. After the Portuguese pointed the way around Africa to Europeans, commercial activity shifted from the Mediterranean routes to those leading to the Atlantic. The consequent decline in the once-thriving trade with European merchants impoverished commercial cities from Iraq to Egypt. Loss of trade revenues forced governments to fall back on land revenues, which weighed heavily on the villagers. At the same time the villagers were increasingly plagued by the nomads, who turned to raiding when the caravan trade slackened. In some districts like Egypt and northern Syria, disease and malnutrition cut the rural population to a fraction of its former size. The population of Iraq had already declined after the destruction of irrigation works by the Mongols. Even in the Ottoman heartland of the Anatolian basin, where there was less brigandage than in the Arab lands, peasants and townspeople were less prosperous in the eighteenth century than their ancestors had been in the sixteenth. By the end of the eighteenth century the Ottoman empire was in a state of near collapse.

Iran, Afghanistan, and Morocco were scarcely better off than the Ottoman empire in 1800. Iran had challenged the Ottomans after 1500, but the Ottoman conquest of the Mamluk domains and Iraq had confined the Safawids of Iran to the immediate vicinity of the Iranian plateau. Though their vigorous proselytization made Iran overwhelmingly Shiite, they failed to persuade their dependents in neighboring Turkestan and Afghanistan to turn away from orthodox Islam. Soon they were in peril from their neighbors, as court luxury and intrigue resulted in the succession of increasingly inept rulers. In the eighteenth century the Safawids were elbowed aside by orthodox Afghans and by Turkomans. The final victors were the Turkoman Qajars, who ruled as Shiites. The Afghans kept their independence after losing their last footholds in Iran, and in 1800 controlled much the same area which the Ghaznawids had held after the rise of the Seljuks. At the other extreme of the Middle East, the Sharifians of Morocco were plagued by Berber uprisings as the nineteenth century opened, for the Berbers disliked the Sharifians' reliance on the Arab tribes and their policy of replacing Berber customary law with the Muslim religious law used by most Middle Easterners.

The only exception to the general trend toward local lawlessness in the late eighteenth century was central and eastern Arabia, previously a hotbed of local strife but now being pacified by the Saudi family. Inspired by a new Muhammad, the puritanical reformer Muhammad ibn al-Wahhab, the Saudis welded the tribes together in an enthusiastic demand for religious reform throughout the Muslim world. However, they were prevented from expanding in the early nineteenth century by the governor of Egypt, who had been assiduously adopting western European military weapons, instructors, and discipline despite the opposition of those accustomed to traditional beliefs and practices.

Thought–Patterns: Islam in Theory and Practice

EARLY MIDDLE EASTERN RELIGIONS AND ISLAM

Almost all early Middle Eastern religions shared a belief that there were many deities, each personifying some aspect of the visible world. However, the belief in many nature-deities began to fade after 1000 B.C. On the Iranian plateau, where the forces of fire and the sun had long been revered, the teacher Zoroaster combined a number of familiar ideas into a new religion in the sixth century B.C. His followers worshiped only the god of light, Ahura-Mazda, who is locked in combat with Ahriman, the god of darkness and evil. Since both Ahura-Mazda and Ahriman are supported by hosts of followers, men and women are not mere suppliants whose only hope lies in propitiating one or the other. Instead, they can actually aid the cause of good and orderliness—or that of evil and confusion. Zoroaster's clear call to moral effort appealed not only to Iranians but also to Mesopotamians who were beginning to question the familiar nature myths; but Zoroastrianism did not become the dominant faith throughout Iran and Mesopotamia until Sassanid times.

While Zoroastrian beliefs were spreading from Iran, Semitic monotheism—the rootstock of Judaism, Christianity, and Islam—was taking shape in the Levant. Even before the Babylonian captivity in the sixth century B.C., which exposed the Hebrew prophets to the currents of thought of Zoroaster's time, they proclaimed that the God of Israel is the only God, the Creator of the entire universe, Who sees everything from the standpoint of eternity and Whose omniscience appears to time-bound human beings to be foreknowledge. God's creation of the universe endows it with a certain reality, but only temporarily, for both the universe and its human inhabitants have only one life. Each human being is fashioned in God's image, embodying those divine attributes which can survive the transition from the scale of eternity to that of time. Thus it is in human nature both to follow and to disobey the rules which God laid down for the universe at its creation, for both eternal and temporal elements are mingled in humanity.

Semitic monotheism was influenced by Egyptian as well as Zoroastrian concepts. The Egyptians believed in a life after death whose character is determined by one's earthly deeds. The influence of this belief is as evident in Christianity and Islam, with their strong emphasis on the final judgment of one's deeds at the end of the created world, as is the Zoroastrian insistence on one's responsibility to strive for goodness against evil. However, Christianity and Islam diverge on the question of how to regulate one's conduct. In Christianity, a small number of broad principles are stressed, and the interpretation of specific rules tends to be somewhat flexible. In Islam, as in orthodox Judaism, a comparatively large number of specific rules are given and their interpretation tends to be flexible only within rather narrow limits.

Despite their differences, Jews, Christians, and Muslims all share a firm belief that God has revealed how human beings should act in order to take their proper place in the universe. They have also contributed to scientific study of the universe, for they have shared the beliefs expressed in the book of Genesis that the first man was given dominion over all other living things (Genesis 1 : 26–28) and that he was told to name all living creatures (Genesis 2 : 19–20). To name them, of course, he had to distinguish them from each other, and the process of making distinctions is the beginning of scientific inquiry. In addition, Jews, Christians, and Muslims have held human beings in such esteem as images of God that the worship of deities in nonhuman form has been effectively destroyed. Nature deities may still be worshiped under the guise of Christian saints and Muslim mystics who are believed to intervene in everyday affairs. However, when they or ordinary men and women appear in nonhuman form in the popular myths and legends of the Middle East, it is generally assumed that some malevolent force has been at work.

Christianity gradually replaced or absorbed the earlier religions of the Mediterranean basin during the first five centuries of the Christian era, while Zoroastrianism was becoming the popular faith of Iran and Mesopotamia. Although these developments affected Arabia only marginally, Zoroastrian, Jewish, and Christian merchants made the Arabs somewhat familiar with the precepts of their respective faiths. The religious upheaval of the seventh century A.D. could therefore draw on ideas which were already subjects of lively speculation. Muhammad always declared that he was carrying on the work of revelation begun in the time of Abraham and continued by the Hebrew prophets and Jesus.

Muhammad instructed his followers that all deeds are to be classified as required, encouraged, permissible, discouraged, or forbidden. In two of the required actions, the duties of daily prayer and of abstinence from food and pleasures during the daylight hours of the sacred month of Ramadan, the believer approaches God in humility; in two others, the duties of almsgiving to needy Muslims and of pilgrimage to the shrine of the Kaaba at Mecca, the believer is brought close to fellow-Muslims. The failure to perform any of these duties will be punished at the time of judgment, unless the believer can plead illness or some other acceptable reason like participation in *jihad,* or holy war against the foes of Islam. Together with the profession of faith, "There is no God but God, and Muhammad is His Prophet," the four duties form the five pillars of Islam.

Other actions, such as jihad, are desirable for salvation but not essential. Their performance will be rewarded in the life to come, but failure to perform them is not punished. A third set of actions, such as marrying or not marrying, is neither rewarded nor punished, being of neutral effect in the struggle for righteousness. The commission of acts such as theft or adultery will be punished, though abstinence from them is not rewarded. The final category is that of deeds such as refusal to believe in God, which are so reprehensible that not only are they punished, but the one who does not commit them is commended and rewarded.

The content of these five categories of actions was clarified in the generations following Muhammad by reference to the Quran, the record of his inspired recitings, and to his ordinary words and actions, the Sunna or practice of Muhammad as described by his companions. In the first years of Islam, the Quran and Sunna provided the Muslim community with its legal code, the Sharia. Since it was soon apparent that the Quran and Sunna did not specifically cover every situation, the principle of analogy came into use. An example of analogy is the argument that the Quran's disapproval of wine extends to all intoxicating beverages. It also came to be widely assumed that when the community of believers, the *umma*, agreed upon a rule of action, the rule should be accepted as valid. This principle of consensus permitted non-Arab peoples like the Berbers to retain many customary practices after conversion to Islam. Moreover, matters like criminal and commercial cases, which directly affected the public peace, were soon put under the jurisdiction of state courts. However, every Muslim government was expected to be guided by the principles of the Sharia. Learned jurists, or *ulama*, applied the rules of the Sharia to Muslims in their personal lives, and pronouncements by leading jurists like the Ottoman Shaikh al-Islam could materially affect the course of events. It was by analogy with the practice of the Sharia that the other Peoples of a Book (Jews, Christians, and Zoroastrians) were expected to have their own court system.

INTELLECTUAL, LEGAL, AND POLITICAL INSTITUTIONS

In the early period of Islamic expansion, as Muslims seized the Hellenized cities of Syria, Egypt, Iraq, and Iran, leading Muslim thinkers became acquainted with Greek speculations on the nature of the universe. Intoxicated with Greek rationalism, some sought to make reason a source of law. However, the orthodox suspected them of claiming that the finite human mind could fully comprehend the infinite God by purely intellectual processes, and successfully confined the sources of law to the Quran, Sunna, analogy, and consensus. Philosophical speculation continued, but consensus was made to operate cumulatively in the world of philosophy as well as in law; once an apparent consensus was reached, it was not to be questioned. The heterodox Shiite community, with its strong reverence for Ali and his descendants, even rejected the principle of consensus in favor of a belief in the continuing ability of its *imams*, or leaders, to reinterpret the meaning of the Islamic law.

As the realm in which speculation was permissible diminished, the center of creative thinking shifted from the Muslim world to western Europe. The brilliant attainments of earlier centuries, when Iranians, Syrians, Spaniards, and other newly converted peoples were striving to harmonize their new faith with the legacy of the past, were not matched despite the support given to scholarship by *waqfs*, or pious endowments. Instead, the reconquest of Spain and Sicily brought Muslim interpretations of Greek and Roman thought to the attention of western Europeans, who promptly began seeking ways to reconcile them with their own concepts.

The wealthy donor who established a waqf or endowment to benefit the community usually dedicated a piece of income-producing real estate to the waqf and chose as administrator a family member whose descendants would continue to maintain the endowed fountain or hospital or school. As time passed, the establishment of waqfs removed large amounts of property from the realm of buying and selling, for waqfs were and still are regarded as sacred and perpetual. Even today the boldest step any Muslim country has taken with respect to them has been to put them under government rather than private administration, a practice for which there are some early precedents.

Waqfs enabled the community of scholars in Islam to be truly international, traveling freely from Herat in Afghanistan to Cordova and Timbuktu. True, the interchange between Shiite and Sunnite scholars diminished after Saladin transformed the Fatimids' al-Azhar in Cairo into a strictly orthodox university. However, both Sunnites and Shiites continued to regard the Sharia code as divinely inspired.

The application of the Sharia was attuned to the principle of justice, the upholding of the innocent against the guilty, as completely as the application of Roman law and its European descendants—but only to justice for the Muslim. The body politic was not united under one law as in the Roman empire, but divided between the Muslims' Sharia courts and the religious courts of the dhimmis. Though governmental decrees were applied to all in the state courts, the influence of the Muslim code, which attributed a protected but inferior status to non-Muslims and to women, tended to lower the position of these two groups in the eyes of the public magistrate, who was invariably Muslim.

Ordinarily, Muslims also had more chances to rise socially and politically than non-Muslims. Rulers took men of all backgrounds into their service as warriors and administrators; guilds took apprentices from outside the families of members. Free men could always advance themselves by acquiring learning or by displaying military ability. Women of all ranks might be brought into a ruler's household. However, Muslim rulers tended to prefer to use slaves, whose ties with their families of origin were broken by the fact of slavery and who could be prevented from having legitimate heirs either by being made eunuchs or by being forbidden to contract legal marriages. The history of the later Ottomans shows the wisdom of such provisions in a family-conscious society, for the efficiency of the Janissaries began to decline as soon as they were allowed to enroll their sons in the corps in the late sixteenth century. Thus the merchant's wealth was far less effective as a political and social force in the Middle East than it was in the Europe of Mamluk and Ottoman days. The use of slaves also weakened the power of those who claimed pride of place because they were descended from conquering Arabs or Turks, from pre-Islamic dignitaries, or even from Muhammad. Birth might strongly affect social position, but it did not completely determine status and occupation. The Middle East seemed to be organized into hereditary groups because of the stratification of society into religious, linguistic, and occupational groupings which reflected early training. Nevertheless, except in royal dynasties and nomad tribes, considerations of birth ordinarily remained secondary.

The ruler who used slaves as administrators did not have to reckon with independent nobles or free townsmen in governing his domains. The only two checks on his authority were an appeal to the Sharia and a flat refusal to obey his commands—both risky, since he might respond by removing the objector. In these circumstances, political thinkers in the Middle East tended to stress the rights of the ruler and the duties of the subject (rather than the ruler's duties and the subjects' rights, as in western Europe).

During the Islamic era, Middle Easterners of all faiths became accustomed to seeing themselves not only as part of a divine plan but also as governed on earth by what Muslim law said relations between people of different religions should be. They also continued to accept martial prowess as a paramount characteristic of the ruler. For five thousand years, scarcely a decade had passed without warfare. The homogeneity of language, religion, and settled outlook that bound monarchs and people together in western Europe was rare in the Middle East, where mountains sheltered diverse linguistic and religious groups and deserts protected the independence of the camel nomad. The resulting need for a strong and loyal army to hold the state together placed its commander so high in state councils that he was usually regarded as the logical candidate for leadership if the ruler faltered. It has therefore been natural for military men to continue to play significant roles in the recent period of transition to the ways of modern life.

The Modern Era: The Northern Tier

THE CAPITULATORY REGIME
(12TH TO 19TH CENTURIES A.D.)

Within a century of Muhammad's death, his followers began to clash with western Europeans in both Spain and France. The first effective western European counterattacks came in the eleventh century, when central Spain, Sicily, and, for a short time, the Levant fell into Christian hands. In Spain and Sicily the western Europeans learned more than they taught, but in the Levant their methods of fortification were eagerly studied by Muslim military engineers and commanders until their expulsion in 1291.

Behind the military shield of the Crusaders, Italian merchants acquired control over the trade between Europe and the Levant. Muslim governments extended the principle of self-rule in private concerns, already applied to their Christian and Jewish subjects, to the Venetians and others who came to trade in their cities. They also granted favorable conditions to encourage the growth of revenue-producing commerce. To retain its share of trade, Byzantine Constantinople gave the Italians similar privileges, which were continued by the Ottomans. The treaties which defined the Italians' position were called capitulations, after the capitulae or chapter-headings in the documents.

After the Portuguese and Spaniards drove the last Muslim rulers from western Europe, they sought to outflank their opponents in northwest Africa and to wrest control of the trade with Asia from the Italian city-states and the Mamluks. The arrivals of Columbus in the Americas in 1492 and Da Gama in India in 1498 opened up new trade routes, whose use soon diminished Mediterranean-Middle Eastern trade. Once the Portuguese seized Hormuz at the mouth of the Persian Gulf in 1507, the sea-borne trade of Persia and Iraq was at their mercy. Though the Venetians aided the Mamluks against them, the Portuguese also seized Socotra near the mouth of the Red Sea. With these bases and others on the African, Indian, and Malayan coasts, the Portuguese became masters of the Indian Ocean. When the Ottomans conquered the weakened Mamluks in 1517, they tried but failed to break the Portuguese stranglehold. Muslim traders could not freely sail the Indian Ocean again until 1622, when the Safawids of Persia used English aid to expel the declining Portuguese from the Persian Gulf.

The profit in overseas trade led other European states to seek their own commercial routes and centers in the Middle East and beyond. The French signed a treaty of friendship and commerce with the Ottomans in 1536. In 1581 the English founded the Levant Company to compete with the French. Soon the Dutch also challenged French leadership. In time, the English, Dutch, and others won the privileges afforded by the capitulatory system to French and Venetian traders. However, the French retained control of the Mediterranean trade, making full use of the favor shown them by the quasi-independent rulers of Lebanon from the seventeenth century onward. Only in Persia and Iraq could the English use their Indian bases to take a leading role. They carried the system of capitulations developed in the sixteenth-century Ottoman empire to Safawid Persia in the seventeenth. The capitulations also came into use in the autonomous dependencies of the Ottomans in northwest Africa, and eventually in Morocco, whose ruler negotiated commercial treaties with Western powers in the late eighteenth century.

While the Atlantic seaboard states were penetrating the Middle East commercially, the Austrians were marching into the Balkans, and the Russians were expanding along the shores of both the Ottoman-ruled Black Sea and the Persian-controlled Caspian. As Ottoman and Persian weakness became visible to Europeans, they took advantage of it by expanding the capitulatory system. In 1740, the Ottomans granted the French far-reaching privileges in return for French diplomatic aid in dealing with Austria and Russia. Henceforth, French subjects could only be arrested in the presence of the French consul and could only be tried in French consular courts under French law. They could travel and trade throughout the Ottoman domains, while paying only a small ad valorem import and export duty. Since the French could also sell their commercial privileges to Ottoman subjects, the Ottomans soon ceased to receive much revenue from foreign trade. The further provision that France must agree to any changes in tariffs made it almost impossible for the Ottomans to raise tariffs, either for revenue or to protect local producers. In addition, local Roman Catholics like the Maronites of Lebanon were to have the same privileges as the French. Similar privileges were granted the British and others. By 1800 this expanded capitulatory system was also in use in Persia and Morocco. Large sections of the urban population quickly found ways to register themselves at foreign consulates as foreign nationals or protégés entitled to tax exemptions and the use of consular courts, which seriously weakened the authority of Ottoman, Persian, and Moroccan officials.

The Ottomans continued to turn to France for support and assistance until the rising young general Napoleon Bonaparte sought to improve France's Mediterranean position by invading Egypt in 1798, on the pretext of aiding the sultan to suppress the insolent descendants of the Mamluks. Ottoman and British forces compelled the French to withdraw within three years. However, the French left behind plans for education and economic development which so impressed the new Ottoman governor that he invited them to return to Egypt as his advisers. They also recovered much of their old position at Istanbul.

Napoleon's activities in Egypt so alarmed the British that they promptly sought control over the foreign relations of Aden at the mouth of the Red Sea and Oman at the mouth of the Persian Gulf. In addition, the British persuaded the new Qajar dynasty in Persia to follow their lead rather than that of France, and supported Persia against Russia. Then, as Russian advances into Ottoman territory continued, France sought to join Britain in supporting the Ottomans against Russia, even though France itself sent troops to Lebanon in 1860 to protect the Maronites under the capitulations. The Ottomans granted Lebanon full autonomy the next year, and the French left, but the Franco-British partnership remained an uneasy one.

THE OTTOMAN EMPIRE AND TURKEY

REFORM BY DECREE (1720–1877). Although fears of Russian and French expansion led Britain to support the Ottomans consistently during the nineteenth century, the Ottoman state could scarcely have survived if its leaders had not striven to alter with the times. In the early sixteenth century the Ottomans had become the first Middle Easterners to adopt a major innovation, the use of artillery, from modern Europe. Eventually they also became the first to begin adapting the institutions of the nation-state.

Austrian and Russian victories after 1690 convinced a few that the traditional Ottoman system needed alterations based on Western models. In 1720 a special Ottoman emissary to France was instructed to inspect French fortresses and factories. In 1731 a description of the Westernization program of Peter the Great of Russia was presented to the court, but the Sharia jurists, or ulama, opposed the new ideas so strongly that few changes were actually instituted. By the time Napoleon invaded Egypt in 1798, continuing Ottoman defeats had brought most Ottoman governmental leaders to agree that Western military institutions should be wholeheartedly adopted. Nevertheless, some still felt it wise to evade ulama disapproval by claiming they were only restoring familiar Ottoman institutions to their pristine vigor. The sultan reorganized the council of state; encouraged schools and a printing press; established permanent embassies in London, Paris, Berlin, and Vienna where young Ottomans could observe Western life firsthand; and began to drill and equip a small force in western European fashion. In 1807 the Janissaries rebelled to protest the new force. The ulama, led by the Shaikh al-Islam, promptly blamed the sultan's innovations for the revolt, and he was dethroned. His successor was soon overthrown by palace intrigues and a cousin enthroned as Mahmud II (1808–1839).

Mahmud II immediately began to establish a European-trained military force which brought unruly Iraq and eastern Anatolia back under effective Ottoman control and in 1826 destroyed the rebellious Janissaries. He also put great effort into recentralizing the Ottoman government and restoring its efficiency, for he saw that a strong government was needed to enforce the modernization essential to Ottoman survival. However, he was never strong enough to insist that the ulama reform their schools so that their students would learn something about the modern world. The new schools and colleges he opened formed an entirely separate system, and many who studied in them had neither contact nor sympathy with the ulama.

Fortunately for Mahmud II, the Shaikh al-Islam he appointed accepted his innovations. Nevertheless, he was concerned about the reactions of the Muslim religious confraternities, or *dervish* orders of religious devotees. The dervish orders practiced rites like singing or dancing, during which they entered an ecstatic state in which they felt themselves to be in communion with God. They were an outgrowth of Sufism, the great mystical strand of Islam, named for the *suf*, an undyed woolen garment worn by many early Muslim mystics to symbolize their noninvolvement in struggles for wealth and power. Such Sufi-influenced religious confraternities became important vehicles of popular religious expression in every portion of the Islamic world by 1400. Most of their members were lay people who returned to everyday life exhilarated by participation in the rites of the order; but as time passed, pious Muslims endowed each order with property administered by full-time members. To prevent the group of full-time dervishes who were closest to the Janissaries from avenging their destruction in 1826 by raising a popular revolt, Mahmud II transferred most of their order's property to governmental administration. However, the successful Greek rebellion of the 1820s and the challenge of the governor of Egypt to his power in the 1830s proved more frustrating to his plans than did the religious confraternities. When he died in 1839, Ottoman fortunes were at a low ebb despite his labors.

Mahmud II's successor proclaimed in 1839 that military conscription of a few men for life would be replaced by conscription of more men for a shorter period, and that government-paid tax collectors would replace the tax-farmers who squeezed as much as they could from the reluctant taxpayers and turned over as little as possible to the government. The objections of those who profited from the old order rendered the decrees largely ineffective. Nevertheless, in the next few years a new French-inspired penal code was introduced, the University of Istanbul was founded, and carefully chosen local assemblies were set up to curb the despotism of local governors.

An even more revolutionary decree was attached to the treaty that ended the Crimean War of 1854–1856, in which Britain, France, Austria, and Prussia aided the Ottomans against Russia. All distinctions among religious communities were abolished, except for the continuance of their respective personal legal codes. Muslims, Christians, and Jews were to be treated alike not only in state courts, but in tax assessment and in military conscription. However, the decree allowed anyone to purchase exemption or hire a substitute for military service. Many local officials maintained the traditional Muslim military monopoly by requiring non-Muslims to choose payment rather than conscription.

The 1856 attempt to remove age-long barriers between religious groups came too late to save the Ottoman empire from dissolution. Efforts to unite the empire by counteracting religious unrest were useless in the face of language-centered movements like Balkan and Arab nationalisms. Furthermore, as long as the capitulations continued, many of the most enterprising residents of the Ottoman state preferred registry as foreign nationals to Ottoman allegiance.

After 1856 the Ottomans began borrowing so lavishly from European bankers for public works and government expenses that they were in financial difficulty by 1875. Consequently, the European powers set up a multinational Ottoman Debt Administration at Istanbul in 1876 to oversee Ottoman finances and ensure the repayment of Ottoman debts to European creditors. To stave off the establishment of complete European control, the new sultan, Abd al-Hamid II (1876–1909; died 1918), reluctantly promulgated a parliamentary constitution based on French and Belgian models. However, as soon as the emergency of a new Russian war gave him an excuse, he suspended both parliament and constitution in 1877. They were not reinstituted until 1908.

With the suspension of the constitution, the era of reform by the initiative of the sultan reached its end. Since the time of Mahmud II, military training, uniforms, and equipment had been considerably modernized. An attempt had been made to abolish legal distinctions between Muslims and non-Muslims, as a step toward building a unified nation-state. However, the traditionalism of the ulama had scarcely been touched, and their schools continued to be separate from the few government military, technical, and professional schools. Henceforth it was the modernized military rather than a modernizing sultan who took the lead in pressing for further reforms.

REGROUPING AROUND THE MILITARY (1877–1923). Abd al-Hamid II's repressive measures alienated his subjects. He tried to counter disaffection by emphasizing the long-dormant claims of the Ottoman sultan to recognition as caliph, and by building railways from Anatolia southeast toward Baghdad and south to Damascus and Medina with German assistance. He also endorsed efforts to unify and strengthen Islam, such as the pan-Islamic movement of Jamal ad-Din al-Afghani, who spent a number of years in Istanbul. In 1889 a number of Istanbul students formed the secret Committee of Progress and Union, which tried but failed to overthrow the sultan in 1896. The leaders fled to Paris, but others founded new societies. One of these, the Fatherland Society of the young Turkish military officer Mustafa Kemal, fused with the Paris group in 1907 in the Committee of Union and Progress. In 1908 the new Committee's Young Turk supporters marched on Istanbul and forced Abd al-Hamid II to restore the constitution of 1876.

Unhappily for the Young Turks, they were not united behind one consistent program. At first they favored a unitary pan-Ottoman state. When Arabs sought a federation which would recognize the differences between Anatolia and Arab Asia, the Young Turks tried to use pan-Islam to bring the Arabs back into the fold. When Arabs began to organize their own anti-Turkish secret societies, some young Turks turned to pan-Turanianism, or the unity of all Turks. They seized on the chance to join Germany in war against Russia in 1914, as a means of uniting with Turks in the Caucasus and Turkestan in a great pan-Turanian state, only to find that Russia would not let its Turkic peoples go.

The Ottoman entry into World War I persuaded Britain to agree reluctantly that the Ottoman empire in Asia must finally be dissolved, as the Ottoman power in Europe and Africa had been dissolved between the Serbian revolt of the early 1800s and the loss of Libya in 1912. Agreements were reached by which Britain would administer the lands from Palestine to Iraq; France would take over Lebanon, Syria, and the part of Anatolia next to Syria; Russia would at last occupy the long-desired Straits; Italy would take southern coastal Anatolia; and Greece would receive western Anatolia with its large Greek population. Only the dry pastures of Arabia and central Anatolia went unclaimed.

When the Russians withdrew from the war after their 1917 revolutions, France and Britain repudiated the agreements letting Russia occupy the Straits. However, the Allies acted on their other agreements as soon as the war ended in 1918. Under the pressure of British, French, and Italian occupation of Istanbul, the sultan accepted a treaty in 1919 which deprived him of most of his lands. The Turks of Anatolia reacted furiously. Led by Mustafa Kemal, they set up a provisional government at Ankara in 1920. Ostensibly it was acting on behalf of the captive sultan, but gradually its members became convinced that a republican government would meet Turkish needs better than the sultanate. In 1922 the sultanate was abolished. By then Kemal had dashed Armenian hopes of independence, driven Greek troops from Anatolia, alarmed the Italians and persuaded the French into withdrawing, and convinced Britain that Turks could still guard the Straits. In 1923 a new treaty recognized Turkish rule over all of Anatolia and the Straits, and also abolished the hated capitulations. Turkey was declared a republic, with Kemal as its first president, and the next year the caliphate was repudiated.

THE TURKISH REPUBLIC (1923–1974). Mustafa Kemal and his followers set six goals for the Turks: republicanism, secularism, populism, nationalism, statism, and reformism. In 1924 the republic established a new constitution, abolished the Sharia courts, and assigned the management of all waqf properties to a minister of religious affairs whose major task was to prevent conservative religious leaders from interfering with his fellow-ministers' plans for modernization. The dervish orders were deprived of legal recognition soon afterward, and the European calendar was adopted in place of the Islamic one. In the next few years the populist goal of equal opportunity for all was promoted through new legal codes, based largely on Swiss models, which outlawed polygamy and gave women equal status with men. Everyone was required to have a family name, so that one Mahmud could be distinguished from another on tax lists or conscription rolls, and Mustafa Kemal was given a special surname by the legislature: Ataturk, or Father of the Turks. The Latin alphabet was adopted in place of the Arabic script, which may use three different forms for one letter, depending on its position in the word. This made it easier to read and write both Turkish and European languages, and effectively confined the study of Ottoman documents or Arabic and Persian literary classics to the highly educated. In 1934 the Turks became the first Middle Eastern people to give women the vote, and soon women began to be elected to the national legislature.

The Turks decided to forgo pan-Islam and pan-Turanianism, and to make their nation out of Anatolia and Istanbul, the region of Rum from which their Ottoman forebears had risen to power and glory. Having expelled almost all the Armenians from Anatolia by 1922, they arranged in 1923 to exchange the Greeks of western Anatolia for Turks living in Greece. Thereafter they shared Anatolia only with a few fellow-Muslim Kurds in the southeast. The Kurds rebelled in 1925, but the uprising was quickly quelled. Soon the establishment of universal military training brought Kurds into the mainstream of Turkish life as "mountain Turks." The greatness of the historical heritage of the peoples of Anatolia was emphasized, and Turkish words were substituted for borrowed Arabic and Persian terms. In the name of the fifth goal—statism or governmental encouragement of economic growth—an agricultural college and a number of model farms were established, banks were opened to finance and operate industries, transport facilities and electric utilities were nationalized and expanded, and profitable state monopolies in consumer goods were established. Finally, to promote reformism or the refusal to be attached to old ways, Ataturk and his companions made speech after speech to as many people as they could reach, explaining that one's earthly life was in one's own hands rather than in those of an overpowering fate and that the changes being made in Turkish life were needed if Turks and Turkey were to survive. Until his death in 1938 Ataturk's ideal remained a civilian government based on popular accept-ance, not a military dictatorship whose reforms could only be imposed and maintained by force.

Although World War II impeded Turkish economic improvement, educational growth, and political liberalization, the tempo of reform picked up once more after 1945. Turkey also allied itself with the United States, for protection against the territorial demands put forth at the end of World War II by the Soviet successors of the Russian empire. The first successful opposition party came into being, as the new Democratic Party challenged the Republican People's Party of Ataturk and his suc-cessors in 1946 and won a legislative majority in 1950. The Democrats used two major issues: urban dislike of state monopolies, and the vil-lagers' deep desire to express their strong Islamic faith more freely. As political leaders realized that secularizing laws had not eradicated re-ligious loyalties, they reopened the intense debate of the 1920s over the role of religion in Turkish life. However, where the question in the 1920s was how far the modernizers could go in controlling public religious expression—and they went very far indeed—the question in the 1950s was how far that control could be relaxed without endangering the new ideal of the nation-state. A number of Ataturk's restrictions were dropped, in-cluding the ban on religious instruction in the schools and religious pro-grams on the state radio network. Between 1950 and 1960 the Democrats extended schools, roads, electricity, and other means of connection with the outside world to increasing numbers of villages, bringing their people into the mainstream of national life, as Ataturk had envisioned. As an ally of the United States, Turkey mechanized its army, thereby promoting further change in Turkish villages as young men returning from military service brought greater familiarity with the machine age. When student demonstrators accused the Democrats of stifling opposition spokesmen through censorship in 1960, the army expelled the Democrats from office, claiming that their orders to quell the students ran counter to Ataturk's tradition of a nonpolitical army.

The army heads promised to withdraw from politics as soon as a new constitution could be enacted and new elections held. The subse-quent 1961 elections presented the Turks with their first experiment in coalition government, for no party had a legislative majority. The 1965 elections restored a single-party cabinet by giving a clear majority to the Justice Party, the effective successor to the outlawed Democratic Party. Many observers were relieved that the enforced departure of the Demo-crats from political life was not followed by decisive Republican victories. They believed that Turkey had avoided establishing a precedent for restoring a defeated party to power by military means, and hoped that the new government under the new constitution would be successful in promoting the well-being of Turkey's people. In 1969 the Justice Party won an even larger majority, but army dissatisfaction with the government's failure to control student opposition to the United States alliance led in 1971 to cabinet changes and imposition of martial law in several provinces. Concern over the treatment of the Turkish Muslim minority on newly independent Cyprus by the island's Greek Orthodox majority was also growing. In 1973 the voters gave the Republicans a plurality. After some hesitation, the Republicans embarked on the experiment of a coalition with the new National Salvation party, which called for continued social reform as an implementation of egalitarian Islamic teaching. A new plane had been reached in the continuing dialogue between the heirs of Kemal, both civilian and military, and the followers of the prophet Muhammad. When Turkey actively intervened on Cyprus in 1974 to prevent its possible absorption into Greece, both nationalists concerned for fellow Turks and believers concerned for fellow Muslims applauded their government's decision, and the Republicans sought new partners.

PERSIA—IRAN AND AFGHANISTAN

PERSIANS AND EUROPEANS (1622–1921). The Safawid shah or ruler of Persia used English military advisers and artillery to help him drive the Portuguese from the Persian Gulf in 1622. However, later shahs did not feel a need to turn to Europe for advice again until the nineteenth century, when the expanding Russian empire began taking over the Qajar dynasty's northern territories. French and British military missions were then brought in to train a standing army. Persian students were sent to Britain, a printing press was set up, and in the 1850s a technical institute staffed by European and Persian teachers was opened. As Russian power in Turkestan made the Qajars decide to cultivate Russian good will, Persians also went to Russia to study. The British began to fear that Persia would fall entirely under Russian domination, once Cossacks began to train units in the Persian army and Russian capital founded a leading bank in the Persian capital of Tehran. Nevertheless, British interests furnished Persia with its first telegraph system and its first regular steamship line, and in 1901 a British subject was permitted to explore for oil in all but the northernmost provinces.

While the Qajars promoted Western scientific and technical studies, their people became involved in the birth of a new religious movement. In 1844 a young merchant proclaimed himself the Bab or gateway to divine truth. He condemned the corrupt lives of many ulama, repudiated many traditional Shiite customs, and proclaimed that everyone, even women, should enjoy the same opportunities. Horrified traditionalists attacked his followers all over Persia. He and several others were executed, Babi teachings were outlawed, and many Babis went into exile. One of the exiled leaders modified the Babi tenets and won converts to the new Bahai movement on an international scale, from Palestine to Germany and the United States. However, other Babis remained in Persia, and their equalitarian ideas contributed greatly to later reform movements.

A more direct response to the challenge of Western power was the pan-Islamic movement of Jamal ad-Din al-Afghani. Al-Afghani first won attention in Kabul for his doctrine of the threefold need for Islamic unity, Islamic strength, and Islamic reinterpretation. He believed that nineteenth-century Muslim weakness resulted from the dead weight of nonessential traditions. Like the Wahhabis of Arabia, he wanted to purify Islam; but unlike them, he stated that Muslims could and should learn how to cleanse their faith by studying the way Christian tradition had been treated in the Reformation era. He also stated that even though all Muslims should work together to revive the caliphate and rebuild Islamic society, the immediate need was for some segment of the Islamic world to strengthen itself in comparison with Europe so that others could learn from its example. In this way he sought to reconcile pan-Islamic ideas with the ideas of nationalism which Muslims were beginning to learn from the West. At the end of the 1860s he left Kabul for Cairo and Istanbul, where he won many disciples during the next decade. The shah of Persia invited him to Tehran in the 1880s, but he aroused so much excitement that he was asked to leave. He then returned to Istanbul, where Abd al-Hamid II sought to use his pan-Islamic doctrine without accepting his pro-nationalist tendencies.

As the nineteenth century continued, the Qajars began to borrow abroad for public works and government expenses, as the Ottomans had done. By 1890 the shah's foreign debts were so large that he sought to pay them by giving a monopoly over the cultivation and sale of tobacco to a European concern. However, inspired by al-Afghani, the ulama and the merchants of Tehran led demonstrations against this European interference, which forced him to repurchase the concession. The merchants were so encouraged that they finally decided to wrest a constitution from the shah's successor. Although their decision was made shortly after some of them were flogged on charges of racketeering, they were also heartened by the Russian revolution of 1905, which forced a constitution on the czar, and by sympathetic British representatives in Tehran. They won the desired constitution in 1906, but Russian pressures soon virtually nullified it.

In 1907 Britain and Russia agreed to divide Persia into three zones of activity, the north for Russia, the south for Britain, and the center for both. During World War I, despite Qajar objections, Ottoman and Russian troops fought in northwest Persia until the 1917 revolutions removed Russia from the conflict. Britain occupied northern Persia in 1918 in an attempt to aid ephemeral anti-Soviet regimes around the Caspian and tried to secure lasting dominance in Persia, but in 1919 the Persian *majlis*, or parliament, refused to accept the treaty the British proposed. The last British troops left Persia early in 1921 as part of Britain's general postwar demobilization. Yet the British continued to develop the oilfields at the head of the Persian Gulf and to make friends with the shaikhs and chieftains of the coastal and mountain tribes. A treaty of Soviet-Persian friendship was signed in 1921, three years after the new Soviet government formally renounced its predecessor's privileges in Persia.

MODERNIZATION UNDER THE PAHLEVIS (1921–1974). Five days before the Soviet-Persian treaty was signed, Colonel Reza Khan of the Cossack Division of the Persian army seized control of Persia's government. In 1925 the majlis made him shah in place of the last Qajar, who had prudently left for Europe after the leading Shiite ulama formally entrusted Reza Khan with maintaining the constitution and the Islamic heritage of Persia. As Reza Shah Pahlevi, he paid close heed to the example of Mustafa Kemal in neighboring Turkey. Like Kemal before 1923, he had to start by strengthening the army so that he could control the country, although his opposition came from Persia's nomad tribes rather than from foreign troops Kemal had faced. Universal military service was established, and families were registered under family names to ensure that as few as possible avoided conscription. Factories were established to furnish equipment and supplies, and public health programs were inaugurated to promote general physical fitness. However, Reza Shah parted company with Kemal in his emphasis on the army. Kemal understood that the ultimate binding force in a united nation must be consensus, not coercion; Reza Shah, faced with a less homogeneous people, thought in terms of force and subordinated the civil to the military.

Like Kemal, Reza Shah realized the need for better transportation and communication networks. Yet he was conscious enough of the risks involved in foreign debts to prefer taxes to loans as a means of paying for them. In another parallel to Kemal, he introduced a civil code modeled largely on that of France. However, he did not dare to destroy the Sharia courts. The Shiite ulama of Persia were still popular because of their opposition to foreign influence, unlike the ulama of Turkey who were discredited by their failure to resist Western occupation in 1918. He therefore confined his secularizing tendencies to such measures as ending compulsory religious instruction in public schools and prohibiting the emotional public commemoration of the death of the caliph Ali's younger son Husain in battle, which had become part of the Shiite year.

During his reign Reza Shah sought to counterbalance Russian and British influence by using German advisers. His new legal codes made possible the abolition of the capitulations in 1928. He largely succeeded in incorporating the tribes into the nation through compulsory military conscription and agricultural settlement. Yet his harsh measures brought bitter opposition and strengthened the army at the expense of civil government. He also failed to weaken appreciably the resistance to change on the part of the Shiite ulama and the wealthy landlords.

Two months after the German attack on the Soviet Union in June of 1941, Reza Shah's pro-German leanings led Russia and its British ally to occupy Iran (as Persia had recently been renamed). Reza Shah promptly abdicated in favor of his son, Muhammad Reza Shah, who joined Russia and Britain as an ally and then turned to the United States to counterbalance them. The United States did join Britain in insisting successfully that Soviet as well as British troops must depart in 1946. However, the United States did not provide Iran with large-scale economic aid. Therefore, in search of income, the majlis nationalized the Anglo-Iranian Oil Company in 1951 in response to the calls of long-time Iranian public servant Muhammad Musaddiq.

When Musaddiq proposed the nationalization of the Anglo-Iranian Oil Company in 1950, he was supported by the Communist-led Tudeh (Masses) party, the Shiite ulama, and a fanatical fundamentalist group called the Fedayin-i-Islam (Devotees of Islam). Since the Fedayin had already assassinated a number of officials for alleged infidelity to the Islamic foundations of the nation, the majlis did not dare oppose a measure which the Fedayin approved. Early in 1951 the majlis passed the nationalization bill and made Musaddiq prime minister. After the oil industry imposed a worldwide boycott on Iranian oil, Musaddiq tried to forestall army opposition by making himself minister of war and dismissing a number of officers; but the landlords who dominated the majlis began to desert him because he was antagonizing the Western leaders who were Iran's safeguards against the Soviets. When he refused to obey the shah's order to resign in 1953, the army defeated his supporters and arrested him. A year later the shah's government reached a settlement with the Anglo-Iranian Oil Company by which an international consortium was formed to operate the nationalized facilities for twenty-five years. However, in 1973 the Shah announced his intention of replacing the consortium with Iranian management immediately, rather than waiting until 1979.

After the Musaddiq era, Muhammad Reza Shah took a more active part in politics and in social and economic reform. He had already tried to weaken the grip of the landlords on the majlis by sponsoring electoral reforms, but at first he made little headway against the landlords and the anti-modernist ulama despite his reliance on the army as a counterweight to their strength. Though he gave his own extensive lands to the state for distribution at low prices to the peasants who were working them, only one other landlord voluntarily followed his example. He therefore sent the majlis home and in 1962 began enforcing a drastic new land law designed to break up all large estates, including those held by religious organizations. The ulama promptly objected.

The continuing strength of the ulama had led the government to take conciliatory steps toward them after World War II, such as allowing modified versions of the celebration of the death of Husain. However, the fear of change which was in part a legacy of the Babi era remained strong. Early in 1963 a wave of ulama-inspired rioting swept through Tehran and other cities in protest against the land reform, the government's proposal to let women vote, and other projected changes. Despite the riots, the government went ahead with land reform and held new parliamentary elections, in which the men and women who voted selected representatives who were known to favor the shah's reforms. Land redistribution was officially declared complete in 1971. The former tenants were encouraged to form village-wide cooperatives and even corporations to improve their productivity. Literacy, health, and reconstruction and development corps were established as branches of the army, to provide needed services in the villages. The resulting improvements in rural life, and the accompanying growth in prosperity in the industrializing cities, made it seem scarcely surprising that the 1971 elections gave more than five-sixths of the legislative seats to the party of the government and only a handful to the other parties which ran candidates. By 1973 average per capita income in Iran had soared to more than five times the 1962 level. As oil revenues climbed in 1973 and 1974, so did government investment in economic development—and in sophisticated military and naval equipment, for the shah was determined that his blueprint for progress should not be interfered with by those inside and outside Iran who regarded monarchy as outmoded.

AFGHANISTAN. In 1809 the British in India persuaded the Durrani clansmen who had ruled Afghanistan since 1747 to conclude their first treaty with Europeans, but as Russia extended its influence into Turkestan, the Durranis tried to use Russia as a counterweight. In 1878–1879 the British in India forced the Durranis to allow them to supervise Afghan foreign relations, and in 1907 Russia accepted British control over Afghan external affairs. Not until 1919 did Afghanistan regain the right to manage its own foreign relations. Two years later, its ruler Amanullah (1919–1929; died 1960) concluded agreements with the Soviet Union, Persia, Turkey, and Britain.

Like Reza in Tehran, Amanullah was affected by the example of Mustafa Kemal. In 1923 he promulgated a constitution and embarked on as many reforms as his government could afford, using German advisers, instructors, and technicians for his educational, public health, industrial, and military programs, as a counterbalance to Soviet and British pressures. For a time he made some headway against those who feared change, but when he spoke of secularizing education and freeing women from seclusion, the ulama encouraged the tribes to rebel. Early in 1929 Amanullah fled, to be replaced before the year was out by the leading Durrani officer in the Afghan army, who issued a less radical constitution specifically recognizing the Sharia as the basis of the law of the land.

Amanullah's attempt to reform Afghanistan along Kemalist lines was premature, for few Afghans of his day knew much about the outside world. However, during World War II Afghans learned enough about Britain, the Soviet Union, and the United States to begin wanting change. After the war the road network and the school system were greatly expanded. Particularly noteworthy was the establishment of a state college for the ulama like those opened in Turkey and Iran after 1945, where future ulama could learn about the modern world in which they would use their Quranic studies. By 1964 the royal government felt it could replace the conservative constitution of 1931 with one which introduced modern legal forms and equality of legal status for all, though it still took the Sharia as its foundation. The first nationwide elections under the new constitution were held in 1965.

After the British withdrew from India in 1947, the Afghans trusted the new state of Pakistan as little as they had the British. They supported the demands for autonomy made by hill tribes on Pakistan's side of the Afghanistan-Pakistan frontier, reverted to the old policy of seeking Russian friendship out of fear of the strength Pakistan might gain from its 1954 alliance with the United States, and sought friendly links with Pakistan's neighbor and rival, India. In addition, they began to develop the Helmand river basin in cooperation with Iran and to seek economic links with other Middle Eastern states. Though Afghan rates of social change and economic growth were slower than those of neighboring Iran, the shah's apparent success in combining reform with stability encouraged the Afghan ruler. In 1973, however, the Afghan king's cousin (a general and former prime minister) took advantage of the king's absence in Europe to proclaim the establishment of an army-led republic in place of the monarchy. The new president promptly revived the issue of the Pakistan border tribes, but he was careful to seek continued friendship with Iran.

The Modern Era: The Arab World

EGYPT

FROM MUHAMMAD ALI TO ISMAIL (1798–1879). The theme of modernization in response to European victories, moving from reorganization of local military forces to a general reorganization led by the army, has been common in the Middle East. Egypt, like Turkey and Iran, exemplifies this trend. Its modernization began when Muhammad Ali, an Albanian officer whom the Ottomans had sent to Egypt after Napoleon's invasion of 1798, established himself as governor of the province by driving the Mamluks from Cairo in 1805. He promptly began hiring French military instructors, engineers, and other technicians, who continued to come to Cairo until his death in 1849.

To raise state income, Muhammad Ali resurveyed the land so that it could be properly assessed, dropped the long-standing practice of exempting waqf lands from taxation, acquired agricultural land for the state by confiscating property for unpaid taxes or irregularities in title, and monopolized most of Egypt's agricultural export trade. He also made heavy agricultural investments, introducing new crops like cotton, draining swamps, digging new irrigation canals and reopening old ones, installing steam pumps to lift water to the fields when the Nile was low, and constructing a dam at the head of the delta to facilitate year-round irrigation there. (The British made the dam more efficient in the 1880s, shortly before they built the first dam at Aswan in upper Egypt.) These steps enabled the peasants to cultivate new fields and to raise more than one crop a year in many areas. Yet as the century progressed, so much land was planted to cotton for export that Egypt began importing rather than exporting grain.

Muhammad Ali used the expanded income of the state to open schools and some factories, and to increase his army and his territories. At first he used mercenary soldiers, but in the 1820s he began conscripting Egyptians for the first time in nineteen centuries. In 1811–1812 he massacred the Mamluks, whose huge estates had made them immune to Ottoman control, and added their holdings to the state-owned lands. At Mahmud II's command, he broke the back of the Saudi-led Wahhabi movement in Arabia between 1811 and 1818. He also seized the northern Sudan, and in the late 1820s aided Mahmud II against the rebellious Greeks, in return for a promise of the governorship of Palestine and Syria. When Greece became independent, the sultan procrastinated about carrying out his promise. Muhammad Ali responded by sending one of his sons to conquer Palestine and Syria in 1831. By 1833 the Egyptians were within 150 miles of Istanbul and still advancing, but European pressures forced them to withdraw from Anatolia late in 1833 and from Syria and Palestine in 1840. Muhammad Ali was then promised that his descendants would continue to be the governors of Egypt.

Muhammad Ali left Egypt thriving agriculturally and strong militarily. However, his first successor dismissed the foreign advisers, closed the schools and factories, gave up the profitable monopolies, and cut the army in half, in order to rid Egypt of foreign influence. Alarmed by this course, his second successor swung back to using French counselors and agreed to construction of the Suez Canal. He also sought to stimulate agricultural production by allowing his subjects to buy and sell agricultural land. The chief results were the building up of large landed estates, as the wealthy acquired both private and public land from impoverished peasants and poorly paid government officials, and the replacement of peasants' grain fields by landlords' cotton fields. As the Egyptian economy became increasingly dependent on the prices of the cotton it sold and the grain it now began to need in the British-dominated world market, British influence in Egyptian affairs soared rapidly.

By the time of Muhammad Ali's third successor, Ismail (1863–1879), European-educated Egyptians were beginning to look at past Egyptian greatness and to wonder why the present was so inglorious by comparison. Ismail responded by prescribing the study of pre-Islamic Egyptian history in the numerous schools he founded, to acquaint Egyptians with their ancestors' ties to Europe. He hoped thereby to win acceptance for steps such as the introduction of a uniform French-influenced legal code for all except personal matters like marriage and inheritance, which continued to be handled in the Sharia and other religious courts. However, European ideas were less attractive to most educated Egyptians than the pan-Islamic message of Jamal ad-Din al-Afghani, who lived in Egypt from 1871 to 1879. Al-Afghani's chief pupil, Muhammad Abdu, became the leading teacher of young Egyptian nationalists for the next twenty-five years.

Although Ismail resembled Muhammad Ali in his large designs and his willingness to study Europe, there was one glaring difference between their administrations. At Muhammad Ali's death, the Egyptian government owed nothing to foreign bankers; but Ismail plunged headlong into debt for projects ranging from Sudanese empire-building to the extension of the railway system and the construction of an opera house in Cairo in celebration of the opening of the Suez Canal in 1869. In 1875, mounting interest payments forced Ismail to raise funds by selling his government's large block of shares in the Suez Canal Company to the British government, and in 1876 Egypt ceased payment altogether on its debts. The European powers then set up a debt commission to control Egyptian finances until the debts were paid. When Ismail objected to the commission's supervision, the powers forced the Ottoman sultan to depose him in favor of one of his young sons.

BRITAIN IN EGYPT (1882–1922). The establishment of the International Debt Commission in 1876 and the deposition of Ismail in 1879 awakened politically conscious Egyptians to the weakness of their position. As the best organized and most cohesive segment of Egyptian society, the army reacted first, taking possession of the government in 1881 under the leadership of an officer who had studied under Abdu. However, the British intervened on the ground that order had disappeared and must be restored, and occupied Alexandria, Cairo, and the region around the Canal. From 1882 to 1922 Britain's representative in Egypt effectively ran its affairs by pressuring Ismail's successors to discharge those officials who refused to follow British advice. A partly elective advisory council was set up in 1883, and political parties began to form.

Between 1880 and 1885 Egypt lost much of the Sudan to a local political-religious movement headed by one who claimed descent from Muhammad. The British led Egyptian soldiers to recover the area, and set up a joint Anglo-Egyptian administration for the Sudan after 1898. They also reformed tax collections and extended the irrigation network. However, Britain's control was unacceptable to Egyptians, who were regaining a self-awareness they had not felt in centuries, under the inspiration of al-Afghani and Abdu. As official head of the Egyptian ulama and rector of al-Azhar (a center of Muslim learning still revered from Morocco to Indonesia), Abdu used his position to promote his belief that purified Islam was the true way to unity and progress.

By 1905, the year of Abdu's death, Egypt was ready for a new revolt against foreign control. The victory of Japan over Russia that year and the success of the Young Turks three years later were widely hailed. The British then blundered seriously by muzzling the Egyptian press, previously the freest in the Muslim world. Anti-British feeling rose still higher at the opening of World War I when the British severed the fictional tie between Cairo and Istanbul, declared Egypt a British protectorate, and conscripted men and animals for war service. When the war ended in 1918, Egyptians united behind another of Abdu's former students in demanding British withdrawal. They formed a *wafd*, or delegation, to carry their cause to London, but the British government would not receive them. The wafd leaders organized nationwide protest demonstrations, for which the British exiled them from Egypt. The Egyptians promptly staged an uprising which led Britain to acknowledge Egyptian independence in 1922. However, London reserved final authority over measures relating to Egyptian defense, the Suez Canal, the future of the Sudan, and Egyptian treatment of foreigners and non-Muslim minorities.

FROM MONARCHY TO REPUBLIC (1923–1974). In 1923 Egypt was proclaimed a constitutional monarchy. After the Wafd political party won the first elections to the new parliament, the king began to take an active part in politics in order to forestall Wafd control. A three-cornered struggle ensued between the king, the British, and the Wafd, in the course of which Egypt won release in 1937 from the capitulatory regime and from British control over Egyptian treatment of foreigners and minorities.

In the 1930s a fundamentalist movement arose, called al-Ikhwan al-Muslimin, the Brotherhood of Muslims. Its members worked in agricultural cooperatives and other Brotherhood-sponsored enterprises, confined their purchases to the products of these enterprises, and vowed unswerving opposition to secularism and modernism. During World War II, when British troops moved into Egypt and other Middle Eastern regions to forestall possible German or Italian moves, Brotherhood influence spread far beyond Egypt's borders. Brotherhood leaders strove to influence postwar policy, but the assassination of an Egyptian prime minister by a Brotherhood member in 1948 led to gradual suppression.

Corruption and inefficiency made the monarchy increasingly unpopular, particularly after the armies of Egypt and other Arab states failed to prevent the state of Israel from coming into being in 1948. Under the leadership of the Revolutionary Command Council led by Colonel Gamal Abdel Nasser, the forces of rebellion came to a head on July 23, 1952, six months after a British refusal to leave either the Sudan or the Suez Canal under Egyptian supervision. Within a week the monarchy collapsed and its last head went into exile. The new regime inaugurated land redistribution and agricultural cooperatives, and laid plans to build a higher dam at Aswan, to cope with the problem of feeding a population which had more than quadrupled since 1850. In 1953 a republic was proclaimed, and in the next two years all the old political parties were outlawed, including the Wafd and the Muslim Brotherhood. In their place the government organized the National Union. A constitution (later replaced) was enacted in 1956, and Nasser was elected president.

The new republic agreed in 1953 to self-determination for the Sudan, which chose independence in 1955. In 1954 the British agreed to withdraw from the Canal Zone within two years. However, when Egypt sought arms from Britain and other Western powers, the arms were refused for fear that Egypt would use them in the intermittent border skirmishes which continued even after the 1949 truce between Egypt and Israel. Consequently Egypt turned to the Soviet bloc and in 1955 began to trade Egyptian cotton for arms from Czechoslovakia. Egyptian raids into Israel accelerated, as did Egyptian attempts to block ships from using the Gulf of Aqaba to reach Israel, which was not allowed by Egypt to use the Suez Canal. When the United States then refused aid for the high dam at Aswan, Nasser cast about for other sources of funds. Soviet assistance eventually played a large part in the construction of the dam, which was dedicated in 1971. However, Nasser's immediate decision was to nationalize the Suez Canal Company. The nationalization took place in July, 1956, a few weeks after the last British troops left Egypt and twelve years before it would have reverted to Egypt under the terms of its charter. Israel, already feeling the results of the Czech arms deal, took alarm. In October, 1956, Israeli troops entered the Sinai peninsula and destroyed the Egyptian fortifications at the mouth of the Gulf of Aqaba. Simultaneously, Britain and France claimed that the Suez Canal was threatened and declared their intent to reoccupy it, only to find both the United States and the Soviet Union opposed. The United Nations arranged a cease-fire and withdrawal, and formed a force to patrol the most sensitive parts of the Egyptian-Israeli frontier on the Egyptian side.

Egypt's successful nationalization of the Suez Canal in 1956 sent Nasser's reputation skyrocketing. By 1962 most other foreign concerns and many private Egyptian enterprises were also nationalized, in an effort to speed economic and social progress by entrusting overall direction to the state. In 1957 the Sharia and other religious courts were abolished, reversing thirteen centuries of separation between Muslims and non-Muslims. Meanwhile, Radio Cairo did all it could to encourage Arabs from Algeria to Yemen to accept Nasser as the leader of the entire Arab world. Early in 1958, Syria joined Egypt in a new United Arab Republic, but the differences between the two partners in size, population, resources, needs, and background led the Syrians to withdraw in 1961. Nasser did not seriously contest the move, although he did discard the National Union in favor of a new and more tightly organized political party called the Arab Socialist Union. His popularity with Egyptians and other Arabs remained high even after a new war with Israel in June, 1967. In that conflict, Israeli forces occupied the entire region between the Israeli border and the Suez Canal out of fear that Nasser's request in May for the withdrawal of the United Nations patrol and his attempt that month to close the Gulf of Aqaba to Israel foreshadowed an attack. From 1967 on, the Suez Canal was closed until Israel could conclude a final peace settlement with the Arabs.

Nasser's continued popularity was evidenced in the 1969 elections, in which only a handful of those who ran as independents against Arab Socialist Union candidates were elected. When he died in 1970 of a heart attack induced by overwork, the streets of Cairo were choked with wailing mourners. His associate and successor, Anwar as-Sadat, continued his policies of seeking aid from every possible source for economic development and attacking Israel verbally more than physically. In 1971 a new federation agreement was ratified by popular referendum in Egypt, Syria, and Libya, which sought to avert the difficulties of the earlier United Arab Republic by recognizing the continued internal sovereignty of each member. Sadat signed a fifteen-year treaty of friendship and cooperation with the Soviet Union in 1971, but in 1972, in a stunning reversal of Egypt's previous reliance on Soviet military instructors, he requested all Soviet military personnel to leave. He also agreed in 1972 to work toward a closer union with Libya, but in 1974 replaced the Ministry for Libyan Affairs in his cabinet with a Ministry for Sudanese Affairs.

In October, 1973, Egypt and Syria launched a coordinated attack upon Israel on the Jewish holy day of Yom Kippur. The attack resulted in Egyptian recovery of part of the east bank of the Suez Canal, but it also resulted in Israeli advances on the Syrian frontier and on the west bank of the Suez Canal before a United Nations Security Council call for a cease-fire halted the fighting. These military actions, in which Egyptian military forces at last had some tangible success against the Israelis, were followed by the opening of the first direct and serious peace discussions between Israel and Egypt since the establishment of the Israeli state. The first fruits of those discussions were an Israeli pullback from the east bank of the Suez Canal in 1974, the establishment of a United Nations buffer force between the Egyptians and the Israelis in the western Sinai, and the commencement of the task of reopening the canal to commerce.

THE MAGHRIB

LIBYA. Of all the regions of the Maghrib, or West, the least attractive to Western merchants a century ago were Tripolitania, Cyrenaica, and Fezzan, the dry coastal provinces of western and eastern Libya and their even drier hinterland. During the nineteenth century the tribes of Cyrenaica and Fezzan remained loosely attached to the Ottoman government in Tripoli, preferring the Ottomans to the European rule then being imposed on neighboring Egypt, Tunisia, and Algeria. A fundamentalist Islamic revival took place, led by Algerian-born Muhammad ibn Ali as-Sanusi, who became acquainted with Wahhabi puritanism in Mecca and settled in Libya after France conquered Algeria. By 1901, when his son and successor died, many Cyrenaicans and Tripolitanians were organized around the Sanusi lodges, which served as both teaching centers and fortresses. When the Young Turks who came to power in 1908 showed signs of opposing a growing Italian interest in the ancient Roman provinces of Tripolitania and Cyrenaica, the government of Italy seized coastal Libya and forced the Ottomans to give up their claims to the entire country in 1911–1912. The Sanusi lodges immediately became the centers of a resistance that was not broken until 1932. Libyans rejoiced at Italy's defeat in World War II and looked forward to independence. After a period of United Nations trusteeship Libya became an independent constitutional federal parliamentary monarchy in 1952, headed by the grandson of the founder of the Sanusi order.

In 1957, the discovery of oil in Fezzan led to increases in government income, in transportation and communication facilities, and in expenditures on agricultural development and social welfare, speeding up the previously slow processes of change. In 1963 Libya was made a unitary instead of a federal state, to facilitate central direction of government programs. In 1964, the king followed the lead of other Maghrib governments by seeking the withdrawal of British and United States troops and bases, which took place from 1966 to 1970. However, monarchical rule came to seem increasingly anachronistic to the newly modernizing Libyan military. In 1969 a group of officers led by Colonel Muammar al-Qaddafi took advantage of the aging king's absence for medical treatment to proclaim the establishment of the Libyan Arab Republic. Four foreign banks were soon nationalized, and by the end of 1973 almost all foreign oil firms were nationalized also. In 1970 Qaddafi, who was a strong admirer of Nasser, agreed to work toward a federation of Egypt, Libya, and the Sudan, where another colonel had also risen to power in 1969. In 1971 Libya became a founding member of the Federation of Arab Republics, together with Egypt and Syria, and formed an Arab Socialist Union which was intended to serve the same function of political integration as its counterparts in Egypt and Iraq. For the next three years Qaddafi strove unsuccessfully to establish full union with a more populous neighbor, first with Egypt and then with Tunisia. In 1974 his colleagues in the Revolutionary Command Council made him their ideological rather than their executive head, reassigning his governmental responsibilities to another of their number.

ALGERIA. As the career of Muhammad as-Sanusi showed, French conquests in Algeria affected all of northwest Africa. When they first landed in 1830, the French intended merely to establish a more pliable local ruler in Algiers, but they soon decided to settle French colonists on Algerias agricultural lands. However, Algerian resistance delayed French control of the coast until 1848, and the tribes of the interior fought until 1884.

In 1863 the French defined Algerian land as individual property instead of following the local practice of regarding it as the collective holding of those who worked it. Formerly, only crops could be disposed of; now the owner could sell the land itself or lose it by defaulting on a mortgage. The land law of 1863 led directly to the acquisition of almost a fifth of the best agricultural land by European settlers. In 1865 the French declared the people of Algeria to be French subjects. As subjects rather than citizens, Algerian Muslims continued to live under their customary laws, legally separate from the settler community. The French set up an excellent school system for the settlers' children, but few Muslims managed to enter it, and fewer still found places in the French administration or the professions. When Algeria became independent in 1962, half its people could speak some French, but only nine percent could read it—and less than three percent could read Arabic with any fluency.

After World War I, Algerian Muslims working in France learned of Mustafa Kemal's activities in Turkey. In 1923 they founded a moderate nationalist movement to work for Algerian autonomy, only to run into European settler opposition. Until 1944, the settlers blocked the granting of full French citizenship to any Algerian Muslim. After World War II, moderate Algerian Muslims requested autonomy within a loose federation with France, but the settlers refused to accept any such arrangement. The French government did promise French subjects a number of the rights of citizens. However, French officials in Algeria implemented the promises so halfheartedly that the moderates rebelled in 1954. In 1956 the moderates finally joined forces with the militants who had been urging revolt for twenty years. Thereafter, both sides resorted to terrorism, making life uncertain for settlers and Muslims alike. Although oil was discovered in the Sahara in 1956, overall economic activity decreased and levels of living gradually declined.

Early in 1962 France finally reached agreement with the Algerians. Most of the settlers promptly left. Dissensions among Algerian leaders then replaced conflicts between Algerians and Frenchmen. During 1963 the dissenters were brought under control by Algeria's newly elected president, who also began nationalizing both foreign and local properties in an effort to force the economy upward. However, rapid population growth and a lack of capital and skills made the prospects bleak. In June, 1965, the Algerian military under Houari Boumedienne expelled the president from office, in the hope that military discipline might succeed where political speeches seemed to be failing. Yet not until 1968 did the French leave their last naval base, and not until 1971 was the property of absentee landowners finally confiscated. Distribution of these agricultural lands to Algerians began in 1972. Dissidents impatient with the continued slowness of modernization tried to overthrow Boumedienne in 1967 and 1968, but without success.

MOROCCO. Unlike Algeria, Morocco was never linked with the Ottomans. In fact, Morocco had held aloof from its neighbors since the days of Carthage and Rome. Even conversion to Islam was not followed by conversion to Arabic culture, although only a third still use the Berber tongue today.

The nineteenth-century Sharifian rulers of Morocco had to cope with the problems of the capitulatory regime, which allowed Westerners to avoid local taxes, control tariff rates, use their own courts, and enable local inhabitants to acquire similar privileges. They therefore chose to confine Westerners to the port of Tangier as much as possible. Nevertheless, by 1900 Westerners were questioning the Sharifians' ability to protect them. Berber resistance to Sharifian policies, such as the imposition of the Sharia in place of customary law, led to widespread disturbances. In 1901, when a number of tribes simply refused to heed a new set of tax laws, the Sharifians had to resort to foreign loans. This proved the prelude to loss of independence, as failure to make payments led to foreign insistence on financial control. In 1906 a general international conference recognized the interest of France and Spain in maintaining Moroccan integrity and independence, leaving the hapless Sharifians no choice but acceptance of foreign guidance. In 1912 the government of France became the special protector of Morocco. Its ruler delegated his powers in the north to a lieutenant, who thereafter dealt with the Spaniards rather than the Sharifians. Tangier was set aside as an international settlement to be governed by its residents, and in the rest of the country French advisers reigned supreme. However, both France and Spain had to deal with Berber uprisings for the next fifteen to twenty years.

The French introduced French law but applied it only to Westerners, and United States nationals continued to use their own consular courts. The Spaniards also left the local legal codes largely untouched. The French even reversed the Sharifian policy of extending the Sharia and recognized the Berber customary law. This antagonized the people of the Arabic-speaking cities, who feared it would delay the unification of Morocco. Berber leaders, on the other hand, disliked the emphasis on Arabic and French in the new schools established after 1912, though they approved the graduates' desire for freedom from French rule. The first formal petition for a lessening of foreign control was presented in 1934, the year when the last Berber uprising was quelled.

By the close of World War II, young Moroccan nationalists had won the support of the educated and of prosperous townspeople, but their programs of modernization were still opposed by the heads of the larger tribes and the leading religious confraternities. In 1953 the French attempted to depose the pro-nationalist Moroccan ruler, Muhammad V, in favor of a more pliable member of the Sharifian line. The people responded with a general uprising which in 1955 forced the French to return Muhammad V to the capital at Rabat and promise full independence. The transfer of power took place early in 1956. Spain was persuaded to emulate France by giving up its protectorate a month later, though it retained a few small coastal enclaves which had been held for generations. Tangier was reintegrated into Morocco late in the year, and foreign control of tariffs, the last relic of the capitulatory system, was abolished in 1957.

Independent Morocco's economic picture was moderately encouraging, but the most productive farms were owned by Europeans, and non-utilization of coal, oil, and water power resources handicapped plans to use the country's iron and other ores for industrial purposes. Muhammad V and his nationalist cabinet quickly began reviving the economy and expanding the educational system, which they intended to use both to modernize the country and to Arabicize the Berbers. They also extended Sharia courts throughout the country and made plans to establish a uniform legal code. New local governing bodies were set up in 1960, in the first nationwide elections. By granting universal suffrage to both men and women, Muhammad V used the elections to further his program for emancipating the women of Morocco. When he died in 1961, his son Hasan continued his modernizing and nationalist policies, promulgating a constitution in 1962 and negotiating United States withdrawal from Moroccan bases in 1963. However, he made it clear that he meant to control the political parties which had emerged during his father's reign. In 1965 he sent the parliament home and suspended the constitution, and in 1967 he eliminated the last political party members from his cabinet in favor of nonparty men. Despite approval of a new constitution and election of a new parliament in 1970, an attempt was made to assassinate him in 1971. A new constitution was presented to the voters in 1972 and again overwhelmingly ratified, but when Hasan invited the three leading parties to participate in a cabinet headed by his sister's husband, only the most conservative party agreed. In 1973 Hasan outlawed the party of his bitterest opponents. As plots against the monarchy continued, Hasan sought greater popular support by ordering almost all foreign-owned enterprises to accept majority Moroccan ownership within two years, and by hosting a major Arab summit conference in 1974.

TUNISIA. When France became interested in Tunisia in the late nineteenth century, a third of its agricultural land lay unused and Algerians were using it as a base against the French in Algeria. Furthermore, like many of his contemporaries, the governor of Tunisia had borrowed so heavily from European bankers that he was near bankruptcy when the French used a border incident as a pretext to establish a formal protectorate between 1881 and 1883. Since Tunisians were already attracted enough to European ideas to have forced the first Middle Eastern constitution on their governor in 1856 (he later rescinded it), they readily accepted the introduction of codes and courts based on European models, the limitation of religious courts to matters of personal status, and the establishment of an elected council.

The French dominated the joint Tunisian-French administration of Tunisia, but Tunisians had much more opportunity to take part in government than did their neighbors in Algeria, which was annexed directly to France. Not until 1907 was a Young Tunisia party formed to work for French withdrawal. It was replaced in 1920 by the Destour (Constitution) party, which split in 1934 into the moderate Old Destour and the more radical Neo-Destour led by lawyer Habib Bourguiba. Tunisians hoped that the German-Italian occupation of their country during World War II would be followed by abolition of the French protectorate, but European settlers in Tunisia blocked their demands until 1954, when France promised internal autonomy. Full independence was finally granted early in 1956 when France acknowledged Moroccan independence. Yet the last French forces did not leave the country until 1963, a year after Algeria gained its freedom.

Bourguiba's long campaign for independence won him such popularity that the newly freed Tunisians made him the first president of their new republic, in 1957. By that time, Tunisia had become the first Arab state to abolish Sharia courts and to enact a code of personal status based on Western models. It also put all waqf lands under a government department. Bourguiba quickly declared a jihad, or holy war, against the poverty which weakened the Islamic community. He called on Tunisians to use the exemption from the month-long fast of Ramadan, an exemption which had always been permitted to participants in jihad. In 1965 he became the first Arab head of state to talk openly of the need to seek accommodation with Israel, and in 1973 he went so far as to open indirect diplomatic contacts with Israel for a brief period prior to the October war.

As Tunisians entered independence, they were fortunate in having the highest educational level in the Maghrib and the largest percentage of townspeople used to the ways of an industrial community. Moreover, many Tunisians were used to seeing themselves as individual members of a nation, rather than merely as parts of a family, through their membership in trade unions and other groups affiliated with the Neo-Destour. Still, Tunisian leaders found it difficult to provide jobs for the rapidly growing population. Impatient with a growing gap between urban and rural productivity even after a decade of steady growth in the officially supported rural cooperative movement, in 1968 the government made all landowners enter cooperatives. However, protests and slowdowns forced the government to make cooperative membership voluntary again in 1969, and many farms returned to private ownership. Thereafter the private sector in agriculture was officially recognized, though cooperatives and state enterprises continued to receive strong encouragement both in the countryside and in the cities. Bourguiba also established the office of prime minister in 1969, apparently intending to use it to groom a successor.

ARAB ASIA AND ISRAEL

At the opening of the nineteenth century, most of Arab Asia was divided among governors who still acknowledged the Ottoman sultan as overlord, but paid him little tribute. After 1830, French, British, and United States missionaries established schools for the region's Christians. From American teachers, Arab Christians learned to think in terms of a united and independent nation whose people shared a common language and history, but did not have a state-supported religious establishment. They spread the idea as widely as they could in competition with the pan-Islamic propaganda of Abd al-Hamid II, who was seeking to use Islam as a bond of union with his Arab subjects in the late nineteenth century, but they had little success. Abd al-Hamid II's opposition soon drove them to Egypt, where they also encouraged rising national consciousness. Thereafter, Arab Muslim army officers, who were learning European techniques in the Ottoman army, took the lead in developing Arab nationalism in Arab Asia.

The tide of Arab nationalism rose rapidly after 1908, when Arabs realized that the reestablished Ottoman constitution was being manipulated to favor Turkish interests at Arab expense. By the opening of World War I, in 1914, the Arabs were ready to join whoever might help them gain independence from Ottoman rule. Husain—Sharif or governor of Mecca and descendant of Muhammad—decided to seek aid from Britain, which already had protectorates in eastern and southern Arabia. This was awkward for Britain, as British aid to an Arab uprising might alienate Muslims in British India, many of whom regarded the Ottoman sultan as the true caliph or successor to Muhammad, and saw Arab antipathy to him as bordering on sacrilege. British administrators in India took care to dissociate themselves from any Arab movements, even when they quietly sent troops to occupy lower Iraq in 1914. The British in Cairo, less squeamish about Indian Muslim sensibilities, faced other problems. In the first place, French plans for Syria and Lebanon would preclude the united independent Arab state envisioned by their correspondent Husain. In the second place, many in Britain wanted to enable persecuted Jews from central and eastern Europe to migrate to Palestine, although it was 1917 before Britain issued the Balfour Declaration favoring the establishment of a Jewish national home there. The British in Cairo finally promised to support a free Arab confederation as long as it did not include either lower Iraq or the region west of a line from Damascus to Aleppo. Shortly afterward, in 1916, the Arab revolt began. However, after the war's end in 1918 the British and French took over all the Arab lands north of the Arabian peninsula as mandates or trusteeships under the League of Nations, leaving Husain with only western Arabia to rule.

LEBANON (1918–1974). By 1918 Arab nationalism was so entwined with Islamic feeling that both Christian Arabs and Western observers doubted the possibility of establishing a united Arab state with equality for all regardless of creed. One reason the French insisted on control of Syria and Lebanon was a desire to safeguard the Maronite community. As mandatory power under the League of Nations, France quickly formed an administrative division with a Christian majority by linking the Maronite region to neighboring Druze and Muslim areas. In 1926 this region was given a republican constitution which allotted legislative seats to Maronites, Orthodox Christians, Sunnite Muslims, Shiite Muslims, Druzes, and other religious groups in proportion to their numbers. Over the years it was also informally agreed that the proportions in the legislature should be left unchanged and that the president should be a Christian, the prime minister a Sunnite, and the speaker of the legislature a Shiite. No formal census was taken after 1932. In 1936 France promised Lebanon independence, but did not formally acknowledge it until 1941, during World War II, and did not withdraw its troops until 1946.

After French withdrawal, most Lebanese continued to agree that the dangers of communal warfare outweighed whatever benefits one group might gain by forcibly upsetting the delicate balance among the communities. Nevertheless, some efforts were made to join Lebanon to Syria by the Lebanese-founded Syrian Nationalist Party and the Syrian-founded Arab Renaissance or Baath party. In the summer of 1958, shortly after Egypt and Syria formed the United Arab Republic, Lebanon came close to civil war over the possibility that the president might seek an unconstitutional second term. Fearing that those who wanted closer ties with the new United Arab Republic might use the situation to achieve their goal, the government requested United States forces to enter the country and help maintain order. The United States troops withdrew three months later, after the election and installation of a new president. The man selected, the Christian commander-in-chief of the army, stepped down at the next election in 1964 in favor of a (Christian) civilian. The presidential election of 1970 was equally uneventful. The Palestinian guerrilla use of mountainous southern Lebanon as a base from which to attack Israel after the 1967 war stretched almost unbearably the ties between those who approved of the guerrillas and those who wanted to avert further Israeli counterattacks on southern Lebanon by forcing the guerrillas out of the country. The resulting violence during and after the 1972 parliamentary elections led to the imposition of martial law for a time. In 1973, government troops redoubled their efforts to bring the guerrillas under control, so as to forestall further Israeli attacks on guerrilla bases in Lebanon. A former Palestinian was even used as prime minister for a time, in the hope that he could persuade the Palestinians to restrain themselves, but that experiment was soon given up as unsuccessful.

SYRIA (1918–1974). In Syria, the Arabs proclaimed Husain's younger son Faisal as king in 1918, but the French expelled him in 1920 and proceeded to rule under League of Nations mandate. They maintained the religious courts of personal status, although in Syria as in Lebanon they introduced civil, criminal, and commercial codes based on French models. In 1930 they granted Syria a constitution, and six years later promised independence; but, again as in Lebanon, independence was not formally proclaimed until 1941 and the last French troops did not leave until 1946.

French departure left Syrians undecided about their role in the Arab world. Some wanted to join with Lebanon, some with Palestine, some with Iraq, and some with Egypt. After 1948 all agreed to hate newly founded Israel, but lack of agreement on whom to join with first led to rapid changes in foreign policy, as one military government after another seized power between 1949 and 1954. During those years the president took refuge in Egypt, where he watched the rise of Nasser. He was so favorably impressed that after his return to Syria he played an important part in bringing about the union of Syria and Egypt in 1958. Syrians rejected the experiment in 1961, believing that their homeland was merely being turned into an Egyptian province, but the pull of Arab nationalism could not be ignored. Another series of coups d'état in 1962 and 1963 raised to power a Baath-influenced government which promptly began nationalizing selected private firms and discussing a loose federal union with both Egypt and Iraq. Factionalism within the Baath movement led to still more coups after 1964, but they had little effect on Syria's general policy of nationalization at home and cooperation with other Arabs abroad. The desire to recover a small but strategic strip of mountainous land along the Syrian-Israeli border, lost to Israel during the 1967 war, only strengthened the Syrian wish for Arab unity. Deprived of bases they had used for almost twenty years, Palestinian guerrillas moved to southern Lebanon and northern Jordan, and only vigorous opposition from the governments of Lebanon and Jordan kept Syrian forces from joining them. Syrians welcomed the Federation of

Arab Republics in 1971, the efforts of Baath leaders to unite with the Arab Socialist Union of Egypt in one political movement, and the establishment in 1972 of a Baath-led national front government, which included almost all the major parties. They also welcomed Soviet support for Euphrates river development, for they hoped that the required technical cooperation with Iraq might lead to other forms of cooperation. The first phase of the Euphrates dam was dedicated in mid-1973. The Baath leaders sought to begin deemphasizing Islam as a bond in Syrian national life with a new constitution that gave equal status to all religions, but they were only able to win enough popular support for its ratification in 1973 by incorporating a provision that the head of state must still be a Muslim.

In October, 1973, in a coordinated military action with Egypt in which contingents from Jordan and several other Arab states eventually joined, the Syrians sought unsuccessfully to recover lands seized by Israel in 1967. Though bitter at their new losses, they were heartened enough by Egypt's recovery of the east bank of the Suez Canal in the postwar negotiations to enter negotiations themselves. In mid-1974, Israel and Syria agreed to a partial Israeli pullback and the establishment of a United Nations buffer force between their armies, in an arrangement negotiated by the same United States intermediary who had worked to bring about the Israeli-Egyptian disengagement, Secretary of State Henry Kissinger.

PALESTINE AND TRANSJORDAN (1918–1948). Soon after receiving the League of Nations mandate over Palestine, the British detached the region east of the Jordan, named it Transjordan, and gave authority over its desert tribes to Abdullah, elder son of Husain. Abdullah built up a British-trained volunteer army as a step toward ruling more of western Arab Asia. After the British relinquished their mandate in 1946, he used his army to annex east central Palestine during the Arab states' war against Israel in 1948–1949, but his plans for further expansion ended when he was assassinated in 1951.

In Palestine itself, the British faced the impossible task of satisfying both the Jewish settlers and the Arab inhabitants. On one hand were the British pledge to enable more Jews to settle in Palestine, the Zionists' dream of an independent Jewish state, the contributions made by incoming Jews to the economy of Palestine, and the tragic plight of Jewish refugees from Hitler's Germany. On the other hand were the Arabs, who objected vehemently to being pushed to one side in their centuries-long homeland. In 1947 the British gave the problem to the United Nations, which formally resolved to settle the Palestine issue by establishing a Jewish and an Arab state, despite the opposition of every Middle Eastern member. The European and Western Hemisphere votes which carried the resolution made Arabs feel that the partition of Palestine was just another Western decision imposed on them against their will, like the earlier League of Nations mandate system. The member states of the Arab League, formed in 1945, served notice that they would not cooperate with the partition plan. When the last British forces left Palestine in May, 1948, a bloody war ensued between the newly proclaimed state of Israel and the states of Egypt, Lebanon, Syria, Iraq, and Transjordan (which Abdullah renamed Jordan after annexing east central Palestine). Truces were signed in 1949 between Israel and Egypt, Jordan, Lebanon, and Syria, but a formal state of war continued and not even a truce was reached between Israel and Iraq. Israel continued to be regarded by Arabs as a parting gift imposed by the West—and, to some extent, so did Jordan, the other fruit of the British mandate in Palestine.

JORDAN (1948–1974). The annexation of east central Palestine left Abdullah, his son, and after 1953 his grandson Husain with the problem of controlling an unruly population, for their nomad supporters now numbered only a third of Jordan's people. The rest of the population was divided equally between inhabitants of the newly annexed lands and Arab refugees from the rest of Palestine, both of whom wanted a united Arab Palestine and cared nothing for Abdullah and his descendants. When the United Arab Republic was formed in 1958, Palestinian Arabs in Jordan hailed Nasser as the new Saladin. Yet Jordan remained in a state of uneasy calm, punctuated at intervals by cabinet crises, parliamentary elections, and outbreaks around the capital by Palestinian guerrillas. The Palestinians, dissatisfied with Husain's unwillingness to support their raids into Israel and despairing of effective aid from any other Arab state, began to coalesce into formal organizations, of which the largest came to be the Palestine Liberation Organization. In 1967 Israeli troops occupied the region west of the Jordan and removed it from Husain's jurisdiction. Then, in 1970 and 1971, Husain's army (enlarged by the universal conscription law of 1966) forced most of the guerrilla leaders to leave Jordan. Although this made him even less popular with the Palestinian refugees, they no longer outnumbered the tribespeople east of the Jordan. His initiation of compulsory education and of voting rights for women in 1966 made him appear more progressive. Nevertheless, his position remained precarious. In the 1973 Arab-Israeli conflict, he was under heavy pressure to open a third front in addition to the Syrian and Suez fighting, but only sent a contingent to the Syrian front. After twenty years of claiming the right to represent Palestinian interests, he finally recognized the Palestine Liberation Organization in 1974 as the legitimate Palestinian representative in future negotiations with Israel, under the pressure of formal recognition of the Palestine Liberation Organization by almost all other Arab and Islamic states at summit conferences in Algeria, Pakistan, and Morocco. The United Nations General Assembly gave the PLO observer status in 1974.

ISRAEL (1948–1974). After 1948, hundreds of thousands of Jewish immigrants from Middle Eastern lands joined the European Jews who formed most of the pre-1948 Jewish population in Palestine. The younger newcomers learned the rudiments of living in an industrial nation-state through universal military training, which was required of women, as well as of men, so that they too would be familiar with the needs and goals of Israeli society. Israel's multiparty parliamentary government functioned at least as smoothly as that of neighboring Lebanon. (Israeli party alignments tended to reflect differing views of the state's role in supporting orthodox Jewish tradition, as those of Lebanon reflected lines between religious groups.) Economic growth was aided by large contributions from abroad, and in 1956 Israel successfully defended its right to continue using the Gulf of Aqaba. Nasser of Egypt tacitly recognized Israel's strength in 1965 when he protested that "certain Arab elements" (probably the Palestinian guerrillas) seemed bent on a new war with Israel before the Arab world was ready. It was ironic that two years later it was his own action in requesting the withdrawal of United Nations forces, and in again blocking the Gulf of Aqaba, which led to Israeli occupation of the formerly Jordanian sector of Jerusalem, the west bank of the Jordan river, part of the Syrian border, the Sinai peninsula, and the east bank of the Suez Canal.

A quarter-century after Israel's formation, most of its people had incomes as high as those of most Europeans, and association with the Israeli economy was raising income levels in the areas occupied in 1967. However, most of those Arabs who had fled in 1948 from the battlefields of Palestine to Egypt, Syria, Lebanon, and Jordan were still in refugee camps, which their hosts tended to regard as a useful diplomatic weapon against Israel. Arab governments insisted on the refugees' right to repatriation, while refugee guerrilla leaders insisted that Jews must accept citizenship in an Arab Palestine rather than confer citizenship on Arabs in a Zionist Israel; but Israel would promise only to provide some—not all—of the funds which would be needed to resettle the refugees in the lands to which they had fled. The elections held in December, 1973, two months after Israel suffered its first significant losses at Arab hands, confirmed the strength of the Israeli public's demand that the security of Israel's borders be the government's first concern. Israeli troops withdrew in 1974 from the banks of the Suez Canal and some of their 1973 Syrian conquests as part of the first stage of peace negotiations with their neighbors. Yet it was clear, as a new cabinet replaced the one that had negotiated the withdrawals, that most Israelis remained unwilling even to consider withdrawing from other areas, especially if Palestine Liberation Organization leaders might come to rule them.

IRAQ. Neither modern schools nor modern nationalism appeared in Iraq as early as they did in Lebanon, Syria, Palestine, or Egypt. The strongly anti-foreign and anti-modern Shiite ulama continued to lead the Shiite half of Iraq's population throughout the Ottoman period, while most of the Sunnite half was controlled by the Arab tribal shaikhs or chieftains of the middle Euphrates and their Kurdish counterparts in the hills along the upper Tigris. Consequently, Arab nationalism at first found few supporters other than army officers and townspeople educated outside Iraq.

At the close of World War I, Iraq was assigned to Britain as a mandate by the League of Nations. Since many Iraqis had been anticipating independence after the Ottomans fell, the news of the mandate triggered an uprising. In 1921, Britain offered the Iraqis self-government as a constitutional monarchy headed by Husain's younger son Faisal, whom the French had driven from Syria, and succeeded in persuading the shaikhs, the ulama, the leading urban families, and the army to accept him. Only the Kurds resisted the new king for long, but the discovery of oil in the Kurdish north in 1927 gave the government too much stake in the region to let it remain restive. A Turkish-style policy of conscripting Kurds into the army was begun. After Faisal's death in 1933, the royal government came to be dominated by Nuri as-Said, who had served under Faisal as an Iraqi volunteer in World War I.

After World War II ended in 1945, Nuri as-Said found it necessary to heed the growing number of townspeople trained in Western ways, as well as established leaders like the shaikhs and the ulama. To meet demands for improvement, the government in 1950 earmarked seven-tenths of all oil revenues for flood control and irrigation works, industrial expansion, urban housing, and other economic projects. Nuri hoped thereby to turn articulate Iraqis from political agitation to economic activity. However, the townspeople still wanted a greater voice in government. Nuri abolished all political parties in 1954 in an effort to quiet his critics, but the sudden enforced silence was deceptive. The next year he added to his unpopularity by signing the Baghdad Pact for mutual defense with Turkey and inviting any interested state to join. By the end of 1955, Pakistan, Britain, and Iran adhered to the pact, but no other Arab state accepted the invitation, for most of the new pact's members recognized the hated state of Israel. Iraqis too resented the pact. In mid-1958 their feelings exploded in the overthrow of the monarchy and Nuri by a group of young army officers who soon withdrew from the Baghdad Pact (which then became the Central Treaty Organization).

The republic established in 1958 resembled that of revolutionary Egypt in insisting on Arab cooperation, national unity, social equality, and more rapid economic development. However, Iraq was troubled by underpopulation rather than overpopulation, such as that which plagued Egypt. As late as 1950 only a fifth of Iraq's cultivable land was in crops. Furthermore, the call for Arab cooperation and national unity alienated the Kurds, who in 1961 began a full-scale uprising. Early in 1963 another military coup brought to power a Baath-influenced group, which made little headway toward peace with the Kurds and was overturned by a non-Baathist group later in the year. A tentative agreement with the Kurds was reached in 1966, but at the end of 1967 the new Kurdish ministers left the cabinet, perhaps partly in protest against the continued use of "Arab Socialist Union" as the name for the only legal political movement. One month later the non-Baathists were overthrown by Baathists, but the Kurds were not reconciled to the new government until 1970. They were then given proportional representation in the national government and recognition of Kurdish as an official national language. The reconciliation broke down when the Baghdad government sought to draw the boundaries of the Kurdish zone strictly on the basis of majority Kurdish population, which would place most of the northern oil-bearing region in the hands of the Arabs who had flocked there in recent years. With possible encouragement from Iran, whose forces had recently clashed with Iraqi border patrols in the Gulf region, the Kurds reopened war with the Baghdad government's forces early in 1974.

Despite the Baathists' return to power and the cooperation with Syria required by the Soviet-supported Euphrates river project, Iraqi leaders were cautious about commitments to other Arab states after an unsuccessful coup in 1965 tried to merge Iraq with Egypt by fiat. Though all Arab states were invited to join the Federation of Arab Republics formed by Egypt, Syria, and Libya in 1971, the fires of Arab nationalism seemed scarcely warm enough to melt the cold fact of economic, geographic, and political circumstances which had bred rivalries among the rulers of Egypt, Syria, and the Tigris-Euphrates valley since the dawn of history.

SAUDI ARABIA.   In most of Arab Asia the educated townspeople and the military usually led in the adaptation of Western ideas and techniques to local circumstances. In the Arabian peninsula, however, Western-educated townspeople and modernized military scarcely existed prior to World War II. There, the chief modernizing forces were Saudi leadership, oil revenue, and motor transport.

The Saudis were seriously crippled by Muhammad Ali early in the nineteenth century. However, after 1902 Abd al-Aziz ibn Saud (1901–1953) brought all of central and eastern Arabia under his control and developed close relations with the British. When Sharif Husain failed to manage Mecca's affairs to the satisfaction of pilgrims to Mecca and Medina after 1918, Ibn Saud struck westward, driving Husain and his family from Arabia by the end of 1925. After the annexation of the holy cities with their profitable pilgrim trade, the extension of his authority over the southern interior was only a matter of time.

Ibn Saud's early successes were based on familiar methods, such as settling his fighting men in agricultural communities around the available water supplies so that they would always be ready for rapid mobilization. In 1923 he granted an oil concession to a British firm, hoping to increase his revenues, but the company gave up the concession after explorations yielded nothing. In 1933 he granted a new concession to Standard Oil of California, but oil was not found until 1938 and the anticipated revenues only materialized after World War II. The Saudi government used these revenues to build highways, provide free medical services, and accelerate programs for finding and tapping underground water supplies so as to settle the tribes on irrigated farmland. Motor buses, jeeps, and airplanes began to replace camel caravans, a railroad was built from the capital of Riyadh to the oil seaport of Dhahran on the east coast, and radio and telephone networks reached every corner of the kingdom.

The Saudis seemed determined to bind their subjects to themselves by assuring their employment in agriculture, oil, or catering to the needs of pilgrims, as the camel trade disappeared. However, some Saudi Arabians became impatient with the personal extravagance of Ibn Saud's successor Saud and other princes, and with continued recognition of the Sharia as the only law of the land. In 1964 the leading members of the royal family and the ulama decided Saud was no longer fit to rule. They replaced him with his younger brother, Faisal (who had also been his prime minister and designated heir). They hoped that more prudent Faisal could better carry out the double task of modernizing and preserving Saudi Arabia. Though an unsuccessful attempt to establish a republic was reported in 1968, the state budget continued to be a matter for royal decree rather than public deliberation.

OTHER ARABIAN STATES. In eastern Arabia, the shaikh of Kuwait emulated the Saudis by using his oil revenue to provide jobs and services, to establish a reserve fund for diversification of the economy, and to aid members of the Arab League who lacked oil income. Similar policies were followed by the other oil-producing principalities, Bahrain, Qatar, and the United Arab Emirates formed by several small shaikhdoms in 1971 after Britain gave up its century-old protectorate over them.

To the south, the region from Yemen to Oman continued to depend on agriculture, herding, and commerce. In 1948, Yemen's *imam* or ruler was assassinated in a coup which was quickly reversed by his heir. The new imam established a road network, a radio station, and the country's first printing press before his death in 1962. He also sought friendship with Communist powers and adhered to the United Arab Republic between 1958 and 1961, for he was concerned over potential border disputes with Saudi Arabia and the British-protected shaikhs of the southwestern coast. Like the ruler of Oman, who was already embroiled in a serious border dispute with the Saudis, the imam was a nonorthodox Muslim. Many Yemenis and Omanis shared their rulers' religious beliefs. However, most of the tribes in Oman's interior were orthodox Sunnites like the Saudis, and most of the people of coastal Yemen were Sunnites who had long resented the dominant Shiites of the mountains. In 1962 a military coup drove a new imam from Yemen's capital and set up a republican government there, while the imam continued to lay claim to power in the mountains. Peace was not finally attained until the royalists agreed to accept and enter the republican government in 1970, the same year that the Omani ruler's more progressive son overthrew him in a coup. By then the British had given up their protectorate over the lands between the new Yemen Arab Republic and Oman. In 1967 these lands became the People's Republic of South Yemen, at the insistence of the modern-minded inhabitants of the port city of Aden, which the British had occupied in 1839. The new government was soon plagued by uprisings in the less modernized countryside. Late in 1972 the People's Republic of South Yemen and the Yemen Arab Republic agreed to merge into one Yemen Republic during the following year. The People's Republic of South Yemen dropped "South" from its name in preparation, but few other tangible steps were taken to implement the merger. Late in 1973 the original one-year schedule was extended indefinitely, as the People's Republic of Yemen became increasingly involved in aiding republican rebels against the Omani ruler, who in turn requested and received support from Iran.

The Task of Modernization

In their efforts to modernize themselves, the peoples of the Middle East have had to strive to replace the old practice of coexistence with the new ideal of cooperation. Formerly, a people could retain independence under a government which confined itself to taxation and the maintenance of order, allowing the members of various social groups to lead their separate lives as long as they did not quarrel openly. However, by the twentieth century a state could scarcely hope to remain free of outside control unless the members of all groups were agreed on a number of common interests and willing to work together under a government which would actively promote those interests. Middle Easterners have tried to bring about such a spirit of cooperation in a number of ways. Three of these have won a large measure of conscious acceptance—the adaptation of Islam, the development of nationalism, and the acceptance of military leadership—but others such as modern transport, health, and education facilities have also been significant.

If ninth- and tenth-century Europeans found comfort in upholding the spiritual superiority of Christianity over Islam as they surveyed the economic, military, and political strength of their Muslim contemporaries, then their descendants could hardly wonder at the tenacity with which nineteenth- and twentieth-century Muslims clung to the belief that Western economic, military, and political strength had not made Islamic ideals outmoded. Most Middle Eastern modernizers received a welcome sense of community from their shared Islamic past. A few wondered whether Islam and modernity were too fundamentally opposed to be made compatible. Modernizing governments could scarcely uphold the caliphate in the face of the widespread drive toward republicanism, nor could they safely assign any of their citizens to the second-class status of the dhimmi. Only in countries like Morocco, where cleavages were not religious, could the Sharia be a unifier. Moreover, governmental preference for trade unions rather than the old-fashioned craft guilds weakened the religious confraternities which were intertwined with the guilds, thereby depriving many persons of opportunities for religious expression which had long been important to them. Some leaders even attacked the confraternities directly, like Ataturk in Turkey. Nevertheless, most modernizers hoped that the principle of consensus, which had always been a widely accepted means of interpreting the Sharia, might prove flexible enough to accommodate the Sharia to modern times. After all, only a few diehards continued to hold that governmental emancipation of slaves had contradicted the Sharia, and every year there were fewer who refused to admit that it was in accord with Islamic principle for women to vote or to work outside the home, or for polygamy to be discouraged and even outlawed.

Middle Eastern modernizers were also agreed on the negative program of destroying the last vestiges of outside domination, but few of them developed a positive agreement on the nature of the newly-freed state until after the foreigners left. Turkish nationalists quickly agreed on Mustafa Kemal's six-point program of republicanism, secularism, populism, nationalism, statism, and reformism, but the Turks were accustomed to a feeling of mastery over their own fate, and their centuries of entanglement in European affairs gave them more knowledge of Europe than other Middle Easterners had. Even Iran was slow to attain a comparable degree of national unity, in spite of its long tradition of pre-Islamic greatness and its preservation of a distinctive identity as a

Shia state. However, a secular nationalism did not appeal to Turkey's Islamic neighbors.

Islam remained a vital element in twentieth-century Middle Eastern nationalism, distressing though that fact was to non-Muslims. This blending of religion and nationalism was scarcely surprising, for *umma*, one of the words most often used to describe the nation, had traditionally meant the community of Muslims rather than the population of a territorial unit. It was therefore difficult for national leaders to make the new interpretation replace the old, although not as difficult as it was for Communists to win a hearing for their ideas. Since most urban Middle Easterners were in small-scale family enterprises, they listened incredulously to calls for a battle of employees against employers. Furthermore, since the politically minded usually wanted a strong and united nation, they could scarcely understand denunciations of nationalism or pleas for a class struggle which would only encourage the existing tendency of various sections of society to fly at each other's throats. The Communists were on firmer ground when they talked of land reform and the need to expel all remnants of Western control. By stressing these two programs, the Communists won followers, but few members, for the doctrines of class struggle and anti-nationalism appealed only to the extremely dissatisfied.

Although Middle Eastern modernizers usually started by borrowing European military weapons and techniques for defense, most of them soon introduced European agricultural, financial, and industrial methods in order to provide the expanded national income needed to support the expensive new military establishments. They also introduced legal codes and constitutions modeled on European lines, in hopes of uniting the nation behind the economic innovations and the military forces by giving equal rights and equal representation to all. However, parliamentary representation tended to express existing cleavages within the body politic more often than it gave voice to a united popular will. When civilian disagreement began to seem detrimental to military goals, military men became unwilling to leave government in civilian hands in one state after another.

The rise of the military to power was illustrated between World War I and World War II in Turkey, Persia-Iran, and Afghanistan. After the debacle of the Palestinian war in 1948–1949, Nasser appeared in Egypt and a series of military coups took place in Syria. In 1958, military leaders took over in Iraq, the Sudan (which returned to civilian rule between 1964 and 1969), and Lebanon (by election for a six-year term). In 1965 Algeria was added to the list, in 1969 Libya and (again) the Sudan, and in 1973 Afghanistan. Of all these miliatry leaders, only Mustafa Kemal of Turkey gave up his military rank and uniform when he entered the government. Nor did his espousal of the principle of civil rule prevent the Turkish army from undertaking a coup in 1960 and watching the civilians closely thereafter. However, the Turkish generals who served as president from 1961 to 1973 resigned their commissions before being nominated for election in the national legislature. In 1973 the legislature refused to accept the army's preferred candidate, but finally agreed to select a member of the upper house who was also a retired admiral.

Whether led by army, king, or parliament, twentieth-century Middle Eastern states could use motorized government forces to outmaneuver and control the previously elusive nomads. Thus the region's newly-utilized oil resources not only provided revenues to governments and contributed to their making and unmaking, but also enabled them to rule the hills and deserts as well as the cities and villages. Oil furnished energy with which to make useful products of other materials. It ran the motor vehicles and many of the ships and trains that were transforming the Middle East from a subsistence economy, in which most people resorted to an exchange of goods only when they needed items they could not hope to obtain locally, to an exchange economy, in which each region concentrated on trading what it could produce most easily for what others could provide most cheaply. As the importance of oil in their economies grew, the principal oil-producing countries of the Middle East joined with Venezuela and Indonesia in 1960 in the Organization of Petroleum Exporting Countries, so as to present a united front in negotiations with the oil companies of the world. Through OPEC they increased their oil revenues substantially in 1965. In 1972 they won acceptance of the principle that each government should participate in every oil company working within its borders, thereby gaining a voice in the operation of the company rather than merely receiving income from it through royalties, leases, concessions, and taxes. In October, 1973, the Arab oil-producing states began using their oil reserves as a diplomatic bargaining counter. They announced that they would gradually cut back overall production and would not sell any oil to the United States or to other states they deemed friendly to Israel until Israel withdrew from the lands it had taken in 1967. Although this announcement came shortly after the Egyptian and Syrian attack on Israel, some economists suggested that its purpose was more economic than political. As oil prices soared in the next few months, not only for the Arabs but also for other oil-exporting countries like Iran, Indonesia, Nigeria, and Venezuela, that suggestion appeared increasingly plausible. The production cutbacks were restored and the embargoes largely lifted after the signing of the Israeli truce agreements with Egypt and Syria in 1974, but the process of implementing participation by host governments in the oil companies was speeded up as OPEC members sought greater control over their own economic future. The question of where best to invest oil revenues began to become acute for those Arabian peninsular states whose own population was too small to absorb productivity all the new income from higher oil prices.

Though the transition from a subsistence to an exchange economy was slow, its beginnings affected every Middle Eastern social unit from the family to the state. As the village household ceased to produce most of what it consumed, both women and younger men could begin to find jobs in the village or the city, jobs in which they would be independent of the family head. In Europe, these economic and social changes were followed by revision of the legal system. However, Middle Eastern states borrowed European legal codes and thereby lifted customary restrictions on women and younger men long before most individuals were actually able to obtain independent positions. The result was a violent clash between parents, who had grown up in a subsistence economy with its traditions of paternal authority, and their sons and daughters, who appealed to the new legal codes and acted with the freedom appropriate to an exchange economy even though the economic and social bases for their assumption of independence were largely lacking.

The villages and cities in which these changes were taking place were growing in population, thanks in part to the introduction of modern public health measures. Those who found life difficult to maintain in their village or their tribe flocked increasingly to the cities in search of opportunity, only to find that there were far more applicants than jobs. Yet the number of job-seekers was not likely to decrease until the experience of a full generation assured parents that almost all the children they brought into the world and cared for would reach maturity, instead of only half of them. Thus economic development became essential to political stability, for only economic growth could thin the ranks of the unemployed who swelled the city mob in almost every capital. Fear of mob power helped explain the drive for industries which could employ city-dwellers almost as much as did the need to increase overall production, the economic advantages of processing domestic raw materials at home, and the desire to demonstrate that Egyptians (for example) could run a steel mill as well as the British—even though Egypt had to import all the raw materials for steel-making until iron and manganese were found near Aswan in 1966.

When Middle Eastern states began to industrialize, they possessed far fewer of what economists call "infrastructures"—the supporting framework of unified legal codes, stable banking and currency systems, well-policed transport networks, and widespread schools which twentieth-century Westerners took for granted—than eighteenth-century Western states had possessed. Consequently, twentieth-century Middle Eastern governments subsidized and controlled industry as nineteenth-century Prussia and Japan and twentieth-century Russia had done, in order to ensure immediate results. They also followed the Prussian, Japanese, and Soviet experiments in using public education to promote national unification. The temptation to use universal public schooling to provide the young with an official interpretation of the basis of the state was very strong where there was no widespread agreement on the relationship of the state to Islam. Yet enforcement of uniformity could lead to a tyranny of the majority, in the absence of the high level of social and economic interchange and cooperation required for true political consensus. The future would depend heavily on the schools. If those in power could win the support of the young, they could carry on their programs with the acquiescence (if not the enthusiasm) of all but a very few intransigents. However, if they failed to convince the new generation of the appropriateness of their plans for the nation's economic, political, and social life, they might be replaced by others; and if the efforts to reinterpret Islam in terms meaningful to the modern world were to fail, Middle Easterners might even follow the Chinese in repudiating their philosophical and political heritage in favor of ideas and practices learned from abroad.

Suggested Readings

A list of historical atlases will be found at the opening of the map section, following the table of contents. A list of suggested readings relevant to the specific area under discussion can be found at the end of Parts Two, Three, and Four. Books dealing with two or more of the major regions to be discussed in Parts Two, Three, and Four will be found in the list of suggested readings at the end of Part Five. Books available in paperback are marked with an asterisk.

Europe

GENERAL

BRINTON, CRANE. *Ideas and Men: The Story of Western Thought,* 2nd ed. Englewood Cliffs, N.J.: Prentice-Hall, 1963.

*McNEILL, WILLIAM H. *The Rise of the West.* Chicago: University of Chicago Press, 1963.

OGILVIE, ALAN GRANT. *Europe and its Borderlands.* Edinburgh: Thomas Nelson and Sons, 1957.

*ROSTOW, WALT W. *The Stages of Economic Growth,* 2nd ed. London: Cambridge University Press, 1971.

SABINE, GEORGE H. *A History of Political Theory,* 3rd ed. New York: Holt, Rinehart and Winston, 1961.

*SJOBERG, GIDEON. *The Preindustrial City: Past and Present.* Glencoe, Ill.: Free Press, 1960.

TO MODERN PERIOD

ARTZ, FREDERICK B. *The Mind of the Middle Ages,* 1st ed. New York: Knopf, 1953.

BAILEY, CYRIL, ed. *The Legacy of Rome.* Oxford: Clarendon, 1924.

*BARK, WILLIAM C. *Origins of the Medieval World.* Stanford, Cal.: Stanford University Press, 1958.

*BOWRA, C.M. *The Greek Experience,* 2nd ed. New York: Praeger, 1969. (Paperback. New York: New American Library.)

*CHEYNEY, EDWARD P. *The Dawn of a New Era 1250–1453.* New York: Harper, 1936.

CLAPHAM, J. H., and EILEEN POWERS, eds. *The Cambridge Economic History of Europe,* vol. I, *The Agrarian Life in the Middle Ages.* London: Cambridge University Press, 1941.

COULBORN, RUSHTON, ed. *Feudalism in History,* 2nd ed. Hamden, Conn.: Archon Books, 1965.

CRUMP, CHARLES G., and ERNEST F. JACOBS, eds. *The Legacy of the Middle Ages.* Oxford: Clarendon, 1951.

DANIEL, NORMAN. *Islam and the West: The Making of an Image.* Edinburgh: University of Edinburgh Press, 1960.

*DAWSON, CHRISTOPHER. *Religion and the Rise of Western Culture.* New York: Sheed and Ward, 1950. (Paperback. Garden City, N.Y.: Doubleday, 1964.)

*GILMORE, MYRON P. *The World of Humanism, 1453–1517.* New York: Harper, 1952.

GRIMM, HAROLD J. *The Reformation Era,* rev. ed. New York: Macmillan, 1965.

*HAMILTON, EDITH. *The Greek Way,* rev. ed. New York: Norton, 1964.

*———. *The Roman Way,* 2nd ed. New York: Norton, 1965.

HAY, DENYS. *Europe: The Emergence of an Idea,* rev. ed. Edinburgh: University of Edinburgh Press, 1968.

*HUIZINGA, JOHAN. *The Waning of the Middle Ages.* London: E. Arnold & Co., 1963. (Paperback. New York: Doubleday.)

LEWIS, ARCHIBALD R. *Naval Power and Trade in the Mediterranean, A.D. 500–1100.* Princeton, N.J.: Princeton University Press, 1951.

———. *The Northern Seas: Shipping and Commerce in Northern Europe, A.D. 300–1100.* Princeton, N.J.: Princeton University Press, 1958.

*LIVINGSTONE, RICHARD W., ed. *The Legacy of Greece,* 2nd ed. Oxford: Clarendon, 1937. (Paperback. London: Oxford University Press.)

*NEF, JOHN U. *Industry and Government in France and England, 1540–1640.* Philadelphia: American Philosophical Society, 1940. (Paperback. Ithaca, N.Y.: Cornell University Press.)

PACKARD, LAURENCE B. *The Commercial Revolution 1400–1776.* New York: H. Holt, 1927.

POSTAN, M.M., and E.E. RICH, eds. *The Cambridge Economic History of Europe,* vol. II, *Trade and Industry in the Middle Ages.* London: Cambridge University Press, 1941.

*STRAYER, JOSEPH R. *Western Europe in the Middle Ages: A Short History,* 2nd ed. Englewood Cliffs, N.J.: Prentice-Hall, Inc., 1974.

*TAWNEY, RICHARD H. *Religion and the Rise of Capitalism.* New York: Harcourt, Brace, 1926. (Paperback. New York: New American Library, 1947.)

MODERN PERIOD

*BECKER, CARL L. *The Heavenly City of the Eighteenth-Century Philosophers,* 2nd ed. New Haven, Conn.: Yale University Press, 1952.

*BRINTON, CRANE. *The Anatomy of Revolution,* rev. and expanded. New York: Vintage Books, 1965.

*Butterfield, Herbert. *The Origins of Modern Science 1300–1800*. London: G. Bell, 1957. (Paperback, rev. ed. New York: Free Press, 1965.)

Langer, William L. *The Diplomacy of Imperialism*, 2nd ed. New York: Knopf, 1960.

*Nef, John U. *Cultural Foundations of Industrial Civilization*. New York: Harper, 1960.

*Nussbaum, Frederick L. *The Triumph of Science and Reason, 1660–1685*. New York: Harper, 1953.

Palmer, Robert R. *A History of the Modern World*, 4th ed. rev. by Robert Palmer and Joel Colton. New York: Knopf, 1971.

*Schumpeter, Joseph. *Imperialism and Social Classes, Two Essays*, trans. by Heinz Norden. New York: Meridian Books, 1960.

See, Henri. *Modern Capitalism: Its Origin and Evolution*, trans. by H. B. Vanderblue and G. F. Doriot. Reprint of 1928 ed. New York: A. M. Kelley, 1968.

*Stromberg, Roland N. *An Intellectual History of Modern Europe*. New York: Appleton-Century-Crofts, 1966.

Thomson, David. *Europe Since Napoleon*, 2nd ed. New York: Knopf, 1962.

Additional suggestions may be found in George Frederick Howe et al., eds., *The American Historical Association's Guide to Historical Literature* (New York: Macmillan, 1961) and in bibliographies listed therein.

The Middle East

GENERAL

Coon, Carleton S. *Caravan: The Story of the Middle East*. New York: Holt, 1951.

Cressey, George B. *Crossroads: Land and Life in Southwest Asia*. Chicago: Lippincott, 1960.

Fisher, William B. *The Middle East: A Physical, Social and Regional Geography*. London: Methuen, 1971.

*Patai, Raphael. *Golden River to Golden Road: Society, Culture and Change in the Middle East*. Philadelphia: University of Pennsylvania Press, 1962.

*Sweet, Louise E., ed. *People and Cultures of the Middle East*, 2 vols. New York: Natural History Press, Doubleday, 1970.

PRE-ISLAMIC PERIOD

Arberry, A.J., ed. *The Legacy of Persia*. Oxford: Clarendon, 1953.

Bevan, Edwyn R., and Charles Singer, eds. *The Legacy of Israel*. Oxford: Clarendon, 1965.

Duchesne-Guillemin, Jacques. *The Western Responses to Zoroaster*. Oxford, Clarendon, 1958.

*Frankfort, Henri. *The Birth of Civilization in the Near East*. Bloomington: Indiana University Press, 1951.

GHIRSHMAN, ROMAN. *Iran from the Earliest Times to the Islamic Conquest.* Harmondsworth: Penguin, 1954.

GLANVILLE, S.R.K., ed. *The Legacy of Egypt.* Oxford: Clarendon, 1942.

*MOSCATI, SABATINO. *The Face of the Ancient Orient.* Garden City, N.Y.: Doubleday, 1962.

*OLMSTEAD, A. T. *History of the Persian Empire, Achaemenid Period.* Chicago: University of Chicago Press, 1948.

*STARR, CHESTER G. *Early Man: Prehistory and the Civilizations of the Ancient Near East.* London: Oxford University Press, 1973.

*TARN, W.W. *Hellenistic Civilizations,* 3rd ed., rev. by author and G.T. Griffith. London: Methuen, 1966. (Paperback. Chicago: World Publishers.)

ISLAMIC PERIOD

*ANDRAE, TOR. *Muhammad: The Man and His Faith,* trans. by Theophil Menzel. New York: Harper, 1960.

*ARBERRY, A.J. *The Koran Interpreted.* New York: Macmillan, 1955.

ARNOLD, SIR T. W., and ALFRED GUILLAUME, eds. *The Legacy of Islam.* Oxford: Clarendon, 1931.

BOSWORTH, C.E. *The Islamic Dynasties: A Chronological and Genealogical Handbook.* Chicago: Aldine, 1967.

*BROCKELMANN, CARL. *History of the Islamic Peoples,* trans. by Joel Carmichael and Moshe Perlmann. New York: Putnam, 1947.

COOK, M. A., ed. *Studies in the Economic History of the Middle East from the Rise of Islam to the Present Day.* London: Oxford University Press, 1970.

FAKHRY, MAJID. *A History of Islamic Philosophy.* New York: Columbia University Press, 1970.

FISHER, SYDNEY N. *The Middle East: A History,* 2nd ed. New York: Knopf 1968.

GABRIELI, FRANCESCO, ed. *Arab Historians of the Crusades,* trans. by E.J. Costello. Berkeley: University of California, 1969.

GIBB, H.A.R. *Mohammedanism: An Historical Survey,* 2nd ed. London: Oxford University Press, 1969.

———. *Studies on the Civilization of Islam,* ed. by Sanford Shaw and William Polk. Boston: Beacon Press, 1962.

*GUILLAUME, ALFRED. *Islam,* 2nd ed. London: Cassell, 1963.

HITTI, PHILIP K. *Capital Cities of Arab Islam.* Minneapolis: University of Minnesota Press, 1973.

*———. *History of the Arabs,* 5th ed. New York: St. Martin's Press, 1968.

HOLT, P.M., A.K.S. LAMBTON, and BERNARD LEWIS, eds. *The Cambridge History of Islam,* 2 vols. London: Cambridge University Press, 1970.

*KIRK, GEORGE E. *A Short History of the Middle East,* 7th rev. ed. New York: Praeger, 1964.

LAPIDUS, IRA M. *Muslim Cities in the Later Middle Ages.* Cambridge: Harvard University Press, 1967.

*LEVY, REUBEN. *The Social Structure of Islam.* London: Cambridge University Press, 1957.

*LEWIS, ARCHIBALD, R., ed. *The Islamic World and the West 622–1492 A.D.* New York: John Wiley, 1970.

ROSENTHAL, E.I.J. *Political Thought in Medieval Islam.* London: Cambridge University Press, 1962.

ROSENTHAL, FRANZ. *The Muslim Concept of Freedom Prior to the Nineteenth Century.* Leiden: Brill, 1960.

VON GRUNEBAUM, GUSTAVE E. *Classical Islam: A History 600–1258,* trans. by Katherine Watson. Chicago: Aldine, 1970.

*———. *Medieval Islam,* 2nd ed. Chicago: University of Chicago Press, 1953. (Paperback. Chicago: University of Chicago Press, 1969.)

———, ed. *Unity and Variety in Muslim Civilization.* Chicago: University of Chicago Press, 1955.

WATT, W. MONTGOMERY. *A History of Islamic Spain.* Chicago: Aldine, 1966.

———. *Islamic Political Thought: The Basic Concepts,* Islamic Surveys No. 6. Chicago: Aldine, 1968.

*———. *Muhammad: Prophet and Statesman.* London: Oxford University Press, 1961.

MODERN PERIOD

BILL, JAMES A., and CARL LEIDEN. *The Middle East: Politics and Power.* Rockleigh, N.J.: Allyn and Bacon, 1974.

BINDER, LEONARD. *The Ideological Revolution in the Middle East.* New York: John Wiley, 1964.

BROWN, L. CARL, ed. *From Medina to Metropolis: Heritage and Change in the Near Eastern City.* Princeton, N.J.: Darwin, 1972.

BULLARD, SIR READER, W., ed. *The Middle East: A Political and Ecomomic Survey,* 3rd ed. London: Oxford University Press, 1958.

FRYE, RICHARD N., ed. *Islam and the West.* The Hague: Mouton, 1957.

GIBB, H.A.R. *Modern Trends in Islam.* Chicago: Octagon Press, 1972.

HADDAD, GEORGE M. *Revolutions and Military Rule in the Middle East,* 2 vols. New York: Robert Speller and Sons, 1965–71.

*HALPERN, MANFRED. *The Politics of Social Change in the Middle East and North Africa.* Princeton, N.J.: Princeton University Press, 1963.

*HUREWITZ, J.C. *Middle East Politics: The Military Dimension.* New York: Praeger, 1969.

*KARPAT, KEMAL H., ed. *Political and Social Thought in the Contemporary Middle East.* New York: Praeger, 1968.

KEDDIE, NIKKI R. *An Islamic Response to Imperialism.* Berkeley: University of California Press, 1968.

LAQUEUR, WALTER Z. *Communism and Nationalism in the Middle East,* 2nd ed. New York: Praeger, 1957.

———, ed. *The Middle East in Transition: Studies in Contemporary History.* New York: Praeger, 1958.

LENCZOWSKI, GEORGE. *The Middle East in World Affairs,* 3rd ed. Ithaca, N.Y.: Cornell University Press, 1962.

LERNER, DANIEL. *The Passing of Traditional Society: Modernizing the Middle East.* New York: Free Press, 1958.

*Lewis, Bernard. *The Middle East and the West*. Bloomington: Indiana University Press, 1964. (Paperback. New York: Harper and Row.)

Longrigg, Stephen H. *Oil in the Middle East*, 3rd ed. London: Oxford University Press, 1967.

McLane, Charles B. *Soviet–Middle East Relations*. London: Central Asian Research Centre, 1973.

Meyer, Albert J., Jr. *Middle Eastern Capitalism: Nine Essays*. Cambridge: Harvard University Press, 1959.

Nolte, R.H., ed. *The Modern Middle East*. New York: Atherton, 1963.

Polk, William R., and R.L. Chambers, eds. *Conference on the Beginnings of Modernization in the Middle East*. Chicago: University of Chicago Press, 1968.

Rondot, Pierre. *The Changing Patterns of the Middle East*, trans. by Mary Dilke. New York: Praeger, 1961.

*Rustow, Dankwart. *Middle Eastern Political Systems*. Englewood Cliffs, N.J.: Prentice-Hall, 1971.

*Smith, Wilfrid Cantwell. *Islam in Modern History*. Princeton: Princeton University Press, 1957. (Paperback. New York: Mentor.)

Spector, Ivar. *The Soviet Union and the Muslim World, 1917–1958*. Seattle: University of Washington Press, 1959.

Stocking, George W. *Middle East Oil: A Study in Political and Economic Controversy*. Nashville, Tenn.: Vanderbilt University Press, 1970.

Vatikiotis, P.J. *Conflict in the Middle East*. London: G. Allen and Unwin, 1971.

THE NORTHERN TIER

OTTOMAN EMPIRE AND TURKISH REPUBLIC

Ahmad, Feroz. *The Young Turks: The Committee of Union and Progress in Turkish Politics, 1908–1914*. Oxford: Clarendon, 1969.

Berkes, Niyazi. *The Development of Secularism in Turkey*. Montreal: McGill University Press, 1964.

Davison, R.H. *Reform in the Ottoman Empire, 1856–1876*. Princeton, N.J.: Princeton University Press, 1963.

*———. *Turkey*. Englewood Cliffs, N. J.: Prentice-Hall, 1968.

Dodd, C.H. *Politics and Government in Turkey*. Berkeley: University of California Press, 1969.

Frey, Frederick. *The Turkish Political Elite*. Cambridge: MIT Press, 1965.

Heyd, Uriel. *Foundations of Turkish Nationalism*. London: Luzac, 1950.

Karpat, Kemal H. *Turkey's Politics: The Transition to a Multi-Party System*. Princeton, N.J.: Princeton University Press, 1959.

*Lewis, Bernard. *The Emergence of Modern Turkey*, 2nd ed. London: Oxford University Press, 1968.

Lewis, Geoffrey. *Turkey*, 3rd ed. London: Benn, 1965.

Makal, Mahmut. *A Village in Anatolia*, trans, by Sir Wyndham Deedes. London: Valentine, Mitchell, 1954.

RAMSAUR, ERNEST E. *The Young Turks: Prelude to the Revolution of 1908.* New York: Russell and Russell, 1970.

ROBINSON, RICHARD D. *The First Turkish Republic.* Cambridge: Harvard University Press, 1963.

ROOS, LESLIE L. and NORALOU P. *Managers of Modernization.* Cambridge: Harvard University Press, 1971.

SUSA, NASIM. *The Capitulatory Regime of Turkey.* Baltimore: John Hopkins University Press, 1933.

SZYLIOWICZ, JOSEPH S. *A Political Analysis of Student Activism: The Turkish Case.* Beverly Hills, Cal.: Sage Publications, 1972.

YALMAN, AHMET EMIN. *Turkey in My Time.* Norman: University of Oklahoma Press, 1956.

PERSIA AND IRAN

ARBERRY, A.J. et al. *The Cambridge History of Iran,* vol. 1 and vol. 5. London: Cambridge University Press, 1968.

AVERY, PETER. *Modern Iran.* New York: Praeger, 1965.

BANANI, AMIN. *The Modernization of Iran 1921–1941.* Stanford, Cal.: Stanford University Press, 1961.

BHARIER, JULIAN. *Economic Development in Iran, 1900–1970.* London: Oxford University Press, 1971.

*BILL, JAMES A. *The Politics of Iran: Groups, Classes and Modernization.* Columbus, O.: Charles E. Merrill, 1972.

BINDER, LEONARD. *Iran: Political Development in a Changing Society.* Berkeley: University of California Press, 1964.

*COTTAM, RICHARD. *Nationalism in Iran.* Pittsburgh: University of Pittsburgh Press, 1964.

ISSAWI, CHARLES, ed. *The Economic History of Iran, 1800–1914.* Chicago: University of Chicago Press, 1971.

LAMBTON, ANN K.S. *Landlord and Peasant in Persia,* rev. ed. London: Oxford University Press, 1969.

RAMAZINI, ROUHOLLA K. *The Foreign Policy of Iran, 1500–1941.* Charlottesville: University Press of Virginia, 1966.

*UPTON, JOSEPH M. *The History of Modern Iran: An Interpretation.* Cambridge: Harvard University Press, 1960.

WILBER, DONALD. *Iran: Past and Present,* 6th ed. Princeton, N.J.: Princeton University Press, 1967.

YAR-SHATER, EDHSAN, ed. *Iran Faces the Seventies.* New York: Praeger, 1971.

ZONIS, MARVIN. *The Political Elite of Iran.* Princeton, N.J.: Princeton University Press, 1971.

AFGHANISTAN

DUPREE, LOUIS. *Afghanistan.* Princeton, N.J.: Princeton University Press, 1972.

FRASER-TYTLER, SIR W.K. *Afghanistan,* 3rd ed., rev. by M.C. Gillett. London: Oxford University Press, 1967.

GREGORIAN, VARTAN. *The Emergence of Modern Afghanistan 1800–1946.* Stanford, Cal.: Stanford University Press, 1969.

NEWELL, RICHARD S. *The Politics of Afghanistan.* Ithaca, N.Y.: Cornell University Press, 1972.

POULLADA, LEON B. *Reform and Rebellion in Afghanistan, 1919–1929.* Ithaca, N.Y.: Cornell University Press, 1973.

THE ARAB WORLD

GENERAL

ABU-LUGHOD, IBRAHIM. *The Arab Rediscovery of Europe.* Princeton, N.J.: Princeton University Press, 1963.

*ANTONIUS, GEORGE. *The Arab Awakening.* London: Hamish Hamilton. 1938. (Paperback. New York: Putnam.)

ARBERRY, A.J., ed. and trans. *Modern Arabic Poetry.* London: Taylor's Foreign Press, 1950.

*BERGER, MONROE. *The Arab World Today.* Garden City, N.Y.: Doubleday, 1962.

DAWN, C. ERNEST. *From Ottomanism to Arabism.* Urbana: University of Illinois Press, 1973.

HAIM, SYLVIA G., ed. *Arab Nationalism: An Anthology.* Berkeley: University of California Press, 1962.

HANNA, SAMI A., and GEORGE H. GARDNER. *Arab Socialism.* Leiden: E. J. Brill, 1969.

*HOLT, PETER M. *Egypt and the Fertile Crescent, 1516–1922: A Political History.* Ithaca, N.Y.: Cornell University Press, 1966.

*HOURANI, ALBERT H. *Arabic Thought in the Liberal Age 1798–1939.* London: Oxford University Press, 1962.

*KHADDURI, MAJID. *Political Trends in the Arab World.* Baltimore: Johns Hopkins University Press, 1970.

*LEWIS, BERNARD. *The Arabs in History,* 3rd ed. London: Hutchinson, 1964. (Paperback. New York: Harper and Row.)

NUSEIBEH, HASAM ZAKI. *The Ideas of Arab Nationalism.* Ithaca, N.Y.: Cornell University Press, 1956.

POLK, WILLIAM R. *The United States and the Arab World,* rev. ed. Cambridge: Harvard University Press, 1969.

SHARABI, HISHAM. *Arab Intellectuals and the West: The Formative Years 1875–1914.* Baltimore: Johns Hopkins University Press, 1970.

EGYPT

*ABD AL-NASIR, JAMAL. *Egypt's Liberation: The Philosophy of the Revolution.* Washington, D.C.: Public Affairs Press, 1955. (The paperback edition of the above book is: Nasser, Gamal Abdel. *The Philosophy of the Revolution.* Buffalo: Smith, Keynes, and Marshall, 1959.)

ABU-LUGHOD, JANET. *Cairo: 1001 Years of the City Victorious.* Princeton, N.J.: Princeton University Press, 1971.

ADAMS, CHARLES C. *Islam and Modernism in Egypt.* London: Oxford University Press, 1933.

BAER, GABRIEL. *Studies in the Social History of Modern Egypt.* Chicago: Universtiy of Chicago Press, 1969.

DEKMEJIAN, R. H. *Egypt Under Nasser: A Study in Political Dynamics.* Albany: State University of New York Press, 1971.

HARRIS, CHRISTINA PHELPS. *Nationalism and Revolution in Egypt: The Role of the Muslim Brotherhood.* The Hague: Mouton, 1964.

HOLT, P.M., ed. *Political and Social Change in Modern Egypt.* London: Oxford University Press, 1968.

ISSAWI, CHARLES. *Egypt in Revolution: An Economic Analysis.* London: Oxford University Press, 1965.

LACOUTURE, JEAN and SIMONNE. *Egypt in Transition,* trans. by Francis Scarfe. New York: Criterion Books, 1958.

*LANE, E.W. *Manners and Customs of the Modern Egyptians,* 3rd ed. New York: Dutton, 1908. (Paperback. New York: Dover Press.)

LITTLE, TOM. *Modern Egypt.* New York: Praeger, 1967.

MARLOWE, JOHN. *Cromer in Egypt.* London: Elek, 1970.

———. *A History of Modern Egypt and Anglo-Egyptian Relations, 1800–1956,* 2nd ed. Hamden, Conn.: Archon Books, 1965.

MAYFIELD, JAMES B. *Rural Politics in Nasser's Egypt.* Austin: University of Texas Press, 1971.

MITCHELL, RICHARD P. *The Society of the Muslim Brothers.* London: Oxford University Press, 1969.

SAFRAN, NADAV. *Egypt in Search of Political Community.* Cambridge: Harvard University Press, 1961.

STEPHENS, ROBERT H. *Nasser, A Political Biography.* London: Allen Lane, 1971.

VATIKIOTIS, P.J. *The Egyptian Army in Politics: Pattern for New Nations?* Bloomington: Indiana University Press, 1961.

———, ed. *Egypt Since the Revolution.* London: G. Allen and Unwin, 1968.

———. *The Modern History of Egypt.* New York: Praeger, 1969.

WYNN, WILTON. *Nasser of Egypt: The Search for Dignity.* Cambridge. Arlington Books, 1959.

NORTHWEST AFRICA (THE MAGHRIB)

General

BARBOUR, NEVILL, ed. *A Survey of North West Africa,* 2nd ed. London: Oxford University Press, 1962.

BERQUE, JACQUES. *French North Africa: The Maghrib Between Two World Wars,* trans. by Jean Stewart. New York: Praeger, 1967.

*BOVILL, E.W. *The Golden Trade of the Moors,* 2nd ed. London: Oxford University Press, 1968.

GALLAGHER, C.F. *The United States and North Africa: Morocco, Algeria and Tunisia.* Cambridge: Harvard University Press, 1963.

*GORDON, D.C. *North Africa's French Legacy, 1954–1962*. Cambridge: Harvard University Press, 1962.

JULIEN, CHARLES-ANDRÉ. *History of North Africa: Tunisia, Algeria, Morocco*. trans. by J. Petrie. New York: Praeger, 1970.

LeTOURNEAU, ROGER. *The Almohad Movement in North America in the Twelfth and Thirteenth Centuries*. Princeton, N.J.: Princeton University Press, 1969.

*MOORE, CLEMENT HENRY. *Politics in North Africa*. Boston: Little, Brown, 1970.

ZARTMAN, I. WILLIAM. *Government and Politics in Northern Africa*. New York: Praeger, 1963.

*———, ed. *Man, State, and Society in The Contemporary Maghrib*. New York: Praeger, 1963.

Libya

EVANS-PRITCHARD, E.E. *The Sanusi of Cyrenaica*, 2nd ed. Oxford: Clarendon, 1968.

FARLEY, RAWLE. *Planning for Development in Libya*. New York: Praeger, 1971.

KHADDURI, MAJID. *Modern Libya*. Baltimore: Johns Hopkins University Press, 1963.

Algeria

CONFER, VINCENT. *France and Algeria*. Syracuse, N.Y.: Syracuse University Press, 1966.

GILLESPIE, JOAN. *Algeria: Rebellion and Revolution*. London: Benn, 1960.

O'BALLANCE, EDGAR. *The Algerian Insurrection, 1954–1962*. London: Faber, 1967.

OTTAWAY, DAVID and MARINA. *Algeria: The Politics of a Socialist Revolution*. Berkeley: University of California Press, 1970.

QUANDT, WILLIAM B. *Revolution and Political Leadership: Algeria, 1954–1968*. Cambridge: MIT Press, 1969.

Morocco

ASHFORD, DOUGLAS E. *Political Change in Morocco*. Princteon, N.J.: Princeton University Press, 1961.

*BARBOUR, NEVILL. *Morocco*. New York: Walker, 1965.

BERNARD, STEPHANE. *The Franco-Moroccan Conflict, 1943–1956*, trans. by M. Oliver et al. New Haven, Conn.: Yale University Press, 1968.

*HALSTEAD, J.P. *Rebirth of a Nation*. Cambridge: Harvard University Press, 1967.

LANDAU, ROM. *Moroccan Drama, 1900–1955*. San Francisco: American Academy of Asian Studies, 1956.

*STEWART, CHARLES F. *The Economy of Morocco, 1912–1962*. Cambridge: Harvard University Press, 1964.

*ZARTMAN, I. WILLIAM. *Destiny of a Dynasty: The Search for Institutions in Morocco's Developing Society*. Columbia: University of South Carolina Press, 1964.

Tunisia

LING, DWIGHT L. *Tunisia from Proctectorate to Republic.* Bloomington: Indiana University press, 1967.

MOORE, CLEMENT H. *Tunisia Since Independence.* Berkeley: University of California Press, 1965.

ARAB ASIA

General

*MALONE, JOSEPH J. *The Arab Lands of Western Asia.* Englewood Cliffs, N.J.: Prentice-Hall, 1973.

Syria and Lebanon

HOURANI, ALBERT H. *Syria and Lebanon: A Political Essay.* London: Oxford University Press, 1946.

HUDSON, MICHAEL C. *The Precarious Republic: Political Modernization in Lebanon.* New York: Random House, 1968.

LONGRIGG, STEPHEN H. *Syria and Lebanon under French Mandate.* London: Oxford University Press, 1958.

PETRAN, TABITHA. *Syria.* New York: Praeger, 1972.

SALIBI, K.S. *The Modern History of Lebanon.* New York: Praeger, 1965.

SEALE, PATRICK. *The Struggle for Syria.* London: Oxford University Press, 1965.

TIBAWI, A.L. *A Modern History of Syria Including Lebanon and Palestine.* New York: St. Martin's Press, 1969.

TORREY, G.H. *Syrian Politics and the Military, 1945–1958.* Columbus: Ohio State University Press, 1964.

ZIADEH, NICOLA A. *Syria and Lebanon.* New York: Praeger, 1957.

*ZUWIYYA-YAMAK, LABIB Z. *The Syrian Nationalist Party.* Cambridge: Harvard University Press, 1966.

Palestine and Israel

BERNSTEIN, MARVER H. *The Politics of Israel: The First Decade of Statehood.* Princeton, N.J.: Princeton University Press, 1957.

BRECHER, MICHAEL. *The Foreign Policy System of Israel: Setting, Images, Process.* New Haven, Conn.: Yale University Press, 1972.

*CHAILAND, GERARD. *The Palestinian Resistance.* Harmondsworth: Penguin: 1972.

FEIN, LEONARD J. *Israel: Politics and People,* rev. ed. Boston: Little, Brown, 1968.

HADAWI, SAMI. *Bitter Harvest: Palestine 1914–1967.* New York: New World, 1967.

LAQUEUR, WALTER Z. *A History of Zionism.* New York: Holt, Rinehart and Winston, 1972.

*———, ed. *The Israel-Arab Reader.* New York: Citadel Press, 1969. (Paperback. New York: Bantam.)

LESLIE, S. CLEMENT. *The Rift in Israel: Religious Authority and Secular Democracy.* London: Routledge and K. Paul, 1971.

PERETZ, DON. *Israel and the Palestine Arabs.* Washington, D.C.: Middle East Institute, 1958.

*QUANDT, WILLIAM B. *Palestinian Nationalism: Its Political and Military Dimensions.* Santa Monica, Cal.: Rand Corporation, 1971.

*SAFRAN, NADAV. *From War to War: The Arab-Israeli Confrontation 1948–1967.* New York: Pegasus, 1969. (Paperback. Indianapolis: Pegasus.)

SEGRE, V.D. *Israel: A Society in Transition.* London: Oxford University Press, 1971.

*WEIZMANN, CHAIM. *Trial and Error.* New York: Harper and Row, 1949. (Paperback. New York: Schocken Books.)

Transjordan and Jordan

PATAI, RAPHAEL. *The Kingdom of Jordan.* Princeton, N.J.: Princeton University Press, 1958.

SHWADRAN, BENJAMIN. *Jordan, A State of Tension.* New York: Council for Middle Eastern Affairs, 1959.

VATIKIOTIS, P.J. *Politics and the Military in Jordan.* London: Cass, 1967.

Iraq

DANN, URIEL. *Iraq under Qassem: A Political History 1958–1963.* New York: Praeger, 1969.

KHADDURI, MAJID. *Independent Iraq,* 2nd ed. London: Oxford University Press, 1960.

———. *Republican Iraq.* London: Oxford University Press, 1969.

LONGRIGG, STEPHEN H. *Iraq 1910 to 1950: A Political, Social and Economic History.* London: Oxford University Press, 1953.

Arabian Peninsula

DOUGHTY, CHARLES M. *Travels in Arabia Deserta,* abr. by Edward Garnett. New York: Heritage, 1931.

HOWARTH, DAVID. *The Desert King: Ibn Saud and His Arabia.* New York: McGraw-Hill, 1964.

KELLY, JOHN B. *Eastern Arabian Frontiers.* New York: Praeger, 1964.

LANDEN, ROBERT G. *Oman Since 1856.* Princeton, N.J.: Princeton University Press, 1967.

LITTLE, TOM. *South Arabia: Arena of Conflict.* London: Pall Mall, 1968.

MACRO, ERIC. *Yemen and the Western World since 1571.* London: Hurst, 1968.

MARLOWE, JOHN. *The Persian Gulf in the Twentieth Century.* New York: Praeger, 1962.

PHILBY, H. ST. JOHN B. *Saudi Arabia.* New York: Praeger, 1955.

SNAVELY, WILLIAM P., and MUHAMMED SADIK. *Bahrain, Qatar and the United Arab Emirates.* Lexington: Lexington Books, 1972.

UNITED STATES GOVERNMENT. *Area Handbook for the Peripheral States of the Arabian Peninsula.* Washington, D.C.: Government Printing Office, 1971.

WENNER, MANFRED. *Modern Yemen, 1918–1966.* Baltimore: Johns Hopkins University Press, 1967.

Additional suggestions may be found in the following works and in the bibliographies listed therein:

AMERICAN UNIVERSITIES FIELD STAFF. *A Select Bibliography: Asia, Africa, Eastern Europe, Central America,* ed. P. Talbot. New York: American Universities Field Staff, 1960, with supplements 1961, 1963, 1965.

CAHEN, CLAUDE, and JEAN SAUVAGET. *Introduction to the History of the Muslim East,* trans. by Mme. Paira-Pemberton. Berkeley: University of California Press, 1965.

HOWARD, HARRY N., et al. *Middle East and North Africa: A Bibliography for Undergraduate Libraries.* Williamsport: Bro-Dart Publishing Co., 1971.

PART TWO

SOUTH ASIA

3

THE FOUNDATIONS OF
SOUTH ASIA

Geographic Foundations:
Regions, Resources, and Peoples

The boundaries of South Asia, like those of the Middle East, can be defined in more than one way. The term "South Asia" will be used here to include India and the neighboring states which have been most strongly influenced by Indian culture—Pakistan, Bangladesh, Ceylon (or Sri Lanka), and the Himalayan states of Nepal, Bhutan, and Sikkim. However, it has also been used to include Afghanistan, which has frequently been associated politically with the region of today's Pakistan, or to include Burma, which was ruled by Britain for several generations as part of its Indian empire.

Although South Asia is just over a third as large as the Middle East, it holds more than three and a half times as many people and therefore has an overall population density more than ten times greater. Like the Middle East, South Asia has a distinctive, ancient, and complex culture made up of many elements. One of these elements is the tradition of rivalry among rulers of its major divisions. Another is the contribution made to its historical development by the long series of invaders from Central Asia and elsewhere. The peoples of both regions also have a lengthy tradition of trading with neighboring peoples and introducing the ways of urban-centered life to them. Unlike the Middle East, however, most of South Asia experienced nearly a century and a half of European rule. When its people began to achieve independence in 1947, no one living in India, Pakistan, or Ceylon could remember the days before British control. Many parts of the three states were as yet scarcely touched by modern ways, it was true; but those who fought for independence, won it, and plunged into the task of making it work had a far more intimate and long-standing association with Western institutions than most nineteenth- and twentieth-century Middle Easterners.

MOUNTAINS AND RIVERS

South Asia is screened from its neighbors by the towering Himalaya mountain range and its westward and eastward extensions, the Sulaimans and the Assam and Burma hills. South of the upland valleys of Kashmir, Nepal, Sikkim, and Bhutan lies the great Indo-Gangetic plain of northern India. Beyond the plain, the peninsula of southern India juts out into the Indian Ocean, and the island of Ceylon lies just off its southeastern tip.

The north Indian plain includes several natural regions, each of which shades gradually into the next. The western part of the plain is watered by the Indus river, its four major eastern tributaries (the Jhelum, the Chenab, the Ravi, and the Sutlej), and its western tributary (the Kabul, which rises in the mountains of Afghanistan). The central plain is watered by the Ganges river and its tributaries such as the Jumna. The Brahmaputra, which waters the easternmost region, rises in Tibet, breaks through the Himalayas into Assam, and shares the delta of the Ganges.

The Indus valley in the western plain is divided into two portions. The lower portion is called Sind; the upper portion, with its five rivers, is called the Panjab. (The word *panch* from which "Panjab" comes is related to *pente*, the Greek word for "five.") East of Sind lies the inhospitable Thar desert; east of the Panjab lie the sloping plains which mark the watershed between the Indus and the Ganges. This watershed, the narrowest part of the north Indian plain, has been the center of many great empires. The region of the middle Ganges has also been a seat of empires, but prior to Britain's conquests, only once did the rulers of Bengal (the Ganges-Brahmaputra delta) extend their domains as far west as the Indus-Ganges watershed.

The north Indian or Indo-Gangetic plain, walled in by the Himalayas to the north, is also bounded by hills on the south. South of the Panjab and the Indus-Ganges watershed lie the Aravallis; south of the watershed and the middle Ganges lie the Vindhyas and their extensions. The hilly region where the Aravallis meet the Vindhyas and the flatter coastal regions of Gujerat to the west and Orissa to the east have historically been closely associated with the northern plain.

The Vindhyas divide the plain from the peninsula, whose heart is the triangular plateau of the Deccan. Two major rivers, the Narbada and the Tapti, flow southwestward from the Vindhyas between the Vindhyas and the Deccan. The Deccan itself is like a massive tilted block sloping west to east. Its western edge rises steeply from the sea in the cliffs known as the Western Ghats, leaving only a narrow coastal plain. Many of the rivers of the central and southern Deccan, such as the Godavari, the Kistna, and the Kaveri, rise in the Western Ghats and traverse the entire plateau to the eastern coastal plain, but some rivers to the north, like the Mahanadi of Orissa, rise on the southern slopes of the hills between the Deccan and the plain. These rivers find an echo in Ceylon, many of whose rivers and streams run northward from the high southern hills of the island.

CLIMATE

The existence of the Himalayan mountain barrier has materially affected the climate of South Asia. The basic climate of South Asia is governed by the seasonal winds, or monsoons. In the warm months of the year, the cool heavy air over the Indian Ocean streams toward the warm land, bringing rain with it; but the winds reverse direction in the cold months when the land is cooler than the sea, and there is little rain. Therefore, most of the rain comes between June and September. However, there is some winter rain in the Sulaimans and the western Himalayas. Furthermore, the rains begin as early as April in Bengal, and the extreme south has rain throughout most of the year. Some southern areas of India receive more than half their rain in the winter months. Southwestern Ceylon and the mountain zone of north central Ceylon also have rain throughout the year, while the mountain-shielded northern and eastern plains of the island receive most of their rain between October and January.

The heaviest rains fall in southern Ceylon, the western coastal plain of India, the Ganges-Brahmaputra delta, and the districts bordering the eastern Himalayas. These four areas average more than eighty inches of rain a year, for they receive the first showers from the spring winds, which generally travel northeastward. The Himalayan wall deflects the spring and summer winds to the northwest, giving the middle Ganges forty to eighty inches of rain per year. The Indus-Ganges watershed receives twenty to forty inches a year, and most of the Indus valley has only five to twenty inches. The Aravalli districts have slightly more rain than the lower Indus valley, for the hills intercept much of the rain that would otherwise reach the Thar desert and Sind. Gujerat, the Vindhyas, and most of the western and southern Deccan receive about twenty to forty inches of rain a year. The northeastern Deccan, most of the eastern coastal plain, and the northern and eastern plains of Ceylon can usually expect forty to eighty inches of rainfall.

In general, except for the well-watered western coastal plain of India, the amount of rainfall diminishes as one goes westward. However, the pattern of seasonal and annual temperature variations is more complex. The Himalayas force the cold air masses that move out of central Asia between October and February to stream westward to the Atlantic and eastward to the Pacific. Since almost none of this cold central

Asian air crosses the Himalayas, only the southern slopes of the mountain wall dip below freezing long enough during the winter to make possible the existence of permanent snowfields which can feed the rivers that flow into the plain throughout the year. The Panjab occasionally has freezing weather, but it almost never freezes south of the line from Sind to Assam. From March to May, South Asia becomes increasingly hot, but temperatures fall when the rains begin. The wetter the area, the cooler it is between June and September. The Western Ghats are the coolest parts of the peninsula then, and the southeastern coast is warmest. The island of Ceylon remains warm throughout the year. Bengal and the northeastern coast of the peninsula are less warm than the southeast, but temperatures increase as one goes westward in the plain, making the Panjab, Sind, and the Thar desert the hottest regions in the rainy season. Thus the Panjab, one of the driest regions south of the mountain wall, also has the greatest contrasts in temperature during the year.

Not only is the Panjab hot and dry in summer and cold in winter; it also suffers from unpredictability of rainfall. The western coastal plain of India, the southern parts of Ceylon, and most of Bengal and Assam are drenched with heavy rains that rarely vary more than fifteen percent from one year to the next. Therefore, the cultivator knows approximately how much rain to expect. However, the rain-bearing winds gradually lose their moisture as they go eastward across the peninsula and westward up the plain. Consequently the amount of rain in the central Deccan, the northeastern peninsula, and the Indus-Ganges watershed may vary as much as thirty percent from one year to another. Variations are even greater in the Aravallis, Sind, the Thar, and the Panjab. Moreover, the year's rain may come all at once in the driest areas. Serious erosion can result from a few days of heavy downpour where soils have been parched by the scorching sun of March, April, and May.

Conditions in the Indus valley closely resemble those in portions of the Middle East. Temperature contrasts in the Panjab correspond to those in the intermontane basins of Afghanistan, Iran, and Anatolia; sparse and unreliable rains mean dependence on mountain-fed rivers and underground water supplies, as in the Nile valley, lower Iraq, and parts of Iran. However, rainfall increases and temperature variations decrease as one moves south or east from the Panjab, so that conditions in much of central India are subtropical. A tropical climate prevails along the Indian coast from Bombay to Calcutta, and in much of Bengal, Assam, and Ceylon.

CONDITIONS OF AGRICULTURE

Soils and vegetation reflect topography and climate. The wetter the climate, the heavier the vegetation is, regardless of whether it is growing on the dark water-retentive soils of the northern Deccan, the lateritic or bricklike soils of many districts of the southern peninulsa and of upland and southwestern Ceylon, or the alluvial soils of the Indo-Gangetic plain, the river deltas, and northeastern coastal Ceylon. Evergreen forest is the natural vegetation where annual rainfall averages more than eighty inches, heavy deciduous forest where average rainfall is forty to eighty inches. Sparse deciduous forest and scrub are found in areas with twenty to forty inches of rain, and scrub or open bush in the driest regions. However, little natural vegetation still exists. Throughout most of the Indo-Gangetic plain, much of the peninsula, and the valleys and plains of Ceylon, human occupancy has replaced evergreen forest with rice paddy, deciduous forest with other cereals, and scrub with crops grown on irrigated land.

Heavy vegetation does not imply fertile soils. The soils of South Asia, like the soils of much of the Middle East, contain relatively little humus because of the rapid rate at which organic matter decomposes in a hot climate. Moreover, the evaporation of water from the soil is nearly impossible in the rainy season and almost uninterrupted during the winter and spring. Therefore many valuable salts and minerals are washed down into the soil away from the plant roots during the wet months, only to be brought all the way to the surface, forming hard crusts, in the dry months. On alluvial soils the crusts can be dissolved by rain or irrigation water, but they are baked solid by the sun on lateritic soils. The low soil fertility which results from such conditions has been a major reason that crop yields per acre in South Asia have generally been somewhat smaller than yields in many other regions, although the unpredictability of the monsoon also plays a part.

Although most of South Asia receives more rain than most of the Middle East, agriculture in South Asia depends heavily on irrigation, since (1) the rains ordinarily come during the warm months when natural evaporation rates are high; (2) the rains tend to come all at once; and (3) the timing and amount may vary widely. A crop can be wrecked if the monsoon rains are too late, too early, too abundant, or too meager. Consequently, irrigation is widely used. Even in the rather well-watered eastern coastal plain of India, up to half the cultivated land is irrigated in some districts. The first British conquerors found dams there that had been used since the tenth century A.D.

The people of the Indo-Gangetic plain use the snow-fed rivers which flow throughout the year for irrigation. From the upper Ganges westward, agriculture depends heavily on irrigation canals. Before the nineteenth century most of these canals were inundation canals, filled only in the flood season. The British supplemented and in some areas replaced the inundation canals with new dam-and-canal systems which made irrigation possible throughout the year. In the foothills and much of the plain, shallow wells whose water is raised by bullocks have been used for many generations, and in the western part of the middle Ganges region, hydroelectricity is now used to pump irrigation water from newly sunk deep wells. In the eastern part of the middle Ganges, most of the irrigation water comes from "tanks," reservoirs made by building earthworks across the paths of natural drainage.

Throughout the peninsula and in northeastern Ceylon, water supplies are more precarious than in northern India because there are no permanent snowfields to feed rivers and underground sources of water throughout the year. Tanks and shallow wells are used in most of the area, supplemented by canals in the delta regions. Wells far outnumber tanks in the northwest Deccan, where water stored in unlined reservoirs would quickly seep away. Only in the eastern and southern Deccan with their hard-baked lateritic soils can water be kept in tanks until it is needed. Even there, the farmer must race with the sun to use the water in a tank before it evaporates. Where rain falls during most of the year, both irrigated and nonirrigated agriculture are less of a gamble than in south central India, with its summer rains, or in northeastern Ceylon, with its winter rains.

THE PRIMARY INDUSTRIES

The people of South Asia still rely almost as heavily as their ancestors did on the growing of field crops. The predominant food crops are wheat in the northwest, rice in Bengal and the coastal plains of southern India and Ceylon, and millet in the Deccan. All three are raised in the middle Ganges. Rice is raised wherever water supplies and temperatures permit, for even though wheat and millet provide more proteins, fats, minerals, and vitamins, rice yields more pounds of edible food per acre than any other crop. Fibers also come from the fields. Bengal raises jute, while cotton is a major crop in the Panjab, the upper Ganges, Gujerat, the Deccan, and the Kaveri valley. In addition, coconut, coffee, tea, and rubber plantations were begun on Ceylon by Europeans, and tea plantations in Assam.

Of the other four primary industries—animal husbandry, fishing, forestry, and mining—animal husbandry is next to agriculture in importance. Domesticated animals have been abundant (almost half as many cattle as people in India, for example) and have been as widely used for farm labor in South Asia as in the middle East. In addition, milk and clarified butter have long been staple foods, although centuries-old prohibitions against killing cattle mean that the great majority of Indians do not eat cattle flesh. However, the cattle of South Asia lack the size and strength of western European, or even Middle Eastern, cattle. Winter rains in the Middle East provide winter pasturage, which is lacking in most of South Asia. Yet the human population of South Asia is so large that little food can be set aside for the cattle during the dry South Asian winter. The shortage of nourishing fodder has lessened the efficiency of South Asian cattle both as workers and as milk producers. It has also made their dung less useful for fertilizer, because of its low content of organic matter. Consequently, few districts in South Asia have developed as efficient an intermingling of crop-raising and animal husbandry as have western Europe or parts of the Middle East.

Fishing and forestry, two other primary industries which provide materials for trade and industry, have not been highly developed. Fish plays only a small part in the diet of those who live inland, partly because of lack of transportation and partly because of traditional reluctance to kill living creatures for food. However, in the coastal districts and Ceylon, fish is a more important food.

Although forests still cover approximately as much land as do rice-fields, natural forests have almost disappeared in heavily populated areas. Nevertheless, forest products have a place in economic life. Hard sal wood from the Himalayan foothills, the Western Ghats, and the eastern Vindhyas has been prized for centuries. The bamboo groves found near villages in all but the driest and coldest areas provide fuel, fodder and raw material for huts, furnishings, tools, and mats and baskets. The even more useful coconut of the southern Indian coasts and Ceylon furnishes food and drink as well as fuel, fodder, and fiber. The hillside forests of Ceylon and the Himalayan states also still provide fuel and materials for buildings, furnishings, and tools.

The last primary industry, mining, did not begin to come into its own until the twentieth century, although South Asia has many important mineral resources. There are large high-grade coal and iron deposits between the Ganges and the Godavari; manganese, aluminum, and chromite in the Deccan; some copper in the north; oil and natural gas in the extreme northwest and the extreme northeast; gold and mica in southern India; graphite in Ceylon; and salt and gypsum in the upper Indus valley and the Aravalli hills. The mountains, the hills, and the Deccan also contain limestones, granites, slates, and other building stones. However, only a few minerals—salt, gold, copper, some iron, and the building stones— were extensively mined or quarried before the nineteenth century.

TRANSPORT AND COMMERCE

Historically, the economy of South Asia was even more predominantly rural, even more dependent on the growing of field crops, than that of the Middle East. In normal years this agricultural economy was not necessarily less flourishing than the more diversified economies of the agricultural-pastoral Middle East and medieval western Europe, in terms of the ratio between what was produced and what was needed for consumption. The great problem of South Asia was the large number of abnormal years, when the rains were late or early, excessive or scanty. Nevertheless, even in the poorest years some goods were available for commerce.

The regions of South Asia have traded with each other and with the outside world since earliest times. Most travel within South Asia has been by land, either on foot or by bullock-drawn cart. Camels have been used in the dry northwest, but the food and water requirements of horses have made them a luxury since their introduction more than three thousand years ago. Raising and keeping horses has been so difficult that the stock has had to be continually replenished from Turkestan or by sea from the Arab lands.

The building of imperial highways has facilitated land travel from time to time in the past two thousand years. However, in the level Indo-Gangetic plain, paths and highways have always been supplemented by the snow-fed rivers from the north, which are navigable all year. The percentage of water traffic increases as one travels eastward to Bengal with its intricate network of waterways, where water transport has ordinarily been more important than land traffic. Bengal with its rivers has been more involved in overseas trade than most of the rest of the north Indian plain, although some trade has been carried on between Sind and the Middle East throughout the past five thousand years.

Before the introduction of the steamship, the annual monsoons were vital to seafaring merchants like the dealers in Arab horses, Ceylonese spices, and Chinese silk. The monsoon winds enabled traders to go east in summer and west in winter with little difficulty, partially offsetting the inconvenience caused by the scarcity of large natural harbors along the coasts of South Asia. The monsoons made it easy for the people of the Indian coastal plains and Ceylon to go overseas. However, the Western Ghats barred the people of the western Indian coastal plain from the interior, except where there were natural openings through the cliffs, like the canyons near Bombay. The people of the eastern Indian coastal plain had only a few hills to cross to reach the interior, but the rivers of the peninsula were too shallow for navigation most of the year, and in the rainy season, the coastal trader would have to fight strong currents and eastward-blowing winds to go upstream, while the people of the interior had little to sell because they did not sow their crops until the rains came. The people of Ceylon were more fortunately situated.

In spite of obstacles to trade between the Deccan and the coastal plains of India, fabrics woven from Deccan cotton found their way to ports on both coasts. Throughout the centuries before the British came, the export of Indian cottons to the Middle East and Southeast Asia formed a staple of Indian Ocean trade, along with Indian and Ceylonese spices, gems, and other light, compact, and valuable items such as Chinese silks. However, bulkier goods like metal wares, building materials, and furnishings generally were not exported.

DISTRIBUTION OF PEOPLES

Although the mainland of South Asia forms a geographic unit, separated from its neighbors by the Himalayan border, it has many divisions. The north includes the uplands (Kashmir, Nepal, Bhutan, Sikkim), the Indo-Gangetic plain (divided into Sind, the Thar, the Panjab, the Indus-Ganges watershed, the middle Ganges, Bengal, and Assam), the hill country of the Aravallis and Vindhyas, and the transitional areas of Gujerat in the west and Orissa in the east. South India includes the Deccan, the southwestern coast, and the Godavari, Kistna, and Kaveri river basins in the east. With such a varied structure it is not surprising to find variety in the life of South Asia. Additional elements of diversity have been introduced from the outside, for even the mountain wall has not kept out all external influences.

There have been few incursions from east and north through the mountain wall. Strong Chinese dynasties sent expeditions into Nepal in the seventeenth and eighteenth centuries A.D., and Burma held Assam briefly in the early nineteenth century, but the great highroads to India have been the passes of the Sulaiman range in the northwest. Aryans, Scythians, Kushans, White Huns, Rajputs, Ghaznawids, and Mughals all streamed from Turkestan to India through Afghanistan. Although Persians and Greeks came from lands farther to the west, they too used the passes of the Sulaimans.

Once over the mountains, each of these peoples entered the Indo-Gangetic plain, and many settled there permanently. Those who stayed in the Panjab often retained ties with Afghanistan and Turkestan, and some of their leaders ruled empires that stretched west as well as east of the Sulaimans. Those who pressed on toward the Ganges usually left Afghanistan behind and turned their eyes still further east and south.

Successive waves of invasion from the northwest affected more than the Indo-Gangetic plain. Each new incursion drove some of the people of the plain southward into the peninsula, across the barriers of the Thar desert, the Aravallis, and the Vindhyas, or even across the sea to Ceylon. Moreover, empire-builders in the north Indian plain often seized additional lands in the hills and the peninsula, introducing even more northern ways into southern life.

Once the refugees and the invaders crossed the hills, they found themselves on the eastward-sloping plateau of the Deccan. The empire-builders of the plain rarely reached beyond the Narbada and the Tapti, but other northerners established themselves throughout the Deccan. However, the trade of the coastal peoples of southern India and Ceylon with the Middle East, East Africa, and Southeast Asia gave rise to flourishing cultures which retained their individuality despite northern influence. These historic factors form the basis of life in South Asia today.

The Formation of Language and Caste Groups

HISTORICAL INTERMINGLING OF PEOPLES

As invasion after invasion poured into the northwest and unsettled the whole of South Asia, the resultant mingling of peoples led to the appearance of distinct linguistic regions. The consequences of the invasions also affected the specifically Indian social structure known as the caste system. To understand these developments, it is therefore necessary to look briefly at the historical record.

Within a few generations of the rise of civilizations in Mesopotamia and Egypt, the Indus valley became the site of a flourishing and highly civilized society. Like its contemporaries with which it traded by way of the Persian Gulf, the Indus civilization relied on large-scale irrigation works. For more than a thousand years its people ruled the dry northwest, but then the Indus cities disappeared and horse-riding, cattle-herding, Indo-European Aryan tribes took control. The Aryans entered the Indus valley at some time between 2000 and 1500 B.C., at the time when other Indo-Europeans were entering Iran.

It is generally assumed that the people of the Indus civilization were related to the Dravidian peoples of the present. Today, small groups of people who use Dravidian languages still exist in the basins west of the Sulaimans and the hills south of the Panjab, where the Aryan conquest would have driven their ancestors. Furthermore, most Dravidians are in southern India. This has been taken to mean that they were pushed southward by the arrival of newcomers in the northern plain.

From the oral traditions preserved in the collections known as the Vedas, the fair-skinned Aryans seem to have disdained the "dark-skinned Dasyus," as they called the earlier inhabitants of the plain. The Dasyus were required to do all the manual labor, while the roles of ruler, priest, and merchant were reserved for Aryans. By 1000 B.C., cities were beginning to dot the north again, as the Aryans extended their rule eastward toward Bengal and southward to the Narbada and Tapti.

The epic of the *Mahabharata* shows that the Aryans fought bitterly not only with the Dasyus but also with each other. When the Persian empire seized the Panjab and Sind in the sixth century B.C., several states were vying for leadership in the Ganges valley. A few were organized as tribal republics, somewhat like the Berber confederations of northwest Africa, but most were organized as monarchies.

Sometime in the fifth or sixth century B.C., Aryans with metal weapons left the Indo-Gangetic plain, landed on Ceylon, and quickly subdued the local inhabitants, known as the Veddahs. The newcomers gradually built up a thriving civilization based on irrigated rice agriculture in the alluvial northern plain. Soon the island became a regular port of call for Middle Eastern and Indian traders on their way to Southeast Asia and China. Tamils from southern India joined the Aryans and through intermarriage formed the Sinhalese people.

The strongest of the north Indian states from the sixth to the fourth century B.C. was the monarchy of Magadha, in the middle Ganges region. It was still flourishing when Alexander of Macedon overthrew the Persian power in northwest India in 326 B.C. However, Alexander's conquest was short-lived, for in 322 B.C. the Indian leader Chandragupta Maurya expelled the Greeks. Using the Panjab as his base, Chandragupta Maurya then united the entire plain from Sind to Bengal into the first great Indian empire, that of the Maurya dynasty. Between 322 and 302 B.C. he added the Vindhyas, the Aravallis, Gujerat, and much of Afghanistan to his domains. His son, and his grandson Asoka, extended the empire southward to a line approximately halfway between the Kistna and the Kaveri. Within forty years of Asoka's death in 232 B.C., the Andhra people of the Godavari-Kistna region regained their independence; but the Maurya empire remained an inspiration to future rulers in the plain.

The revolt of the Andhra signaled the collapse of the Maurya empire. By the second century B.C. the northwest was again ruled by Greeks, and the rest of the empire was divided among a number of rulers. Rivalries among them bred a weakness which allowed various central Asian tribes to enter northwest India, as did the Saka in the last century B.C. and the Kushan in the first century A.D. The Kushan drove the Saka into Gujerat and across the Narbada river, where they remained in power until the rise of the second great Indian empire, the Gupta dynasty of the fourth and fifth centuries A.D. The Kushan disappeared by the third century A.D., when the Sassanids briefly reestablished Persian rule in the Panjab.

Soon after the Guptas appeared in Magadha in the fourth century A.D., they conquered the Panjab, the former Saka territories, and Bengal. However, they did not reach south of Bombay. Powerful though they were, they could not overcome the four flourishing Dravidian kingdoms of the south—the Pallava who had taken over the territory of the Andhra, the Kerala on the west coast, the Chola in the Kaveri basin, and the Pandya at the tip of the peninsula. Much of the southerners' wealth and strength came from the trade they had carried on for centuries with Egypt, Mesopotamia, Southeast Asia, and China, either directly or by way of the flourishing entrepôt of Ceylon.

None of the rulers of the north Indian plain were able to subdue the Deccan and the south during the first ten centuries A.D.—not even the White Huns from central Asia, who ruled from the Panjab to the Narbada in the late fifth and early sixth centuries A.D., or the energetic ruler Harsha, who reigned from Gujerat to the Brahmaputra in the early seventh century A.D. The Deccan remained a separate seat of empire under the Chalukya, who were probably related to the Gurjara tribe that entered India from the northwest in the sixth century A.D. Late in the eighth century the Chalukya began to face the rivalry of a people who eventually defeated them, the Rashtrakuta, who spoke the Dravidian Kannara language. To the south and east, the Pallava crossed the Kaveri occasionally between the sixth and tenth centuries A.D., but the Chola, Pandya, and Kerala retained their independence. On Ceylon, new Tamil arrivals from south India came to pose an increasing challenge to the continued dominance of the Sinhalese.

During the centuries of Chalukya and Rashtrakuta power in the center and Pallava, Chola, Pandya, and Kerala rule in the south, the situation in the north was highly confused. In the west, the expanding Arabs seized Sind and the western Panjab by 715 A.D., only to find their way eastward blocked by the Thar desert and the newly arrived Gurjara in the center of the plain. The Gurjara in turn were challenged on the south by the Rashtrakuta and on the east by the Pala rulers of Bengal, who at times held large portions of the Ganges valley. By 1000 A.D. the Gurjara were too weak to prevent a Muslim advance. However, in the peninsula a resurgent Chola dynasty toppled the Pallava, fatally weakened the Rashtrakuta, and overpowered the Kerala and Pandya during the ninth and tenth centuries, bringing all of south India under one rule for the first time. In the early eleventh century, the Chola added most of Ceylon to their south Indian empire. They sent large expeditionary forces to Pala-ruled Bengal and the distant island of Sumatra. The Sinhalese managed to eject the Chola a few decades later, but their Tamil neighbors on Ceylon established and maintained a control over the island's northern plains which lasted until the Portuguese arrival in the sixteenth century.

While the people of the Chola-ruled peninsula concentrated on southeastern Asia, Gurjara weakness allowed Muslim invaders to seize the plain. The Turkish Ghaznawids completed the conquest of the Indus valley, joining it to Afghanistan and part of Turkestan as the Kushan had done. The Persian Ghurids who replaced the Ghaznawids in 1186 quickly swept down the Ganges and overthrew the successors of the Palas in Bengal, driving the petty princes of the plain north to the Himalayan foothills or south to the Aravallis and Vindhyas. The princes of the central hills barely maintained themselves against the Turkish Mamluk or slave dynasty which replaced the Ghurids in 1206 and proceeded to march south to the Narbada. However, the princes had a brief respite from the attacks of the Delhi Sultanate (the collective name for the series of Turkish slave dynasties which reigned in the central plain from 1206 to 1526) in the mid-thirteenth century, when the rulers of Delhi had to cope with the Mongol invasions of Afghanistan and the Panjab.

During the thirteenth century the Chola empire fell apart and the Rashtrakuta were driven southward by the Aryan Maratha people, who took over the northern Deccan with the help of dispossessed Aryans fleeing the Delhi Sultanate. As the fourteenth century opened, the Delhi Sultanate extended its control south to the Kaveri in a series of rapid campaigns which left only the Pandya independent. However, Bengal, Gujerat, and the new Bahmani kingdom in the Deccan soon broke away under Muslim rulers who paid only nominal allegiance to Delhi, and local leaders established control in Orissa and the lower Godavari valley. Below the Kistna, the new empire of Vijayanagar united the Dravidians of the south against the threat of Muslim domination. In 1398 a brief but devastating incursion from Turkestan crippled the Delhi Sultanate so that resurgent local princes recovered control in the Aravallis in the next century. Before 1500 the Bahmani kingdom split into five rival states, but the rivals managed to unite against Vijayanagar, raze its capital in 1565, and annex its northern territories. The remainder of once-proud Vijayanagar was soon divided into a number of petty states.

By the time Vijayanagar fell, the northern plain was already ruled by the Mughal dynasty, the last great empire to be founded by invaders from the northwest. In addition, the first western European traders had appeared along the coast. The Mughals were led into the northern plain by Babur, a descendant of the leader who had plundered Delhi in 1398. Babur overthrew the Delhi Sultanate in 1526, with the help of some of the Ottoman artillerymen who had defeated the Mamluks of Syria and Egypt barely a decade earlier, and went on to conquer Bengal by 1529. Ten years later his son was driven back toward Turkestan by an Afghan, Sher Khan, who had served the sultans of Delhi in the eastern part of what had once been Magadha but was now known as Bihar. His short but eventful reign as Sher Shah was followed by the return of Babur's son, who reconquered much of the plain with the aid of the Persian Safawids.

Babur's grandson Akbar (1556–1605) extended the limits of his empire from the Sulaimans on the west to the Mahanadi on the east, and from the Tapti in the south to the Brahmaputra on the north. Akbar's grandson Shah Jehan (1628–1658) reached down to the Kistna, only to rouse bitter resistance among the Maratha of the Deccan. In the mid-seventeenth century the Maratha leader Sivaji laid the foundations of a confederation that dominated central India for almost two hundred years. The first Maratha campaigns were directed against Shah Jehan's son Aurangzeb (1658–1707). Aurangzeb's incessant campaigns brought all but the tip of southern India to acknowledge his rule at some time during the last thirty years of his reign. However, as soon as his armies moved out of a newly conquered district to fight elsewhere, the district would refuse to continue to pay him allegiance. By the end of his successor's reign the strength of the Mughal empire was exhausted.

Between 1707 and 1757 the Mughals lost control over all but the district around the capital at Delhi. Neither the Muslim governors in the plain nor those south of the Godavari paid the Mughals more than lip-service. The Maratha controlled the central part of India, while local princes ruled in Rajasthan—"Land of Kings"—as the region of the Thar desert, the Aravallis, and the western Vindhyas had come to be called. No one—Mughal, Maratha, princeling, or governor—expected foreigners from overseas to rule almost all of South Asia within another hundred years. The Afghan incursion of 1739 worried the ruler at Delhi more than the small but growing power of the British. Yet European rivalry for Indian and Ceylonese trade, which began after 1600 when the Dutch and English challenged Portugal's century-old supremacy in the Indian Ocean, eventually resulted in British rule.

LINGUISTIC DIVISIONS

The outcome of these marches and countermarches was the formation of the present-day language groupings of South Asia. Sanskrit-using Aryans replaced Dravidians in the north and absorbed the Veddahs of Ceylon, only to be joined on Ceylon by Dravidian-speaking Tamils and driven south and east in India by the Saka, the White Huns, and the Gurjara. The latter in turn were displaced by Muslim Arabs, Turks, Persians, Afghans, and Mughals. The ranks of the Muslims continued to be swelled by new arrivals from many lands until the time of Akbar. Then the stream dwindled to a trickle, for orthodox Sunnites from Anatolia, the Arab world, and Turkestan rarely chose to travel through the domains of the now militantly Shiite Safawids.

The fruit of the Aryan invasion was the establishment of the two major linguistic divisions of India, the Aryan and the Dravidian. Aryan languages hold sway from the Himalayan foothills to a line drawn from Goa to the mouth of the Mahanadi. They also predominate in the southern and central portion of Ceylon.

The dominance of Aryan languages in northern and central India was probably given indirect support by the experience of Muslim rule. Most of the Muslims who migrated to India after the time of the Ghaznawids were accustomed to speaking and writing in Persian, an Indo-European language related to Sanskrit, and therefore to the Aryan tongues which grew out of Sanskrit. On Ceylon, however, the early blend of Sanskrit and Tamil into the basically Aryan Sinhalese tongue was rivalled rather than supported by later Tamil invaders. Aryan languages have not spread to the higher slopes of the Himalayas or the hills that border Assam and Burma. The peoples there still speak the Tibeto-Burman languages of their ancestors, who left southwestern China for the mountains many centuries ago.

Almost all who use Dravidian languages in India are in the south, which was rarely under Aryan or Muslim control. The areas inhabited by the speakers of the four major Dravidian tongues, Malayalam, Kannara, Telugu, and Tamil, were recognized in the provincial divisions established in the Republic of India during the 1950s: Kerala (Malayalam), Mysore (Kannara), Andhra (Telugu), and Madras (Tamil). At that time Dravidians made up about a fourth of the population of the Republic of India.

When independence came in 1947–1948, Aryan languages were spoken by about two-thirds of the people of the new India, more than nine-tenths of all Pakistanis, and about seven-tenths of the people of Ceylon. In India and Pakistan, those who spoke the different Aryan languages could understand each other to some extent, but they wrote in a variety of scripts and used vocabularies ranging from the Persian-flavored tongues of the Indo-Gangetic plain to the Dravidian-influenced ones of central India.

The Panjabi, Sindhi, Rajasthani, Hindustani, and Bihari tongues shared Persian influence. Most of those who used them had come to accept the Persianized Hindustani developed at the Mughal court as the language of literature and public affairs. Those who wrote in the Nagari alphabet called it Hindi; those who used the Arabic script, introduced by the Muslims, called it Urdu. However, the Bengali, Oriya, Marathi, and Gujerati languages had long traditions of separate development in Bengal, Orissa, the northern Deccan, and Gujerat. The citizens of the new India who used them resisted as fiercely as the Dravidians all proposals to make Hindi the national language. Similarly, the numerous Bengalis of East Pakistan protested against the desire of West Pakistanis to make Urdu the official tongue of Pakistan. Since Bengali was spoken by about 55 percent of the people of Pakistan at the time of its formation, and since Bengali, Oriya, Marathi, Gujerati, and the four major Dravidian languages were spoken by approximately half the people of the new India, prospects were scarcely bright for rapid linguistic unification in either country on the basis of Hindi or Urdu. Although Sinhalese was at least the majority language in Ceylon, Tamil resistance at first forced Ceylon, like India and Pakistan, to accept the continued widespread use of English in higher education and the upper levels of government.

THE CASTE SYSTEM

The combination of natural geographic regions and a succession of invasions has left South Asia with more than a dozen languages, each used by millions. Even the Oriya, the smallest of the Indian language groups listed above, number more than the Norwegians and

Swedes combined. Yet the caste system, the social system which both unites and separates the people of South Asia, has been as important as the linguistic divisions inherited from the past.

Our knowledge of pre-Aryan South Asia is very slight. However, the caste system probably resulted from the mingling of Aryan practices and ideas with those of the Dravidians. The caste system gradually developed in the Indo-Gangetic plain and spread southward into the peninsula during the twenty-five-hundred years or so after the Aryans first arrived. It is distinguished by three major features: eating patterns, marriage patterns, and occupational patterns.

EATING PATTERNS.   Over the centuries, increasingly rigid rules were laid down for the preparation and consumption of food—what might be eaten, who might prepare it, in what vessels it might be cooked and eaten, who might share it. These rules developed partly out of belief in the power of food to transmit various qualities to those who eat it—as many peoples have believed a warrior's bravery is enhanced by eating the heart of a wolf or a lion—and partly out of conviction that the touch or even the glance of some individuals could pollute the food and the cooking and eating utensils of others, a conviction resembling the fear of the "evil eye" found from the Mediterranean to the China Sea. Both of these beliefs may well have been Dravidian in origin. The constant fear that a touch, a shadow, or a glance might contaminate a clay vessel, which unlike a metal one could not be satisfactorily purified for reuse, was a boon to the maker of cheap pottery; but it was fatal to the rise of a far-flung trade in ceramics or the development of the pride in a beautiful ceramic piece displayed in China or the Middle East. Rules concerning eating patterns were also affected by the Aryan practice of the sacrificial meal, which only the members of the family could eat because it honored their ancestors.

The Aryans apparently accepted indigenous beliefs about the impropriety of killing living creatures for food at an early stage in this process of formulating rules for the use of food. Although the Aryans ate beef and other kinds of meat freely when they entered the Indus valley, a few centuries later they had almost ceased to eat the flesh of cattle and were beginning to avoid the use of other kinds of flesh.

MARRIAGE AND FAMILY PATTERNS.   Eating patterns naturally influenced marriage patterns. The accepted customs with regard to who might prepare food and who might consume it—summed up in the term "commensality" or "state of sharing the same table"—meant that each person could only eat the food cooked by a limited number of other persons. Therefore, it was almost essential to marry within the commensal group. The normal range of matrimonial choice was effectively restricted by the inconvenience to a man of having a wife whose cooking he could not

eat for fear of ritual pollution, which only extensive and expensive ceremonies could remove. Other rules required each person to marry outside
the group of those regarded as his or her immediate kin. These rules ensured widespread mixing within the commensal group.

Although marriage beyond the limits of the commensal group was
rare, the men of many castes were permitted to marry women of castes
which were only slightly lower than their own. The parents of the prospective bride ordinarily accepted such an alliance readily even though it
generally entailed a higher than usual dowry. This practice created difficulties for lower-caste men, who found the women of their castes marrying upward. It also made it hard for upper-caste parents to find proper
husbands for their daughters. This in turn tended to encourage either female infanticide or polygamy in certain groups, since it was thought an
unbearable disgrace to have an unmarried daughter.

The Aryans who took over the Indo-Gangetic plain and spread their
influence southward stressed the patrilineal tie between father and son
as the strongest bond within the family. A father expected all his sons,
with their wives and children, to remain with him. Father, sons, grandsons, and even great-grandsons lived together as a joint family, holding
their property in common and sharing the products of their labor as their
ancestors had done when herding was the Aryans' only occupation. In
practice, these joint families usually split up after the death of the father
—each son receiving an equal share of the family's jointly held and
jointly managed property. In later times, the practice of equal division
led to a fantastic fragmentation of landholdings in many parts of South
Asia.

Over the centuries, the Aryan patrilineal joint family became the
pattern for society as a whole. However, it was not adopted rapidly.
Certain marriage and adoption customs still followed in south India seem
to indicate that the Dravidians originally saw the ties between mothers
and their children as the strongest bonds within the family. The Dravidians' sons and daughters therefore inherited from their mothers, not
from their fathers. The bitterness of the struggle between Aryan patrilineal and Dravidian matrilineal concepts of family organization can be
seen in the division between "right-hand" and "left-hand" groups within
certain south Indian castes. The right-hand groups retain some customs
associated with inheritance through the mother, but the left-hand groups
avoid these customs and favor the tie between father and son.

By the sixth century B.C. women were already beginning to be
severely restricted. The value of their contribution to daily household
life was fully appreciated. Their ability to bear sons was recognized as
essential. Not only were a man's sons his best insurance against want,
but only his lineal descendants could validly perform the rites required
at his death to ensure his safe passage to the next life. However, women

were treated as inferior and expected to be obedient to their husbands in all things. Among the higher castes in India, the wife was even supposed to die with her husband. Sometimes she did so literally, on the funeral pyre, in the rite called *sati;* sometimes she did so figuratively, by giving up all but the barest necessities and pledging never to remarry.

A wife and the sons she could bear were so important to a man's present and future welfare that few Indian men cared to remain single. Yet the number of potential wives was limited by the prohibition of the remarriage of widows on the ground that a widow who remarried was disloyal to her first spouse. Consequently, girls were married at earlier and earlier ages, until finally a girl could be both married and widowed before she reached the age when she could bear children. The absurdity of thus removing girls from the marriage market before they reached puberty seems to have been disregarded entirely. However, the strictness of the rules against a widow's remarriage and the accompanying growth of child-marriage may have been linked with the spread of the patrilineal system. If there actually was a contest between father-centered and mother-centered patterns of family organization, those in the patrilineal system might well have insisted on maintaining the dominance of the husband at all costs.

OCCUPATIONAL PATTERNS.   It is not known whether pre-Aryan society had begun dividing into commensal groups which married within their own ranks, or how much pre-Aryan society had begun to reserve certain occupations for certain families. However, it is reasonably certain that when the Aryans first arrived they largely took over the roles of ruler, priest, and merchant, and did not practice agriculture or the artisan crafts for many centuries. Almost undoubtedly, one consequence of the Aryan invasion was the establishment of the broad division between the upper three castes—Brahmin (priest), Kshatriya (ruler or warrior), and Vaisya (merchant)—and the Sudra or laboring caste. The men of the upper three, or "twice-born," castes were entitled to wear a sacred thread which showed that they were eligible for the second or spiritual birth that resulted from studying the sacred traditions of the Vedas. The men of the lower caste could not be invested with the sacred thread, and traditionally they were not allowed to explore the Vedic literature.

The broad division of society between the twice-born and the Sudras did not coincide entirely with the division between Aryans and non-Aryans during the early centuries of Aryan rule in the plain. In all three of the upper groups there was some intermingling with the corresponding Dravidian groups. Aryan and Dravidian priests exchanged ideas and observations; Aryan and Dravidian rulers formed allegiances; Aryan and Dravidian merchants traded with each other. This intermingling may account for many of the differences between the early

Aryans and their descendants. Yet the "dark-skinned Dasyus" remained Sudras for the most part, and when their leaders formed powerful states in Bengal or the south, where Aryan rule had not yet been established, they were referred to by the Aryans as Sudra kings.

As the generations passed and the food-handling and matrimonial rules became ever more rigid, the divisions between those who could marry and share food came to coincide clearly with the occupational divisions imposed by Aryan supremacy. The Aryans who went to Ceylon in the sixth century B.C. also took with them the fourfold division of Brahmin, Kshatriya, Vaisya, and Sudra. However, they never elevated Brahmins above Kshatriyas to the degree practiced in India, and they did not draw as sharp a line between clean and unclean laborers as came to be done in India.

In India, strong traditional aversion to contact with blood, death, and grime eventually placed certain occupational groups like leatherworkers, who had to touch dead animals, outside the pale of acceptability. Leatherworkers, butchers, and others whose work was held to be polluting, like street-sweepers and washers of soiled clothing, were regarded throughout India as untouchable. Their mere presence was regarded as contaminating in the south, where untouchables might have to remain a full seventy feet from a Brahmin or even refrain entirely from moving about in daylight. However, no member of a recognized caste group would ever think of performing the tasks assigned to the untouchables, which gave them the slight comfort of knowing that their services were needed and their meager livelihood was secure. Over the years the untouchables divided themselves into occupational groupings which developed food-handling and matrimonial rules that corresponded closely to those of the recognized castes, though they were usually much less restrictive. In recent years, as part of the effort of social reformers to break down the barriers of caste, neutral terms like Panchama (fifth grouping) have begun to be used to refer to these people, rather than the old word for untouchable, the terms "scheduled castes" and "depressed castes" which came into official use during the British era, or even Mahatma Gandhi's term Harijans (children of God).

Each group in the caste system performed a specified share of the tasks necessary to the maintenance of society. The members of each group were held together largely through intermarriage (although wives might be brought in from lower groups), and at the same time separated from the rest of society by the food-handling rules. Some of the rigidities of the caste system may be related to the possibility that the food-handling rules came from the Dravidians. If the Dravidians were concerned to prevent others from polluting their food, they may have been the ones to refuse to eat with the Aryans rather than vice versa. The Aryans might well have reacted by adopting even stricter food rules than those observed by their Sudra subjects, with the priestly Brahmins upholding the strictest rules of all in order to justify their claims to purity. If these suppositions are correct, the defensiveness felt by the Aryans might help explain the eventual hardening of the caste system into an extremely rigid set of prescriptions and prohibitions.

RIGIDITIES AND FLEXIBILITIES. The rigidity of the walls around those who shared the same occupation, food rules, and marriage rules often imposed hardships on individuals and the joint families to which they belonged. Yet this rigidity made the society of South Asia unusually flexible in absorbing groups of newcomers. By treating powerful invaders as Kshatriyas, accepting them as rulers, expecting them to marry among themselves, and leaving them to themselves socially, the people of South Asia could get along with the Saka, Kushan, Gurjara, and other conquerors with little friction. Until the Muslim period, most invaders were quite willing to accept Kshatriya status. One well-known example is the Rajput caste group, many of whose members are descended from the Saka. The priests who accompanied the conquerors were similarly fitted into the social order by acceptance of their claims to supernatural authority. The very name of the Magi Brahmin caste group shows that its earliest members must have been associated with the priests of ancient Iran. Uncivilized tribespeople, on the other hand, were treated as Sudras or even untouchables. They were brought within the fold of civilized society by being assigned certain tasks but forbidden to mingle with higher caste groups at meals or in marriage. Thus the caste system which was so inflexible in some ways could be highly adaptable in others.

The transformation of outsiders into new caste groups took place first in the Indo-Gangetic plain. Similar developments occurred in south India once northern priests and rulers began to extend their influence into the peninsula. The local priestly hierarchies were accepted as Brahmins; the small local warrior groups (the southern kingdoms lived by overseas trade rather than by conquest) became Kshatriyas. The local merchants became Vaisyas, at least to the north of the Godavari. Farther south the merchants were often ranked as Sudras, perhaps because northerners tended to associate dark skin with Sudras rather than with the twice-born upper castes. Thus south India has very few Kshatriyas and Vaisyas in comparison with the north. The local artisans and cultivators became Sudras, and those whose occupations entailed contact with blood or grime were regarded as untouchable, lacking in caste status. However, the untouchables of south India soon developed as elaborate a system of occupational, food, and marriage rules as the untouchables of the north.

In such a social system even the introduction of a new occupation cannot be disruptive for long, since those who follow it fall naturally into the pattern of an intermarrying, commensal, occupational group and thus form a new caste group. As long as a great majority continues to accept the caste system, it cannot even be successfully opposed, as various Indian reformers have found to their dismay in the past twenty-five centuries. Jains, Buddhists, Sikhs, and other opponents of the caste system have simply been left to themselves, maritally, socially, and occupationally. They have been treated in effect as caste groups even though they have repudiated caste rules. Followers of foreign religions have been similarly treated. Jews, Christians, Parsis (Zoroastrians), and Muslims all actively opposed caste restrictions when they first arrived in India, but eventually they too resigned themselves to being regarded as separate castes. Some have even adopted a few caste practices, as have many members of India's own originally anti-caste groups. In Ceylon, where the caste system was well entrenched by the time Buddhism was introduced, it simply continued to exist in spite of Buddhist teaching. However, Buddhist opposition to caste divisions may have helped to prevent the raising of barriers between castes to as high a level as came to prevail on the mainland of India. In Nepal, where Buddhists and Hindus have lived side by side for over two thousand years, the caste structure has not been as rigid as in India.

ENFORCEMENT OF CASTE RULES. The caste system is the solution developed in South Asia for the problems of transmitting a specific form of sedentary life to already sedentary peoples and to peoples who were not yet sedentary. It contrasts markedly with Middle Eastern solutions to the same problems, which have relied on spatial rather than social separation. In the Middle East, those who cared little for village or city life took to the hills and deserts as pastoralists. In South Asia, most of the corresponding groups became Sudras, or possibly untouchables. In the Middle East, each village was usually homogeneous, and although many sorts of people lived in the cities, most city-dwellers lived in carefully segregated homogeneous residential districts. In South Asia, each village had to contain members of a number of caste and untouchable groups because certain types of everyday work were only performed by members of certain groups. Contemporary students of South Asian societies often find more than twenty groups represented in a village of eight or nine hundred people, although the majority in each village come from not more than two or three groups.

Thus one's caste group has been the dominant factor in one's life in South Asia, rather than one's clan or village as in the Middle East. In the Middle East the elders would invite malcontents to leave the household or the village and seek their fortunes in the city or the wilderness, but the separation was only spatial, and one who returned successful or repentant was usually reaccepted. Furthermore, the Middle Eastern guild was open to those not born into membership, unlike the South Asian caste.

Traditionally, the individual in South Asia was born into an occupation. True, agriculture was open to members of all recognized caste groups, and members of most caste groups were free to enter any one of several occupations. However, the lower a person's rank was, the more limited his or her range of choice tended to be.

If a man or woman performed a forbidden task, or married improperly, or did not obey the rules for eating and social intercourse, he or she could be expelled by the caste group. A person who was driven from the caste group for infringing its rules was called an outcaste. No one in or out of the caste would have anything to do with such a person, who thus would have neither livelihood nor companionship. It was possible to win reinstatement, but the process was so arduous and expensive that few would willingly risk having to undergo it. Among both recognized castes and untouchables, the rules and divisions of caste were maintained by the social pressure of the fear of becoming an outcaste.

The operation of social pressure was not left to chance. Every caste group, whether part of a recognized caste or part of a body of untouchables, had a governing body called a *panchayat* among lower groups and a *sabha* among the upper castes. The panchayat or sabha was empowered to interpret the rules of the caste group and to decide whether or not they had been broken in a given case. Any unorthodox action was almost certain to be brought to the attention of the panchayat or sabha by someone who feared possible pollution through association with the one who had gone beyond the accepted limits of behavior.

The effective size of a caste group was limited to the group of families who recognized the jurisdiction of the same caste panchayat or sabha. This is why many caste groups have names like Nambudri Brahmin or Baghel Rajput, indicating that their members form a subdivision of the general group of Brahmins or Rajputs. Although the caste system spread throughout South Asia, a specific caste group was ordinarily confined to one linguistic region. A panchayat or sabha could hardly operate effectively if those subject to it spoke different languages or lived too far apart for ready communication. Some caste groups, notably those engaged in commerce, came to be represented in many parts of South Asia, but most caste groups were and are restricted to one linguistic region. One may speak in theory of Brahmins, Kshatriyas, Vaisyas, Sudras, and Panchamas (the former untouchables), but in practice, the functioning associations are the Saraswat Brahmins of the Panjab, the Chandel Rajputs of the middle Ganges, the Baniya merchants of Gujerat, the Meda basketmakers of Mysore, or the Cakkiliyan leatherworkers of Madras. These functioning associations are usually referred to in India as *jati*.

Among the upper castes, who were perhaps less fearful for their position than the lower groups, the sabhas seem to have been less formal and to have met less frequently than the panchayats of the lower groups. Often a lower group appears to have organized itself more tightly so that it could enforce adherence to standards appropriate to a higher caste group, in the hope that virtuous behavior would eventually raise its members' position in the eyes of others. The noted Indian anthropologist M.N. Srinivas calls this "Sanskritization," or acceptance of the standards laid down for the twice-born upper castes in classical Sanskrit literature. Whenever outside observers in recent centuries have noticed the attempts of caste groups to move upward in the scale, they have noted the efforts of Sudras and untouchables to win acceptance by adopting upper-caste rules against eating meat or allowing widows to remarry. Thus, although the caste system has limited individuals and families, it has not permanently limited the entire group. A caste group could elevate its status over a period of approximately four to six generations by faithfully following the patterns of behavior of a caste group of higher status. However, in order to succeed, its members had to be patient about maintaining those patterns in the teeth of disparagers until those who could remember their great-grandparents' complaints about "social climbers who were only scum when I was a child" had departed from the scene. Riots may still take place in Indian villages if Sudra or Panchama weddings resemble upper-caste weddings too closely for some upper-caste members to tolerate. Nevertheless, the discovery that the courts now tend to side with the lower-caste victims (rather than tending to support the upper-caste attackers, as in the pre-British era, or tending to sentence attackers and victims alike for breaking the peace, as in the British era) has put a damper on such actions.

CASTE IN THE VILLAGE AND THE CITY. As the dominant feature of social organization in South Asia, the caste system deeply affected family, village, and urban life. Caste rules determined the function and status of the family and told its members whom they might marry and with whom they might share food. Caste panchayats and sabhas kept family members from breaking caste rules by threatening expulsion from the caste for improper behavior.

Caste rules ensured that most families included people brought up in other villages. The almost universal requirement that a man marry outside the circle of his immediate kin usually meant he could not marry anyone who was thought to have the same male ancestor. Because the members of a given caste group in a given village were ordinarily descended from one caste member who had entered the village generations earlier, they were by definition immediate kin and could not intermarry. Consequently, most village men had to bring in wives from other villages, and most village girls had to move to other villages when they married. How this system of uprooting women from their home villages relates to the struggle between father-centered and mother-centered forms of family organization is still unclear, but it could have helped ensure that a wife would have no one nearby to uphold her in disputes with her husband or his family. In addition, the influx of wives from outside the village constantly brought other villages' ways of doing things to the attention of both the village and the family. It thereby contributed to the growth of uniformity within each geographic and linguistic division of South Asia.

The caste system marked out the division of labor within the village. Those who produced food provided the priests, weavers, smiths, potters, carpenters, barbers, washers, sweepers, and herders (if any) with food in exchange for their services. In return, most priests and workers refrained from cultivating the soil. The workers were, in effect, servants to the entire village, although some claimed equal status with the cultivators. A number served as general laborers, working for whoever needed them. Some, like the sweepers, were paid by the village as a whole; others, like the carpenters, were paid directly by the joint families they served. Either way, the payments rarely made their recipients wealthy. Even a Brahmin family head might be poor, if he lived in a well-behaved village whose people rarely made missteps that would require them to undergo the purification rites which only a Brahmin priest could perform.

The importance of caste meant that the panchayat or assembly of the village elders did less to keep order than did the elders in a Middle Eastern village, since the villagers looked to caste rather than village panchayats to enforce most of the rules by which they expected each other to live. Village panchayats were usually concerned only with maintaining harmonious relations between the caste groups in the village and raising the revenues assessed by the rulers of the territory in which the village was located. Thus they resembled Middle Eastern city governments in miniature, dealing with self-governing groups of households more than with individual households.

Indian caste and village panchayats were small in comparison to the body of elders in a Middle Eastern or a Ceylonese village, which ordinarily included all or most of the family heads. As the name ("panch"="five") indicates, the Indian panchayat consisted of a handful of men. In some regions the village panchayats were chosen by lot, but often they were informally chosen on the basis of prestige, which left out all but the wealthiest or most virtuous members of lower caste groups and excluded untouchables altogether.

Indian village panchayats whose members were chosen on the basis of reputation tended to be self-perpetuating, even though the means of selection resembled a type of informal periodic general election in which many caste members (but no untouchables) took part. Those who had the opportunity to help select the panchayat knew perfectly well who was respected or influential and who was not. Furthermore, most potential electors were attached to one of the more important men in the village through family ties, tenancy, or indebtedness, and each such person's relatives and dependents naturally followed his lead in the public meetings at which the selections were made.

In many ways, the traditional South Asian city was only the village on a larger scale. Again, caste rules governed all activities, and the tasks to be performed were parceled out among the caste groups. Furthermore, the mode of livelihood for all was the exchange of services and payments, as in the village. However, payment was rarely made in food in the city, and merchants and administrators rather than cultivators were the food-providers, bringing food into the city by trade and taxation. In both Middle Eastern and South Asian cities, the rulers' primary function was to maintain harmony among a number of almost-autonomous associations: guilds and religious groups in the Middle East, caste groups in South Asia. Thus the Muslim conquerors of India in the eighth century and thereafter could apply many of the methods of control learned by their ancestors in the Middle East, as long as they were willing to accept the caste groups of India as the equivalents of the religious and occupational groupings with which they were familiar. The introduction of Muslim public law made remarkably little difference to the general workings of government, in spite of the disparity in viewpoints between Muslims and those who lived by the precepts associated with the caste system.

Thought-Patterns: Hinduism and Its Opponents

HINDUISM AND RELATED BELIEFS

BRAHMINISM AND THE ROLE OF THE PRIESTHOOD. The way in which most Indians look at the world is embodied within the complex of beliefs and actions called Hinduism. As far as is known, Hinduism is a synthesis of the ideas and practices of the Aryan invaders with the ideas and practices of the peoples who came under their rule in the northern plain before 1000 B.C. The early traditions preserved in the Vedas indicate that the Aryans thought the universe was controlled by deities who manifested themselves in natural phenomena. Agni, the spirit of fire, was one of the more important of these deities, which is not surprising in view of the early connections between the Aryans and the Iranian peoples whose worship of fire was eventually incorporated into Zoro-astrianism.

The Aryans considered their offerings to the deities to have special potency. Their belief that properly made offerings were important to the deities' welfare may also be related to the origins of Zoroastrianism, whose followers believed human offerings of good deeds to be essential to the victory of the good Ahura-Mazda over the evil Ahriman. The Aryans thought the deities were so dependent on human offerings that when the priests performed the sacrificial rituals correctly, the deities were bound to grant the request of the maker of the offering. This conviction gave the priests, or Brahmins, great power in Aryan society, for by omitting some detail of ceremony they could nullify the effect of the sacrifices they made for anyone of whom they disapproved.

The Brahmins were so powerful that the religion of the early Aryans is commonly called Brahminism. The early Aryan priesthood was not yet organized entirely along caste lines, for one of the oldest Sanskrit scriptures states that a man who lives a pure life and is versed in Brahmin teachings should be accepted as a true Brahmin regardless of his origin, but the Brahmins were well on the way to becoming a closed caste by 1000 B.C. However, they were also well on the way to accepting a number of beliefs and practices which probably came from the Dravidians, with the result that the religion of the descendants of the Aryans had changed from Brahminism to Hinduism by the sixth century B.C.

HINDUISM AND THE ACCEPTANCE OF THE MEANINGLESSNESS OF PHE-NOMENA. Hinduism is separated from Brahminism by the full acceptance of certain doctrines about which the Brahmins had long been speculating, as is clear from the Sanskrit scriptures of the Vedas and from the Upanishads, which are commentaries on the Vedas. These doctrines probably came to the Brahmins' attention through conversations with the priests of the earlier Indian traditions. Of these doctrines, the basic one concerns the nature of the universe itself. The Hindu distinguishes between ultimate reality and the phenomena of the perceivable universe to a degree rarely found outside India. To a Hindu, the true essence of the universe has no phenomenal qualities. It is not a divine personality, as Jews, Christians, and Muslims believe. It is not a real seed from which a real tree unfolds, as the Chinese say in one of their expressive images of the relationship between fundamental reality and the perceivable world. To use another image, the Hindu sees the essence of the universe as an unfathomable ocean, on which the phenomenal world floats like flotsam and jetsam that has no organic link with the ocean on which it spins and tosses. The image of the ocean does not indicate the origin or nature of the phenomenal universe, except as one makes the same leap of faith as the Hindu and assumes that the flotsam and jetsam of the world around one has no reality because it is not part of the ocean on which it lies. Nevertheless, the image is useful.

The fundamental reality, the essence of the universe, is called *Brahman* (soul) or *Brahma-tat* (that which is). The phenomenal universe is *lila*, play, sport, a jest (one might say) of the deities, who themselves are only manifestations of Brahman, waves on the surface of the boundless ocean of Brahma-tat that even at their greatest do not begin to indicate the true nature of the depths. The waves play with flotsam and jetsam; the deities play with the world of human beings.

Like every game, the sport of the deities has its rules. It can also be played over and over again. In other words, the phenomenal universe is cyclical. Each time the universe appears and disappears, the same general sequence of events occurs. The universe degenerates from the pristine freshness of creation to the chaos of destruction, and is not renewed until the deities decide to play another game. From the human standpoint the game is long, being measured in kalpas, or periods of 4,320 million years, but to the deities it seems very short.

Since it is only a game, the phenomenal universe lacks reality. To think it has reality is *maya*, illusion or delusion. In fact, the Sanskrit word "maya" and the English word "measure" have the same root, for all measurement is based on what the Hindu calls the delusion, maya, that there is actually something to be measured. Instead of studying the phenomenal universe, the Hindu strives to sink into the depths of the ocean of true reality. One should cease to pay attention to the appearances floating on its surface and should regard oneself as in reality a bubble of foam on the top of a wave—part of the ocean, not part of the flotsam and jetsam. To cling to the appearances of the phenomenal world is to deny one's true nature by acting as though one belonged to the flotsam and jetsam. Such beliefs discouraged close attention to natural science and human history, and indeed, what is known of the pre-modern history of India comes mainly from sacred writings, accounts by foreign travelers, the annals of Muslim kingdoms, and archaeological studies, not from Hindu historians.

MEANS OF ACHIEVING RELEASE. Although life in the visible world is an illusion, it is still a game, with rules one can scarcely ignore. Perhaps the most important rule is *karma*, or consequence. Every action by which one indicates attachment to the world has the consequence of binding one to remain in it. As long as one performs such actions, one is part of *samsara*, the wheel of existence, and one's death is promptly followed by a rebirth, which is the consequence of not having broken the bonds of maya with which one is chained to the wheel. Westerners usually call this rebirth the transmigration of the soul, which is misleading because the "soul" that undergoes rebirth is not a unique and permanent entity, as it is in ordinary conversation among those reared in the atmosphere of Judaism, Christianity, or Islam. It is merely an impermanent bundle of consequences which eventually ceases to lead a separate existence and returns to the ocean of the infinite. To the Hindu, the soul does not look forward to resting in the bosom of the Lord with others like itself; the soul *is* the Lord. Once one fully accepts this belief, one will break away from the human activities that rivet one's attention to the surface rather than the depths of the limitless ocean to which one belongs. One can then be reabsorbed into Brahman.

The name for reabsorption into the ocean of Brahma-tat through giving up attachment to the world is *moksha*. Although moksha is often translated as "salvation," it would be better to use "release," for it means the release of the individual from samsara, the wheel of existence, through the breaking of the bonds of karma, consequence. One achieves moksha by ceasing to be attached to the phenomena among which one moves. Nonattachment may be achieved in any of three ways. One may give up worldly actions and live as an ascetic; one may give up worldly emotions and devote oneself in loving worship (*bhakti*) to a deity in whom one becomes absorbed as the froth is absorbed in the ocean wave; or one may give up worldly ambitions and continue to live in the ordinary world. The person who chooses the last path must pay no heed to the consequences of his or her deeds, in the sense of calculating their probable effects upon the future through the operation of karma, for such calculation is itself a sign of attachment to the world. This viewpoint somewhat resembles Middle Eastern ideas of predestination, in which one's deeds are the result rather than the determiner of one's fate, and the Hindu of active temperament who follows the path of renouncing the fruits of action can be as zealously energetic as a fervent seventh-century Muslim or sixteenth-century Calvinist. A notable example is Mahatma Gandhi, who relied strongly on the teaching of one of India's great literary masterpieces, the "Bhagavad-Gita" or "Song of the Lord" in the epic poem of the *Mahabharata*. The concept of achieving release by acting without counting the costs in advance finds its highest expression in the "Bhagavad-Gita."

All three ways—asceticism, loving worship, and action without attachment—lead equally to release, but the way of disciplined asceticism has been the one most stressed by Hindus. It even became part of the ideal life-pattern for men of the twice-born castes. Each Brahmin, Kshatriya, or Vaisya male has customarily been encouraged to pass through four stages between the time he receives the sacred thread and the time he dies. First he should be a student of the Vedas, learning to play the part assigned him in the world. Then he should be a householder, marrying and raising a family. After his children have grown, he should become an ascetic hermit, meditating on his true nature as part of Brahma-tat. Finally he should become a wandering ascetic, demonstrating by indifference to discomfort that he has realized his oneness with the underlying essence of the universe.

PROTESTS AGAINST CASTE: JAINISM AND BUDDHISM. The incorporation of asceticism into the life cycle of the upper castes indicates how skillfully the caste system was adapted to the basic Hindu view of the world. According to the rules of the game of existence, karma determined the form in which one would be reborn. A caste member who lived a life of passion and cruelty might be reborn into a wandering tribe or even as a wild beast. Yet if he or she lived by the rules in this new existence, a new rebirth at a higher level might be achieved. In a sense, each rebirth was a fresh start. The result of an individual life was a bundle of consequences which had to be reborn. The nature of that bundle of consequences determined where it would reemerge on the wheel of existence; but the newborn individual began with a clean slate. The karma of his or her past life had been eliminated by rebirth into a new condition—Brahmin, Sudra, elephant, cobra, or demon. Once reborn, one could start anew.

Many Hindus held that in theory an individual could achieve moksha through nonattachment no matter what the estate to which he or she had been born, but in practice most Hindus believed that only men of the Brahmin caste could seriously anticipate release. Consequently, the goal of every individual who was not a Brahmin male was to live so uprightly as to deserve rebirth at that level.

Some groups, like the Jains and Buddhists, repudiated the assumption that only Brahmin men could attain release. The Jain and Buddhist faiths were founded in the sixth century B.C. by men of the Kshatriya caste who condemned Brahmin ascendancy and with it the entire caste system. The Buddhists insisted that release, which they termed *nirvana* or extinction, was possible for everyone regardless of birth. The Jains agreed that anyone who lived a karma-free life might attain release, but they were less hopeful than the Buddhists in estimating how many might eventually free themselves from the wheel of life and death.

Both Jains and Buddhists grew in numbers up to the time of Asoka Maurya, who patronized all religions in his desire to spread a sense of mutual moral responsibility among his subjects. The Buddhists spread from their founder Gautama's birthplace in the Himalayan foothills westward through the Indus valley and beyond the Hindu Kush into Central Asia; eastward through Bengal toward Burma; and southward to Ceylon, where the Sinhalese trace their conversion to missionaries of Asoka's time. As they grew, they began to divide into two major streams of interpretation, the Theravada, or teachers' way, and the Mahayana, or greater vehicle.

Theravada Buddhists insisted that everyone must work out his or her own release, as Gautama had done. One must rid oneself of attachment to the world; that was all there was to it. If one could not do this, then one should strive to acquire merit by aiding the world-renouncing monks and nuns, who were closer to achieving release. The acquisition of merit would improve one's chances of becoming capable in the next life of withdrawing from worldly involvement through entering the monastic order.

Most of the Mahayana Buddhists also held in theory that final release must be the fruit of one's own efforts. However, Mahayana teachings offered the ordinary person so much aid from *bodhisattvas* (beings who have attained release from illusion, but who choose to stay in the world and help others find release also) that in practice many Mahayana Buddhists came extremely close to relying on faith in the powers of the bodhisattvas as the means of obtaining release.

Mahayana teachings attracted more followers in India than did the more austere Theravada doctrines, but eventually both forms of Buddhism were either reabsorbed into Hinduism or replaced by the religion of the Muslim invaders of the eighth century A.D. onward. Where reabsorption took place, it relied primarily on the simple device of regarding the Buddha as a manifestation of the widely worshiped creator-god Vishnu. Both Buddhists and Hindus could accept this idea because they shared the belief that all deities were merely varying appearances of one underlying reality. However, Buddhism remained the religion of the Sinhalese—perhaps in half-conscious resistance to the pressures from Hindu Tamil south India on Buddhist Sinhalese Ceylon—and of many in the Himalayan foothills. In recent years it has even returned to India. Many from the ranks of the former untouchables have turned to it since India's independence in 1947, as a genuine yet indigenously Indian form of protest against caste restrictions.

Neither Jains nor Buddhists succeeded in remaking Indian or Sinhalese social structures, which were already fashioned along caste lines when the teachers of these religions came to protest them. In Ceylon, the caste system readily made room for Buddhist monks at a level equivalent to that of Brahmins, as advisers to rulers and subjects alike. In India, the Buddhists were for the most part brought back into the caste system through their reabsorption into Hinduism. The Jains, who were fewer in number, were simply treated by the Hindus as though they were a separate caste. However, the extremes to which the Jains carried their tenet of *ahimsa,* or nonviolence to living creatures, contributed strongly to the general Hindu tendency to stress nonviolence to other living beings. Jain teachings reinforced the Hindu belief that all beings were equally a part of Brahma-tat and a result of karma, and that proper behavior toward animals was as necessary to release as proper behavior toward people. This belief is most familiarly expressed in the rules prohibiting cattle-slaying and confining the eating of flesh to non-Brahmins.

HINDUISM AND CASTE. Despite the Buddhists' belief that release was attainable from any state, the Hindus insisted that rebirth as a Brahmin was a prerequisite to moksha, even though all states of phenomenal existence were equally part of lila, the divine sport. This insistence was their heritage from the Brahminical past, stemming from the elevation of the priesthood in Aryan days. However, the ordering of society required that there be others besides priests. There must be rulers to protect and administer, merchants to exchange goods, workers to produce goods, and laborers to provide essential services. Each was needed for the functioning of the whole, the continuance and completion of the game of life. As a result there was a sort of equality within what ordinary observers saw as inequality. Each group had its role to perform. Each group was equally part of the cosmic order, whether it ranked high or low in the eyes of those (still blinded by maya) who imagined a difference in rank between weavers and butchers or rulers and peasants. Consequently each group had its own rule of life to follow. Each member of each group was born into it because of failure to escape from karma; but if one faithfully obeyed the rules for members of one's group, one would show that one was detached enough from earthly desires to subordinate all trace of individuality to the demands of the game of which one was a part. By surrendering oneself to the performance of the duties of one's caste group, one recognized the unreality of any distinction between oneself and others. In time, that recognition would enable one to achieve moksha by being born as a Brahmin male, observing the four *ashrama*, or stages—student, householder, hermit, and wanderer—and being absorbed at death into the depths of the ocean of Brahma-tat.

The obligation of the individual was to heed his or her *dharma*, or duty, the law of his or her current being. Dharma, which means both "law" and "duty," was the name given to the rules of human behavior; but there were many dharmas, not just one. The dharma of the priest was to behave as a priest; that of the ruler, to behave as a ruler; that of the sweeper, to behave as a sweeper; that of a *thug*, or ritual murderer, to behave as a thug. Each was equally bound to follow dharma. The priest must give up chicken, lamb, and fish, which others ate freely because no rule required them to abstain. The ruler must tell falsehoods if necessary to preserve the state, although others were enjoined to be strictly honest. The sweeper must meekly accept poverty and scorn. The thug must kill in spite of government ordinances and the general abhorrence for being a cause of death. Thus everyone from ruler to criminal had a recognized place in society. The concept of dharma became an almost perfect device for encouraging the individual always to act predictably, thereby preserving society from disrupting surprises.

The concept of the multiform dharma, whose content varies with one's role in the community, is an interesting means of drawing the distinctions between private and public ethics over which Westerners agonize every time the public good seems to require an action that is regarded as wrong for a private individual to perform. With their concept of a uniform law, Westerners have condemned such behavior as underhanded, but Indians accepted it as part of the nature of the universe, at least until they began to Westernize. Interstate relations in pre-modern India were unashamedly of the dog-eat-dog variety. Indian writers called this the law of the fishes, stating that smaller individuals would invariably be swallowed by their larger fellows unless they could grow or could develop some effective defense.

The multiform dharma enjoined everyone to follow the specific set of rules for the caste group into which he or she was born. To follow another set of rules was to court disaster, for the consequence of thus asserting oneself against the natural order would certainly set back one's progress toward release. No Sudra should strive to act as a Kshatriya; no Vaisya should seek to be a Brahmin; and conversely, no ruler should behave like a merchant or an artisan. The man who refused to live by the dharma of his group, in token of recognition that all contribute equally to the lila which is life, not only entangled himself in karma; he also endangered all his associates, unless they cut themselves off from him by making him an outcaste. For the woman who was made an outcaste, life could be even harder than for the outcaste man, for she was usually even less prepared to fend for herself without the support of family and *jati*.

Under the multiform dharma, some groups were enjoined to slay and others to heal, some to build and others to scavenge, some to seclude their women and others to provide temple prostitutes. The aggregation of dharmas was unified by the belief that all of them were parts of the set of rules by which the game of the gods and goddesses must be played. It was the task of the Brahmins and Kshatriyas to uphold each dharma by spiritual and temporal sanctions. The Brahmins performed their rites only for the virtuous, and anyone who had been made an outcaste was required to undergo the ceremonies prescribed by the Brahmins before reentering organized society.

The Kshatriya's chief task was to enable those within the state to follow out their dharmas, upholding the decisions of caste-group panchayats and arbitrating in intercaste disputes. To carry out this task, the ruler had to use every means to preserve the state, including warfare, judicious alliances, and internal and external intelligence agencies; for unless the state continued to exist, its inhabitants could not pursue their respective modes of life without interruption.

HINDUS AND MUSLIMS

The Kshatriya's functions were completely political: to maintain internal order and to preserve external safety. Foreign conquerors like the Sakas, the Muslims, and the British soon found that their Hindu subjects expected them to perform the same functions in the same way as a Kshatriya. Most governments in India, like most governments in the Middle East, did little more than maintain armies, arbitrate quarrels between the various segments of society, and levy taxes to pay their soldiers and administrators. However, governments in India usually gave some financial aid to the pursuit of learning, and a few supported public works. Those rulers who undertook public works, like Asoka, concentrated on dams, canals, wells, forts, and the roads which enabled armies to move swiftly against rebels or invaders. As in the Middle East, officials were often granted the income from the regions they administered because it seemed an easier means of payment than collecting everything at the center and then redistributing it; as in the Middle East, the independence this gave provincial and local officials invited enterprising governors to rebel whenever the central authority showed signs of weakness.

Most people cared little about the rise and fall of dynasties, for their lives were governed by the village and the caste group, neither of which was much affected by a change of ruler. Feelings of loyalty to a specific state were lacking, although the idea existed that there should be a state, with a definite area and a functioning government. Few large empires lasted more than three or four generations. Even the rulers of small states rarely tried to establish a personal relationship with their subjects by taxing individual households instead of villages. Apparently the Afghan Sher Shah and the Mughal Akbar in the sixteenth century A.D. were the first to collect revenue directly from the cultivators in the countryside. Yet even they did not try to supervise internal village affairs, but continued to hold village leaders responsible for maintaining local order. Whether Hindus or Muslims were ruling, Indian political life continued to consist of many closed and self-perpetuating corporations, one of which was responsible for supervising the relations between the others and preventing outside interference with their internal workings. That organization corresponded closely to the theory of the multiform dharma.

Sher Shah's and Akbar's continued reliance on village authorities to preserve order shows that these two rulers accepted at least part of India's traditional social and political organization. Most Muslim rulers followed policies similar to those of Hindu rulers. The Muslims let the caste groups run themselves and concentrated on finance, war, and administration, which they had learned in the Middle East to regard as the major concerns of government. They also took up the law of the fishes with zest and practiced it against both Hindu and Muslim states.

In using existing patterns of government, Muslim rulers usually felt they were following the Quran by protecting the non-Muslim dhimmis over whom they ruled as long as the dhimmis did not rebel or refuse to pay taxes. The Quran even provided for the dhimmis to run their own affairs except when they came into conflict with Muslims, in which case Islamic law must prevail. Muslims had successfully ruled largely Christian populations on this basis in the early years of Islam and had eventually won the religious as well as the political allegiance of most of their subjects. The first Muslim conquerors may well have hoped for similar results from similar methods in India. However, the analogy was imperfect. The basic world-views of Muslim rulers and their non-Muslim subjects in the Middle East were similar, as Muhammad had recognized when he told his followers to respect Jews and Christians; but in India, the world-views of the Muslims and their Hindu subjects were diametrically opposed at a multitude of points.

From the beginning to the end of the period of the Muslim dynasties, Muslims argued heatedly over whether a Hindu could properly be treated as a dhimmi, a protected person, since Hindu beliefs diverged so markedly from those of the Christians and Jews specified in the Quran as worthy of tolerance. Christians and Jews agreed with orthodox Muslims on the existence of one divine Person, the Creator of one purposeful world whose human inhabitants were distinguished from animals by the possession of individual souls. Each soul had one life to prove its worthiness to dwell eternally with other souls in the presence of their Maker, by living according to the single law of God and respecting equally all who obeyed Him. However, Hindus postulated an impersonal unity from which purposeless universes rose and to which they returned in an unending cycle. Hindus saw no line between human and animal comparable to that drawn by Muslims; they repudiated the idea of a permanent individual soul; and they accepted the concept of rebirth. They looked toward the reabsorption of an unreal self into a fathomless reality, of which that self was as much a manifestation as any of the numerous deities they worshiped. Furthermore, they accepted as many laws as there were groups within society. Despite the belief that all groups contributed equally to the life of the phenomenal world, Hindus drew such sharp social distinctions between caste groups in everyday life that the caste system appalled orthodox Muslims almost as much as did the bewildering variety of Hindu gods and goddesses.

Practical considerations dictated to the first Muslim conquerors of Sind that Hindus, being a majority, should be treated as dhimmis regardless of whether they were theoretically accepted as such. As Muslim dominion spread beyond the northwest, where additional waves of Muslim invaders and local memories of Buddhist opposition to caste made almost the entire region turn to Islam, the conversions which took place in the plain and the peninsula were scarcely numerous enough to enable Muslims to campaign successfully against Hinduism. Yet practical considerations counted for nothing with fanatics, who periodically desecrated or destroyed Hindu temples, scattered their priests, and commanded their worshipers to renounce idolatry.

Outside the northwest, conversions were numerous enough to give Muslims a majority only in eastern Bengal. Buddhism had lingered there until the Muslims conquered the successors of the Palas, so that Bengalis were open to a new form of anti-caste preaching. In other regions, many groups which were weary of their low social position turned to Islam, but there were not enough to upset the Hindu ordering of society. The Hindu majority merely treated the Muslims as a separate caste. A number of Muslim converts from Hinduism even retained many practices of the caste system, not only with regard to occupational specialization but also with regard to marriage and food-handling. In Ceylon, Arab and Persian traders made a few converts to Islam, but Muslims made little impression on the caste systems of either Sinhalese or Tamils.

One of the most conciliatory Muslim rulers in India was the Mughal Akbar, who lifted the poll tax on non-Muslims, befriended the Rajputs and relied on their political and military support, and used large numbers of Hindus in his government. However, his great-grandson Aurangzeb sought to reestablish an orthodox Sunnite Muslim polity, reimposing the poll tax, expelling Hindus from high office, and destroying Hindu temples that had been built without Mughal permission. Aurangzeb's insistence on orthodoxy led nonorthodox Shiite Muslims as well as Hindus to oppose him. He spent over half his reign campaigning against insurgents and even tried to subjugate the last Hindu-ruled domain south of the Kaveri to deprive his Hindu subjects of the hope of its support.

Aurangzeb was an exception, like the few fanatics among pre-Mughal Muslim rulers. Most Muslim officials scarcely paid attention to Hindu worship or the caste system. The vast majority acted like Kshatriyas, contenting themselves with maintaining internal order, external security, and the revenues. As in the Middle East, tax collection was often entrusted to private individuals, who made fortunes as tax-farmers by collecting more than they had to turn over to the officials who granted them the concession. Some Muslim rulers, like Firuz Shah of Delhi in the late fourteenth century, obtained a number of capable slaves and used them as administrators, in imitation of Ottoman and other Middle Eastern examples. However, more rulers used free men, who were paid by being granted the right to collect part of the land revenue. Akbar and the others who used this method sought to tie the rank and income of each official to his position, so that he lost them when he left his post, rather than keeping either the title or the land-revenue grant and passing them on to his heirs. The attempt did not always succeed. Thus both Muslim and Hindu governments in India were similar to their Middle Eastern contemporaries, despite wide differences in Muslim and Hindu theory.

This does not mean the coming of Islam did not affect the life of India. Rulers might be tolerant, but even in a foreign tongue the public daily calls to prayer—"There is no God but God, and Muhammad is His Prophet"—constantly reminded Hindus of the presence of an alien faith. Some tried to absorb it as they had earlier done with Buddhism. They stressed the ideal of loving devotion to the One True Reality, which was part of Hinduism, in hopes of finding a bond of union with Islamic monotheism. A few, like the Sikhs, repudiated the caste system in an effort to overcome Muslim objections to their faith. However, the differences between the Creator and the Uncreating were too marked for Hindu attempts at absorption to win many Muslims, other than those already inclined toward the pantheistic mysticism of the Sufi movement.

The call to prayer was not the only constant reminder of differences between Hinduism and Islam. The Hindus' knowledge that Muslims killed and ate cattle did not improve relations, especially when the cattle were driven to slaughter through a Hindu-inhabited street; nor were anyone's nerves soothed if Hindus played music outside a Muslim place of worship during times of prayer, when Muslim ritual forbade the use of music.

Many Hindus reacted to the Muslim conquest by withdrawing still farther into the shell of caste. They hardened the lines between groups and placed even more restrictions on women to keep their daughters from being taken into Muslim households. They even forbade as contaminating the overseas travel which had sustained the Chola and their predecessors, lest contact with non-Hindus lead to conversion from Hinduism. However, religious passions ran less high on the island of Ceylon, which remained free from Muslim rule, and the existing barriers of caste were not reinforced in comparable ways.

The relationship between ordinary Hindus and Muslims in India was frequently strained, even when the greatest cordiality was being displayed by Muslim rulers to their Hindu subjects and by Hindu mystics to their Muslim counterparts. A Hindu-Muslim synthesis offered fruitful possibilities at the top of the political pyramid and in the fraternity of mysticism, but below these exalted heights there was much bitterness on both sides. Muslims could not accept the premises on which Hindu life was based; Hindus found the Muslims too numerous to ignore. They could not understand why Muslims refused to be absorbed into the Hindu way of life, as previous conquerors and reformers had been. By the time Mughal rule gave way to European control, the longstanding antagonisms which came to be typified in Sivaji and Aurangzeb had already made it highly unlikely that India could be united under a leadership which was either dominantly Muslim or largely Hindu.

4

BRITAIN IN SOUTH ASIA

Establishment and Maintenance of British Rule

EUROPEAN RIVALRIES (1498–1764)

The first direct voyage between Europe and India was made by the Portuguese captain Vasco da Gama, whose arrival on the southwestern coast of India in 1498 was followed in 1510 by the Portuguese capture of Goa and in 1517 by the establishment of a Portuguese garrison at Colombo on Ceylon. The Portuguese promptly sought to win local supporters through conversion and intermarriage. They even succeeded in placing a Sinhalese convert to Christianity on the throne of southewestern Ceylon and in claiming the region for Portugal when he died in 1597 without leaving any heirs. By the time the Mughal Akbar was succeeded by his son in 1605, the Portugese held not only Goa and southwestern Ceylon, but also the island of Bombay, a number of other points along the western coast, and ports near the mouths of the Kaveri and the Ganges.

The Portuguese were unable to retain all these outposts in the face of pressures from other European trading nations in the seventeenth century. Trade-minded Protestant Englishmen and Dutchmen refused to recognize the papal pronouncement of 1493 dividing the non-European world into Portuguese and Spanish spheres of influence. When Spanish involvement in European affairs gave the Dutch and English a chance, they set out to break the Spanish and Portuguese monopolies in the New World, Africa, the Indian Ocean, and the South China Sea. In 1600 and 1602 the English and Dutch formed their East

India Companies, which were licensed to carry on all English and Dutch trade from India eastwards.

Although the Dutch entered the Indian Ocean a bit later than the English did, they were even more eager to weaken Spain. England had ensured its independence of Spain by defeating the Spanish Armada in 1588, but the Dutch did not force Spain to acknowledge their independence from the Spanish crown until 1648. The Dutch therefore not only sought trading privileges in the Indian Ocean, as the English did; they also attacked the possessions of Portugal, which from 1580 to 1640 were included in the Spanish empire.

In Ceylon, the Dutch formed an alliance with the Sinhalese kingdom of Kandy to the east of the Portuguese, and by 1658 succeeded in expelling the Portuguese from Ceylon. They then proceeded to establish a new legal system based on their own Roman-Dutch code, to introduce new crops, to restore irrigation works, and to bring in Tamils from northern Ceylon to help cultivate the soil. In 1665 a serious internal revolt led their Kandyan ally to ask their aid. For almost a century thereafter, Dutch influence in Kandy was strong.

In India, the Mughals soon became aware of Portuguese naval power. Later they learned of Portuguese persecution of Muslims through the courts of the Inquisition, which came to Goa in 1540. The Mughals therefore welcomed English, Dutch, Danish, and French traders as a counterbalance to Portuguese control of the seas. In 1612 the Mughals granted the English East India Company the right to trade at Surat in Gujerat, at that time a major port and until then an exclusively Portuguese preserve. In 1639 the Company leased the site of Madras from one of the petty Hindu rulers who sprang up in the south after the fall of Vijayanagar. During the same period the Company was also establishing trading rights in the Ganges valley and the Mahanadi delta. The Dutch East India Company followed closely, entering Surat in 1616. By 1661 English-Dutch rivalry was so intense that the English allied themselves with the declining Portuguese against the Dutch. In token of the alliance, the Portuguese ceded Bombay to Charles II of England.

As the seventeenth century progressed, the English East India Company's officers decided to strengthen their positions. Unlike their contemporaries in the Middle East, who traded in regions ruled by dynasties that might be weak but were still functioning, they had to find means of surviving amidst a number of warring claimants to power. The experience of Maratha raids on Surat in 1664 and 1670 and the decline of Mughal authority during Aurangzeb's long campaigns made Company men fear losses of goods to plunderers, emboldened by the lessening of public order. A fort had already been built at Madras. Bombay became a second Company fortress when Charles II transferred the island to the Company in 1668. The terms of transfer gave the Company at Bombay all the rights of sovereignty, including the right of coinage and the right to declare war and make peace. By 1700 a third fort was built, near Calcutta in Bengal.

The English East India Company in Bombay, Madras, and Calcutta was, in effect, a government as well as a trading company. It exercised full sovereignty in Bombay. At Madras, which the Company had leased from a petty prince who attached no limiting conditions to the contract, James II of England allowed it to set up a municipal government in 1687; and in 1715, after Mughal governors replaced the former rulers of the area, the Mughal court recognized the Company's right to administer Madras. In fact, by 1735 the Mughal representatives in the region were also permitting the Company to administer the nearby towns. Meanwhile, in 1698 the provincial government in Bengal recognized the Company as the official tax collector for Calcutta and two neighboring villages—the first instance in which the Company exercised control over Indians by virtue of Mughal recognition rather than English charters.

While the English were establishing themselves at Madras, Bombay, and Calcutta, the French joined them at Surat, in 1668. By 1674 local Muslim authorities granted the French East India Company land on which to establish settlements at Pondichery, near Madras, and Chandernagore, near Calcutta. French successes in both India and Europe led the Dutch and English to combine against them in the 1690s.

French preoccupation with European and American affairs left the French East India Company without support until the 1740s. It even withdrew from Surat. However, Mughal provinces neither paid tribute nor showed obedience to Delhi. They made war on each other, on the Maratha confederacy, and on local Hindu chieftains, with little deference to the wishes of their nominal overlord. Into this tangle and confusion came two remarkable Europeans, Clive of Britain and Dupleix of France, each of whom saw the situation as a rare opportunity to strengthen his country by acquiring power in India. The outcome of the resulting land and sea battles determined the fate of India and its immediate neighbors for generations.

At first the British and French attacked each other directly. During the general European conflict of the War of the Austrian Succession (1740–1748), British naval vessels in the Indian Ocean captured French merchant ships. The French appealed to the Muslim ruler of the region behind Madras, the Nawab (governor) of the Carnatic, the southeastern coast, to require the British to release their ships. The appeals were fruitless, for the Nawab had no navy. France then sent a naval squadron to the Indian coast, where it aided French land forces in seizing Madras. The British asked the Nawab for help, on the ground that as the representative of Mughal authority he was bound to protect their position. The Nawab agreed and sent an army, but his troops proved worthless against the small but disciplined French force. Dupleix thereupon took a new look at the situation.

Dupleix saw clearly that the British could control the seas. Moreover, they had centers of power in the west and in Bengal as well as in the Carnatic. However, Dupleix concluded that the French could establish themselves too firmly to be uprooted, if they could win the support of strategically placed Indian princes in return for lending the small but evidently superior armies of the French East India Company to the princes in their wars with their neighbors. He promptly offered aid to two men, a rival of the Nawab of the Carnatic and a candidate for control of Hyderabad in the Deccan. Madras was returned to the British by the peacemakers in Europe, but by 1750 Dupleix's new allies ruled both the Carnatic and Hyderabad.

The British at Madras awoke to the situation too late to prevent Dupleix's allies from recognizing him as governor of much of the eastern coast, but in the next two years the British made alliances with three Hindu powers, the ruler of Tanjore on the east coast, the ruler of Mysore to the west, and part of the Maratha confederacy. The British thereby followed a cardinal rule of traditional Indian diplomacy, seeking allies on their neighbors' opposite borders in true Kshatriya style. Under Clive's leadership the allies seized both the new Nawab and his capital. Dupleix was recalled to France not long after, in 1754.

In 1755 Clive learned that the new Nawab of Bengal was menacing British holdings there. The Nawab feared that the British intended to overthrow him as they had recently overthrown his colleague in the Carnatic, for the British at Calcutta favored one of his rivals and were strengthening their fortifications. He insisted that the new fortifications be demolished. When this was not done, he seized Calcutta outright in 1756. Clive and his men promptly sailed from Madras to Bengal and recovered Calcutta early in 1757. Clive then allied himself with the Nawab's rivals, while the Nawab turned to the French, for France and Britain were then involved in the Seven Years' War (1756–1763). However, some of the Nawab's generals were secretly won over by the arguments, promises, and financial inducements put forward by Clive and his Indian allies. As a result, the Nawab's armies were routed at the battle of Plassey in 1757 and another Nawab took his place. The British also captured all the French positions. At the end of the Seven Years' War the French were given back Pondichery, Chandernagore, and a few other places, but in 1769 the French government dissolved the French East India Company. The Company's disappearance marked the end of French influence in India for a time.

In 1760 the new Nawab's son-in-law took his place. The British traders at Calcutta soon quarreled with him over their illegal extension of the commercial privileges granted them by the Mughals. The Mughals had exempted official British East Company trade from paying duties, but Company merchants were also refusing to pay taxes on the trade they conducted as private individuals in their spare time. Fighting broke out in 1763. When the British defeated the Nawab and his allies in 1764, they captured the titular Mughal emperor. Clive restored the emperor to Delhi in exchange for formal recognition of the British East India Company as official supervisor of revenue collection not only in Bengal but also in neighboring Orissa and Bihar. Thereafter, as Clive wrote in 1767, whoever held the office of Nawab was merely a convenient figurehead whom the Company could use to object to other Europeans' activities.

The newly growing power of the Company was recognized as far away as Ceylon. There, a Malayalam-born ruler of Kandy strove to strengthen his position as the founder of a new dynasty by making friends with Company representatives in Madras. In 1760 he fomented uprisings against Dutch rule around Colombo. The Dutch quelled the revolt, forced Kandy to cede its coastal domains, and thereafter ruled all of Ceylon except the mountainous southern interior still held by Kandy.

EARLY BRITISH EAST INDIA COMPANY RULE (1764–1793)

The British East India Company's position as revenue collector of Bengal enabled the Company's men to fill their own pockets as they collected taxes, fees, and gifts. Company men in India concentrated so hard on their private welfare that they neglected the affairs of the Company, and it nearly went bankrupt. The *nabobs*, or newly rich Company men returned from India, soon became well known in Britain, and so did their bribe-taking and other means of using the Company's position to profit themselves. Finally the British Parliament passed a Regulating Act, in 1773. The Act required the Company to render semi-annual reports to the British government; recognized the Company's governors as the chief authorities in Bombay, Madras, and Calcutta; established a Supreme Court at Calcutta and a four-man council to work with the governor there; and gave the governor at Calcutta (then Warren Hastings) a nominal authority over his colleagues in Bombay and Madras. The new Supreme Court soon began judging Indian cases, though the Act confined its jurisdiction to British subjects.

While British power was growing in Bengal, the British at Madras formed an uneasy alliance with the Marathas and the Nizam (viceroy) of Hyderabad against Haidar Ali, a Muslim who seized the Hindu-ruled state of Mysore in 1761. When Haidar Ali proved too strong for the small British forces, the British signed a treaty with him in 1769. In 1775 Hastings found himself at war with the Marathas, who took a French adventurer into their service after the French entered the American Revolutionary War in 1777. Three years later Haidar Ali seized the aid offered him by the French and extended his sway over the Carnatic. However, when peace was finally made in 1782, Hastings managed to require Haidar Ali to give up his gains and return to Mysore.

By the time Hastings left India in 1785, the British, in effect, ruled Bengal. Not only did they collect the taxes in the province; under Hastings they also took over the administration of justice. The Company had long since established legal systems for the local people in Company-ruled Bombay and Madras, where no Indian ruler laid claim to jurisdiction. These legal systems owed most of their provisions to Muslim and Hindu tradition. However, the courts of Bengal remained under the Nawab until Hastings established district-level civil and criminal courts. In each of these courts, a Company-appointed officer was to render judgment, assisted by local advisers who would inform him concerning the private laws of Hindus and Muslims and the modified Islamic public law that had been in effect throughout most of India since the Muslim conquest. The efficiency with which the British enforced the decisions of their judges led a growing number of disputants to take an all-or-nothing chance in the Company courts, rather than resort to the older practice of private bargaining and compromise. As a result, lawyers became a numerous and influential group in Bengal during the next few decades.

Hastings' struggles with the members of his council in Calcutta and his fellow governors in Madras and Bombay led to the passage of a new India Act in 1784. The new Act strengthened the Calcutta governor-general's control over Bombay and Madras, and it cut his council to three. It also made him responsible to two masters: the Company's board of directors in London, and a newly established board of control made up of members of the British government. Hastings resigned the next year, 1785. In 1791 his successor Lord Cornwallis was given the right to override his council in Calcutta if he thought it necessary.

When Cornwallis arrived in Calcutta in 1786, he promptly began to reorganize the Company administration. He revised the structure of the Company's army so that all its commissioned officers would be British. He also insisted that all high officials in the civil administration be British, and he raised the salaries of civil administrators so as to lessen the temptation to take bribes. The success of the army reorganization was shown during an inconclusive war with Haidar Ali's son Tipu Sultan in 1791–1792. Tipu Sultan sought French assistance, for France and Britain were at war once more, now that the French Revolution had commenced, but the British repelled his attacks. The success of the reorganization of the civil administration was shown by the record of integrity made by the Indian Civil Service in later years.

Before Cornwallis left India in 1793 he inaugurated other important changes. He separated revenue collection in Bengal from the administration of justice, giving the two sets of tasks to two different sets of officials rather than leaving them both to the tax collectors. He also elevated the position of the *zamindari*, the individuals recognized by the Mughals as responsible for seeing that the villages paid their land taxes. In past years the zamindari had been scarcely more than tax collectors, but Cornwallis made landlords of them by simply refusing to let the courts uphold any of the other claims to land which Bengalis were accustomed to recognizing, such as the right to cultivate a given plot of land or to collect the products of its trees.

The recognition of the zamindari as the only owners of land was part of a "Permanent Settlement," in which the zamindari were required to pay the same amount in taxes each year instead of having the amount raised (or lowered) by periodic reassessments. They were also required to pay promptly or have their lands confiscated and auctioned to the highest bidder. Cornwallis hoped the zamindari would concentrate on raising their incomes by encouraging agricultural improvements, like the English landlords of his day, but his hopes were not fulfilled. The strict enforcement of the provision for auctioning the lands of zamindari who failed to pay a year's taxes led to a rapid turnover of zamindari rights. Many zamindari therefore felt too uncertain of the future to consider making sizable investments. In addition, most zamindari preferred living in the cities as absentee landlords to remaining in the countryside and improving the land. Population was growing, the number of families seeking land to cultivate was growing, and many zamindari increased their incomes simply by raising rents, expelling those tenants who said they could not afford the higher rates, and taking new tenants in their places. Not until 1859 did the British protect the cultivators of Bengal, Orissa, and Bihar by stating in the Bengal Cultivators' Act that a person who had cultivated the same plot of land for twelve successive years could renew the lease on it permanently. Thereafter, villagers were less fearful of being expelled from their land in favor of people who wanted land so badly that they would promise to pay exorbitant rents.

In the other regions controlled by the British East India Company in the time of Cornwallis and his successors, the Company did not repeat what came to be regarded as the mistake of promising never to change the amount of the land tax. It also assessed the land tax either on the villages or on the individual peasants, not on the local equivalents of the zamindari. The Company's contracts with the peasants or villages for the payment of taxes specified that the amount to be paid would be altered periodically in the light of changing land values. This system of periodic reassessment made revenues keep pace with the government's needs and the taxpayers' ability to pay far better than did the Permanent Settlement in Bengal.

EXPANSION OF COMPANY DOMAINS (1793–1826)

When Cornwallis sailed for Britain in 1793, the Company's authority was still confined to Bombay, Madras, the few southern coastal districts seized in the struggles with the French, and Bengal, Orissa, and Bihar. The independent Muslim rulers of Mysore and Hyderabad divided most of the south between them; the Afghans held the Indus valley; the central Ganges was ruled by a Company ally, the Nawab of Oudh; and the Maratha dominated the rest.

The situation was altered greatly in the next twelve years. When the Dutch Republic became a satellite of revolutionary France, the British seized Dutch Ceylon and the Cape of Good Hope at the southern tip of Africa in 1795–1796, in order to protect their growing Indian empire. Tipu Sultan and the Maratha both received French support as Napoleon rose to power in revolutionary France. To forestall any resurgence of French power in India, the Company's governor-general from 1798 to 1805, Richard Wellesley, took vigorous action. Mysore was restored to its former Hindu rulers, but its northern territories were given to the Nizam of Hyderabad in return for assistance to the Company. The rest of the south was annexed to the Company-ruled lands around Madras. The friendly rulers of Hyderabad and Oudh were required to accept new treaties of alliance, sometimes called subsidiary treaties, which left the control of their foreign affairs to the British East India Company. Finally, Wellesley forced the Maratha leaders in the Deccan, together with a few Rajputs, to accept similar subsidiary treaties with the Company. While Wellesley was thus bringing most of India into close relations with the Company, the Sikh leader Ranjit Singh and his once-pacifist followers took up the arts of war and wrested most of the Panjab from Afghan rule. The Sikhs of the Panjab remained formidable neighbors to the British in Delhi until Ranjit Singh died in 1839.

In 1817, two years after the Napoleonic wars ended, the Maratha tried and failed to throw off the Company yoke. The Company annexed much of western India to the region controlled from Bombay and required both the Maratha and the Rajputs to accept new subsidiary treaties. The mountain state of Nepal had already been forced to accept a subsidiary alliance in 1816. In 1826, when the seizure of Assam by the king of Burma seemed to threaten the Company's position in Bengal, the eighth governor-general occupied not only Assam but most of coastal

Burma. The rest of the Burma coast was taken by Company armies in 1852.

BRITISH STUDY OF INDIAN LANGUAGES AND TRADITIONS

The nature of British rule in eighteenth-century India was markedly affected by the fact that their rule started when the still-functioning Mughal provincial government accepted the privately run British East India Company as its agent for collecting the revenues of the province of Bengal. It was also influenced by the fact that it began before the age of steam and electricity shrank the distances between European governments and their nationals overseas, or multiplied the output of European factories and the demand for materials and markets.

Partly because of these factors, Company men did not see their task as one of reshaping Indian life. They were as eager as any other empire-builders to promote long-lasting, profitable trade between the land from which they came and the land to which they went. In addition, they were quite willing to assume that it was essential to commercial growth to put an end to the constant warfare by winning control over the warring local governments. (They also thought commercial growth required the continuance of a Company monopoly over British trade with India and points east, but Parliament withdrew that privilege between 1813 and 1833 despite their arguments.) However, Company men in India were far from home, and most of them did not have families in India unless they established Indian households. They tended to regard Indian culture favorably. They respected India's ancient literature; they admired its handicrafts, such as the hand-loomed textiles which were important in world trade in the seventeenth and eighteenth centuries; and they accepted its customs with little criticism.

Many Company judges took great interest in establishing the nature of the legal system they were supposed to apply in the Company's courts, although their own presuppositions about the equality of all before the law made them pay less regard to caste and class than earlier magistrates had done. Company men were encouraged to study Sanskrit, Arabic, and Persian, not only because of need for more systematic knowledge of local law, but also because of the curiosity aroused by resemblances between the languages of Europe and the ancient Aryan language, Sanskrit. Warren Hastings, for example, learned Persian, Arabic, and Bengali. He supported Englishmen who studied Sanskrit, and he helped to found the Asiatic Society of Bengal.

As the years passed, a number of Company men studied the relationships between the languages of Europe and northern India. They came to recognize a historical kinship between Indo-Aryans and Europeans. Their studies inspired other Western scholars, and many Europeans began to take a warm interest in translations from the Sanskrit into English, French, German, and other languages. German scholars were especially attracted to the literatures of India, from which they learned to think in terms of relativity. These evidences of western European interest in Indian culture made it easy for Indians to be equally interested in Western ideas. Indian and Briton could meet on a plane of friendship and mutual respect in intellectual life, if not in political affairs. The interest taken by Britons in Indian ideas was an important factor in the relative amicability with which Indians eventually accepted a number of British ideas, although it was scarcely the conclusive factor.

For the peoples of the Ottoman empire and East and Southeast Asia, where Europeans did not display the same kind of cousinly interest, the originators of modern Western thought were alien in a way in which they were not alien in Aryan-permeated India. To most Europeans, Islam was an offensive offshoot of the Judeo-Christian tradition, to be disdained as it had been since before the Crusades. Moreover, Chinese and Japanese acceptance of the basic reality of the phenomenal world seemed naive to those accustomed to distinguishing temporal from eternal matters; and the mingling of Chinese, Indian, and Islamic elements in Southeast Asian culture appeared to many Westerners as an uncritical series of imitations uninformed by any unifying principle. Middle Easterners and East and Southeast Asians naturally reacted to such rebuffs, in contrast to the reciprocal interest displayed by Indians and Westerners.

EARLY HINDU AND MUSLIM REACTIONS TO COMPANY RULE

After a hundred years of warfare, the Indian society into which the British came as conquerors in the eighteenth century was yearning for the past. For centuries the Hindus had been tightening their restrictions on themselves as a means of retaining their individuality despite Muslim rule. Now many Muslims, distressed at the decline of Mughal power, were turning to leaders like Shah Waliullah of Delhi (1703–1762), who sought to purge Islam of alien elements that had crept into it. Other Muslims merely sat back and bewailed the loss of their authority to the British. When the British took over Bengal, the former Muslim officials continued to look back to the Mughal era, and many of them refused to work with the new British officials.

The Hindus made the transition to serving their new overlords with much less difficulty than did the Muslims. Since Hindus had continued to hold many lower-level administrative posts throughout the Muslim era, they were used to working under rulers who did not share their way of life. The Hindus of Bengal took up the study of English eagerly. At first they used English to enter the civil service, but as more and more Bengalis decided to use Company courts, English also became necessary for entry into the growing legal profession. Young Bengali lawyers then began to study English law as well as Hindu and Muslim law, so that they could appeal more effectively to the English judges before whom they pleaded their clients' cases.

Similar patterns recurred as the British acquired new Indian domains. Muslims sighed for the days of Mughal ascendancy and largely abstained from intercourse with the British; Hindus studied the British with some of the same close and sympathetic attention with which the British studied them, for the Hindus hoped that their new masters would prove to be like the friendly Akbar rather than the intolerant Aurangzeb. As a consequence, a few Hindus were ready to listen carefully to British suggestions in the early nineteenth century, when social reform movements in Britain and missionary work by evangelical Protestants in India began to stimulate reform-mindedness in Company circles. These Hindus applauded when Company administrators outlawed *sati* (the sacrifice of a widow on her husband's funeral pyre) and *thagi* (the ritual strangling of travelers as an offering to Kali, the goddess of destruction), and established English-language schools to compete with existing schools of Muslim and Hindu learning.

The most outstanding early-nineteenth-century student of the West in India was a Bengali, Raja Ram Mohan Roy (1772–1833), who was a Company official for a time. A Brahmin, he was deeply learned in the religious lore and the classical tongues of both India and the West. After leaving the Company's service, he settled in Calcutta with the intent of synthesizing what was best in the Indian heritage with what was most constructive in Western thought and practice. He helped found India's first collegiate institution of Western learning in 1816. He upheld freedom of speech and advocated freedom of the press, which already held a place in Indian life by the 1820s. He opposed the custom of sati, the inequities of the caste system, and the worship of a multitude of gods. In 1828 he founded the Brahma Samaj, or Divine Society. The Brahma Samaj sought to combine the rigorous use of reason upheld in the Upanishadic commentaries with the ethical system of Christianity, which seemed eminently reasonable to Raja Ram Mohan Roy and his followers.

After Roy died, the ideals of the Brahma Samaj were taken up by the Tagore family, whose most notable member was the poet Rabindranath Tagore (1861–1941), winner of the Nobel Prize for literature in 1913. The Tagores, like others who supported the nineteenth-century renaissance of learning and the arts in Bengal, were themselves the products of British rule. They were among those who had become zamindari under the Permanent Settlement, had realized large incomes as their land increased in value, and could therefore afford works of charity and patronage.

REFORMS AND FURTHER EXPANSION IN INDIA
(1828–1856)

As the nineteenth century progressed, the British East India Company continually modified the tax-collecting and judicial systems that were evolving in the territories it controlled. During the governorgeneralship of William Bentinck (1828–1835) these processes of evolution became so rapid that they almost turned into revolution. A spirit of liberalism was rising in Britain, and Bentinck, a man experienced in India and deeply committed to the principles of the evangelical and utilitarian movements, was able to put through many reforms under its influence. He had the sympathy of a large part of the British Parliament, which decided in the Charter Act of 1833 to define the office of the governor-general more clearly by separating it from the governorship of Bengal and by forbidding the Company to take part in nongovernmental activities like trade. The Act also added a member to the governorgeneral's council whose specific task was to advise him concerning modifications in the legal system.

While Bentinck was in office, exploratory studies were made of the problems involved in organizing and codifying the multitude of laws administered in Company courts. More Indians were included in the civil administration, although Englishmen and Scotsmen continued to hold almost all the higher positions. Most of these men were trained in England at a college established in 1806 to educate potential members of the Company's Indian Civil Service. Under Bentinck, English replaced Persian as the language of government records, and witnesses were permitted to testify in the courts in their everyday speech instead of having to use Persian. These changes encouraged the development of both English and the Indian vernacular tongues, at the expense of Persian and its Indian offshoots Urdu and Hindi. Furthermore, Bentinck decided to alter the Company's educational policy by promoting the study of English. Since the time of Hastings, the Company had financed Sanskrit, Persian, and Arabic studies, on the ground that the Company needed Indians who were learned in Hindu and Muslim law to assist British judges in Bengal; and since 1813 Parliament had stipulated that the Company should spend 10,000 pounds per year on the instruction of Indians. The decision to use those funds for instruction in English and the intellectual heritage of western Europe, rather than Sanskrit, Persian, and Arabic, may have been

Bentinck's most significant innovation. In future years, Indians raised on the ideas of Locke, Bentham, and Mill were to expect these ideas to be applied in India as well as Britain. Bentinck also forbade female infanticide and the rites of sati and thagi.

In the years following Bentinck's administration, the British in India became concerned over their northwest frontier. The Panjab fell into disunity after Ranjit Singh died, and the Russians were advancing toward Afghanistan. When an attempt to force Afghanistan to accept British leadership was ignominiously defeated in 1842, the British realized they had to control the Indus valley if they were to influence Afghanistan in future. Between 1843 and 1849 they conquered and annexed both Sind and the Panjab. They also persuaded the *maharaja* or ruler of Jammu and Kashmir, where a local Hindu prince had taken advantage of the decline of Sikh power to set up an independent state, to accept a subsidiary treaty.

Having safeguarded its frontiers, the Company government embarked on what might be called internal expansion, under James Dalhousie, governor-general from 1848 to 1856. Dalhousie brought several regions under direct Company control by using the longstanding though nebulous Indian traditions concerning the authority held by a paramount ruler over subsidiary rulers and the undeniable fact that the British East India Company was the paramount power in India. In 1831 Mysore had already been taken from its ruler and put under the Company on the ground that its ruler was administering it poorly. Mysore remained under British administration for fifty years before being returned to its ruling house, whose heads thereafter conducted themselves unimpeachably. Oudh in the central Ganges valley was taken over because of maladministration in 1856 and was never returned to its former rulers. Dalhousie also annexed several portions of central India under the customary Indian doctrine of lapse, which provided that a subsidiary state reverted to the paramount power at the death of the last member of its ruling family. Since Dalhousie refused to follow the Indian practice of recognizing adopted sons as full heirs, these annexations produced bitter resentment among adopted princes who thereby lost what they believed to be their rightful inheritance.

Dalhousie did not confine himself to internal expansion. His term of office was as notable for innovations as was Bentinck's. New members were appointed to the governor-general's council to advise him on legislative questions. The establishment of telegraph lines and a new postal system enabled private individuals as well as government officials to communicate rapidly and cheaply with one another all over India. In extension of programs begun in Bentinck's time, public works administrations were set up in the British-ruled provinces, speeding up the construction of a network of improved roads and an extended system of irrigation and transport canals, and preparing the way for the building of the great dams of later years. Most important of all, the introduction of railroads opened up new possibilities for villagers and townspeople by enabling goods and people to move freely throughout India.

The railroads begun in Dalhousie's time extended from one corner of India to the other by 1875. By weaving together the economic life of all of India to an unprecedented extent, the railroads promoted the idea of India as one country as much as did Dalhousie's practice of treating India as a political unit. When Dalhousie applied the principle of paramountcy, when he brought representatives from the Company administrations at Bombay and Madras into his council at Calcutta, and when he encouraged those who were attempting to codify the laws used in British India, he assumed that India could be regarded as one. He thereby encouraged others to make the same assumption.

THE UPRISING OF 1857 AND THE END OF COMPANY RULE

The number and rapidity of the innovations introduced by Dalhousie and his predecessors alarmed many Indians. A year after Dalhousie left, the Indian *sepoys*, or soldiers, in the Company's army at Meerut near Delhi broke out in what the British termed the Sepoy Rebellion or the Indian Mutiny. The rebels seized Delhi and proclaimed the sovereignty of the Mughals. Many in the north supported them, but the Panjab, Bengal, and the areas south of the Narbada remained relatively quiet. By the end of 1858 the British were once more in full control, but not through the British East India Company. The British Parliament was so roused by the news of the rebellion that it abolished the Company and placed British India directly under the Crown, making the governor-general, the provincial governors, and their councils agents of the Crown instead of the Company.

The British government quickly made clear to the princes that London expected to maintain the Company's subsidiary treaties with them, but promised not to interfere with their boundaries and assured them that adopted heirs would be recognized in future. These promises effectively froze the boundaries of the states of Princely India, as these regions were called in contrast to British India. No alterations were made in the territories held by the princes until Britain left India in 1947. The princes continued to accept British resident advisers as before, but they did not always accept the advice they were given on internal administrative matters. Neither the pre-1858 reforms of Hastings, Cornwallis, Bentinck, and

Dalhousie nor the further reforms introduced after 1858 affected most of Princely India. When the British left and the princely states were embodied in India and Pakistan, they proved to be a thorny problem for the new governments.

TRANSITION FROM COMPANY RULE TO
CROWN RULE IN CEYLON (1795–1848)

When Crown replaced Company in India, the Crown's officers could use the experience of Ceylon as a guide, for Ceylon had become a crown colony more than half a century before. The first British East India Company administrators sent there from Madras in 1795 had ignored local sentiment and provoked an uprising by using Tamils from Madras to help them govern the Sinhalese. When news of the revolt reached London, Parliament required the Company at Madras to share the responsibility of ruling Ceylon with the British government. The first and only governor under this joint administration promptly replaced the Tamils with Sinhalese.

The joint Company-Parliament administration ended in 1802, when Ceylon was made a crown colony. In 1803 the British invaded Kandy. A Sinhalese minister in the Kandyan court had invited the British to help him topple the Malayalam dynasty when they arrived in 1795. The British refused, but he provoked them into driving the king from Kandy in 1803 by instigating attacks on merchants from British-held Ceylon. The king returned in 1811, but in 1815 his mistreatment of merchants led the British to invade Kandy again. This time the British took over the kingdom, promising to retain its religious and legal institutions. However, they modified their promises in 1818 when Kandyan nobles and monks united in an anti-British uprising. After suppressing the revolt the British proclaimed a reform of abuses. They reserved the right to introduce what they called necessary changes into Kandyan institutions and to protect the interests of all religions, not just Buddhism. The nobles were still used as administrators, but under closer supervision than before. Christian missionaries were allowed to work in Kandy, and the Roman-Dutch code of laws enforced in the coastal areas was also applied there.

Christian missionaries had been active in the lowlands since Portuguese days. Under Dutch and British rule the missionaries concentrated increasingly on providing Western education. At first they taught only the children of the small Christian community, but soon they began to teach others. By the mid-nineteenth century large numbers of Ceylonese were attending both mission and government schools to study the English language that would enable them to enter the government, the flourishing commercial houses, or a profession like medicine or law.

Like the Dutch and Portuguese on Ceylon, the British at first required their Sinhalese and Tamil subjects to fell trees, build roads, catch elephants, collect cinnamon, and provide other labor services. However, Parliament began to object to this and other aspects of the Ceylonese situation, and sent out two investigating commissions, one for administrative and one for judicial affairs. In 1832 the commissioners recommended strongly that the Ceylonese be given more personal freedom and more civil and political rights and responsibilities. Not all the recommendations were adopted, but by 1845 forced labor and the government cinnamon monopoly were ended. An appointed legislative council of nine officials and six private individuals (three European, one Eurasian, one Sinhalese, one Tamil) was created to advise the governor—who took twelve years to appoint the first six nonofficial members.

When the legislative council was established, officials' salaries were cut as an economy measure. Soon the officials began using the permission given them many years before to own land and sell its produce. They established great coffee plantations in the hills of Kandy and proceeded to concentrate on their plantations rather than their governmental duties. As a result, essential irrigation works were neglected in much of the lowland region. In addition, large numbers of Sinhalese from the coast and Tamils from the mainland were brought to Kandy to work on the plantations. Dissatisfaction with these conditions led the Kandyan nobles to crown a new king and raise a revolt in both Kandy and the southwest in 1848, but the revolt was soon quelled.

REFORMS UNDER CROWN RULE IN INDIA

In British India, economic change proceeded rapidly after 1858 as communication, transport, and irrigation systems spread over the countryside, making possible the beginnings of modern industry. By 1900 the British completed most of the public works they carried out before leaving India. Most of these dams, canals, roads, railroads, and other projects were constructed under the supervision of the governor-general's executive council member for public works, whose position was created in 1874. The construction of hydroelectric installations and the local transport networks needed to bring the more remote villages into the mainstream of economic and political life was largely left for the new governments of independent India and Pakistan.

In the realm of law, a penal code and codes of civil and criminal procedure were enacted for British India between 1859 and 1861. As the years passed, more and more Indian magistrates were appointed to the courts. In education, a university was established in Calcutta in 1857, the year of the uprising. Within the next thirty years, four more universities were founded. The number of private and public elementary and secondary schools grew steadily though slowly after 1858. Education at the lower levels was given in the local languages, but English was introduced at an early stage, and at the universities the only courses not given in English were those on Indian classical literature.

In the realm of administration, the principle that Indians were to be eligible for every office had been laid down in 1833, when the Company was still administering British India, and reaffirmed in 1858 when the Company was replaced by the Crown. However, practice could be quite divergent from principle, as the question of entry into the Indian Civil Service shows. To enter the I.C.S., whose members were the only persons eligible for high administrative and judicial posts, it was necessary to pass a competitive examination. Until 1922 the examination was held only in Britain, making it difficult for Indians to compete. To compound their difficulties, the maximum age for taking the examination was set at twenty-two in 1859, reset at twenty-one in 1866, and lowered to nineteen in 1877. Not until 1879 were Indians allowed to enter the I.C.S. without examination if the governor-general approved their candidacy. Even then, those who did so were put in a separate category whose members were not eligible for the highest positions. Finally, in the 1880s, provincial and subordinate or technical civil services were established which were open to qualified Indians without restriction. The provincial and subordinate services gave the graduates of the new universities some outlet for their talents, but the I.C.S. retained the most important posts, and the I.C.S. continued to be dominated by its British members long after entrance examinations began to be held in India. As late as 1939, fifty-five percent of the members of the I.C.S. were British; and at the opening of 1947, the year of independence, over forty percent were still British.

The first small step toward introducing Indians to British parliamentary procedures was the Indian Councils Act of 1861. The executive councils of the governors and the governor-general continued to be entirely British, but half of the men appointed to assist the central and provincial executive councils in making legislation were to be chosen from outside the civil administration, and some of those selected were Indians. In the 1870s, government-appointed local boards were set up to supervise health programs, education, and other public business. However, they had so little real authority that the ablest were not attracted to them even after they were made partly elective in the 1880s. In 1892 the central and provincial legislative councils were expanded in size, and the governor-general asked the larger municipalities, the universities, and other organized bodies like the commercial associations to nominate candidates for nonofficial seats in the provincial councils. This procedure came close to the principles of election and representation, but outright election was not introduced in response to Indian demands until 1909.

During the half-century after 1858, Indians showed a steadily growing interest in political activity. That interest reached a climax between 1899 and 1905, when Lord Curzon was governor-general of British India and viceroy, or representative of the Crown, to the princely states. Curzon's attempts to strengthen government control over the five public universities in 1904 aroused all university-educated Indians, who feared this might foreshadow a restriction of the opportunities available to them in their own country. When Curzon decided in 1905 to partition the unwieldy province of British Bengal, which included many neighboring districts as well as the delta region of Bengal itself, protest demonstrations erupted throughout the province and sympathetic demonstrations were quickly organized in other provinces. However, the immediate cause of Curzon's resignation in 1905 was not the demonstrations, but a disagreement over the government's relation to the Indian armed forces.

From the earliest days of Company power in India, the British had recruited, trained, and used local troops. All three presidencies, as Calcutta, Bombay, and Madras were known in the Company era, had their own forces. Most of the troops who rebelled in 1857 were in the armies of the Calcutta presidency; those of Bombay and Madras stayed relatively quiet. After 1858, the British began recruiting Hindu soldiers from all castes instead of only the upper castes. They also increased the size of the non-Hindu contingents, most of whom were drawn from the Sikhs, the Pathans of the Afghan border, and the Gurkhas of Nepal. The number of British soldiers was increased until there was one for every two Indian soldiers, instead of the one-to-five ratio of 1856, and only British troops were used as artillerymen. In addition, the armed forces of the princely states were informally brought into the system of imperial defense, and an overall commander-in-chief was appointed. Yet the governor-general's council continued to include a military officer, who of course was outranked by the commander-in-chief, to advise the government on military matters. When the British government at London proposed to drop the military member of the council, Curzon feared this would lessen civilian control of the military, and he resigned in protest.

Curzon was succeeded as governor-general by Lord Minto, who served until 1910. In 1909 the British Parliament enacted a series of political reforms on the recommendation of Minto and the Secretary of State for India in London, Lord Morley. The Morley-Minto reforms introduced the elective principle into provincial and central government and thus prepared the way for the parliamentary governments which took control in 1947. They also marked a turning point in Britain's relations with India. In the later nineteenth century the British concentrated on extending the economic, social, educational, administrative, and legal reforms and innovations begun in the period of Company rule. (These reforms and innovations accompanied comparable changes elsewhere in Britain's domains. The first liberalizations in Britain's own electoral laws came in

1832, during Bentinck's reform administration; the second came in 1867, the year Canada became a self-governing dominion and six years after the first Indian Councils Act. The first railroads in Britain were built just before Dalhousie's term. Irish tenants' grievances against absentee landlords were redressed in 1870, eleven years after the Bengal Cultivators' Act. The Morley-Minto reforms came within eight years of the establishment of self-governing dominions in Australia, New Zealand, and the Union of South Africa.) However, from 1909 to their withdrawal in 1947 the British concentrated increasingly on dealing with rising Indian demands for self-rule.

Local Struggles for Independence

REFORM MOVEMENTS IN HINDUISM

As the nineteenth century progressed, the Brahma Samaj founded by Raja Ram Mohan Roy proved to be too intellectually oriented to appeal to most Hindus. Only its catholicity of approach had much influence. Its proclamation that truths were to be found in every major religion opened the way for Indians in later years to examine Western ideas on the basis of reason rather than emotion and to adopt many features of the Western Christian ethical system without feeling that they thereby destroyed their individuality.

Most Hindus of the late nineteenth century found the puritanical Arya Samaj movement more appealing emotionally than the Brahma Samaj. The Arya Samaj was founded in 1875 by Dayananda Sarasvati (1824–1883), a Brahmin from Gujerat with its strong Jain traditions. Dayananda condemned the accretions grafted onto the Vedic teachings by the Upanishadic commentators, exhorting his fellow Hindus to return to the simple orthodoxy of the early days when men and women had been equal and neither caste restrictions nor untouchability had existed. He even extended his preaching to Indian Muslims, establishing the Sudhi (purification) movement to reconvert those whose ancestors had turned from Hinduism to Islam. He founded the Cow Protection Association to save cattle from slaughter as a sign of Hindu reverence for life. He and his followers also founded many schools in northern and western India. Dayananda prepared the way for the half-religious, half-political career of his fellow-Gujerati, Mahatma Gandhi. The Arya Samaj made no claim to synthesize the best in East and West, for it upheld the superiority of a purified Hinduism, but its doctrines of equality owed a profound if unacknowledged debt to the spirit of western Europe.

A course of deliberate synthesis was undertaken by the mystic

Ramakrishna Parahamsa (1834–1886), who strove in his spiritual ecstasies to identify himself with each great religious tradition in turn and then sought to impart his insights to disciples. His most notable follower was Vivekananda (1862–1902), who was a Kshatriya rather than a Brahmin like his master. Vivekananda founded the Ramakrishna and Vedanta mission societies, whose combination of philanthropy and teaching strikingly resembles the nature of Christian mission work in nineteenth-century India. He proclaimed not only that all religions contain elements of truth, as Raja Ram Mohan Roy had done, but that they are in fact essentially the same. This was a radical statement to make to orthodox Hindus, who had long thought all non-Hindus outside the pale. The degree to which his teaching was accepted in India, on the ground that it was consistent with the same catholicity of belief that had reabsorbed Buddhism, was one more link in a chain of willingness to study Western ways without prejudging them on the basis of their origin. The foundation of the Theosophical Society in 1875 was also important in making Indians receptive to Western ideas, for the Society's leaders, Mmes. Blavatsky and Besant, drew their inspiration from the Sanskrit scriptures and thereby unintentionally reassured Indians anew that the West from which India was learning was willing to learn from India in return.

THE INDIAN INTERMEDIARIES AND THE INDIAN NATIONAL CONGRESS

The spiritual reactions of the Hindus to Western overlordship in India partly resembled their reactions to the Muslim conquest, including strivings for both self-purification and synthesis. Not all their reactions were spiritual, but since Hindu tenets affected every aspect of life, many nonspiritual reactions to British rule had religious overtones. Several of the mutinies of Hindu soldiers in Company armies came from fear of being made outcastes if they obeyed orders which had some bearing on caste rules. In 1806, soldiers in the south mutinied over an order to cease using caste marks, and in 1824, soldiers in Bengal mutinied against going to Burma by sea rather than land. Even the great uprising of 1857, which resulted largely from dissatisfaction with Company programs of political and economic centralization, was touched off in part by rumors that some new cartridges were greased with the fat of cows (sacred to Hindus) and pigs (abhorrent to Muslims). However, the rise of a new class to positions of leadership was more important to India's future than were the mutinies.

The Mughal rulers, and the Muslim and Hindu princelings who had assumed authority when the Mughals declined, lost prestige as the British took over the reins of government from them. Within Indian society, power and prestige gravitated to the class of the intermediaries, the persons who acted with and for the British in their dealings with the bulk of the population. Most of the intermediaries were upper-caste Hindus, although the Parsis took the lead in Bombay. Intermediaries came into being in all three centers of British power—Bombay, Madras, and Calcutta—but they first became numerous in Bengal, the first large region where the British won full control.

Originally, the intermediaries learned English so that they could work with the British, but a number followed the early example of Raja Ram Mohan Roy by going on to deeper study of British thought and practice. Some were landholders like the Tagores, who as tax-collecting zamindari were intermediaries as much as any record keeper in a Company office. Some were merchants, like the Parsi community in Bombay. As more positions in the civil service were opened to Indians over the years, more and more intermediaries were officials in the government. The number of government posts grew rapidly in the time of officials like Dalhousie, whose inauguration of new government activities like irrigation and transport services brought whole new departments into being. Another growing group comprised the professionals—the lawyers, who had to use English fluently once it became the language of the higher courts in 1835; the teachers, who instructed potential lawyers and officials; the journalists, who sought to influence both their fellow Indians and their British rulers; and those who learned to practice Western medicine.

As British power spread over India, the intermediaries sprang up everywhere in a pattern which was to be transferred with greater or lesser fidelity to every other European-held region in Africa and Asia between 1840 and 1940, from French-ruled Senegal and British-ruled Sierra Leone to Dutch-ruled Indonesia. All over India, the English-speaking few were united by a sense of a common relationship as mediators between the British and their own people. The English language which they used replaced Persian and Urdu as the hallmark of those who were influential in government circles. The intermediaries were literate in English, which enabled them to communicate readily through the mails and the press, and their reading of English literature acquainted them with English pride in England and the English people. Soon the intermediaries began to develop a strong affection toward their own people and a belief that India too could become a great and united nation.

Gradually the intermediaries drew together to work for the nation they envisioned. Even before the uprising of 1857, the Bombay Association had been formed in India to petition Parliament for governmental reforms, and the London Indian Society was established to lobby in the imperial capital. The London Indian Society was founded by a Bombay Parsi and a Bengali who later became the first president of the Indian National Congress.

In 1877 another Bengali leader toured northern India as far west as the Panjab, holding meetings to protest the British decision to lower to nineteen the age at which the Indian Civil Service examination had to be taken. However, the real organization of a nationalist movement did not occur until the 1880s, when the growth of the railroad network made all-India congresses feasible. The immediate background for the first Indian National Congress in 1885 was the furor aroused by a measure introduced into the governor-general's council in 1883. This bill, the Ilbert Bill, would allow all Indian judges to try cases involving Europeans, as Indian judges were already doing in the cities of Calcutta, Bombay, and Madras. British residents in India who were engaged in private business rather than government affairs protested loudly, for they feared that Indian judges would not listen sympathetically to their cases. Protest meetings, petitions, and agitation in the press forced the government to concede that in cases involving Europeans, half the jury should be European.

The Ilbert Bill agitation dramatically demonstrated two things to Indian observers. It showed that organization and protest paid off in results and that social discrimination against Indians could affect their political and economic position. Social discrimination had become increasingly evident as more people came from Britain to India. Many of the newcomers brought their families, and most of the families accepted the tendency of most Indians to treat them as a separate caste. They shunned association even with the only Indians who sought it, the intermediaries—who were precisely the ones to feel the discrimination most keenly because they had absorbed the largest amount of Western thinking on human equality.

The Ilbert Bill agitation went far to convince the intermediaries that they must act to protect themselves from becoming permanent social, economic, and political inferiors in their own country. In 1884 the National League in Calcutta, the Mahajan Sabha in Madras, and the Presidency Association in Bombay were formed by Western-educated Indians eager to break the British monopoly of top-level governmental and economic positions. At the instigation of a sympathetic retired British Indian Civil Service officer, these organizations united in the Indian National Congress at Bombay in 1885. The formal proceedings of the Congress, held in English, were largely confined to mild requests for more Indian participation in government and expressions of loyalty to India and the purposes of British rule. Most of the seventy who attended were Hindus, although a few were Parsis and two were Muslims. However, none of them believed their religious affiliation should affect their political life. From the beginning, the Congress declared itself the representative of all Indians regardless of geographical origin or religious background, a truly national body committed to the principle of governmental neutrality in religious affairs. In their conviction that the united nation of which they dreamed could only be achieved under a secular government —as in their reliance on the Western-educated for leadership, their later campaigning for complete foreign withdrawal, and their strong desire to have the institutions of Western representative constitutional government applied to the social and economic transformation of their homeland—the members of the Congress provided a model which would be followed in the twentieth century by nationalist movements not only in British-ruled regions from Ghana and Kenya to Burma and the Caribbean, but also from French-ruled Africa to Dutch-ruled Indonesia.

MUSLIM REACTIONS

It was the tragedy of the Indian National Congress that in later years some of its own leaders would give Muslims reason to think of it as a Hindu association. However, the Muslims of India were uneasy long before 1885. The British conquest deprived Muslims of the political power which had been their claim to recognition in India, and most of the leading Muslims reacted to British rule by ignoring it as much as possible. Some Muslims entered Company armies, and some advised Company judges, but few turned to economic activity as Hindus and Parsis did. Almost none learned English so that they could serve in the Company's civil administration. When the uprising of 1857 began in the Company's armies, it quickly won support from Muslims who sought to use it to restore the titular Mughal ruler in Delhi to power. This attempt to bring back the past typified the early Muslim reaction to the British. Not until it failed did Muslims seriously begin to seek a basis on which to cooperate with the British, as the Hindus were already doing.

One of the few Muslim Indians to enter the Company administration before 1857 was Sayyid Ahmad Khan (1817–1898). In the 1860s, Sayyid Ahmad Khan tried earnestly to promote understanding between his fellow Muslims and the officials of the new British government under the Crown. He also sought to persuade Muslims to take more interest in commerce and administration. A trip to Europe in 1869 convinced him that his fellow Muslims needed to study the ideas and practices of the West. He returned to India believing fervently that the use of reason, enjoined by early Islamic theologians, would enable Muslims to select and use the most valuable components in the Western tradition—a belief much like Raja Ram Mohan Roy's reliance on the use of reason as stressed in the Upanishads, and potentially equally fruitful.

In 1875 Sayyid Ahmad Khan founded Aligarh College, to enable and encourage Muslims to study English and acquire the learning available in that language. However, there was little communication between the department of Quranic studies, whose professors taught in Arabic, and the other departments, in which English was used. As a consequence, the students rarely managed to synthesize their Islamic heritage with their English studies. Instead, Muslim and Western thought remained in separate compartments in their minds, as the pan-Islamic leader al-Afghani foresaw from Cairo not long after Aligarh opened. The Muslim graduates of Aligarh and of similar institutions rose to prominence in British India, but as a body, they were uncertain whether they belonged to the Islamic or the British world. The one thing they were sure of was that they were not part of Hindu India.

In plain terms, the policy of Sayyid Ahmad Khan and his followers was to cooperate with the British so that the British could stay in India and keep its Muslim minority from being engulfed by the Hindus. Muslim leaders were alarmed by the resurgence of Hinduism evidenced in movements like the Arya Samaj, the Sudhi or reconversion movement, and the Cow Protection Association. Furthermore, many Muslims were distressed by the decline of Persian and Urdu as the languages of cultivated men, and by the growth of vernacular literatures which promoted local patriotisms that almost always looked back to a pre-Muslim past.

Sayyid Ahmad Khan refused to take part in the Indian National Congress. He foresaw that it would eventually work for an independent government based on the representative principles learned from Britain, and he saw no hope for the Muslims under a government based on majority rule, for they would always be outnumbered three to one. His influence and his arguments were so strong that not many Muslims took the opposite stand. Nevertheless, a few Muslims did join the Congress in search of a basis for friendly cooperation with the Hindus. The zenith of Muslim participation in the Congress came in 1890, when 156 out of 702 delegates were Muslims, but thereafter their numbers dwindled rapidly. By 1905 only 17 out of 756 delegates were Muslims.

THE INDIAN NATIONAL CONGRESS, THE ALL-INDIA MUSLIM LEAGUE, AND THE MORLEY-MINTO REFORMS OF 1909

Although Sayyid Ahmad Khan's influence helped to lessen the number of Muslims who were willing to unite with Hindus to weaken the British, the activities of Hindu leaders like Bal Gangadhar Tilak (1856–1920) contributed even more to Muslim uneasiness. Tilak, a prominent figure in western India in the years before World War I, was well versed in English and Sanskrit as well as in his native Marathi language. As a member of the Deccan Education Society, an association dedicated to the teaching of Indians, he helped establish Ferguson College in 1885 and also taught law there. In addition, he was known for his commentary on the "Bhagavad-Gita," the classic Indian expression of the achievement of release through a life of action.

In 1890 Tilak entered politics, assuming the editorship of a Marathi newspaper and of an English-language newspaper which circulated throughout India. His editorials upheld the virtues of orthodox Hinduism. Although Dayananda had opposed child marriage as an unhappy folly, Tilak praised it as the tradition of centuries. Although Congress admired British institutions and proclaimed that it would use peaceful measures to increase Indian participation in government, Tilak revived the memory of the martial Sivaji's fight against the Mughals and founded gymnastic societies to train Hindu youths in warlike exercises. Tilak also formed cattle-protection societies to promote Hindu solidarity. Tilak's aim was self-rule. His willingness to use any available means to expel the British led him to appeal to Hindu sentiment without regard for difficulties that might arise later. Nevertheless, every call for loyalty to Hindu standards tended to encourage militancy against Muslims and against all proposals for social reform.

In 1899 a new political figure appeared in western India, Gopal Krishna Gokhale (1866–1915). Like Tilak, Gokhale was a Chitpavan Brahmin conversant with English, Sanskrit, and Marathi; like Tilak, Gokhale had joined the Deccan Education Society and taught at Ferguson College. Both men wanted to see the people of India free and able to live with dignity and a measure of security. However, Gokhale was as convinced of the advisability of moderation as Tilak was of the need for action. Tilak wanted self-government first and social reform afterward; Gokhale believed that India could only attain true self-rule through co-operation with Britain, using British power to achieve the social reforms needed to unite the country behind a program of reasoned modernization. Gokhale thought India could not be free until it was remade; Tilak felt India could not be remade until it was free.

Gokhale began his political career as a member of the governor's legislative council at Bombay, but in a few years moved to the central legislative council in Calcutta. His moderate ideas appealed to Indian National Congress members more than those of Tilak, and Gokhale remained the acknowledged leader of the Congress until he died in 1915. Still, Tilak had a growing band of supporters, whose Hindu fanaticism worried many Muslims. When the partition of Bengal was announced in 1905, Tilak threw himself wholeheartedly into the protests of the Bengalis. He coined the word *swaraj* (self-rule) to go with the Bengali *swadeshi* (self-produced) movement to boycott foreign goods, and he openly approved the mass protest meetings organized by Bengali leaders. In the next three years, terrorist movements sprang up in Bengal, the Panjab, and the Maratha region, and finally Tilak was imprisoned for encouraging them. He left prison in 1914, just in time to take over the Congress after the death of Gokhale.

Gokhale was almost as stirred as Tilak by the Bengali reaction to the 1905 partition plan. He promptly condemned the British for their disregard of public opinion. For the first time, the Indian National Congress officially favored dominion status and responsible, representative government for India. In response to the Congress demands and the terrorists' activities, the Liberal party cabinet which replaced the Conservatives in Britain late in 1905 initiated the studies that led to the Morley-Minto reform act of 1909, with its provisions for representative government.

The Morley-Minto reforms provided that sizable Indian minorities should be elected to the central and provincial legislative councils of British India, and that one member of each executive council, central and provincial, should be Indian. In the Bengal legislative council the elected Indians would actually be a majority. However, the elections were not to be conducted on the basis of single-member territorial constituencies like Congressional districts in the United States. Each elected member of the central and provincial councils was chosen by a special group—landowners, chambers of commerce, trade associations, universities, local governmental councils. Some members of the central legislative council were chosen by Muslim voters. The elected members of the legislative councils could only present their constituents' desires and complaints to the executive councils. They could not require the executive councils to carry out their resolutions. Thus the Morley-Minto reforms made the government of British India partly representative of the electorate, but they did not make it responsible to Indian voters.

Few prominent Muslims supported Congress demands for representative, responsible government. Muslim leaders, most of whom still came from the landowners and the aristocracy, were convinced that the swaraj, or self-rule, envisioned by the Congress meant the death knell of the Indian Muslim community unless preventive measures were taken. They therefore formed the All-India Muslim League in 1906 to protest against simple territorial representation. At their insistence, the Morley-Minto reforms provided for the representation of various groups rather than simple territorial constituencies. The principle of communal electorates was introduced by the separate representation given to Muslim landholders, on the ground that they would be underrepresented in terms of the property they owned unless they had their own representatives for whom only they could vote. This was true enough, and anxious Muslim leaders were somewhat comforted by the granting of their request, but the demand for separate electorates foreshadowed the demand for separate states a generation later.

CEYLONESE PARALLELS (1848–1919)

British policy in Ceylon in the decade after 1848 corresponded to that of Dalhousie in India in the same period. Canal and road networks were improved, and a railroad from Colombo to Kandy was started. To revive the village councils, they were given authority to maintain local irrigation networks. In 1871 the authority of the village councils was extended to other local affairs, and councils with elected majorities were set up in the largest towns. Urban dwellers thus began to experiment with European methods of city government.

During the late nineteenth century, government schools increased in number and enrollment, although private Buddhist, Hindu, Christian, and Muslim schools far outstripped them in influence. The continuing growth of English-language mission and government schools challenged Buddhist and Hindu leaders to provide better schooling for their followers. Networks of Buddhist and Hindu educational institutions were established among Sinhalese and Tamils. Both Buddhist and Hindu teachers sought to increase their followers' enthusiasm as well as to teach them to read and write. As a result, not only did literacy rates rise among Hindus and Buddhists, but their intolerance increased toward adherents of other religions.

In Ceylon after 1848, as in India after 1858, the center of opposition to British rule shifted from the tradition-minded to the Western-educated. Increasing complaints were heard about the appointive nature of the legislative council, its weakness, and its overwhelmingly British membership. These complaints persuaded British governors that it would be easier to groom the Kandyan nobles as administrators than to use the Western-educated. The young Ceylonese who learned Western ways in government and mission schools deplored as an anachronism the perpetuation of the Kandyan nobility, but their complaints were ignored. In Ceylon as in India, the British were looking for enlightened leaders in the old aristocracy, when actually these individuals were to be found in the new Western-educated middle class. In 1889 a second Sinhalese and a Muslim were added to the governor's council, but otherwise Ceylon's governmental structure remained almost unchanged until the era of World War I. Between the 1850s and World War I the energies of both government officials and private British residents in Ceylon were primarily devoted to the plantations which supplied world markets with coffee, tea, cinchona, rubber, and coconut products.

Growing prosperity enabled the Ceylonese middle class to increase in numbers and wealth. After the Russo-Japanese war of 1904–1905 and the extension of the elective principle in India in 1909, the educated members of the Ceylonese middle class protested vigorously against the system of appointing the members of the governor's council from each of the various racial and cultural groups on the island. Though they still had no political organizations comparable to the Indian National Congress, they followed the Congress's lead in requesting elections based on territorial rather than communal constituencies. In 1912 the British finally allowed a minority of the nonofficial members of the legislative council to be elected—but on a communal basis, in line with the provisions of the Morley-Minto reforms in India.

During World War I, Ceylonese dissatisfaction rose to the surface in the 1915 riots. Some of the few Arab-descended Ceylonese Muslims exchanged blows with Buddhists who had interrupted a Muslim religious service by playing music. The British feared the fighting would lead to an attack on themselves and therefore jailed a group of prominent Buddhists. One of those imprisoned, D.S. Senanayake, later became the first prime minister of independent Ceylon. Soon after the 1915 riots, the first political parties began to be formed. Of these, the most significant was the Ceylon National Congress, formed in 1919 on the model of the Indian National Congress, with the goal of a secular state in which both major linguistic and religious groups would feel secure.

FROM THE MORLEY-MINTO REFORMS TO THE MONTAGU-CHELMSFORD REFORMS OF 1919

Active agitation for self-rule died down after Tilak was sent to prison and the Morley-Minto reforms went into effect. The British won some good will by annulling the partition of Bengal and moving their seat of government from Calcutta to the old capital at Delhi. Minto's successor as governor-general and viceroy received warm expressions of esteem from Indians when he publicly sympathized with the Indians in the Union of South Africa in their struggle against discriminatory regulations there. Although some terrorist activity continued, little else of political significance occurred between 1911 and the outbreak of World War I in 1914. However, World War I proved almost as great a watershed in Indian affairs as did the uprising of 1857.

Before 1857, British statesmen spoke freely of the time when educated and enlightened (i.e., Westernized) Indian leaders would again rule their own country; but after 1857, the British lost confidence in the good will of the Hindu and Muslim princes, who seemed to them the natural leaders of India, and began to act as if they expected to remain in India for many generations. The British were not looking for leaders in the new class of the intermediaries. Until after World War I the British seemed unaware that India as well as Britain was experiencing the rise of members of the newly affluent and newly educated middle classes to positions of leadership once held by the aristocracy. Instead, the British in India continued to expect India's future governors to come from the upper classes, and they continued to be disappointed by the lack of interest shown by most of the princes and nobles in Western methods.

The members of the Indian National Congress, all of whom were intermediaries, continued to be regarded by the British as persons of little influence in the country at large, despite the evidence afforded by the agitation against the partition of Bengal. The British paid little heed to Congress demands that Indians be allowed a voice in framing policy, until the era of Minto and Morley, and even then few British leaders believed that Congress spoke for the majority of Indians. By the time the British began listening to moderates of Gokhale's type, Gokhale was dead, and Tilak was rallying Indians to his program of swaraj first, reform later. While he lived, Gokhale insisted that Indians should wait until World War I was over to press their demands on the British, but by the end of 1916, the year after Gokhale's death, Tilak controlled the Congress. A trip to Britain convinced Tilak that its people were far more receptive to Indian suggestions than were the British in India, and thereafter he encouraged the Congress to appeal to the Parliament in London rather than to attack the government in Delhi.

During the war years, Indians discovered that western Europeans were as capable of plunging themselves into the holocaust of general war as Indians had been in the past. Indians were inspired by the success of Indian arms in the Middle Eastern theater, by the realization that Russia was throwing off the despotism of the czars, and by the hope that Britain would apply to India the idealism embodied in Woodrow Wilson's principle of the self-determination of peoples. Indians were also encouraged by the growth of Indian industry. In 1914 India was already the world's fourth largest maker of cotton textiles. In addition, the Parsi family of Tata, from Bombay, had opened the first Indian steel mill in the iron and coal country on the Bihar-Orissa border, a mill which eventually became the largest single steel plant in the British Commonwealth. The enlargement of these and other enterprises during and after World War I made India the world's eighth largest industrial power in the 1930s.

Rising belief in the ability of Indians to chart their own course in the modern world led to the formation of the Home Rule League in 1916 to call for self-rule as soon as peace was restored. For a brief period, the Muslim League even joined the Congress in supporting the Home Rule League demands. A number of Muslim leaders, influenced by pan-Islamic ideas, were greatly distressed to find Indian troops fighting the Ottomans in the Middle East. They therefore formed the Khilafat (Caliphate) movement to uphold the Ottoman sultan's continued right to rule despite his support of Germany and Austria. The distress of Muslim leaders at living under a government which was at war with the Ottomans even made them join the fight for swaraj, although it meant veering away from their previous policy of upholding British rule as a protection against Hindu engulfment. However, Muslim leaders continued to insist that separate constituencies were necessary to safeguard Muslim interests, and Tilak had to accept the principle of communal electorates in order to win the Muslims as allies.

The British responded to the combined demands of the Congress and the Muslim League by promising postwar reforms. The contributions made to the British cause in World War I by Indians in and out of the armed forces were deeply appreciated in Britain. That appreciation helped pave the way for the first tentative steps toward responsible government, the enactment in 1919 of the Montagu-Chelmsford reform act.

The Montagu-Chelmsford reform act, which went into full operation in 1921, divided the duties of the British government in India between the center and the provinces. It also divided the central legislative council into two houses, both with Indian majorities elected directly by those who owned enough property to have to pay a set amount of taxes every year. Certain seats were set aside for representatives of the Muslim electorate, as in the Morley-Minto reform act. The powers of the executive councils in the provinces were divided into two categories: reserved subjects like finance and police, for whose conduct the governor was responsible to the central government, and transferred subjects like health, agriculture, public works, and local government. The ministers for the transferred subjects were made responsible to the provincial legislative councils, which now were to have elected Indian majorities. Since finance was a reserved subject, the freedom of every minister was somewhat limited. Nevertheless, several provincial departments of public works carried out important irrigation projects between 1921 and 1934, and advances were made in a number of other fields.

GANDHI'S RISE TO LEADERSHIP

By the time the Montagu-Chelmsford reforms went into effect in 1921, the march of events had overtaken the British. New terrorist violence in the Panjab, where the Sikhs sought to force the British to guarantee them self-rule, led to the Rowlatt Acts of early 1919. These acts empowered the police to intern suspects without trial and enabled judges to dispense with juries in political cases. A century before, such measures would have been accepted as part of the ruler's prerogative, but by 1919 the British system of legal safeguards for individual freedom was so deeply rooted in India, and Indians had learned the lessons of political organization so well, that the Rowlatt Acts provided the nationalist leaders with a grievance over which they could raise a general storm of protest.

When the Rowlatt Acts were passed by the legislative council in Delhi, Tilak was in London seeking Parliamentary approval of responsible government for the provinces of British India. The task of leading the protest therefore fell to Mohandas Karamchand Gandhi (1869–1948), a disciple of Gokhale who was later given the title *Mahatma,* or great soul, by his followers. Gandhi, a Vaisya from the Jain-influenced province of Gujerat, was a lawyer trained in Britain. At the close of 1914 he had returned to India after twenty-one years in South Africa, during which he had led the Indians there to a real, though incomplete, victory over the restrictions imposed on them by the government of the Union of South Africa. In so doing he had forged a weapon against injustice which he called *satyagraha*, truth-force, the method of nonviolent non-cooperation combined with the belief that truth would prevail if means as well as ends were morally sound. Soon after his return to India he began to lead small satyagraha movements against local injustices. These efforts, and his work in South Africa, made it natural for the leading figures in the Congress to ask him to launch a series of protest meetings against the Rowlatt Acts.

Gandhi called upon Indians to engage in an India-wide *hartal*, or voluntary closing of places of business, a weapon long used by urban merchants to force local officials to heed their protests against actions they considered unjust. To his distress, the hartal movement led to violence in the Panjab. Four Europeans were killed by a mob at Amritsar in April, 1919. Three days later the high-strung Amritsar military commandant, General Dyer, ordered his troops to fire on a crowd of ten thousand in a public park, killing 379, by official estimate.

The Amritsar Massacre, as Dyer's action was quickly named, became a *cause célèbre* in both India and Britain. Indians and many Britons attacked Dyer, but other Britons defended his action. However, when the Indian National Congress met in Amritsar in December, 1919, it did not yet realize how numerous Dyer's defenders were. Although Tilak called for continued militancy against the British because the Montagu-Chelmsford reforms were insufficient, Gandhi asked for cooperation in putting the reforms into effect because cooperation would demonstrate Indians' ability to act responsibly. The Congress compromised by resolving to cooperate but to continue protesting the meagerness of the reforms.

Gandhi's willingness to cooperate with the British turned into unwillingness in 1920 when the House of Lords formally refused to condemn Dyer. Gandhi preached all over India against what he called "this satanic government," appealing to moral principles in a way which mortified liberal Britons as much as it appealed to Indians. He also sought a basis for cooperation with the Muslims, whose Khilafat movement was reviving in protest against the harsh terms imposed at Paris on the Ottomans.

In the summer of 1920 the Congress resolved to begin an all-India campaign of complete civil disobedience: resignation from government offices, boycott of government elections, withdrawal from government schools and colleges. It also made the vitally important decision to reorganize itself along linguistic lines. Since 1915 the Telugu-speaking Andhra members of the Congress had been asking the Congress to form linguistically homogeneous subunits which would facilitate local work by bringing together those who were propagandizing in the same language. They had won Tilak's support in 1917, but Gandhi did not agree until 1920. The leaders of the Congress, almost all of whom were from the north, scarcely realized that the Dravidian-speaking peoples of the south could fear Aryan linguistic domination in a united India as much as Muslims feared Hindu dominance. When the Congress leaders accepted the practical arguments for linguistic organization, few of them were aware of how desperately anxious the Andhras were to have the principle recognized.

The reorganization of the Congress so that Andhras, Bengalis, and other linguistic groups could work out their own local programs and activities was crucial in transforming the Congress from a rather small middle-class group to a mass movement with millions of members. Linguistic reorganization was as vital as Gandhi's appeals to Indian moral sentiments, for linguistic reorganization enabled Gandhi to spread his message of unity to all, making the call for swaraj truly national. It also contributed to the eventual rearrangement of the federal Republic of India into linguistically homogeneous states—along lines which usually paralleled the divisions made earlier within the Congress organization, wherever a town in which two or more languages were spoken had to be assigned to one or another state.

Revitalized by Gandhi's program of satyagraha and reorganized so that it could take its message directly to the people, the Congress embarked in 1920 on its attempt to win swaraj by noncooperation. Voters and students boycotted elections and schools, but few civil servants were willing to jeopardize their livelihood by resigning their posts. The British government gave no sign of accepting Congress demands, and in 1921 nonviolence began to give way to violence.

Gandhi called off the satyagraha campaign in 1922 in protest at his followers' actions and went willingly to prison to expiate his miscalculation. He came out in 1924 to wield an even greater power over public sentiment. As a Vaisya rather than a Brahmin, he chose the peasant's garment rather than the ascetic's robe when he put off Western dress and took up a life of poverty. Through his enlistment of the hearts and consciences of those around him he won the love and support of the ordinary people of India in his lifetime as no one had ever done before— or been able to do, before the advent of the railroad and the printing press.

Gandhi appealed to the highest sentiments of caste Hindus by his religious devotion, his vegetarianism, and his espousal of *ahimsa,* or nonviolence. His respect for all men and women extended his influence from the caste Hindus to the untouchables, who were then taking heart from the career of the Western-educated untouchable B.R. Ambedkar, later the first minister of law in independent India. Gandhi called the untouchables Harijans (children of God), because of their patient endurance of the restrictions placed on them. His efforts to persuade caste Hindus to remove those restrictions led many of the Harijans to begin turning to him as well as to Ambedkar in hope of improving their lot. However, few Muslims were impressed by Gandhi despite his vehement declarations that Muslims were as Indian as Hindus and must be accepted as such. Many Muslims saw in his vegetarianism the same sentiments that led to anti-Muslim cow-protection societies. His praise of ahimsa seemed a rebuke to their own martial past. Even his campaign to end untouchability troubled some Muslims, who feared that his success would deprive them of millions of potential allies against the dominance of caste Hindus.

Indian business leaders and industrialists welcomed Gandhi's insistence that every patriotic Indian should use *swadeshi* (self-produced) goods. They secretly deplored his insistence that swadeshi meant cottage rather than factory industry, but they applauded his opposition to government control of economic life even while they balked at his call for a rural society based on agriculture and village handicrafts. His efforts to apply moral principles to politics helped save India from large-scale civil warfare until the eve of independence, undermined British confidence in the righteousness of their own position, and won India a unique place in world opinion.

Gandhi's call for peace between Hindus and Muslims was not the only voice heard in the 1920s. In 1923, while he was in prison, the militant Hindu Mahasabha society was founded to build up Hindus' physical fitness and reconvert Muslims. Shortly afterward, the Khilafat movement collapsed when the Turks abolished the caliphate. Communal riots, which dated back at least to the 1870s, became bloodier and more frequent as Muslim fears of Hindu domination grew. Sometimes the Muslims attacked first; sometimes the Hindus did.

The future leader of the Pakistan movement for a separate Muslim state, Muhammad Ali Jinnah, saw the strength of Muslim sentiment and decided to leave the Congress, to which he had belonged for some years. He revived the moribund Muslim League and formed the Independent Party, which competed for votes with the Congress-backed Swaraj Party. Despite his efforts, Swaraj Party victories continued at the polls, and communal riots continued in the cities and the countryside. Finally, in 1927, the British appointed the seven-member Simon Commission to seek a plan of governing India which would satisfy all the interested parties.

In appointing the Simon Commission, the British laid themselves open to criticism by not including any Indians. In response, the Congress, the League, and other interested Indians called an all-India conference in 1928. The Indians who attended were invited to draft their own constitutional proposals. The majority approved a report requesting dominion status, full self-government, and the abolition of separate communal electorates. Neither Jinnah nor many of the other Muslims present accepted the recommendation to abolish communal electorates. However, some Muslims agreed to it and thereafter worked with the Congress in hopes of establishing a true Hindu-Muslim partnership in a secular state.

The more ardent enthusiasts in the Congress, like the young Jawaharlal Nehru, did not like the conference request for dominion status. They wished the right to secede completely from the British Commonwealth. Gandhi persuaded them to accept the conference report only by promising to lead a second mass civil disobedience campaign if dominion status were not achieved by the end of 1929. The British promised in 1929 to grant dominion status eventually and to include Indians in future constitutional discussions, but these promises did not fully meet Congress demands. Gandhi therefore went ahead with the passive resistance campaign, in order to avoid a split between moderates and enthusiasts.

Gandhi astutely chose to protest the salt tax. Not only did every villager feel this tax, but it resembled the hated salt tax of pre-1789 France enough to make protests against it strike a sympathetic chord among both Britons and Western-educated Indians. In the spring of 1930, Gandhi and a coterie of followers walked the one hundred seventy miles from his home to the sea, made salt on the seashore in defiance of the law, and quietly awaited the results: demonstrations, arrests, and the imprisonment of Gandhi. Meanwhile the Simon Commission published its report, recommending fully responsible government in the provinces and a continuance of merely representative government at the center. At Simon's urging, the British government agreed to hold a roundtable conference of British and Indian leaders soon after the report was published.

ROUNDTABLE CONFERENCES AND REFORMS

The first British-Indian roundtable conference met from November, 1930, to January, 1931, with sixteen representatives from Britain, sixteen from Princely India, and fifty-seven from British India—but not one from the largest Indian political group, the Indian National Congress. A second conference was held at the end of 1931. By that time Gandhi was free again, and it was obvious that his hold on Indian minds and hearts was greater than ever. He alone represented the Congress at the second conference. However, both the untouchable leader Ambedkar and the Muslim representatives refused to accept Gandhi's claim to speak for a united India. Neither Ambedkar nor the Muslims would agree to Gandhi's proposal to abolish separate communal electorates, which had been granted in 1919 to untouchables as well as Muslims on the ground that their needs and grievances would go unheeded if their candidates had to compete with caste Hindus.

When the British declared in 1932 that they would continue the separate untouchable electorates as Ambedkar wished, Gandhi undertook a fast in protest against the British decision and the untouchables' willingness to accept it. Ambedkar finally capitulated, though not until Gandhi's life was despaired of, and agreed that the untouchables ought to be included in the ordinary voters' roll with the caste Hindus. Gandhi won his point: the leaders of the new India ought to look toward a union of all. In the long run Ambedkar won too, for it proved easier to rouse the consciences of caste Hindus on behalf of the untouchables when the untouchables agreed to regard themselves as part of the Hindu community than it had been when the leaders of the untouchables insisted on their separateness. After 1932 the Congress consistently overrode orthodox Brahmin objections and insisted that untouchability must become a thing of the past.

A third roundtable conference late in 1932 proved as fruitless as the first two in reconciling the conflicting views of the Congress, the League, the princes, and the British. The British cabinet then produced its own proposals. In the long and heated discussions which ensued, a number of Parliament members attacked the proposed reforms as damaging to both the British people and the toiling, illiterate, impoverished masses of India. Nevertheless, most of the proposals were embodied in the Government of India Act of 1935, which came into effect in the provinces of British India in 1937.

The India Act of 1935 provided for the inauguration of responsible government in the provinces. A provincial governor could override the actions of his cabinet ministers, but the British made it clear that they did not expect the governors to use their veto power. Responsible cabinets were set up in all the provinces of British India by the end of 1937. Two new provinces were created, making a total of eleven "governors' provinces" with elected legislatures and with cabinets responsible to the legislators. Some of the provinces were given bicameral legislatures. Six regions, most of which were inhabited by comparatively isolated tribes like the Nagas of the northeast, remained directly under the governor-general's rule as before.

The India Act of 1935 also provided for bringing the princely states into a voluntary all-India federation with the provinces. This federation was to operate somewhat as the provinces had been operating since 1919, with some powers reserved to the governor-general and others transferred to a bicameral legislature. The federation never came into being, for World War II interrupted the process of persuading the princes to join it. However, the Act set forth a basic pattern for central-provincial relations which was closely followed in the federal constitutions later enacted by the republics of India and Pakistan.

RISING MUSLIM FEARS OF HINDU DOMINATION

The satyagraha movement which helped produce the India Act of 1935 weakened the restrictions on Indian women and broke down many of the restrictions of caste, as men and women of all castes cooperated in passive resistance and underwent imprisonment together. Yet satyagraha was accompanied by more and more clashes between Hindus and Muslims. Most Muslims abstained from the hartals and other satyagraha demonstrations, to the disappointment of ardent nationalists. Hindu attacks on Muslims multiplied in 1931 and 1932. In response, a group of young Indian Muslims called in 1933 for a separate Muslim national state in the Indus basin so that the umma, the community or nation of the Muslims, could govern its own internal affairs. Their demands went only one step beyond the request of the poet Muhammad Iqbal, former president of the Muslim League, who had asked in 1930 that the Muslim-majority region in the northwest be made an almost completely autonomous member of a loose all-India federation.

Until 1937, Jinnah and most other Muslim League leaders accepted Iqbal's suggestion as more practicable than the establishment of a completely separate Muslim state. However, League attitudes began to change when League leaders found that the Congress refused to recognize the League as the true representative and sole spokesman of the Muslim community. The India Act of 1935 retained the whole system of communal electorates, with separate constituencies for Muslims, Sikhs, untouchables, and some smaller groups. In 1937, the first provincial elections under the Act gave the Congress a majority in the legislatures of five of the eleven provinces of British India, a plurality in two more, and effective control in still another through the victory of a friendly party. A coalition government took power in Assam, and Muslim-oriented parties controlled the Panjab and Bengal. At this point the real break came between League and Congress.

In the interest of effective cabinet government, Congress leaders insisted that all members of the cabinets they formed must be loyal to the Congress. Although the Congress freely appointed its own Muslim members to office, it refused to include League members in its cabinets, to the dismay of Jinnah and other League leaders. Jinnah had campaigned for the League with considerable success in the provinces with large Muslim minorities. He was hoping to establish the type of Congress-League coalition cabinets which the Congress refused to consider. Now Jinnah had to choose between leading the League into the Congress (which would have delighted Congress leaders by strengthening their claim that Indians formed a united nation politically despite religious differences) and leading the League away from the India which the Congress claimed to represent. He chose the latter course.

CEYLONESE PARALLELS (1919–1939)

While dreams of Indian unity were being shattered by Hindu-Muslim antagonism, dreams of Ceylonese unity were foundering on Sinhalese-Tamil rivalry. In 1920 the Ceylon National Congress persuaded the British to include Ceylonese in the executive council, to expand the legislative council, and to have almost a third of the legislative council elected from territorial constituencies. The proportion of elected representatives was raised to almost half in 1923. When the Simon Commission was sent to India in 1927, a parliamentary commission was also sent to Ceylon. It recommended that the legislative and executive councils be replaced by a single state council; that at least four-fifths of the council members be elected by universal male and female suffrage from territorial constituencies; and that the heads of the council's committees on home affairs, agriculture, local administration, health, education, public works, and communications be the ministers of the corresponding government departments. Parliament accepted these recommendations in 1929. In the first state council elections of 1931 a majority of those elected were Sinhalese, but the council chose both Sinhalese and Tamils as ministers.

In spite of these encouraging developments, a number of Tamil leaders left the Ceylon National Congress during the 1920s and 1930s to form their own organization, for they feared that otherwise Tamils might lose their community identity. Many Tamils boycotted the 1931 elections in protest against the abolition of communal representation. The selection of Tamil ministers mollified them somewhat, but after the 1936 elections when the Sinhalese council majority chose only Sinhalese ministers, the Tamils were again dismayed. The resultant outcry led to more British investigations and discussions, which were interrupted by World War II.

INDIAN NATIONAL CONGRESS, MUSLIM LEAGUE, AND COMMUNISTS DURING WORLD WAR II

At the outbreak of World War II in Europe in 1939 the British governor-general declared British India to be at war alongside Britain, without consulting Indian leaders. In protest, Congress members resigned from all parliamentary offices. The ensuing deadlock lasted until the war ended in August, 1945, despite efforts on both sides to break it. When the Congress offered cooperation if a responsible federal government were established in British India, the British refused, in view of Muslim opposition to the form of federation the Congress proposed. When the British promised full dominion status and elections for a constituent assembly as soon as the war should end, the Congress refused to agree to wait that long for Indian freedom. Both the British and the Congress found that before final arrangements for independence could be made, they would have to take account of the demand for communal self-government put forward by the Muslim League on behalf of India's millions of Muslims.

When the Congress ministries in the provinces of British India decided to resign late in 1939 to protest the governor-general's failure to consult Indian leaders before declaring India to be at war, Jinnah called for a Muslim day of thanksgiving for deliverance from Congress tyranny. Jinnah and the League then proceeded to take advantage of the Congress's self-imposed withdrawal from politics. Without active Congress competition for Muslim support, the League became in fact what it had long claimed to be in theory, the representative of the overwhelming majority of Muslims. In 1940 the League called officially for a separate Muslim state comprising Bengal and Assam in the east and the Panjab, Sind, Baluchistan, and the North-West Frontier Province in the west. It did not openly claim Kashmir and such Muslim-ruled princely states as Hyderabad, for these states belonged to Princely India rather than to the British-ruled territories, and the princes would have to agree to any changes affecting their domains. Throughout the war years, the League strengthened itself in preparation for the anticipated struggle against all who might object to any partition of India.

The withdrawal of the Congress from formal political life between 1939 and 1945 also gave opportunities to the Communists. After Hitler invaded the Soviet Union in 1941, the small Communist party in India switched overnight from opposition to friendship toward the British. Between 1941 and 1945 the Communists built up support in industrial centers like Calcutta and crowded rural areas like the Godavari valley and Kerala. In both Kerala and the Godavari valley they exploited Dravidian lower-caste antagonism to the northern-dominated Congress with its largely Brahmin leadership. However, the number of Brahmins in Communist ranks often made it hard to convince others of Communist antagonism to upper-caste domination. A small Communist party was also founded on Ceylon in 1943, but it soon split into three parts, one loyal to Moscow and two committed to their own differing interpretations of Marx.

Although Congress leaders abstained from parliamentary affairs during World War II, they kept up their campaign to expel the British.

Shortly after Japan and the United States entered the war at the end of 1941, the British proposed to grant dominion status to India when the war ended, but the Congress leaders called on the British to quit India immediately. They then launched a new civil disobedience campaign. The British promptly arrested most of them and imprisoned them until the closing months of the war.

A few months after the quit-India movement failed, a former Congress president who had broken with Gandhi and fled from India turned up in Japanese-occupied Singapore as the head of the Japanese-sponsored Indian National Army, pledged to liberate India from British rule. The Indian National Army scarcely affected the fighting, but the promptness with which the British arrested, tried, and sentenced its leaders as traitors after the war shows that it did alarm them—perhaps even enough to help convince them that they ought to begin to meet Congress demands more rapidly.

DECISION TO WITHDRAW

In June, 1945, the British governor-general attempted to form an Indian executive council for British India with equal numbers of Muslims and caste Hindus, as well as representatives of the Sikhs and the untouchables. The attempt failed when the League insisted that all Muslims in the executive council must be League members, while the Congress, which refused to give up its claim to be an Indian rather than a Hindu party, insisted on nominating some of its own Muslim members. When the war ended in August, Britain's newly installed prime minister, who as a young man had gone to India with the Simon Commission, instructed the government in India to hold elections early in 1946 for the central and provincial councils. The governor-general was also directed to set up an all-Indian executive council at the center and to call a constituent assembly as soon as possible. At the same time, the British put a new constitution into effect in Ceylon. It expanded the elective council and added an upper house to it, half of whose members would be chosen by the lower house and half by the governor. Elections for the new lower house were held in March, 1946.

When the government of Britain promised a constituent assembly for India, the Muslim League again put forward its proposals for a separate Muslim state. Neither the British nor the Congress leaders were willing to partition India between Hindus and Muslims after a century of looking at India as a unit. Nevertheless, the Congress continued to act as if the British were the main obstacle to establishing an independent India. In the 1946 electoral campaigns, the Congress denounced the British, but failed to court the Muslim community. As a result, Congress candidates carried the general (i.e., caste Hindu) constituencies, but

League candidates won all but sixteen of the approximately five hundred seats allotted to Muslims in the central and provincial assemblies.

When the newly elected central assembly met in February, 1946, Jinnah warned that Muslims would fight if necessary to establish Pakistan. In response to this alarming statement, the British government sent out a cabinet mission in March to consult with Indian leaders. The cabinet mission proposed a three-level federation with strong provincial governments, intermediate regional groupings of provinces, and a weak central government. The mission hoped that the regional groupings would satisfy Muslim demands by enabling Muslim-majority provinces to work closely with each other on matters of common interest. The princely states were to be fitted into the system through a loose association with the center, much like their existing association with the viceroy.

Both the League and the Congress accepted the cabinet mission's proposals, although with misgivings. In the campaign for the constituent assembly, League and Congress candidates won over ninety percent of the seats assigned to Muslims and Hindus respectively. However, the League took alarm when Jawaharlal Nehru stated that he believed the constituent assembly was free to alter the cabinet mission proposals, for there were too few League members in the assembly to block any Congress moves. Therefore the League members refused to take their seats when the assembly met in December, 1946. By July of 1946 Jinnah himself had already repudiated the three-level concept, and the League was calling on Muslims to take direct or violent action.

From August 16 to August 19, 1946, direct action took forty-seven hundred lives in Calcutta as Muslims attacked Hindus. The Hindus retaliated vigorously, for the League calls for violence had forewarned them. From August, 1946, to February, 1947, conflicts between Muslims and Hindus took twelve thousand lives in the Indo-Gangetic plain. The Sikhs of the Panjab also prepared for action. For decades they had supported a movement for greater autonomy, and they were not disposed to see either Hindus or Muslims rule their homeland.

The communal clashes of late 1946 forced both the British and the Congress to concede that partition was the only feasible course even though it distressed all who had dreamed of a united India. In February, 1947, the British government declared that it planned to withdraw within sixteen months. In June the governor-general proclaimed that the British would agree to partition and would leave by the end of the year. The British also promised dominion status to Ceylon, which formally became a self-governing member of the British Commonwealth in February, 1948. During the early summer of 1947 the provincial assemblies of the Indian provinces with large Muslim populations voted on partition. Boundary commissions were set up to determine the borders in the Panjab and Bengal, where Muslims were a majority in some districts, but not in others. The British Parliament passed the India Independence Act in July, setting August 15 as the independence date. The final transfer of authority from Britain to the new states of India and Pakistan took place at midnight, August 14, 1947. On August 16 the decisions of the boundary commissions were made known.

5

THE ERA OF INDEPENDENCE

The Experience of Partition and Independence

Although the decisions of 1947 did divide the mainland of South Asia, in a sense it was no more divided than before. Throughout the British period, the more than six hundred princely states, ranging in size from a few acres to thirty-two thousand square miles, had remained apart from British India. They were linked to the Crown through subsidiary treaties, but they were affected little by developments in British India. Only a few of the princes accepted any appreciable number of the governmental innovations suggested by their British advisers, and most of the people of the princely states did not feel the full effect of the economic unification brought about by the railway system. However, all the princely states agreed to join one of the two new nations. As a result, the former division between British India and Princely India was replaced by the new division between India and Pakistan. The Himalayan states of Nepal, Bhutan, and Sikkim came to be associated closely with India, somewhat as they had been earlier with the British in India. The chieftains of the tribal states on the northwest frontier acceded to Pakistan, and so did the Baluchistan chieftains south of Afghanistan who had signed subsidiary treaties with the British in the third quarter of the nineteenth century. Almost all the remaining states eventually acceded to India. The state of Kashmir presented special problems because of its Hindu ruler, its largely Muslim population, and its position adjoining both India and Pakistan. Soon after independence, both India and Pakistan became involved in Kashmir's affairs and ended up dividing it between them, even though both claimed the right to govern all of it.

The exalted mood in both India and Pakistan at the time of independence was dampened by the sobering experience of partition. The British withdrew against a background of bloody communal warfare, the warfare Gandhi had feared ever since he had sought to win Muslim friendship by supporting the Khilafat movement of the early 1920s. The reality of partition did not halt the bloodshed. The weeks following partition saw massacres far bloodier than those which horrified observers in Calcutta a year before, as the Panjab erupted in a three-sided orgy of hatred. Sikhs, Muslims, and Hindus gave vent to the pent-up feelings of generations in a holocaust of murder and arson that drove more than eight million from their homes in both India and Pakistan by November 21, and sent another three million refugees in their wake from then to July, 1948. Even then, forty million Muslims were left in India and over ten million Hindus in Pakistan.

Partitioned Bengal came close to erupting like the Panjab, as Hindus from eastern Bengal arrived in Calcutta and started to attack the Muslim community. However, the venerated Gandhi went to Calcutta and started a fast in protest against the killing of Muslims. The disturbances ceased immediately. Anti-Muslim feeling also ran riot in Delhi as refugees arrived from the west with reports of their terrifying experiences. Therefore Gandhi left for Delhi as soon as Calcutta was quiet. He embarked on a new fast on behalf of the Muslims of Delhi, but before he had achieved his goal of ending communal strife, he was shot to death in January, 1948, by a young member of the Hindu Mahasabha who objected to his concern for the fate of Indian Muslims. The news of the manner of Gandhi's death shocked the Hindus deeply. The killing of Muslims stopped immediately, while the Hindu Mahasabha was put under a cloud that took years to lift.

COMPARISON OF INDIA, PAKISTAN, AND
CEYLON AT INDEPENDENCE

Both India and Pakistan felt the consequences of partition, but those consequences were far worse for Pakistan. In the first place, India was one continuous unit whose regions were connected by functioning overland transport and communications networks. However, Pakistan was divided into two widely separated portions, eastern and western, whose communication with each other depended heavily on sea and air facilities. The shifting waterways of the Ganges-Brahmaputra delta had made the building of roads and railroads into East Bengal (the new East Pakistan) prohibitively difficult; and even if such highways and railways had existed, the inflamed state of public opinion in both India and Pakistan during the early days of independence would hardly have allowed Pakistanis to use Indian facilities to move between the two portions of their country. Ceylon was also less fortunate than India, since its railway network was not as highly developed as was that of India.

A second advantage which the new India had over Pakistan and Ceylon was that India contained all four of the major cities of South Asia—Delhi, Calcutta, Madras, Bombay—together with their administrative, financial, commercial, industrial, and educational institutions. Pakistan had only one important cultural and economic center, the city of Lahore in the Panjab, and Lahore was devastated in the riots following partition. Pakistan was therefore left with Karachi in the west and Dacca in the east, neither of which had ever been more than merely a provincial center. Colombo on Ceylon was not devastated like Lahore or inundated with refugees like Delhi and Calcutta, and continued to serve effectively as the nerve center of the island; but it too was little more than a local center.

India and Pakistan each received a total of nearly six million refugees in the first year of independence. However, this was about one out of every thirteen or fourteen Pakistanis and less than one out of every sixty Indians. Moreover, the nature of the refugee populations differed. Many of the Hindus who fled to India were townspeople—professional persons, merchants, artisans, laborers, people in service occupations—whose skills were useful for India's industrialization program. The Sikh villagers who left western Pakistan for India were welcomed by their fellow Sikhs to lands newly vacated by Muslim villagers fleeing to the Pakistani side of the Panjab boundary, and most of the Sikh townspeople found places in India's growing cities. On the other hand, many of the Muslims who went to Pakistan were villagers with only agricultural skills. These skills were useful, but they were not as immediately needed in the new state as the skills possessed by the Hindus whose departure deprived Pakistan of many of the doctors, lawyers, bankers, wholesalers, retailers, skilled workers and others who had previously served the inhabitants of the territory. Though a number of Muslims left the towns of India for Pakistan, Pakistan's professional persons and urban workers were proportionately far fewer than India's in the years just after independence.

The personnel problems of the new Indian and Pakistani administrations reflected the longstanding differences in Muslim and Hindu reactions to British rule. Pakistan was reasonably well provided with military officers, but so short of civilian personnel that it had to employ a large number of British citizens, former Indian Civil Service members, until it could recruit and train enough Pakistanis. Although India and Ceylon were scarcely oversupplied with experienced and capable administrators, neither of them needed to resort to such expedients.

Corresponding differences appeared in the economic situations of

India and Pakistan. Undivided India had been the world's eighth largest industrial producer. It had numerous cotton and jute mills, and enterprises like the Tata iron and steel complex in Bihar. Post-partition India inherited all but a minute portion of pre-partition India's factory industry and ninety-five percent of its developed hydroelectric capacity, while Pakistan with its near monopoly of the world's jute crop had not a single jute mill. Ceylon was somewhat more industrialized than Pakistan, but its few small factories employed only 54,000 of its more than seven million people in 1953.

With such disadvantages, it was remarkable that Pakistan survived. Its first governor-general was Muhammad Ali Jinnah, who guided the state through its troubled early days. The strain of the first few months of independence overtaxed him so greatly that he died of a heart attack in September, 1948. His long-time lieutenant, Liaquat Ali Khan, then prime minister, promptly took over the leadership of the state.

Both India and Pakistan thus lost their most prominent pre-independence leaders in the same year. However, what followed the death of Jinnah differed profoundly from what followed the death of Gandhi. The assassination of Gandhi served to unite the people of India; the death of Jinnah served only to confound the people of Pakistan. Even before independence, Jawaharlal Nehru had succeeded Gandhi as the political head of the nationwide Congress movement. Although Nehru did not aspire to Gandhi's spiritual leadership, his acknowledged political power put him in a far better position than Liaquat Ali Khan to carry on as his nation's leader after his mentor died. Nehru also stayed in power longer than Liaquat Ali Khan, providing a continuity which was very helpful to the new state in establishing habits of loyalty. In October, 1951, Liaquat Ali Khan was assassinated by a disgruntled Pakistani tribesman from the region bordering Afghanistan, but Jawaharlal Nehru led the Congress to victory in the first three nationwide elections in independent India, winning control of the central legislature in 1952, 1957, and 1962. He died in 1964, and within two years he was succeeded by his daughter Indira Gandhi.

Ceylon also lost its most prominent pre-independence leader when its first prime minister, D.S. Senanayake, died after being thrown from a horse in 1952. Though an opposition coalition took command in 1956, and though it was 1965 before Senanayake's son Dudley became prime minister, political continuity seemed nearly as assured as in India in the 1950s and 1960s. When the widow of the leader of the 1956 coalition succeeded him as prime minister after his assassination in 1959, and then replaced the younger Senanayake in 1970, it began to appear that there was even continuity in electoral reversals. However, in 1973 the death of Dudley Senanayake from a heart attack put an end to his hopes of regaining power.

The patterns of economic, social, and political organization which the leaders of the new states of India, Pakistan, and Ceylon chose as models were generally those with which they had become familiar in the British period, although local circumstances necessitated modifications. The leaders of Ceylon seemed to have the easiest task in one way, since at least half their people were literate. The leaders of India and Pakistan, working with people of whom not more than one in six could read any language, faced tremendous problems as they struggled to use their knowledge of the modern world to elevate the position of their people.

When independence came, more than three-fourths of the people of South Asia lived in small, congested villages, many of which lacked a reliable source of clean water or a road that could be used throughout the year. The problems of Pakistan's modernizers were increased because many of the ulama, those learned in Muslim law and theology, were still as opposed to modernization as were many of their counterparts in Middle Eastern lands. The problems of modernizers in India, and to a lesser extent in Ceylon, were multiplied by the restrictions which caste rules placed on most of their people. Caste restrictions were still powerful in the hundreds of thousand of villages, even though they had been weakened in the cities. Nevertheless, the processes of modernization begun in the two hundred years preceding independence were too far advanced to be arrested. The leaders of each government set to work to inspire their people with a new dedication to expand their economy, reform their social relationships, fashion a truly democratic government, and assume their proper place in the world at large.

Problems of the New States

EXTERNAL POLICIES

The place of South Asia in world affairs had been recognized as early as 1919, when British India had been a signatory to the peace treaties after World War I and a founding member of the League of Nations even though it was not yet an autonomous dominion like Canada or Australia. British India had also been a founding member of the United Nations in 1945. India, Pakistan, and Ceylon remained associated with the British Commonwealth, even after becoming republics in 1950, 1956, and 1972 respectively. (However, Pakistan withdrew in 1972 when Commonwealth members recognized the newly formed state of Bangladesh in east Bengal, after India had helped it secede from Pakistan.) They welcomed the technical assistance offered by members of the

Commonwealth, the United States, and other powers through mecha-
nisms like the Colombo plan of 1950. They also became active in the
United Nations, but selected different paths in world affairs.

India chose nonalignment. It sought to remain independent of the
power blocs led by the United States and the Soviet Union, accepting
aid from all sides and making itself sufficiently acceptable to rival powers
so that its leaders could moderate between them. The significance of
India's services as a mediator was very great at times, at least until
Chinese Communist attacks in the 1960s began to make India seem less
neutral than before. However, the pledges of aid which were received
from the United States and Britain during that period came to be offset
by Soviet support in India's continuing rivalry with Pakistan, as evidenced
in the Indo-Soviet friendship treaty of 1971.

Pakistan, on the other hand, began by choosing overt alignment
with Britain and the United States in the Central Treaty Organization
(originally the Baghdad Pact) in the Middle East, and also in the South-
East Asia Treaty Organization. Pakistan's choice was motivated partly
by an overwhelming fear of India's intentions and partly by alarm over
Afghani interest in the mountain tribes of the northwest. Displays of
friendship between India and Afghanistan did nothing to dispel that
alarm. In the early 1960s, as Chinese Communist insistence on satisfactory settlement of boundary claims with India and Chinese Communist denunciations of Indian policy mounted in intensity, Pakistan began to look to the People's Republic of China for a measure of diplomatic
support. The signing of a boundary treaty between Pakistan and the
People's Republic of China in 1963 marked a definite shift toward a more
independent course for Pakistan. That shift was underlined in 1972 when
Pakistan withdrew from the British Commonwealth and the South-East
Asia Treaty Organization. The People's Republic of China demonstrated
its friendship for Pakistan by vetoing United Nations membership for
Bangladesh until in 1974 India returned the Pakistani soldiers taken
prisoner by Indian troops in Bangladesh at the end of 1971. However,
Pakistan remained linked with Turkey, Iran, and Britain in the Central
Treaty Organization, and in 1973 began to seek closer relations with
economically growing Iran as a counterweight to Indian and Soviet
friendship with Afghanistan. Iran responded with economic aid and
also with military aid against rebellious groups on the Pakistani side of
the frontier between Pakistan and Iran.

It was hardly surprising that Pakistan set its course in a direction
different from that taken by India. Pakistan's early alignment with Britain
and the United States, like its later approaches to the People's Republic
of China, was only one more expression of the deep cleavages between
the Muslim and Hindu communities. During the British period the Muslims had grown so alarmed at the thought of becoming a permanent

minority in a state run by and for the majority that they had insisted on a separate state when the British withdrew. They won their point, but the leaders of independent Pakistan in the west continued to feel greater apparent need to maintain their independence from India than from Britain, particularly after Bangladesh came into being with Indian aid and allied itself closely with India. That feeling was heightened still more when India exploded its first nuclear device underground in 1974, shortly after the last prisoners of the India-Pakistan-Bangladesh conflict of 1971 had been repatriated.

At first Ceylon also chose continued close association with Britain, allowing Britain to continue to use naval bases on the island. However, a change in government led to a change in policy. In 1957 the British were asked to withdraw from the bases, and thereafter Ceylon sought to follow a nonaligned course, although it did remain in the Commonwealth. Ceylon avoided taking sides among the larger states, in the hope of inheriting part of India's role as a mediator, but its efforts to help resolve matters such as the Sino-Indian border dispute had only limited success.

THE PRINCELY STATES AND NEPAL, BHUTAN, AND SIKKIM

The states of what had once been Princely India posed problems to both India and Pakistan in the early years of independence. Though the princes were nominally free to go their own way when the British left, their states were tied economically to neighboring regions in the new states. In addition, a century of habit had accustomed the princes to allowing the paramount power to manage their external affairs. The princes therefore yielded to the urgings of British, Indian, and Pakistani leaders to associate themselves with one of the two new states. Before independence came, the chieftains of Baluchistan and the northwest frontier had agreed to join Pakistan, while all but three of the princely states adjacent to India had given India control of their communications, defenses, and foreign affairs.

The three princes who did not accede to India immediately were the Muslim rulers of Junagadh and Hyderabad and the Hindu ruler or maharaja of Kashmir. The ruler of Junagadh, on the west coast north of Bombay, acceded to Pakistan, but he fled when his predominantly Hindu subjects rose in rebellion. In November, 1947, his council invited the Indian government to enter, and three months later Junagadh's people voted overwhelmingly to associate themselves with India.

In the Deccan, the Nizam of Hyderabad apparently hoped to make his large and populous state independent. However, he was at a double disadvantage: his state was landlocked and most of his people were Hindus. He refused to commit himself to either India or Pakistan until

November, 1947, when he said only that he would not accede to Pakistan. In the next few months, fanatical Muslims from Hyderabad raided neighboring Indian territories, eventually provoking a military response. In September, 1948, the Indian army occupied Hyderabad, and in November the Nizam accepted association with India.

To the north, the Hindu maharaja of the largely Muslim state of Jammu and Kashmir also refused to choose between India and Pakistan. Each of the two was eager for Kashmir, for its territory lies across the headwaters of three of the rivers of the Panjab. Pakistan's eagerness was sharpened by anxiety, for in the western Panjab life itself depends on the three Kashmiri rivers. Shortly after independence the maharaja agreed to let Pakistan manage some of his state's means of communicating with the outside world. Soon, Pakistani tribesmen from the northwestern frontier began to cross into Kashmir. Fighting broke out in October, 1947, between the maharaja's forces and the incoming tribesmen. The maharaja promptly turned to India for aid. When the government at Delhi insisted that he must accede to India in order to qualify for assistance, he agreed, and Indian troops were rushed to Kashmir.

By the time the Indians arrived, pro-Pakistanis in western Kashmir had organized an Azad (Free) Kashmir government and declared that Kashmir belonged to Pakistan. India charged Pakistan with aggression in the United Nations Security Council, Pakistan brought countercharges, and the Security Council set up a commission to bring about a cease-fire and plebiscite. In January, 1949, the commission obtained a cease-fire between the Pakistani irregulars and the Indian regular troops in Kashmir, but no plebiscite was held. Instead, each government maintained control of the area on its side of the cease-fire line, while continuing to claim the right to rule the rest of the state also.

Kashmir's political life had been complicated since the 1930s by the existence of two strong political parties among the Muslim population. One party was in sympathy with the Muslim League, the other with the Indian National Congress. The head of the pro-Congress party became a hero to most Kashmiris when he was imprisoned for agitation against the maharaja. Shortly after independence he was released, and in October, 1947, the maharaja accepted him as his prime minister. However, the pro-League party supported the Azad Kashmir government in the area held by Pakistan. In 1952 the pro-Congress prime minister in Indian-held Kashmir had the maharaja deposed by the legislature in favor of his son. Then an even more pro-Congress political leader became prime minister. A constituent assembly was called, and a constitution was drafted which clearly stated that the princely state of Jammu and Kashmir was part of India. When the constitution went into effect in January,

1957, the government of India declared that Kashmir was now completely integrated into India except for the area held by Pakistani troops.

Pakistan did not accept Indian claims to Kashmir. To Pakistanis, the Indians were taking two conflicting positions, supporting Hindu majorities in Junagadh and Hyderabad yet refusing a plebiscite in Muslim-majority Kashmir. The government at Delhi paid no heed to Pakistani protests, for the integration of Kashmir had become a point of honor with Indian leaders. While India controlled most of Kashmir, the Congress could contend that Muslims were satisfied to live in a secular state with a Hindu majority. Until and unless it seemed that a plebiscite would favor India, no plebiscite was likely to be held in Indian Kashmir. Yet the Kashmir plebiscite was as much a point of honor with Pakistan as the integration of Kashmir was with India, for if a vote showed that Kashmiri Muslims were unsatisfied, then one of the chief arguments for the formation of Pakistan would be reconfirmed.

Although agreement on the use of the Kashmiri rivers was finally reached in 1960, the Kashmiri issue remained a deeply emotional one for both India and Pakistan, for it was intimately bound up with the question of whether or not partition was justified. Pakistan therefore welcomed the negotiations with the People's Republic of China which culminated in a boundary treaty early in 1963. By agreeing with Pakistan on the location of the border between China and Azad Kashmir, the People's Republic of China gave tacit recognition to Pakistan's claims to an interest in Kashmir. After fourteen years of waiting in vain for their Western allies to give substantial support to their calls for a plebiscite in Kashmir, this was a soothing balm to many troubled Pakistanis. However, India sought to dampen Pakistani hopes in August, 1965, attacking along the sixteen-year-old cease-fire line in retaliation for allegedly serious Pakistani incursions into Indian-held territory. A cease-fire was arranged in January, 1966, through the mediation of the Soviet Union, but charges and counter-charges of violations of its terms delayed its implementation. When open warfare broke out once more between Indian and Pakistani forces in December, 1971, in the region of eastern Bengal, Pakistan again sought to increase its holdings in Kashmir, but again in vain. Thereafter, Kashmir's political leaders began to reconcile themselves to an Indian allegiance, and even to complain that Pakistan was interfering in Kashmiri affairs by continuing to seek a plebiscite.

India's actions in Junagadh, Hyderabad, and Kashmir in 1947–1948 apparently forewarned the French, for shortly afterward they asked the Indian government to administer their few small territories along the coast of India. However, the Portuguese paid no attention even after India quietly took control of a few small landlocked Portuguese holdings.

Pro-Indian inhabitants of Goa, the last possession of the Portuguese, attempted to win freedom from Lisbon by a satyagraha movement in 1955, but to no avail. Indian troops then blockaded the colony to prevent the Portuguese from trading in India for food and other necessities. At the end of 1961 the Indian army finally expelled the Portuguese from Goa, ending the blockade and freeing troops to meet the increasingly grave Chinese threat along the Himalayan boundary.

The Himalayan states of Nepal, Bhutan, and Sikkim presented a different situation from the princely states. They had traditionally been closely linked with the Chinese empire, as well as with the empire of Britain. The rulers of Nepal continued to send periodic missions to Peking until just before the emperors of China were overthrown in 1911–1912, although Bhutan and Sikkim had by then accepted British direction of their foreign affairs. Britain formally recognized Nepal's right to manage its own external relations in 1923, though its control over Nepal's access routes to the sea gave it much influence in Nepali affairs. Neither the British, the Indian National Congress, nor the hereditary rulers of the three mountain states expected them to be absorbed bodily into the new India. However, strains soon developed between independent India and the three Himalayan states over just what their position as a political buffer and cultural transition zone between India and China should mean. Sikkim and Bhutan were too small to refuse to continue allowing their foreign relations to be directed from New Delhi, but Nepal successfully asserted its freedom from Indian management of its affairs. In 1950 the hereditary Rana prime ministers of Nepal agreed to a trade treaty with India which was unfavorable to long-range Nepali interests. Before the end of the year, the king dismissed the Rana line and took over the direction of Nepal's affairs himself. In 1956 he signed a treaty of trade and friendship with the People's Republic of China, despite Indian objections. Thereafter, Nepal worked to counterbalance Indian pressures through the development of relations not only with the People's Republic of China but also with countries in every continent. Bhutan also began to assert its right to be recognized as a separate state, becoming a member of the United Nations in 1971.

Sikkim, the smallest state, was least successful in asserting itself, in part because of the problems inherent in governing a state in which only a quarter of the people see themselves as indigenous (the rest are recent immigrants from Nepal). In 1973 the hereditary ruler of Sikkim and the leaders of its indigenous and Nepali political movements invited India to supervise Sikkim's day-to-day governmental administration temporarily, while they concentrated on working out a new electoral system which would give the Nepali majority greater opportunity for representation in the National Council. The first elections under the new system were held in 1974. Shortly thereafter the new assembly stripped the ruler of his power, and Sikkim became an associate state of India with representation in the Indian national legislature.

PROVINCIAL REORGANIZATION

The quasi-autonomous relationship of the states of former Princely India to India and Pakistan did not last long. Within five years they were absorbed into one or the other, and within ten years the boundaries of the provinces of India and Pakistan had been redrawn so that no trace was left of the former outlines of the princely states.

The frontier chieftains of Pakistan were soon merged into the provinces of Baluchistan and the North-West Frontier, and in 1955, Baluchistan and the North-West Frontier Province were united with West Panjab and Sind into one province, West Pakistan. Pakistan administered Azad Kashmir separately. The formation of West Pakistan meant Pakistan had only two provinces, a novelty in the history of federations. The two new provinces were more nearly balanced in population than the former ones had been, for the province of East Pakistan (formerly East Bengal) had somewhat over half the people of Pakistan. However, the integration of the Pathan regions into West Pakistan led to friction with Afghanistan. In 1955 Afghanistan began to give active diplomatic support to the demands of Pakistan's frontier tribes for greater autonomy, even asking for the creation of an independent state of Pushtunistan for the tribes which shared the Pushtu language with many of their Afghan neighbors. The two-province arrangement was maintained for fourteen years. Then in 1969 West Pakistan was again divided into four provinces. Thus when East Pakistan broke away to become the new state of Bangladesh at the end of 1971, the remaining state of Pakistan was still organized as a federal government.

In India, one of the Congress Party's ablest organizers quickly brought many small states directly under the administration of the provinces they adjoined. The other small states were grouped into five states' unions. When India's new constitution took effect in 1950, both the states' unions and the provinces became full-fledged states of the Indian federal republic. The largest princely states, Mysore, Hyderabad, and Kashmir, also became states of the Indian federal republic in 1950, although Pakistan refused to admit that Kashmir belonged to India. Except in Kashmir, the rulers of the princely states were given pensions when the constitution went into effect, and their rule was replaced by republican institutions. The peaceful way in which this resolution was accomplished aroused the admiration of observers.

Since the 1950 constitution allowed the Indian parliament to alter state boundaries, the central government was able to make some radical changes in response to public sentiment. The Telugu-speaking Andhras, who had spearheaded the drive for linguistic reorganization of the Congress a generation earlier, also spearheaded the drive for linguistic reorganization of the states. At first the central government resisted all arguments, but in December, 1952, an Andhra leader fasted to death to protest Delhi's refusal to consider forming an Andhra province. The wave of riots which accompanied and followed his fatal fast convinced the central government that it must act. In 1953 the Andhra state was created out of parts of Hyderabad and Mysore, and a States Reorganization Commission was established to study the overall situation.

When the States Reorganization Commission reported in 1956, it advised a full-scale reorganization along linguistic lines in the Dravidian south. Changes were also recommended in the boundaries of some central and northern states. The adoption of the commission's report made India a federation of fourteen states and six specially administered districts (the capital, the Indian-held island groups of the Indian Ocean, and certain tribal areas on the Himalaya and Burma frontiers).

The commission weighed carefully the strength of linguistic sentiment against the dangers of division inherent in that sentiment. However, linguistic reorganization also allowed the central government to erase the last traces of some of the former princely states. The complete disappearance of Hyderabad, which had already been diminished by the formation of Andhra, was the most striking and significant example.

The 1956 adoption of the commission's report gave the users of the four major Dravidian languages the separate states they wanted, but it did not satisfy those who used the two Aryan languages of Gujerati and Marathi. The Gujeratis and Marathas continued to be united in one state, Bombay, even though they wanted separate states. After long and bitter protests, Bombay state was finally divided into Gujerat and Maharashtra in 1960. The 1956 report also ignored the desire of the Sikhs in the eastern Panjab for a separate state. The Sikhs cloaked their demand in a linguistic guise in order to increase its acceptability in Delhi, but Delhi was as sensitive to religious communalism in the Panjab as in Kashmir. The long-rebellious Naga tribes of the eastern Himalayas obtained a state in 1963, but the Sikhs were not granted one until 1966. In 1968 a sub-state was agreed upon for the restless hill tribes of eastern Assam. In 1972 it became a full-fledged state, as did two other eastern hills areas previously administered directly from Delhi. Religious communalism also reared its head in once-Portuguese Goa, where the large Christian minority made clear its preference for a separate state rather than inclusion in neighboring Maharashtra. Economic concerns began to lead toward a new wave of separatism after 1970. Leaders in the wealthier part of Andhra initiated a campaign for separation from the poorer, ex-Hyderabad portion of the state, but were persuaded to end it late in 1973. Demand for a separate state also began to strengthen among the hill peoples of the Bihar-Bengal-Orissa border region.

In Ceylon and Nepal, the internal administrative boundaries which existed at the time of the British departure were left largely unchanged. With no princely states to be absorbed, with existing provinces and districts largely prescribed by natural geographical divisions, and with unitary rather than federal governments, within which provincial and district boundaries had relatively little political significance, there was little effective pressure for alteration.

LINGUISTIC DIVISIONS

The question of language was vitally important from the outset in India, Pakistan, Ceylon, and Nepal. In India, neither those who spoke Dravidian languages nor those who used Bengali, Oriya, Marathi, or Gujerati were willing to accept Hindi as the sole official language of government administration and higher education in India, although the authors of the constitution envisioned the replacement of English by Hindi within less than a generation. English was associated with foreign rule, but Hindi was associated with control from Delhi. In all of the states of India, early education was given in the local languages, and secondary and higher education were increasingly offered in local languages. Most of the leaders of newly free India received much of their education in English, and the use of English served as a bond between them, but many of the young people who were receiving their education in their own languages would expect to make their way in later years without a thorough knowledge of a second language. This threatened the Indian union with grave problems, for one who knew only his or her own language would find it difficult to work effectively with people from other states. As early as the 1962 elections, it was becoming clear that political parties hesitated to select monolingual candidates even for district office. Yet when the provisions of the 1950 constitution for replacing English entirely with Hindi were scheduled to go into effect at the opening of 1965, riots and demonstrations in the Dravidian south forced the government to delay the final changeover indefinitely.

Pakistan faced a similar dilemma. Urdu, the common language of the educated in western Pakistan, was not accepted in the Bengali-speaking eastern wing. When the first constitution-makers discussed using Urdu as the sole national language, Bengalis objected so strongly that the idea was dropped. English remained the common language of Pakistani leaders even though it was the language of their former overlords. Bengalis continued to feel that their language and culture were slighted, even though all civil servants were required to know both Bengali and Urdu and to serve tours of duty in both wings. Their desire for a state in which both their cultural and their economic interests would be given a higher priority eventually led to the separatist movement which gave rise to the new state of Bangladesh in 1971.

In Ceylon, there were differences of interest between Sinhalese and Tamils. The Tamils of the north and east worried about their position as a permanent minority of about twenty-three percent; the Sinhalese, though a seventy percent majority, worried about the greater use made by Tamils of the schooling provided by the British, which gave the Tamils an edge in business and the professions. The Sinhalese also worried about the possibility that the large Tamil community in India might intervene in Ceylonese affairs on behalf of their fellow Tamils. The ruling party in post-independence Ceylon tried to play down these linguistic differences (and the religious differences which accompanied them, for most Sinhalese-speakers were Buddhist and most Tamil-speakers were Hindu). However, in 1956 the pressures of the electorate forced it to change its policy from one of support for the continued recognition of both Sinhalese and Tamil as national languages to the recognition of Tamil as only a regional language. Despite this change, the party lost that year's election, and its more strongly Sinhalese-oriented successors made Sinhalese the only official language throughout Ceylon between 1956 and 1964. After the completion of a treaty with India in 1964 providing for the repatriation to India of a number of the more recent Tamil immigrants, the language issue became somewhat less intense. In 1966, after another change in government, Tamil was again recognized as a regional language in the north and east; but according to the new constitution of 1972, all judicial proceedings throughout the country were to be in Sinhalese. Tamils protested, but to no immediate avail.

In Nepal, as in India, there were a dozen or more widely differing languages, some based on Sanskrit and others not. However, the use of the Sanskritic Nepali language as the national language has met less resistance than the use of Hindi in India. This may be in part because its heavy infusion of Tibeto-Burman loan words makes it less strange to the ears of Nepal's Tibeto-Burman speakers than Hindi is to the Dravidian speakers of India.

CONSTITUTIONAL DEVELOPMENT

The constitutional development of India, Pakistan, Ceylon, and Nepal, like their linguistic problems and their handling of provincial boundaries, displayed both similarities and contrasts. When independence came, Ceylon already had a constitution setting up a unitary government which was parliamentary in form. Its provinces had no autonomous powers, and its cabinet ministers were required to resign if they lost the support of more than half the lower house of the legislature. This constitution proved satisfactory enough so that it was only slightly altered prior to 1972. At that time, Ceylon ceased to be a dominion with a governor-general representing the British crown and became a republic with a president, renaming itself Sri Lanka (the worthy and resplendent). The constitution of the new Sri Lanka established a one-house national assembly and made Buddhism the state religion. Previously, Ceylon had been a secular state.

By contrast with Ceylon's experience, in Nepal the royal government promulgated constitutions three times between 1948 and 1962. The first was a parliamentary constitution issued by the Ranas, the hereditary prime ministers who had run Nepal's affairs since 1845. It was never fully implemented and was withdrawn after the king expelled the Ranas from power in 1950–1951 with the cooperation of the newly formed Nepali Congress Party. The second, also parliamentary in form, was withdrawn after the king decided in 1960 that he did not wish to share power with the Nepali Congress, which had won a clear majority in Nepal's first parliamentary elections in 1959. The third provided for directly elected village councils and indirectly elected district, zone, and national councils. Nationwide class organizations were also established for peasants, laborers, women, students, youth, and children, and later for ex-servicemen as well, as a substitute for political parties. The Nepali Congress in effect went into exile thereafter. Occasional street demonstrations in the capital called for liberalization of the constitution, as in 1972, but the royal government paid them little heed.

Both the experience of Ceylon and that of Nepal contrasted with the experiences of India and Pakistan, which in turn contrasted with each other. At the time of partition in 1947, both India and Pakistan had constituent assemblies elected by the members of the provincial assemblies within their respective territories. Both used the constituent assembly as the central legislature until the constitution was drafted. Both constituent assemblies drew heavily on the India Act of 1935. Both states declared themselves republics, acknowledging the British crown only as a symbol of Commonwealth unity. Both constitutions established federal governments, carefully enumerating the spheres of central and provincial activity. Both federations were highly centralized, with residual powers going to the center rather than the states, and the central government had clear authority to take over state governments if necessary. Both constitutions accepted the parliamentary form of government, in which cabinet ministers must resign if they lose the support of more than half the legislators.

In other ways the experiences of India and Pakistan were not alike. India put its first constitution into effect in 1950 and proceeded to carry out its provisions without any fuss. A draft constitution was ready in Pakistan in 1950, but the constituent assembly did not approve it, for it gave too little autonomy to the Bengali wing to suit Bengali representatives, and it paid little heed to the Islamic basis on which the nation was supposedly founded. The assembly wrangled over various proposals until the governor-general of Pakistan sent it home in 1954. He then proposed to promulgate a constitution himself and to amalgamate the provinces of western Pakistan into one, but the Federal Court declared that he could not do so under the terms of the independence act which established Pakistan. Therefore, the provincial legislatures elected a second constituent assembly in 1955.

The new assembly quickly unified West Pakistan and in 1956 accepted a constitutional draft. The 1956 Pakistan constitution gave the two states of the federal union a great deal of autonomy. It did not attempt to establish a single national language, and it did include provisions to encourage Islamic studies and to bring the law of the state into line with the Sharia, the law of the Quran and Sunna.

Political leaders in Pakistan soon discovered that the provision for harmonizing the law of the state with the Sharia was practically unworkable because of differences in interpretation. Some people wanted to enact the entire body of Sharia law as enforced in states like Saudi Arabia, while others repudiated such proposals as fatal to the modernization of social and economic life. The more rigidly orthodox Muslims had already made their position clear by attacking the property and persons of the reforming Ahmadi sect in the Panjab in 1953. The realization that it would not be easy to harmonize state law with the Sharia contributed to rising dissatisfaction with the implementation of the constitution. In 1958, after only two years, the constitution was abrogated and a military government established. A new constitution, promulgated in 1962, made few concessions to the orthodox. It provided for a small advisory commission drawn from the ulama, but it allowed the president to choose the members of the commission. It also made cabinet members responsible to the president rather than to the legislature.

The 1962 presidential constitution lasted less than a decade. In 1969 it too was abrogated, for rising discontent in East Pakistan was forcing reconsideration of its provisions. When that discontent resulted in the division of the state into Pakistan in the west and Bangladesh in the east in 1971, Bangladesh adopted a provisional constitution which established a unitary parliamentary government, in which the prime minister would be responsible to the national assembly. The permanent constitution which went into effect at the end of 1972 retained the unitary parliamentary form. In 1972 Pakistan adopted an interim constitution which retained a federal structure, and in 1973 it adopted a permanent constitution which declared Pakistan to be a federal Islamic republic and reestablished a parliamentary rather than a presidential form of government.

POLITICS

PAKISTAN. The difference in the fates of the Indian and Pakistani constitutions of 1950 and 1956 was only one indication of the differences in the political development of the two countries. Both central governments unhesitatingly used their constitutional right to take over state governments. Whenever a state government lost ability to maintain order, the central government stepped in, as was to happen in the Indian states of Kerala and West Bengal when rioting broke out against the actions of a Communist-led cabinet and legislature. It became constitutionally acceptable in India for the chief minister of a state who lost his or her legislative majority to ask for president's rule in order to prevent possible public disorder in the period between the dissolution of the state assembly and the holding of new elections, as was done in Orissa in 1973. In 1972 and 1974, for example, the Indian government took over the Andhra and Gujerat state governments because of local rioting. Successive Pakistani governments took control of states even oftener. In 1973 alone the president of Pakistan dismissed two out of four provincial governors for failure to quell local disturbances.

The comparative instability of political parties in Pakistan contributed to the frequent dissolution of state governments there. Few Pakistani leaders had done as much planning for an independent state as had the leaders of India, for the first strong demand for Pakistan came only seven years before the actual formation of the state. Most of the energies of Pakistan's leaders therefore had to be devoted to arguing for the existence of Pakistan, not to planning what it would be like after its inception. Furthermore, many Pakistani leaders came from the tradition-minded landlord group rather than the modern-minded middle class and were unused to thinking in terms of constructing a modern nation-state. After the deaths of Jinnah and Liaquat Ali Khan, most of the remaining political figures proved remarkably inept. In 1954 the Muslim League was ignominiously defeated by a coalition of opposing factions in the provincial elections in eastern Pakistan; shortly after the 1956 constitution went into effect, a new party defeated the League in West Pakistan.

The League's swift decline was largely attributable to the inability of leading politicians to put aside personal differences in the interest of a coherent program, as Gandhi had long since taught the politicians of the Indian National Congress to do. In Pakistan's first eleven years, cabinet followed cabinet in quick succession both at the center and in the states. At the same time, day-to-day administration was hampered by a shortage of qualified personnel. The civil service was also affected by the temptation to accept bribes, an inclination which was all too natural where poorly paid officials, not yet steeled to put the general welfare above personal advantage, wielded power to grant export licenses, assess property for taxation, and otherwise influence the lives of the wealthy.

During the months after the first constituent assembly was dissolved in 1954, the governor-general brought Muhammad Ayub Khan, commander-in-chief of the armed forces, into the cabinet for a short time. Four years later, in 1958, the president of the republic requested him to take complete control. Ayub Khan began by proclaiming his intention to cleanse the country of corruption. Soon he abolished political parties, abrogated the constitution, and became a military dictator. The army he commanded gave him the largest reservoir of disciplined, Western-trained men in Pakistan, because of the course of development followed by the Muslims of British India and by the Pakistani movement.

Corruption diminished sharply under Ayub Khan. In 1959 it was decided to move the capital north from Karachi to the new city of Islamabad. In 1960 a program of "basic democracy" was inaugurated, in which the people were to vote for the members of their local governing bodies. These bodies were to choose members of district councils, which in turn selected members of regional councils. The regional councils chose members for the provincial councils, which then elected members for the national council. However, all councils above the local level also included members appointed by the civil administration, and the appointed members tended to take the lead in discussion. The elected representatives of the people promptly made Ayub Khan president for five years and requested that he promulgate a new constitution, which came into effect in 1962. The new constitution retained the basic-democracy system, based on indirect elections at all but the local level. It also made the cabinet responsible to the president rather than to the legislature. An effort was made to placate Bengali sentiment by specifying Dacca as the main seat of the legislature.

Ayub Khan hoped to govern without the mechanism of political parties, but soon found that disorganization in the national assembly and public objections to continued curbs on political activity were too great to ignore. Consequently, political parties were again permitted to form in 1962, but only the party supporting the president, an offshoot of the old Muslim League, made serious efforts to broaden its base and develop a constructive program. The other parties, including a second League offshoot and the Jamaat-i-Islami (a fundamentalist Muslim group which strongly resembled the Muslim Brotherhood of Egypt and the Fedayin-i-Islam of Iran in its call for a return to the Sharia as the basis of the state), concentrated on bringing down the president. In the 1964 elections for the local-level basic democrats who would select a new president in 1965, the opposition parties campaigned for the sister of the revered Jinnah, who promised to return to parliamentary rather than presidential government. It was perhaps a measure of the parties' sterility that the one name they could agree to support was Jinnah, and of either their desperation or their daring that they would run the first woman candidate for president in any Muslim republic. It was certainly a measure of the difference that prolonged exposure to the West had made in attitudes that even the Muslim fundamentalists would rally behind a woman. It was also a measure of the parties' appeal to dissatisfied elements—and of the freedom of the elections—that they garnered more than a third of the electors' seats. However, the fact that Ayub Khan won clear majorities in East as well as West Pakistan was taken as a measure of the progress of national unification.

Unfortunately for that unity, the strenuous efforts made by the Ayub government in its early years to eliminate corruption and to channel development funds into the poverty-ridden east were not maintained. As early as 1965 there was talk of the "twenty-two families" who controlled the economy—one of them headed by Ayub's brother—and though Ayub had indeed won a slim majority in the east, much of his support had come not from the Bengalis but rather from Muslims who had fled from eastern India in 1947. In 1966 Sheikh Mujibur Rahman of the Awami League in East Pakistan called for greatly increased provincial autonomy within a minimal federal structure. He was accused of treason and jailed, but popular outcry forced his release, and Bengali demands for a new constitution mounted. In the west, too, discontent grew as the "twenty-two families" were revealed to be in control of two-thirds of the country's industry. Former foreign minister Zulfikar Ali Bhutto was jailed for a time in 1967 for his protests against the Ayub government. Rioting in late 1968 and early 1969 led Ayub to resign power to his chief of staff, Muhammad Yahya Khan, who abrogated the constitution in 1969, divided West Pakistan into four provinces again, and called for elections to a new constituent assembly in 1970. Sheikh Mujibur's Awami League won 160 of the 162 seats assigned to the east, and Bhutto's People's Party of Pakistan won 81 of the 138 assigned to the West. The assembly never met, however, for Yahya refused to accept the Awami League's constitutional proposals. The League then proclaimed independence for East Pakistan, as Bangladesh (Free Bengal). After eight months of strife in eastern Bengal between Yahya's West Pakistani garrison there and Mujibur's Bengali supporters, the Indian government sent troops to Dacca in December, 1971, and Yahya was forced to concede defeat. India's intervention was avowedly undertaken so that the millions of refugees who had swarmed into western Bengal during 1971 could return home to a free Bangladesh, which they did in the next three months. However, the Indian government was also unquestionably relieved to be able to expel the West Pakistanis, who had been running guerrilla training camps for tribespeople from India's eastern hill country.

The defeat in the east forced Yahya to resign. As head of the majority party in the west, Bhutto became the new leader of the truncated state. Martial law was lifted when the interim constitution was proclaimed in April, 1972. The constituent assembly members elected from the provinces of the west in 1970 began to consider the draft of a permanent constitution, adopted in April, 1973. Bhutto's government took over the management of a number of the largest firms held by the "twenty-two families," nationalized the major insurance firms, and dismissed hundreds of officials for corruption, in a bid for continued popular support.

During 1972 the Bhutto government released the few Indian soldiers taken prisoner on the Kashmir-Sind front in the 1971 conflict and put into effect a cease-fire line agreed on with India. However, all through the year it refused to recognize formally the independence of Bangladesh. This in turn delayed the return of Pakistani soldiers taken prisoner by Indian troops in the territory of Bangladesh at the end of 1971. The Indian government argued that in order to obtain the release of prisoners, the Pakistani government must admit that Bangladesh was an independent state and had a voice in their fate. Agreement was finally reached among Pakistan, India, and Bangladesh in 1974. After Pakistan formally recognized Bangladesh, clearing the way for it to join the United Nations, all prisoners of war were returned to their homelands.

BANGLADESH. In the first months of Bangladesh's existence as an internationally recognized state, Sheikh Mujibur Rahman virtually embodied its government within himself, much as Muhammad Ali Jinnah had done earlier in Pakistan. He defined his aims for Bangladesh as nationalism, secularism, democracy, and socialism. He soon fixed a lower ceiling on landholdings and nationalized the major properties of the former "twenty-two families," but these steps were too moderate to suit more doctrinairely Marxist socialists, particularly among students and intellectuals. Leaders of one Marxist group were taken into custody after some of their members assassinated some of Sheikh Mujibur's followers in mid-1972. However, most of Sheikh Mujibur's political opponents concentrated on preparing for the elections scheduled for March of 1973 under the new permanent constitution. They attacked him for moving too slowly toward socialism, complaining that the constitution did not establish a genuinely socialist state. They also attacked him for tying Bangladesh too closely to India, as shown by his signing of a mutual defense pact with India and by his agreement to coordinate Bangladesh's economic planning with that of India. Nevertheless, his party won an overwhelming victory at the polls. Clearly, the Islamic sensibilities of most of Bangladesh's people were not unduly offended by Sheikh Mujibur's adoption of a still undefined secularism as one of his four guiding principles, and most of Bangladesh's people continued to be hopeful about the results of the steps taken up to then in the names of nationalism, democracy, and socialism. However, growing unrest among those whose first bouyant hopes were unfulfilled led to a constitutional amendment late in 1973 permitting the declaration of a state of emergency and the assumption by the government of near-dictatorial powers in case of war, external aggression, or internal disturbance.

INDIA. The collapse, first of the Muslim League, then of the parliamentary system, and finally of the federal union itself in Pakistan was not matched by developments in India. In general, the Congress Party continued to hold power at both the state and national levels in India after the enactment of the constitution of 1950. Strong local parties frequently challenged its power, particularly in the south. Opposition parties or coalitions even won local elections, as the Communists and their allies did in Kerala in 1957 and West Bengal in 1967. However, opposition parties rarely won two successive elections. Wherever the Congress lost an election, its leaders moved promptly to regain power by tightening up their own organization, broadening their appeal, and splitting their opposition as much as possible. By the time of the third general election in 1962 it was clear that India was developing a party structure which was neither one-party nor competitive in the Western sense. Instead it was dominated by a mainstream party of consensus which stayed in power by two primary means: keeping factionalism within itself to a minimum, and undercutting opposition parties through a policy of adopting the most constructive features of their programs. The Congress Party's ability to resolve internal conflicts was sorely tested in 1964 when Nehru died after seventeen years as prime minister, and a successor had to be chosen. The test was passed when moderate Lal Bahadur Shastri was selected shortly afterward. When Shastri died in January, 1966, immediately after concluding the Kashmir cease-fire agreement with Ayub Khan, the unity of the Congress was even more sharply tested. However, the party's leadership passed the test again by agreeing to choose as the new prime minister the daughter of Jawaharlal Nehru, Indira Gandhi, a political leader in her own right and one respected in south India as the only important Congress member to leave Delhi to travel through the south during the linguistic riots of the previous year.

Although the Congress majority in the central legislature was diminished in the fourth general election of 1967, and although the Congress came out of that election year with control of only eight of the seventeen state governments, Indira Gandhi survived the subsequent challenge to her leadership by some of the very Congress members who had made her prime minister in 1966. The Congress divided into two wings, one supporting her and one opposing her, and fought out the conflict in the national elections called for 1971. Indira Gandhi's wing won an overwhelming victory, carrying over two-thirds of the seats in the lower house of the federal legislature. Thus she had a free hand to follow through on promises to use the power of the state to provide better credit terms to farmers and other small and medium entrepreneurs, and to end the pensions paid since 1947 to the former princes. The popularity of these measures, and the additional popularity which she gained as a result of India's successful intervention on behalf of Bangladesh, enabled the Congress to capture almost all the sixteen (out of twenty) state governments for which elections were held in 1972.

As part of their strategy for gaining, retaining, or regaining power, Indian politicians in all parties chose their candidates with care. In sensitive areas, caste affiliation often played a role. Sometimes the technique of matching was used, as in pitting Chitpavan Brahmin against Chitpavan Brahmin in Maharashtra; sometimes the technique of opposition was used, as in setting lower-caste Nadar against upper-caste Vellala in Madras. Either technique tended to perpetuate rather than obliterate distinctions made on grounds of caste. Consequently, the politicians were acting in contradiction to the spirit of the Indian constitution, which envisioned a lessening in the individual's consciousness of caste distinctions. (The constitution not only forbade the practice of untouchability; in the hope that caste restrictions would wither away if deprived of legal recognition, it also declared that the state would give no support to the decisions of caste bodies. Still, as private associations, caste bodies could own and manage property, lay down rules of conduct for their members, and fine or expel those who broke the rules. The rules could not be enforced at law, but neither could an outcasted individual seek reinstatement in court.) When India's politicians found caste affiliations useful, caste distinctions took a new lease on life. Although fears of defilement by touch or glance were fading, most people retained a strong distaste for the idea of marrying people from other caste groups or exchanging family visits with them; and in the complicated business of Indian politics, caste-bloc votes were often vitally important.

Despite the part played in Indian politics by caste divisions, India's first five general elections were peaceful. Opposition to the socialist preferences of Congress leaders appeared in the Swatantra Party formed by business leaders. Religious communalism raised its head in parties like the strongly Hindu-oriented Jana Sangh, whose founders sought to return to a caste-based society led by Hindus, somewhat as fundamentalist Islamic groups in the Middle East like the Muslim Brotherhood sought to return to the traditional Muslim-led society with its differentiations between Muslims and dhimmis. Several Marxist parties, ranging from pro-Peking or pro-Moscow to ruggedly independent in attitude, put up local competition which was often effective for a time, particularly in Kerala and West Bengal. Language-centered local-autonomy movements (like the Dravida Munnetra Kazhagam in the Tamil south around Madras) came to dominate some areas and win representation in New Delhi, but through the use of ballots rather than the bullets which Kurdish leaders in Iraq resorted to in order to win representation in Baghdad. Nor could the Congress government use universal military training to counteract local separatism, as Turkey and Iran had done, as long as some caste members still believed the touch of others could be ritually polluting. Nevertheless, the Congress remained firmly in control at the center. Though Congress governments at the state level strengthened Indians' faith in the electoral process by meekly leaving office when defeated at the polls, they also effectively used that process to return themselves to power. One of the most stunning examples was the Congress sweep in West Bengal in 1972, after a decade during which Communist-dominated coalitions of opposition parties had periodically swamped Congress candidates. Still, the willingness of Congress to abide by the results of elections was highly significant for the development of a politically united and stable nation, in which all but the most intransigent of opposition movements would be willing to accept constitutional limitations instead of breaking out in riots, uprisings, and coups d'état. By 1971 even the Jana Sangh was softening enough to declare its acceptance of a secular state as an appropriate framework within which to uphold the ideal of a harmonious society based on the recognition of differences among social groups.

CEYLON (SRI LANKA). A similar willingness to abide by electoral results was shown in Ceylon. The United National Party of Ceylon, which was formed on an avowedly noncommunal basis by D.S. Senanayake of the Ceylon National Congress and which successfully contested the elections of 1946, was weakened by rivalries among his would-be successors after his accidental death in 1952. A rise in the price of rice, and an increase in pro-communal feeling among the Buddhist Sinhalese majority, led to a defeat at the polls in 1956 at the hands of a coalition of pro-Buddhist Sinhalese leaders and members of the small but talented and vocal Marxist groups. Young Buddhist monks took an active part in the campaign, which coincided with the twenty-five-hundredth anniversary of the release of Gautama Buddha from the world. They feared that the secularism of the United National Party and its receptivity to Westernization would damage the prospects of Buddhism in Ceylon. The younger monks' denunciations of the United National Party in their sermons contributed heavily to the party's defeat, though older monks tried to discourage their political activity by remonstrating that such actions showed attachment to the world. Yet the victorious coalition's promotion of Sinhalese interests, and its 1957 expulsion of the British from naval bases on Ceylon, were not enough to satisfy some. A Sinhalese Buddhist zealot assassinated Prime Minister S.W.R.D. Bandaranaike in 1959. New elections continued the coalition government under his widow Sirimavo Bandaranaike, in 1960.

When the time came for elections again, in 1965, a growing uneasiness over Marxist influence led the political activists among the Buddhist monks to shift their support to the United National Party under Senanayake's son Dudley. Somewhat to the amazement of those who expected the Marxists to try to hang onto power at all costs, the Bandaranaike coalition bowed gracefully to the resulting electoral defeat. However, the return of Sirimavo Bandaranaike's coalition to power in the next election of 1970 was followed by a reapportionment of legislative seats which would probably make it harder for the United National Party to repeat its 1965 comeback. The Bandaranaike government also won wide approval for its affirmations of the Buddhist and Sinhalese foundations of the state, which were formally enshrined in the new Sri Lanka constitution of 1972. Nevertheless, the avowedly socialist policies of the Bandaranaike government were not radical enough to suit a number of Ceylonese, who found their lot worsening in both rural and urban areas as population growth pressed ever harder on available resources. In the spring of 1971 a large-scale outbreak of youthful dissidents was quelled only with difficulty. Though the 1972 constitution promised state action for the well-being of all, the translation of those promises into actual jobs, goods, and services was not an easy task. By the end of 1972 the Bandaranaike government felt secure enough to release most of the young people who had been jailed after the 1971 outbreak, but it still had to come to terms with Tamil opposition to its pro-Sinhalese Buddhist policies, as expressed through the newly formed Tamil United Front. In 1973, the funeral of United National Party leader Dudley Senanayake became the occasion for a large-scale but relatively peaceful expression of discontent at the continued slowness of economic development. Shortly afterward, the government sought to muffle criticism by making the country's largest newspaper chain a public corporation, with a close friend of the prime minister's son-in-law as editorial adviser.

ECONOMIC GROWTH

The leaders of South Asia naturally turned much of their attention to economic matters, for they were convinced that their states could hardly survive unless the living standards of their people were raised.

They feared that poverty and unemployment would breed discontent, which might give rise to sufficient political unrest to break up the state. Furthermore, successful nationwide economic development programs could create a nationwide community of interest which would help hold the state together in spite of divisive factors such as linguistic differences, religious differences, and differences between those who prefer new ways and those who cling to the old. Therefore, all the governments of South Asia inaugurated a series of five-year development plans, India in 1951, Sikkim in 1954, Pakistan and Ceylon in 1955, Nepal in 1956, Bhutan in 1961, and Bangladesh in 1973. These plans were designed to promote general economic growth by diversifying the economy so that most people would live by exchanging goods and services rather than by subsistence agriculture. The planners tended to emphasize industrial growth even more than agricultural growth, not only to increase overall production and individual incomes, but also, at least in India and Pakistan, to furnish items to the armed forces. Because economic development was seen as a matter of national concern, government leaders in every state stressed the need for governmental action, rather than complete reliance on private enterprise to give the economy the needed impetus.

The evident need for industry led every South Asian government to favor it. With three-fourths to nine-tenths of the population in the countryside, the number engaged in agriculture was believed by most planners to be too great for efficient farming. In India and Pakistan particularly, planners tended to think that in the long run, agricultural productivity could not be greatly increased until families could move off the land. If jobs could be provided in industry and other urban occupations, more people could earn a living without farming. They might then be more willing to sell their land, so that the myriad tiny scattered plots could be consolidated into larger fields on which better seed and equipment would produce more and better crops with less labor.

By 1960 or so, India, Pakistan, and to some extent Ceylon were finding that industry responded so well to state encouragement that industrial expansion was beginning to be financed by reinvestment of industrial profits, rather than by borrowing from government funds raised through taxes. However, agriculture was growing far more slowly than industry in the three countries. Despite a gradual rise in rural incomes, there was a real danger that their economies would become dual economies, in which urban income levels would be many times higher than rural income levels. Consequently the three governments stepped up the programs for rural development which they had established as they embarked on their first five-year plans.

The rural improvement programs stressed amenities such as improved water supplies and productivity-increasing measures such as the use of improved seeds. They also prompted the building of more and better roads over which villagers and produce could travel to market. Above all they emphasized schools, in which villagers could be introduced to the habits of thought and behavior appropriate to an exchange economy and a modern nation-state. In Nepal, the establishment of the village councils and the class organization for peasants in 1962 signaled rising governmental concern for rural development. However, in Ceylon, not even the evident need for rural workers of all types could induce most of the unemployed urban youth to volunteer for service in the rural areas, even while they were protesting in 1971 and again in 1973 that Ceylon's economic growth was too slow.

Another aspect of rural development was land reform, which included not only the redistribution of large landlord holdings to those who worked them but also the consolidation of small fragmented holdings into larger and more compact units. Until Ayub Khan took control, Pakistan's implementation of both types of land reform was slow by comparison with India, whose less landlord-dominated leaders did not hesitate to use the power of the state to compel the reorganization of landholdings. The states of India, Pakistan, Ceylon, and Nepal all enacted tenant-protection laws between 1947 and 1957. However, implementation of these and other land-reform programs proved to be another matter. Lands held by landlords who fled as refugees when partition came in 1947 could be easily redistributed among former tenants in the Panjab and Bengal, but landlords who stayed in either Pakistan or India proved harder to displace. In both the Indian and the Pakistani Panjab, for example, the number of tenants decreased and the number of owners increased, but landless agricultural laborers increased even faster than landowners. After Bangladesh seceded from Pakistan, both Bhutto and Sheikh Mujibur promised greater attention to land redistribution. In Ceylon, as late as 1971, over half the rural population owned no land at all or less than half an acre, and legislation to restrict the size of private landholdings was not approved until 1972. Even then, foreign-owned plantations were specifically exempted. When food shortages led in 1973 to a government decree permitting public control of all cultivable land, only land not currently in use was actually taken over for redistribution by the land reform commission. The commission encouraged the establishment of cooperative farms. In Nepal, where the emphasis shifted from land redistribution to provision of better rural credit facilities in 1965, there was little change in the number or size of landholdings. Everywhere in South Asia there was resistance to the consolidation of small holdings as long as subsistence agriculture still dominated. Families continued to want pieces of several kinds of crop land to supply their own needs, rather than thinking in terms of concentrating on one piece of land to grow one type of crop for the market.

India made the greatest gains in industrialization in the first years of independence, for India had by far the largest industrial base with which to begin. Indian planners also relied far more heavily from the start on government management. A number of private Indian financiers and industrialists claimed that the Indian economy would have moved even faster if the Indian government had concentrated on expanding transport and communications facilities, public utilities, and educational opportunities, rather than competing with private enterprise. Whether this was correct for India or not, industry in Pakistan grew rapidly during the first and second five-year plan periods, and the Pakistani government took little part in managing industries outside the fields of armament and national defense. Progress during the third plan period was not so dramatic. In particular, resentment at the failure of private industry to meet the needs felt by people in the eastern wing contributed strongly to the establishment of Bangladesh. The new state promptly declared its intention of nationalizing basic transport, industrial, and banking facilities, so that future industrialization would be directed more toward benefiting society at large. In the west, too, the new Pakistan government declared its intention of forcing managerial reforms, for the scandal of the "twenty-two families" had bitten deeply into people's minds. Large-scale nationalization began in 1974. Both Bangladesh and Pakistan used Islamic teachings on social justice to justify their movement toward public management, much as many Middle Eastern governments had done in earlier years. Elsewhere in South Asia, the government of Ceylon had already moved toward nationalization of industries during the first Bandaranaike period, taking over transport, banking, insurance, and petroleum facilities between 1958 and 1964. The government of Nepal, on the other hand, provided credit and utilities services for private (mostly foreign) industrial investors, rather than trying to establish factories itself.

Economic development in the states of South Asia was aided by funds from many sources. The first steps toward international cooperation to promote economic growth in South and Southeast Asia were taken at the meeting of Commonwealth representatives at Colombo, Ceylon, in 1950, that established the Colombo plan. The plan brought together governments which could offer personnel, tools, and money, and governments which had plans for putting personnel, tools, and money to work. The states of South Asia received and gave aid through international agencies, such as the United Nations with its Economic Council for Asia and the Far East, the International Bank for Reconstruction and Development, and, after its formation in 1966, the Asian Development Bank. Both through these multimember agencies and through more direct arrangements, the states of South Asia received assistance from Britain and other Commonwealth members, the United States, western

European states, and, after 1955, the Soviet Union and its eastern European allies. Between 1958 and 1961 the People's Republic of China tried to undercut the competing influences of the West, the Soviet Union, and even India by giving aid to Ceylon, Pakistan, and Nepal. These various sources of aid were vital, for in all the newly independent states of South Asia, many items which were needed for efficient use of resources (such as elaborate machine tools or complex chemical compounds) had to be purchased abroad. Since none of these states yet had the capacity to produce enough export items to pay for all the imports they needed to build their economies, much of the aid went to purchase imports which helped to increase total production more rapidly than would otherwise have been possible.

The easiest form of aid for a recipient government to use was the simple grant. However, most international agencies could not afford to make grants without expectation of repayment; few donor governments were prepared to ask their taxpayers to support any sizable program of aid based on grants; and few recipient governments—whether in South Asia or in any other region of the world—were willing to be placed in the position of receiving an outright gift from a powerful donor state, which might seem to obligate them to support its international policy or give special consideration to its nationals. Consequently, both recipients and donors tended to prefer loan arrangements, which required repayment, rather than grants which did not need to be repaid. No-interest, low-interest, and even regular-interest "soft" loans—loans which could be repaid in the recipient's currency—were generally regarded at first as easier for recipients to handle than "hard" loans which had to be repaid in an internationally accepted currency like the dollar or the pound sterling. Barter agreements, by which the donor was bound to accept stated amounts of a recipient's products in return for stated amounts of machinery or other goods and services from the donor, were also regarded favorably by recipients at first. Yet not many donor states outside the Communist group were willing to engage in them, and some recipients complained after a few years that the goods received were not always of the quality desired.

Most donor states and international agencies were reluctant to make many soft loans because they would then have to find means of using the repayment installments within the recipient country. After a few years, some recipient countries which received large amounts of aid, like India, also began to question the long-range effects of soft loans and of programs like United States Public Law 480, under which surplus grain was sent from the United States to the recipient country to be sold (at low prices, to ease local food shortages) for local currency which in turn was to be used locally. As more and more local currency came to be held by foreign donors, recipient governments began to be concerned over their loss of control over their own currency supply. Some even began to fear that a donor state which might wish to manipulate a recipient state's economy could use large holdings of the recipient's currency to do so. As a result, recipients came to regard loans and grants from international agencies as far more acceptable than loans and grants from individual states. They also began to negotiate hard loans whenever the proposed project appeared likely enough to lead to an increase in export capacity so that the installments on the hard loan could be met. Though aid continued to be generally regarded as necessary to rapid economic growth, recipient governments, donor states, and international agencies remained wary about the forms it took. The financial difficulties experienced by Middle Eastern states in the late nineteenth century, as a result of taking out too many hard loans (the only kind then available) for projects and purposes which made too little contribution to export capacity to make repayment possible, were all too well remembered in capitals around the world.

The complexities of protecting financial independence while seeking needed aid may be illustrated by India. In 1973, India negotiated an agreement with the United States on the return of Public Law 480 funds to Indian control. In 1974, India entered agreements with Iran, which was already aiding Afghanistan and Pakistan, by which India would send technical personnel to help with Iranian development plans while Iran sold oil to India on unusually easy terms. India had learned from experience the advisability of working out mutually acceptable exchanges, in preference to loans or to purchasing large amounts of foreign products with Indian currency.

Both the recipients and the donors of foreign aid in South Asia have expected that total production will eventually be large enough so that the people of the region can afford to buy all the imports they need, without recourse to grants, barter agreements, and soft loans. However, that time is unlikely to arrive soon unless rates of population growth drop sharply. As long as the population of any relatively poor country continues to grow rapidly, most of any increase in industrial and agricultural output must go into merely keeping people alive, and little is left to invest in productive enterprise or to use to improve living and working conditions. The Indian, Pakistani, Bangladesh, and Ceylonese governments have actively encouraged parents to limit the size of their families, but these efforts are unlikely to succeed until experience convinces people that most children really will reach maturity. This is especially true in India, since Hindus generally believe every man should have at least one son to succeed him. Furthermore, the rapid increase in life expectancy as public health services expand means that the adult population is growing, as more adults live into their forties, fifties, and sixties. Between 1891 and 1961 the total population of South Asia nearly tripled.

Scarcely any leveling-off was yet in sight in the 1970s, to the dismay of economic planners.

ALTERATIONS IN SOCIAL PATTERNS

In South Asia, as elsewhere, there have been close links between patterns of social behavior and programs for industrialization and rural development. The caste system, which provided for division of labor in a subsistence economy, has obstructed the facility of movement appropriate to an exchange economy. This was one of the reasons the Indian government refused to uphold caste restrictions and insisted that all individuals be given equal treatment regardless of caste, creed, or sex. Equalization before the law was justified by appealing to respect for individual dignity. A certain form of respect for individual dignity was inherent in the caste system, insofar as it assumed that each member of each caste group had his or her proper and essential role in society. Indian leaders strove diligently to build new equalitarian attitudes on that foundation. Though Pakistan, Ceylon, and Nepal were less affected by the workings of the caste system than was India, they also found it advisable to take steps to ensure the legal equality of all citizens, women as well as men.

Despite Fatima Jinnah's 1964 campaign for the presidency, Pakistani women were generally less active in public life than Indian women were. Women played important parts in the pre-independence Indian National Congress, and after 1947 Indian women continued to enlarge their position in the community, taking part in rural development programs, voting in elections, entering industry and the professions, and acquiring greater personal freedom than they had had since the time of the Aryan conquest. The selection of Indira Gandhi as prime minister in 1966, dramatic though it was, was only one of a multitude of individual breaches made in the ancient but crumbling walls of restriction. India's women were assisted by the enactment of federal statutes governing marriage and inheritance, but otherwise they had to depend primarily on their own efforts. In Ceylon, too, the selection of a woman as prime minister demonstrated that the legal and political equality of women was not merely fictional. Though women in Nepal did not yet have full legal equality with men as the 1970s opened, the new legal code promulgated by the king in 1963 gave them rights of inheritance and divorce which they had not previously had.

Indian women were freer to venture into public life partly because of the introduction of factory industry, in which women as well as men could find employment. Even before 1900, the rise of factories in India was presenting problems associated with urbanization: poor sanitation, overcrowded housing, broken family ties, and unemployment—which meant people were available to take part in mass demonstrations (with or without a small payment from demonstration organizers) and perhaps even do a little looting at the expense of those against whom the demonstration was directed. Pakistan and Ceylon began to experience similar problems in the 1950s, but industrialization both there and in India was accompanied by increased personal freedom for both men and women.

In the countrysides of India, Pakistan, Bangladesh, Ceylon, and Nepal, the gradual replacement of a subsistence economy by an exchange economy and the slow but steady improvement of transportation facilities lessened the risk of famine in any given area. It also began to tie village levels of living to prices in world markets. Prior to World War I, the general standard of rural life in most of South Asia was probably rising, but then a decline set in, largely because increases in rural population were not matched by increases in agricultural productivity per worker. Not until after independence was the downward trend reversed by the renewal of work on transportation networks, irrigation systems, and other facilities which enabled villagers to produce more goods and exchange them more readily for the goods produced by others. In the late 1960s, the introduction of new strains of high-yield rice and other seeds promised a "green revolution" which Indians hoped would make their country self-sufficient in food grains, and which other South Asians also anticipated would improve their agricultural productivity. However, only the few cultivators who had moved from subsistence to commercial farming benefited from the new seeds at first. Growing worldwide energy shortages, which made it increasingly difficult for the poorer nations either to manufacture or to import needed fertilizers and insecticides, also hampered the spread of the "green revolution."

HINDRANCES AND SPURS TO CHANGE

The changes which took place in the cities and villages of South Asia between 1750 and 1950 were profound. The ties of the joint family were stretched, though not entirely broken, as individuals accepted the Western-inspired idea that they ought to recognize the worth of economic and political units other than those bounded by kinship and religion, and began to place the welfare of fellow-workers and fellow-nationals above the demands of relatives and coreligionists for positions and perquisites. The workings of the caste system were modified by the impracticability of maintaining customary restrictions on physical contact between members of different caste groups in an age of railroads, buses, and factories. (Still, most public eating places in India continued to employ Brahmin cooks because food prepared by a Brahmin could not contaminate anyone in a ritual sense.) Yet caste affiliations did not lose meaning after independence. Recognition of the value of caste solidarity in political maneuvering maintained a consciousness of caste affiliation, strengthening distinctions between caste groups although not necessarily increasing the restrictions on their members. Furthermore, caste groups continued to seek higher status by adopting restrictions associated with higher groups. The attempt of untouchable groups to rise in the social scale by emulating upper-caste behavior increased the restrictions on their members' personal liberty at the same time that the legal abolition of untouchability and the practical difficulties of maintaining it were decreasing the external limitations on their freedom of action. Simultaneously, the scholarships and other privileges given by the Indian government to the former untouchables and other disadvantaged groups put low social status at something of a premium. In some caste groups this led to a struggle and even an outright division into two formally separate groups between those who wanted to Sanskritize, or seek higher status, and those to whom government benefits made continued low status attractive.

The features of the caste system associated with ritual-pollution concepts declined measurably from 1850 to 1950, and even more sharply thereafter. Nevertheless, throughout mainland South Asia the overall level of religious activity tended to rise rather than to fall. The building of railroads enabled pilgrims to travel to the shrines of Hinduism in far greater numbers than ever before, while the followers of Raja Ram Mohan Roy, Dayananda, and Vivekananda used the printing press as well as personal preaching to encourage deepened devotion among their fellow-Hindus. In Ceylon, the growth of religious schools promoted a rise in communal feeling among members of all faiths.

In response to British conquest and Hindu resurgence in India, Muslims clung fervently to their faith. However, their fervor often seemed directed toward Islam as a mark of separateness from the Hindus they had once ruled, rather than as a religion with a positive content of its own. The Muslims' insistence that they were distinct from their former Hindu subjects helped account for the difference in Muslim and Hindu responses to British rule. The Hindus had long been accustomed to maintaining their separateness from Muslim overlords who paid little heed to their ideas on philosophy or public affairs. In the ten centuries from the Arab invasion of Sind to the British seizure of Bengal, Hindus learned to work with rulers of an alien faith and outlook. However, the Muslims had only been conquered by other Muslims. Consequently Muslims in British-ruled India found it as hard to accept defeat at British hands as did their brethren in the Middle East. In fact, Muslims in India displayed the same tendencies toward militarism and negative nationalism as other Muslims undergoing comparable experiences, to say nothing of the same mixture of pan-Islamic ideas, activism, and attempts to purify and reinterpret the Islamic tradition. They often deliberately sought out connections with the Muslim Middle East (as in the Khilafat movement of the decade up to 1924) in an effort to assert their Islamic nature. Pakistan's post-1971 turn toward Iran reflected this continuing desire for Islamic identification, as well as a recognition of common concern over the friendship of Afghanistan, India, and the Soviet Union. On the other hand, the Hindus of India acquired a self-confidence which enabled them to study Western thought without rancor, for the Hindus found that the linguistic relationships between the language of their scriptures and the tongues of Europe made the scholars of the West accept them as kin.

Only a few Hindus like Raja Ram Mohan Roy were deeply affected by Western ideas at first, but their numbers grew with every generation, until the vast majority of independent India's leaders were convinced that every aspect of Indian life had to be reshaped to make room for ideas and practices learned from the West. Even the rising young leaders in the states of India, who emphasized the importance of local traditions, were seeking to spread the benefits of industrialization and universal education to larger numbers, not to halt modernization. In Ceylon, the opposition displayed by Sinhalese Buddhist leaders to secularism and Western alliances was accompanied by the desire for extension of educational and economic advantages to a larger percentage of the people. The same desire fueled the uprisings which plagued the Bandaranaike government in 1971 and led to the establishment of the Sri Lanka constitution in 1972. In Nepal, Sikkim, and Bhutan, the number of modernly educated leaders was still small by comparison with Ceylon or India; but they too shared the desire for educational and economic advances along modern lines.

The commitment to a modern society which was made by Muslim leaders in the regions that became Pakistan and then divided into Pakistan and Bangladesh was as fervent as that of their counterparts in India or Ceylon. However, they had not yet reconciled those concepts with Islamic thought as well as Indian and Ceylonese leaders had integrated them with Hindu and Buddhist philosophy. The Muslims had no Raja Ram Mohan Roy, and no Jamal ad-Din al-Afghani or Muhammad Abdu. Even Sayyid Ahmad Khan had stressed European contributions in just a few fields of endeavor and had kept Quranic studies separate from Western learning in the university he founded. Only with the rise of Zulfikar Ali Bhutto and Sheikh Mujibur Rahman, each of whom sought to integrate the social teachings of Islam with the social teachings of Marxism in a blend which owed much to formulations of Arab socialism in lands like Egypt and Tunisia, did the calls of the poet Muhammad Iqbal for development of both self and society within an Islamic framework appear to be leading to a usable blend of Islamic belief and modernizing practice.

Still another problem faced by leaders in all the states of South

Asia stemmed from the reverence traditionally paid to the learned in every South Asian society, and from the expectation (which tended to accompany that reverence) that the learned would live by overseeing the labors of others rather than by working themselves. Rural-development programs in particular were hampered by the all-too-common tendency of well-educated government officers to order rather than to persuade and to describe in words rather than to demonstrate in action, when working with largely illiterate villagers. Few young college graduates were willing to leave the towns and cities for rural service, even though the need was desperate. For one thing, their education was still largely a literary one, which gave them little of the practical training needed for truly effective service. For another, the villages offered them few amenities or amusements. Efforts were made to enlist paid volunteers for definite terms as schoolteachers and village workers, but in India, Pakistan, and Bangladesh, as in Ceylon, the results were not highly encouraging.

Under British rule the peoples of South Asia had developed an increasing individual and corporate self-awareness, in response to British encouragement of two concepts deeply rooted in Western experience: the worth of the individual, and the value of the corporate life of the nation of which the individual is a part. The idea of the individual as a permanent entity, which underlay Western beliefs concerning human dignity, was absent in Hinduism and Buddhism. Yet Hindu and Buddhist belief in the equal impermanence of all individuals proved to be as compatible with equalitarian doctrine as Muslim concepts of the soul. The experience of economic and political unification, which led western Europeans to consider the nation-state the most important social unit to which they belonged, was new to the peoples of South Asia, but the farther it progressed, the more likely it was to reach eventual fruition in integrated nation-states.

Where corporate self-awareness became directed toward the geographic unit as the home of the nation, it heralded the unity sought by the Indian National Congress or the Ceylon National Congress. Where it became directed toward those who shared the same religion or language, it bred divisive sentiments whose strength was shown both in the formation and in the division of Pakistan, in the realignment of the states of India along linguistic lines, and in the course of Ceylonese politics. The full ramifications of the rise in corporate self-awareness are still undiscerned, but one thing seems sure. In a world in which the expansion of literacy and growth of mass media are broadening people's opportunities to learn about each other, the national, religious, and linguistic self-awareness of South Asians is likely to increase, no matter how much this may distress those who still hold the traditional Hindu and Buddhist belief that all self-awareness, corporate or individual, is only maya, illusion.

Suggested Readings

Books available in paperback are marked with an asterisk.

South Asia

BAILEY, FREDERICK G. *Tribe, Caste and Nation.* Manchester: Manchester University Press, 1960.

BROWN, W. NORMAN. *India, Pakistan, Ceylon,* rev. ed. Philadelphia: University of Pennsylvania Press, 1964.

*———. *The United States and India, Pakistan, Bangladesh,* rev. and enlarged. Cambridge: Harvard University Press, 1973.

DUMONT, LOUIS. *Homo Hierarchus: The Caste System and Its Implications,* trans. Mark Salisbury. Chicago: University of Chicago Press, 1970.

HARPER, EDWARD B., ed. *Religion in South Asia.* Seattle: University of Washington Press, 1964.

HUTTON, J.H. *Caste in India,* 4th ed. London: Oxford University Press, 1963.

*LEACH, E.R., ed. *Aspects of Caste in South India, Ceylon and Northwest Pakistan.* London: Cambridge University Press, 1960.

MADDISON, ANGUS. *Class Structure and Economic Growth: India and Pakistan Since the Moghuls.* New York: W. W. Norton, 1971.

*MANDELBAUM, DAVID G. *Society in India,* 2 vols. Berkeley: University of California Press, 1970.

*MARRIOTT, McKIM, ed. *Village India: Studies in the Little Community.* Chicago: University of Chicago Press, 1955.

*MASON, PHILIP, ed. *India and Ceylon: Unity and Diversity.* London: Oxford University Press, 1967.

*MAYER, A.C. *Caste and Kinship in Central India: A Village and Its Region.* Berkeley: University of California Press, 1965.

MISRA, B.B. *The Indian Middle Classes.* London: Oxford University Press, 1961.

MUNSTERBERG, HUGO. *Art of India and Southeast Asia.* New York: Abrams, 1970.

*SMITH, DONALD E., ed. *South Asian Politics and Religion.* Princeton, N.J.: Princeton University Press, 1966.

*SPATE, O.H.K. *India and Pakistan: A General and Regional Geography,* 3rd ed., rev. London: Methuen Press, 1967. (Paperback. New York: Barnes and Noble.)

*———. *India and Pakistan: Land, People and Economy.* New York: Barnes and Noble, 1972.

SRINIVAS, M.N. *Caste in Modern India, and Other Essays.* Bombay: Asia Publishing House, 1962.

*———. *Social Change in Modern India.* Berkeley: University of California Press, 1966.

TINKER, HUGH. *The Foundations of Local Self-Government in India, Pakistan and Burma.* New York: Praeger, 1968.

———. *India and Pakistan: A Political Analysis.* London: Pall Mall, 1967.

WILCOX, WAYNE A. *India, Pakistan, and the Rise of China.* New York: Walker, 1964.

*WISER, W. and C. *Behind Mud Walls, 1930–1960,* rev. ed., with 1970 supplement. Berkeley: University of California Press, 1972.

Pre-Independence India

TO MODERN PERIOD

AHMAD, AZIZ. *An Intellectual History of Islam in India.* Edinburgh: Edinburgh University Press, 1969.

Alberuni's India, trans. E.C. Sachau, abr. ed., ed. by Ainslie T. Embree. New York: Norton, 1971.

ALLAN, JOHN, et al. *The Cambridge Shorter History of India,* ed. by H.H. Dodwell. Delhi: Chand, 1969.

*BASHAM, A.L. *The Wonder That Was India,* 3rd rev. ed. London: Sidgwick and Jackson, 1967. (Paperback. New York: Grove Press.)

*BROWN, DONALD M. *The White Umbrella: Indian Political Thought from Manu to Gandhi.* Berkeley: University of California Press, 1958.

*BROWN, W. NORMAN. *Man in the Universe: Some Continuities in Indian Thought.* Berkeley: University of California Press, 1966.

*CONZE, EDWARD. *Buddhism: Its Essence and Development.* New York: Harper and Row, 1965.

*DEBARY, W. THEODORE, et al., comps. *Sources of Indian Tradition,* new ed. New York: Columbia University Press, 1964.

DREKMEIER, CHARLES. *Kingship and Community in Early India.* Stanford, Calif.: Stanford University Press, 1962.

EDWARDES, S.M., and H.L.O. GARRETT. *Mughal Rule in India.* London: Oxford University Press, 1962.

IKRAM, S.M. *Muslim Civilization in India,* Ainslie T. Embree, ed. New York: Columbia University Press, 1969.

KARVE, IRAWATI. *Hindu Society: A New Interpretation.* Berkeley: University of California Press, 1960.

MAJUMDAR, RAMESH-CHANDRA, et al. *An Advanced History of India,* 3rd ed. London: Macmillan; New York: St. Martin's Press, 1967.

METCALF, THOMAS R., ed. *Modern India: An Interpretive Anthology.* New York: Macmillan, 1971.

*MOORE, CHARLES A., ed. *The Indian Mind.* Honolulu: East-West Center Press, 1967. (Paperback. University Press of Hawaii.)

MORELAND, W.H., and A.C. CHATTERJEE. *A Short History of India,* 4th ed. London: Longmans, 1957.

*Nehru, Jawaharlal. *The Discovery of India,* 2nd ed. New York: John Day, 1947. (Paperback. Garden City, N.Y.: Doubleday.)

Nilakanta Sastri, K.A. *History of India,* 3 vols. Madras: S. Viswanathan, 1950–1952.

——. *A History of South India,* 3rd ed. London: Oxford University Press, 1966.

*Panikkar, K.M. *A Survey of Indian History,* 4th ed. Bombay: Asia Publishing House, 1966.

Qureshi, I.H. *The Muslim Community of the Indo-Pakistan Sub-Continent, 610–1947: A Brief Historical Analysis.* The Hague: Mouton, 1962.

*Rawlinson, Hugh. *India: A Short Cultural History,* rev. ed. London: Cresset Press, 1948. (Paperback. New York: Praeger.)

*Spear, Percival. *A History of India,* Vol. II. Baltimore: Penguin, 1966.

——. *India: A Modern History,* rev. ed. Ann Arbor: University of Michigan Press, 1961.

Spellman, John W. *Political Theory of Ancient India.* London: Clarendon, 1964.

The Song of God: Bhagavad-Gita, trans. and interpreted by Franklin Edgerton. New York: Harper & Row, 1964.

*Thapar, Romila. *A History of India,* Vol. I. Baltimore: Penguin, 1968.

*Wheeler, Sir R.E. Mortimer. *The Indus Civilization,* 3rd ed. London: Cambridge University Press, 1968.

MODERN PERIOD

Ahmad, Aziz. *Islamic Modernism in India and Pakistan, 1857–1964.* London: Oxford University Press, 1967.

*Bondurant, Joan V. *Conquest of Violence: The Gandhian Philosophy of Conflict,* rev. ed. Berkeley: University of California Press, 1965.

Bose, N.S. *The Indian Awakening and Bengal.* Calcutta: Firma K.L. Mukhopadhyay, 1960.

*Brecher, Michael. *Nehru: A Political Biography,* abr. ed. Boston: Beacon Press, 1962.

——. *The Struggle for Kashmir.* New York: Oxford University Press, 1953.

*Brown, Donald M. *The Nationalist Movement: Indian Political Thought from Ranade to Bhave.* Berkeley: University of California Press, 1965.

Brown, Judith M. *Gandhi's Rise to Power.* London: Cambridge University Press, 1972.

*Chaudhuri, N. *Autobiography of an Unknown Indian.* Berkeley: University of California Press, 1968.

Cohn, B.S. *The Development and Impact of British Administration in India.* New Delhi: Indian Institute of Public Administration, 1961.

Edwardes, Michael. *Nehru: A Political Biography.* New York: Praeger, 1971.

*Erikson, Erik H. *Gandhi's Truth.* New York: Norton, 1969.

*Fischer, Louis. *The Life of Mahatma Gandhi.* New York: Harper & Row, 1950. (Paperback. New York: Macmillan.)

*——, ed. *The Essential Gandhi: An Anthology.* New York: Random House, 1962.

*GANDHI, MOHANDAS K. *Autobiography: The Story of My Experiments With Truth*, trans. by Mahadev Desai. Washington, D.C.: Public Affairs Press, 1954. (Paperback. Boston: Beacon Press.)

GILLION, KENNETH L. *Ahmedabad: A Study in Indian Urban History.* Berkeley: University of California Press, 1968.

*HARDY, P. *The Muslims of British India.* Cambridge: Cambridge University Press, 1972.

HEIMSATH, CHARLES H. *Indian Nationalism and Hindu Social Reform.* Princeton, N.J.: Princeton University Press, 1964.

IQBAL, SIR MUHAMMAD. *Poems from Iqbal*, trans. by V.G. Kiernan. London: J. Murray, 1955.

KABIR, HUMAYUN, ed. *Green and Gold: Stories and Poems from Bengal.* New York: New Directions, 1959.

KUMAR, R., ed. *Essays on Gandhian Politics: The Rowlatt Satyagraha of 1919.* Oxford: Clarendon Press, 1971.

McCULLY, BRUCE T. *English Education and the Origins of Indian Nationalism.* Gloucester, Mass.: P. Smith, 1966.

METCALF, THOMAS R. *The Aftermath of Revolt: India, 1857–1870.* Princeton, N.J.: Princeton University Press, 1964.

MISRA, B.B. *The Administrative History of India, 1834–1947.* Bombay: Oxford University Press, 1970.

*NANDA, B.R. *The Nehrus, Motilal and Jawaharlal.* London: G. Allen and Unwin, 1962. (Paperback. Chicago: University of Chicago Press.)

O'MALLEY, L.S.S., ed. *Modern India and the West.* London: Oxford University Press, 1968.

ROBERTS, PAUL E. *History of British India Under the Company and the Crown*, 3rd ed. London: Oxford University Press, 1958.

SAYEED, KHALID B. *Pakistan: The Formative Phase, 1857–1948*, 2nd ed. London: Oxford University Press, 1968.

*SEAL, ANIL. *The Emergence of Indian Nationalism.* London: Cambridge University Press, 1968.

SHILS, EDWARD. *The Intellectual Between Tradition and Modernity: The Indian Situation.* The Hague: Mouton, 1961.

SINGH, HIRA LAL. *Problems and Policies of the British in India, 1885–1898.* Bombay: Asia Publishing House, 1963.

STOKES, ERIC. *The English Utilitarians and India.* London: Oxford University Press, 1969.

*TANDON, PRAKESH. *Punjabi Century, 1857–1947.* Berkeley: University of California Press, 1968.

THOMPSON, E.J., and G.T. GARRATT. *Rise and Fulfillment of British Rule in India.* London: Macmillan, 1934.

WOLPERT, STANLEY A. *Tilak and Gokhale: Revolution and Reform in the Making of Modern India.* Berkeley: University of California Press, 1962.

Independent India

BHATIA, KRISHAN. *The Ordeal of Nationhood: A Social Study of India Since Independence, 1947–1970.* New York: Antheneum, 1971.

*Embree, Ainslie T. *India's Search for National Identity.* New York: Knopf, 1972.

Franda, Marcus F. *Radical Politics in West Bengal.* Cambridge: MIT Press, 1971.

Harrison, Selig S. *India: The Most Dangerous Decades.* Princeton, N.J.: Princeton University Press, 1960.

Hunter, Guy. *The Administration of Agricultural Development: Lessons from India.* London: Oxford University Press, 1970.

Kochanek, Stanley A. *The Congress Party of India: The Dynamics of One-Party Democracy.* Princeton, N.J.: Princeton University Press, 1968.

Lamb, Alastair. *The China-India Border.* London: Oxford University Press, 1964.

Mahar, J. Michael, ed. *The Untouchables in Contemporary India.* Tucson: University of Arizona Press, 1972.

Malenbaum, Wilfred. *Prospects for Indian Development.* New York: Free Press, 1962.

*Maxwell, Neville. *India's China War.* London: Cape, 1970. (Paperback. New York: Doubleday.)

Menon, V.P. *The Story of the Integration of the Indian States.* New York: Macmillan, 1956.

———. *The Transfer of Power in India.* Princeton, N.J.: Princeton University Press, 1957.

Murphy, Gardner. *In the Minds of Men.* New York: Basic Books, 1955.

*Palmer, Norman D. *The Indian Political System,* 2nd ed. Boston: Houghton-Mifflin, 1971.

*Park, Richard L. *India's Political System.* Englewood Cliffs, N.J.: Prentice-Hall, 1968.

Park, Richard L., and Irene Tinker, eds. *Leadership and Political Institutions in India.* Princeton, N.J.: Princeton University Press, 1959.

Patterson, G.N. *Peking Versus Delhi.* London: Faber and Faber, 1963.

*Rudolph, L.I. and S.H. *The Modernity of Tradition: Political Development in India.* Chicago: University of Chicago Press, 1967.

Rudolph, S.H. and L.I., eds. *Education and Politics in India.* Cambridge: Harvard University Press, 1972.

*Smith, Donald E. *India as a Secular State.* Princeton, N.J.: Princeton University Press, 1963.

Stern, Robert W. *The Process of Opposition in India.* Chicago: University of Chicago Press, 1970.

Tandon, Prakesh. *Beyond Punjab: A Sequel to Punjabi Century.* Berkeley: University of California Press, 1971.

*Tyson, Geoffrey. *Nehru: The Years of Power.* New York: Praeger, 1966.

Verba, Sidney, et al. *Caste, Race and Politics: A Comparative Study of India and the United States.* Beverly Hills, Calif.: Sage, 1971.

Weiner, Myron. *The Politics of Scarcity: Public Pressure and Political Response in India.* Chicago: University of Chicago Press, 1962.

———, ed. *State Politics in India.* Princeton, N.J.: Princeton University Press, 1968.

Independent Pakistan

AYUB KHAN, MUHAMMAD. *Friends Not Masters: A Political Autobiography.* London: Oxford University Press, 1968.

BHUTTO, ZULFIKAR ALI. *The Myth of Independence.* London: Oxford University Press, 1969.

BINDER, LEONARD. *Religion and Politics in Pakistan.* Berkeley: University of California Press, 1961.

CALLARD, KEITH. *Pakistan: A Political Study.* London: G. Allen and Unwin, 1957.

———. *Political Forces in Pakistan, 1947–1959.* New York: Institute of Pacific Relations, 1959.

FELDMAN, HERBERT. *From Crisis to Crisis: Pakistan, 1962–1969.* New York: Oxford University Press, 1972.

JAHAN, ROUNAQ. *Pakistan: Failure in National Integration.* New York: Columbia University Press, 1972.

PAPANEK, GUSTAV F. *Pakistan's Development: Social Goals and Private Incentives.* Cambridge: Harvard University Press, 1967.

SAYEED, KHALID B. *The Political System of Pakistan.* Boston: Houghton Mifflin, 1967.

WHEELER, RICHARD S. *The Politics of Pakistan: A Constitutional Quest.* Ithaca, N.Y.: Cornell University Press, 1970.

*WILCOX, WAYNE A. *Pakistan: The Consolidation of a Nation.* New York: Columbia University Press, 1963.

ZIRING, LAWRENCE. *The Ayub Khan Era: Politics in Pakistan, 1958–1969.* Syracuse, N.Y.: Syracuse University Press, 1971.

Independent Bangladesh

NICHOLS, MARTA R., and PHILIP OLDENBURG. *Bangladesh: The Birth of a Nation*, ed. by Ward Morehouse. Thompson: Interculture Associates, 1973.

Ceylon

*ARASARATNAM, S. *Ceylon.* Englewood Cliffs, N.J.: Prentice-Hall, 1964.

JAYAWARDENA, VISAKHA KUMARI. *The Rise of the Labor Movement in Ceylon.* Durham, N.C.: Duke University Press, 1972.

KEARNEY, ROBERT N. *The Politics of Ceylon.* Ithaca, N.Y.: Cornell University Press, 1973.

LUDOWYK, E.F.C. *The Modern History of Ceylon.* London: Weidenfeld & Nicholson, 1966.

RYAN, BRYCE. *Caste in Modern Ceylon.* New Brunswick, N.J.: Rutgers University Press, 1953.

WRIGGINS, WILLIAM H. *Ceylon: Dilemmas of a New Nation.* Princeton, N.J.: Princeton University Press, 1960.

Himalayan States

CHAUHAN, R.S. *The Political Development in Nepal, 1950–1970.* New York: Barnes and Noble, 1972.

COELHO, U.H. *Sikkim and Bhutan.* New York: Barnes and Noble, 1972.

JOSHI, B.L., and L.E. ROSE. *Democratic Innovations in Nepal.* Berkeley: University of California Press, 1966.

*KARAN, PRADYUMNA P., and W.M. JENKINS, JR. *The Himalayan Kingdoms: Bhutan, Sikkim and Nepal.* Princeton, N.J.: Van Nostrand, Reinhold, 1963.

ROSE, LEO E., and MARGARET W. FISHER. *The Politics of Nepal.* Ithaca, N.Y.: Cornell University Press, 1970.

Additional suggestions may be found in the following works and in the bibliographies listed therein:

American Universities Field Staff. *A Select Bibliography: Asia, Africa, Eastern Europe, Latin America.* New York: American University Field Staff, 1960, with supplements 1961, 1963, 1965.

JACOB, LOUIS A., et al. *South Asia: A Bibliography for Undergraduate Libraries.* Williamsport: Bro-Dart Publishing Company, 1970.

*MAHAR, J. MICHAEL. *India: A Critical Bibliography.* Tucson: University of Arizona Press, 1966.

PART THREE

EAST ASIA

6

THE FOUNDATIONS OF EAST ASIA

Geographic Foundations: Regions and Resources

MOUNTAINS AND PLAINS

Like the terms "Middle East" and "South Asia," the term "East Asia" and the older term "Far East" which it is gradually replacing may be interpreted in several ways. East Asia may refer to all of Asia east of the Himalayas and the Assam and Burma hills; it may mean the region east of India and south of Siberia; or it may indicate, as it does here, the region east of India, south of Siberia, and north of the eastward extension of the Himalayas. That region presently includes the Republics of China and Korea, the People's Republics of China, Korea, and Mongolia, and the constitutional monarchy of Japan. The peoples of China, Korea, Mongolia, and Japan differ in many ways, but a common inheritance from the Chinese past binds them together as effectively as the Islamic heritage unites the divergent peoples of the Middle East.

The extensive mountains and deserts which separate East Asia from the rest of Asia form a cultural as well as a geographic boundary. Although Chinese civilization has deeply affected Southeast Asia, the peoples of that region have also been profoundly influenced by centuries of intellectual and commercial intercourse with the trading states of India. This differentiates them markedly from the Japanese, the Koreans, and the peoples of China's northern and western borderlands, all of whom have historically been much more closely related to the Chinese world than to any other.

East Asia is separated from the states of South Asia by the Himalayas, which rise southeast of the Pamirs, the "Roof of the World" in the center of Asia. The Himalayas form the southern border of the plateau of Tibet, which is bounded on the north by the Altyn Tagh and Kun Lun ranges. The eastern extensions of the Altyn Tagh and the Kun Lun, in the Nan Shan and Tsing Ling ranges, form the dividing line between northern and southern China. East of Tibet, the high Szechwan and Yunnan plateaus lie between the Tsing Ling and the steep-sided mountains and hills—eastern extensions of the Himalayas—that divide China from Southeast Asia; and east of Szechwan and Yunnan lie the basins of the T'ung-t'ing and P'o-yang lakes and the valleys and coastal plains of south China.

These mountains and basins are part of a complicated network that sprawls eastward from the Pamirs to the Pacific. To the north of the Kun Lun and the Altyn Tagh lies the Tarim basin, whose northern border is the Tien Shan range. Both the Tarim basin and the Dzungarian basin, which lies between the Tien Shan and the Altai range, have long been passageways for traders and nomads. The plateau of Mongolia, the central part of which is called the Gobi Desert, is north and east of Dzungaria. It is bordered by the Nan Shan on the south and the Khingan or Hsingan mountains on the east. To the east of the Khingan mountains is the plain of Manchuria.

Although the rivers of Manchuria flow to the sea, like the rivers of Szechwan, Yunnan, and the T'ung-t'ing and P'o-yang lake basins, Manchuria is almost as completely surrounded by mountains as the regions of interior drainage from Tibet to Mongolia. The mountains of Siberia and Korea lie north, east, and south of the Manchurian uplands. Even the Sea of Japan resembles an intermontane basin, bounded by the ranges of Korea, Siberia, and the islands of Sakhalin, Hokkaido, Honshu, Shikoku, and Kyushu. In fact, all the seas of East Asia are surrounded by mountains. The Yellow Sea lies between the mountains of Korea, the Liaotung (or Kwantung) peninsula in southeast Manchuria, and the Shantung peninsula northeast of the Tsing Ling; the East China Sea lies between the mountains of southern Korea, Kyushu, the Ryukyu islands, Taiwan (Formosa), and the hilly coastal provinces of Chekiang and Fukien in south China; and the South China Sea lies between the peaks of the south China province of Kwangtung, Taiwan, the Philippines, Indonesia, the Malay peninsula, and Vietnam.

The people of the north China plain, the first people in East Asia to develop a city-based society, were surrounded by the hills and basins of south China, the mountains and plateaus of the west and north from Tibet to Mongolia, mountain-rimmed Manchuria, the ranges of Korea, and the chain of islands from Sakhalin to Taiwan. North China's leaders have historically put their greatest effort into the task of spreading their concept of civilized life within the natural boundaries of East Asia, leaving intercourse with the world beyond the mountains to those who lived away from the north China plain. Nomads like the Huns and Avars, not the Chinese, crossed central Asia to Europe in the early Christian era. Turkish and Mongol peoples, not Chinese, entered Russia, the Middle East, and India. The Burmese, Thai, and Vietnamese peoples left southern China for Southeast Asia. Chinese from the southern provinces and Japanese reached Southeast Asia too; but northern Chinese rarely ventured that far except on diplomatic missions.

The civilization of northern China has always been a magnet to the people in the areas surrounding it. The tribes of Manchuria, the Mongols, the Uighurs and other Turkic peoples of Dzungaria and the Tarim basin, and the Tibetans developed distinctive societies within the mountain walls enclosing their high and arid homelands. The Turkic peoples were even converted to Islam by their cousins across the mountains in Turkestan. Yet the influence of Chinese ways has remained strong.

The difference between Korean life and north Chinese life has been far less than that between north Chinese and Mongol, Uighur, or Tibetan life. However, differences do exist, for the problems of the Korean peninsula differ in both size and type from those of the north China plain, hundreds of miles away across Manchuria and the Yellow Sea. Still greater differences exist between Chinese and Japanese life. The sea has isolated Japan from China, as the mountains isolated Tibet or the Tarim, though the mountainous nature of the four main islands of Japan (Kyushu, Honshu, Shikoku, and Hokkaido) has encouraged the use of sea rather than land transport for short as well as long journeys. Even within China, there are noticeable differences between life in the northern plain and life in the valleys of the center and south.

RIVERS AND NATURAL REGIONS

The importance of mountain ranges in the growth of East Asia is matched by the importance of rivers. The Huang Ho, or Yellow river, has bound northern China together for centuries. As it flows eastward in a curving course from the Kun Lun to the Yellow Sea, the Huang Ho carries silt from the dry and easily eroded loess soils of the provinces of Kansu, Shensi, Shansi, and western Honan to eastern Honan, Shantung, Hopei, and Kiangsu. Kiangsu also receives silt from the Huai river, which rises in the Tsing Ling range, but sinks into the soil before reaching the sea, and from the Yangtze, the longest of China's rivers. The Yangtze flows southward from the Kun Lun and then turns east, crossing Szechwan, Hupei, Anhwei, and Kiangsu on its way to the sea.

The T'ung-t'ing and P'o-yang lakes act as natural storage basins for the water of the Yangtze, making the danger of flood along its banks much less than in the lower Huang Ho valley. Over the centuries, the silt brought downstream by the Huang Ho has raised its bed as much as fifty feet above the surrounding plain. If human neglect or a natural disaster causes a break in the natural and artificial dikes that keep the Huang Ho in its channel, the resulting flood may devastate many square miles. Such floods have been so numerous that the river is often called "China's Sorrow." The most destructive floods have occurred when the Huang Ho changed course. Until 1191 A.D., it entered the sea north of Shantung, but then it shifted to a new channel which entered the sea south of Shantung. In 1852 it returned to its northern bed. Shortly after the opening of the Sino-Japanese war of 1937–1945, the Chinese deliberately cut the dikes in an effort to use the resulting flood to halt the Japanese advance into the north China plain; but by 1947 the dikes were replaced with the help of United States engineers, and the river returned again to its northern channel.

The Huang Ho with its heavy load of silt and its frequent shallow places is not as usable for navigation as is the Yangtze. Boats can use the Yangtze from central Szechwan to the sea, although they may have trouble with the swift currents in the Yangtze gorges between Szechwan and Hupei. The major tributaries of the Huang Ho, the Wei in Shensi and the Fen in Shansi, are also less navigable than the Yangtze's major tributaries, the Han in Hupei, the Yuan in Kweichow and Hunan, the Siang in Hunan, and the Kan in Kiangsi. The Huai river in Honan, Anhwei, and Kiangsu can be navigated in the stretches between its rapids and its shallow places. Other navigable streams are the Hsi (West) river in Kwangsi and Kwangtung, the Min in Fukien, the Chientang in Chekiang, the Hai in northern Hopei, the Liao in southern Manchuria, and the Sungari of northern Manchuria, which flows northward to the Amur river that has separated Russia from China since the mid-nineteenth century.

Rivers also play some part in transportation in Korea and Japan. However, like the rivers of the south China coast, the Korean and Japanese rivers are too short and too full of rapids and waterfalls to be easily navigated. Their coastal plains are also rather small, with two notable exceptions—the Kanto plain around the modern Japanese capital of Tokyo and the Settsu plain around the former Japanese capital of Kyoto. The numerous harbors along the mountainous shorelines have generally been more useful than the rivers for all but purely local trade in Japan, Korea, and southeastern China.

The mountains, plateaus, and river valleys of East Asia form a number of natural communication units. There are the intermontane plateaus of the west and north—Tibet, the Tarim, Dzungaria, and Mongolia—which have no river outlets to the sea. There is the Huang Ho drainage basin, reaching from the loessland to the sea. Within the Huang Ho basin, the Kansu corridor, Shensi, Shansi, and Shantung can be clearly distinguished from Hopei and Honan in the great north China plain, which merges with the coastal plain of the Yangtze in Kiangsu. The Yangtze valley with its outlet at Shanghai comprises another natural unit, in which Szechwan, Hunan and Hupei in the T'ung-t'ing lake basin, Kiangsi in the P'o-yang lake basin, Anhwei, and the coastal provinces of Kiangsu and Chekiang form distinguishable subunits. In the south, the Yunnan plateau, Kwei-chow, and Kwangsi and Kwangtung are natural units also. To the north and east of the Huang Ho basin lie Manchuria, whose two major rivers, the Liao and the Sungari, are divided only by gently rolling uplands; the Korean peninsula, separated from Manchuria by the Yalu river; and the islands of Japan, Hokkaido to the north and Kyushu, Honshu, and Shikoku around the Inland Sea. Longstanding historical associations bind these regions to one another, but each has its own special characteristics, for the development of each has been affected by climate, soil, and other resources as well as by the presence or absence of mountains, rivers, and plains.

CLIMATE

Climate in the regions of East Asia, like climate elsewhere, depends largely on four factors. One is distance from the sea, with which are associated the amount of rainfall received and the degree to which rainfall and temperature vary over time. Another is distance from the equator, with which the annual temperature pattern is associated. A third is topography or landforms, which can affect amount of rainfall received. The fourth is position on the continent, which is associated with the timing of the rainy season. On the western side of the Eurasian land mass, much of Europe and almost all the Middle East receive more than half their rain in the cold winter season, but most of the rain of south Asia comes in the warm summer months. In East Asia also, most of the rain falls between May and September, when cool air flows from the Pacific to the heated interior of Asia. There is less rain in the winter when the winds reverse direction, except in western Honshu, where the winter winds that cross the Japan Sea from the continent bring even more rain than those of summer. Southern China, southern Korea, and Japan have some rain throughout most of the year, but in the north and west there is almost none between October and April.

The best-watered portions of East Asia are the hills and mountains of Japan, Korea, and south China, which average forty to eighty inches of rain per year. Parts of northern Japan and Korea, together with the strip between the Yangtze river and the Nan Shan and Tsing Ling mountains, receive thirty to forty inches; the north China plain and parts of Manchuria receive twenty to thirty inches. Settled agriculture can thus be practiced in all of these regions. However, Tibet, the Tarim, Dzungaria, and Mongolia are much drier, which makes settled agriculture extremely difficult except where there are mountain-fed springs and rivers. Where average rainfall is smallest, annual variability is greatest, so that in some districts a torrential downpour may be followed by years of drought. Therefore nomadic pastoralism is the commonest mode of living in Tibet, the Tarim, Dzungaria, and Mongolia, as it is in drought-ridden portions of the Middle East. The nomad tribes herd camels in the driest areas, yaks in the highest and coldest places, and horses in the less inhospitable districts, supplementing the larger animals with sheep and goats.

The mountain barrier which stretches from eastern Tibet to the Tsing Ling range and northern Korea keeps northern China and the interior relatively dry in summer by intercepting most of the water vapor carried by the winds from the Pacific toward the center of the continent. In winter, the same mountain barrier keeps the regions south of it from feeling the full force of the chill stream of air that comes out of central Asia. From November to March freezing temperatures are common north and west of the mountains, falling to –40 degrees Fahrenheit (–40 degrees Centigrade) in the far interior. Snow falls in most of Japan and Korea, although the nearby sea keeps south China and the coasts of south Korea, Kyushu, Shikoku, and southern Honshu from experiencing it. In the summer, too, the dry interior has greater extremes of temperature than do the moist coastal lowlands and hills. Even on the Tibetan plateau, where 10,000-foot elevations would lead one to expect coolness, temperatures of 90 degrees Fahrenheit (32.2 degrees Centigrade) have been recorded—and so have fluctuations of 80 degrees Fahrenheit (26.6 degrees Centigrade) between noon and midnight of the same day. Nearer the sea, daytime and nighttime temperatures do not differ so markedly.

In South Asia, the Panjab has the highest and lowest temperatures and the least (and least reliable) rainfall. Temperature variations lessen as one moves east or south from the Panjab, while amount and reliability of rainfall increase. In East Asia, the Gobi Desert of Mongolia can be used as a similar point of reference. On the whole, temperature variations diminish and the amount and reliability of rainfall increase as one moves east or south from the Gobi. However, the cold weather is less sustained in the Gobi than in Tibet, where the subsoil, although not the surface, remains permanently frozen. The southernmost parts of China, Korea, and Japan become somewhat warmer than the Gobi in summer.

PRIMARY INDUSTRIES

The mountain barrier that stretches from eastern Tibet to the Tsing Ling range, the Shantung peninsula, northern Korea, and northern Honshu forms a line of demarcation between two distinct climatic regions, maritime (relatively mild and wet throughout the year) and continental (relatively dry, with marked seasonal variations in temperature and rainfall). This mountain barrier also separates the wide plains and basins of the north from the smaller ones of the hillier south. The soils, the vegetation, and the modes of livelihood found in the regions of East Asia reflect these differences in climate and topography.

In mountainous, rainy Japan and Korea, soils are usually shallow except in river flood plains, where the streams deposit the silt they carry down from the mountains. Heavy rains may leach or dissolve many valuable soil nutrients, carrying them far down into the ground and necessitating the use of fertilizers to raise crop yields. The deepest and richest East Asian soils are in the river basins of China: the yellow loess of the upper Huang Ho basin, the red-brown soils of the upper Yangtze basin, and the alluvial soils of the river flood plains from the Liao to the Hsi. However, the thin red soils of the south China hills are as leached and eroded as soils in Korea and Japan. In regions of interior drainage like Mongolia, salt crusts which inhibit plant growth may form on the surface. The natural vegetation of the regions south of the Tsing Ling-Honshu mountain barrier is forest, but the Huang Ho valley and the drier regions to the north are natural grasslands, which shade off into drought-resistant scrub growth in the driest areas. Most of the high plateau of Tibet supports only grasses and mosses.

Most East Asians live within seven hundred and fifty miles of the sea. Soils are reasonably fertile, the weather is warm at least six months of the year, and water supplies are ample for agriculture—the first of the five primary industries. At least seven-tenths of the people of East Asia still live by agriculture. Yet barely a quarter of Korea's hilly surface is in crops, hardly more than a sixth of mountainous Japan, and only an eighth of mainland China. Vast areas of mountain and desert are too steep or too dry for agricultural use. Even if Manchuria, Mongolia, Dzungaria, the Tarim, and Tibet are excluded, almost three-quarters of the rest of China has been left uncultivated because of topographical or climatic problems.

Rice is the major crop in the maritime areas. Along the south China coast two or even three crops may be grown in a year, but in the rest of south China and in southern Korea and Japan the summer rice crop is followed by something like wheat or barley which requires less water and warmth, in effect establishing a rotation of crops. Tea is widely grown on the hillsides of southern China, Korea, and Japan. In northern Japan, northern Korea, and the basins of the Liao, the Sungari, and the Huang Ho, the warm season is too short to grow more than one staple crop a year. Wheat and barley are widely grown where the weather is warm enough, but in the coldest areas millet, kaoliang (a type of sorghum common in north China), and soybeans are the chief crops. Vegetables and melons are raised everywhere. In the past few centuries, corn (maize), white potatoes, and sweet potatoes from the New World have become secondary crops in much of East Asia. Cotton grows from the Yangtze valley northward, and silkworms have customarily been raised in all but the coldest regions.

Silk, cotton, tea, rice, wheat, millet, barley, vegetables, fruits, nuts, and other agricultural products have traveled on East Asian trade routes for thousands of years. Yet prior to the twentieth century, agriculture was generally practiced on a subsistence rather than a commercial basis. It also remained largely dependent on human labor. The scavengers of the house and yard—pigs, dogs, chickens, ducks, and geese—can be found everywhere in the agricultural regions. However, far fewer cattle have been used in most of East Asia than in South Asia or the Middle East. Cattle have been especially scarce in the hilly regions south of the Tsing Ling-Honshu mountain barrier, where the lack of level land makes terracing the hillsides necessary. It is both difficult and uneconomical to use cattle in small terraced fields.

The Chinese never learned from their pastoral neighbors to use dairy products, as Indians and Middle Easterners did. Consequently, cattle have not been regarded as steady food-suppliers either by the Chinese or by the Koreans and Japanese who learned their agricultural techniques, but merely as food-consuming work animals. Thus animal husbandry, the second primary industry, has been important only in the dry north and west. There it has been all-important because of the scarcity of croplands, forests, fisheries, and mines.

The third primary industry, forestry, depends on the wooded hill-sides of Manchuria, Japan, Korea, and southern China. The more accessible slopes were largely denuded by the nineteenth century, but reforestation programs, particularly in Japan, have enabled forest products from paper to plastics to play an expanding role in twentieth-century East Asian life. In the cultivated portions of East Asia many trees have been planted around the villages to furnish fruit, nuts, and food for the fiber-producing silkworm. They also furnish shade and beauty.

The natural and planted forests which cover three-fifths of Japan and three-fourths of Korea provide Japanese and Koreans with ample wood for buildings, furniture, and fuel. However, wood has long been much more scarce in China. The wood available for building there has been eked out with clay, bamboo, and reeds in agricultural regions, or felt and dried dung in pastoral areas. Grass, fallen leaves, and dung have been used for fuel whenever high temperatures were not required; and since at least the fourth century A.D. the Chinese have used coal to produce hot fires for baking, smelting, and the firing of ceramics. The use of coal has enabled the Chinese to use more of their scarce wood for buildings and furnishings than do the peoples of other largely deforested regions like the Middle East, where wood was the major fuel for hot fires. Thus the great buildings of China usually had wooden beams and pillars, unlike the stone and brick architectural monuments of India and the Middle East; but only in Japan and Korea were entire temples and palaces constructed of wood.

The fourth primary industry, fishing, has been important in East Asia for centuries. Not only have fish been taken from the seas and rivers, but fish have been raised as a crop throughout the region south of the Tsing Ling-Honshu barrier. Fish, fresh or salted, have been consumed most extensively in the islands of Japan, but even the Chinese, who eat less than a tenth as much fish per person per year as the Japanese, eat more fish than the people of the United States. Only the pastoral nomads of the interior have never relied on fish as a major source of protein.

The mineral resources which support the fifth major primary industry, mining, are fairly large and diversified. There is coal in many parts of China, Korea, and Japan. Iron is found in Kwangtung, the Yangtze valley, north Korea, and northern Japan, with the largest deposits in southern Manchuria and neighboring provinces of China. Most of the iron deposits are fairly close to workable coal supplies. Copper and silver are found in the southern interior of China, northern Korea, and most of Japan. Until Europeans began to bring precious metals to East Asia from the New World in the sixteenth century, Japan supplied most of the region's silver and much of its gold. Tin is present in southwest Honshu, but it is more abundant in Yunnan and other parts of south China. Other important mineral deposits include aluminum in Manchuria, gold and graphite in north Korea, lead and zinc in Honshu and the Yangtze valley, antimony in Manchuria and south China, tungsten in north Korea and south China, sulphur and manganese in Honshu, mercury in south China, and petroleum, found along a line from Dzungaria and Szechwan to northern Honshu. However, only coal, iron, copper, tin, silver, gold, and mercury were exploited before the nineteenth century. China has the resource base to support a major industrial complex, but Japan and Korea must import some of the raw materials needed for heavy industry. Within China, the resources of the Yangtze valley and neighboring districts have been utilized longest, but those of Manchuria have been most highly developed.

TRANSPORT AND COMMERCE

Most of the products of East Asia's pastures, fields, forests, fisheries, and mines have been processed and used near their point of origin, although the ancient Romans wore Chinese silk and the Safawids of Persia prized Chinese porcelain. In those times, goods from north and south China were transported to other regions of Asia by caravans of pack animals which traversed the grasslands and oases that fringe the Mongolian, Dzungarian, and Tarim basins. However, animals were rarely used for transportation in agricultural regions because of the expense and difficulty of feeding them in districts whose human inhabitants needed all the food they could raise. Instead, goods were carried on the backs of human beings, except where ships could be used. In the basins of the Yangtze and the Hsi and along the coasts of south China, the Korean peninsula, and the islands of Japan with their many natural harbors, water transport was almost as important as land transport, but boats could not be used easily on the smaller rivers with their many rapids and falls. Some of the trade between China and Korea was carried on by land, but most of it went by sea, as did all trade with Japan.

The major land routes worked out by the peoples of East Asia became the bases of the railway lines built in more recent times in China, Japan, Korea, and Mongolia. By the 1930s, Japan had built one of the only two railroad networks in Asia which was comparable in density to European railway systems. (The other was in the Ganges valley.) Nevertheless, Japan still uses the sea for much of its domestic commerce, as well as all of its foreign trade except the small quantities of goods carried by air.

Social Organization:
Kinships of Ancestry and Residence

NOMAD TRIBES

Although trade flourished in East Asia, until recent times most of its people lived in small self-sufficient communities, producing most of what they consumed at home and making as few exchanges as possible with the outside world. Some of them still live in such communities, usually agricultural, but occasionally pastoral.

Though the flocks and herds of Tibet, the Tarim, Dzungaria, Mongolia, and Manchuria differ in composition from those of the Middle East, their masters have been equally dependent on the animals' milk, meat, hair, wool, hides, and dung. Like Middle Eastern nomads, East Asian nomads have traded with the agriculturalists of the oases, the mountain valleys, and the great river basins. Historically, they have raided and even conquered the settlements whenever a breakdown of central authority enabled them to do so, much like Middle Eastern tribes. However, they rarely crossed the mountains into Korea, and only the Mongols ever attempted a full-scale invasion of the Japanese islands.

Chinese rulers were generally stronger in comparison to their nomad neighbors than Middle Eastern rulers, for China was larger in population and territory than most Middle Eastern states. Furthermore, China's cities lay wholly within settled agricultural country, rather than being separated by stretches of nomad-held desert country as in the Middle East. Nevertheless, if allowances are made for these important differences, the relations between nomad, city, and village in China can be compared in part to relations between nomad, city, and village in the Middle East. With no natural defenses between the Huang Ho valley and the neighboring steppe, China was always vulnerable to the incursions of nomad raiders who occasionally turned conquerors. By the sixteenth century, China's rulers were so attuned to regarding the nomad frontier as their major defense problem that they paid little heed to European traders on the coast. Not until the nineteenth century did China's rulers realize that they could no longer deal with Europeans as they were accustomed to dealing with the nomads to the north.

As nomads of the steppe, where constant vigilance was essential to survival, most of the Turkic and Mongol nomads of the north were organized on a permanent rather than a shifting basis. Every patrilineal household was headed by the father of the family. The tribe and its divisions and subdivisions each had recognized leaders. Within this framework an ambitious chieftain could weld the tribe together not only to attack other tribes or farming villages—isolated farmsteads have been as rare in northern China as in the Middle East—but to conquer cities and force their administrators to acknowledge the tribe as overlord. At times, nomad tribes succeeded in controlling part or all of agricultural China for generations. Most Chinese raised few objections to their rule. Like the Middle Eastern village, the Chinese village was largely self-sufficient in social and political as well as economic affairs. Consequently its people were little affected by changes of masters at the imperial or even the provincial capital, many miles away and several administrative layers above.

FAMILY AND CLAN

Traditional Chinese, Korean, and Japanese villages consisted of a number of patrilineal households. Ideally, each household included the father, his male descendants, and their wives and children, and would stay together under the leadership of the eldest son after the father died. In practice, younger sons often left the home before the father's death. In China the family property was usually divided among all the sons when the father died, so that they could set up independent households, but in Japan the eldest son usually received all or almost all the family property. If a Japanese younger son received much property, it was generally understood that he and his descendants would remain closely linked with the eldest son's household and would give it their service and support.

In China, Korea, and Japan, some younger sons of village households left for the cities, and some became hired laborers in other village households. However, at least in China, those who left the parental roof to work did not forfeit their inheritance. Only the youth who was adopted by a sonless couple lost his interest in the property of the household of his birth. Through adoption he broke all his ties with his own ancestral line and formed new ones with the ancestral line of the household he entered.

Consciousness of belonging to a specific ancestral line was very strong. In China, for example, all the descendants of a common ancestor regarded themselves as members of the same clan, with lifelong mutual obligations. The member households of the clan came together in the rites performed at births, at marriages, at the birthdays of the eldest members of the clan, at funerals, and at the yearly festivals honoring deceased ancestors. When misfortune came, the individual or the household turned naturally to the clan for aid.

Many Chinese and Korean villages were composed wholly or largely of households of one clan. Since a man was not usually allowed to marry a woman of the same clan, girls in such villages had to move to a different village when they married, not just to a different household. Even if a bride remained within the village of her birth, she was required to break her ties with the household of her childhood, for by marrying into her husband's household she was in effect adopted into it. Her parents took no part in the ceremonies at the groom's home, and in many areas she could only visit them at specified times. These rules were intended to make it easier for her husband's parents to train her to obey them as her new parents.

In China, Korea, and Japan, the purpose of marriage was to continue the family line. It was therefore regarded as the business of the elders of the household, not of the couple themselves. The couple's parents arranged their children's marriage through intermediaries or go-betweens, who presumably would not be embarrassed by close questioning about the prospective bride or groom, or by bargaining over the gifts to be exchanged. Once formally begun, the marriage relation was governed by the groom's parents. They insisted uncompromisingly on the importance of filial piety, obedience to parents, for they were concerned about the possibility that the bride might draw her husband's attention from them and make him unwilling to remain and support them.

The duty of the child to obey the parent both before and after marriage has been a principle of East Asian life for many centuries. The groom was constantly reminded to serve his parents as he had done before his marriage, so that in future his children would learn to follow his example and serve him. The new bride was even more constantly reminded that she was now the daughter of her husband's parents and must obey them accordingly. Even if her husband died, she would still be part of her husband's household. In most cases she had brought children into that household, children whom she could not take out of it unless the household head assented, which he rarely did. She would therefore have to leave her children motherless as well as fatherless if she left. Consequently the remarriage of widows was discouraged in China, Korea, and Japan as strongly as in India, although widows were not cut off from society in other ways as much as in India. Nevertheless, widows remarried often enough so that those in positions of authority, who wished to reward filial piety as a pillar of the social order, customarily erected monuments in memory of deceased widows who had filially remained with their dead husband's parents.

The remarriage of widowers was not restricted, for it brought new members into the household. A man could also take a second fully recognized wife while his first wife still lived, if she had no children and the household could afford the expense of arranging a second marriage. Annulment was impossible, since it would undermine the filial piety of daughters-in-law by offering them the possibility that their ties to their parents-in-law might legitimately be broken. An unsatisfactory daughter-in-law was simply sent back to her parents, who could then scarcely hope to arrange for her anything better than becoming a secondary wife or concubine to someone else. To have a daughter returned was a terrible disgrace, for it showed that she had not been reared to be properly obedient, and parents would go to almost any lengths to avoid it.

Within the household, the bonds between parents and children were ideally strongest, those of brothers (as sons of one father) ideally next in strength, and those of wives and husbands weakest. The strains and restraints which the system placed on both men and women were great. The stress was greatest for the new wife, who had to shift her allegiance to a new set of parents. If the strains became too great to bear, her one effective method of protest and escape was suicide, which was generally accepted in East Asia as the final recourse of both men and women faced with unresolvable conflicts.

VILLAGE AND CITY

In the villages of East Asia, each household produced most of what it consumed and consumed most of what it produced, exchanging what little was left for material goods, personal services, and governmental protection. The head of each household ran its internal affairs. Each household cooperated with and assisted other households in its clan or family line. It also cooperated with other households in its village to avert outside interference and to do tasks like maintaining dikes and irrigation canals which obviously benefited everyone.

Like agricultural villages in the Middle East and South Asia, the East Asian village usually had a recognized governing body. Ordinarily the village elders came from all the clans or family lines in the village, or even from all the households. As in similarly organized Middle Eastern villages, one elder was usually chosen either by his fellows or by government officials to be responsible for the relations between the village and the government.

In traditional India and the Middle East, villages largely ran themselves. Government officials merely collected levies (in labor, crops, or coin) and settled any disputes that proved too difficult for the village elders to handle. In East Asia the general situation was rather similar. However, in periods of strong government the villagers of China, Korea, or Japan were often made collectively responsible for one another. All the households, not just the headman and the elders, would then be directly involved in preventing troubles which might provoke government intervention.

Under the neighborhood system, as this collective responsibility system was called, each village was divided into neighborhoods of five or ten households. Each neighborhood, like each village in India or the Middle East, was then required to furnish a given number of army recruits or a specified amount of labor, produce, or money, even if some households had to provide more than their share because others gave less. Thus the system effectively ensured that each household would exert heavy pressure on its neighbors to contribute their share. When efficiently enforced, the neighborhood system may have led to fairer assessments than the all-village type of collective responsibility, which gave village elders a chance to assess their friends lightly and their foes heavily.

The collective responsibility of the neighborhood included the maintenance of order as well as the collection of levies. When the system was in full operation, anyone in a neighborhood who failed to report a neighbor's punishable offense was tried and punished as though he or she had committed a similar crime. This usually resulted in a rapid reporting of offenses, but it could also lead to neighborhood conspiracies of silence.

The neighborhood system meant that in East Asia, the territorial group of the neighborhood rather than the occupational grouping of the caste or the religious grouping of the millet came to supplement kinship groupings within the village. This experience with territorially based organization was a form of political training. In recent generations it contributed to the rise of well-defined territorially based nationalisms in the region, although the high level of cultural homogeneity attained during centuries of relatively uninterrupted development was probably more important. The neighborhood system of collective responsibility partially prepared Chinese, Koreans, and Japanese to accept the theory of common neighborhood interest underlying the establishment of street cells in Communist states or voting wards and precincts elsewhere. In this respect they differed markedly from the members of religious and caste communities in the Middle East and South Asia, who generally assumed they shared more ties with people living at a distance from them than they did with many of their immediate neighbors.

The neighborhood system was also used in the cities, where it supplemented household and clan kin groups and guild occupational groups. Like guilds in other societies, those of East Asia were largely hereditary. This was truest in Japan, where hereditary modes of occupational and political organization were far better regarded and upheld than on the mainland, but even in Japan, the hereditary nature of the guilds was modified by the widespread practice of adopting promising young men from other families. Over the years the descendants of the original members might be completely replaced by men brought into the guild by adoption, for even in heredity-minded Japan the ongoing household rather than the blood line was the basis of social organization. Unlike the orthodox Hindu household, which could only adopt members of the same kinship group, the Japanese, Korean, or Chinese household could adopt anyone from any clan.

Kinship, occupational, and neighborhood groups were the major concern of the officials responsible for maintaining peace and collecting levies in East Asia's cities. Like city governors in India or the Middle East, East Asian city officials let these self-perpetuating associations run their own affairs as long as public order and the public treasury were not endangered. However, differing traditions in China, Korea, and Japan meant that there were variations in the ways officials viewed themselves and their states.

Historical Development:
The Formation of China, Korea, and Japan

CHINA

FROM SHANG TO CH'IN (15TH TO 3RD CENTURIES B.C.). Twentieth-century archaeologists are finding evidence that the inhabitants of the grasslands of Turkestan, Dzungaria, and the Kansu corridor may have carried wheat, bronze, iron, wheeled vehicles, and even the concept of writing from the early civilizations of Mesopotamia and the Indus to the people of the Huang Ho valley in northern China. Yet other aspects of early Chinese civilization were distinctively East Asian in origin, such as rice cultivation, the making of silk, patterns of pottery decoration, and the use of long-bladed hoes rather than animal-drawn plows to till the soil. By the end of the fifteenth century B.C. the people of north China had fashioned these elements into a distinctive culture. For the next several centuries this culture was dominated by a group of rulers in the center of the north China plain. These rulers were known to later Chinese as the Shang dynasty.

Statues, bronze vessels, and other relics show that the people of Shang times were already skilled in metallurgy and writing. Shang writing was unmistakably the ancestor of the writing systems used in later centuries by the Chinese, the Koreans, and the Japanese. Like the later systems, Shang writing used one symbol for each idea to be expressed rather than for each sound, as in the scripts of India or the Middle East, and many modern Chinese, Korean, and Japanese word-signs or characters are clearly modifications of Shang word-signs. The Shang rulers sacrificed to the spirit of the earth and other nature deities. They were also greatly concerned about winning their ancestors' aid, or at least avoiding the ancestors' displeasure. Apparently the ancestors were thought to have joined the spirits of nature at the time they died.

As the eleventh century B.C. closed, the Shang were overthrown by their hardier neighbors in the Wei valley to the west. The victors, who called themselves the Chou dynasty, attributed a variety of evil deeds to the declining Shang and claimed that the spirit of heaven had given them a mandate to replace the Shang. The early Chou kings divided most of their large new domains among family members and loyal supporters. However, the bonds of loyalty between the kings and their nobles weakened in later generations. The nobles did not challenge the right of the Chou kings to perform the sacrifices to the spirits of nature, but in almost every other way they ignored the Chou. They ruled their states to suit themselves and did not aid the Chou when nomad tribes entered the Chou capital in the Wei valley in the eighth century B.C. and forced the Chou to move eastward.

Despite the lack of effective central government, a phenomenal rise in wealth and population took place in the north China plain between the eighth and the fourth century B.C. The adoption of the iron-tipped ox-drawn plow increased agricultural production and made great irrigation projects and transport canals both possible and profitable. Trade and town life grew as agriculture expanded, and copper coins replaced cowrie shells and bolts of silk as media of exchange. At the same time, the growing use of horses among the nomads of the steppes to the north forced the states to build long defensive walls for protection from raiding parties and to create their own cavalry forces. The introduction of the horse into China prepared the way for more effective political unification by enabling the Chinese not only to fight the nomads but also to communicate more rapidly than ever before over long distances within China itself.

In the midst of these centuries of ferment, the teacher K'ung-tzu (Confucius) questioned the common practice of assigning the tasks of government on a hereditary basis. Confucius insisted that noble character, not noble birth, was the true mark of the nobility which rulers should possess. He believed that the best government would be one made up of the most virtuous men in the state. At the time, few heeded him. More rulers listened to the legalists, who thought government should be based on strict and impartial laws rather than the virtues of individuals. These were times of chaos, in which the old hereditary order was being challenged by three groups: the nomads, the princelings who were founding new states on the northern and southern fringes of the Chou domains, and the upstart merchants of the towns, who wanted a better position in society than the low rank assigned them by the hereditary nobles. The legalists believed that these challenges could only be met by a strong government which would proclaim and enforce a single specific code of behavior, using the principle of collective neighborhood responsibility and replacing the aristocracy of blood with a system of rank based on military merit. They were convinced that strength required centralization, and they scoffed at Confucius' proposal that the ruler should merely appoint men of virtue and leave the conduct of affairs to their discretion.

The rulers who paid most attention to the legalists were the Ch'in, who by the fourth century B.C. had taken over the Wei valley lands once held by the Chou. In 221 B.C. the Ch'in finished the conquest of the states of the Huang Ho and lower Yangtze valleys. Soon they conquered three new areas: Szechwan in the west, the strip from the Tung-t'ing lake to the lower Hsi river in the south, and the lower Liao valley in the northeast. The man who led the Ch'in to victory titled himself Ch'in Shih Huang-ti, "Ch'in's first imperial ruler." He promptly divided the empire into thirty-six provinces with centrally appointed governors and built a network of post roads so that he could supervise them effectively, much as the Persians far to the west had done three centuries earlier. He standardized weights, measures, coinage, and the length of wagon axles (so that carts from every part of China could follow the pairs of ruts which served as secondary roads throughout the empire). He even tried to standardize thought, burning as many writings of the various nonlegalist schools of political philosophy as he could find and burying alive the scholars who approved them. He also had the existing defensive walls united into one fourteen-hundred-mile barrier against the nomads, the famed Great Wall of China. However, four years after he died in 210 B.C. the Ch'in dynasty was overthrown by opponents of his more drastic measures of unification, which had included the uprooting and resettling of whole villages. A bitter struggle ensued between a member of the old aristocracy and a peasant's son who took advantage of the fluid situation. The peasant's son won out, and founded the Han dynasty in 202 B.C.

GLORY AND COLLAPSE: HAN CHINA (202 B.C.–290 A.D.). By the time the Han came to the throne, the memory of the small independent states of the pre-Ch'in era had faded enough so that the Han could reestablish a measure of centralized control. At first the Han bowed to previous custom by assigning large areas to their leading followers as privately ruled realms, but by 154 B.C. the Han were appointing the officials who administered the affairs of these realms, as well as those who administered the lands the ruler held directly. However, the Han still received no taxes from private realms, which seriously hampered them as government expenditures rose. Furnishing a standing army to fight the nomads and maintaining a bureaucracy to run the provinces and realms became increasingly expensive, yet the income of the dynasty from crown lands and taxes on trade remained approximately the same.

Unlike western European monarchs in early modern times, the Han did not encourage trade as a means of raising revenue, for they inherited a bias against merchants from the legalist tradition of the Ch'in era and the Confucianists of the latter Chou era. The Confucianists deplored the merchants' unvirtuous striving for profit; the legalists deplored their failure to produce any material goods and their inclination to travel rather than to stay in one place where they could be controlled like peasants or artisans. In line with these ideas, the Han regarded merchants as dangerous and formally excluded them from taking part in government or buying land. Merchants were subjected to inhibiting controls and exactions, which were often interpreted and enforced arbitrarily and capriciously. They therefore had to think constantly in terms of propitiating the officials so that they could stay in business. They were not as fortunate as their contemporaries in the Roman Mediterranean world, who could think in terms of carrying on their business under a set of rules which clearly specified the upper as well as the lower limits of their obligations to the government.

Shortly after the centralization of the Han administration, the Han ruler Wu-ti (141–87 B.C.) began expanding the empire. In the south, the regions of Yunnan, Kweichow, Fukien, and Annam (northern Vietnam) were added to the former Ch'in lands. In the northeast, northern Korea was brought under Chinese rule. In the northwest, the acquisition of control over the tribes of Inner Mongolia and the Tarim basin eventually enabled the Chinese to trade with the Parthian and Kushan empires which lay between the western borderlands of China and the worlds of the Mediterranean and India. Of the mainland regions controlled by China in the twentieth century A.D., only Tibet remained wholly outside the Han domains. However, not for centuries did immigration from the Huang Ho and Yangtze valleys make the south China coast a Chinese-speaking region, and the tribes of Yunnan and Kweichow were still resisting Chinese rule in the nineteenth century A.D.

In the south, the mingling of the northern Chinese immigrants with the local peoples soon led to the formation of spoken dialects which were quite different from northern speech, but since the symbols used to write Chinese expressed thoughts rather than sounds—as though !! stood equally for "crown," "corona," and "Krone," or (!!) for "Caesar," "Kaiser," and "Czar"—the written language remained an effective means of communication for the literate. The continued use of the same written language held the vast empire together culturally even after it fell apart politically in the second and third centuries A.D., and the writings of the educated kept alive the tradition of imperial unity. The ideas of Confucius had become widely known after Han Wu-ti began to patronize them officially. By the third century A.D. most literate Chinese were familiar with the Confucian idea that true imperial unity could only be achieved under the guidance of an elite body of educated officials, who served their ruler faithfully and by their virtuous example inculcated obedience in ordinary people.

Shortly after 180 A.D., rebellions led by two religious sects broke out among poverty-stricken peasants in heavily peopled Shantung and Szechwan. Several generals were sent to quell the revolts. The mission was eventually accomplished, but instead of restoring the rebellious areas to the Han, three of the generals partitioned the entire Han empire among themselves. There was a brief reunification between 280 and 290 A.D., but it was followed by total collapse.

The fall of the Han was a shock to the Chinese. It stemmed primarily from internal factors. Palace-bred rulers lost the ability to keep a balance between the power of their civil administrators and the power of their personal retainers. The dynasty also failed to build up nonagricultural revenues to meet rising expenses, as natural increases in population in times of peace necessitated increased outlays on administration and the few services the state provided. However, the nomads who hovered along the imperial borders quickly took advantage of China's weakness after the Han fell.

DIVISION, REUNION BY SUI AND T'ANG, AND REDIVISION (290–960 A.D.). After Han Wu-ti subjugated the northern nomads, the tribes began to learn enough about the ways of settled life to rule as well as raid the agricultural regions. From 290 A.D. on, they poured across the Great Wall, setting up a host of petty dynasties north of the Yangtze. Some of the invaders retained their tribal languages and customs, but many of them, like the powerful Northern Wei (386–550 A.D.), gave up the old

tribal ways and became almost indistinguishable from their Chinese subjects. Thousands of Chinese fled southward across the Yangtze to escape
barbarian rule, thereby hastening the Sinicization of the south. Numerous
Chinese leaders in the south founded short-lived dynasties, like the
Southern Ch'i (479–502 A.D.), and tried vainly to reconquer the north.
The empire was not finally reunified until 589 A.D., when a northern
dynasty established control over all of China south of the Great Wall.
The new imperial dynasty, the Sui, was established by an individual who
claimed Chinese ancestry, but was probably partly Mongol.

The victorious Sui reasserted the control of the central government
as far south as Vietnam. They also moved successfully against the natives
of Taiwan and the tribes which controlled the Kansu-Tarim trade route.
However, they failed to capture northern Korea, which had been independent for three hundred years, and they met with a serious reversal at
the hands of the Turks to the northwest. After less than thirty years, the
Sui were overthrown in 618 by one of their officials, who also claimed
Chinese descent but was probably of mixed Chinese-nomad origin. The
new dynasty took the name of T'ang. Like the Han who succeeded the
Ch'in, the T'ang who followed the Sui built up a powerful empire, even
greater than that of the Han. Not only did the T'ang control the former
Han domains; they were also recognized as overlords by the rulers of
Tibet and a unified Korea. They even attracted the interest of the Japa-
nese, who until then had been in touch with the mainland chiefly through
Korea.

The first T'ang rulers refined the use of three important means of
control which had been successfully tried in earlier times. The first means
was government ownership of land. When the government held the land,
each family was allowed to cultivate an area whose size depended on the
size of the family. In return the family provided the government with a
corresponding amount of labor and agricultural produce. To maintain this
system, periodic censuses were needed to ascertain the composition of
each family, assign each family suitable fields, and prescribe the amounts
of labor and produce each family should furnish the government. The
second means of control was the neighborhood collective responsibility
system. The third was the establishment of special colonies on the
frontiers and in other strategic areas, whose obligations to the government were fulfilled by giving military service. The early T'ang applied
these three methods to much of China, but like their predecessors, they
received no taxes from the extensive lands still held by great private
families, temples, and other religious institutions.

The early T'ang dynasty thoroughly overhauled the machinery of
the imperial government. They expanded the system of state-sponsored
schools and civil service examinations, which the Han had started rather
haphazardly and the Sui had revived more systematically. They rebuilt
the post roads; set up an orderly hierarchy of provincial, prefectural, and

district officials, all of whom were under central government control; divided the central government's tasks between separate policy-making and policy-enforcing bodies; and founded the boards of censors, whose task was to ensure the continued efficiency of the entire system by inspecting and criticizing the actions of every member of the government from the lowliest district magistrate to the emperor himself.

Despite these sweeping reforms, the T'ang had to undertake another reorganization within little more than a century, for the return of peace and unity was followed by a number of changes in Chinese life. Peaceful conditions contributed to an economic growth within China which stimulated overseas trade. Arab merchants, replacing the Persians of earlier years, settled at Canton under T'ang protection. The T'ang were no fonder of merchants than the Han, but the T'ang were willing to profit from the taxes that could be levied on commerce and therefore replaced the old restrictive policies with policies of encouragement. Economic expansion also enabled individuals who were not hereditary aristocrats to acquire the wealth and leisure that would enable their sons to study successfully for the civil service examinations, which only the landowning aristocracy could previously afford. Soon the old aristocracy and the new gentry merged into a ruling class which stressed education rather than birth as its distinguishing criterion, but which continued to regard land ownership as desirable. In addition, population growth made the government's scheme of periodic land redistribution unworkable in its original form. After a generation of experimentation it was replaced in 780 A.D. by a system of private ownership and a tax on all land, levied on whoever owned it. This tax was the final blow to the privileged position of the old aristocracy, but it did not affect the temples and other religious institutions, most of which continued to be exempt from taxation.

The series of experiments which led to the revenue-producing reform of 780 was related to other problems faced by the dynasty. The T'ang had had to hire nomad mercenaries to crush a mid-eighth-century rebellion. Thereafter they were never able to dispense with the services of the nomads, whose extravagant demands helped to impoverish the government. When new peasant uprisings broke out late in the ninth century, the T'ang fell victim to their military commanders as the Han had done. During the first half of the tenth century, China was divided into a number of warring states. However, the provinces of the north were finally reunited by a new dynasty, the Sung, which added the south to its territories between 960 and 980 A.D.

URBANITY UNDER THE SUNG (960–1279 A.D.). The founders of the Sung had observed that heavy reliance on generals tended to lead to division of the empire. Therefore, they resolutely subordinated the military to the civil arm of government. This policy preserved them from the ambitions of their generals, but it made them too weak to recover northern Vietnam, which used the fall of the T'ang to win independence as northern Korea had used the fall of the Han. The Sung could not even maintain the line of the Great Wall. The Tibetan Hsi Hsia dynasty ruled Kansu, and the Mongol Liao dynasty ruled the Liao valley, during much of the early Sung period.

The Sung centralized the administration even more highly than the T'ang had done, but the expense of maintaining and supervising the strong military forces needed to protect the northern borders proved too great for the treasury. In the early twelfth century the Sung helped the Chin dynasty of northern Manchuria to overthrow their mutual foe, the Liao. To the distress of the Sung, the Chin then swept southward to the Wei and Huai rivers in 1127 A.D. The Chin used Chinese methods to administer their new domains, but they retained their own language and alphabetic script (which they had borrowed from Middle Eastern sources) to distinguish themselves from their Chinese subjects.

Although the Chin took their northern territories in 1127 A.D., the Sung soon rose to new heights of prosperity and artistic refinement, for by the twelfth century the south had grown so in wealth and population that it was even more flourishing economically than the north. Consequently, the south alone could support a larger bureaucracy during the Southern Sung era (1127–1279) than the whole country had had before. The leisure class and the military establishment of the Southern Sung were also larger than those of the early Sung.

Economic growth during the Southern Sung era can be compared in part to the beginnings of the commercial revolution in western Europe at the same period. The amount of coal used to smelt iron in twelfth- and thirteenth-century China increased sharply. The abacus was invented for use in calculation, and paper currency was developed for convenience. Commerce grew so that private merchants began to form guilds on a nationwide rather than a local or provincial basis and to challenge the tradition of government monopoly over most of the trade between the provinces. Foreign trade also increased both the overland trade to the north and west and the overseas trade to the east and south. The rising value of overseas commerce led Chinese merchants to go abroad themselves, instead of letting Koreans continue to manage the trade with Korea and Japan while Arabs and other outsiders monopolized trade with Southeast Asia and India.

The enrichment of the cities by trade led to a proliferation of the goods and services available in them. Soon the attractions of urban life became so great that the gentry left their landed estates and clustered in the cities. Peaceful arts like gardening replaced the warlike recreation of hunting as the favored amusement of the upper classes. The members of the civil service, most of whom came from the landowning gentry, began to temper their natural interest in agriculture with an interest in urban pursuits. Then, in the latter thirteenth century, this highly cultivated, wealthy, commercial-minded society fell to the Mongols, who under Genghis Khan had already overrun not only the Chin domains in the Huang Ho valley but the entire region from Mongolia to Turkestan.

BARBARIAN RULE: THE MONGOL OR YUAN DYNASTY (1271–1368 A.D.). The Mongols, whose activities as rulers of China also affected the history of Korea and Japan, were the first nomad conquerers to seize all of China. However, the Mongols were by no means the first rulers of nomadic origin to govern agricultural regions south of the Great Wall. For centuries, nomads had used their superior cavalry to capture portions of the Huang Ho valley whenever the central government of China was weak. They had learned to use Chinese methods and personnel to administer Chinese villages and towns, but they had also discovered that to stay in power they must retain their own warlike abilities. They had to preserve their riding and hunting skills by living in the steppe part of the time as well as in their new domains.

The Mongol cavalry easily seized most of the north China plain during the lifetime of the first great Mongol leader, Genghis Khan, but the Mongols found it necessary to learn new tactics and develop new weapons when they reached the south with its ricefields, waterways, and narrow valleys. Whether or not the first primitive cannon were used in besieging the walled cities of south China, by the end of the Mongol era, cannon were in regular use. The Mongols entered Yunnan in 1253, sending the Thai people who had previously ruled that area farther south into Southeast Asia, and they appointed Muslim administrators who converted many of the Yunnan tribes to Islam. However, they did not overthrow the Sung and reach Canton until 1279, more than halfway through the reign of Genghis' grandson Khubilai (1260–1294).

Khubilai Khan named his dynasty the Yuan in 1271 and proceeded to use the administrative machine of the defeated Sung. In fact, he centralized the imperial government still more by tightening his control over the provincial governors. Since he believed that Chinese officials might try to rebel, he staffed his administrations with men from many parts of the far-flung Mongol domains and even from more distant regions. The foreign character of the Yuan administration is graphically illustrated by the fact that after seventeen years in the service of Khubilai Khan, the Venetian Marco Polo was more familiar with the Persian language of many of his fellow-administrators than he was with the language of the Chinese whom he had been helping to govern.

Khubilai Khan's reliance on non-Chinese administrators was extremely unpopular. The continued use of foreigners as officials helped to produce local revolts from the 1340s onward. Other factors prompting the revolts were an over-issuance of paper currency and a series of disastrous floods and famines. In 1368 A.D. the Mongols were driven from their capital at Peking by the founder of the Ming dynasty, whose base was in the Yangtze valley, and by 1382 all of China from the Great Wall to Yunan was under Ming rule.

REACTION TO BARBARIAN RULE: THE MING (1368–1644 A.D.). The Ming were far more ethnocentric than the T'ang or even the Southern Sung had been. They were hyperconscious of their role as the protagonists of Chinese cultural superiority over the nomads, whose recent conquests had shocked and alarmed Chinese leaders. Although great naval expeditions were sent to investigate ports where Chinese merchants traded in Southeast Asia, India, and Arabia in the early fifteenth century, the Ming never followed them up with subsequent expeditions. The scholar-bureaucrats disapproved of the expeditions because they were initiated and led by the eunuch attendants of the imperial court, whose participation in state affairs the scholar-bureaucrats in every dynasty sought to curb. Moreover, the expeditions used up revenues which the scholar-bureaucrats thought would be better used for defenses against the northern nomads; and the expeditions appeared to lead only to the entrance of more foreign goods and ideas, which the scholar-bureaucrats thought unnecessary or even harmful to the all-embracing, all-sufficient Chinese way of life. Chinese distaste for all things foreign was apparently heightened by the bitter experience of being not only conquered by nomads but actually governed by outsiders, even though the outsiders were used within the familiar Chinese administrative framework.

The Ming claimed that their government followed T'ang models, although in fact they used Yuan patterns for the most part. They modified the administrative hierarchy and the examination system somewhat, in order to keep favoritism at a minimum. In 1417 they published definitive official editions of the classical works studied by those preparing for the civil service examinations, in the hope of discouraging students from accepting unorthodox interpretations. Still, not every degree-holder received his diploma through study, for the lower degrees could be obtained without passing the examinations. The son of a high official could inherit the right to a diploma; the wealthy man could purchase one. Only the few who held the highest degree were assured of holding office, for the number of posts was limited, and the highest degree was almost never granted except through the examination. However, the possession of any degree was worth a great deal. Any diploma gave its holder the privileged status of the educated man, who among other things was rarely forced to endure corporal punishment or heavy taxation. In return, the diploma-holder was expected to take part in the unpaid but prestigious tasks performed by those who were eligible for office but not actually in the civil service. These tasks included supervising local irrigation facilities and transport networks, training local militia, settling local quarrels, and maintaining schools, charitable institutions, and public shrines.

The Ming revived the longstanding Chinese dynastic custom of treating all foreigners as vassals bearing tribute to their superior, the emperor of China, and requiring of them the three deep kneelings and nine complete prostrations of the kowtow ritual. Foreigners were treated as vassals even when they were obviously traders rather than official emissaries, as in the south Chinese ports. Their interest in trade was recognized, but they were not allowed to trade until they offered tribute to the local government officials. Even when the Ming paid the Mongols and Turks not to attack their northern borders, they maintained the fiction of the vassal rendering homage by receiving gift-bearing emissaries from the northern nomads and then giving far more valuable gifts in return. In fact, one of the purposes of the fifteenth-century naval expeditions was to induce as many states as possible to acknowledge the supremacy of China by sending tribute to the Ming capital.

The fall of the Southern Sung and the destruction wrought by the Mongols weakened Chinese overseas traders so greatly that Korean and Japanese merchants began to replace them even in Chinese ports. When the first tribute mission came from Japan in 1401, the Ming promptly protested formally about the piratical activities of many Japanese traders along the China coast. However, these complaints did not stem from concern for Chinese merchant interests. The unquestionable fact that the rise of commercialism in the Southern Sung had been followed immediately by the disasters of the Yuan era had only confirmed traditional anti-merchant attitudes among Confucian-trained rulers and officials. Furthermore, the major concern of the treasury was the land tax, not the customs tariff. The Ming were only concerned about the safety of their frontiers on sea against the Japanese (and later against Portuguese and other Europeans), and on land against the nomads beyond the Wall. When new nomad movements boded ill for the peace of northern China, the Ming moved their capital from the Yangtze valley north to Peking in 1421. Thereafter they concentrated on their landward defenses, sparing as little as they dared for maritime defense and nothing for a new round of overseas expeditions.

The Ming overstrained their resources in the 1590s by sending troops to defend their Korean neighbors successfully against an invasion by Japan, whose leaders were then in an expansionist mood. In the next few decades, numerous local rebellions showed that Ming strength was declining. In 1644 a powerful bandit chieftain entered the Ming capital just as the last Ming emperor despairingly hanged himself. Yet the bandit did not found the next dynasty. The leaders of a state set up a

generation earlier by the seminomadic Manchu tribe in northern Manchuria took advantage of the situation. When a distressed Ming general
invited the Manchu to cross the Wall and overthrow the bandit, they
accepted with alacrity and proceeded to take over the Ming domains for
themselves.

SINICIZED BARBARIAN RULE: THE MANCHU, OR CH'ING (17TH AND 18TH
CENTURIES A.D.). The Manchu who conquered China in the seventeenth
century were related to the Chin dynasty of five centuries before. The
Manchu first rose to power in Manchuria, in the upper Liao valley
between the Chinese-settled south and the nomad tribes to the north.
There they could study Ming administrative forms. As the Ming declined, the Manchu seized part of southern Manchuria in 1618 and began
to practice ruling over Chinese in the Chinese fashion. In 1644 they
entered Peking and took over the government, but they did not capture
the last claimant to the Ming throne until 1662, and they had to pursue
him into Burma to seize him.

In the process of quelling revolts in southern China, the Manchu
took Taiwan in 1683. The Ming had not ruled Taiwan, but Ming loyalists
and others used it as a base from which to raid the Fukien coast until
the Manchu occupied it. In the north the Manchu enrolled the tribes of
inner Mongolia as allies against those of outer Mongolia. Even before
1644 the Manchu had established close ties with the southern Mongols,
for they recognized fully the importance of controlling the steppe. In the
mid-eighteenth century the Manchu added Dzungaria and the Tarim
basin to their domains, giving the name Sinkiang (new province) to
these Turkic-inhabited regions. At the same period Tibet was incorporated into the Manchu empire as a protectorate after a century of experimenting with other methods of control.

Before the Manchu crossed the Wall in 1644, they took the name
Ch'ing for their dynasty. The Ch'ing learned well the lessons of the past.
They separated themselves from their subjects by elaborate rules designed to prevent every Manchu from following Chinese modes of life
and to keep each fit for military service. They trained and used Chinese
to quiet small local rebellions; but until the nineteenth century, Chinese
troops were never gathered in large armies as the Manchu and their
Mongol allies were, for the Ch'ing feared that a large Chinese force
might start an uprising. Yet the Ch'ing left the Ming administrative
system almost unchanged. They merely inserted themselves into it by
establishing the principle that Manchu and Chinese were to be equally
represented in the top levels of administration. In much of the central
administrative hierarchy, single positions were made into two offices, one
for a Manchu and one for a Chinese. Manchu governors-general were
appointed to oversee groups of provinces. Manchu military officials were

designated to assist—and watch—the Chinese civil governors. By these means the Ch'ing succeeded in striking a delicate but practicable balance between offering able Chinese an attractive field for their talents and offering ambitious Chinese an opening for rebellion.

The Ch'ing took care to enlist the support of the scholars by patronizing scholarly activities, for the Ch'ing wished the scholars to continue to encourage their ablest pupils to travel the path to public office through the examination system as they had under the Ming. The Ch'ing subsidized scholarly enterprises ranging from the writing of dictionaries, encyclopedias, geographies, and histories to the collecting of rare works. (In the late eighteenth century the Ch'ing also used the search for rare works to ferret out and destroy writings which cast reflections on the Ch'ing or on any previous nomad dynasty.) The scholars responded with a loyalty which lasted until the last days of the Ch'ing at the opening of the twentieth century. In large part, the Ch'ing owed their success to their skill in combining the maintenance of distinctions between Manchu and Chinese with a high degree of receptivity toward traditional Chinese attitudes and governmental patterns. Thus the Chinese entered the fateful nineteenth century still convinced of the superiority of their civilization, which even their Manchu rulers accepted, only to find that neither Manchu nor Chinese could maintain China's superiority in the face of western European strength and of the internal strains resulting from the doubling of the population since 1644.

KOREA

The mountainous peninsula of Korea was inhabited at least as early as 2000 B.C. by tribes who trickled into it from northern Asia. These tribes had traditions of hereditary aristocratic rule and worship of the spirits of nature, some of whom were considered the ancestors of various tribal leaders. Their languages were Altaic or Turkic-Mongol and used agglutinative prefixes and suffixes to express shades of meaning.

By the third century B.C. the people of northern Korea learned the arts of government and agriculture and the use of bronze and iron from the Chinese, partly through trade and probably partly from Chinese who fled to Korea during the wars of the late Chou period. The state of Choson, which the north Koreans founded, was conquered by Han Wu-ti in 109–108 B.C. For the next four hundred years, northern Korea was ruled by Chinese. The Chinese introduced the Koreans to the Chinese script, which was very difficult to use for an agglutinative language because its ideographs expressed only the unshaded meanings of the word-roots. Koreans in the south learned agriculture, writing, and the use of metal from the Chinese and soon began setting up small independent kingdoms.

When nomad victories over Chinese forces broke the link between north Korea and the Huang Ho valley at the close of the third century A.D., the south Korean kingdoms seized the northern districts for a time. Most of the peninsula soon came under the control of a new state, Koguryo, whose capital was in the north. Inspired by the heritage of Han China, the Koguryo rulers gave up their aristocratic tribal organization for the bureaucratic administration introduced by the Chinese and established institutions of Chinese learning. However, the south was still divided among tribally organized kingdoms like Silla, where society was divided between those whose ancestry made them eligible for leadership and those whose ancestry made them ineligible. During this period from the third to the sixth century A.D., the south was in closer touch with Japan than was the north.

When China was reunified, its rulers tried but failed to conquer Korea. After Koguryo repulsed the Sui, the T'ang renewed the attack, only to find it necessary to take Silla as an ally. By the time Koguryo fell in 668, Silla was strong and well-organized enough to force the T'ang to leave all but the northern one-fourth of the peninsula. The T'ang had to recognize the autonomy of the rest of Korea, which was ruled by Silla. In return, Silla paid tribute regularly to China and modeled its institutions on those of the powerful T'ang, as the Japanese were also doing in the seventh century A.D.

Although the new provinces, perfectures, and districts of seventh-century Silla were supervised by a carefully organized central government, the administrators continued to be drawn from the hereditary upper class. Only the greatest families were eligible to provide the highest officials. Even when an examination system was finally introduced in 788, the right to take the examinations was confined to members of the upper class. However, during the ninth century this aristocratic order was undermined by the rise of a merchant class enriched by the growth of the Korean-controlled trade between Korea, China, and Japan. In 901 a successful revolt led to the formation of the Koryo dynasty, which by 936 brought all of Korea under its control. The Koryo ruled until 1392.

Since the civil wars which preceded the Koryo victory wiped out the old aristocracy, the Koryo decided to establish a new one. In theory the right to take the civil service examinations was opened to all, but in practice the new aristocracy monopolized government office by effectively restricting the time and opportunity which commoners had for education. Since the entry of Chinese merchants into Korean trade was weakening local merchants—who were the only commoners wealthy enough to afford much formal education—the aristocracy met little opposition. The Koryo, like Silla before them, sent tribute to China's rulers in acknowledgment of their superiority. (Tribute was sent to both the Chin and the Southern Sung after 1127.) They did not acknowledge Mongol overlordship until 1258, but during their last years in power, they became so dependent on the Mongols that when the Mongols fell, the Koryo court began to consider attacking the Ming who had expelled them. Eventually an expedition was launched, but one of the generals assigned to lead it perceived the hopelessness of the idea and preserved Korea from Ming retaliation by rebelling. In 1388 he seized the capital and in 1392 the throne, founding the Yi dynasty, which lasted until 1910.

By the time the Manchu replaced the Ming in 1644, the Yi were already in their third century of rule. The first Yi rulers had revoked most of the land-tax exemptions granted by their Koryo predecessors, but they did not interfere with the tradition that only landholders took the examinations required to enter government service. The Yi lacked the strength to insist that their landowner-officials give them the kind of deference paid by Chinese landowner-officials to their rulers. However, the self-perpetuating administration which the Yi headed was stable enough to withstand internal factionalism, Japanese invasion, economic decline in the wake of the invasion, and the reappearance of tax-free estates. The Yi even survived a series of major revolts in the nineteenth century. Through these vicissitudes the Yi continued to uphold the Chinese tradition. They used its classics as the basis for the examinations; they clung to its external details even while they denied its spirit by limiting government services to a hereditary class; and they sent tribute to its rulers, first the Ming and then the Ch'ing. The Yi were as shocked as the Ch'ing when they discovered that the age-old Chinese system of international relations no longer worked in the circumstances of the nineteenth century.

JAPAN

RISE AND DECLINE OF THE IMPERIAL COURT (TO 1185 A.D.). From 3000 or 4000 B.C. on, the Japanese islands were inhabited by tribes, many of which came from northeast Asia by way of Korea. Others came from southeastern Asia by way of the Ryukyus. By approximately 200 B.C. these tribes had learned the use of bronze and iron and the Chinese techniques of rice-growing from newcomers who were continuing to arrive by way of Korea. In the third century A.D., when western Japan first appeared in Chinese records, one of its many clan heads was already beginning to be acknowledged by the rest as a religious leader. In the next several centuries Japanese rulers occasionally sent embassies to some of the dynasties in China, but the Japanese relied primarily on their close relations with southern Korea for contact with the mainland.

During the fourth and fifth centuries A.D. the Yamato clan of the Settsu plain extended its control over western and central Japan. Since the Yamato claimed descent from the sun, as other tribal groups claimed descent from other natural forces, the Yamato rulers were the high priests or priestesses of the sun-worshiping cult. Sun worship became the chief of the many nature cults of the island as the Yamato conquered their neighbors.

The Yamato used tribal principles of organization to incorporate everyone from agricultural worker to military aristocrat into one society based on a complex combination of hereditary titles and imperially conferred rank. The system soon became so difficult to manage that in the sixth century the Yamato rulers began confining themselves to the role of high priests or priestesses and leaving administrative tasks to others. When the Sui reunified China, the Yamato began to study Chinese methods of government in the hope of bringing order into the confusion of their administration. Shortly after the T'ang replaced the Sui, the Japanese state was remodeled along T'ang lines. On paper, hereditary aristocratic titles were replaced by imperially bestowed official ranks, an elaborate post road system was established, and agricultural land (the chief source of taxes) was declared to be state property to be periodically redistributed to the able-bodied who would provide the government with goods and services in return for the right to cultivate the soil. However, the new ranks were given almost entirely to holders of old titles; most of those appointed to office in the provinces were local men with hereditary claims to leadership. The tax system collapsed during the ninth century as powerful families were granted exemptions to keep them friendly to the throne. The post roads also fell into disrepair, although southern Kyushu and northern Honshu were added to the imperial domains before 900 A.D. The introduction of Chinese concepts concerning the seat of government proved more successful. In 710 the Yamato founded a capital city modeled on the T'ang capital. It was built with the aid and advice of Japanese scholars and artists who had accompanied the periodic embassies sent to China and who had spent one to twenty years studying every aspect of T'ang civilization. A second capital, Kyoto, was founded in 784, probably to enable the imperial clan to escape the influence of the leaders in the numerous temples and monasteries that had sprung up about the first capital of Nara. No additional cities were built, for Japan was still almost wholly agricultural. The Yamato also accepted the principle of masculine rule from China. After 784 no empresses succeeded to the throne, except in one brief period almost a thousand years later.

During the ninth century the court ceased to send embassies to the T'ang. Not only were the T'ang declining, but the Japanese had studied China so intensively that they were ready for a period of quiet assimilation. Private trade with the mainland continued, but no more formal embassies were sent for over five hundred years. As the embassies to the mainland ceased, the Chinese-inspired imperial government of Japan changed. The tax and post road systems fell into disuse, while the court nobility in effect replaced the imperial clan as managers of Japanese affairs. The court nobles, led by the Fujiwara family, acquired this leadership through their possession of influence in the capital and landed estates in the countryside.

As the rule of the court nobles displaced the T'ang-inspired bureaucratic system, the nobles appointed men to manage their rural holdings so that they could remain in the capital. Many of the estate managers came from families with long traditions of local leadership. Soon these men began to maneuver for local power, either in their own interest or in that of the nobles they served, and they started raising private armies for both defensive and offensive purposes. The estate managers still provided the court nobility with income in return for continued exemption from imperial taxes, but as they built up followings of *samurai* (mounted warriors), they also began to form alliances among themselves. The court nobles then began to bring these warrior bands to the capital to use in their own struggles for power. Finally, in 1185, the largest warrior band took control of the capital and made its members stewards alongside the court nobles' estate managers throughout the country. The victorious band came from Kamakura, in the Kanto plain.

STRUGGLE AMONG THE WARRIORS: KAMAKURA TO THE ESTABLISHMENT OF TOKUGAWA (1185–1603 A.D.). With the victory of the Kamakura warriors the central government of Japan passed from the chief court nobles, who had taken it from the emperor, to the acknowledged leader of the estate managers. Yet the theoretical supremacy of the court and the role of the emperor as high priest were unquestioned, much as the priestly function of the Chou was unquestioned in China when their vassals ceased to heed their commands. The leader of the estate managers was not given formal imperial recognition until seven years after he established his privately-run government. In 1192 the emperor appointed him *shogun*, or generalissimo, head of the imperial military forces. Since the first shogun and his successors used Kamakura as their headquarters, the period of their rule is called the Kamakura shogunate (1185–1333).

In 1274 and 1281 the Kamakura had to face the efforts of the powerful Mongols to conquer Japan, the only full-scale invasions launched against the islands before the twentieth century. The Mongols amassed huge fleets, with Korean cooperation, but failed to overcome Kamakura resistance. Although the shogunate threw back the invasions—with the help of a great storm in 1281 which largely destroyed the Mongol fleet— it did not survive much longer. The ties of loyalty which bound the first stewards to the shogun wore thin as the generations passed. When one emperor took up the sword to claim that he should rule as well as reign, the Kamakura government quickly fell. However, another military man soon ended the emperor's experiment and set up a puppet emperor who made his military sponsor shogun in 1336.

By the time the Kamakura fell, the Japanese had fully assimilated what they had learned from China. They had rejected what seemed unsuitable to them and adopted or adapted what they could effectively use. The examination system was an early and notable casualty in this process. The Chinese emphasis on family loyalty as the basis of the state was another casualty, since loyalty between lord and vassal was the fundamental political bond for the warrior bands. Chinese Confucianist suggestions concerning the fallibility of dynasties and the possibility that Heaven might decree their replacement were ignored, as being incompatible with Japanese concepts of loyalty. Nevertheless, as rising production and trade led to improved communications and greater leisure, Chinese artistic and literary influences spread. The history of Japanese writing shows the strength of Chinese influence. By the late ninth century the Japanese developed two phonetic systems for writing the agglutinative Japanese language. However, those phonetic systems were left to the women, while the men continued to study and write either in pure Chinese or in a difficult mixture of Chinese and Japanese written in Chinese characters. (The same sort of thing happened in Korea in the fifteenth century.) The prestige of Chinese learning made Japanese warriors proud to master it, unlike their western European counterparts who tended to look down on literary accomplishments.

The replacement of the Kamakura by the Ashikaga shogunate in 1336 showed that the Japanese court had, in effect, discarded Chinese-style bureaucratic rule in favor of asking the warriors to maintain order, since they had the strength to enforce obedience. The Ashikaga shogunate never controlled as much of Japan as the Kamakura, but the local leaders of warrior bands continued the tradition of military rule, whether or not they gave allegiance to the shogunate.

The local warrior leaders continued Japanese internal economic expansion by protecting local markets and encouraging trade. They also recognized the *za,* groups of merchants and artisans which functioned like guilds. As long as the za paid certain fees, stipulated in advance, the warriors let their members carry on their trade without further exactions. This arrangement contrasted sharply with the situation in China, where guild members might be subjected to unscheduled exactions at any time. By the sixteenth century, money rather than barter was used in all but the smallest transactions in Japan, and many towns had grown up around castles, temples, marketplaces, harbors, and post stations on the roads.

Increasing numbers of Japanese traders had visited Korea since the eleventh century and China since the twelfth. In the fourteenth century they began using the excellent swords made in Japan not only as articles of trade but as weapons, forcing reluctant Chinese and Korean city governors to let them trade. As the fifteenth century progressed, Japanese thronged China's shores, defying Ashikaga efforts to monopolize the lucrative Chinese trade by entering tributary relations with the Ming in 1401. Japanese merchant adventurers even sailed to Southeast Asia, where they met the Portuguese in the sixteenth century.

By 1500 A.D. many Japanese merchants were going abroad in the service of *daimyo*, local warrior lords whose power was based on the loyalty of their armed retainers or samurai. The daimyo were discovering that trade brought in money, which could hire, equip, and maintain warriors to conquer and administer their weaker neighbors' domains. The resultant warfare was carried on through the sixteenth century almost without reference to the Ashikaga, who finally disappeared in 1573.

In their struggle for power, the daimyo paid little heed to traditional class distinctions. Merchants were too helpful as financiers to be disdained; commoners were too useful in warfare to be ignored, particularly after the Portuguese introduced firearms to Japan in the 1540s. Temples and trading towns also built up military forces in self-defense. However, only the wealthier daimyo could afford cannon or the stone walls necessary for defense from cannon-shot. By 1590 a process of ruthless elimination begun by Oda Nobunaga (d. 1582) enabled a man of peasant stock, Toyotomi Hideyoshi, to force all the daimyo to become his vassals and persuade the emperor to give him a high civil office. Hideyoshi sought to end the turbulence of the past by requiring all commoners to give up their arms and by prohibiting warriors, townspeople, and peasants from changing their status, but he overreached himself when he invaded Korea. Although his armies were successful at first, they met disaster as soon as the Ming sent Korea aid. After Hideyoshi died in 1598, his young son inherited his post, but he was soon displaced by one of Hideyoshi's vassals, Tokugawa Ieyasu. In 1603 the emperor made Tokugawa Ieyasu shogun.

TOKUGAWA JAPAN (17TH AND 18TH CENTURIES). Like the Ch'ing in China, Tokugawa Ieyasu studied the lessons of the past with care, and he constructed his government in accord with what he observed. He recognized the existing political reality of the daimyo, who ruled their domains as petty sovereigns. Many daimyo were left in control of their lands and followers and merely took an oath of allegiance to Ieyasu. Others kept their followers, but were shifted to different domains. Even some who had opposed Ieyasu were left in power, but he carefully placed daimyo loyal to himself in the domains surrounding their lands. Central Japan from Kyoto to the Kanto plain was reserved for Ieyasu and his closest followers. Ieyasu constructed the strongest fortified castle in the country in his own capital of Edo (now Tokyo), established a second great fortress in the heart of Kyoto and destroyed most of the palace used by Hideyoshi, and forbade anyone else to build or repair a castle unless Edo first approved the plans.

The Tokugawa interfered little with internal domain affairs. However, to forestall possible rebellion, Ieyasu and his immediate successors placed restrictions on the daimyo. Each daimyo had to leave his wife and children in Edo at all times as hostages for his good conduct and had to spend alternate years or half-years in Edo. The expense of keeping one establishment in his domain and one in Edo drained his purse so that he could scarcely afford to equip a rebel army, even if he thought he could hide his plans from Tokugawa spies. He was forbidden to contract marriage or form any relationship with another daimyo without the shogun's permission. He also had to accept the general rules established for all domains. Any breach of these rules was followed by dispossession from part or all of his lands, or by reassignment to a smaller domain. The Tokugawa did not fully trust any of the daimyo; but they trusted least the families of Ieyasu's former opponents, who were called the "outside lords." The outside lords (most of whom were outside physically as well as politically, being in the north and west) were never included in Tokugawa councils as were the "inside lords," the descendants of Ieyasu's earlier supporters.

The Tokugawa did not stop with regulating the daimyo. They sought to stabilize all of society by vigorously applying Hideyoshi's plan to freeze the class structure. Sharp distinctions were drawn between sword-bearing samurai and commoners, and between food-producing peasants, goods-producing artisans, and nonproductive parasitic merchants. Placards enjoining all classes to practice loyalty and filial piety were posted even in the smallest hamlet, as had long been done in China, so that the literate few could read them to the illiterate many.

By the 1630s these placards also contained prohibitions against the Christian faith introduced by the Portuguese. After considering the risks to which continued entry of foreign goods and ideas could expose their carefully planned system, the early Tokugawa decided to root out Christianity, which in the Roman Catholicism of the Portuguese acknowledged the spiritual authority of a prelate in Europe. The Tokugawa also restricted foreign trade to one port on the western island of Kyushu. Chinese and Dutch merchants could trade there on very limited terms, but no other foreigners could enter the country. The daimyo nearest Korea welcomed Korean traders despite the restrictions; the daimyo nearest the Ryukyus conquered the northern part of the chain and traded with Chinese merchants who went there. However, even these two daimyo did not disobey the shogunate's command that in future, no

Japanese was to be permitted to leave Japanese territory or reenter it from abroad—an edict which left Japanese merchants in Southeast Asia stranded when it went into effect in 1637.

The Tokugawa tried to mold Japanese life into a set pattern and then hold change to a minimum. Yet their own alternate-attendance system, which required the daimyo to divide their time between their domains and Edo, helped to integrate Japan's economic life at the national level and thereby make obsolete the political compartmentalization of the domains. The alternate-attendance system brought good roads to every part of Japan. It stimulated urban growth along the most frequently used routes and made Edo larger than any European capital in the early 1700s. It promoted the growing money economy, as daimyo sold their domains' products to raise funds for their trips to and from Edo and for their households there. The need for money led daimyo to encourage villagers to raise cash crops in large enough quantities to herald the start of commercial agriculture. Meanwhile, prosperous urban merchants evaded all the restrictive sumptuary laws by which the shogunate tried to limit their expenditures. From the late seventeenth century on, city life was as gay and opulent in Japan as it had been in the China of the Southern Sung.

Unlike China and Korea, Japan entered the nineteenth century in a state of ferment. Its economy was growing, not stagnating like theirs. As a result, its society was feeling stresses somewhat like those which disrupted early modern Europe, not resting content with the existing order as were China and Korea. Furthermore, a variety of intellectual movements had prepared leading Japanese to embark on a nationalist course, while the leaders of China, at least, were not prepared by their philosophic traditions to accept the presuppositions of modern nationalism.

Thought-Patterns:
The Search for Harmony with Heaven and Earth

ORGANIZATION OF THE UNIVERSE

The earliest Chinese, Koreans, and Japanese of whose religion anything is known seem to have believed that the universe resulted from the interaction of natural forces controlled by powerful spirits. The universe was not illusory to them, as it was to thinkers in ancient India, nor was it a temporary creation, as it was to Muslims, Christians, and Jews. The universe was simply the expression of the forces of nature as affected by the spirits which inhabited nature. Some of these spirits were found in natural phenomena, like heaven, the sun, earth, water, grain, or mountains. Some of them were the ghosts of persons whose life-force was so strong that it continued to operate after their bodies died. At first it was assumed that only the ancestors of the aristocracy were powerful enough in the world of spirits to be worthy of propitiation, but eventuallly those on every social level revered their ancestors in the hope of receiving the ancestors' assistance, or at least avoiding their curse.

By Chou times the Chinese distinguished fairly clearly between the spirits of nature and the spirits of human beings. They worshiped natural forces, such as those of heaven, earth, and grain, as deities, and they revered their forebears as ancestral spirits. However, if more were known about pre-Chou China, it might be discovered that the first Chinese mingled ghosts and deities as thoroughly as Koreans and Japanese were doing when they were first discussed in Chinese writings. Not only did Japan's imperial clan claim descent from the sun, but every Japanese and Korean clan regarded a certain natural force as its ancestor. The remark that the Chinese made deities of their ancestors while the Japanese made ancestors of their gods and goddesses is too simple to be accurate, but it is true enough to be partly useful.

Chinese, Koreans, and Japanese shared a belief in the reality of the visible universe which was so strong that they made no allowance for activity or interest in any other sphere. They did not assume a sharp division between the illusory and the truly real as Indians did, or between the temporal and the eternal as Middle Easterners did. To Chinese, Koreans, and Japanese, even the spirits they worshiped operated within the universe they lived in, although the spirits might often be in regions unknown to human beings. Most Middle Easterners assumed a struggle between good and evil, in which were contrasted the temporal and eternal. Most Indians assumed that the illusory and the ultimate were irreconcilable; but most East Asians thought of opposites as supplementing each other rather than being constantly at war. What could be more opposite than cold and heat? Yet each has its uses, and out of their mingling come the various degrees of temperature.

Building on the belief that opposites are complementary, the Chinese classified every natural phenomenon from food to the winds of heaven as *yang* (e.g. male, sun, south, hot, bright, active) or *yin* (e.g. female, moon, north, cold, dark, passive). Neither the yang nor the yin classification meant a thing was good or bad. What was bad was an overdose, like being burned or frozen. Goodness meant balancing each with the other, tempering liberality with prudence to avoid wastefulness, tempering thrift with generosity to avoid miserliness.

The Koreans and Japanese borrowed the Chinese system of classification into yang and yin, but they did not fully accept the Chinese assumption that the same thing might be good in some situations and bad in others. Instead they retained a strong belief that certain actions were unclean in and of themselves, regardless of circumstances, and that any such actions must be followed by ritual purification to avert divine anger.

EARLY RELIGION

With their belief in a real world in which real spirits had a real influence over the outcome of events, early Chinese, Koreans, and Japanese tended to think in terms of searching for the best place for themselves in the world they saw around them. They concluded that they should fit themselves into the rhythmic pattern of the universe, living so as to be in harmony with the basic triad of heaven, earth, and human society. In the Western world and the Middle East, the belief that human beings live simultaneously in society, in the natural world, and in the supernatural or eternal realm would correspond roughly to this East Asian triad. However, Jews, Christians, and Muslims have assumed that the finite natural and social worlds could never harmonize perfectly with the infinite and transcendent supernatural, while no such assumption was ordinarily made by Chinese, Koreans, and Japanese. To them, all three members of the triad—heaven, earth, and human society—were part of the same realm, not of different realms.

Traditional East Asian religious and philosophical systems sought accord with the natural order of the universe. However, Chinese, Koreans, and Japanese followed differing paths toward that goal. Until the time when the Yamato court began to borrow ideas wholesale from China, the Japanese followed the path of Shinto, the way of the deities. Shinto involved displaying reverence for all the powers of nature, including ancestral spirits, and avoiding any act which would displease them. When acts disturbing to the unseen powers could not be avoided—chopping down a tree to build a house, moving a corpse to its burial place—propitiatory and expiatory rites were performed to ward off the spirits' wrath. Most Shinto rites, which included sacrifices, prayers, and ablutions, had both a hopeful and a fearful aspect—hopeful that the deities and spirits would be kind if properly worshiped, fearful of their anger if they were neglected or scorned. As might be expected from the similar antecedents of the Korean and Japanese peoples, the early popular religion of Korea was much like Shinto. However, Korean popular religion gradually turned toward fear, while Japanese religion tended to incline toward hope. Japanese hopefulness was later demonstrated in Buddhist rosaries made of smiling Buddha-heads, not of miniature skulls as in India.

The Chinese shared a related set of beliefs which they termed *feng-shui*, wind and water, and which Western observers have termed geomancy. Feng-shui required that every building be carefully located so as to be in accord with the local pattern of winds and streams—a wise precaution in a land of storms and floods, although carried out on somewhat different principles from those used by Western architects and engineers concerned with wind stress and water action. Every Chinese villager also did homage to the deities of the soil and grain, but only the emperor, whose title was Son of Heaven, could sacrifice to the spirit of heaven. No Chinese emperor of historic times was ever regarded as a literal descendant of heaven. However, his title and his exclusive right to sacrifice to heaven may possibly have come from a time when the Chinese, too, made ancestors of their deities.

TAOIST AND CONFUCIAN PHILOSOPHY AND PRACTICE

Early East Asian popular religions sought to harmonize the relations between human beings and the world of which they were part, so that they would not upset its workings. As religion shaded into philosophical speculation, first in China and then in Korea and Japan, many carried this search for harmony over into the doctrine of *Tao*, the Way. To them, Tao was the way of naturalness. Artifices were to be avoided, for they set one against nature rather than joining one with nature. The true way was *wu-wei*, not-striving, by which the Taoists or followers of Tao meant taking everything that came, including death, as part of the natural course of events. This open-hearted acceptance of things as they are, neither praising nor condemning nor attempting to change them, somewhat resembles the concept of the multiform dharma in traditional India. When Indian thought first came to China in the form of Buddhism, not only the Taoists but also many others regarded it as similar to Taoism. However, the Chinese soon began to realize that the Indian origin of Buddhism made its teachers see the world as an unreal illusion to be left behind, and that therefore Buddhism was different from Chinese beliefs, which proceeded from the assumption that the world was real and ought to be enjoyed.

Taoist insistence that spontaneity was the way toward harmony with nature ran counter to the current of the times, for all complex large-scale societies depend on artifices such as metallurgy, writing, and political organization. Many were attracted to Taoism, particularly among those not in public office, but its adherents rarely ran society. Instead, the leaders of society came to be inspired by the doctrines of Confucius, who in the troubled era of the later Chou period called on men and women to attain harmony with the natural order by practicing virtue.

To Confucius and his followers, one could best achieve harmony with heaven and earth by being in harmony with other people. They focused on society as the realm in which human energy could be most fruitfully used, unlike the Taoists, who concentrated on the natural world, or the popular religions, which emphasized the realm of spirits. The Confucianists stressed the proper maintenance of the five relationships between ruler and minister, father and son, elder and younger brother, husband and wife, and friend and friend. They believed that upholding the five relationships was the best way to promote social harmony, which would enable people to live together in cooperation not only with one another but also with the forces of nature and with the deities and spirits. The forces of nature would respond to such cooperative human efforts as irrigation works; the deities and spirits would rejoice when men and women lived in harmony. In short, Confucianism was essentially as hopeful as Taoism.

When Confucius was teaching his first followers, the five relationships were assuredly not being properly upheld. Minister deserted ruler, son betrayed father, brother fought brother, wife and husband quarreled, and friends broke their pledges to one another. Therefore the Confucianists said that the men who held positions of authority should use the power of example to promote the needed virtues of benevolence, righteousness, considerateness, integrity, and loyalty. Since these virtues were rare, a man would have to be carefully trained in them if he were to serve as an example to others. The Confucianists brought together a set of books from which a man could learn the nature of each virtue and how it should be practiced, and they recommended that every prospective official be examined on his knowledge of those books before being given office. These were the arguments underlying the civil service examination system introduced by the Han. Unquestionably, the Han decision to favor the Confucian school was vitally affected by Confucian emphasis on hierarchical rank, the preservation of order, and the observance of rules that would make their subjects' behavior more predictable and less disruptive.

The Confucianists believed that the ability to become virtuous was inherent in everyone, not just in a few as the aristocracy would have others believe. Though they laid greater stress on the instruction of men, who were expected to take the lead in public affairs, they also provided for the instruction of mothers, wives, and daughters in the proper performance of their duties to their families and neighbors. Stories of virtuous women were compiled, to be read by the few women whose families could afford to give private instruction to them and their brothers while they were still children, or to be told or read aloud to others. As Confucius' chief follower Mencius put it, "Every man can be a Yao or a Shun." (Yao and Shun were two legendary sage-kings known to all Chinese; Mencius' own mother became enshrined as a model for other women because of the care she took in rearing him after his father's death.) Therefore every man should be free to take the examinations and enter government service. However, the Confucianists made a few exceptions. Merchants and their sons, and a few other occupational groups such as actors, were excluded from the examinations because the Confucianists thought they were so contaminated by selfishness and greed that no amount of study could make them altruistic. Together with the fact that an individual had to spend all his time in study to become proficient enough in the difficult Chinese written language to pass the examinations, the limitations on merchant families effectively restricted the group which could take the examinations to the sons and protégés of wealthy landowners. Still, a merchant could make his descendants eligible by becoming a landholder. Furthermore, most clans had at least one member who could afford to support the education of a promising boy. Such education was regarded as an investment, for advancement to high office brought opportunities to acquire land as a reward for service and to receive fees of various types, as well as giving prestige to the individual, his household, and his clan. Besides, most officials were more lenient with members of a colleague's clan than with members of clans which contained no officials.

Once in office, the official was to use precept and example to guide those beneath him into the way of social harmony, which included paying taxes and other levies as well as keeping public order. He was to be like a father, chastising when necessary, but reserving the use of chastisement until all other means had failed. His ability to cope with the problems which arose in his sphere of action was measured in large part by the presence or absence of discords inharmonious enough to reach his superiors' ears. Occasionally the disputes he had to resolve were based on honest misunderstandings which investigation and explanation could dispel; but as dynasties rose and fell, most officials came to feel that any dispute which the parties could not resolve themselves by mutual agreement or through some nonofficial degree-holder's mediation was itself evidence of their lack of virtue. Virtue, after all, was harmony with a universe which was basically one rather than conformity to a standard laid down by the Infinite for the finite. By the time Western concepts came to China in the nineteenth century, many officials cared little how a dispute was settled as long as the disruption it produced was stilled.

Since there were many diploma-holders and few positions in the latter Ch'ing era, ambitious degree-holders usually had to win the favor of higher authorities to obtain a post. The most effective way to do this was to contribute handsomely to the funds at the disposal of the authorities for public (and occasionally private) use. To recover such expenses, officials often accepted presents from those involved in disputes which fell within their jurisdiction. Bribery even touched the supervisory officials of the central government, who ceased to be effectual in ferreting out and dismissing officials whose favor could be purchased. The maintenance of an outward semblance of harmony was preferred to all other considerations, with results not unlike those produced by partly similar circumstances in the later Ottoman empire. By the end of the eighteenth century, many government officials in both China and the Ottoman Empire were anxious only to give capricious rulers no excuse to replace them. They vacillated between local factions, accepting presents from all sides but rarely satisfying any one group for long, in unsuccessful attempts to avert complaints by local residents to their superiors. In China, these complaints came largely from would-be office-holders who used local grievances to bring themselves to the attention of higher officials, while in the Ottoman domains they came largely from leaders of the religious communities, who did not see themselves as potential government administrators but were primarily interested in the well-being of their coreligionists. Yet in spite of all the maneuvering for position which took place in actual practice, the ideal of a genuinely peaceful society, living in harmony with the universe under the benevolent guidance of men selected for virtue rather than wealth or power, inspired Chinese until the close of the dynastic period.

During the long span of China's development, many other concepts were woven into the noble ideal of the harmonious society. One was the Mandate of Heaven, the belief that heaven could and would decree the overthrow of the Son of Heaven himself if he were not virtuous. By justifying successful revolutions, the Mandate of Heaven concept undoubtedly encouraged many who were distressed by the floods and famines that occurred when dynastic governments lost their efficiency after a century or two and failed to keep up the dikes and levees. Another important concept was the belief that the Son of Heaven was sovereign not only over the Chinese but also over all other peoples, so that every nation must acknowledge him in order for the universe to be truly harmonious. This belief was the foundation on which the Chinese rested their tributary system of international relations. As long as the only world the Chinese knew from experience was East Asia, where their size, wealth, strength and cultural advancement were unmatched, the facts of political life and the belief did little violence to each other—except during the Yuan period, when China briefly belonged to an imperial system that extended far beyond East Asia.

THE RECONSTRUCTION OF BUDDHISM

By the end of the Han dynasty in the third century A.D., the Chinese had developed the basic concepts that they held until the twentieth century. They strove for harmony with the universe through the unselfish practice of the five major social relationships: ruler and minister, father and son, brother and brother, husband and wife, friend and friend. They believed these relationships would best be promoted by officials whom the ruler chose for the ability to demonstrate a knowledge of virtuous behavior. They also believed the ruler himself was subject to heaven's decree, even though he was master of all humanity. The collapse of the Han and the dismemberment of the empire dealt the supporters of these ideas a serious blow, for the whole hierarchically ordered system fell apart when there was no emperor to serve as its head.

In the period of barbarian incursions from the north which followed the Han collapse, the cheery hopefulness of the Confucianists seemed inadequate to many Chinese. Even the Taoists, who were less tied to a specific political system, failed to meet the need of the Chinese for consolation in a time of trouble. Instead, the Chinese turned to the Buddhist doctrines brought to the ports of south China by missionary Indians and overland to north China by missionary Indians and converted barbarians.

Confucianists were scandalized by the Buddhist practice of monasticism, which prevented those who followed it from engaging in the five relationships. Such a clash was natural between a doctrine oriented toward society and one oriented away from society. Taoists were equally scandalized by the Buddhist assumption that one's goal was to escape the world around one as illusory, rather than to unite with it as real. Still, the richness of Buddhist teaching appealed to those of a speculative turn of mind, for it opened up the vast sophisticated realm of Indian thought.

Most of the Buddhist teachers who came to China in the early Christian era from India and Central Asia taught the Mahayana doctrine. This doctrine states that the ordinary person could attain release by receiving aid from the *bodhisattvas*, those who were ready to leave behind the wheel of life and death but who remained in the world to help others to attain release. With their vows of helpfulness to all living beings, the bodhisattvas were attractive figures to distressed Chinese, alarmed for the future now that the great Han empire had crashed in ruins. The Buddhists themselves modified their doctrine by saying that sons and daughters could acquire merit on behalf of their parents and deceased ancestors. Through entering monastic life or giving gifts to monasteries, a devoted son or daughter could speed his or her forebears toward the desired goal of release. The theological justification for this belief in the transferability of merit is extremely abstruse, but the practical one is obvious: it fitted Buddhism neatly into a society whose cardinal sin was the denial of obligations to others and particularly to one's ancestors.

By the time the Sui and the T'ang reunited China, Buddhism was as completely woven into the fabric of Chinese life as were Confucianism and Taoism. All the protests of the Confucianists, whose importance revived as the empire was reunified, failed to destroy Buddhism. Ordinary Chinese continued to seek the aid of specialists in Taoism when illness was to be cured by restoration to harmony with nature. They continued to heed the Confucianists in matters of social intercourse. However, they sought the ministrations of Buddhist priests and monks at the time of death, when the soul of the departed was being judged to determine whether it would rise or fall in its next existence, for the Chinese accepted the doctrines of karma (consequence) and rebirth even more widely than those of maya (illusion) and nirvana (release or extinction).

One might almost say the Chinese assigned the task of harmonization with each component of the triad of heaven, earth, and human society to a different system of thought and belief: Buddhism for heaven, Taoism for earth, and Confucianism for human affairs. However, this was not quite true. Those educated most thoroughly in the Confucian classics insisted that their doctrine was all-sufficient and that Buddhism and Taoism were worthless superstitions. During the later T'ang and the Sung eras, Confucianists strove to compete with the attractions of Buddhist philosophy by grafting onto their teaching a metaphysical explanation of the universe which used familiar Chinese terms like yang and yin, but owed much to Indian concepts introduced by the Buddhists. Otherwise, the officially supported Confucian system of thought remained largely unaltered between Han and Ch'ing times. After the T'ang, the only rulers who failed to acknowledge the supremacy of the Confucianists were the Yuan, who filled government posts with adherents of foreign religions like Islam and Christianity. Yet even the Yuan retained much of the Confucian state structure, stressing the precepts which upheld the prerogatives of the Son of Heaven.

Buddhism also took hold in Korea, where the continuance of a hereditary class structure showed that the Confucian ideas brought to nothern Korea by the Han were only partly assimilated. In Korea as in China, Confucianism and Buddhism became part of a triad of doctrines: Confucianism (in modified form) for social harmony, Buddhism for harmony with the universe, and the cults of local deities and spirits for harmony with the world immediately present to the senses. A similar triad eventually developed in Japan, taking the form of Buddhism, Shinto, and a modified Confucianism. In fact, Buddhism was a more important vehicle of Chinese civilization than Confucianism, in Japan. The period of greatest Japanese cultural borrowing from China, the seventh and eighth centuries A.D., was also the period of greatest Buddhist influence in China. A person could even enter some branches of the T'ang civil service by being examined on Buddhist or Taoist writings rather than the Confucian classics. However, the patronage given to Buddhism by the one woman who ever tried to claim the title of emperor of China for herself, early in the T'ang era, helped to discredit Buddhism in Confucian eyes thereafter.

JAPANESE MODIFICATIONS OF CHINESE BUDDHISM AND CONFUCIANISM

Buddhism was seldom challenged in Japan between the seventh and the seventeenth century. The upper classes almost ignored the teachings of the Shinto cults. Shinto and Buddhism sought to absorb each other's followers, each one claiming that the deities of the other were really manifestations of its own. This technique had worked for the Hindus in India, where they and the Buddhists started from the same premises, but it did not work in Japan, where Shinto assumed the reality of the visible universe while Buddhism assumed its unreality. As the Japanese became more confident of their ability to match Chinese accomplishments—witness the export of manufactured goods like swords and fans—many of them returned to the religion of their ancestors. However, they now combined its practice with the practice of Buddhism.

Under the influence of Taoism, with its emphasis on spontaneity, Chinese Buddhism had developed the Ch'an or meditation sect out of one line of Buddhist speculation. The Ch'an teachers thought the way to attain the release one sought was simply to discipline oneself until one suddenly realized there was nothing to seek. One was already released, if one could believe it, for illusion is all in one's mind. In the East Asian context of a real world, this meant one could live in harmony with reality, though in the Indian context of an illusory world it meant one could live without attachment to phenomena.

Few Chinese accepted Ch'an Buddhism. Its emphasis on disciplining the will rather than the intellect grated on the sensibilities of a people long attuned to a belief that intellectual activity was superior to all other forms of behavior. However, Ch'an teachings flourished in Japan. The Ch'an stress on will rather than intellect appealed strongly to the warriors, who found as much satisfaction in Ch'an teaching as peasants and townspeople found in the bodhisattvas worshiped by those who preached reliance on the aid of these benign figures for release. As Zen Buddhism, the half-Taoist Ch'an teachings became the inspiration of Japan's ruling class in the Kamakura and Ashikaga shogunates.

In Kamakura times a Japanese named Nichiren founded the only Buddhist sect ever to attach itself so firmly to one social body, the Japanese people, that its leaders attacked all other Buddhist sects as harmful to the well-being of the nation. It was scarcely accidental that this sect arose at the time the Mongols defeated Korea, foreshadowing the one recorded attempt to invade Japan before the twentieth century. Fear of conquest heightened the self-consciousness which Japan's isolation from the mainland always encouraged, just as resentment of Yuan use of non-Confucianized outsiders encouraged strong attachment to all things Confucian and opposition to all things non-Confucian in the China of the Ming and Ch'ing.

Under the personal discipline of Zen, the warriors finally united Japan at the end of the sixteenth century, only to find they needed a doctrine of social responsibility. They required every Japanese family to register at a Buddhist temple, but Buddhism was too concerned with the individual, and to a lesser extent with his or her family, to be useful in promoting loyalty to the society beyond the family. The Tokugawa therefore turned to Confucianism.

As an enjoiner of social harmony through the stabilization of the social order in a unified state, Confucianism fitted Tokugawa realities better than it had ever fitted earlier Japanese political life. (The social mobility afforded by the examination system was still ignored.) The supremacy of Confucian doctrine was bolstered by the continued prestige in Japan of all things Chinese. The Tokugawa used Confucianism to justify the rule of the samurai as the superior or princely man of Confucian doctrine, and to explain the low standing assigned to merchants in spite of their evident prosperity. Tokugawa Confucianists also emphasized loyalty to one's overlord as the cardinal virtue, not just one of several. They were doubtless grateful to Chinese authors for mentioning the relationship of ruler and minister first in the list of the five major social relationships, even though the family nature of three of the rest betokened the overriding importance of the family in the Chinese Confucian system.

In Japan as in China, Confucianists sought to draw lessons for the present from the experience of the past. Like the Japanese court of the seventh and eighth centuries, or the scholars of Silla in Korea, the Tokugawa samurai emulated Chinese Confucians by studying and writing history. They promptly discovered that the powerless emperor in Kyoto, descendant of the sun-goddess, ought in theory to exercise the authority actually held by the shogun. The resulting tensions were as much a part of eighteenth-century Japanese ferment as the breaking down of class barriers which occurred whenever impecunious samurai married the daughters or adopted the sons of merchants in lieu of paying the debts they incurred as they followed their lords to and from Edo.

The peoples of East Asia entered the nineteenth century still convinced that they were living in a real world, despite fifteen hundred years of Buddhist preaching. They believed that in this real world they should seek harmony with heaven, earth, and their fellows, and that they could attain the desired harmony through Buddhism, the original local cults, and Confucianism. The ways of western Europeans were to disturb them profoundly, for Western ways were based on belief in a universe divided into two realms, eternal and temporal. Westerners were used to choosing between good (or eternal) and bad (or temporal), in courts, in legislatures, and in religious life, not to resolving conflicts by acknowledging the partial justifiability of all claims, like East Asians. When the first Europeans reached East Asian waters in the sixteenth century, only their goods won much acceptance. European ideas had but little effect before the second wave of European overseas expansion in the nineteenth century.

7

THE WESTERN IMPACT
ON EAST ASIA

Early Contacts with Europeans

PORTUGUESE AND JESUITS IN CHINA AND JAPAN
(16TH AND 17TH CENTURIES)

If one takes seriously the claims of certain traders listed in Han records as tribute-bearers from Rome, the earliest Sino-Western contacts were in the second century A.D. However, the first period in which Chinese and western Europeans had a chance to know each other directly was the Yuan era, during which merchants like the Polo family and missionaries like William of Rubruck came to China from Europe. Europeans were deeply impressed by China's size and wealth, but the Chinese saw little of their European visitors, who had more to do with the Mongols than with the Chinese. The Chinese did not become aware of Europeans as a distinct group of people until the sixteenth century, when the Portuguese arrived from their newly seized bases in the Indian Ocean to seek trade with China and Japan.

The first Portuguese landings were made along the China coast. To the Ming rulers in Peking they were merely sea-borne barbarians who came from farther away than the Japanese and who resembled the Japanese in their willingness to resort to arms if local authorities tried to restrict them. As barbarians, they were to be brought within the tributary system or else expelled.

The Portuguese sent a mission to Peking in 1517, three years after their first arrival in south China, but the Ming refused to accept the Portuguese overtures. The Ming were hearing too much about Portuguese piracy and conquest in Southeast Asia to be in a receptive mood. For forty years the Portuguese made technically illegal and frequently piratical visits to south China. On some of the later visits they helped Chinese officials to suppress Chinese pirates operating near Canton. Finally, in 1557, they were granted informal permission to reside on the isolated peninsula of Macao and to trade in Canton under Chinese governmental supervision.

By the time Portuguese traders were allowed to reside in Macao, other Portuguese had reached Japan. Portuguese firearms immediately found a market there, for the Japanese were then in the midst of the struggle for supremacy among the daimyo. The Portuguese, whose expeditions had been partly motivated by anti-Muslim feeling, introduced Roman Catholic Christianity to the Japanese through the Jesuit missionary Francis Xavier in 1549. They also sought to place missionaries in China, but did not succeed until 1582 when the Jesuit Matteo Ricci arrived at Macao on his way to Peking, bringing recent European scientific advances with him as well as Christian teaching.

The Jesuits' path in Japan was smoothed by the outward resemblances between Christianity and Buddhism, and by the desire of the daimyo to trade with the Portuguese, who refused to trade where missionaries were not welcome. Ambitious daimyo eagerly accepted the guns, the methods of fortification, and the trade opportunities offered by the Portuguese, for guns, forts, and money could help the daimyo master their neighbors. In return they gave the Jesuits freedom to preach in their domains. Hundreds of thousands of Japanese embraced Christianity by the 1630s, when the Tokugawa decided to get rid of the foreign religion. All of them were Roman Catholics, for the Protestant Dutch who joined Portuguese and Spanish traders along the Japanese coast after 1600 were uninterested in proselytization.

Once Hideyoshi and the Tokugawa completed the reunification of Japan and the construction of an effective government, the growing importance of Western trade and Western ways began to alarm many Japanese leaders. They feared that either the Portuguese or the Spaniards, who had recently taken the Philippines, would conquer Japan by using their superior firearms, their growing knowledge of the islands, and their close relationship with the Christian Japanese and with the daimyo of the trading centers of Kyushu and western Honshu. These specific fears, together with the general desire to promote social stability by keeping out disruptive influences, led the Tokugawa to limit Japan's contacts with the outside world to a carefully controlled minimum, expelling all Europeans except the nonproselytizing Dutch.

After 1638 Japan's only contact with Europe was through the Dutch traders allowed to stay on the island of Deshima in Nagasaki harbor. The Dutch were required to make periodic reports to the shogunate on the affairs of the outside world. These reports were one of the few ways in which the Tokugawa learned what was happening outside their boundaries. Yet the Tokugawa remained supersensitive to affairs in the world beyond Japan and the possible effects of Western ideas on Japanese life. Corn and potatoes came into Japan; the Dutch reported on foreign events. However, the Dutch were closely guarded on the way to and from Edo lest they disturb the enforced peace of the countryside, and the content of their reports was only revealed to the select few who the Tokugawa thought should have such knowledge. After 1630, all books which even mentioned Europe or Christianity were absolutely proscribed. In 1695 a multivolume Chinese description of Peking was rejected because one passage referred favorably to the virtuous behavior of the Jesuit Matteo Ricci during his stay there.

DUTCH LEARNING IN JAPAN (18TH CENTURY)

In 1720 the Tokugawa relaxed the rule against books which mentioned Europe and Christianity enough to allow Japanese who were reading in Chinese books about the advances Western scientists were making in astronomy to import Western books on scientific and technical subjects. However, the only European language which even the most enterprising eighteenth-century Japanese could study was Dutch, and the Dutch were no longer as prominent in European scientific circles as they had once been. Therefore the Rangaku (school of Dutch learning) which grew up in the latter eighteenth century was somewhat limited in what it could learn about European studies in astronomy, mathematics, botany, anatomy, and medicine, even from the most gifted of the physicians who came to serve the little Dutch community at Nagasaki.

Rangaku, Dutch learning, was a challenge to the Tokugawa order, for it introduced a habit of drawing conclusions from direct observation which was quite unlike the prevailing tendency to assume one's conclusions and then interpret one's observations in line with them (witness the refusal to admit the reality of the cultural refinement achieved by merchants, because they were assumed to be at the bottom of the social scale). There were other challenges to the Tokugawa system. Ironically, some came from the Confucian tradition the Tokugawa wished to use to promote orderliness, as various Confucian schools debated over the source of the moral law or as Japanese Confucian scholars undertook the historical studies which brought the emperor's court at Kyoto into the foreground for the first time in centuries. The revival of interest in Shinto doctrines, many of which were linked with the priestly role of the imperial house, provided a set of challenges to Tokugawa authority that stemmed from Japanese tradition. Nevertheless, Rangaku was significant because it prepared at least a few Japanese to cope with the problems raised in the nineteenth century by the technologically based power of the West. Rangaku accustomed its adherents to the idea that the West had something to teach, as well as to a few of the concepts which underlay Western science and technology. Perhaps even more importantly, it accustomed them to the idea that they could learn and use what the West had to teach without losing their identity as Japanese.

The concepts introduced by the followers of Rangaku did much to lay the foundation for Japan's rapid modernization-by-Westernization in the latter nineteenth century, but other factors also contributed to Japan's readiness to modernize. The life of Tokugawa Japan already resembled that of the nation-states of early modern Europe, with a central government which was all-powerful over what it chose to regulate and an economy which was increasingly geared to nationwide commerce rather than local subsistence. In addition, the Japanese not only shared a common cultural heritage, but had long been conscious that it was distinct from the cultures of others. Above all, as the appearance of the school of Dutch learning shows, Japanese intellectual leaders—unlike their counterparts in China—were fully aware that a knowledge of other cultures could be valuable. Japanese scholars assiduously studied the language of the Chinese and later the Dutch for the sake of learning, but until the nineteenth century no Chinese scholars regarded the study of any other language as worth their time and effort for scholarly purposes, unless they were among the very few who took enough interest in the background of Buddhism to study Sanskrit.

EUROPEAN MERCHANTS AND MISSIONARIES IN CHINA (17TH AND 18TH CENTURIES)

Before the mid-nineteenth century, the Chinese inquired little about the peoples of the West or their ideas of the universe. The Ch'ing had gained power by using, not displacing, the principles of the Chinese-run Confucian state which the Ming had restored after the deviations of the Yuan, and the Ch'ing upheld the universal superiority of Confucian learning at least as firmly as the Ming. The early Ch'ing bowed to Western learning only in the field of astronomy, where the Ming had preceded them in using the knowledge of the Jesuits.

The scholarly attainments of Ricci and the Jesuits who followed him to China had soon attracted favorable attention at the capital. After the Jesuits succeeded in correcting the Chinese calendar, they were given an effective monopoly of the post of court astronomer in Peking. The second Ch'ing emperor granted freedom of religious observance to worshipers in Roman Catholic churches, which by his time were to be found throughout China south of the Wall. However, when the papacy refused to allow the Jesuits to accept the socially all-important rites of ancestral sacrifice as compatible with Christian teaching, the Ch'ing responded in 1724 by expelling all the missionaries except a few who were retained for astronomical work. In both China and Japan the rulers eventually decided that Christianity was potentially subversive because in its Roman Catholic form it inculcated a loyalty to someone outside the Chinese (or Japanese) system. Therefore they strove to terminate its practice (in Japan) or at least its foreign connection (in China).

By the time the Ch'ing expelled the missionaries, Dutch, English, and French ships had joined the Portuguese along the China coast. The Dutch were at first unable to win Chinese permission to compete with the Portuguese at Canton. Therefore they used Taiwan as a base from 1624 to 1662, when they were driven out by a supporter of the vanished Ming. The Ch'ing restricted China's trade with Europeans to the Portuguese at Macao and Canton from 1655 to 1685, in part because the Ming partisans were using Taiwan as a base from 1662 to 1683 and the Ch'ing wished to restrict all trade to protect their control of the south China coast. To acquire permission to trade, the Dutch sent tribute-bearing envoys to Peking and provided part of the fleet that seized Taiwan for the Ch'ing in 1683. After Taiwan fell, the Ch'ing opened several ports and allowed Dutch, English, and other non-Portuguese Europeans to trade.

While western Europeans knocked at the sea gates of China, the Russians who were then colonizing their way across Siberia clashed with Manchu troops in the valley of the Amur. The Ch'ing sent Jesuits to negotiate in Latin with the Russian representatives, for none of the Manchu or Chinese officials could use a language which could be understood in Moscow. The Russians and the Jesuits concluded China's first treaty with a European power in 1689 at Nertchinsk, north of the Khing-an mountains. The Russians brought a thousand troops to the scene of the negotiations, but the Ch'ing sent ten thousand. The treaty excluded the Russians from the Amur valley. However, it provided for tribute (actually trade) missions to Peking which were expanded in scope by an additional treaty in 1727. It was drawn up as a treaty between equals, for when a Ch'ing embassy traveled to the Russian court, its members kowtowed to the ruler just as Russian envoys kowtowed in Peking. The treaties of 1689 and 1727 enabled the Russians to study the overland approaches to China and to establish residents in the Ch'ing capital who could inform them about Chinese affairs. Meanwhile, western Europeans were confined to the sea frontier, which was less important than the land frontier in Chinese eyes, and they rarely visited Peking. Consequently, the Russians were to be in an advantageous position in the nineteenth century.

THE CANTON TRADE AND THE TRIBUTARY
SYSTEM (1757–1839)

As the eighteenth century opened, the Dutch held an authorized monopoly of Japan's limited contacts with Europe. The trade between China and the West was divided between the Russians to the north and the Portuguese, Dutch, English, and French to the south. The European traders in south China were later joined by merchants from Denmark and Sweden, but the British were decidedly in the lead by the time the first ships from the new United States reached Canton in 1784.

During the early eighteenth century the southern trade gravitated toward Canton, which was the closest major Chinese port to European bases in Southeast Asia and India. In 1757 the Ch'ing made Canton the only port in which Europeans could trade. There they granted a monopoly over the profitable European trade to a small group of Chinese merchants who paid well for the privilege. The membership of this licensed monopoly group, the Co-hong, fluctuated between four and thirteen (the government-set maximum). The Co-hong merchants were given official rank, and the European merchants were required to present their complaints, requests, and other communications to the Co-hong merchants for transmission to the imperial officials in Canton. No European was allowed to communicate directly with a member of the Ch'ing bureaucracy, or indeed with any Chinese except the few employed in the various aspects of the Canton trade.

As in the expulsion of missionaries, the Ch'ing were taking steps similar to those taken by the Tokugawa a century earlier. However, there was one important difference. The Ch'ing did not request the Europeans to report to them periodically on world events, as the supposedly more isolationist Tokugawa did.

The Europeans at Canton were closely restricted. They could only trade with the licensed Co-hong merchants. Since they could only communicate with the government through these same merchants, they had little hope of breaking the Co-hong monopoly. They were expected to pay fees to the customs officials over and above the established tariffs, and the size of those fees fluctuated with the current financial situation of the customs men, not with the value of the cargo being brought in for sale. Europeans could reside permanently in Macao, but they could only stay in their warehouses on the Canton waterfront for limited periods and they were not allowed to enter the city itself. Although they were unwilling to admit the assumption, they were assumed by the Ch'ing to be under the jurisdiction of Chinese law, with its concept of collective rather than individual responsibility and its long tradition of regarding unsettled disputes as evidence of lack of virtue on both sides.

These restrictions were galling to the British, who dominated the Canton trade through their own government-licensed monopoly, the British East India Company. Not only did the Co-hong monopoly limit the commercial activities of Western nationals, but use of the Co-hong as intermediary between Westerners and Ch'ing officials indicated that Westerners were regarded as inferior beings, unworthy to approach an imperial official directly. From 1787 onward the British government tried to alter the Canton system by sending official emissaries to establish formal diplomatic relations with Peking, but to no avail. The situation remained uneasily quiescent as long as British merchants going to China had to be licensed by the East India Company, for the Company could keep British traders from taking matters into their own hands by threatening to withdraw their Company licenses. However, when the British Parliament abolished the Company monopoly of Britain's China trade in 1833, open conflict soon followed. Private British merchants flocked to Canton and immediately began objecting to the restrictions placed on them by Ch'ing officials. Neither Company nor Crown could control them, for the Company had lost its monopoly and the Crown had no formal relations with the Ch'ing, all its missions having been turned away. The British government sent an official representative to Canton, but the Canton authorities refused to deal with him except through the licensed Chinese merchants.

The restrictions imposed on Westerners at Canton seemed natural to the Ch'ing, who were only following centuries-old Chinese tradition when they insisted on treating all non-Chinese as barbarians (except the Mongols, who were honored as cousins and allies of their Manchu neighbors). Like their predecessors, the Ch'ing assumed that foreigners wanted intercourse with China in order to enjoy the benefits of its superior culture. This assumption was supported by the fact that China's foreign trade was largely in luxury goods, exchanging silks, porcelains, and fine teas for furs, pearls, rare animals, and opium. Therefore the Ch'ing felt that foreigners ought to expect and be expected to remain on a lower plane in all their dealings with Chinese in general and with China's government in particular.

The Ch'ing were able to maintain this tributary system as long as they were strong enough to make it risky for Europeans to challenge them, which was still the case in 1792 when Ch'ing forces defeated the warlike Gurkhas of Nepal. However, the Ch'ing came to be plagued by internal weakness after 1800. A growth in population and a rise in agricultural tenancy as increasing numbers competed for land, which almost always accompanied the long periods of peace enforced by powerful dynasties in China, had begun to breed disaffection comparable to that which had helped topple almost every preceding dynasty. Serious rebellions in the outlying areas of Kansu, Taiwan, and Kweichow drained much of the imperial treasure between 1781 and 1797. More and more revolts sapped its military, administrative, and financial resources in succeeding years, in yet another round of the dynastic cycle Chinese historians had described so often in the past. Internal weakness alone would have made it difficult for the Ch'ing to uphold the tributary system in the face of Westerners' demands for the same treatment they would receive in the West with its full-grown consular and diplomatic services and its highly developed systems of commercial law. The extensions of the capitulatory system forced on the weakening Ottoman empire in the eighteenth century showed how vulnerable a large but internally divided empire might be, in the face of a determined drive by Westerners to gain special privileges within its borders. The combination of Ch'ing internal weakness and the rapid rise in Western technological superiority in the early nineteenth century eventually made the maintenance of the Chinese empire's tributary system impossible.

Western Pressure on China

OPENING OF CHINA TO WESTERN TRADE (1839–1844)

By the 1830s, British trade in China was heavily dependent on the exchange of opium grown in India for the tea, silks, and porcelains desired by Europeans. Like the furs the Russians brought, opium was one of the few commodities which were salable in self-sufficient China. The Ch'ing raised moral objections to opium, and they attacked the opium trade as the exchange of useful products for a useless and evil thing. However, the British paid little heed to Ch'ing protests. British merchants needed a product to trade for Chinese goods, and their purchases of Indian-grown opium were profitable to the British East India Company. Finally, after more than a century of ineffectual attempts to ban the importation of opium, Peking dispatched the honest and able Chinese official Lin Tse-hsu to stamp out the opium trade at Canton in 1839.

Lin Tse-hsu soon confiscated and destroyed the opium then in the Canton warehouses, but he failed to convince either the British traders or the official British representative at Canton that each British merchant should post a bond which would hold him responsible not only if he imported opium but also if any other British merchant did so. The ensuing series of skirmishes turned into open warfare in 1840 and lasted until 1842. During the war, British naval forces blockaded the mouth of the Yangtze and forced the Ch'ing to agree to negotiate at Nanking.

In the Anglo-Chinese treaty of 1842 and a supplementary treaty signed in 1843, the Ch'ing agreed to open four additional ports, called "treaty ports," to British residence and trade. Shanghai, at the mouth of the Yangtze, was the most northerly of these. The Ch'ing ceded the island of Hongkong to the British in perpetuity. They paid indemnities for the cost of the war and the value of the opium seized by Lin Tse-hsu. They also abolished the policy of licensing only certain merchants to trade with the British and established a low uniform tariff which could only be changed if both parties agreed. The British were given legal jurisdiction over their own nationals in criminal cases. The Ch'ing recognized the right of official British representatives to communicate directly with Ch'ing officials and promised that the British would receive any further privileges that might be granted other foreigners in future. The similarity of the tariff, criminal jurisdiction, and most-favored-nation clauses to provisions in the Ottoman capitulatory treaties is worth noting. The expanded capitulatory system of the late eighteenth century in the Middle East provided the model for Western powers as they sought means of increasing their nationals' commercial activity in China, and later in Japan, Korea, and Siam.

The Ch'ing voluntarily extended most-favored-nation treatment to all foreigners, promising each state that its nationals would be given any privilege which was yielded to nationals of any other state, in hopes of using the foreigners to counterbalance one another. In 1844 the Ch'ing signed a treaty with a representative of the United States, who succeeded in extending extraterritoriality to civil as well as criminal cases. The Ch'ing also signed a treaty with the French, who asked for a statement of toleration for Christianity. The emperor promulgated the toleration statement separately rather than embodying it in the treaty, but the first tentative step had been taken toward adding Western protection of the empire's Christian subjects to the extraterritoriality, tariff, and most-favored-nation-clause parallels to the Ottoman capitulations.

The governments recognized by the Ch'ing gradually procured concessions, or perpetual leases and even outright grants of land, on which their nationals could build in the treaty ports. Within the concessions, the consuls rather than the Chinese authorities held sway. Thus the relatively few Chinese who resided in them could live under foreign jurisdiction much as those who registered as foreign nationals or protégés with Western consulates in the Ottoman empire were able to do, heightening the resemblance between the Chinese situation and the capitulatory system. There might be as many as eight such tiny foreign-run municipalities alongside the Chinese city, as eventually occurred at Tientsin in the north. In some places the representatives of several governments held joint authority over everyone in a specified area, as in the International Settlement at Shanghai, which grew to have a sizable Chinese population over the years. Local authorities did not welcome the concessions, which could weaken Ch'ing control at the local level. The concessions were merely (and sometimes barely) tolerated, at the behest of Peking, which was hopefully groping for a means of using the treaties to bring these insistent barbarians from overseas into a proper tributary relationship, like that accepted by Koreans and many Southeast Asians.

DISSATISFACTION, TREATY REVISION, AND THE TIENTSIN INCIDENT (1844–1870)

The Sino-foreign treaties of the 1840s did not prove satisfactory to either side. The Ch'ing objected to the leniency with which foreign consuls judged the few cases they bothered to take up under the extra-territorial clauses. The Ch'ing also complained about the near-piracy practiced by some Westerners of various nationalities. The foreigners objected to the regulations prohibiting them from engaging in any activity outside the treaty ports. As early as 1854 the British began requesting a new treaty. The French joined them in 1856, after the Kwangsi authorities arrested a French priest who was illegally preaching in the province and executed him for suspected sedition. Hostilities broke out late in 1856 when Canton officials boarded a vessel owned by a Hongkong Chinese, searched it for pirates, hauled down the British flag, and imprisoned most of the crew. British and French forces captured Canton in 1857. The British, French, United States, and Russian consuls at Canton then sent simultaneous notes to Peking, requesting treaty revisions. When no satisfactory answer was received, the British and French sailed north and captured the Taku forts below Tientsin on the Hai river. In 1858 the Ch'ing negotiated almost identical treaties with British, French, United States, and Russian representatives at Tientsin.

The Tientsin treaties of 1858 enabled the foreign powers to send their ministers to the capital without the kowtow ritual. The treaties permitted foreigners to travel in the interior and to practice and preach Christianity. Eleven new treaty ports were opened to trade and residence, and foreign vessels were allowed to trade on the Yangtze. The Ch'ing also agreed to pay indemnities to Britain and France.

The treaties were to go into effect when duly ratified copies were exchanged in Peking. The Russians, using the overland route, accomplished this with no difficulty. The United States agreed to make the exchange at a small coastal city north of Tientsin. However, when the Ch'ing tried to prevent the British and French from coming to Peking by way of Tientsin, the British and French seized the Taku forts a second time and marched inland to Peking in 1860. The Manchu court fled hastily, leaving one unhappy prince and his entourage to cope with the conquerors, who looted and burned the beautiful Summer Palace outside the city. At this point the Russians stepped in. Since 1850 the Russian governor-general in Siberia had been founding settlements along the Amur, in spite of the terms of the treaty of Nertchinsk. In 1858 he had used the Ch'ing preoccupation with the British and French to persuade the Ch'ing to give up the north bank of the Amur. Now the Russian representative in Peking, with a magnanimity which did not deceive the hapless imperial prince, offered to save Peking from destruction in return for the Maritime Province—the lands bounded by the Amur, its southern tributary the Ussuri, and the sea. The offer was accepted. The Russians emerged from the struggle of 1856 to 1860 not only with the new privileges received by Britain, France, and the United States, but with a sizable slice of the lands once claimed by the Ch'ing.

The Ch'ing at first refused to recognize that the tributary system had collapsed, and they looked for ways to make the new treaty system fit the patterns inherited from the past. Not until 1860 showed that the barbarians could seize the capital of China did the Ch'ing begin in earnest to study the ways of Western diplomacy. Even then, their aim was to use the Westerners' own presuppositions and rules to prevent them from altering the structure of China's internal life as radically as they were changing the form of its external relations.

Between 1860 and 1870 the speed with which the Ch'ing learned to cite chapter and verse from Western international law to support their own position was watched with bemused interest by Western diplomats, who hoped this might presage Westernization in other spheres. However, many merchants and missionaries observed the same process with fascinated horror, for they realized that the Ch'ing could use the precepts of international law to prevent them from spreading their influence across the land more rapidly by stretching the treaty clauses. The new Ch'ing policy of obeying every treaty clause proved most effective in persuading Western governments not to let their nationals go beyond the letter of the treaties, and for a time there was real cooperation between the Ch'ing and the Western diplomats. Then came the Tientsin incident of 1870.

Lurid misrepresentations of the missionary activities of French Roman Catholic priests and nuns led the Chinese officials at Tientsin to request permission to make an immediate official inspection so that they could disprove the charges and quell the growing popular unrest, but the French consul intemperately refused. When the gathering mobs heard of the refusal, they felt their worst suspicions had been confirmed. Infuriated, they killed every French national they could find, whether priest, nun, or lay person. The Tientsin massacre, as the French called it, led to the return of mutual suspicion between the representatives of the Ch'ing and the Western nations.

INTERNAL STRIFE AND THE RISE OF PROVINCIAL
LEADERS (1780s TO 1890s)

By the time the Ch'ing began using the Western concept of a family of sovereign and equal states to preserve China's internal integrity, affairs inside China had already taken a serious turn. The number and size of local rebellions had swelled since the 1780s to the point where the system set up by the Ch'ing in the seventeenth century could no longer cope with the rebels. The limited local Chinese forces that supplemented the small Manchu and Mongol garrisons stationed in key areas were insufficient to handle local unrest by themselves. Wherever Manchu or Mongol garrison members succumbed out of boredom to the opium habit, as many did, rebellion became almost endemic. For all its emphasis on harmony through compromise, in practice the Confucian state system provided no effective means of expressing the deep-rooted discontents that grew out of a combination of expanding population and increasing exactions by both landlords and government, except the rebellions staged by the secret societies which always flourished in China at such times. In the 1850s local insurrections became regional ones. The Muslims of Yunnan set up an independent state, the Miao tribes of Kweichow rebelled, and rebel movements challenged Ch'ing power both north and south of the Yangtze.

In the south, the rebels were led by a Chinese who tried the civil service examinations, failed, and then came briefly under the influence of Protestant Christian missionaries. In 1850 he proclaimed himself head of the T'ai-p'ing (great peace) dynasty and stated that he had the Mandate of Heaven to overthrow the Ch'ing. By the fervor with which he preached such novel doctrines as equality not only between men but even between men and women, and by the thoroughness with which he organized his followers, he led the way for the T'ai-p'ing to sweep through most of southern China, reaching Nanking in 1853 and making it their capital. As Manchu forces were withdrawn from the north to cope with this serious menace to Ch'ing survival, the north was convulsed by rebellions which were collectively termed the Nien Fei movement. The T'ai-p'ing tried to utilize the unsettled condition of the north. Their forces reached the vicinity of Tientsin, but they were unable to establish a working relationship with the Nien Fei and had to retire to Nanking. In desperation, the Ch'ing granted the requests of Chinese provincial officials for permission to raise, train, equip, and lead local Chinese armies against the T'ai-p'ing and later the Nien Fei. This modification of previous practice was to have momentous importance.

Most of these new provincial Chinese armies followed the pattern established by Tseng Kuo-fan, governor of Hunan. Their members were drawn from the settled peasantry, in opposition to the landless from whom the rebels won support. They were indoctrinated with massive doses of Confucian ideology, in opposition to the foreign-influenced doctrines of the T'ai-p'ing. The troops were given Western as well as Chinese weapons, for the superiority of Western firearms was recognized, and the men were paid both generously and promptly—a rarity for Chinese armies, which usually had to keep themselves alive in part by living off the country. The provincial armies did not suppress the T'ai-p'ing until 1864 or the Nien Fei until 1868, but by 1860 they had restored enough control to the central government's representatives to enable the Ch'ing to reassert their claim to authority by revitalizing the familiar Confucian state structure. However, the Ch'ing also had to cope with the destruction wrought during the fourteen years of the T'ai-p'ing rebellion, when two-thirds of China's provinces underwent such devastation that twenty million people perished.

The way the T'ai-p'ing were suppressed was of great importance to the course of events in the next several decades. The emphasis placed on upholding Confucian ideology against the slightly Christianized doctrines of the T'ai-p'ing contributed strongly to the marked suspicion and hatred shown to foreign ideas in the half-century between the fall of the T'ai-p'ing and the fall of the Ch'ing in 1912. Foreign ideas, and especially Christianity, were treated as enemies of the Chinese way of life. The formation of the anti-T'ai-p'ing armies by provincial rather than central officials was also significant, since it made the provinces more independent of the center. With armies of their own, governors could maintain order without calling on Peking for aid. Although the governors remained loyal to the Confucian ideal of a united empire at first and did not consciously use their new strength to oppose Ch'ing policies, by 1900 that situation was beginning to change.

Another significant result of the T'ai-p'ing era was the climate of opinion produced by the success with which the provincial armies used limited amounts of Western arms while maintaining their Confucianism untarnished. This experience encouraged Chinese to think they could borrow Western technology without borrowing any part of the system of ideas out of which that technology had arisen. Throughout the half-century after the T'ai-p'ing fell, the standard Chinese reaction to the West was "Western utility—Confucian essence," or using Western techniques for their utility while maintaining Confucian doctrine for its value. It was naive of the Chinese to assume that the value of Confucian doctrine could go unchallenged when the mode of behavior that went with another doctrine was openly recognized as having more utility than the mode of behavior that went with Confucianism, but since the Chinese had experienced less large-scale intercultural interchange than any other numerous body of civilized people in Asia, their innocence is understandable. Only a few recognized that it was necessary to know and use Western ideology in order to use Western technology. Those few therefore opposed Western technology as disruptive, or else accepted the ideology that went with it. At first the individuals who were willing to adopt Western ideas as well as Western techniques attempted to prove that the Western ways of thinking could be found within the Confucian heritage, but when this finally proved unworkable because of the great differences in the bases of the Western and Confucian systems, they accepted Western thought in place of Confucian ideology.

The attempt of the Ch'ing to revitalize the Confucian state system in the 1860s, using the familiar technique of discharging corrupt officials and insisting on loyalty and honesty, gave the dynasty enough of a new lease on life to bolster Chinese confidence in the possibility of retaining the essential spirit of the Confucian system within China, while using Western diplomatic techniques to defend China from Western territorial and spiritual encroachment and employing Western arms for defense from internal and external attack. In the generation after 1860, Western-style arsenals, shipyards, and machine-tool factories were set up; Western-style coal mines, iron mines, and railways were opened to supply them with raw materials; and Western-style technological institutes were founded to train the men to run the mines, the railways, and the factories, shipyards, and arsenals. Almost all these innovations were carried out by the provincial authorities, who were therefore in a position to ignore Peking in later years. They were even more independent of the imperial court than their counterparts in previous eras of dynastic decline, when the provinces were separated from the capital by journeys of days or even weeks in length rather than linked to it by the metal thread of the Ch'ing central government's new telegraph system.

Western Pressure on Japan

OPENING OF JAPAN TO WESTERN TRADE (1853–1868)

The tidings of the first Anglo-Chinese war and the forcible opening of China arrived in Edo with the next Dutch reports. The news helped persuade the Tokugawa that their policy of isolation was outliving its usefulness as a defensive measure. Russian, British, and United States vessels had appeared sporadically in Japanese waters during the preceding century. Since 1806 the Russians had been raiding Sakhalin, just north of thinly populated Hokkaido. In 1853 the Russians added Sakhalin to their domains, and in that same year the ships of United States Commodore Perry arrived in the forbidden waters of Edo bay. Reluctantly the Tokugawa decided that they could no longer maintain a policy of complete isolation and that it would be preferable to begin by establishing relations with a government whose territories were more distant than those of the czar. However, the Tokugawa shogunate intended to revive the seclusion policy as soon as possible.

In 1854 the shogunate promised to allow limited United States contacts with Japan. During the next two years the British, the Russians, and the long-resident Dutch were granted similar treaties, in which the terms of intercourse were expanded to include consular representation and some extraterritorial jurisdiction. The shogunate found it difficult to persuade the imperial court to agree to these treaties, but was finally successful. Then the United States requested the exchange of diplomatic representatives between the two countries, full extraterritorial jurisdiction, the right of foreigners to practice the Christian religion, a uniform and mutually agreed upon tariff, and most-favored-nation treatment. The news of the second Anglo-Chinese war alarmed the Tokugawa into agreeing to such a treaty in 1858 and negotiating similar treaties with the Dutch, the Russians, the British, and the French. However, many objections were raised at the imperial court in Kyoto to approving the actions of the shogun at Edo. The court was supported by the outside lords, some of whom were sincerely anti-foreign, but many of whom saw the treaty issue as a chance to topple the Tokugawa from their position of power. By 1862 the Tokugawa were so torn between their recognition of the impossibility of returning to seclusion and their awareness of the hostility of most of the daimyo that they tried to curry favor with the daimyo by relaxing the alternate-attendance system. This step only hastened their downfall by freeing the outside lords from the fear of what their families might suffer if they defied Tokugawa orders against building up their personal military establishments or attacking foreigners.

The court finally decided to accept the treaties informally, but only until Japan was strong enough to expel the Western barbarians. A date was even set for the beginning of the expulsion: June 24, 1863. The followers of two outside lords, Choshu in western Honshu and Satsuma in southern Kyushu, began attacking the few Westerners to be found on Japan's roads and waterways. The Western powers retaliated swiftly. In 1863 United States and French warships fired on the naval defenses of Choshu, while a British squadron bombarded the Satsuma city of Kagoshima. In 1864 a combined British, French, Dutch, and United States naval expedition leveled the Choshu coastal forts. The emperor formally ratified the treaties.

The lord of Satsuma was so impressed by the ease with which the British bombarded his possessions that he immediately requested the British to furnish him with an example of a modern naval vessel. Similarly, the allied bombardment of Choshu was followed by a request from the lord of Choshu for military instructors and weapons. Choshu then proceeded to build up a peasant conscript army, which was already strong enough by 1866 to defeat the forces of the Tokugawa when they tried to destroy this evidence of disobedience to their longstanding decrees against military preparations on the part of the daimyo. The Tokugawa did not recover from this stunning defeat of Tokugawa samurai by Choshu peasants. (The Choshu troops were led by samurai and equipped with more modern arms than the Tokugawa forces, but still they were peasants.) At the close of 1867 the last Tokugawa shogun resigned, hoping that voluntary resignation might win him a place as one of the counselors of the newly enthroned young emperor, but 1868 showed the emptiness of that hope. The shogunate was abolished; the Tokugawa forces were defeated and scattered when they tried to oppose the rise to power of Satsumu, Choshu, and the other outside lords; and the imperial court moved to the long-established political and economic center of the nation at Edo, which was renamed Tokyo, or Eastern Capital.

As the sign of what was called the Meiji Restoration (after the courtesy title of Meiji given the young emperor), the emperor's advisers called in 1868 for the abandonment of unsuitable practices from the past, the study of everything that was valuable regardless of its origin, and a broader participation in the discussion of affairs of national importance. The emperor's advisers were convinced that Japan's greatest need in the new era it was entering was to maintain its national integrity and become an accepted member of the Western family of nations, instead of a part of the Chinese tributary system. The West could defeat China even on its home ground; therefore, the West must be Japan's first concern. Most of the emperor's advisers were younger samurai from the domains of Satsuma and Choshu. During the next thirty-five years they guided Japan toward the goal of equality with the West so successfully that Japan became the ally of Britain, the greatest naval power of the West. Furthermore, the Western powers gave up the special privileges which Japan had granted their nationals in the early treaties.

END OF TOKUGAWA RULE AND EARLY
WESTERNIZATION (1868–1877)

When Japan signed its first treaty with the United States in 1854, it entered the period of reopened foreign contacts with what, under the circumstances, was a distinct advantage over China and Korea, for Japan was in such internal ferment that the old ways were being protested rather than upheld. Those Japanese who objected to the existing state of affairs were groping for something to replace the Tokugawa order, not for a way of restoring it to its original purity. Scholarly historical studies were turning their attention to the imperial institution as a means through which to effect alterations. At first, the outside lords who led the battle against the Tokugawa had little more in mind than taking the place of the Tokugawa family as rulers. However, their followers and successors had more extensive ideas of what was needed. They turned to the West in search of the techniques and the knowledge required to make Japan a part of the state system of the Western world, as their forebears had turned to China a thousand years before in search of the techniques and knowledge needed to make Japan part of the Chinese system of tributary states. The replacement of the Tokugawa shogunate with a centralized imperial government was part of the search.

The first step toward regaining Japan's independence of action was the recognition that government by locally autonomous units was inapplicable to the emergencies of the day. In 1869 the leading daimyo voluntarily restored their domains to the crown, which then appointed them as its administrators in their districts. In 1871 the numerous domain units were abolished in favor of a small number of prefectures, administered by men who might or might not be of daimyo rank. This tightening of central control made it easier for the government in Tokyo to form and execute national policy.

The Meiji leaders knew that more was needed than mere administrative reorganization. A literate populace capable of comprehending governmental directives was required. In 1871 the government proclaimed universal primary education as its goal, and by 1900 Japan's literacy rate was as high as any in the world. An obedient populace that would carry out the government's decrees was also required. Therefore, the new ministry of education emphasized loyalty to the sun-descended imperial line. Later this emphasis gave rise to State Shinto, the formal recognition of the deity of the emperor and the divine origin and civilizing mission of Japan. The proponents of State Shinto in the 1890s saw it as a means of binding all Japanese together in unquestioning obedience to their ruler's commands as promulgated by the organs of government. A populace that shared the burdens of defense and finance equally and unitedly was regarded as preferable to the existing distinctions between the duties of various classes. The Meiji leaders saw that class distinctions perpetuated divisive tendencies, and they feared that such distinctions might encourage a conservatism among the privileged which could block progress toward acceptance by the West. Consequently, universal military conscription was introduced in 1872, ending the samurai monopoly of the right to carry arms, and in 1873 a flat-rate land tax was adopted. The new tax was to be paid in money, not in produce, and it was to depend on land value rather than the size of the current crop.

These measures dismayed the more conservative samurai. The government sidetracked them temporarily by sending an expedition to

Taiwan in 1874 in retaliation for the killing of sailors from the Ryukyus by some Taiwanese. The Chinese subsequently recognized Japanese overlordship in the Ryukyus. However, the conservatives rebelled outright in 1877, the year after the government forbade samurai to continue showing their rank by wearing two swords in public. The rebels were protesting against the government's abolition of the centuries-old class barriers and against the loss of income and position they suffered when the daimyo-samurai system of administration was abolished. Their rebellion was of no avail. The new conscript army was too strong for them to overcome.

PROGRAM FOR MODERNIZATION (1877–1894)

While the Meiji government worked toward universal literacy, universal military service, and the abolition of class privilege, it also built railways and opened Western-style banks to provide credit facilities, for railways and credit were needed to encourage the rise of the industries which were required to outfit and equip the new army. The government started some industries itself, in fields where private businessmen hesitated to enter for lack of experience. The proceeds of the land tax were invaluable to the government as it started to promote modern factory industry. Later, the fact that the government continued to rely on the land tax, while business and industrial profits went relatively untaxed and were therefore available for reinvestment, was nearly as valuable for the growth of Japanese manufactures. Japanese industry expanded so rapidly that Japan's exports of manufactured goods were worth over fifty times as much in 1895 as they had been in 1870. However, Japanese governmental efforts would have meant little if economic growth had not been encouraged by Japanese traditions of admiration for frugality, hard work, and the effort to reflect credit on oneself and one's associates by displays of proficiency.

The internal strength and unity achieved through these economic and political measures were not enough, in the eyes of the Meiji leaders. Strength and unity were only means to the real end, which was to put Japan on a par with the powers of the West so that they would not engulf Japan. To that end, many aspects of the general Western system of government were adopted at least in part. Measures which could further national unification were particularly stressed. Codes of criminal, penal, civil, and commercial law patterned on Western models were adopted in the 1880s and 1890s, so as to nullify Western excuses for retaining extraterritoriality. Earlier, in the 1870s, Christian teaching had been permitted, as a token of the cessation of official hostility to foreigners. In addition, the government and the newly started private newspapers of the 1870s campaigned with indiscriminate zeal against a variety of aspects of Japanese life. The more Westernized Japanese realized that Westerners thought many Japanese customs uncivilized. However, many Japanese must have wondered why eating raw fish was less civilized than eating rare roast beef.

The Meiji leaders followed not only Western legal models but the Western pattern of constitutional government, in which a formally elected body which theoretically represented the interests of all the people of the nation was called together periodically to discuss and approve the basic outlines of government policy. The intention to adopt constitutional government was announced in 1880, in part to afford some satisfaction to dissident former samurai who felt they were not being given a proper share in government, and in part to forestall the possibility that the government would have to forfeit prestige by bowing to popular demands for representative government if it did not act soon.

The Meiji constitution was finally promulgated in 1889. It was modeled on the German constitution, which suited the preconceptions of those in power in Japan. By 1889 several ambitious leaders had formed political parties, but the constitution gave them only a limited field for their activities. The emperor retained supreme authority, which meant in practice that his advisers exercised it. The legislature, or Diet, was powerless to object effectively either to cabinets or to budgets. Cabinets were to be selected by the emperor and responsible to him, not to the Diet, and the preceding year's budget allocations would automatically be continued if a new budget were not approved. Elections for the lower house of the Diet were conducted on the basis of a franchise so limited that scarcely half a million men could vote. (The franchise was somewhat liberalized in the next thirty years.) The upper house was chosen partly by election, partly by imperial appointment, and partly by hereditary position. Moreover, the cabinet was not all-powerful. Even if an ambitious politician managed to be appointed to it, which was rare before World War I, he could not hope to oppose the wishes of the military.

The constitution of 1889 gave the highest officers of the army and navy independent access to the emperor through a Supreme War Council. This meant they did not have to obey the cabinet if they could find a way to claim imperial sanction for their actions. In 1900 the ministers of war and navy were even required to be officers on the active list. This rule was formally modified in 1913, but the practice remained. As active officers, the ministers of war and navy were under the orders of the Supreme War Council, which could command them to resign whenever the policies of the cabinet displeased the Council. Thus the army and navy high command could at any time force a cabinet reorganization which would get rid of offending cabinet members and their ideas. In short, the Supreme War Council came to be able to control the cabinet rather than be controlled by it.

Since the Supreme War Council rather than the legislature dominated the cabinet, the legislators were powerless to act effectively. As early as the 1890s many of them cynically decided to sell their votes to the rising industrialists—hence the low taxes on industry—and to those members of the civil and military services who cared to buy a favorable vote now and then. Others protested against the role allotted the legislature. However, the dissident factions buried their differences when Japan and China went to war over Korea in 1894. The Sino-Japanese war, like the Taiwan expedition twenty years earlier, rallied all Japanese to the banner of national interest.

Korea and China: Japan's Proving Grounds

PRESSURES ON KOREA AND CHINA (1876–1890)

Observing that the West respected the language of political modernity, the Japanese adopted a constitution and a set of modern legal codes. Observing as well that Westerners respected the language of force, the Japanese turned to Korea to display their strength and to prevent that strategic area from being seized by a power which might emulate the Mongols by using it as a base from which to invade Japan.

A few Jesuits and other Europeans had entered Korea since the sixteenth century, but not until the 1860s did the British, Russians, and French seek to open trade. The Koreans feared foreign intrusion too much to accede to the requests, and in a wave of anti-foreignism they nearly wiped out the small Roman Catholic community. The French sent a punitive expedition, but it was too small to be effective. Emboldened by their success in driving away the French, the Koreans fired on United States and Japanese vessels which approached Korea in the early 1870s. The Koreans claimed that they could not have relations with states outside the Confucian orbit, since Korea was a tributary state of China. When Japan inquired of the Ch'ing concerning the Korean claim, the Japanese were told that Korea was a Ch'ing dependency, but that China did not control Korean affairs. Japanese envoys then proceeded to Korea, where they were granted the right to trade in three ports and exchange ministers with the Korean government. The Japanese interpreted the signing of the treaty as Korea's acknowledgment of its own sovereignty, as did other powers which signed similar treaties in the 1880s. However, neither Korea nor China admitted that Korea was a sovereign state rather than a Ch'ing dependency.

The Japanese opening of Korea in 1876 came in the midst of a period of renewed pressures on China. Five years after the Tientsin incident of 1870, a British subject was killed while exploring the route between Yunnan and the Ch'ing tributary state of Burma. The British promptly required the Ch'ing to apologize, to pay an indemnity, and to open ten more treaty ports. When the British conquered the kingdom of Burma in 1885, they required the Chi'ng to sign a treaty recognizing British control of Burma. In 1890 the British replaced the Ch'ing as protectors of the tiny state of Sikkim on the southern slope of the eastern Himalayas.

Britain and Japan were not the only powers challenging Ch'ing claims. During the 1870s the Russians made inroads into Sinkiang. These inroads were partially reversed by monetary payment in 1881, the year the Ch'ing finally acknowledged the Japanese annexation of the Ryukyus. When the French installed a protectorate in Annam (Vietnam) in 1885, they fought a short and bloody undeclared war to force the Ch'ing to recognize the new situation. Even the Portuguese won a concession. After more than three hundred years of occupation, Macao was formally ceded to them in perpetuity.

SINO-JAPANESE WAR OF 1894–1895

The events of 1876 opened a struggle between China and Japan for control of Korea. When the Japanese acquired the Ryukyus, the Ch'ing realized that Japan had withdrawn from the Confucian tributary system and was acting in accord with the rules of the Western system of sovereign states. The Ch'ing therefore persuaded Korea to sign treaties with the United States, Britain, Germany, Italy, Russia, and France so that these Western powers would recognize and uphold Korean integrity against Japanese encroachment. The treaties opened Korea to Western trade and missionary enterprises enough to alarm most Korean leaders for the future of the Korean version of the Confucian state, but not enough to bring new leaders to the fore who would be able to maintain Korean independence if the existing order collapsed. The Koreans did not intend to give up the tributary system. They declared their dependence on China in every treaty they signed. Nor were the Ch'ing repudiating the Koreans as dependents. They sent a Chinese resident adviser to Seoul in token of their overlordship, and they were granted partial control over the foreign borrowings of the Korean government.

The Japanese did not want either China or the West to control Korea. They wished to bring Korea into their sphere by inducing Korea to accept their tutelage in adopting Western ways. Therefore, they supported the reform-minded group around the Korean queen, who opposed the anti-foreignism of the man acting as regent for the young king of Korea. The reform party tried to overthrow the regent, with Japanese aid, but Chinese soldiers put down the uprising. In 1885 China and Japan agreed that neither would send troops to Korea without notifying the other. When a new outbreak came in 1894, China and Japan dutifully notified each other that troops would be sent.

The Chinese and Japanese troops which arrived in Korea in 1894 soon began to attack each other. To the world's amazement, Japan won easily. Despite China's partial adoption of Western arms, the Chinese were no match in anything but personal bravery for the far better drilled and equipped Japanese. In the Sino-Japanese peace treaty of 1895, China not only gave up her protectorate over Korea, but ceded Taiwan, the Penghu (or Pescadores) islands, and the Liaotung peninsula in southern Manchuria to Japan. China also promised to pay an indemnity and to sign a commercial treaty, which was to grant the Japanese all the privileges held by Westerners in China and open seven more treaty ports.

The Japanese victory was a shock not only to China but to Korea, which became the plaything of Japan and Russia. Before the Sino-Japanese war, Korea had been tossed back and forth between Japan, which supported modernization, and China, which supported the Confucian system still preferred by Korea. Now Korea found itself between Japan and Russia, both of which were bent on a modernization Korea did not yet desire.

The Western powers were also surprised, but they soon recovered and began to treat Japan as an equal and a rival in East Asian affairs. Russia was particularly dismayed at the Japanese acquisition of the Liaotung peninsula, for it had long coveted that region. The Russians persuaded Germany and France to join them in putting pressure on Japan to give up the Liaotung peninsula in return for a larger indemnity, and Japan felt compelled to accept the proposal. Japan and Russia also agreed to give joint support to Korea if any other power tried to gain a foothold there. These arrangements were unwelcome to Japan's leaders, but they consoled themselves by persuading the Western powers to assent to the abolition of extraterritoriality, which took effect in 1899, and the abolition of external controls over Japanese tariff rates. The final recovery of tariff autonomy in 1911 made Japan the first Asian nation to achieve the goal of freeing itself from overt Western control. The acquisition of most-favored-nation privileges in China in 1895 had already made the Japanese the first Asians to be formally recognized anywhere as having the same status as Westerners, when it came to receiving special consideration.

CONCESSIONS FORCED ON CHINA BY WESTERN POWERS (1895–1898)

Russia, Germany, and France did not go unrewarded for intervening on behalf of the Ch'ing in 1895. The Ch'ing gave France a number of commercial privileges along the Annam (Vietnam) border. To pay the indemnity, Franco-Russian and Anglo-German loans were accepted, which proved lucrative for the European banking houses involved. The Ch'ing also granted Russia the right to build, administer, and protect a railway line through Manchuria. Russia was to operate this Chinese Eastern Railway as part of the Trans-Siberian Railway to Vladivostok, on the Japan Sea opposite northern Honshu. The Chinese could purchase the Chinese Eastern Railway after thirty-six years, but if they did not, it would revert automatically to China after eighty years.

The concessions made to France in the south and Russia in the north seemed to many to signal the opening of a period in which any part of the Ch'ing empire might legitimately be sought. When robbers killed a German missionary in Shantung in 1897, Germany demanded and got a ninety-nine-year lease of the peninsula's best harbor, Kiaochow Bay, and the right to build two railways, to mine coal, and to be given first chance to furnish any foreign loans needed for activities in Shantung province. Early in 1898 Russia leased the southern tip of the Liaotung peninsula for twenty-five years and received the right to connect it by rail to the Chinese Eastern Railway. Soon France leased Kwangchow Bay in southern Kwantung for ninety-nine years. Britain leased the port of Weihaiwei in northern Shantung, from which to watch both the Russians and the Germans, and obtained a ninety-nine-year lease on lands adjacent to the territory permanently ceded to Britain in 1860 opposite the island of Hongkong. Before 1898 ended, the Ch'ing also contracted a new Anglo-German loan.

CONVULSIONS IN CHINA (1898–1901)

The events of 1895–1898 seriously threatened Chinese sovereignty. In response, a number of Chinese became interested in the Western ways recently adopted in Japan. Some tried to show that the values of the West were really present in Confucian thought, if the classics were rightly interpreted. These men stressed the values associated with the rational inductive study of the universe and the values associated with the unification of a people under a central government which was strong because it heeded the freely expressed desires of those it ruled. Twenty years later Ch'en Tu-hsiu, who eventually founded the Chinese Communist party, called on his fellow Chinese to make friends with "Mr. Science" and "Mr. Democracy," as he referred to these two concepts.

The proponents of scientific study and representative constitutional government won the ear of the emperor in 1898, after the alarms raised by the Chinese Eastern Railway concession to Russia, the German entry into Shantung, and the Russian, French, and British leases on the coasts of Manchuria, Kwangtung, and Shantung. In the "Hundred Days of Reform" from June 11 to September 16, 1898, edict after edict issued from

Peking. The first edicts asked for more railways and more institutions of Western learning, but the outpouring of reform decrees abruptly halted soon after the emperor demanded the abolition of unnecessary government posts. The attempt to abolish sinecures threatened a number of politically powerful civil and military officials. They promptly turned to the empress dowager, who declared her nephew incompetent and took over the government. Other empresses in times past had acted as regents for minor princes, but it was highly unusual for an empress to act for an emperor who had already been formally enthroned. However, the officials had grown accustomed to working under her when she had previously been regent, first for her young son and then for her nephew in his youth, and many of them preferred her familiar policies to her nephew's innovations.

The empress dowager, who remembered fleeing Peking in 1860, was inclined to sympathize with the strong anti-foreign movement which appeared among the Shantung peasantry in 1898. The governor of Shantung openly favored the anti-foreignism of the Righteous Harmonious Fists, or Boxers as the Westerners called them. In protest, Western diplomats exerted enough pressure on the Ch'ing to force the empress dowager to reassign the Shantung governor to a province in the interior, late in 1899. The next governor of Shantung, Yuan Shih-k'ai, was a protégé of the man who had followed Tseng Kuo-fan as the leader of the "Western utility—Confucian essence" school. He put down the Boxers in Shantung, but by then they had spread into the neighboring provinces. The outcome was the anti-foreign Boxer uprising of 1900 in north China, whose virulence provoked the "Western" powers (including Japan) into sending a combined expedition to Peking to rescue foreign nationals there.

The governors of the provinces near Peking supported the Boxers, at the behest of the empress dowager. However, the governors of the provinces from Shantung southward weighed the Westerners' power against that of their superiors and decided to behave as if the empress dowager were acting under the duress of the Boxer occupation of Peking, where in fact the Boxers and the imperial troops were jointly besieging the foreign legations. The governors in the center and south did not countenance anti-foreignism in the territories they controlled. They even persuaded the foreign powers to accept their claim that the Boxers were insurgents. The European powers and Japan agreed to the polite fiction of "Boxer insurgency" largely because they could not decide what to do if the Ch'ing dynasty were toppled. Because they could not determine whether to divide China among themselves (on lines on which they could not agree) or to establish a new government (set up by a method on which they could not agree), it was simpler to continue recognizing the Ch'ing. The United States, which also took part in the expedition to Peking, agreed to the fiction of "Boxer insurgency" because it made it easier to persuade the other powers not to lay definite plans to partition China and thereby make trade by United States nationals more difficult.

When the foreign expedition reached Peking in August, 1900, the Manchu court fled to the city for the second time in the life of the empress dowager. For the second time in forty years the Ch'ing had to accept terms dictated to them from their own capital. The major provisions of the settlement signed in 1901 included payment of indemnities; destruction of all forts between Peking and the sea; temporary suspension of civil service examinations in districts where foreigners had been attacked; tariff revision; and permission for the foreigners to fortify and garrison the legation quarter in Peking. (Chinese reacted to the last item much as people in the United States would react if a group of foreign powers captured Washington, D.C., and demanded the right to fortify and garrison the entire embassy district. The people of the United States took a long time to cease vilifying the British for their treatment of Washington, D.C., in the War of 1812.) Except for loans accepted from various banking groups and except for the privileges given Japan after the Russo-Japanese war of 1904–1905, these were the last concessions granted by the Ch'ing, who were replaced by the Republic of China early in 1912. In 1908, the United States returned the unused part if its indemnity funds to set up a Western-style university in Peking and to send Chinese students to the United States for graduate work.

THE RUSSO-JAPANESE WAR OF 1904–1905 AND THE ANNEXATION OF KOREA

The Russians occupied all of Manchuria in the course of their participation in quelling anti-foreignism in China in 1900. Even after the 1901 settlement was signed and foreign troops began to leave Peking, Russian troops stayed in parts of Manchuria that were far from the routes of the newly opened Chinese Eastern Railway and the projected South Manchuria Railway. Alarmed, Britain and Japan drew together in the Anglo-Japanese alliance of 1902. During 1903 Japan negotiated in vain with Russia, seeking Russian acknowledgment of Japan's interest in Korea in return for Japanese recognition of Russia's interest in Manchuria. Early in 1904 the Japanese attacked Russian ships and troops stationed in Manchuria, hoping to force Russia to agree to the desired terms. Japan's victories were costly, however, and Japan soon requested the good offices of the United States in obtaining a peace treaty.

The Russo-Japanese treaty of 1905 enabled the Japanese to take over the southern three-fourths of the South Manchuria Railway route and all Russia's privileges in the Liaotung peninsula, once they won the consent of the helpless Ch'ing government, over (and on) whose territory the fighting had taken place. Russia also recognized Japan's paramount interest in Korea, granted Japanese fishermen the use of certain Siberian coastal waters, and ceded the southern half of Sakhalin to Japan.

The Ch'ing government not only transferred the south Manchurian concessions to Japan, but opened sixteen new treaty ports. The Ch'ing also agreed to permit Japanese to guard the South Manchuria Railway and the new Japanese-built railway that linked the South Manchuria Railway to Korea, which was rapidly falling under Japanse control. During the Russo-Japanese war, the Japanese occupied Seoul and forced Korea to accept Japanese advisers for its financial and international affairs and Japanese police inspectors for its provinces. Before 1905 ended, the Japanese placed a resident adviser in Seoul, as the Ch'ing had done a generation earlier. Japan also won United States recognition as the sole legitimate spokesman for Korea in international affairs. When the Korean king sought to call the world's attention to his country's plight by sending a delegation to the Second Hague Peace Conference of 1907, the Japanese required him to abdicate and established a formal protectorate over Korea. When a Korean assassinated a former Japanese resident adviser for Korea in 1909 in Manchuria, Japan responded by annexing Korea outright in 1910. Meanwhile, Japan and Russia secretly agreed in 1907 that each would respect the other's East Asian interests: Japanese interests in Korea and southern Manchuria, Russian interests in northern Manchuria and outer Mongolia. By the time the Ch'ing fell in 1912, both Japan and Russia were busily consolidating their positions in the lands north and east of the Great Wall.

Internal Unity and the Power to Resist

The fact that the Ch'ing were toppled from within, not from without, points up the fact that most of East Asia was more successful than the Middle East, South or Southeast Asia, or Africa in retaining independence prior to World War I. Only a minute fraction of the people of East Asia came under direct Western political control, in Hongkong, Macao, and the concessions in the treaty ports of China. Even after allowances are made for the degree to which East Asian governments were hampered by the Western acquisition of treaty port concessions, extraterritorial privileges, tariff controls, foreign advisers, legation guards, and the like—all of which continued to affect the life of China until World War II—the amount of independence East Asian states enjoyed contrasts markedly with the situation in most of the Middle East and South and Southeast Asia after the 1830s, or in most of Africa after the 1880s. The foreign personnel who were hired by the Ch'ing to run the maritime customs service after the T'ai-p'ing era were responsible to the

Ch'ing, not to the Western governments which kept watch over the foreign debt administrations in Egypt and the Ottoman empire after 1876. The one East Asian state which failed to keep its independence was Korea, which in 1910 came under the rule of Japan, the most Westernized state in East Asia.

One reason the European powers failed to take over East Asia was the degree of unity which existed within the East Asian states. China, Korea, and Japan were sizable but compact and thickly populated territorial units, unlike states in the Middle East where deserts separated the regions of heavy settlement, or states in Southeast Asia and in Africa south of the Sahara where villages tended to be relatively uncrowded and to have only minimal links to central governments. Moreover, China, Korea, and Japan were inhabited by sedentary peoples who had not undergone invasions massive enough to displace them from their homes or transform their cultures, as had happened to many other peoples from Southeast Asia through India and the Middle East to most of Africa at one time or another. Even the nomads whose entry into north China made thousands flee south beyond the Yangtze became so well blended into the northern Chinese population that they left scarcely any significant cultural trace behind them after a few generations, except insofar as the spread of Buddhism in both north and south China may be attributed to the general unrest caused by their incursions. As a result of a long history of settled life within clearly defined boundaries, China, Korea, and Japan were far more united in religion, language, and political life when the time came to resist Western encroachments than were the states of most other regions.

When Westerners first began sailing to East Asia, the religious beliefs of most of its peoples were firmly established. The Muslim Turks to the west of the mountain barrier between eastern and central Asia had converted the Turks of Sinkiang and neighboring areas to Islam, and the Yuan dynasty had introduced Islam to the tribes of Yunnan. Even after the bloody suppression of Muslim uprisings in both Yunnan and Sinkiang in the 1860s and 1870s, enough survived to give twentieth-century China as many Muslims as twentieth-century Turkey or Egypt. In addition, a form of Buddhism known as Lamaism had spread from its place of origin in Tibet to the Mongols during the Yuan era. In Lamaism, great reverence is given certain living individuals in every generation, in the belief that these individuals are reincarnations of the most important bodhisattvas. The Chinese had long been accustomed to a threefold blend of Confucian, Taoist, and Buddhist practices and precepts. Similarly, the Koreans had learned to mingle Buddhism and Confucianism with their local cults, and the Japanese were beginning to include more Confucian concepts in their outlook, which was based on Buddhist and Shinto ideas and insights.

The first Westerners to reach Japan and Korea found that almost everyone in those two states spoke a language intelligible to his or her fellows. Although only two-thirds of China's people spoke mutually intelligible dialects, all but a few of the other third spoke languages descended from the parent Chinese tongue. Furthermore, the nonphonetic ideographic nature of the Chinese script meant that all literate Chinese read and wrote the same language even though its words might be pronounced differently. Only the relatively small tribal peoples (including Tibetans, Turkic Muslims, Mongols, Manchu, and hill tribes in Yunnan and Kweichow in the south) did not yet regard themselves as Chinese; in the south, some of the more settled of them were already on the way toward assimilation into Chung-kuo, the Middle Kingdom, the age-old Chinese name for the empire of China.

China was indeed the Middle Kingdom in East Asia when the Portuguese, Dutch, and British arrived. On all sides, from Japan and Korea to Mongolia, Tibet, Burma, and Annam (Vietnam), China's neighbors had always recognized its cultural superiority, even when they were attacking its rulers. As those around China formed states of their own, they did so through a dual process of accepting Chinese influence while developing their own consciousness of being non-Chinese. They acknowledged their debt to China for instruction in the arts of government by entering into tributary relations with the Chinese emperor, but by distinguishing themselves from the Chinese while they learned from China, they developed further toward the kind of nationalism found in the modern West than did China. The Chinese of Ming and early Ch'ing times were conscious of themselves as different from the peoples around them. However, they had yet to acknowledge that there could be a civilization equal or superior to their own in subtlety and complexity. Even after the Yuan era, the Chinese still thought more in terms of bringing outsiders into their culture than they did of keeping outsiders out of their nation.

This difference between China and its neighbors contributed to the striking differences between nineteenth-century Chinese and Japanese reactions to the West. The Japanese had already passed through a period of intensive borrowing in their relations with China, and they had assimilated their borrowings so completely that, in regard to cultural matters, they had been able to turn their backs on the Chinese and go their own way. Experience had therefore prepared them to engage in another threefold cycle of imitation, assimilation, and self-assertion, and that is almost exactly what they did in the nineteenth and twentieth centuries. Having discovered and acknowledged Western strength, they imitated the West, assimilated and modified its ways to fit their own traditions, and asserted their independence of Western leadership. However, the Chinese behaved toward the West as they had previously behaved toward the northern barbarians whenever the barbarians broke through China's defenses. The Chinese accepted the fact of temporary and partial rule by the new barbarians of the West, while striving to bring the newcomers into the Chinese cultural orbit. Only when they realized that the West would not acknowledge China's cultural superiority did they begin to pay serious attention to Western ways, and when they did, they turned to Japan's experience for guidance in what to adopt and what to reject. During the twentieth century the Chinese have been undergoing a process of imitation, assimilation, and self-assertion much like that begun in nineteenth-century Japan, although the Chinese have followed a somewhat different path from the Japanese.

Thus the three major states of East Asia enjoyed a degree of unity unmatched in Middle Eastern, South Asian, Southeast Asian, or African states when Westerners reached their shores. East Asians were accustomed to thinking in terms of an overall political unit which encompassed equally all who lived in a given territory, partly because there were few distinctions of language or religion to sunder the body politic. Consequently, Chinese, Japanese, and even Koreans were better prepared to resist outright Western conquest than were the peoples of the Middle East, South and Southeast Asia, or Africa. However, the West's failure to conquer any sizable portion of East Asia cannot be attributed only to the powers of resistance displayed by China, Japan, and Korea. The fact that Japan was not occupied by a Western state until after its defeat in World War II—by which time Japan was as modern as much of the Western world—was primarily a consequence of Western lack of interest in Japan. Most of the Western powers also had little interest in Korea, although the Japanese annexation of Korea was undertaken in frank competition with the West and in imitation of Western policies toward unmodernized states. The focus of Western attention was China, with is vast area and its hundreds of millions of people. Yet China did not fall under Western domination in the way India or the Arab world did. No one Western power was strong enough to master all of China regardless of other Westerners' desires, as the British did in India; and the various European states which wished to divide China among themselves never did so, partly because they were never able to reach a mutually satisfactory agreement on the lines of partition, as they did in Africa.

8

EAST ASIA IN THE TWENTIETH CENTURY

Study in Frustrations:
The First Phase of the Chinese Revolution

FORMATION OF REPUBLICANISM IN CHINA (1895–1917)

The fact that the Western powers did not topple the Ch'ing made many Chinese leaders breathe more easily for a time. The school which held that Western values were contained in the Confucian classics took a new lease on life. The empress dowager, apparently thoroughly chastened, plunged into preparations for introducing an educational system constructed on Western lines in place of the Confucian-centered examination system, which the Boxer settlement of 1901 had suspended in much of northern China. The empress dowager also abolished the distinctions hitherto made between Chinese and Manchu, and promised a Western-influenced legal code. After the Russo-Japanese war, in which Japan with its constitution defeated constitution-lacking Russia, she even talked of a constitutional monarchy with elected parliaments at both the national and provincial levels. A thoroughgoing ten-year campaign against the growing of opium in China was mounted, encouraged by the British promise to stop the importation of opium into China when the campaign was successfully completed.

The apparent revitalization of the Ch'ing after 1900 did not please those Chinese leaders who had gone beyond a belief that the Ch'ing could maintain the Confucian tradition. A few believed that China's Confucian heritage was still usable, if only the decaying Ch'ing were replaced by a truly Chinese government patterned on the principles of

Confucius. However, increasing numbers were attacking the whole monarchical system inherent in Confucian doctrine and advocating a republic which could incorporate the principle of popular rule. The Confucianists and the republicans agreed in opposing the Ch'ing, but they disagreed on what should follow the fall of the dynasty.

The opponents of the Ch'ing united in anti-dynastic associations which had three major sources of support: the anti-dynastic secret societies which had been rampant since the 1780s; the Chinese merchants living abroad in Southeast Asia and the United States who deplored the weakness of their native land; and the Chinese students in Japan. Hundreds of young Chinese flocked to Japan after the Sino-Japanese war and the Boxer uprising, seeking the secret of the success with which the Japanese had modernized without ceasing to be themselves. Many, like Chiang Kai-shek from 1908 to 1911, went as students on government scholarships; but many went without such assistance, like Ch'en Tu-hsiu in 1902 and Chou En-lai from 1917 to 1919. Most of the Chinese students returned from Japan eager to achieve results comparable though not necessarily identical to what they had seen in Japan, and to do so as rapidly as possible. Others remained abroad to work for the anti-Ch'ing associations they joined while in Japan. Still others, like Mao Tse-tung in Hunan, learned about the Japanese example secondhand from students who had been in Japan and from newspapers, magazines, and books.

The anti-Ch'ing or anti-Manchu associations made dozens of attempts to kindle revolt in various parts of China between 1895 and 1910. Many of the attempts were inspired by Sun Yat-sen. Sun, born in Kwangtung province, received much of his early education from Christian missionaries. As he reached manhood, he became convinced that China must Westernize. The failure of his first attempt at revolution in 1895 forced him to spend most of the next fifteen years outside China. At first he relied on the secret societies and the contributions of Chinese merchant families abroad, but in 1905 his movement joined the various associations of Chinese students in Japan in the T'ung Meng Hui, or United League. The T'ung Meng Hui espoused the republican ideal which Sun had adopted some time before and which expressed the desire of most of the students.

In 1911 a combination of provincial and anti-foreign sentiment came to the republicans' aid. The Ch'ing alienated the leaders of Szechwan and the south by trying to use a large foreign loan to bring the provincially owned railways under a central administration. Late in the summer, outbreaks occurred in Szechwan. These outbursts merged in October with a revolt by the troops stationed in the tri-city industrial complex of Wuhan (Hankow, Wuchang, and Hanyang) in the central Yangtze valley. The leaders of the soldiers' revolt wanted a republic. By December a provisional republican government was set up in the south, with Sun as president. By February, 1912, the republicans persuaded Yuan Shih-k'ai, the strongman of the Ch'ing, to convince the advisers of the boy emperor (the empress dowager and her nephew had died in 1908) that he should abdicate.

During the spring of 1912 Yuan became doubly China's ruler. Not only did the Ch'ing entrust him with supreme authority when the boy emperor abdicated, but the grateful provisional republican assembly elected him president in place of Sun. As president, Yuan called for nationwide elections. However, he strengthened his position by having the leading advocate of parliamentary government assassinated before the new national assembly met in 1913.

Sun's followers in the new Kuomintang or Nationalist party, which held a large number of seats in the national assembly, reacted strongly to the assassination of their colleague. They also opposed Yuan's continuing to borrow from abroad even though China was already heavily in debt to foreign bankers. They attempted to overthrow him in 1913, but failed. Yuan's response was to dissolve the assembly in 1914 and proclaim a constitution giving himself full powers. During 1915 Yuan leaned increasingly on his grant of authority from the Ch'ing. He even proclaimed himself the founder of a new dynasty. However, he quickly found that the leaders and men of the provincial armies in the south would not accept this. He gave up his plans early in 1916 and died shortly afterward, leaving the government of China for all practical purposes in the hands of the provincial military commanders.

Although the nineteenth-century leader Tseng Kuo-fan would surely have disowned them for failure to live up to Confucian ideals, the provincial military commanders of the early Chinese republic were the heirs of the system he had inaugurated, under which provincial officials raised, outfitted, and paid their own troops to protect their own people. The commander of the troops which had rebelled against the Ch'ing in October, 1911, took over as president in 1916, having been made vice-president by the elected parliament in 1913. In 1917 he reconvened the parliament and sought to dismiss the Anhwei general, who had become prime minister shortly before Yuan died. However, he found it necessary to call in the Yangtze-valley general against the Anhwei general. The Yangtze-valley general then expelled the republican government from Peking and tried to restore the Ch'ing dynasty. The other generals were incensed. Within twelve days they restored the republic and brought back the Anhwei general as prime minister. The president then resigned, to be replaced by the Kiangsu general, whom the parliament had elected vice-president when it reconvened.

Sun Yat-sen was disgusted by this shuffling of offices among the generals. In September of 1917 he left Peking for Canton, taking with him the Kuomintang members of the parliament. At Canton he established a government which claimed to be the only rightful constitutional government of the Republic of China, but it took ten years and a major conflict between the Kuomintang and the generals before the foreign powers were convinced of the justice of the Canton government's claims.

The birth of the Republic of China had been hailed by the Western powers, which promptly offered loans to the new government. The fall of the Ch'ing was also hailed by leaders in outer Mongolia and Tibet, who quickly declared their independence of China for fear that otherwise their people would be overrun by the renascent Chinese. China unwillingly promised Russia in 1913 to recognize the new government in outer Mongolia as autonomous, although not independent, and in 1919 sent troops into the region to put down a government formed by the Mongols. China also unwillingly negotiated an agreement with Britain in 1914, recognizing Tibet as autonomous and demarcating the boundaries between Tibet and its neighbors in Afghanistan, India, Nepal, Bhutan, Sikkim, and Burma, but China never ratified that agreement. When World War I began in 1914, China declared its neutrality. Japan declared war on Germany, and promptly occupied the German concessions in Shantung despite Chinese protests.

EXPANSION AND CHECKMATE: JAPAN, CHINA, AND RUSSIA (1895–1925)

While China was finally deciding on a republican form of government, Japanese expansion surged forward. With the acquisition of Taiwan and the Penghus, or Pescadores, in 1895, Japan emerged from the Sino-Japanese war in full command of the sea approaches to most of China, Korea, and Siberia. As a result of the brief Russo-Japanese conflict of 1904–1905, Japan was able to add southern Sakhalin, the Liaotung peninsula, the South Manchuria Railway line, and all of Korea to its domains. Meanwhile, the defeated Russian government had to face rising discontent at home, and the dying Ch'ing were discredited still further by their failure to act to recover control in Manchuria.

The pre-1914 territorial expansion of the Japanese empire was made possible by continued growth in the size and strength of its industrial and military establishments. That growth depended on several conditions: continued increase in agricultural productivity, maintenance of financial stability, mobilization of the nation's human resources through education and universal military conscription, and continuance of orderly government. The Japanese peasant took care of the first by making good use of improved techniques; the leaders of the Japanese government took care of the remaining three.

The leaders of Japan were not to be found in the Diet or the political parties. After 1889, as before, the most important figures in the

Japanese government were the small group of former samurai who had guided the Meiji Restoration. These men, most of whom had come from Satsuma and Choshu, formed an informal oligarchy known as the *genro*, or elder statesmen. From 1868 to 1918, the members of the cabinet were almost invariably genro or men approved by the genro. A few genro went into political parties as a means of controlling them, but the result was the strengthening of the genro rather than the parties. Not until the last weeks of World War I was a cabinet headed and selected by a leader who had risen through support from the parties rather than from the genro, and even he had won a measure of acceptance from the remaining genro. Japan's economic growth, its high literacy rate, the self-discipline and national loyalty of its people, and its nearly thirty years of experience with parliaments, parties, and elections were not sufficient to ensure that party government would replace oligarchic government in 1918 or thereafter. The necessary condition of the subordination of the military to the civil arm of government was lacking, and events in China as well as in Japan led the Japanese military to take matters into their own hands increasingly in the years after World War I.

By the end of World War I, Japan's economic power increased greatly. The trade opportunities opened to Japanese industrialists by the wartime withdrawal of European manufactures from Asian markets transformed Japan from a debtor nation, buying more abroad than it could sell, to a creditor nation, selling more than it bought. At the same time, few Japanese entrepreneurs were troubled by labor union agitation for wage increases commensurate with increases in productivity. Employers continued to treat their workers paternalistically, and employees continued to accept the dependence on their employers implied in paternalism. Coupled with low tax rates for industry, the carryover of paternalism from the still numerous family enterprises to the new industrial giants enabled industrialists to invest a high proportion of their companies' incomes in further expansion.

The Japanese also expanded their territorial empire during the war years. Not only did they seize the German concessions in Shantung, but they obtained additional concessions from the government of Yuan Shih-k'ai. Early in 1915 Japan presented the Republic of China with a series of twenty-one demands, arranged in five groups. The demands were designed to give Japan the leading position among the powers involved in China's affairs. The Japanese requested the transfer of the German privileges in Shantung to Japan; the extension of Japan's privileges in southern Manchuria for ninety-nine years instead of twenty-five, together with permission for Japanese subjects (including Koreans) to enter the region, travel and reside in it freely, exploit its minerals, and lease or own land; the establishment of a joint Sino-Japanese company to run the chief group of iron and coal mines and steel works in the central Yangtze valley; a Chinese pledge not to concede any more coastal areas to other powers; and sweeping promises to give preference to the Japanese in all Chinese projects involving foreign participation, particularly in Fukien province opposite Taiwan. The Chinese granted most of the first four groups of demands, under protest, but accepted very few of those in the fifth group. It was rumored that Yuan only consented in return for Japanese promises to recognize his assumption of the imperial title.

When the generals who succeeded Yuan at the head of the Peking government finally decided in 1917 to enter World War I on the Allied side, the move was unpopular with the Chinese because it put China on the same side as Japan. When China entered the war, it abolished German, Austrian, and Hungarian extraterritorial jurisdiction, thereby driving a wedge into the façade of Western privilege. China also used its membership in the Allied ranks to bid for the return of the German concessions in Shantung to China at the peace table, but without success. Since Australia refused to consider including in the treaties a clause upholding the principle of racial equality, as Japan desired, Japan was even less willing than it might otherwise have been to give up the Shantung concessions.

Japan did not keep the Shantung privileges for long. Japan's use of the Allied intervention in Siberia in 1918 was widely disapproved. The avowed object of the expedition was to remove supplies and prisoners of war from Siberia, now that the new Soviet government had signed a separate peace treaty with Germany. However, the Japanese attempted not only to block the Soviet government from acquiring authority in eastern Siberia but to win control of the region for themselves. These and other Japanese activities made the Anglo-Japanese alliance unpopular in both Canada and the United States. Meanwhile, Britain and the United States were increasingly concerned over the burgeoning naval race between themselves and Japan in the Pacific. In 1921 these factors led to a dual conference in Washington, D.C., on naval affairs and Far Eastern problems. The five-power naval conference established a 5:5:3:1.75:1.75 ratio among the navies of Britain, the United States, Japan, France, and Italy, and substituted a four-power alliance of Britain, France, Japan, and the United States for the Anglo-Japanese treaty. The nine-power conference on the Far East agreed on a treaty which reaffirmed the integrity of China, the equal right of all nations to trade with China, and the united interest of the signers in encouraging governmental stability in China. In many ways the nine-power treaty resembled the 1906 agreements reaffirming Moroccan integrity and independence which had preceded the French and Spanish occupation of Morocco, but there were two crucial differences. The recognized Chinese government in Peking, though ineffective, was still receiving revenue enough through the maritime customs service so that foreign lenders were not pressing for general foreign supervision of China's finances; and the powers most interested in partitioning China into spheres of interest had not reached agreements on doing so, as the French had done with Britain, Italy, Spain, and Germany before moving into Morocco. The nine powers did not offer to give up the territorial concessions they had won in the past, but the conference did result in China's being allowed to raise its tariffs. The nine powers also set up a commission to study the problem of extra-territoriality, in preparation for discussing its future abolition. During the Washington meetings, diplomatic pressure induced Japan to restore all the Shantung privileges to China in 1922, except for the right to control one railway for fifteen years. Late in 1922 the last Japanese troops also withdrew from Siberia.

The Soviet Union, having already aided outer Mongolia to rid itself of both Chinese and anti-Soviet Russians in 1921, appeared in eastern Siberia soon after the Japanese left. The consolidation of Soviet power there was shortly followed by Soviet negotiations with both Japan and China. The 1925 Soviet treaty with Japan did little more than re-affirm the 1905 settlement. The 1924 Soviet treaty with China was more significant. It implemented Soviet declarations of 1919 and 1920 repudi-ating czarist imperial gains, giving up extraterritorial jurisdiction (which chiefly affected the numerous pro-czarist refugees in China), restoring to China the Russian leaseholds in the foreign settlements of Tientsin and Hankow, and returning the unused portion of the 1901 indemnity. The Soviets did retain the czarist-built Chinese Eastern Railway and the privileges associated with it. They also insisted that China reaffirm the autonomy of outer Mongolia, which later in 1924 proclaimed itself the Mongolian People's Republic. During the next fifteen years, the new Mongolian government successfully eliminated the power of the heredi-tary nobility and of the priestly establishment of Lamaism. However, its efforts to induce Mongol herders to enter collectives were frustrated by their opposition, which was encouraged in the 1930s by Japanese agents who hoped to extend Japanese influence into the region.

FERMENT IN CHINA (1912–1923)

The Soviet Union's entry into eastern Siberia came at a time of ferment in China. The course run by China's first parliament had been rough. It was snuffed out by the ambitious Yuan Shih-k'ai, reinstated after his death, and mauled and manipulated by the warlords, the generals of the provincial armies. Finally it split in two: one part remaining in Peking under warlord control and one part withdrawing to Canton under

Sun Yat-sen. The Canton parliament soon found it was almost as much at the mercy of the Kwangtung general as the northern government was dominated by whichever northern general currently occupied Peking with his army. By the time the Chinese parliament was five years old, it was obvious that a parliament alone could not revitalize China.

It was also obvious that the attempt to enable Chinese to use Western techniques freely and easily by finding Western values in the Confucian heritage had been nearly as superficial as the "Western utility—Confucian essence" school. Neither of these movements was solving the problems China faced as it was forced against its will to leave the hierarchical Confucian tributary state system for a world of sovereign equals. A new beginning was needed. The result may be compressed into the line, "Select the best from East and West." Chinese who wanted to use Western techniques began to accept the Western values associated with them on their own merit, without trying to prove those values to be Chinese except insofar as being true made them universal. Yet even those who were most drawn to Western ways were still too attached to the Chinese heritage to be able to ignore it. They therefore took care to look for what was still usable from the past under the new circumstances of a twentieth-century republic.

One of the first and most significant results of the "Select the best from East and West" school of thought was the *pai-hua,* or common-speech, movement led by Chinese like Ch'en Tu-hsiu who went abroad to study after 1900 and returned before or during World War I. Having accepted the importance of universal literacy as a means of enabling every man to be a sage like Yao or Shun (and every woman, too, for the woman's rights movement was another product of the age), the youthful returned scholars insisted that it was necessary to stop writing in the terse and highly conventionalized style of the ancients and start writing in the ordinary spoken language. Otherwise, it would be difficult to extend literacy to all. The young scholars also felt the use of the vernacular would free the minds of Chinese from the patterns of the past, so that they could indeed "select the best." The pai-hua movement was an immediate success. All varieties of books and periodicals were soon being written and published in pai-hua. Within seven years of the inception of the movement in 1915, the pai-hua style of writing was used in all of the pitifully few public elementary and secondary schools in China.

The supporters of the pai-hua movement were animated by a fervent Chinese patriotism. The depth of their desire for continuity with the Chinese past was vividly demonstrated by their failure to promote a changeover from the Chinese ideographic script to a phonetic script using the Latin letters used in the West, as well as a changeover from the classical to the vernacular style of writing. True, the existence of many monosyllabic words of almost identical sound made development of a usable Latin-based script difficult, but the Vietnamese had already shown it was possible for such a language to be written in the Latin alphabet, and usable Latin-based scripts were worked out for Chinese by a few enthusiasts. However, even today these scripts are only used to aid in the learning of the characters, somewhat as Japanese have long used their syllabic scripts as aids in the study of Chinese characters. It would appear to have been the longing not to break completely with the past, more than the difficulty of the changeover, that made the young Chinese scholars behave differently from the Turkish leaders in the 1920s—clinging to rather than rejecting the script in which their heritage was recorded, and rejecting rather than adopting the script which would facilitate their study of Western languages. Yet the patriotism of the young Chinese scholars combined a strong attraction for the magnificence of China's heritage with a bitter sense of betrayal, for that magnificent heritage had failed to meet the needs of the present. Consequently, the young scholars and their students fastened on the land and the people as the primary foundation on which the new state of China should be constructed. They became even more fervent than the pre-1912 revolutionaries in their belief that if only the combined will of the Chinese people could be made strong enough, ways could be found to achieve all their goals.

Patriotism brought the young scholars and their students close to the small but growing urban commercial classes who were developing similar feelings. Since 1905 the merchants and the few industrialists of China had periodically protested what they saw as foreign insults to China by boycotting the goods of the offending country, and the newly organizing factory workers were beginning to oppose the foreign ownership and management of many of the industrial plants in China. When the Peking government formally accepted the transfer of Germany's privileges in Shantung to Japan early in 1919, the students and the commercial classes joined to protest the government's spinelessness in what became known as the May Fourth movement. By demonstrations in Peking and other major cities, the students, workers, and merchants forced the government to refuse to ratify the Versailles treaty, which the diplomats had reluctantly accepted. This success heartened the patriots, and so did the Japanese retrocession of almost all the Shantung privileges in 1922. By 1923 the student-worker-merchant combination was more than ready for a concerted drive on all foreign privileges, once a dynamic leadership should appear. The degree to which the Chinese could bury their differences in order to work together against foreign encroachment had already been shown in 1918 when representatives of the rival Peking and Canton governments had come together and selected a joint delegation to represent China at Versailles.

MARXISM AND NATIONALISM IN CHINA (1918–1931)

Between 1912 and 1922 China's students and scholars were in a state of intellectual upheaval, seeking to build a new foundation of enduring values for the life of the new China. The dismissal of the Confucian past was followed by a keen interest in the philosophical schools current in the West, most notably in the pragmatism of John Dewey, who insisted that the ability to make practical applications was the test of the truth of an idea. A number of Chinese studied under Dewey at Columbia University, and at their invitation he lectured in Peking in 1919 and 1920. Pragmatism attracted many Chinese because its habit of seeking what was workable fit into their habit of seeking what was harmonious. However, the victory of Marxism under Lenin in Russia turned the eyes of Chinese intellectuals in a new direction.

Marxism attracted many young Chinese after World War I because it claimed to combine the much desired virtues of both science and democracy. It provided definite answers to all the puzzling questions of the past and present. In particular, it explained China's weakness as that of a downtrodden colony whose affairs were being run by all the Western powers and Japan as well. Marxism-Leninism also stressed the desirability of recognizing and using every possible opportunity to further the supposedly inevitable revolution, an emphasis which appealed to the strong streak of reliance on the power of the will in most of those Chinese who desired change. In addition, the Leninist form of Marxism preached the leadership of the many by the trained and dedicated few, a concept which bore some similarity to the Confucian scholar-bureaucracy. Finally, Marxism-Leninism was as bitter as the most virulent Chinese in its manifold denunciations of the rulers of the countries most involved in China's affairs. It was not surprising that from 1918 onward young Chinese studied Marxism. At first they sharply criticized its rigidities. Even the future Communist leader Mao Tse-tung, in an early article calling for a "great union" of "small unions" of peasants, workers, women, youth, and other groups with special grievances against the old order, indicated that the voluntarism and agrarian communitarianism of the Russian anarchist Peter Kropotkin appeared to him to be more comprehensive than Marxism-Leninism. However, when the Soviet Union began promising in 1919 to give up its special privileges in China, Chinese students of Marxism grew positively enthusiastic. In 1920, Marxist study groups were formed in Peking by Ch'en Tu-hsiu and others, in Hunan by Mao Tse-tung and others, in several other parts of China, and in France, where Chou En-lai arrived that year to study.

Representatives from these groups held the first Communist party congress in 1921.

The treaty embodying the Soviet renunciations was signed at Peking. However, the Soviet Union did not ignore the rival government of Sun Yat-sen at Canton. While Marxist doctrines attracted Chinese students (although not Chinese merchants), Sun was impressed by the organizing ability which had given the Marxists victory over the czars. He had tried unsuccessfully to win recognition and assistance for the Canton government from Britain, France, and the United States. In 1923 he decided to turn to the Soviets. A few months before the Sino-Soviet treaty was agreed on in Peking, the Soviets struck a bargain with Sun to help him reorganize his political party, the Kuomintang.

The Soviets saw cooperation with Sun as a prime opportunity to win China for the world revolution. They planned to place members of the new Chinese Communist party in key Kuomintang party posts while they were reorganizing the Kuomintang, thereby putting the Communists in a position to take over the government when the Kuomintang came to power. At the Soviets' behest and with Sun's permission, the Chinese Communists became Kuomintang members. Soviet advisers streamed into Canton, while Kuomintang members like Chiang Kai-shek, a follower of Sun since the days of the T'ung Meng Hui, studied Marxist doctrine and tactics in the Soviet Union. The Kuomintang adopted the cell-congress form of organization, in which only the leader of each small cell of party members met other cell leaders in periodic congresses and which the Soviets had found useful for clandestine work. (The cell-congress mode of organization later frustrated Communist attempts to take over the Kuomintang by infiltration.) The Three Principles of the People—the three principles of nationalism, democracy, and economic betterment that Sun had begun enunciating before the Ch'ing fell—were reinterpreted so as to bring them somewhat more in line with Marxist proclivities. Sun's plan for a period of tutelage, for learning the practices of democratic government at the local level under Kuomintang instruction before experimenting anew with constitutional government, was also modified in some details. A military school, headed by Chiang but with Chou En-lai as a political instructor, was set up at Canton to provide Sun's government with its own army so that it could put an end to the rule of the generals.

Both officers and men in the Kuomintang armies of 1925 onward were indoctrinated with patriotic fervor strongly flavored with Marxist-Leninist anti-imperialism and the three principles of Sun Yat-sen. However, Chiang also saw that they were reminded of the maxims of Tseng Kuo-fan. Like many Chinese, Chiang could not accept a complete break with the past. He approved of republicanism, but he tended to see it as a way to enable the people to transfer the Mandate of Heaven from one government to another without the destruction and bloodshed of rebellion, rather than as a way to enable them to take active part in making governmental decisions. Loyalty and obedience were still the primary virtues.

By the time Sun died in 1925 the new Kuomintang army had freed the Canton government from the control of the south China warlords. In 1926 the Canton government's forces marched northward, entering Nanking in 1927 and Peking in 1928. The victorious Kuomintang made Nanking their capital and renamed Peking "Peiping" (northern peace) to symbolize their victory.

As the Kuomintang troops marched northward, the Communist members of the Kuomintang served as an advance guard. The Communists led the work of organizing students, peasants, and workers against the warlords of the north. They accused the warlords not only of standing in the way of the achievement of the triple goal of national unity, democratic government, and increased strength and well-being, but also of being subservient to the foreign powers which were China's real enemies. At the same time, the merchants and industrialists were won over by those Kuomintang members who shared Chiang's belief that the attainment of Sun Yat-sen's triple goal required a return to some of the traditional virtues. At the halfway mark of the northward march in 1927, these two factions of the Kuomintang, Left and Right, turned on each other. Under Chiang's leadership the right wing won. The Communists were expelled from the Kuomintang and stamped out ruthlessly in the cities where they had their major following. Only those who were working in areas which Chinese central and provincial governments had always had difficulty in policing, like Mao Tse-tung in rural Hunan, escaped relatively unscathed.

The right-wing victory made Chiang the undisputed successor to Sun as head of the Kuomintang. Chiang then persuaded one northern warlord after another to accept his leadership. This move brought all of China's former domains under the nominal rule of Nanking, except for the autonomous regions in outer Mongolia and the Tibetan plateau. However, it also meant that Chiang's government at first had scarcely any control in the north, for the warlords refused to put their armies under the central government. During the first three years of Chiang's rule, the Kuomintang government spent most of its energy trying to force the northern generals to give up their private armies, but it was only partially successful. Meanwhile, the Communists regrouped in the south, establishing a base of operations in the hilly borderland between Kiangsi and Hunan provinces. Under Mao Tse-tung they set up a Chinese Soviet Republic late in 1931. Once more there were two governments struggling

for power in China; once more, the one that would finally win the
struggle would be the one whose leaders were willing to make a more
complete break with the past.

THE KUOMINTANG-COMMUNIST-JAPANESE
TRIANGLE (1928–1937)

By the time the Chinese Soviet Republic was formed in 1931, the
government at Nanking was organized along the lines laid down by Sun
for the period of tutelage. Executive, legislative, judicial, civil service
examination, and control or censorial councils were set up, their chair-
men and vice-chairmen comprising the state council. All of these bodies
were selected by the Kuomintang, so that the councils derived their
authority from the self-chosen leaders of the nation rather than from a
popular elective process.

The Kuomintang government continued the reassertion of Chinese
sovereignty which had begun with the abrogation of German, Austrian,
and Hungarian extraterritorial privileges during World War I. The Sino-
Soviet agreement of 1924, repudiating treaty-port leaseholds and extraterritoriality, was followed by the British return of leaseholds in two
Yangtze-valley cities during the Kuomintang march to victory in 1927.
China regained its tariff autonomy in 1930. By then all the powers except Britain, France, Japan, and the United States either gave up their
extraterritorial privileges or promised to give them up as soon as every
other power agreed to do so.

The Kuomintang government set about constructing the transportation network needed to make China truly a political unit. It promulgated
China's first fully comprehensive modern legal code, providing for equal
treatment of men and women and recognizing individual rather than
collective responsibility. The Kuomintang government also tackled the
problem of the poverty-stricken peasantry, decreeing a maximum-rent
law. However, neither the new rent law nor the new legal code was ever
put into effect in the rural areas. Chiang lacked the strength to enforce any
decree which ran counter to the personal wishes of the warlords, whom
he had perforce recognized as governors in the provinces as the late
Ch'ing and the early republic had done, and most of the warlords were
either uninterested in the reforms proposed by the Kuomintang government or actively hostile to them. Even those few surviving warlords who
did actively promote schools, roads, and other carriers of modernization
within the provinces they governed tended to ignore the central government's decrees, for they wanted to gain for themselves whatever credit
their subjects might be giving anyone for improvements in their lot.

The Kuomintang regime was not left free to remold Chinese life
as much (and as little) as its leaders felt necessary in the circumstances

of the modern world. Not only did it face the warlords and the Communists, neither of whom was it ever able to master entirely, but it had to face the Japanese. As soon as Chiang became head of a more or less united China, Japanese army leaders took alarm lest the apparently strengthening Kuomintang deprive them of their positions in Manchuria, whose iron and coal were increasingly valuable to Japan's heavy industry. The Japanese used their remaining toehold in Shantung to try to block Chiang in 1928, but in vain. In September, 1931, the Japanese troops stationed in the Liaotung peninsula (also know as Kwantung) and along the South Manchuria Railway fanned out from their bases and occupied all of Manchuria, to the rage of China and to the horror of the League of Nations and the United States. The Chinese united in boycotting Japanese goods, but the Japanese took military action at Shanghai and near Peiping, forcing the Kuomintang government to accept a truce in 1933. The Japanese made a great show of giving up their extraterritorial privileges in the puppet state of Manchukuo, which was founded in Manchuria in 1932 under their auspices.

Harassed by the Communists and thwarted by the continued power of the warlords, the Kuomintang government had to choose which enemy to deal with first. It chose to attack the Communists rather than the Japanese. During the next two years, Kuomintang forces drove the Communists out of Kiangsi on the "Long March" of six thousand miles, in which the Communists moved across Hunan, Kweichow, and Szechwan into northern Shensi, where they set up their government at Yenan in 1935.

The Long March decimated Communist ranks. It also enabled Nanking to establish effective control in Kweichow and Szechwan for the first time, as Kuomintang forces passed through those two provinces in pursuit of the head of the Chinese Soviet Republic, Mao Tse-tung, and his leading general, Chu Teh. However, not all Chinese agreed with Chiang's policy of attacking internal enemies first and dealing with external foes later. In particular, the Shensi garrison commander felt Chiang ought to fight the Japanese first and use the Communists against them. The Shensi commander's father had been killed in Manchuria by the Japanese, and he himself had been driven from Manchuria by them. When Chiang flew to Shensi in 1936 to tell him to move on Yenan, he imprisoned Chiang in his quarters until Chiang agreed to accept a policy of cooperation with the Communists. In February, 1937, Yenan and Nanking reached an informal understanding.

The first step toward cooperation between Chiang and Mao was hailed with joy by almost every Chinese who heard of it. The students were especially elated. Since 1931 they had chafed not only under the indignity of Japanese control of Manchuria but under the Kuomintang's increasing restrictions on freedom of expression. They hoped that Kuomintang-Communist cooperation would mean a lessening of controls at home as well as a stronger policy toward Japan. The Japanese were less pleased. Some Japanese army leaders in Manchuria were so alarmed at the possibility that the Kuomintang-Communist pact might mean Soviet support for China against Japan that they took matters into their own hands as they had in 1931 and began fighting Chinese troops near Peiping in July, 1937.

SOVIET REACTIONS (1928–1941)

The possibility that Chiang Kai-shek might win full control of China had been as unwelcome to the Soviets as to Japan, for a strong and determined China would put an end to Soviet as well as Japanese influence north of the Great Wall. The Soviets broke off relations with Nanking in 1929, when the governor of Manchuria took over the Chinese Eastern Railway's telegraph network and arrested the Soviet agents who worked out of the consulates along the railway line. However, the Japanese entry into Manchuria soon gave the Soviets even greater reason for alarm.

The Soviets did not welcome Japan's seizure of Manchuria or the subsequent Japanese capture of a neighboring Chinese province north of the Wall. The League of Nations condemned Japan's actions, but Japan simply withdrew from the League in 1933. The Soviets were also distressed when Japan forced Chiang to establish a demilitarized zone south of the Wall, and when the Japanese tried to make friends with the Mongols and Tibetans. The Soviets dared not refuse to sell the Chinese Eastern Railway to the Japanese-supported puppet government in Manchukuo in 1935, but they were keenly aware that the loss of the Chinese Eastern Railway threatened the security of much of the Trans-Siberian Railway. Therefore, the Soviets concluded a mutual assistance pact with the Mongolian People's Republic in 1936 and sent troops which helped the Mongols turn back a Japanese incursion in 1939. In addition, they strove to link isolated Sinkiang as closely as possible to Soviet Turkestan, whose people were related in speech, religion, and ethnic origin to the people of Sinkiang. Until Hitler invaded European Russia in June, 1941, the Soviets also aided Chiang, thereby enabling him to resist Japan until the Japanese attacks on the United States and Britain in December, 1941, provided him with new allies. The Soviet aid to Chiang disturbed Japanese leaders so much that they sought a neutrality pact with the Soviet Union. They gained it just before Germany invaded Russia, more to the Soviets' relief than to their own in the next few months.

Elimination of Japan and the Kuomintang from Mainland China

VICTORY OF THE MILITARISTS IN JAPAN (1918–1937)

Both the desire and the ability of Japanese army officers to act on their own in China in the 1930s stemmed from the internal situation in Japan. In 1918, when the Meiji constitution was twenty-nine years old, the first party cabinet was installed. This was the first cabinet which was not dominated by oligarchs from the Meiji era, which had formally ended when the Meiji emperor died in 1912. However, it did not depart radically from precedent, nor did the party cabinets which followed it between 1918 and 1931. The parties continued to derive their chief strength from business and from those government officials who chose to enter the elective side of political life. The vote was extended to all adult males in 1925, but this step was accompanied by the passage of a peace preservation law which made it a crime to speak slightingly of the emperor, the imperial system of government, or the "Japanese way," a catchall phrase which could include almost anything.

Prime Minister Kato, under whom the suffrage and peace preservation laws were enacted, had previously pressed the Twenty-One Demands on Yuan Shih-k'ai in China in 1915, when he was foreign minister. By 1925 he was convinced that Japan should seek friendship with a reviving China, but most of the Japanese military were equally convinced that Japan's interests required that Japan dominate China. The more idealistic of them described their desire for domination as a yearning to guide China along the path to modernization which Japan had followed. In the early 1920s they had some excuse for feeling that China needed guidance, for battles between the warlords were raging in every province.

The bulk of the Japanese military were drawn from the country-side, where most Japanese still lived. They were distressed over the poverty of the peasants under high taxes, high rents, high prices for their needs, and low prices for their crops, as contrasted with the affluence of the industrialists and financiers who influenced political affairs. Between a desire to help the peasantry and a desire to dominate China, many military officers decided that the party cabinets must go, since they looked on amicably at the Kuomintang's climb to power, yet did almost nothing for the peasants.

Most of those who actively opposed the party cabinets' leniency toward China were army rather than navy officers. The navy was highly conscious that Japan's industrial establishment would be imperiled if the powers friendly to China decided to blockade Japan, for Japanese industry depended heavily on raw materials from outside the four main islands of Japan. A number of army officers even came to feel that the constitutional structure of Diet and cabinet should go, leaving the military as the emperor's sole spokesmen to his people. Curiously, in view of their fanatical allegiance to the symbol of the emperor, the officers who supported this plan to revive the experience of seven centuries of shogunal rule were strongly influenced by Marxism. Most of them wanted the state to control industry, so as to lessen the role of industrialists and financiers in government.

With such feelings rampant in army circles, it was hardly surprising that the Japanese troops in Shantung tried to halt Chiang's progress to Peking in 1928, or that shortly afterward the Japanese in Liaotung (Kwantung) assassinated the reigning Manchurian warlord in an unsuccessful effort to take over Manchuria before it acknowledged Chiang's authority. When the Kwantung army plans for Manchuria were frustrated by the refusal of the party cabinet to follow the army lead in 1928, anti-cabinet feelings heightened in the army; and when it seemed that the next prime minister might request the abolition of the Supreme War Council's independent access to the emperor, a step which would place the military under cabinet control, a young fanatic shot and fatally wounded the prime minister late in 1930. By then the parties were weakened by the desertion of many of their former supporters in the bureaucracy, who wished to become an independent force, and a three-way struggle for control of internal and external policy was taking place among politicians, bureaucrats, and military leaders.

Impatient younger officers in Japan planned two coups d'état in 1931, but both moves failed because of premature disclosure of the plans. The equally impatient Kwantung army leaders were more successful, for they not only planned but carried out the coup by which they won effective control of all of resource-rich Manchuria. Control was exercised through three agencies: a puppet government headed by the last member of the Ch'ing dynasty, whom the Kwantung army made ruler of Manchukuo (land of the Manchu) in 1932; the posts of Japanese ambassador to Manchukuo, governor of the leased Kwantung or Liaotung territory, and commander of the Kwantung army, all of which were held by one Japanese military officer; and the South Manchuria Railway Company, a primary instrument for Japanese economic development even after its "return" to Manchukuo as part of a "relinquishment" of extraterritorial and other privileges. The Japanese military saw to it that the resources of Manchuria and Korea were developed according to an overall plan. By 1941, north Korea and central and south Manchuria contained the largest and most productive heavy industrial complex in East Asia.

The successful coup in Manchuria encouraged fanatics in Japan. In May, 1932, the last party leader from the 1920s to act as premier was murdered by a group of young officers. The assassins then surrendered voluntarily and used their trial to publicize their opinions. The newspaper-reading public received their protestations of patriotism with considerable sympathy, which encouraged those who shared the assassins' ideas. At the same time, their willingness to use violence intimidated those both in and out of public office who did not share the fanatics' distaste for party government. For the next few years no party man served as prime minister, but even nonparty cabinets moved too slowly against the businessmen and the Chinese to satisfy the impatient junior officers. Early in 1936 the young fanatics seized central Tokyo and killed not only high civilian officials but many of their own more moderate superior officers. Alarmed at such insubordination, the remaining senior officers moved promptly and efficiently to crush this insurrection. However, almost all the remaining political party leaders were frightened into silence, even though elections for the lower house of the Diet in 1936 and 1937 showed overwhelming voter support for those who opposed the drift toward militarism; and most of the bureaucrats cast their lot with the military for the sake of personal safety. After that it was a foregone conclusion that the cabinet would not object to bold moves when the Kwantung army again became involved in fighting in north China in 1937, for fear that a Sino-Soviet alliance might expel the Japanese from Manchuria.

JAPANESE VICTORIES IN CHINA (1937–1941)

At first the war with China went well for the Japanese. By the end of 1937 they occupied the major cities of most of the north China plain and the lower Yangtze valley. Within another year they seized Canton in the south and the Wuhan industrial complex in the center. Yet Chiang did not give up. When Nanking fell in 1937, the Kuomintang government moved to Hankow; when Hankow fell in 1938, the government moved still further up the Yangtze to Chungking in Szechwan. The Japanese did not really control the occupied regions, for all across the north China plain as far south as the Yangtze valley the Communists formed guerrilla forces to harass them. The Communists organized the villagers into local supply teams and used the peasants' willingness to accept their leadership in this patriotic task to propagandize in their own behalf.

The Kuomintang government was well aware of the propaganda

element in Communist guerrilla activity, but it lacked leaders who could rally the peasantry as effectively as did the Communists. Before 1937 it had concentrated on winning political and financial support from merchants and industrialists in the eastern cities; after 1938, when its chief source of revenue was the land tax paid by the wealthy landlords of Szechwan, it scarcely dared compete with the Communists for peasant loyalty for fear of losing its income. As the war continued, the struggle became more and more three-cornered, with each participant—Kuomintang, Japanese, and Communists—grimly determined to get rid of both the others.

The Japanese occupation, which led eventually to the establishment of a Japanese-controlled puppet government in east central China, made the extraterritorial privileges of Britain, France, and the United States actually valuable to the government of Chiang. Since Westerners were subject only to their own consuls, they could shelter Chinese from Japanese troops. They could also observe what occurred in Japanese-held areas and report it to the outside world, as long as Japan continued to desire peace with Britain, France, and the United States. This situation ended abruptly at the end of 1941 when Japan declared war on the Western powers (a formality not observed when large-scale operations began in China in 1937). At the opening of 1943 the Western powers formally gave up extraterritoriality and the other privileges they had acquired and held in the century since 1842. Only Hongkong and Macao remained as symbols and reminders of China's former weakness. Japan had already formally ceded its extraterritorial privileges in Manchuria to the puppet government it had set up there in 1932.

JAPAN OVERMATCHED: WORLD WAR II (1939–1945)

The opening of World War II in Europe, in September of 1939, introduced new elements into the East Asian situation. Attracted by the military orientation of Hitler's Germany and Mussolini's Italy and impressed by Hitler's swift conquest of western and northern Europe, Japan signed the Tripartite Pact with Germany and Italy in September, 1940. (By that time, Japan's political parties had dissolved themselves completely and, supposedly, voluntarily.) The ambitious military, frustrated in China, hoped to profit by the German defeat of the French and Dutch in Europe and the expected defeat of Britain.

The military believed that the weakening of Britain, France, and the Netherlands afforded Japan a unique opportunity to obtain control of the great natural resources of these nations' Southeast Asian possessions, thereby ensuring supplies of militarily strategic raw materials like rubber and providing materials, markets, and investment opportunities for the Japanese economy. In September, 1940, the German-dominated government of Vichy France allowed Japan to use French airfields in northern French Indochina in the war on China. Ten months later, Vichy France permitted Japan to occupy bases in southern French Indochina also. In protest, the United States froze all Japanese assets in the United States, bringing Japan's trade with the United States to a standstill.

Not only was the United States becoming increasingly interested in Britain's struggle against Germany, and therefore in blocking expansion by Germany's allies, but the United States was also alarmed for the fate of China. In line with one of the cardinal principles of United States foreign policy since the inception of the republic, Washington's chief interest was the maintenance and extension of the freedom of every state's nationals in general (and of Americans in particular) to trade and travel in every country with as little restriction as possible, either by their hosts or by third parties such as imperial governments. That principle had led to the original Monroe Doctrine of opposition to European reentry into Latin America in 1823. It had also led to establishment of control over the Philippines in 1898 to prevent them from falling into the hands of the expanding Japanese, support of China against the European powers and Japan in the Boxer era, and opposition to Japanese activities in China after the Manchurian occupation in 1931. In 1941 the same principle led to United States opposition to growing Japanese interest in French Indochina and other European colonies in Southeast Asia. (The United States wished to see Southeast Asia freed as soon as possible from all foreign control, now that it was planning to leave the Philippines in 1945.) That principle also led to opposition to the establishment of Communist governments around the world because of the restrictions they almost invariably placed on travel and trade, both by their own people abroad and by foreigners within their borders.

The Japanese military tried in vain to persuade the United States to change its stand, but they were unwilling to give up their plans for further expansion, as the United States demanded. Moreover, they found that Britain and the dominions of the British Commonwealth froze Japanese assets in their territories, and that the Dutch in the Netherlands East Indies set up stringent controls on trade with Japan. The Japanese military finally decided on a three-part plan. They would knock out of action as much of the United States' Pacific fleet as possible in one blow at the naval base of Pearl Harbor in Hawaii, seize Southeast Asia, and negotiate a favorable peace with a chastened Washington. Japan could then consolidate its gains into a Greater East Asia Co-Prosperity Sphere, an enlargement of the New Order in East Asia already established in Manchuria and eastern China.

The Japanese military carried out the first two parts of their plan, but not the third. The United States set grimly to work to drive them from their conquests. By the end of 1942, United States submarines and planes were already sinking enough Japanese ships to cripple the Japanese war effort; by the end of 1944, United States bombers ranged freely over Japanese cities. The end was clearly in sight. Yet many of the military refused to talk of surrender, for they feared that the demand of the United States and its allies in the United Nations for unconditional surrender meant the United Nations would abolish the imperial institution itself. Their fanatical devotion to the imperial system as they understood it was so great that they came close to believing its destruction by others would destroy Japan. They almost preferred the self-destruction of a fight to the end. They only agreed to surrender in obedience to the emperor's personal command, which was finally given on August 14, 1945, after the Soviet Union entered the Pacific war and after the United States dropped atomic bombs on Hiroshima and Nagasaki.

During the closing weeks of the Pacific war, Japan tried to use the good offices of the Soviet Union as a still-neutral power. By that time, however, the Soviets had already agreed to enter the war in return for Western promises to persuade Chiang to agree to continued autonomy for the Mongolian People's Republic, restoration of the Chinese Eastern and South Manchuria Railways to the Soviet Union, and internationalization of the port of Dairen in the Liaotung peninsula. The West had also agreed to Soviet acquisition of southern Sakhalin and the Kurile islands northeast of Hokkaido.

On August 8, 1945, the Soviet Union denounced its neutrality pact and declared war on Japan. The Soviets occupied all of Manchuria and the part of Korea north of the thirty-eighth parallel, accepting the surrender of Japanese troops in those regions. They carried off the portable items in the Japanese-built Manchurian industrial complex and turned over captured Japanese military supplies to the Chinese Communist guerrillas, who had been operating against the Japanese in north China since 1937 and were then preparing for a final showdown with the Kuomintang. The Soviets signed a treaty of alliance with Chiang, internationalizing Dairen, restoring the Manchurian railways to the Soviets, and calling for a plebiscite in the Mongolian People's Republic, which promptly declared its independence in January, 1946. The Mongolian People's Republic launched a program of industrialization, with Soviet and later with Chinese Communist assistance. By the 1960s the new factories were attracting so many people from the harsh countryside to the cities that the government was requiring some to return to their home districts. From 1956 on, the Mongolian government also moved once more to establish herding and farming collectives. In 1959, almost the entire countryside was reorganized into collectives, each of which then came to serve as a governmental as well as an economic unit.

COMMUNIST TAKEOVER IN CHINA
AND KUOMINTANG RETREAT TO TAIWAN (1945–1949)

By the time Japan surrendered to the United Nations, the erst-while three-cornered struggle in China was already, in effect, a Kuomintang-Communist duel. Since January, 1941, Kuomintang and Communist troops had fought openly. In this renewal of the struggle of the 1930s, the Kuomintang was clearly at a growing disadvantage from every standpoint but that of military equipment. The best Kuomintang troops had fallen in the early struggle with Japan. Repressive measures taken against critics of the Kuomintang, on the ground of need for wartime unity, were alienating both intellectuals and business people. Skyrocketing inflation during the period of incessant shortages in the remote strongholds of Szechwan, Kweichow, and Yunnan was demoralizing both business people and bureaucrats. Increasing bureaucratic corruption and inefficiency were eroding what popularity the Kuomintang government retained as a symbol of resistance. Meanwhile, the Communists under Mao Tse-tung were combining recruitment of the peasants of the north with moderation toward landlords and business people and encouragement of free discussion among intellectuals, which won them growing support on all sides.

In 1944 the United States began trying to bring the rivals together in some sort of united government. In January, 1946, a consultative conference representing all political parties was finally held. Chou En-lai served as chief negotiator for the Communists. Agreements were reached for a step-by-step progression from a military truce to the inclusion of members of all parties in the state council, the formation of a parliament with control over the executive branch, and the integration of the Communist troops into the national armed forces. The truce agreement specified that both Communist and Kuomintang troops would be stationed in Manchuria, which was still occupied by the Soviet forces that had moved in to accept Japanese surrender and loot the industrial establishment. Communist troops from neighboring provinces moved in immediately. When Kuomintang troops arrived somewhat later, they had to fight their way in.

Disagreements over implementation of the 1946 program led to Kuomintang expulsion of the Communists from Nanking, in February, 1947, and to the resumption of full-scale civil war. With its near-monopoly of air power, the Kuomintang might still have had a chance of victory, but it chose to build its strategy around the cities rather than compete in the rural areas with the Communists. It also expended its best troops in a hopeless campaign to drive the Communists from Manchuria, disregarding the counsel of United States military advisers.

By the end of 1948 few Chinese had much confidence in Kuomintang leadership, and fewer still placed their faith in the smaller demo-cratic parties formed since the 1930s. Western democratic forms seemed irrelevant to Chinese society, and the attempts of Chiang and those around him to persuade China's scholars, teachers, and writers that se-lecting the best in East and West meant returning to Confucian values and retaining Western techniques struck most intellectuals as an ana-chronistic throwback to the days of Chiang's hero Tseng Kuo-fan. In-stead, the intellectuals tended to adopt some form of Marxism, out of desire to adopt both Western techniques and the values necessary to support them while still asserting Chinese superiority and attacking the West from which the new techniques came. As Marxists, they could regard themselves as being at the head of the world revolution rather than at the rear of the capitalist procession. They could also satisfy their yearning for a link with the past, if they followed the Communist lead in regarding the earthy folk culture of ballads, dances, and so on as a more truly Chinese heritage than the rarefied literature and art of the Confucian-minded scholar-bureaucrats. Thus a large number of those who inherited the role of the Confucian scholars as leaders of public opinion had deserted the Kuomintang by the end of World War II. Nor did the peasants care to see the Kuomintang remain in power. Peasants were still paying exorbitant rents in Kuomintang-held regions, but the Communists were enthusiastically implementing the Kuomintang's own rent-control law of 1930, to the relief of landlords who had feared con-fiscation and were therefore mollified by this show of relative friend-liness. The moderate policies followed by the Communist government at Yenan made merchants, industrialists, and financiers as credulous as the landlords concerning Communist intentions. Most of the ill-paid urban workers were delighted by Communist promises to end inflation and increase their real income.

As a result of these various military, intellectual, social, economic, and psychological factors, the Communists were able to drive Chiang from the mainland and to set up the People's Republic of China in September, 1949. Only the islands of Taiwan and the Penghus, or Pesca-dores, recently recovered from Japan, remained in Kuomintang hands, together with a few islets scattered along the China coast which the Communists could not seize because at the time they had no navy. For a while it was questionable whether the Kuomintang government would survive at all. The United States government, dismayed by corruption in the Kuomintang, was not inclined to support it. In January, 1950, Presi-dent Truman even declared that the United States did not intend to furnish any further military aid or advice to the Kuomintang forces on Taiwan. However, the situation was restudied when war broke out in Korea in June, 1950. President Truman then declared that the United States would actively oppose a Chinese Communist conquest of Taiwan—

and, in an effort to keep the newborn People's Republic of China from entering the Korean conflict, also requested the Kuomintang government to refrain from naval and air attacks on the mainland. The United States commitment to defend Taiwan was reiterated in a mutual security treaty with the Republic of China which was signed in 1954 and ratified in 1955.

Power Struggles in Korea

KOREA UNDER JAPANESE RULE (1910–1945)

The Korean war of 1950–1953 was of crucial importance for East Asia. Korea was the last East Asian state to open its ports to Westerners. It passed in turn from Chinese to Russian and then to Japanese domination, being annexed in 1910 by the expanding Japanese. The Koreans tried to resist, but the well-armed Japanese went ahead with their programs of land survey, agricultural improvement, forestry, railway and highway networks, sanitation and public health work, and promotion of vocational education and the study of the Japanese language as a preparation for becoming loyal subjects of the emperor of Japan. The distressed Koreans saw no way out of their imprisonment until Woodrow Wilson's call for the self-determination of peoples gave them hope that they might somehow regain their independence if they could only bring their plight to the attention of the peacemakers in Paris after World War I.

In March, 1919, the Koreans astonished the world with the first display of coordinated nationwide peaceful demonstrations against external imperial rule. The Japanese response was a savagely effective campaign of repression which forced every leading Korean either into prison or into exile. Among the exiles was Syngman Rhee, who left immediately after representatives of his compatriots elected him president of a provisional republican government in April, 1919. In 1920 the Japanese made some concessions to Korean sentiment. They placed civilians rather than military men in high posts in their administration in Korea, and they began to build more elementary schools, although they made little provision for secondary or higher education for Koreans.

Japan's treatment of Korea improved somewhat in succeeding years, but Japan's control of Korean economic life grew tighter every year as Japanese acquired land and founded industrial and commercial concerns. Furthermore, the Japanese insisted as persistently as ever that Koreans must accept the emperor of Japan as their own ruler. Only outside Korea could Koreans express their desire for freedom. Some followed Rhee's leadership, some espoused the Communist cause from their places of exile in the Soviet Union, and some followed other leaders, but all Korean expatriates continued to call for Japanese withdrawal until it finally came in the autumn of 1945.

CONFLICT IN DIVIDED KOREA (1945–1953)

According to agreements reached between the United States and the Soviet Union early in 1945, the United States accepted the surrender of Japanese troops south of the thirty-eighth parallel in Korea, while the Soviets accepted the surrender of the Japanese in the north. However, neither the victorious powers nor the Koreans in exile had reached agreement on the method by which Korea should regain the independence that all agreed Korea ought to have. Since the Soviets and the Korean Communists had prepared themselves to establish a government run by Koreans in the north, the Soviet occupation forces were ready to work with the "people's committees" set up by Koreans returning to their homeland from the Soviet Union. Since the United States was not correspondingly prepared, it set up a military government in the south and continued to use experienced Japanese for a time before finally turning to Koreans. In March, 1946, a joint Soviet-American commission met to set up a provisional government for a united Korea, but the commission broke up in May over the Soviet refusal to let most of the nationalist groups operating in the south participate in the provisional government. The United States military government then began to set up a provisional government in the south, calling together a half-elected, half-appointed legislature at the close of 1946. Meanwhile, the Soviets continued to expand the role of the people's committees in the north. No agreement was reached on how to mesh these institutions into a single government.

In 1947 the United States took the Korean question to the United Nations, which called for nationwide elections to a provisional constituent assembly. The elections were held early in 1948, but only in the south, for the United Nations representatives who went to Korea to supervise the balloting were refused entrance into the north. The provisional assembly adopted a constitution for the Republic of Korea and elected Syngman Rhee as president. The new Republic of Korea was recognized as the legitimate government of Korea by all of the United Nations except the Soviet Union and its eastern European satellites, in August, 1949. (At that time the United Nations was still predominantly composed of the states of Europe, the Middle East, and the Americas which had been at war with Germany and Japan.) The Soviets responded by recognizing a People's Democratic Republic of Korea under Kim Il-sung as the proper government of the country, with headquarters in the north. Both the Soviet Union and the United States then began withdrawing their troops, in effect leaving the two regimes to fight it out between themselves.

The government of the Republic of Korea severely restricted those who did not support the policies of Syngman Rhee. Consequently the northerners, who controlled slightly more than half the area but only a third of the population of Korea, found that their program of internal subversion in the south was unsuccessful. On June 25, 1950, the Soviet-trained and Soviet-equipped northerners crossed the thirty-eighth parallel in an attempt to reunite Korea by force of arms. The United Nations Security Council, from which the Soviets absented themselves in protest against the countinued presence of the Nationalist Republic of China months after the formation of the People's Republic of China on the mainland, called immediately for assistance to the Rhee regime. Most of the assistance came from the United States, but it did not come soon enough to prevent northerners from pushing southward rapidly. However, during the autumn of 1950, United Nations forces turned the tide and pushed toward the Yalu river which divides Korea from Manchuria. The People's Republic of China then served informal notice that it was prepared to move. The Chinese Communists feared that their friendly Communist neighbor with its Japanese-built links to Manchuria might be replaced by the anti-Communist Rhee government. When United Nations troops pressed on, massive numbers of Chinese joined the north Koreans and carried the war southward again. In response, General MacArthur of the United States, commander of the United Nations forces, obliquely threatened to bomb the People's Republic of China if a satisfactory settlement was not reached. President Truman removed MacArthur from command, for he regarded MacArthur's words as going beyond the orders under which MacArthur was operating. In June, 1951, United Nations forces again crossed the thirty-eighth parallel, inflicting heavy losses on the Chinese. Negotiations between the conflicting parties were opened the next month. After two years during which fighting continued, it was agreed in July, 1953, that non-Korean questions such as the fate of Taiwan were not to be included in the truce settlement, that prisoners of war were not to be repatriated against their will, and that the truce line should be the militarily more defensible cease-fire line rather than the thirty-eighth parallel.

SEPARATE DEVELOPMENT (1953–1974)

After the truce was signed, each of the two Korean regimes continued to claim to be the rightful government of all Korea. The soldiers of the two governments glared at each other across the line while their superiors strengthened their forces. The north, which the Japanese had developed more intensively than the south, rebuilt and expanded its war-devastated industrial establishment with Soviet aid. All agricultural land was collectivized, after an initial distribution to peasant families. In the south, distribution of land to the peasants proceeded more slowly, but factories (previously almost nonexistent) began to be built with United States technical and financial support. Literacy spread rapidly in both north and south, in large part through the teaching of the phonetic Korean script. Yet, although Koreans still shared the same language, they were not sharing the same political experiences or the same government.

Purges and regimentation in the north were nearly matched by repression in the south as each government sought to root out potential or actual subversion. Nevertheless, Syngman Rhee's opponents elected one of their leaders vice-president of the Republic of Korea in 1956. Redoubled efforts to put down this too-effective opposition brought student-led riots and demonstrations against Rhee in 1960. The army supported the rioters, and Rhee was forced to leave the country. (He died in exile in 1965.) The opposition party came to power briefly, but in May, 1961, it was replaced by an army-led regime. The army was impatient with the parliament's slowness in tackling corruption and economic development. As in much of the Middle East, the massive doses of modernization administered to the Korean army after 1950 made it the largest group in the country accustomed to discipline and the use of machines. In 1962, after brief experiments with parliamentary and military rule, voters in the Republic of Korea approved a return to the presidential form of government. When the voters selected a president in 1963, they elected by a narrow margin the leading figure in the military government of the preceding two years, Pak Chung-hi. Pak's support came primarily from his home region and the rural areas. The town-dwellers whose opposition had earlier helped to topple Rhee preferred Pak's chief opponent. However, Pak was again elected president in the election of 1967 and reelected in 1971, each time with an increasing percentage of the vote and with urban as well as rural support.

Korea had been compelled by Japan to enter the modern world against its will, but now that it was free from Japanese rule, it was torn against its will into two states. Under the energetic leadership of Kim Il-sung, the people of the north were brought to follow the Communist path toward modernization and unity. The ancient symbol of the Chollima, or winged horse, was used after 1959 to inspire the people to speed toward a fully Communist society through a socialism based on collective farms and a mixture of cooperative and state-owned enterprises. As his Soviet allies ceased to be willing to support active efforts at reunification, Kim turned to the People's Republic of China for diplomatic support from 1963 to 1965, and stepped up the propaganda campaign against the government of Pak in the south. However, from 1966 to 1969 he turned back toward the Soviet Union, whose economic aid was enabling northern Korea to achieve a per capita income nearly as high as that of the rapidly-growing south by 1970. In 1967 and 1968 he sought to infiltrate the south with small bands of guerrillas, but economic growth there effectively counteracted the appeal of the northern efforts to mount an uprising. In 1970 Kim turned toward Peking once again, but in 1971 the number of border incidents along the 1953 truce line declined rather than rose, and in 1972 the Kim government agreed to hold talks with the Pak government on possible forms of cooperation. The talks were welcomed by Koreans on both sides of the line, for they had found it understandably difficult ever since 1945 to accept or adjust to their first experience with political division in more than a thousand years. By the end of the year the talks had proceeded well enough to lead to the drafting of new constitutions in both north and south, and to the establishment of a north-south coordinating committee to prepare for eventual peaceful reunification. The new constitution for the south, which established a national conference for unification and gave the president almost dictatorial powers, was ratified and put into effect before the close of 1972. Under its terms, Pak was elected president once more, this time for a six-year term. Legislative elections in 1973 gave Pak's political opponents as many elective seats as his supporters, but the new constitution's provisions for presidential appointment of a third of the legislative body ensured him a two-thirds majority. Those who were brave enough to circulate petitions in 1974, requesting a strengthening of the legislative branch, were promptly arrested. Both unification and democratization seemed to be receding once more into the distant future.

Japan After World War II

OCCUPATION AND REFORM (1945–1952)

Koreans in the post-1945 era might well be inclined to look at their former Japanese rulers with a bitterness resembling that of post-1918 Arabs toward the Turks. In East Asia after World War II, as in the Middle East after World War I, the vanquished oppressors were shorn of their conquests. Yet they remained under one government and recovered from the ravages of war with amazing rapidity, while their liberated former subjects found themselves divided and weakened because of great-power rivalries. Japan soon reopened trade with both halves of Korea, but not until twenty years after World War II ended could Japan establish diplomatic ties with a Korean government—the Republic of Korea recognized by many of Japan's other trading partners —because of the virulence of Korean hatred toward Japan. Even then, student riots in Seoul and other cities protested the south Korean ratification of the final treaty in August, 1965.

The Japanese entered the postwar era disheartened by the collapse of the imperial system they had known since Meiji times. The downfall of the imperial system was formally recognized on January 1, 1946, when the emperor publicly disclaimed descent from the sun goddess. The Japanese were so benumbed by defeat that they received the entering occupation troops from the United States with scarcely a murmur, accepting the authority of General MacArthur as Supreme Commander of the Allied Powers with a lack of resentment which astounded Americans.

The occupation leaders plunged immediately into what they saw as their twin tasks of demilitarization and democratization. In demilitarization, the armed forces were demobilized, the remaining war industries dismantled, and the leading military men indicted as war criminals. All who had held high political or economic positions while the militarists were in control were deprived of their positions, on the assumption that they had supported the war. Many of these men continued to exert important influence from behind the scenes. However, removing them from their posts gave opportunities to younger leaders and to men previously eclipsed because of anti-militarist leanings. Thus the purge was as much a part of democratization as of demilitarization, and so was the breaking up of the great holding companies, or *zaibatsu*, which had previously controlled most of Japan's heavy industry. The zaibatsu were mammoth combines each of which included financial and commercial enterprises as well as industrial plants.

The occupation authorities supervised the rewriting of the constitution in 1946. The new, democratized constitution made the cabinet responsible to the Diet. It also abolished not only the independence but the existence of the military arm of government, in a formal renunciation of the right to use armed force. The renunciation of arms in Article IX won immediate and wide acceptance in Japan, for it carried overtones of an assumption of moral leadership in the world at large which could enable Japanese to wipe out the bloodstains on their recent past.

In other democratizing moves, political and economic power was extended to new groups through legal guarantees of equal rights for women, including the right to vote, and through a vigorous land reform program. By 1950 more than ninety-five percent of Japan's farmers owned at least some of the land they worked. Nearly two-thirds owned all they used, instead of a little over one-third as in the 1930s. To promote greater public participation in political discussion, the educational system was reorganized. The number of years of compulsory schooling was increased from six to nine. Many more Japanese youths were enabled to go beyond the nine-year level than the one-sixtieth who had previously reached senior secondary school, and all traces of indoctrination in the divinity of the emperor and the divine mission of Japan were removed from the curriculum. As part of the drive to broaden the political and economic power base, the previously weak and restricted labor unions were encouraged. However, when the unions turned to organizing general strikes for political purposes, the government promptly discouraged those activities.

Almost all these constitutional, legal, and social changes took place between 1945 and 1950. Most of them were widely accepted, for many Japanese had desired them throughout the militarist period, when free expression of such desires was unsafe. By the time of the Korean conflict, the occupation had long since accomplished what its leaders felt could be done to broaden Japanese participation in Japan's affairs. Yet occupation forces were not free to leave until the victorious powers could agree on the terms of a peace treaty with Japan. The outbreak of war in Korea convinced the United States and its Western allies that the peace treaty must be made, so that Japan could undertake its own economic recovery and manage its own political and social reorganization.

In September, 1951, forty-nine of the fifty-one states that had been at war with the Japanese empire signed a peace treaty with Japan in which the Japanese renounced control over all but the home islands. By that time, the United States had arranged to administer the Ryukyus and Bonins, though it recognized residual Japanese sovereignty there; the Soviets had occupied southern Sakhalin and the Kuriles; and the Kuomintang ruled Taiwan and the Penghus, or Pescadores. Japan also promised to seek membership in the United Nations as a peace-loving state. (It was admitted late in 1956, two months after the Soviet Union finally terminated its state of war with Japan.) In April, 1952, Japan signed a separate treaty with the Republic of China under Chiang, carefully avoiding any promises not to recognize or negotiate with the People's Republic on the mainland. In addition, Japan signed a mutual security pact with the United States in 1952. The occupation ended, but United States troops remained in bases on Japanese soil, even after the Korean truce of 1953. It proved more difficult for Japan to reach a formal peace treaty with the Soviet Union. Only in 1973 did an agreement begin to seem possible, after the Japanese foreign ministry hinted that Japan might give up its continued claim to several of the southernmost Kuriles held since 1945 by the Soviets.

INDEPENDENT REVITALIZATION (1952–1974)

Shortly after fighting opened in Korea, Japan began to build defense forces under the guise of a National Peace Reserve. This step was highly unpopular with those of all ages and shades of opinion who were weaving a new mystique of Japanese superiority around the constitutional renunciation of armament. Rearmament became a burning political issue as the rather fluid party structure of postwar Japanese politics began to solidify into two major groups—a single dominant conservative party called the Liberal Democrats, which favored private rather than state-run enterprise, and a Socialist party, which consistently held about a third of the seats in the lower house of the Diet from 1955 to 1969—and a scattering of radicals to the extreme left and right in the more vigorously Marxist parties and the superpatriotic associations. At times, even the vital question of how to expand foreign trade paled beside the rearmament issue. Foreign trade was essential to a Japan in which a growing majority of the people now lived in towns and cities. Every cabinet sought to widen Japan's circle of trading partners in both the developed and the developing nations, through formal international agreements with states from Canada and the Soviet Union to Indonesia and Brazil, and through informal encouragement of private trade throughout the world, even in states not formally recognized by Japan. In the name of facilitating Japanese competition in foreign markets, some of the component units into which the zaibatsu had been forcibly divided were even permitted to recombine, though in a somewhat looser form than before. The need for reliable trade channels was underscored heavily late in 1973, when the Arab oil embargo threatened Japanese industries severely. The government hastened to declare its sympathy for the Palestinian cause, while Japanese business firms quickly completed negotiations on new agreements to develop petroleum and natural gas reserves in Iraq and Soviet Siberia. Nevertheless, there were times when the rearmament issue took the center of the stage away from questions of trade, and the spring of 1960 was one of those times.

Early in 1960 the Liberal Democrats used their two-thirds majority to push a revised mutual-security pact with the United States through the Diet, in the teeth of adamant opposition from the Socialists, who claimed that the new pact encouraged rearmament. The unpopularity of rearmament enabled the Socialists to win support from students, labor unions, and many others in a series of demonstrations demanding the resignation of the cabinet. After weeks of pressure, the cabinet did resign, but not until the new pact had actually taken effect. A few months later, a member of one of the small but tightly knit superpatriotic groups which favored the pact as a step toward rearmament assassinated a Socialist leader publicly.

The superpatriots and the radical Marxists clashed violently in the streets over many issues after 1945, although the world press paid them little attention until 1960. There were probably few more injuries in these street riots than there had been in street fights between Japanese men relieving their tensions in the amusement quarters of the cities of Tokugawa and Meiji Japan. Still, the fact that public issues rather than private brawls provided the occasion for the fighting had some significance. Like the rapid growth of such socially constructive voluntary organizations as parent-teacher associations, it was a demonstration of the interest of ordinary Japanese in expanding their role in their nation's affairs. This did not mean that many Japanese were politically active a great deal of the time. Most urban Japanese men continued to put most of their effort into advancing within the company or the governmental agency they joined when their formal schooling ended. They also continued to regard leaving one company or agency for another as akin to a samurai's disloyalty to his lord in feudal times, a betrayal of the employer to whom one owed one's entry into the world of work. Most urban Japanese women continued to concentrate primarily on family matters, though increasing numbers of them also worked in factories, offices, and agencies. Most rural Japanese, both men and women, continued to pay more attention to work and family than to local or national politics. What the increased interest of most Japanese in political affairs did mean was that Japanese now saw their destiny as being in the hands of the whole people, rather than in the hands of a few leaders, far more than they had done a century before. Nor could the United States occupation be given most of the credit for that change. Rather, it was the indoctrination in one's duty to the nation in the public schools from the Meiji era onward, and the political experiences of the years from the 1880s to the 1930s, which had convinced most Japanese that they had a personal responsibility to see that Japan should never again become economically disturbed enough to tempt militarists or enable revolutionaries to oust seemingly inept civilians, and to see that Japan should never again become friendless enough to be forced to undergo another occupation by even the best-intentioned foreigners. They therefore sought to fulfill their responsibility by turning out in large numbers for almost every election.

The Liberal Democrats' retention of overwhelming Diet majorities, even though Socialists gradually came to win control of many major city governments, was largely the result of careful ticket balancing in terms of factors like place of origin, social and economic viewpoint, and nationwide party standing. Japan's three- to five-member legislative constituencies made it essential to have an appropriate number of slightly differing candidates who were popular among different groups in each constituency, rather than one or two overwhelmingly popular candidates who might actually take votes from other candidates of the same party. The Liberal Democrats were also aided to some extent by lags in redistricting as Japan became more and more urban, since they tended to win more votes in rural areas than in cities. Still, the Liberal Democrats remained the largest overall vote-getters, winning nearly fifty percent of the votes cast in 1972, compared with about twenty percent for the Socialists. The Liberal Democrats also remained skillful manipulators of the nominating process, from the standpoint of maximizing the number of seats won for the number of votes cast. They obtained 282 out of 486 seats in the lower house in 1972, while the Socialists obtained 118.

The small groups of Marxist and superpatriotic extremists drew many of their supporters from among those young Japanese who were finding it difficult to obtain the training and experience they needed for the kinds of jobs they wanted, in spite of the economic boom which raised per capita income in Japan to southern European levels by 1960 and almost to British levels by 1969. (Industrial growth and the use of chemicals in agriculture also raised pollution levels to such a degree that a national environmental improvement program had to be established in 1971.) Other dissatisfied young men and women turned to politically active religious groups like Soka Gakkai, the Value Creation Society, an offshoot of Nichiren Buddhism, the militant sect formed in the thirteenth century. In 1959 Soka Gakkai began electing members to the upper house of the Diet. In 1962 its candidates polled four million votes and became the third largest group in the upper house, after the Liberal Democrats and the Socialists. In 1964 Soka Gakkai established the Komeito or Clean Government Party, which won its first 25 seats in the lower house in 1967 and nearly doubled its numbers there in 1969 by capturing eleven percent of the popular vote, mostly at Socialist expense. However, Komeito candidates won only 29 places in the 1972 elections, as the Socialists regained a number of seats, while the previously rather unsuccessful Communists nearly tripled their representation from 14 in 1969 to 38 in 1972, in the wake of that year's establishment of diplomatic relations with the People's Republic of China.

Komeito's combination of what it termed humanistic socialism and a nationalism which was tempered by calls for world federalism sometimes made it hard to predict how its parliamentary members would vote. Like the Socialist party, it usually opposed the reigning Liberal Democrats on issues such as continued budget increases for the self-defense forces, in the name of humanistic socialism. It also opposed continuation of what it termed the restrictive mutual security treaty with the United States, in the name of national freedom of action. Yet it supported the

Liberal Democrats on other issues more often than it opposed them. Still, the party's dream of a world federation which would render large armies unnecessary was clearly more appealing to Japanese who were seeking lasting values in a world of change than were the calls of superpatriots for achieving national self-determination through greatly expanding the defense forces. In 1970 novelist Yukio Mishima, who favored rearmament, dramatically committed suicide in the former samurai style at the headquarters of the National Peace Reserve to protest Japan's apparent decline in the martial virtues.

The Japanese government gradually recovered the administration of the Ryukyus and the Bonins. The government also expanded the all-volunteer National Peace Reserve, as the number of United States troops and bases was diminished by successive renegotiations of the terms of the mutual security pact, and in 1973 drafted Japan's first comprehensive defense plan since 1945. Nevertheless, every anniversary of the atomic bombing of Hiroshima and Nagasaki brought forth renewed appeals from Japanese in all walks of life for peace through worldwide disarmament. Many Japanese agreed with the Komeito, the Socialists, and the Communists in hoping that the higher courts would uphold a 1973 decision by a district court judge that the placement of a land-to-air missile base in a Hokkaido forest preserve by the National Peace Reserve contravened Article IX.

The Second Phase of the Chinese Revolution

CONSOLIDATION OF COMMUNIST POWER (1949–1953)

The burgeoning economy of Japan was of special interest to its neighbor, the People's Republic of China. If normal trade could be resumed, the mills and factories of Japan could furnish many items which were still in short supply on the mainland even after years of intensive rehabilitation of existing enterprises and feverish addition of new ones. When Mao Tse-tung, Liu Shao-ch'i, Chou En-lai, Lin Piao, the aging Chu Teh, and the other Communists who had worked with them in Kiangsi and Yenan for almost twenty years took over the government of Manchuria, inner Mongolia, north China, and south China from the Kuomintang between 1945 and 1949, they faced a task of staggering magnitude. They had made themselves responsible for modernizing the minds and lives of hundreds of millions of Chinese, most of whom outside the cities had scarcely been touched by many of the currents of modernization that had affected the students and the urban classes. Now the Chinese Communists had to bring these millions out of the family- and village-centered life they had previously known into a nationwide community in which national loyalty would take precedence over local and family ties, and in which both agriculture and industry would be oriented toward producing for the needs of the entire society rather than for the subsistence of the household.

The manifold problems of transforming social, economic, political, and intellectual life were tackled with an energy and directness rarely seen before in China, or indeed in any other state before 1949 except Meiji Japan, Bolshevik Russia, and the Turkey of Mustafa Kemal Ataturk. The Yenan years had shown the value of setting up propagandist organizations which cut across family ties and then requiring attendance at their frequent meetings, as a means of replacing family loyalties with loyalties to wider groups. In the new People's Republic of China, federations for women and youth sought with considerable success to wean these two groups from attachment to the family system in which they had always played subordinate roles. Workers' groups in factories, block groups in cities, village groups in rural areas brought men and women together on a basis other than that of family membership. In succeeding years most of the government's numerous campaigns —some repressive, some constructive—were carried out through these groups.

The party members and sympathizers who led the various groups used weekly or even daily meetings to promote the active cooperation of every group member with the policies of the party. All attempts to remodel rural life—the confiscation of landlord holdings in 1950–1951 and their redistribution to the landless; the encouragement of agricultural cooperatives in the next few years; the pooling of the land of individual households in collective farms in 1955–1956; the formation of agricultural communes in 1958 (in which the initial intention was to treat agricultural workers almost like soldiers, with military drill, labor brigades, and a replacement of the home by dormitories and mess halls) —relied heavily on the variety of people's organizations which had been created. People's organizations were similarly used to force business people and industrialists to let the state take over their firms, and to carry out campaigns against those foreign-trained professors in the universities who did not support the new regime enthusiastically, against sabotage and waste and pilfering in the factories, against flies and mosquitoes in the streets and roadways, and against all counterrevolutionary tendencies.

The Korean conflict was a windfall for the Communist government as it sought to mobilize China's human and natural resources. The Chinese soldiers who fought in Korea were scarcely the volunteers they were claimed to be. However, the Chinese Communists' concern for the safety of Manchurian industries was real, and it was far from difficult for them to whip up a violent "Resist America, Aid Korea" campaign throughout China once the largely United States forces of the United Nations approached the Yalu. "Resist America, Aid Korea" became the watchword in everything: factory output, agricultural production, road-building, literacy programs, and remorseless campaigns to force all who were tainted by any contact with the United States-led West to repent their sins or suffer the consequences. Under the circumstances it was hardly surprising that the Communist regime refused to enter normal relations with Britain until after the Korean truce, even though Britain recognized the Communists almost as soon as they came to power. Nor was it surprising that they sharply restricted foreign travel and residence to those whose presence they found useful, like Soviet and other instructors and technicians, potentially friendly news commentators from every country, and a few carefully chosen diplomatic, trade, and cultural missions.

The estimates of how many former landlords and others were executed by people's courts for past and current crimes between 1949 and 1953 range from half a million to fifteen million, or from one out of every six hundred adults to an improbably high figure of one out of every twenty adults. Perhaps five to fifteen million persons, or one out of every twenty to sixty adults, were sent for a few weeks to a few years of political and personal reeducation in the reform labor camps which thereafter became a lasting feature of the Chinese scene. Millions of others bowed more quietly to the constant pressure to profess devotion to the regime. By 1953 the Communists had a tighter grip on China than they might have had without the accident of what for them was the right war in the right place at the right time, even though they seem to have had little to do with its inception. The Korean conflict also enabled them to put an end to the autonomy of the Tibetan plateau in 1950–1951 with fewer objections from other states than might have been raised if attention were not being focused on Korea. It was true that once the United States Seventh Fleet began to patrol the Taiwan strait, Communist hopes of occupying Taiwan lessened; but the closeness of the Seventh Fleet to the China coast furnished new material for "Hate America" campaigns, as did the fact that the fleet was protecting a government in which many mainland Chinese had lost faith by the time the Communists took over.

INTERNAL DEVELOPMENT AND EXTERNAL POLICY (1953–1974)

After the Korean truce, the Chinese Communists began to feel more confident of their position. They had eliminated their worst foes, and they believed their new order was secure. In 1953 they inaugurated their first five-year development plan. In the next few years agricultural production rose by one-sixth and industrial production doubled, but the rising population, measured in 1953 as 582 million (of whom all but six percent were Chinese in language and culture), meant that per capita output increased less sharply. In 1954 a new constitution was promulgated, reestablishing most of the familiar provincial, district, and subdistrict framework in place of the regional military administrations of the first five years. It provided for elective congresses and councils at all levels, and added the organizational refinement of autonomous areas for locally strong non-Chinese peoples such as the Mongols in the north, the Uighurs in the west, and the Miao in the south. The democratic parties founded in the Kuomintang era, and even a self-proclaimed "patriotic Kuomintang," continued to exist. However, elections were little more than a ratification of previous Communist party selections, for a committee of Communist party members and supporters nominated a single slate of approved candidates for every election.

After the death of Stalin in the Soviet Union in 1953, Mao Tse-tung became the senior statesman of world Communism, in terms of his length of service as head of a major state. The course of Sino-Soviet negotiations demonstrated the change in Mao's position. The Sino-Soviet agreements of early 1950, recognizing the independence of the People's Republic of Mongolia and providing for military, political, and economic cooperation, and the 1952 Soviet renunciation of all the Manchurian privileges regained from Chiang except the use of Dairen in the Liaotung peninsula, were negotiated by Mao in Stalin's capital. However, the Soviet agreements of 1954 to withdraw from Dairen and join China in constructing a railway link between the two states across Sinkiang were negotiated by Stalin's successors Khrushchev and Bulganin in Mao's capital. Even Chiang became a convenient scapegoat on whom to blame ills, more than a dangerous foe, once it became clear that his United States defenders had no intention of bombarding the mainland as long as he was left alone.

Taking note of the apparently promising outlook in the spring of 1957, Mao decided to venture onto the path of decreasing doctrinal vigilance—a path trod in 1956 by Khrushchev in his denunciation of Stalin—and "let a hundred flowers bloom together, let the hundred schools of thought contend" as they were said to have done in the latter Chou, so that free criticism of weaknesses in implementing the Communist program might suggest ways to improve its effectiveness. He got more than he bargained for: the program itself was criticized from top to bottom. A few would say that this was his real desire, since it brought anti-Communists into the open so that they could be identified and removed. In any case, the fall and winter saw a renewal of repression as those who had spoken most freely were isolated and intimidated into recanting. Some even interpreted the formation of the highly regimented communes in 1958 as, in part, an attempt to shut off opportunities for private discussion, but many other considerations were involved in that step. These other considerations included: a need to increase production; a belief that the dormitories and mess halls would release women from housework for more productive labor; a hope that dormitories, nurseries, and work brigades would further weaken the bonds of family; a desire to ensure that the state received, for distribution in the crowded and growing cities, all food produced beyond the minimum needs of the peasants; a wish to encourage industrialization in the countryside, to relieve the pressures on the cities and the transport networks; and possibly even a plan to slow down population growth by separating men and women. (In 1961 the government began to encourage men and women not to marry until the age of twenty-five or thirty.) However, injudicious plans such as the anti-sparrow campaign—whose result was the loss to insects of more grain than sparrows had ever eaten—led to grumbling. To meet complaints, much of the regimentation was dropped. By 1960 the peasants were allowed to live as separate families, to have small private gardens, and to sell produce from their gardens. In addition, the unwieldy communes (sometimes encompassing dozens of villages) were in effect broken down into units which corresponded closely to the traditional groups of four to eight villages whose people were accustomed to trading and intermarrying with one another.

The easing of restrictions on the personal life of commune inhabitants did not mean relaxation of doctrinal watchfulness. If anything, the Chinese Communists became more rigidly Stalinist than ever before, perhaps because drastic Stalinist methods were useful in a state just beginning to industrialize, perhaps because officially-inspired Stalin-like glorification of Mao was regarded as an indispensable unifying device. The more openly Khrushchev interested himself in satisfying the consumer at home and seeking to influence rather than overthrow existing governments abroad, the more bitterly Mao denounced such policies as revisionist and the more loudly he called for concentration on production at home and assistance to active revolutionaries abroad. Chinese Communists even began trying to persuade Soviet technical advisers in China to support the Chinese line. This disagreement over tactics had been foreshadowed as early as November, 1949, when Liu Shao-ch'i had indicated that China's experience provided a better model for Asian, African, and Latin American peoples than did Russia's experience. In 1960 Khrushchev withdrew all Soviet economic and technical aid to the People's Republic of China, hoping to force Mao to moderate his stand. However, the numerous conferences held in the next few years did not succeed in resolving the conflicts between Soviet and Chinese Communist interpretations of Marxism-Leninism, not even after October, 1964, when Khrushchev was replaced and the first Chinese atomic test in Sinkiang served notice that his policies had not halted China's technological advance. There was no formal rupture in diplomatic relations between the governments of Communist China and the Soviet Union, but each sought to win other Communist parties to its view of the world situation. The chief visible result, other than direct animosity between Peking and Moscow, was the renewed determination of the Chinese leaders not to rely on foreign aid to support their economic development. They felt that they had been burned once, when Soviet aid was withdrawn in 1960; and they not only took great pride in repaying ahead of time the Soviet loans contracted for in the 1950s, but they also avoided taking out loans from any state thereafter. They advised other developing countries to follow their example. Even though they themselves engaged in agreements to provide goods and services to other developing countries, they made a point of ensuring that Chinese goods of high quality were exchanged for their partners' products if the agreement was a barter agreement. If the agreement was a loan agreement, they sought to turn the payment received back into the borrower's economy, either by gift where a gift might seem acceptable or by Chinese purchase of local goods, in order to avoid acquiring a large fund of local currency under Chinese control.

As part of the maintenance of control at home, in 1954, in 1958, and again in 1960 the Chinese Communists heavily bombarded the few small islands held by the Kuomintang along the Fukien coast and used by the Kuomintang as centers for observation and infiltration. The Communists also enforced rigid discipline in Tibet, causing the Dalai Lama, the spiritual leader of Tibetan Buddhism, to flee across the Himalayas to India in 1959. As their interest in affairs in Tibet and Sinkiang increased, the Chinese sent patrols into Indian-held regions in the western Himalayas which would give them easier access to western Tibet and western Sinkiang. They even built roads in these regions. The government of India protested, pointing to the Anglo-Chinese boundary convention of 1914, but the Chinese Communists replied that the convention was unratified and therefore meaningless. Between 1959 and 1963 they emphasized their point by concluding boundary agreements with their other southern neighbors from Pakistan to Burma. They also signed a border agreement with Mongolia, thereby hinting that they did not regard their northern boundaries as satisfactory either. Despite the border agreement and the economic aid which Mongolia received from Peking, Mongolia continued to lean toward Moscow as a needed counterweight to Chinese pressures; and after Mongolia signed a new treaty of friendship and cooperation with the Soviets in 1966 which permitted Soviet troops to be stationed in Mongolia, the Chinese stopped sending assistance.

In the fall of 1962, Chinese and Indian troops clashed openly in both the western and the eastern Himalayas. The Soviet Union, desiring friendship with both states, called vainly for negotiations. This only provoked more Chinese Communist denunciations of Khrushchev for setting the interests of a non-Communist bourgeois nationalist government on a par with those of a Communist comrade. No negotiations were held, but the chastened Indian army ceased to challenge Chinese control in the western Himalayan regions claimed by Peking. The Chinese could now freely send Chinese colonists into Tibet, as had been done to some extent in Sinkiang and inner Mongolia since the last years of the Ch'ing. They could also enforce the dissolution of the old monastery-centered social structure of Lamaism in Tibet, as the Mongolian People's Republic had done in the 1930s in Mongolia. Disgruntled Tibetan refugees in India might try to interfere, and even to attempt unsuccessfully in 1974 to take over neighboring Bhutan as a base, but the old Lamaist structure was effectively shattered in Tibet. On China's northern border, the years after 1960 saw an increasing concentration of troops on both the Soviet and the Chinese side, and an increasing number of border incidents in Dzungaria to the west and the Amur and Ussuri valleys to the east. In addition, Peking occasionally made pointed public references to the czarist imperialist seizure in the nineteenth century of regions previously ruled by China. To some it seemed like more than sheer coincidence that the Sino-Soviet dispute had come to the surface in the year which marked the hundredth anniversary of the Russian acquisition of the Maritime Province. Others wondered whether the arrangements the Soviet Union began to make after 1965 for Japanese participation in the development of Siberian resources might foreshadow a Soviet-Japanese understanding. By the 1970s this prospect seemed real enough to be a factor in Peking's foreign policy. In 1972 the People's Republic of China received the president of the United States as a guest and agreed to sign a formal treaty with Japan. In 1973 it exchanged liaison officers with the United States as part of its effort to prevent the formation of an informal partnership among the United States, Japan, and the Soviet Union which could be detrimental to Chinese interests.

By 1965 Mao's concern for building up to greater heights the will of China's people to remold every aspect of Chinese life—in particular, their will to repudiate all forms of individualism and of the elitism which still made many Chinese regard manual work as a sign of inferiority—led him to turn against his long-time associate Liu Shao-ch'i. Liu's support for the modification of the commune program in 1960 made him appear to Mao to be willing to compromise with individualism, by using higher income and other personal incentives to increase production rather than by insisting on exclusive reliance on will-power and the socialist incentive of improvement in the position of the whole group. Liu also appeared to Mao to be willing to foster elitism, by promoting formal technical education more than practical working experience. With the support of army leader Lin Piao, Mao called on the youth of China in 1966 to serve as Red Guards, attacking all vestiges of individualism and elitism, and heaping public humiliation on those revisionists in high places who were taking the road back toward capitalism. For two years there were no secondary school and college classes, as the Red Guards were encouraged to go from place to place to carry on this Great Proletarian Cultural Revolution against all revisionist and capitalist tendencies. Party members at all levels were required to admit past failings. In many cases they were also forced to yield provincial or local leadership to military officers through the mechanism of revolutionary committees composed of army members, party members, and representatives of popular organizations such as the Red Guards.

Liu was finally demoted from his government and party posts in 1968 and, in effect, was forced into an involuntary retirement within the walls of the old imperial palace in Peking where the leading Chinese Communists lived and worked after 1949. He died of cancer in 1973. From 1969 onward many Red Guards were assigned to productive labor in the countryside, to continue their education through manual work rather than through academic training. University admissions policies were altered so that in general a student could enter college only after working for more than a year and had to be recommended by his or her fellow-workers. Office workers, teachers, and others whose work was not manual were expected to work periodically in factories or fields, in a further effort to underline the equal importance and dignity of working with hands or with the head. Those who still seemed unconvinced of the dignity of manual labor were required by local courts, to which their neighbors or their fellow-workers or the still-zealous Red Guards reported them, to undertake manual work as part of a period of self-remolding in the forced labor camps. For some this was at least the third time since 1949 that they had been sent to such camps, to stay for the weeks or months it might take for them to reeducate themselves enough to satisfy the directors of the camps that they were purged of self-interest and ready to work selflessly for the good of all. Then in 1971 Lin Piao followed Liu Shao-ch'i into political oblivion, as Prime Minister Chou En-lai prepared to receive as a guest in Peking President Nixon of the United States, the very power against which Chinese on the mainland had been exhorted to struggle since the days of "Resist America, Aid Korea" twenty years before. By that time the party had been reorganized and was beginning to recover its badly shaken morale. However, since approximately five-eighths of those who were serving in 1971 on both the provincial party committees and the provincial revolutionary committees were either military officers or political officers attached to military units, there were obviously close ties between party and army. These ties may have formed a basis for the accusation of plotting to seize power from Mao which was publicly leveled against Lin, after his death in an airplane crash was reported late in 1971. Yet Lin's death did not put an end to close working relationships between party, army, and government. By the end of 1972 over half the cabinet ministers in Peking were men whose abilities had first been recognized in the People's Liberation Army, and who had only been moved to civil posts after the opening of the Great Proletarian Cultural Revolution six and a half years before.

In 1973 the restoration to an important post of one of the first party leaders ousted in the Great Proletarian Cultural Revolution signaled a further rehabilitation of the party. At the tenth official congress of the Chinese Communist Party in August, 1973, Lin Piao was formally denounced, and Teng Hsiao-p'ing and others who had been disgraced during the Great Proletarian Cultural Revolution were reelected to the central committee of the party. Still, no general accusations were leveled against the military, and the new central committee had a number of military members. It also included some younger people, one of whom, Wang Hung-wen, had risen to prominence in Shanghai during the Great Proletarian Cultural Revolution. Wang was the first party deputy chairman to come from the post-1949 generation. With party affairs apparently in order once more, party leaders turned in late 1973 and 1974 to denouncing the continuance of Confucian tendencies in Chinese thinking. Since these denunciations were often coupled with praise for the centralizing policies of the first Ch'in emperor as "progressive in their day," it was possible to see in the new campaign a warning against the perils of too-great decentralization, as well as a veiled threat against relying on personal connections. Party leaders began to transfer military officers to other provinces and replace them with civilians in provincial committees. In 1975 a new state constitution put all armed forces under the party chairman, Mao.

THE KUOMINTANG ON TAIWAN (1945–1974)

By the time United States President Nixon visited Peking in 1972 the Communists were virtually certain that Chiang's hopes of returning to the mainland were no more than the daydreams of an exile. After expelling Communist delegates from Nanking in 1946, the Kuomintang had called an all-parties national convention which drew up a constitution establishing an elective parliamentary government in place of the existing Kuomintang-chosen one. However, the Communists and many of the small democratic parties boycotted the convention. Nationwide parliamentary elections were held in 1947, but local Kuomintang leaders, unwilling to let non-Kuomintang candidates win, caused many irregularities. Many of the parliament members went to Taiwan in 1949, thereby giving Chiang's government its claim to continue to be recognized as legitimate ruler of China, a claim which was finally denied by the United Nations when it seated the People's Republic of China in place of the Republic of China in 1971.

The United States did not formally recognize Taiwan as Chinese territory after Japan renounced all claim to it in the 1951 peace treaty, even when the United States committed itself in 1954 to defend Taiwan and the Penghus, or Pescadores. This curious situation was tied to the United States' unwillingness to see the People's Republic of China lay successful claim to the island during and immediately after the Korean conflict. It also left the door open to the possibility of a later readjustment by which Taiwan might become an independent state, if the people on the island ever decided to move in that direction. Meanwhile, Taiwan supported a national government, staffed almost entirely by the leaders of the nearly two million mainlanders who fled in 1949 to join their then more than six million fellow Chinese on the island, and a largely elective provincial and local system of government in which the islanders came to play the majority role after an initial period of control by the mainlanders. It also supported a large military establishment, in which Taiwanese played a growing part, as aging mainlanders left active service.

Not all Taiwanese were satisfied with their situation as part of the Republic of China. A small Taiwanese independence movement began in 1948 as a protest against Kuomintang exploitation of the newly recovered island, and some Taiwanese even grumbled that they had been given better treatment by the Japanese than by the Kuomintang. Mainlander-islander relations improved gradually after the Kuomintang-led government moved to Taiwan, as the Kuomintang rid itself of corrupt and inefficient officials, expanded the school system, carried through a successful redistribution of land, and used United States aid to build up both agriculture and industry on the foundations laid by the Japanese. One Taiwanese independence leader even made his peace with the Kuomintang government and returned to Taiwan from his self-imposed exile in Japan late in 1965. Others returned later. Nevertheless, the independence movement persisted, to the dismay of Kuomintang leaders still committed to the belief that there was only one China, in which it was their task to implement the threefold program of Sun Yat-sen on the solid basis of the Confucian virtues of loyalty and obedience. After the expulsion of the Republic of China from the United Nations in 1971, the Kuomintang government moved to give more voice

to Taiwanese in its decisions, in a renewed effort to avert the possibility of a revolt. At the same time, however, Chiang's son was made
premier. Kuomintang leaders were unhappy when Japan recognized the
People's Republic of China in 1972, for Japan was Taiwan's largest
trading partner; but it soon became clear that trade with Japan would
scarcely be affected by the severing of formal relations between Tokyo
and Taipei.

China, Japan, Korea, and Mongolia: Comparisons and Contrasts

The unwillingness of either the Kuomintang or the Chinese Communists to admit that the Chinese people might actually live under
two separate governments, one on Taiwan and one on the mainland,
arose from centuries of regarding all who shared Chinese culture as
one people who belonged in one state under one government. It was
not merely a result of Western-introduced ideas of sovereignty. Before
the nineteenth century the development of East Asia was relatively
uninterrupted by invasions, other than the movements within the mountain walls of nomad groups whose members normally acknowledged
the superiority of Chinese culture even though they did not adopt it.
The three settled peoples of East Asia, the Chinese, Koreans, and Japanese, each had a tradition of unity and a consciousness of being distinct
from the other two, long before Western ideas of nationalism were introduced. Furthermore, each was accustomed to expressing its unity and
distinctness through a single government, a common language, and a
common set of religious beliefs and social practices. The Mongols also
had a consciousness of distinctness, a common language, a common set
of religious beliefs and social practices, and a sense of unity based on
the codification of Mongol law by Genghis Khan, but politically they
had been kept divided by the policies of their Manchu neighbors since
the seventeenth century.

As Japanese, Koreans, and Mongols studied China's culture, they
were perhaps more consciously aware of themselves as separate peoples
than were the Chinese, who concentrated on studying their own heritage.
However, as the twentieth century progressed, the strength of the hold
of China's past on China's present could be gauged by the convulsions
that China continued to experience in seeking a means of exchanging the
old for the new without giving up its ancient claims to uniqueness and
leadership. The Chinese Communists' boast that they would provide
college education for all within less than a generation was but one
illustration of this desire to prove in a new context that everyone could
be a Yao or a Shun, and that China would lead the way in showing
how to achieve this goal. The first efforts to universalize higher educa-

tion were channeled into institutions like the half-work-half-study universities opened in the communes in 1958. The unwitting students, eager for the recognition given the educated, were told they were doing college-level work when the actual level was nearer late elementary or early secondary schooling, as the government later tacitly acknowledged when it began referring to these institutions as schools for adult education. The major intent of these schools, as shown by their other name of Red-and-expert universities, was to improve their students' skills in manipulating Communist concepts and performing productive tasks. Another intent, pursued with redoubled zeal after the Great Proletarian Cultural Revolution began in 1966, was to force those who still thought in terms of academic tradition to break with the past and acknowledge the value of working with the hands as well as with the head.

Looking at mainland China somewhat fancifully, the Communists might be called the new Ming, devoted to the cause of Chinese supremacy after a period of smarting under the realization that non-Chinese did not necessarily accept Chinese ways. They might also be called the new Ch'in, reorganizing China ruthlessly on a more tightly integrated basis than that of the preceding system; or the new T'ang, seeking to synthesize the heritage of the past with the foreign ideas introduced during a period of dynastic collapse. However, the Communists stressed the "folk past," not the "gentry past" as the Kuomintang did, under the pressure of the need to replace the old order with its emphasis on the elite by a new order in which those below the elite level would take a more active part. The Communists might even be called the new Ch'ing, though they were more successful than the Ch'ing in confining free access to the mainland of China once again to the single southern "treaty port" area of British-held Hongkong and Portuguese-held Macao, and in limiting travel and residence elsewhere to a carefully selected few.

The same problems of xenophobia, national integration, and cultural adaptation were also faced by Koreans, by Mongols, and by Japanese, who may have been more reassured about the possibility of civilian control of the military in a democratic state by President Truman's dismissal of General MacArthur than by all the lectures given them during the occupation era. Still, the problems of Korea, Mongolia, and Japan were not on the same scale as those of China, either in terms of the number of people involved or in terms of the break with the past. Koreans, Mongols, and Japanese had all had experience with acknowledging China's cultural leadership, while the Chinese had scarcely considered the possibility that they might not be the center of the civilized world. Some would question whether they have yet considered it seriously. Nevertheless, their neighbors' substitution of Western for Chinese models in the nineteenth and twentieth centuries forced the Chinese to seek a means of recovering their lost leadership. The Chinese experimented with a number of formulas, all of which deliberately used some Western methods and equally deliberately repudiated others. Gradually they realized that they could not regain their ancient power unless they accepted so many Western ideas and techniques that they could no longer retain much of their Confucian heritage. In this they differed from most of those in other regions of the world who still saw themselves as heirs to Islamic, Hindu, or Buddhist traditions, but who also still believed that the strands of Western scientific and democratic thought could be woven into the fabric of those traditions to create genuinely modern yet not unfamiliar materials for their peoples' use. After a century of debate in China over the degrees of compatibility and incompatibility between Confucianism and the new ideas from the West, the Communists who repudiated the Confucian past most completely made themselves the masters of the destinies of most Chinese. They promptly set about doing their utmost to convince the peoples of the earth that the new China represented the hope of the world of the future, as the old China had represented the height of human achievement in the East Asia of the past.

Suggested Readings

Books available in paperback are marked with an asterisk.

East Asia

BECKMANN, G.M. *The Modernization of China and Japan*. New York: Harper, 1962.

*CROWLEY, JAMES B., ed. *Modern East Asia: Essays in Interpretation*. New York: Harcourt, Brace, and World, 1970.

*IRIYE, AKIRA. *Across the Pacific: An Inner History of American-East Asian Relations*. New York: Harcourt, Brace, and World, 1967.

MAKI, J.M., ed. *Conflict and Tension in the Far East: Key Documents, 1894–1960*. Seattle: University of Washington Press, 1962.

MAY, E.R., and J.C. THOMSON, JR., eds. *American-East Asian Relations: A Survey*. Cambridge: Harvard University Press, 1972.

MUNSTERBERG, HUGO. *Art of the Far East*. New York: Abrams, 1968.

REISCHAUER, EDWIN O., and JOHN K. FAIRBANK. *East Asia: The Great Tradition*. Boston: Houghton Mifflin, 1960.

———, and ALBERT M. CRAIG. *East Asia: The Modern Transformation*. Boston: Houghton Mifflin, 1973.

———.*East Asia: Tradition and Transformation*. Boston: Houghton Mifflin, 1965.

ROZMAN, GILBERT. *Urban Networks in Ch'ing China and Tokugawa Japan*. Princeton, N.J.: Princeton University Press, 1974.

China

GENERAL

CH'EN, SHOU-I. *Chinese Literature: A Historical Introduction*. New York: Ronald, 1961.

CRESSEY, GEORGE B. *Land of Five Hundred Million: A Geography of China*. New York: McGraw-Hill, 1955.

ELVIN, MARK. *The Pattern of the Chinese Past*. Stanford, Cal.: Stanford University Press, 1973.

*FEI, HSIAO-TUNG. *China's Gentry*, rev. ed. Chicago: University of Chicago Press, 1953.

*MESKILL, JOHN, ed. *An Introduction to Chinese Civilization*. New York: Columbia University Press, 1972.

*POSNER, ARLENE, and A.J. DE KEIJZER, eds. *China: A Resource and Curriculum Guide*. Chicago: University of Chicago Press, 1973.

*SCHURMANN, FRANZ, and ORVILLE SCHELL, eds. *The China Reader*, 3 vols. New York: Vintage, 1967.

*SULLIVAN, MICHAEL. *The Arts of China.* Berkeley: University of California Press, 1973.

*TREGEAR, T.R. *A Geography of China.* Chicago: Aldine, 1966.

WILLMOTT, W.E., ed. *Economic Organization in Chinese Society.* Stanford, Cal.: Stanford University Press, 1972.

*YANG, CH'ING-K'UN. *Religion in Chinese Society.* Berkeley: University of California Press, 1961.

TO MODERN PERIOD

*BALAZS, ETIENNE. *Chinese Civilization and Bureaucracy*, ed. A.F. Wright, trans. H.M. Wright. New Haven, Conn.: Yale University Press, 1964.

*BIRCH, CYRIL, ed. *Anthology of Chinese Literature from Earliest Times to the Fourteenth Century.* New York: Grove Press, 1967.

BUCK, PEARL S., trans. *Shui Hu Ch'uan: All Men Are Brothers*, 2 vols. New York: Grove Press, 1957.

*CHAN, WING-TSIT, trans. and comp. *A Source Book in Chinese Philosophy.* Princeton, N.J.: Princeton University Press, 1969.

*CHANG, KWANG-CHIH. *The Archaeology of Ancient China.* New Haven, Conn.: Yale University Press, 1963.

CHI, CH'AO-TING. *Key Economic Areas in Chinese History*, 2nd ed. New York: Paragon Book Reprint Corp., 1963.

CH'Ü, T'UNG-TSU. *Han Social Structure.* Seattle: University of Washington Press, 1973.

*CREEL, H.G. *The Birth of China.* New York: Ungar, 1964.

*————. *Chinese Thought from Confucius to Mao Tse-tung.* Chicago: University of Chicago Press, 1965.

————. *The Origins of Statecraft in China.* Chicago: University of Chicago Press, 1970.

*DAWSON, RAYMOND, ed. *The Legacy of China.* Oxford: Clarendon, 1964.

*DEBARY, WILLIAM T., ed. *Self and Society in Ming Thought.* New York: Columbia University Press, 1970.

*DEBARY, WILLIAM T., et al., comps. *Sources of Chinese Tradition.* New York: Columbia University Press, 1960.

*FAIRBANK, JOHN K., ed. *Chinese Thought and Institutions.* Chicago: University of Chicago Press, 1964.

FENG, YU-LAN. *A History of Chinese Philosophy*, 2nd ed. in English, trans. Derk Bodde, 2 vols. Princeton, N.J.: Princeton University Press, 1966.

*FITZGERALD, CHARLES P. *China: A Short Cultural History*, 3rd ed. New York: Praeger, 1966.

*GERNET, JACQUES. *Daily Life in China on the Eve of the Mongol Invasion*, trans. H.M. Wright. New York: Macmillan, 1962. (Paperback. Stanford, Cal.: Stanford University Press.)

Ho, Ping-ti. *The Ladder of Success in Imperial China.* New York: Columbia University Press, 1964.

——. *Studies on the Population of China, 1368–1953.* Cambridge: Harvard University Press, 1959.

*Hsiao, Kung-chüan. *Rural China: Imperial Control in the Nineteenth Century.* Seattle: University of Washington Press, 1960.

*Hucker, Charles O. *The Traditional Chinese State in Ming Times.* Tucson: University of Arizona Press, 1968.

——, ed. *Chinese Government in Ming Times: Seven Studies.* New York: Columbia University Press, 1969.

Hudson, Geoffrey, F. *Europe and China: A Survey of Their Relations from the Earliest Times to 1800.* London: E. Arnold, 1931.

*Irwin, Richard G. *The Evolution of a Chinese Novel: Shui-hu-chuan.* Cambridge: Harvard University Press, 1953.

*Kracke, Edward A. *Civil Service in Early Sung China, 960–1067.* Cambridge: Harvard University Press, 1968.

*Latourette, Kenneth S. *China.* Englewood Cliffs, N.J.: Prentice-Hall, 1964.
——. *The Chinese, Their History and Culture,* 4th ed. New York: Macmillan, 1964.

*Levenson, Joseph R., and Franz Schurmann. *China—An Interpretative History.* Berkeley: University of California Press, 1969.

Michael, Franz. *The Origin of Manchu Rule in China.* Baltimore: Johns Hopkins Press, 1942.

*Moore, Charles A., ed. *The Chinese Mind.* Honolulu: East-West Center Press, 1967.

*Mote, Frederick W. *Intellectual Foundations of China.* New York: Knopf, 1971.

*Munro, Donald J. *The Concept of Man in Early China.* Stanford, Cal.: Stanford University Press, 1969.

Needham, Joseph. *Science and Civilization in China,* 7 vols. projected; 5 vol. issued to 1974. London: Cambridge University Press, 1961–1973.

*Nivison, David S., and A.F. Wright, eds. *Confucianism in Action.* Stanford, Cal.: Stanford University Press, 1959.

Perkins, Dwight H. *Agricultural Development in China, 1368–1968.* Chicago: Aldine, 1969.

*Sullivan, Michael. *A Short History of Chinese Art.* Berkeley: University of California Press, 1967.

*Waley, Arthur. *Three Ways of Thought in Ancient China.* London: G. Allen, 1963. (Paperback. New York: Doubleday.)

*Wittfogel, Karl A., and Chia-sheng Feng. *History of Chinese Society: Liao, 907–1125.* Philadelphia: American Philosophical Society, 1949.

*Wright, A.F. *Buddhism in Chinese History.* Stanford, Cal.: Stanford University Press, 1965.

*——, ed. *The Confucian Persuasion.* Stanford, Cal.: Stanford University Press, 1960.

*——, ed. *Studies in Chinese Thought.* Chicago: University of Chicago Press, 1962.

MODERN PERIOD

*BIANCO, LUCIEN. *Origins of the Chinese Revolution, 1915–1949,* trans. Muriel Bell. Stanford, Cal.: Stanford University Press, 1971.

BOORMAN, HOWARD L., ed. *Biographical Dictionary of Republican China,* 4 vols. New York: Columbia University Press, 1967–1971.

BOYLE, JOHN H. *China and Japan at War, 1937–1945: The Politics of Collaboration.* Stanford, Cal.: Stanford University Press, 1972.

CH'EN, JEROME. *Yuan Shih-k'ai,* 2nd ed. Stanford, Cal.: Stanford University Press, 1972.

*CHESNEAUX, JEAN. *Peasant Revolts in China, 1840–1949,* trans. C.A. Curwen. New York: W.W. Norton, 1973.

*CH'IEN, TUAN-SHENG. *The Government and Politics of China.* Cambridge: Harvard University Press, 1961. (Paperback. Stanford, Cal.: Stanford University Press.)

CHOU, SHU-JEN. (Lu Hsun). *Ah Q and Others,* trans. Chi-chen Wang. New York: Columbia University Press, 1941.

*CHOW, TS'E-TUNG. *The May Fourth Movement.* Cambridge: Harvard University Press, 1964. (Paperback. Stanford, Cal.: Stanford University Press.)

*CLUBB, O. EDMUND. *Twentieth Century China.* New York: Columbia University Press, 1964.

*COHEN, WARREN I. *America's Response to China.* New York: John Wiley and Sons, 1971.

*FAIRBANK, JOHN K. *Trade and Diplomacy on the China Coast: The Opening of the Treaty Ports, 1842–1854.* Cambridge: Harvard University Press, 1964. (Paperback. Stanford, Cal.: Stanford University Press.)

*———. *The United States and China,* 3rd ed. Cambridge: Harvard University Press, 1971.

*FEIS, HERBERT. *The China Tangle.* Princeton, N.J.: Princeton University Press, 1964.

FEUERWERKER, ALBERT. *The Chinese Economy, 1912–1949.* Ann Arbor, Mich.: Center for Chinese Studies, 1968.

———. *The Chinese Economy, Circa 1870–1911.* Ann Arbor, Mich.: Center for Chinese Studies, 1969.

GILLIN, DONALD. *Warlord: Yen Hsi-shan in Shansi Province, 1911–1949.* Princeton, N.J.: Princeton University Press, 1967.

*HARRISON, JOHN A. *China Since 1800.* New York: Harcourt, Brace, and World, 1967.

*HO, PING-TI, and TANG TSOU, eds. *China in Crisis,* 2 vols. in 3 books. Chicago: University of Chicago Press, 1968.

HSU, IMMANUEL C.Y. *China's Entrance into the Family of Nations: The Diplomatic Phase, 1858–1880.* Cambridge: Harvard University Press, 1960.

———. *The Rise of Modern China.* London: Oxford University Press, 1970.

*HSUEH, CHUN-TU, ed. *Revolutionary Leaders of Modern China.* London: Oxford University Press, 1971.

HUGHES, ERNEST R. *The Invasion of China by the Western World,* 2nd ed. New York: Barnes and Noble, 1968.

*ISAACS, HAROLD R. *The Tragedy of the Chinese Revolution*, rev. ed. Stanford, Cal.: Stanford University Press, 1951.

ISRAEL, JOHN. *Student Nationalism in China, 1927–1937*. Stanford, Cal.: Stanford University Press, 1966.

*LEVENSON, JOSEPH R. *Confucian China and Its Modern Fate*, 3 vols. Berkeley: University of California Press, 1964–1966.

*———. *Liang Ch'i-ch'ao and the Mind of Modern China*. Cambridge Harvard University Press, 1965. (Paperback. Stanford, Cal.: Stanford University Press.)

———. *Modern China: An Interpretive Anthology*. London: Macmillan, 1970.

———. *Revolution and Cosmopolitanism: The Western Stage and the Chinese Stages*. Berkeley: University of California Press, 1971.

*LEVY, MARION J. *The Family Revolution in Modern China*. New York: Atheneum, 1968.

LO, JUNG-PANG, ed. *K'ang Yu-wei, A Bibliography and a Symposium*. Tucson: University of Arizona Press, 1967.

MENDEL, DOUGLAS. *The Politics of Formosan Nationalism*. Berkeley: University of California Press, 1970.

*MICHAEL, FRANZ, and CHUNG-LI CHANG. *The Taiping Rebellion*, Vol. I. Seattle: University of Washington Press, 1966.

PYE, LUCIAN W. *Warlord Politics*. New York: Praeger, 1971.

*SCHIFFRIN, H.Z. *Sun Yat-sen and the Origins of the 1911 Revolution*. Berkeley: University of California Press, 1968.

SCHWARTZ, BENJAMIN. *In Search of Wealth and Power: Yen Fu and the West*. Cambridge: Harvard University Press. 1964.

*SHARMAN, LYON. *Sun Yat-sen, His Life and Its Meaning: A Critical Biography*. Stanford, Cal.: Stanford University Press, 1968.

*SHIH, VINCENT Y.C. *The Taiping Ideology*. Seattle: University of Washington Press, 1967.

*TAN, CHESTER C.L. *The Boxer Catastrophe*. New York: Columbia University Press, 1955. (Paperback. New York: Norton.)

*———. *Chinese Political Thought in the Twentieth Century*. New York: Doubleday, 1971.

TENG, SSU-YU. *The Taiping Rebellion and the Western Powers*. London: Clarendon, 1971.

———, and JOHN K. FAIRBANK, eds. *China's Response to the West: A Documentary Survey, 1839–1923*. New York: Atheneum, 1963.

TIEN, HUNG-MAO. *Government and Politics in Kuomintang China, 1927–1937*. Stanford, Cal.: Stanford University Press, 1972.

*TSOU, TANG. *America's Failure in China, 1941–1950*, 2 vols. Chicago: University of Chicago Press, 1963.

*TUCHMAN, BARBARA. *Stilwell and the American Experience in China, 1911–1945*. New York: Macmillan, 1970.

*WAKEMAN, FREDERICK. *Strangers at the Gate: Social Disorder in South China, 1839–1861*. Berkeley: University of California Press, 1966.

*WALEY, ARTHUR. *The Opium War Through Chinese Eyes*. Stanford, Cal.: Stanford University Press, 1970.

*WRIGHT, MARY C. *The Last Stand of Chinese Conservatism: The T'ung-chih*

Restoration, 1862–1874. New York: Atheneum, 1966. (Paperback. Stanford, Cal.: Stanford University Press.)

*———, ed. *China in Revolution: The First Phase, 1900–1913.* New Haven, Conn.: Yale University Press, 1968.

YOUNG, ARTHUR N. *China's Nation-Building Effort, 1927–1937.* Stanford, Cal. Hoover Institution Press, 1972.

COMMUNIST PERIOD

*BARNETT, A. DOAK. *China on the Eve of Communist Takeover.* New York: Praeger, 1963.

*———. *Communist China: The Early Years, 1949–1955.* New York: Praeger, 1964.

BOORMAN, HOWARD L., et al., eds. *Moscow-Peking Axis: Strengths and Strains.* New York: Harper, 1957.

*Bulletin of the Atomic Scientists. *China After the Cultural Revolution.* New York: Random House, 1970.

CHANG, CHU-YUAN. *The Rise of the Chinese Communist Party, 1921–1927.* Lawrence: University Press of Kansas, 1971.

CHENG, CHU-YUAN. *The Economy of Communist China, 1949–1969.* Ann Arbor, Mich.: Center for Chinese Studies, 1971.

*COHEN, A.A. *The Communism of Mao Tse-Tung.* Chicago: University of Chicago Press, 1964.

ECKSTEIN, ALEXANDER, et. al., eds. *Economic Trends in Communist China.* Chicago: Aldine, 1968.

FLOYD, DAVID. *Mao Against Khrushchev.* New York: Praeger, 1964.

*HARRISON, JAMES P. *The Long March to Power: A History of the Chinese Communist Party, 1921–1971.* New York: Praeger, 1972.

*HINTON, HAROLD C. *An Introduction to Chinese Politics.* New York: Praeger, 1973.

*———. *China's Turbulent Quest,* new and enlarged ed. New York: Macmillan, 1972.

*HINTON, WILLIAM. *Fanshen: A Documentary of Revolution in a Chinese Village.* New York: Monthly Review Press, 1967. (Paperback. New York: Random House.)

*———. *Hundred Day War: The Cultural Revolution at Tsinghua University.* New York: Monthly Review Press, 1972.

*HOUN, FRANKLIN W. *A Short History of Chinese Communism.* Englewood Cliffs, N.J.: Prentice-Hall, 1967.

*JOHNSON, CHALMERS A. *Peasant Nationalism and Communist Power: The Emergence of Revolutionary China, 1937–1945.* Stanford, Cal.: Stanford University Press, 1966.

KLEIN, DONALD, and ANNE B. CLARK. *Chinese Communism: A Biographical Dictionary, 1921–1965.* Cambridge: Harvard University Press, 1971.

KOLATCH, JONATHAN. *Sports, Politics and Ideology in China.* New York: Jonathan David, 1972.

LEWIS, JOHN W., ed. *The City in Communist China.* Stanford, Cal.: Stanford University Press, 1971.

LEYDA, JAY. *Dianying, Electric Shadows*. Cambridge: M.I.T. Press, 1972.

*LIFTON, ROBERT J. *Revolutionary Immortality: Mao Tse-Tung and the Chinese Cultural Revolution*. New York: Random House, 1968.

MACFARQUHAR, RODERICK, et al. *Sino-American Relations, 1949–1971*. New York: Praeger, 1972.

*MEHNERT, KLAUS. *Peking and Moscow*, trans. Leila Vennewitz. New York: New American Library, 1964.

*MEISNER, MAURICE. *Li Ta-chao and the Origins of Chinese Marxism*. Cambridge: Harvard University Press, 1967. (Paperback. New York: Atheneum.)

*MYRDAL, JAN. *Report from a Chinese Village*. New York: Pantheon, 1965. (Paperback. New York: New American Library.)

*NORTH, ROBERT C. *Chinese Communism*. New York: McGraw-Hill, 1966.

*———. *Moscow and Chinese Communists*, 2nd ed. Stanford, Cal.: Stanford University Press, 1963.

*OKSENBERG, MICHAEL, ed. *China's Developmental Experience*. New York: Praeger, 1973.

ROBINSON, THOMAS W. et al. *The Cultural Revolution in China*. Berkeley: University of California Press, 1971.

*SCALAPINO, ROBERT A., ed. *Elites in the People's Republic of China*. Seattle: University of Washington Press, 1972.

*SCHRAM, STUART R. *The Political Thought of Mao Tse-Tung*, rev. ed. New York: Praeger, 1969.

*SCHURMANN, FRANZ. *Ideology and Organization in Communist China*, 2nd ed. Berkeley: University of California Press, 1970.

*SCHWARTZ, BENJAMIN. *Chinese Communism and the Rise of Mao*. Cambridge: Harvard University Press, 1966. (Paperback. New York: Harper.)

*———. *Communism and China: Ideology in Flux*. Cambridge: Harvard University Press, 1968. (Paperback. New York: Atheneum.)

*SNOW, EDGAR. *The Long Revolution*. New York: Random House, 1972.

*———. *Red Star Over China*, rev. ed. New York: Grove, 1968.

TANG, PETER, and JOAN MALONEY. *Communist China: The Domestic Scene, 1949–1967*. So. Orange, N.J.: Seton Hall University Press, 1967.

*TOWNSEND, JAMES R. *Political Participation in Communist China*. Berkeley: University of California Press, 1967.

*TREADGOLD, DONALD W., ed. *Soviet and Chinese Communism*. Seattle: University of Washington Press, 1967.

*VOGEL, EZRA. *Canton Under Communism*. Cambridge: Harvard University Press, 1969. (Paperback. New York: Harper.)

*WALLER, DEREK J. *The Government and Politics of Communist China*. London: Hutchinson, 1970. (Paperback. New York: Doubleday.)

WELCH, HOLMES. *Buddhism Under Mao*. Cambridge: Harvard University Press, 1972.

WU, YUAN-LI, ed. *The People's Republic of China: A Handbook*. New York: Praeger, 1971.

*YANG, CH'ING-K'UN. *The Chinese Family in the Communist Revolution*. Cambridge: M.I.T. Press, 1959.

*——. *A Chinese Village in Early Communist Transition*. Cambridge: M.I.T. Press, 1959.

(The paperback edition of the above two books is distributed as one volume, *Chinese Communist Society: The Family and the Village*. Cambridge: M.I.T. Press.)

YU, FREDERICK C.T. *Mass Persuasion in Communist China*. New York: Praeger, 1964.

*ZAGORIA, DONALD S. *The Sino-Soviet Conflict, 1951–1961*. Princeton, N.J.: Princeton University Press, 1962. (Paperback. New York: Atheneum.)

Mongolia and Inner Asia

BAWDEN, C.R. *The Modern History of Mongolia*. London: Weidenfeld & Nicholson, 1968.

GROUSSET, RÉNÉ. *The Empire of the Steppes: A History of Central Asia*, trans. N. Walford. New Brunswick, N.J.: Rutgers University Press, 1970.

LATTIMORE, OWEN. *Inner Asian Frontiers of China*, 2nd ed. Boston: Beacon Press, 1962.

——. *Nomads and Commissars: Mongolia Revisited*. London: Oxford University Press, 1962.

LI, TIEH-TSENG. *The Historical Status of Tibet*. New York: King's Crown, Columbia, 1956.

PETROV, VIKTOR P. *Mongolia: A Profile*. New York: Praeger, 1970.

RICHARDSON, H.E. *Short History of Tibet*. New York: Dutton, 1962.

RUPEN, ROBERT A. *The Mongolian People's Republic*. Stanford, Cal.: Hoover Institution Press, 1966.

SAUNDERS, J.J. *The History of the Mongol Conquest*. London: Routledge & K. Paul, 1971.

SHAKABPA, TSEPON W.D. *Tibet: A Political History*. New Haven, Conn.: Yale University Press, 1967.

STEIN, R.A. *Tibetan Civilization*, rev. ed., trans. J.E.S. Driver. Stanford, Cal.: Stanford University Press, 1972.

WHITING, ALLAN S. *Sinkiang: Pawn or Pivot?* East Lansing: Michigan State University Press, 1958.

Korea

BRANDT, VINCENT S.R. *A Korean Village: Between Farm and Sea*. Cambridge: Harvard University Press, 1971.

CHUNG, JOSEPH S. *The North Korean Economy*. Stanford, Cal.: Hoover Institution Press, 1973.

CHUNG, KYUNG CHO. *Korea: The Third Republic*. New York: Macmillan, 1971.

CONROY, HILARY. *The Japanese Seizure of Korea, 1868–1910*. Philadelphia: University of Pennsylvania Press, 1960.

HAN, SUNGJOO. *The Failure of Democracy in South Korea.* Berkeley: University of California Press, 1973.

HAN, WOO-KEUN. *The History of Korea,* rev. ed., trans. Kyung-shik Lee, ed. G.K. Mintz. Honolulu: University of Hawaii Press, 1972.

*HATADA, TAKASHI. *A History of Korea,* trans. B.H. Hazard and W.W. Smith. Santa Barbara, Cal.: American Bibliographical Center, 1969.

HENDERSON, GREGORY. *Korea: The Politics of the Vortex.* Cambridge: Harvard University Press, 1968.

HULBERT, H.B. *The History of Korea,* ed. C.N. Weems, 2 vols. New York: Hillary House, 1962.

KANG, YOUNGHILL. *The Grass Roof.* Chicago: Follett, 1966.

KIM, C.I. EUGENE and HAN KYO. *Korea and the Politics of Imperialism, 1876–1910.* Berkeley: University of California Press, 1967.

LEE, CHONG-SIK. *The Politics of Korean Nationalism.* Berkeley: University of California Press, 1963.

LI, YUK-SA, ed. *Juche: The Speeches and Writings of Kim Il Sung.* New York: Viking, 1972.

McCUNE, GEORGE M. *Korea Today.* Cambridge: Harvard University Press, 1950.

McCUNE, SHANNON. *Korea's Heritage: A Regional and Social Geography.* Rutland, Vt.: Charles E. Tuttle, 1956.

OSGOOD, CORNELIUS. *The Koreans and Their Culture.* New York: Ronald, 1951.

*PAIGE, GLENN D. *The Korean People's Democratic Republic.* Stanford, Cal.: Hoover Institution Press, 1966.

PIHL, MARSHALL R., ed. *Listening to Korea: A Korean Anthology.* New York: Praeger, 1973.

*REES, DAVID. *Korea: The Limited War.* New York: St. Martin's, 1964. (Paperback. Baltimore: Penguin.)

RUDOLPH, PHILIP. *North Korea's Political and Economic Structure.* New York: Institute of Pacific Relations, 1959.

SCALAPINO, ROBERT A., and CHONG-SIK LEE. *Communism in Korea,* 2 vols. Berkeley: University of California Press, 1967.

SCALAPINO, ROBERT A., ed. *North Korea Today.* New York: Praeger, 1963.

SOHN, POW-KEY, et al. *The History of Korea.* Seoul: Korean National Commission for UNESCO, 1970.

SUH, DAE-SOOK. *The Korean Communist Movement, 1918–1948.* Princeton, N.J.: Princeton University Press, 1967.

WEEMS, BENJAMIN B. *Reform, Rebellion and the Heavenly Way.* Tucson: University of Arizona Press, 1964.

Japan

GENERAL

BAILEY, JACKSON H., ed. *Listening to Japan: A Japanese Anthology.* New York: Praeger, 1973.

HALL, JOHN W., and RICHARD K. BEARDSLEY, eds. *Twelve Doors to Japan.* New York: McGraw-Hill, 1965.

*ISHIDA, TAKESHI. *Japanese Society.* New York: Random House, 1971.

NAKANE, CHIE. *Japanese Society.* Berkeley: University of California Press, 1970.

SINGER, KURT. *Mirror, Sword, and Jewel: A Study of Japanese Characteristics.* New York: George Braziller, 1973.

VARLEY, H. PAUL. *Japanese Culture: A Short History.* New York: Praeger, 1973.

TO MODERN PERIOD

ANESAKI, MASAHARU. *History of Japanese Religion.* Rutland, Vt.: Tuttle, 1971.

*BELLAH, ROBERT N. *Tokugawa Religion.* Glencoe, Ill.: Free Press, 1957. (Paperback. Boston: Beacon Press.)

BOXER, C.R. *The Christian Century in Japan, 1549–1650.* Berkeley: University of California Press, 1967.

———. *Jan Compagnie in Japan, 1600–1811,* 2nd rev. ed. New York: Oxford University Press, 1968.

BROWN, DELMER M. *Money Economy in Medieval Japan.* New Haven, Conn.: Yale University Press, 1951.

CRAIG, ALBERT M., and DONALD SHIVELY, eds. *Personality in Japanese History.* Berkeley: University of California Press, 1970.

DORE, RONALD P. *Education in Tokugawa Japan.* Berkeley: University of California Press, 1965.

*DUUS, PETER. *Feudalism in Japan.* New York: Knopf, 1969.

FREDERIC, LOUIS. *Daily Life in Japan at the Time of the Samurai, 1185–1603,* trans. Eileen M. Lowe. New York: Praeger, 1972.

HALL, JOHN W. *Japan: From Prehistory to Modern Times.* New York: Delacorte, 1970.

*KEENE, DONALD. *Anthology of Japanese Literature from the Earliest Era to the Mid-Nineteenth Century.* New York: Grove, 1955.

*———. *The Japanese Discovery of Europe, 1720–1830,* rev. ed. Stanford, Cal.: Stanford University Press, 1969.

*———. *Japanese Literature: An Introduction for Western Readers.* London: Murray, 1953. (Paperback. New York: Grove.)

KIDDER, J.E., JR. *Japan Before Buddhism.* London: Thames and Hudson, 1966.

*MORRIS, IVAN. *The World of the Shining Prince: Court Life in Ancient Japan.* New York: Knopf, 1964. (Paperback. Baltimore: Penguin.)

*MURASAKI, SHIKIBU. *The Tale of Genji,* trans. Arthur Waley, 2 vols. New York: Modern Library, 1960. (Paperback. New York: Doubleday.)

*REISCHAUER, EDWIN O. *Japan: The Story of a Nation,* rev. ed. New York: Knopf, 1970.

*SANSOM, SIR GEORGE B. *A History of Japan to 1867,* 3 vols. Stanford, Cal.: Stanford University Press, 1958–1963.

———. *Japan: A Short Cultural History,* rev. ed. New York: Appleton-Century-Crofts, 1962.

SHELDON, CHARLES D. *The Rise of the Merchant Class in Tokugawa Japan, 1600–1868.* Locust Valley, N.Y.: Augustin, 1958.

TSUNODA, RYUSAKU, et al., comps. *Sources of Japanese Tradition.* New York: Columbia University Press, 1958.

MODERN PERIOD

AKITA, GEORGE. *Foundations of Constitutional Government in Japan, 1868–1900.* Cambridge: Harvard University Press, 1967.

ALLEN, GEORGE C. *A Short Economic History of Modern Japan,* rev. ed. New York: Praeger, 1963.

*BEARDSLEY, RICHARD K., et al. *Village Japan.* Chicago: University of Chicago Press, 1969.

BEASLEY, W.G. *The Meiji Restoration.* Stanford, Cal.: Stanford University Press, 1972.

*———. *The Modern History of Japan.* New York: Praeger, 1966.

BORTON, HUGH. *Japan's Modern Century,* 2nd ed. New York: Ronald Press, 1970.

*BUNCE, W.K. *Religions in Japan.* Rutland, Vt.: Charles E. Tuttle, 1955.

*BUTOW, R.J.C. *Tojo and the Coming of War.* Princeton, N.J.: Princeton University Press, 1965. (Paperback. Stanford, Cal.: Stanford University Press.)

CRAIG, ALBERT M. *Choshu in the Meiji Restoration.* Cambridge: Harvard University Press, 1961.

*DORE, RONALD P. *City Life in Japan.* Berkeley: University of California Press, 1963.

*———, ed. *Aspects of Social Change in Modern Japan.* Princeton, N.J.: Princeton University Press, 1967.

DUUS, PETER. *Party Rivalry and Political Change in Taisho Japan.* Cambridge: Harvard University Press, 1968.

FEIS, HERBERT. *Japan Subdued.* Princeton, N.J.: Princeton University Press, 1961.

*FUKUZAWA, YUKICHI. *Autobiography,* trans. Eiichi Kiyooka, authorized rev. ed. New York: Columbia University Press, 1966.

HACKETT, ROGER F. *Yamagata Aritomo in the Rise of Modern Japan, 1838–1922.* Cambridge: Harvard University Press, 1971.

HAROOTUNIAN, HARRY, and BERNARD SILBERMAN, eds. *Modern Japanese Leadership.* Tucson: University of Arizona Press, 1966.

HIRSCHMEIER, JOHANNES, S.V.D. *The Origins of Entrepreneurship in Meiji Japan.* Cambridge: Harvard University Press, 1964.

IKE, NOBUTAKA. *The Beginnings of Political Democracy in Japan.* New York: Greenwood Press, 1969.

*JANSEN, MARIUS B. *The Japanese and Sun Yat-sen.* Cambridge: Harvard University Press, 1967. (Paperback. Stanford, Cal.: Stanford University Press.)

*———. *Sakamoto Ryoma and the Meiji Restoration.* Princeton, N.J.: Princeton University Press, 1961. (Paperback. Stanford, Cal.: Stanford University Press.)

*KEENE, DONALD. *Modern Japanese Literature: An Anthology.* New York: Grove, 1960.

*LOCKWOOD, W.W. *The Economic Development of Japan.* Princeton, N.J.: Princeton University Press, 1954.

MARSHALL, B.K. *Capitalism and Nationalism in Prewar Japan.* Stanford, Cal.: Stanford University Press, 1967.

MAXON, YALE CANDEE. *Control of Japanese Foreign Policy.* Berkeley: University of California Press, 1957.

*MORLEY, JAMES W., ed. *Dilemmas of Growth in Prewar Japan.* Princeton, N.J.: Princeton University Press, 1971.

NORMAN, E.H. *Japan's Emergence as a Modern State.* New York: Institute of Pacific Relations, 1940.

*REISCHAUER, EDWIN O. *The United States and Japan,* 3rd ed. Cambridge: Harvard University Press, 1965. (Paperback. New York: Viking.)

*SANSOM, SIR GEORGE B. *The Western World and Japan.* New York: Knopf, 1951.

SCALAPINO, ROBERT A. *Democracy and the Party Movement in Prewar Japan.* Berkeley: University of California Press, 1953.

——. *The Japanese Communist Movement, 1920–1966.* Berkeley: University of California Press, 1967.

SCHEINER, IRWIN, ed. *Modern Japan: An Interpretive Anthology.* New York: Macmillan, 1974.

SHIVELY, DONALD H., ed. *Tradition and Modernization in Japanese Culture.* Princeton, N.J.: Princeton University Press, 1971.

SILBERMAN, BERNARD. *Ministers of Modernization: Elite Mobility in the Meiji Restoration, 1868–1873.* Tucson: University of Arizona Press, 1964.

*SMITH, THOMAS C. *The Agrarian Origins of Modern Japan.* New York: Atheneum, 1966. (Paperback. Stanford, Cal.: Stanford University Press.)

——. *Political Change and Industrial Development in Japan: Government Enterprise, 1868–1880.* Stanford, Cal.: Stanford University Press, 1965.

SMITH, WARREN W. *Confucianism in Modern Japan.* Tokyo: Hokuseido Press, 1959.

STORRY, RICHARD. *The Double Patriots.* Boston: Houghton Mifflin, 1957.

*TANIZAKI, JUNICHIRO. *The Makioka Sisters,* trans. E.G. Seidensticker. New York: Knopf, 1957. (Paperback. New York: Grosset and Dunlap.)

WARD, ROBERT E. *Japan's Political System.* Englewood Cliffs, N.J.: Prentice-Hall, 1967.

*——, ed. *Political Development in Modern Japan.* Princeton, N.J.: Princeton University Press, 1968.

SINCE WORLD WAR II

Asahic Shimbun. *The Pacific Rivals.* New York and Tokyo: Weatherhill and Asahi, 1972.

*COLE, ROBERT E. *Japanese Blue Collar: The Changing Tradition.* Berkeley: University of California Press, 1971.

*DORE, RONALD P. *British Factory—Japanese Factory.* Berkeley: University of California Press, 1973.

———. *Land Reform in Japan*. London: Oxford University Press, 1966.

FUKUI, HARUHIRO. *Party in Power: The Japanese Liberal Democrats and Policy-Making*. Berkeley: University of California Press, 1970.

*GIBNEY, FRANK. *Five Gentlemen of Japan*. New York: Farrar, Straus and Young, 1953.

*IKE, NOBUTAKA. *Japanese Politics: Patron-Client Democracy*, 2nd ed. New York: Knopf, 1972.

KAWAI, KAZUO. *Japan's American Interlude*. Chicago: University of Chicago, 1964.

LANGER, PAUL F. *Communism in Japan*. Stanford, Cal.: Hoover Institution Press, 1972.

*MAKI, J.M. *Government and Politics in Japan*. New York: Praeger, 1962.

*MARUYAMA, MASAO. *Thought and Behavior in Modern Japanese Politics*, ed. Ivan Morris. New York: Oxford University Press, 1966.

*McNELLY, THEODORE. *Politics and Government in Japan*, 2nd ed. Boston: Houghton Mifflin, 1972.

MORRIS, IVAN. *Nationalism and the Right Wing in Japan: A Study of Postwar Trends*. New York: Oxford University Press, 1960.

*SCALAPINO, ROBERT A., and J. MASUMI. *Parties and Politics in Contemporary Japan*. Berkeley: University of California Press, 1962.

*VOGEL, EZRA F. *Japan's New Middle Class*, 2nd ed. Berkeley: University of California Press, 1971.

WEINSTEIN, MARTIN E. *Japan's Postwar Defense Policy, 1947–1968*. New York: Columbia University Press, 1971.

WHITE, JAMES W. *The Soka-Gakkai and Mass Society*. Stanford, Cal.: Stanford University Press, 1970.

WOODARD, WILLIAM P. *The Allied Occupation of Japan, 1945–1952, and Japanese Religions*. Leiden: E.J. Brill, 1972.

Additional suggestions may be found in the following works and in the bibliographies listed therein:

American Universities Field Staff. *A Select Bibliography: Asia, Africa, Eastern Europe, Latin America*. New York: American Universities Field Staff, 1960 with supplements 1961, 1963, 1965.

GILLIN, DONALD, et al. *East Asia: A Bibliography for Undergraduate Libraries*. Williamsport: Bro-Dart Publishing Co., 1970.

*HUCKER, CHARLES O. *China: A Critical Bibliography*. Tucson: University of Arizona Press, 1962.

*SILBERMAN, BERNARD S. *Japan and Korea: A Critical Bibliography*, 2nd ed. Tucson: University of Arizona Press, 1962.

PART FOUR

SOUTHEAST ASIA

9

THE FOUNDATIONS OF SOUTHEAST ASIA

Geographic Foundations: Regions and Resources

REGIONS OF EXCHANGE

The Middle East, South Asia, and East Asia are not completely isolated from each other by the mountains and deserts that separate them. For centuries the dry, high region from Mongolia to Turkestan has been traversed by Turkic and Mongol horse nomads, Chinese and Persian traders, and Buddhist and Muslim pilgrims. This region—variously called Central Asia, High Asia, and Inner Asia—possesses considerable natural unity in terms of resources, climate, and economic and social life. However, its tribally organized peoples have lacked strong traditions of political unity. Consequently, they have been controlled by their powerful neighbors as often as they have been free. Only Genghis Khan and his successors united them for any length of time, and only a part of the Mongol people has succeeded in establishing a sovereign state in the twentieth century. The rest of the Mongols, and all the Turkic peoples of Central Asia, inhabit lands which have been under Russian or Chinese administration for generations. Moreover, Central Asia is far from the seas used by Westerners. Its people have therefore acquired most of their knowledge of the modern world from neighboring Russians and Chinese, not from Portuguese, Spaniards, English, French, Dutch, or Americans, all of whom have displayed far more interest in Southeast Asia, the other region through which people, ideas, and goods have passed between East Asia, South Asia, and the Middle East. The term "Southeast Asia" denotes the region south and east of the Burma, Assam, and south China hills. It includes Burma,

Thailand, Laos, Cambodia, Vietnam, the Philippines, Indonesia, Malaysia, Singapore, and Brunei. This region has long been a meeting place of the Indian and Chinese influences which formerly led some Europeans to refer to all of it as Indochina.

MOUNTAINS, RIVERS, AND ISLANDS

Southeast Asia is separated from China by forbiddingly steep hills extending from the Himalayas to the China Sea, and from India by the low mountain chain which forms the watershed between the Brahmaputra basin in India and the Irrawaddy basin in Burma. This mountain chain, the Burma-Java arc, then sinks beneath the sea to rise again in Sumatra, Java, and the lesser islands east to Timor.

The Irrawaddy and its longest tributary, the Chindwin, rise on the southern slopes of the Himalayan extension, as does the Menam in Thailand. Between the Menam and Irrawaddy basins lie the complex Shan hills, which contain the narrow valley of the torrential Salween river. The Salween starts in eastern Tibet, like the Yangtze, but it enters the Indian Ocean rather than the China Sea. The mountain chain between the Salween and the Menam continues southward through the Malay peninsula, where it meets the mountain chains that run southwesterly from the Philippines, Celebes or Sulawesi, and Borneo or Kalimantan. East of the Menam lie the hills that mark the watershed between its drainage basin and that of the Mekong, the longest river of Southeast Asia.

Like the Salween, the Mekong rises in eastern Tibet and parallels its southward course for a time. Then it turns east, skirting the Korat plateau in northeastern Thailand, descends to the plains of Cambodia (marked off from the Menam valley by the Cardamon hills), and reaches the sea in southern Vietnam. Between the central Mekong and the China Sea lie the Annamite mountains, which form the watershed between the Mekong and the Red river. The Red, like the Menam and the Irrawaddy, rises on the southern side of the Himalayan extension.

These five major rivers and the mountains which define their drainage basins form the mainland part of Southeast Asia. Since mainland Southeast Asia is next to southern China, Chinese influences have naturally been strongest in this area. Most of its people speak largely monosyllabic languages brought from China by Burmese, Thai, Vietnamese, and other relative newcomers. Most also follow Buddhism, but usually in a form learned from Ceylon rather than from China. However, Indian and Islamic influences have been stronger than Chinese in the Malay peninsula and the islands. The one major exception is the Philippine archipelago, which Spain seized before Indian and Islamic influences had had time to penetrate deeply. In the Malay peninsula and the islands, the people still speak the agglutinative Indonesian languages of the Malayo-Polynesian family, which were used throughout Southeast Asia two thousand years ago.

The river valleys were the goal of the Burmese, Thai, and Vietnamese, who took the valleys from earlier inhabitants and established compact rice-growing societies like those of southern China, leaving the hillier lands to later arrivals and remnants of earlier groups. They took little interest in maritime affairs, regarding the shallow and protected Andaman and South China seas as even greater barriers than the south China hills. However, the Indonesian-speaking peoples whom they displaced were accustomed to sea travel. Many chose to sail to the Malay peninsula or to the islands to join their fellow Malayo-Polynesians. To them, the sea was as much a highway as was a river like the Mekong, at least from December through June when the sailor was free from the danger of the great storms known as typhoons.

The lower Mekong basin is a natural commercial center. The great tides of the delta help seagoing ships to travel within less than sixty miles of the falls near the border between Cambodia and Laos. Moreover, the level of the lower Mekong is relatively constant. The Red river, the central Mekong, the Menam, the Salween, the Irrawaddy, and the Chindwin all fluctuate sharply in volume because of seasonal rainfall. However, the natural storage basin of the Great Lake in Cambodia, like the T'ung-t'ing and P'o-yang lakes of the central Yangtze valley, receives the overflow of the swollen Mekong in the flood season and discharges the stored water in the drier months, greatly moderating the fluctuations of the lower Mekong. The swamp lands of eastern Sumatra have performed a similar function for the rivers which flow eastward from the mountains of western Sumatra. Some eastern Sumatran river outlets were important ports a thousand years ago, until silt began to clog them. Then they were replaced by ports in northern Sumatra, the Malay peninsula, and northern Java, which were nearly as close as eastern Sumatra to the straits of Malacca and Sunda, the shortest passages between the Indian Ocean and the China Sea.

CLIMATE, SOILS, AND VEGETATION

In spite of difficulties, water transport has remained the major means of communication in most of Southeast Asia. Only the most mountainous areas have been served entirely by land transport, which has tended to be carried on by men and also women rather than animals. This has been partly because of the terrain and partly because of a failure to regard milk-giving animals as a steady source of food. Indians taught Southeast Asians many things, but not the use of milk and butter. Until ice cream was introduced in the larger cities, Southeast Asians were nearly as uninterested in dairy products as were the Chinese.

The popularity of ice cream, where available, points up a major characteristic of Southeast Asia's climate: it is warm throughout the year. Most of its people enjoy temperatures near 80 degrees Fahrenheit (26.7 degrees Centigrade) at all times, for their homelands straddle the equator and are surrounded by the moderating influences of the sea. Although the highlands are cooler than the coastal plains, frost is almost unknown. Even in mountain-shielded interior areas like the Korat plateau or the central Irrawaddy basin, temperatures rarely sink below 60 degrees Fahrenheit (15.5 degrees Centigrade) or rise above 100 degrees Fahrenheit (37.7 degrees Centigrade). On the mainland the warmest months are March, April, and May—just before the rainy season; but in the Malay peninsula and the islands, only the interior of northern Luzon in the Philippines experiences comparable temperature variations, and Luzon, like most of the mainland, is more than fifteen degrees north of the equator.

The general pattern for the mainland and the Philippines is one of heavy rainfall between June and September, when cool, moisture-laden winds travel from the oceans to the land, as in India or China. Nearness to the sea means some rain in other seasons, at least on the seaward slopes of the mountains; but the central Irrawaddy, the Menam basin, the Korat plateau, the Red river valley, and northern Luzon do experience drought from time to time in the dry months. In the Malay peninsula and Indonesia, close to the equator, there is little seasonal variation in rainfall. In the southernmost islands from Java eastward, the heavy rainfall associated with the warmer months comes in January and February, when the winds of the southern hemisphere converge on the heated land mass of Australia.

Annual rainfall is fairly reliable throughout the area. The range of variability is greatest in the central Irrawaddy, the Menam valley, the Korat plateau, western Cambodia, and northern Sulawesi, the only regions which receive less than sixty inches of rain per year. Even there the rainfall is as dependable as in the central Ganges valley or the north China plain. However, the constant high temperatures evaporate water rapidly, making irrigation necessary for successful agriculture wherever rainfall averages less than sixty inches on the mainland or less than eighty inches in Indonesia, as it generally does from central Java eastward.

Climatic conditions seriously affect the soils, vegetation, and agriculture of Southeast Asia. Heavy rainfall and high temperatures speed up chemical decomposition and the leaching out of valuable plant nutrients, producing lateritic or bricklike soils in much of the region. Once stripped of forest cover, these soils harden in the sun to a bricklike consistency.

Soils are truly fertile only in the silt-enriched river valleys and in areas like Java where large amounts of volcanic ash with its abundance of soluble minerals have been deposited in the past few thousand years. Consequently only these regions have developed the great concentrations of population ordinarily associated with the growing of flooded-field rice, the staple cereal of the region. Where there is enough rain, as on the mountains of Java or the Philippines, the hillsides are terraced, and each terrace becomes a rice paddy as it fills with rainwater; where there is not enough rain, as in central Burma, the rivers are used for irrigation purposes during the wet season.

The natural vegetation of most of Southeast Asia is forest. Sixty percent of the region is forested, with evergreen rain forest near the equator; deciduous trees, such as teak, where rainfall varies seasonally; and mangrove swamps along the coasts where river-borne silt provides the mangrove with some soil. However, that does not mean the soil is naturally fertile. The infertility of the soil forces thousands of people to live by shifting cultivation—clearing a patch of ground by fire, thus fertilizing it with the ashes of the trees; raising a crop or two of yams or some other staple food; moving to another patch, and another and another, while the forest reclaims its own; and returning after ten years or more to repeat the process, in a regular cycle. Shifting cultivation works when the cultivators are few and the intervals long, but if population growth shortens the intervals, it self-defeatingly results in the replacement of forest by fire-resistant grasses. Therefore twentieth-century governments have tried to prohibit it both in Southeast Asia and in tropical and subtropical Africa, where similar climate and soil conditions have also made it widely practiced for centuries. Nevertheless, it is still carried on in portions of many African states, and in areas of Southeast Asia nearly equal in total size to Thailand.

COMMERCE AND THE FIVE PRIMARY INDUSTRIES

Despite problems of soil and climate, agriculture is the most important primary industry of Southeast Asia, and probably has been since the Malayo-Polynesians came in the centuries immediately before and after 2000 B.C. The chief crops have been rice in the lowlands and yams in the forest clearings. Spices, nuts, fruits, and vegetables have been scarcely more than condiments for the staples and whatever protein foods were available.

Fishing has probably been the second most important primary industry. Fresh and preserved fish have given Southeast Asians most of their animal proteins. The rivers, the seas, the swamps, the Great Lake— even artificial ponds in some regions like heavily populated Java—have furnished those near them with a wide variety of fish and other seafood.

Forestry has also been significant, for wood has been the major building material. Only the most calculatedly impressive buildings, those dedicated to the deities, were made of stone in earlier times. In addition, the forest has provided furnishings, implements, and such fuel as has been needed to cook food, bake pottery, and work metal.

Animal husbandry has been important too, providing the oxen used as work animals in drier regions and the water buffalo used in wetter areas. It has also furnished animal proteins, in the form of eggs, chickens, pigs (among non-Muslims), and dogs, which have been officially praised in northern Vietnam because they produce two litters per year rather than only one as pigs do. However, there has been little dairying.

Until the late nineteenth century, mining was perhaps the least important of Southeast Asia's primary industries. Still, tin for bronze was obtained in the Red river valley, the Malay peninsula, and the islands just south of it; gold and iron were found in the Malay peninsula; and iron was also mined in Luzon and the Annamite range. In the nineteenth and twentieth centuries, prospectors unearthed nickel, zinc, tungsten, and chrome in the Shan hills; chrome and manganese in the Philippines; phosphates in Cambodia; oil in Burma, Sumatra, and Borneo; tungsten and aluminum in the Malay peninsula; and coal almost everywhere, but particularly in the Red river valley and western Sumatra.

The diversified primary industries of Southeast Asia have long furnished material for brisk internal trading. However, only a few Southeast Asian products, such as tin and spices, were exported to other regions in any quantity before the nineteenth century. It was Europeans who first began to exploit teak forests on a large scale and to introduce commercial production of rice in the Irrawaddy, Menam, and Mekong deltas, rubber in the Malay peninsula and Indonesia, coconut products in Indonesia and the Philippines, and abaca (Manila hemp) in the Philippines. Like Central Asia, Southeast Asia has historically been a transit area. All but a few of its products have traditionally been consumed almost entirely within its own confines. Southeast Asia seems to have exported fewer ideas or techniques in the historic period than did the Middle East, which has been both a transit zone and an exporter of cultural patterns from the most ancient times through the Islamic era. However, the Chinese appear to have learned the techniques of growing rice from early Southeast Asians. Trade across the Indian Ocean introduced Southeast Asian root crops and musical instruments to eastern Africa. From there they spread throughout much of the rest of tropical and subtropical Africa after the first centuries of the Christian era.

Historical Development:
Indian and Chinese Influences on Local Rulers

SOUTHEAST ASIA IN THE LAST CENTURIES B.C.

The peoples of early Southeast Asia appear to have been Veddoids, resembling the early Veddah people of Ceylon. Like the Veddahs, they had barely begun to practice shifting cultivation when they were overrun and largely absorbed by newcomers from the north who introduced settled agriculture. The Malayo-Polynesians who moved into the region from Southeast China after 2000 B.C. continued to exchange goods and ideas with those who stayed behind in the south China hills. After 1000 B.C. they learned the use of bronze and iron from the villagers of south China, who in turn were in touch with the cities of north China.

The Malayo-Polynesians were capable sailors who spread the use of the types of bronze and iron tools, ornaments, and ceremonial objects they knew throughout Southeast Asia. Not only were they in touch with south China when the Chou were ruling the north, but then or later they went to India and as far afield as southern Arabia and Madagascar, where their descendants are still found. In return, Arabian and Indian traders visited Southeast Asia, as shown by archaeological finds ranging from a Roman lamp in Thailand to Hittite and Roman beads in the Malay peninsula.

The Dravidians of early India may have been related to the Malayo-Polynesians. If they were, then the welcome which Malayo-Polynesians gave to Hinduism and Mahayana Buddhism in the first centuries A.D. would not be as surprising as earlier Chinese cultural dominance might make it seem. Both Hinduism and Mahayana Buddhism synthesized Dravidian and Aryan beliefs and practices. Shared myths and preconceptions would have made the ways of even a partly Aryanized India seem more acceptable to Malayo-Polynesians than patterns of thought developed in north China, particularly when the Indian ways were introduced by the Dravidians of the trading states of south India. The inhabitants of Southeast Asia learned much from Chinese technology, but in other matters they came to lean toward India. Indian patterns affected institutional and intellectual life in most of Southeast Asia, except in the Red river valley where Chinese patterns prevailed. There, the advance guard of a new wave of invaders related to the Chinese in language and culture began to settle in the last few centuries B.C. Between the death of Ch'in Shih Huang-ti and the rise of the Han, the Chinese overlord of Canton seized the Red river basin, and in 111 B.C. it was incorporated into the Han domains as Annam, the "pacified south."

RISE OF INDIAN-INFLUENCED COMMERCIAL EMPIRES
(1ST TO 13TH CENTURY A.D.)

By 100 A.D. the lower Mekong basin was the heart of a flourishing Malayo-Polynesian commercial empire, known as Funan to the Chinese rulers who later received tribute from its court. After 100 A.D. the state of Champa grew up along the fertile but narrow coast between Funan and the Chinese-ruled Red river basin of Annam. In the Malay peninsula, small but strategically placed states like Kedah arose. The borders of Kedah, which lay at the northern entrance to the Malacca strait, marked the southeastern limit of the power of Funan. As early as the third century A.D. the soldiers of Funan crossed the Gulf of Siam and captured the isthmus of Kra, and at times Funanese influence may have extended as far west as the lower Irrawaddy valley.

The Malayo-Polynesian Mon people of the central Irrawaddy basin used land as well as sea routes to reach India in that period, while traders from India crossed the region on their way to and from China as early as the second century B.C. Consequently the Mon were familiar enough with Indian developments to make their later court chroniclers feel justified in cherishing the tradition that the Indian ruler Asoka Maurya sent Buddhist missionaries to Burma as well as to Ceylon. However, the first state in what is now Burma of which there is any definite record is a west-coast state of the fourth century A.D. At that time the Mon were already retreating before the incoming Pyu people, who were related in language and culture to the Chinese. The Pyu were leaving southern China in the face of the arrival of thousands of Chinese who were fleeing the nomad successors of the Han in the north.

Early in the sixth century the heartland of Funan in the Mekong basin fell to the Khmer, a Malayo-Polynesian people closely related to the Mon. Meanwhile small states were beginning to appear in the islands of Indonesia. Almost as soon as Funan was overthrown, Java and Sumatra began a rapid rise to prominence. The most advantageously situated state was Srivijaya in eastern Sumatra, alongside the Malacca and Sunda straits. The dynasty which arose in Srivijaya during the seventh century profited from the increase in Indian Ocean trade which followed the restoration of unity and peace in China and the Middle East by the rising T'ang dynasty and the expanding Muslims, and Sumatra replaced the Mekong as Southeast Asia's commercial center.

In the eighth century the Sailendra dynasty on Java began to contest Srivijaya's leadership. The Sailendra, who may have been descended from the vanquished rulers of Funan, even attacked the Khmer and Champa on the mainland. During the ninth century, after a Javanese rival took over Sailendra lands and married a Sailendra princess, the last Sailendra prince moved to Sumatra. There he married a Srivijaya princess and founded a new dynasty. Thereafter central and east Java were left to the rivals of the Sailendra until their commercial competition led the Sailendra to destroy their capital in 1006. Meanwhile, the Chola rulers of south India became impatient with Sailendra restrictions on trade through the Malacca and Sunda straits. In 1025 the Chola successfully raided the Sailendra capital. The Sailendra recovered from the blow and maintained themselves until late in the fourteenth century, but by the end of the thirteenth century their power was negligible. Independent rulers in the Malay peninsula, like the one who sent expeditions to Ceylon in 1247 and 1270, no longer acknowledged Sailendra control of the east side of the Malacca strait. Furthermore, in 1286 the new Singhasari rulers of Java weakened Sailendra's Sumatran power by setting up a puppet kingdom just north of the Sailendra capital.

THE ARRIVAL OF THE PYU, BURMESE, THAI, SHAN, AND LAO (4TH TO 13TH CENTURY A.D.)

At first the shift of Southeast Asia's external commerce from the Mekong to Sumatra did not seem to weaken the mainland peoples, who continued to resist the penetration of their homelands by the peoples of the south China hills. These newcomers were being squeezed out of south China by increasing numbers of Chinese settlers, who by Sung times made southern China even more populous and productive than the north.

In the Irrawaddy basin, the Mon began to be pressed not only by the Pyu but by the newly arriving Burmese during the seventh century. When the new Thai kingdom of Nanchao in Yunnan destroyed the Pyu capital in the ninth century, the Burmese took advantage of Pyu weakness to set up their own kingdom in the Irrawaddy valley at Pagan. In the eleventh century the Burmese seized the Mon capital and united the Irrawaddy valley. At that time and in later years many Mon left for neighboring areas, but not until eight hundred years later did the Mon who remained in Burma cease to struggle against Burmese control.

The Shan hills complex separated the Irrawaddy basin so markedly from the Menam-Mekong region that neither affected the other greatly before the twelfth and thirteenth centuries. The Khmer successors of Funan soon split into a northern and a southern half. The northern kingdom was located in the upper part of the Mekong valley; the southern established its capital at Angkor near the Great Lake. During the ninth to the eleventh century, Angkor extended its sway over the Korat plateau, the lower Menam basin, and the Malay peninsula down to the northern limit of Srivijaya influence. Yet the Khmer did not succeed in taking Champa. After a thousand years of Chinese rule, the Annamese, or Vietnamese, of the Red river valley won their independence in 939 A.D., and they too wanted Champa. Champa prudently sought China's good will as a counterweight to its neighbors' ambitions. It thereby survived until the fifteenth century, when the Ming turned their attention to the northern nomads instead of the Nanyang, the "southern seas" that had been of vital interest to China since T'ang times.

Southeast Asian rulers began to cultivate good relations with the Chinese rulers of Annam as early as the third century A.D., when both Funan and Champa started sending emissaries to the overlords of southern China. By the fifth century, rulers in the Malay peninsula, Sumatra, and Java were sending embassies to China; and Srivijaya and the Sailendra continued the custom. The wisdom of the policy was demonstrated in the early eleventh century, when Sung China befriended Champa against the expansive tendencies of China's former Vietnamese subjects, but gave Mataram on central Java no aid against the tribute-paying Sailendra. The northern and southern Khmer also sent tribute to Chinese rulers. However, the ninth-century Pyu received no aid from the declining T'ang against the Thai of Nanchao despite their protestations of homage, or for that matter against the Burmese, who established relations with China soon after uniting the Irrawaddy valley in the eleventh century. Between the ninth and thirteenth centuries, Shan, Thai, and Lao peoples left Nanchao for the Shan hills. In the hilly lands between the Irrawaddy and the Mekong they established petty states which were ready to take advantage of the confusion wrought in Southeast Asia by the Mongols in the latter thirteenth century.

MONGOL AND MING PRESSURES
(13TH TO 15TH CENTURY A.D.)

When Khubilai Khan and his successors replaced the Sung, they tried to solidify the extremely vague authority claimed by the Sung over the affairs of Vietnam, Champa, Angkor, Pagan, Srivijaya, and Java, on the basis of the tribute missions which these states had sent to China for centuries in return for trade privileges and formal recognition as rulers of their domains. Undoubtedly the Mongols were partly inspired by anxiety. They believed a Sung prince had escaped to the Nanyang, and they may have feared that he would use the flourishing Chinese merchant community there to rally the kingdoms of Southeast Asia to the Sung cause. Chinese traders had even entered the still almost cityless Philippines in the eleventh century.

Whatever fears the Mongols had were scarcely allayed by the near-unanimity with which the Southeast Asian kingdoms rebuffed Mongol invitations to continue tributary relations. Consequently between 1280 and 1300 the Mongols captured Pagan and dethroned its rulers; sent expeditions into the Shan hills to require the Shan chieftains to keep the peace;

raided Vietnam and Champa, forcing them to acknowledge Mongol over-lordship; received tribute from the Thai of the upper Menam, who had been joined by many of their fellow-Thai from Nanchao after the Mongols incorporated that kingdom into their domains in 1253; encouraged the Thai to harass Angkor; and launched an attack on Java. Only Srivijaya escaped, as did Ceylon, whose rulers had responded fairly amiably to the missions of Khubilai Khan.

The Singhasari ruler of much of Java became so alarmed at the news of the Mongol claims that he sought to rally rulers from the Malay penin-sula to Borneo against the Mongols, but he spent so much time and energy on alliance-building that he became vulnerable to rebellion. He was over-thrown just before the Mongols landed in 1293. The Mongols did not stay long. After they left, another dynasty, Majapahit, came to power instead of the discredited Singhasari line and extended its control to parts of Sumatra.

This great Mongol activity altered the political face of Southeast Asia, even though it was halted by the weakening of Mongol strength which accompanied the Chinese revolts that finally brought the Ming to power in 1368. The rise of Majapahit in Indonesia was one such change. In Burma the fall of Pagan allowed the Shan to seize central Burma and establish a capital at Ava, while the Mon set one up at Pegu. Not until 1539 and 1555 did the Burmese overthrow Pegu and Ava, reuniting the Irrawaddy basin. Mongol encouragement of the Thai led the Thai to seize the entire Menam basin from the Khmer. In 1350 the Thai founded the kingdom of Ayuthia, and after 1430 Khmer power waned in the face of Thai attacks. Angkor was abandoned a few decades later. The Thai, whose chronicles record that they were using cannon in 1411, also expanded into the northern Malay peninsula as Majapahit waned in the fifteenth century. Mongol encouragement of the Lao led to the formation of a separate Lao state in 1353. The Mongol weakening of Champa made it easier for the Vietnamese to conquer most of the country in the fourteenth and fifteenth centuries, despite an interruption caused by Ming seizure of Vietnam.

The early Ming were disposed to claim as much for China as had the Mongols. They gladly accepted tribute from Majapahit, Angkor, Ava, and Champa, believing the renewal of tributary relations to be a sign of their possession of the Mandate of Heaven. In 1405 they also received tribute from the new trading state of Malacca, whose founder was carving out an independent domain in the Malay peninsula. The Ming sent out naval expeditions to persuade more rulers to accept Chinese overlordship in re-turn for recognition and to assert China's authority and protection over Chinese overseas. One Ming expedition even intervened in eastern Su-matran affairs in 1407, seizing the port of Palembang from half-pirate, half-merchant Chinese who had recently taken it over, and bestowing it on more reliable Chinese. Nearer home, the Ming sought to weaken the

Shan chieftains by intervening in their quarrels. The Ming also tried to regain control of the Red river valley, but they only held Vietnam from 1407 to 1428. Altogether, the Ming made clear their view of Southeast Asia as a sphere of political as well as economic influence for China, before renewed nomad attacks forced them to turn their attention northward rather than southward.

The shift of official Chinese interest away from Southeast Asia did not lessen unofficial Chinese activity. Chinese from the coastal provinces of Kwangtung and Fukien continued to settle in every part of the area. Gradually they won control of much of its internal trade, although they continued to divide its external trade with merchants from India and the Middle East.

RENEWAL OF INDIAN INFLUENCE: ISLAM AND TRADE (13TH TO 16TH CENTURY A.D.)

By the fifteenth century, when the Chinese government ceased to focus much effort on Southeast Asia, Muslims ruled most of India. The consequent development and application of caste rules against overseas travel meant that the Indian merchants who came to Southeast Asia were Muslim rather than Hindu, as they had been a few centuries earlier. Thus Southeast Asian trade with India began to reinforce the Muslim influences which had first reached Southeast Asia shortly after the seventh-century conversion of the Arabs and Persians who sailed its seas to China. Whether Islam was more attractive when presented by Indians rather than by the less familiar Arabs, or whether Southeast Asians were attracted primarily by the mystical teachings of the Sufis who spread out along the trade routes used by their fellow Muslims in the late thirteenth century, northern Sumatra was already being converted to Islam by the time the Mongols invaded Java. In the next two centuries, rulers of seaport city-states from Arakan in western Burma through Malacca to eastern Java accepted the principles and practices of Islam to some degree.

When the fervently anti-Muslim Portuguese arrived in Southeast Asia shortly after 1500 A.D., they had less success against their Muslim competitors' faith than against their trade. The Portuguese and their Dutch successors could only propagate Christianity east of Borneo. Late in the sixteenth century the Spaniards found that many people in Mindanao in the southern Philippines had already been won to Islam by zealous traders. Even the people of Champa turned Muslim by the time their state fell to Vietnam. Their descendants in Vietnam and Cambodia are still the only sizable body of Muslims on the mainland east of Arakan. Between Arakan and Champa, in Burma, Thailand, Laos, and Cambodia of today, earlier formal professions of Hinduism and Mahayana Buddhism had given way to the simpler doctrines of Theravada Buddhism in the twelfth and thirteenth centuries. Neither Islam nor Christianity, which was introduced by the western Europeans who gradually replaced Indians in the external trade of the mainland after 1500, made much headway against Theravada Buddhism, which came to mainland Southeast Asia from Ceylon.

Thus the Southeast Asia of the sixteenth century presented a complex picture. In the Red river valley and along the coast to the south, recently taken from Champa, the Vietnamese upheld the traditions they had learned from China. Outside Vietnam, Southeast Asian societies consisted essentially of court and countryside, with a sprinkling of Chinese and other resident merchants. In the Mekong valley, the Lao (cousins to the Thai) had established small states. In the hills between the Lao and the Vietnamese lived tribes who had fled there to escape the privilege of being ruled by anyone, Chinese, Vietnamese, or Lao. The people of the Shan hills, who were also kin to the Thai, were acquiring a knowledge of Buddhism and the arts of statecraft from the Thai and Burmese to the south. The Irrawaddy basin was still divided between Burmese and Mon, with the Mon currently free from Burmese rule. A variety of tribes lived in the hills between the Irrawaddy and the Brahmaputra. Small trading states, in which Islam was gaining converts, existed in the coastal district of Arakan and on the western coast of the narrow strip of land between the Bay of Bengal and the Gulf of Siam. The Thai held the Menam basin and part of the Korat plateau; the Khmer still ruled the lower Mekong valley. The Thai had driven the Khmer from Angkor, but the Vietnamese were just on the verge of entering the Mekong delta.

In the Malay peninsula the rulers of the Malay states were free from Sumatran and Javanese overlordship. The last great Javanese empire, Majapahit, had long since passed its prime. Muslim rulers in northern Sumatra and the Malay peninsula were attempting to enforce Islam in the countryside, but in most of Java and in its immediate neighbors like Madura and Bali, the court cults of earlier years still held sway. However, both Indian and Islamic influences were scarce in the islands northeast of Java—notably in Borneo, where the descendants of the Chinese soldiers left behind by the Mongol expedition of 1292 claimed to have introduced the first rudiments of civilization. Unified rule was lacking in the Malay peninsula and the islands. These divisions probably made it easier for Europeans to establish themselves in the Malay peninsula, Indonesia, and the Philippines than on the mainland, where the late sixteenth century saw a resurgence of strength as the Burmese reunified the Irrawaddy valley and drove eastward toward the Thai, while the Vietnamese expanded into the Mekong delta at Khmer expense.

Thought-Patterns and Social Organization:
The Roles of Hinduism, Buddhism, and Islam

HINDUISM AND MAHAYANA BUDDHISM AS COURT CULTS

Two thousand years ago, when Indian travelers and traders began to bring some knowledge of Hinduism and Mahayana Buddhism to Southeast Asia, its societies were made up of the metal-using Malayo-Polynesians and the earlier Veddoid peoples whom they had absorbed. These societies were organized into small rice-growing village communities which depended on mutual cooperation to maintain the terraces (in hilly regions) and dikes (in river valleys) that kept the rice fields filled with the life-giving water from the rains or the overflowing rivers. Most of these societies recognized descent and inheritance through the female rather than the male line, like some of the early inhabitants of Ceylon and probably of India, and like many African societies.

The people of early Southeast Asia did not possess a highly differentiated social structure, and their lives were not yet complicated by the rise of cities. However, they did recognize leaders, who were regarded as maintainers of harmony between human society and the powers of nature. This attitude toward the leader somewhat resembled the expectation of the Chinese, from whom came much of the early cultural inspiration of Southeast Asia, that the emperor should influence those below him and please Heaven above him by the propriety of his behavior. The Southeast Asians also revered natural forces and the spirits of their ancestors, as did the Chinese. Still, they were not so powerfully drawn to Chinese ways that they were prepared to ignore the equally sophisticated culture of India once they became acquainted with it. In the age of Rome and the Han, both Southeast Asian and Indian merchants began to ply back and forth regularly along the trade routes from China to the Middle East, carrying ideas as well as goods. The decline of Rome increased Indian interest in Southeast Asian trade; the acceptance of Indian religious and literary traditions increased Southeast Asian interest in India.

The Southeast Asians of two thousand years ago discovered that the Indians also revered their ancestors and the powers of nature (as manifestations of ultimate reality). In addition, at least among Hindus, the Indians regarded their "leaders," the Kshatriyas, as the upholders of the laws by which the deities expected men and women to live. Moreover, the Hindu Indians still relied on the incantations and sacrifices of the priestly Brahmins to maintain the ruler's position as a god-ruler, a deity incarnate in human form. In this, the Indian states differed markedly from the Chinese empire, whose rulers were increasingly relying for support on the Confucian literati, with their tendency to concentrate on human affairs. The Hindu belief that all phenomena were merely illusory appearances also differed significantly from the Chinese belief in the reality of the visible universe. In Southeast Asia, the Hindu system with its greater recognition of the ruler's spiritual or even magical functions seems simply to have been more suited as a vehicle of civilization than the Chinese system. Since Southeast Asians were not yet literate or organized into large societies, they had little use for bureaucracies in the Chinese fashion, but they did regard their leaders as mediators between the human and spirit worlds. In addition, Southeast Asian rulers seem to have found Indian political theory, with its emphasis on the absolute authority of the god-ruler, more attractive than the Chinese concept of an emperor whose delegation of authority to the educated somewhat limited his personal power. Moreover, the doctrine of karma, with its clear indication that every action has consequences, offered a readily understood sanction for human conduct.

In India, with its host of competing states constantly jostling each other, the god-ruler ordinarily had to spend much time and energy on strictly human matters like administration and foreign affairs. However, in early Southeast Asia, with its small and widely separated communities, local rulers were generally free to concentrate on improving their relationship with the spirit world through elaborate, costly, time-consuming rituals. Not till later did they build defensive walls around their capitals, gather armies, and make war; and when they did begin to fight their neighbors, they measured success and failure in terms of prestige and the simple display of power at least as much as in terms of economic or territorial gain. In many ways they resembled their contemporaries in Africa south of the Sahara. Most African rulers were left relatively free for far longer than Southeast Asian rulers to concentrate on ritual mediation between their people and the forces of the natural world, for population pressure built up less rapidly in economies not based on intensive irrigated agriculture.

Southeast Asian rulers began wanting to use written records to keep track of their expanding peoples early in the Christian era, but it was several centuries later that African rulers in the grasslands south of the Sahara began to feel the need of introducing written records, or of establishing a bond of union which could bring together people from many bloodlines. Not until after 1000 A.D. did royal courts in the West African grasslands begin to adopt the Islamic religious and cultural patterns which Muslim Middle Eastern traders had made familiar in both western and eastern Africa for several centuries, somewhat as Southeast Asian rulers had earlier adopted Hindu and Mahayana Buddhist religious and cultural patterns which Indian traders had made familiar in Southeast Asia for several centuries. As late as the nineteenth century, most East African governments (other than those in the Arab-founded coastal cities) still preferred to depend on the trained memories of selected persons rather than make the changeover to the use of written records. Their populations were small enough to make this feasible, and they still found the time-honored rituals satisfactory enough not to wish to exchange them for the Muslim and Christian religions of the Arabs and Europeans with whom they traded. Only the rulers of the Ethiopian plateau, whose trade with the Middle East antedated the Christian era, had a literate tradition older than that of any Southeast Asian state.

As trade grew between the merchants and rulers of India and Southeast Asia, the self-proclaimed god-rulers of Southeast Asia eagerly welcomed the assistance of Indian Brahmins (not all of whom were freely entitled to claim that status in India) in fulfilling their subjects' expectation that their behavior would be ritually correct enough to ensure the continuance of the natural rhythm of the universe. The astrologers who are the spiritual if not lineal descendants of the Brahmins still advise heads of government from Burma to Indonesia concerning propitious times to inaugurate new policies and dedicate new buildings. The founders of Funan and Champa were only the forerunners of a host of rulers who used Hindu rites to enhance their prestige among their own subjects and among other rulers for more than a thousand years.

Mahayana Buddhist doctrines, which shared with Hinduism the idea that every act which indicates one's acceptance of the world as real will result in one's being born into the world again, also came to be used as a prop to Southeast Asian thrones. Though the Mahayana Buddhists lacked a hereditary priesthood, their monks could also serve as counselors to rulers. Moreover, in India they had already developed the theory that the genuinely good ruler must have derived the ability to rule well from being a manifestation of one of the bodhisattvas, the beings whom they believed had achieved readiness to enter the state of nirvana but chose to remain in the world to aid others to reach it also.

In Southeast Asian states whose rulers depended on Hindu rites to maintain their authority, the ruler was regarded as a manifestation of one of the major deities, usually Vishnu the creator or Siva the destroyer. In states whose rulers turned to Mahayana teachings the ruler was regarded as a reincarnation of a leading bodhisattva. (When Khubilai Khan, the Mongol ruler of China, formally proclaimed that he was a reincarnation of the Jina-Buddha, the Singhasari ruler of Java declared himself a reincarnation of the Bhairava-Buddha, probably in order to counteract any influence which Khubilai Khan's move might have in Southeast Asia and to establish a basis for an anti-Mongol alliance.) Over the centuries, some dynasties switched back and forth between Mahayana and Hindu cults several times, as various calamities seemed to indicate that the current form of royal ritual was displeasing to the deities, or as the successes of a ruler who followed some other cult seemed to display its greater efficacy.

It made little difference to the rice-growing peasants in the villages which cult their rulers followed. They cared only that the rhythm of the universe was not disrupted. As long as their rulers were visibly exerting themselves to maintain that rhythm through increasingly complex ritual observances, the particular cult the rulers followed was of no great importance to the peasants. In fact, the various cults were probably almost indistinguishable to untutored peasants. All of the cults required the building of large temple-shrines, of which the greatest remaining examples are Angkor Wat, raised in Cambodia by the Khmer for a ruler who was believed to be an incarnation of Vishnu, and Borobudur, raised in Java by the Sailendra for a ruler who was believed to be a bodhisattva. While the rulers lived, they worshiped at these shrines; when the rulers died, they were buried in the same shrines, to be worshiped by their successors in an intricate mixture of ancestor worship and the Hindu or Mahayana cult to which they belonged. As long as the rhythm of the universe continued, the peasants' chief concern with their rulers' cults was the requirement that they give up a portion of their produce and their time to supply the needs of those who built and maintained the temple-shrines.

Little effort seems to have been made to carry the teachings of any of the court cults to the villagers. The average villager continued to worship the spirits of his or her ancestors and the familiar nature deities as before. Even the ordinary resident of the capital was not much affected by the religion of the court. The artisans or the laborers helped build the palace or the temple, but they did not worship in the shrine; they and their families merely watched the ceremonial processions which periodically went back and forth between shrine and palace. Not until the missionaries of Theravada Buddhism and Islam arrived in Southeast Asia were either villagers or townspeople drawn into active participation in a religious community which included people in distant villages and cities as well as those they knew personally. Nevertheless, some features of the court cults filtered down into the lives of the commoners, as demonstrated by the frequent invocation of the aid of Siva at rice-planting time in the Malay peninsula even today.

POLITICAL AND ECONOMIC ORGANIZATION IN THE COMMERCIAL EMPIRES

In the Southeast Asian states of the early Christian era, the court relied on inspirations which were largely of Indian origin, while outside the court the beliefs and practices of former days continued almost unchanged. The court looked upward and outward; the rest of society did not. The closest tie between court and countryside was the peasant's acceptance of an obligation to furnish labor and produce so that the court could carry on its rituals and build its temple-shrines. Even in the capital city, the ordinary resident merely furnished labor, manufactures, and an appreciative audience to the court. The capital was normally the only important city in a traditional Southeast Asian kingdom, since its major purpose was to maintain the court and the court cult. It was neither an economic nor an administrative center, to the degree that cities in older and more populous states were.

Administratively, the court needed only a rudimentary governmental organization to collect the produce and enforce the labor service needed to maintain the court. The villages were largely self-governing, and there was little reason to fight over land in a relatively unpopulated region. Before Europeans arrived, the Thai and the Vietnamese were the only Southeast Asian peoples to develop a central administration in which specific duties were assigned to specific ministers; the rest continued to use royal councils in which several ministers' responsibilities might overlap. The Vietnamese learned the arts of government during the thousand years the Chinese ruled them; the Thai ruled in Yunnan on the borders of China for several centuries before the Mongol onslaught impelled them southward to the Shan hills and the upper Menam and Mekong valleys.

Economically, almost all Southeast Asians continued to till the soil, while most of the remaining few became artisans. In the earlier and simpler days before the rise of courts, trade with the outside world was carried on by the people themselves at least as much as by outsiders, and local trade was carried on primarily by local people. Later, external commerce became concentrated around the courts, which used foreign trade to supply themselves with luxury goods. The courts did not wish to take time from their religio-political activities to be active in commerce. In this, they contrasted with the courts of Africa south of the Sahara. African rulers were almost always interested enough in the revenues to be gained from trade to be willing to devote time and attention to its control, and to confine foreign traders' activities primarily to external commerce. However, Southeast Asian courts from Burma to Java let external trade fall into the hands of the foreign merchants—Chinese, Indians, and Middle Easterners—who brought in the goods they wanted. As time passed, these foreign merchants also came to dominate local trade. They had a wider commercial network on which to draw for goods and markets than local merchants had, and local merchants received no real encouragement from the rulers. The rulers let foreign merchants live by their own laws in the capitals and in such lesser cities as existed. The rulers did not interfere with their activities in the city or the countryside as long as desired foreign luxuries were furnished to the court; the foreign merchants used their connections with the world outside Southeast Asia to win increasing control over the internal as well as the external commerce of the region. Nevertheless, the economic power of foreign merchants was never as complete in the Malay peninsula and Indonesia, with their strong seagoing traditions, as it came to be on the mainland, where rice-growing absorbed the time and energy of most of the people.

The seizure of commercial leadership in Southeast Asia by outsiders began by the seventh century A.D., as Muslim, Chola, and T'ang merchants flocked increasingly to each other's ports by way of Southeast Asia. By the time the Portuguese arrived in the sixteenth century, much if not most of the region's trade was carried on by Arabs, Indians, and most particularly Chinese, under a system resembling the capitulatory regime of the nineteenth-century Ottoman empire. As in the Ottoman empire, the permission given foreign merchants to compete on the same terms as local merchants gave them an actual advantage because of their wider commercial networks. Moreover, the foreign traders' governments occasionally intervened on their behalf in a pre-gunboat prototype of gunboat diplomacy, as the Cholas and the early Ming did. This state of affairs was accepted without question, for the notion of a sovereign territorial state in which all should share the same cultural outlook, loyalties, and rules of behavior was not yet part of the thinking of Southeast Asians. As long as their needs were supplied, they did not care that individuals whose final cultural and political allegiance lay elsewhere were supplying them.

In economic and political as in religious life, the view of most Southeast Asians traditionally encompassed the village and the court, each of which had little to do with the other. Even after the religious upheavals of the twelfth century onward, when Theravada Buddhism and Islam not only replaced Mahayana Buddhism and Hinduism in the courts but entered the life of the villages as well, economic life continued to follow the familiar pattern of indigenous villagers, nonindigenous merchants, and indigenous court. Rulers continued to rely on their religious and social prestige to maintain their subjects' loyalty, rather than on the rationality and efficiency of their administrations. The average ruler cared about efficiency only in the army, which had to be competent to preserve the state from rebellion or invasion. Rebellions were rare except where there were antagonisms between earlier and later settlers, as there were between Mon and Burmese, but invasions became frequent as each court in turn sought to enhance its prestige at its neighbors' expense.

POLITICAL STRUCTURE IN VIETNAM

Vietnam was the one striking exception to the general religious, economic, and political pattern just outlined. From 208 B.C. to 939 A.D. the Red river valley was ruled by Chinese who at first contented themselves with ruling through local leaders. However, they imposed their newly

developed bureaucratic system of government after a briefly successful
rebellion led by the Trung sisters in 40 A.D. For the next nine centuries
Vietnam was ruled according to Confucian ideas. Three short-lived attempts were made to throw off Chinese domination in the sixth century
A.D., but the Vietnamese did not win independence until 939, after the
fall of the T'ang.

By 939 A.D. the Vietnamese were accustomed to dealing with the relations of heaven, earth, and human society through a blend of Confucian, Mahayana Buddhist, and local beliefs and practices, much as the
Koreans amalgamated Confucianism, Buddhism, and local cults under
somewhat similar circumstances. The Vietnamese were as accustomed
as the Koreans were to using the Chinese written characters, which were
more suited to the monosyllabic Vietnamese language than to the poly-
syllabic Korean tongue. The Vietnamese were also used to studying the
Confucian classics in order to pass through a centrally administered examination system into high public office. After they achieved independence from China, they accepted the Confucian system of governing
through enlightened men who would use persuasion rather than force
whenever possible; and they applied the Confucian principle of respect
for worth rather than birth more fully than the Koreans. So successfully
were the Vietnamese welded into a united people, capable of using
Chinese ideas and techniques to throw off Chinese rule (paralleling recent
uses of Western ideas and techniques to end Western control in many
countries), that the teachings of Islam and Theravada Buddhism did not
attract them in later years. Instead they retained their Chinese-inspired
religious and political system intact until the nineteenth century, when
the French shattered their belief that the system could maintain their independence from outside control.

THERAVADA BUDDHISM AND SOCIAL STRUCTURE
IN MAINLAND SOUTHEAST ASIA

The villagers of the Irrawaddy, Menam, and lower Mekong valleys
had few contacts with their rulers' courts during the first ten centuries
A.D., whether they were of the older Mon-Khmer group or newcomers
like the Burmese, who adopted the Mon written language, religious beliefs, and governmental methods. Still, what knowledge they did gain of
the court cults prepared them by the eleventh or twelfth century to absorb a more sophisticated set of religious concepts than the animistic
nature worship they still followed.

Disorders in twelfth-century Burma led three Buddhist monks (two
of them Mon) to leave the Burmese court and seek safety in Ceylon.
Their Sinhalese hosts persuaded them that everyone, not just a favored
few, could leave the cycle of rebirths behind by accumulating merit and

eventually entering the monastic life. The three became convinced that the Theravada insistence that everyone must work out his or her own release offered more hope than the Mahayana reliance on bodhisattvas for aid. When they returned to Burma, they began to propagate the Theravada doctrines zealously, not only in the court but among the people. (It is difficult to determine the relation between the zeal of the two Mon monks to enable as many as possible to escape the troubled world and the fact that the Burmese had just declared their cultural independence of the Mon by putting their written records into their own language.) So effective was their preaching that within a hundred years almost all the Burmese, Mon, and Khmer villagers and townspeople of the Irrawaddy, Menam, and Mekong valleys were converted. The Thai peoples who entered Southeast Asia in large numbers after the Mongol conquest of Nanchao in 1253 also adhered to Theravada Buddhism, which the Mon of the lower Menam taught them along with the phonetic script that the Mon and Khmer had originally adapted from Indian sources.

The acceptance of Theravada Buddhism in mainland Southeast Asia tended to reinforce the traditional economic and social independence of women, even though it was widely assumed that only men could actually attain final release. This seeming paradox was related to family patterns, which did not stress father-son ties above all others. Inheritance might be through the mother or through both parents, and most sons and daughters left their parents and founded new homes when they married. Rarely did more than one son or daughter remain at home after marriage to support the parents as they grew old.

Theravada Buddhism simply strengthened the previous tendency of men to care little about attempting to control what women did. Since every man had to win his own release, women's actions could not affect his attainment of release. Men began to concentrate so much on achieving the release which they alone could win that they paid even less attention than before to questions of family relationships and commercial activity. Boys attended monastery schools, which sprang up from the Chindwin to the Mekong as men who chose the monastic life settled down in small centers in or near villages, like the monks of Ceylon. As the boys grew to manhood they often took vows themselves for a while, though few remained permanently in a monastery. Girls—ineligible for immediate salvation—were left to learn how to bargain and to run a household from their mothers. When they married, they made far more daily decisions in the households they set up than a young wife could ordinarily hope to do in the larger patrilineal families of China, India, or the Middle East.

People in the West have tended to believe that individualism is closely linked to economic growth. Theravada Buddhism is highly individualistic in that it teaches that everyone must achieve his or her own release. Yet most people in Theravada Buddhist mainland Southeast Asia have cared little about amassing riches. To acquire wealth, it was necessary to become involved with the world, but everyone's goal was to withdraw from the world so as to win release from the cycle of rebirths. Even the building of shrines and monasteries, a highly meritorious activity in the Theravada scale of values, was left almost entirely to the rulers. It was rarely done by individual donors like those whose portraits adorn many European churches. In Southeast Asia, individualism was embedded in a system of thought that regarded mundane affairs as ultimately insignificant and therefore left the individual free because his or her actions did not matter. Individualism therefore did not encourage a striving for worldly achievement, as it did in the context of Semitic monotheism, with its belief that earthly happenings did possess some measure of importance in the divine plan. By discouraging involvement in worldly affairs, Theravada Buddhism may actually have helped outsiders like the Chinese to acquire control of the commerce of mainland Southeast Asia between the twelfth and fifteenth centuries. If so, then Theravada Buddhism also reinforced the tendency of the societies of mainland Southeast Asia to be divided into a small upper class concentrated around the ruler and a large lower class clustered in the villages.

ISLAM AND SOCIAL STRUCTURE IN THE
MALAY PENINSULA AND THE ISLANDS

Theravada Buddhism became the religion of the cities and villages of mainland Southeast Asia, but it scarcely touched the shifting cultivators in the hills between the valleys, few of whom had anything to do with the outside world. Similarly, in the Malay peninsula and the islands, neither the missionaries of Islam nor the propagators of the earlier court cults had much effect on religious life outside the settled agricultural areas before the Europeans came. Even the court cults were unknown in the Philippines, which lacked elaborate courts or any written records other than the accounts of the Chinese merchants who began to reside there in Sung times. When the Spaniards arrived in the Philippines in the sixteenth century, tribal organization and animistic beliefs still held sway, except in the islands nearest Indonesia.

The strategic location of the Malay peninsula and Indonesia on the main trade routes between the Indian Ocean and the South China Sea contributed to the early appearance of Indian-inspired courts and court cults, which eventually led to a division of labor between indigenous ruling class, nonindigenous merchants, and indigenous peasant and laboring class which corresponded closely to that on the mainland. However, the Chinese did not become as numerous in relation to the Indian and Arab communities in the Malay peninsula and Indonesia as they became in most of the mainland during the twelfth to the fifteenth century.

Most of the Indian merchants in the Malay peninsula and Indonesia came from Mahayana Buddhist Pala-ruled Bengal or from Hindu regions like Gujerat and the Chola empire, not from the land of the Sinhalese whose longstanding ties with Burma formed the background for the introduction of Theravada Buddhism to the mainland in the twelfth century. After the twelfth to the fourteenth century, when Muslims captured Bengal, Gujerat, and most of the Chola lands, the rulers of the Malayan and Sumatran principalities discovered that most of the traders who came to their ports were Muslims. Soon these rulers began to patronize Islam, and some even adopted its creed and tried to propagate it among their subjects. Still, Islam remained a religion of the ports for many years.

To the rulers who adopted Islam, conversion was largely a means of encouraging trade. To the villagers of the coast and the interior who eventually accepted it also, it gave a more satisfactory explanation of the universe than simple animism or the little they understood of the court cults. Sufi mysticism rather than Sunni orthodoxy struck the deepest response among ordinary Malays and Indonesians, whose slight knowledge of Indian religion had already accustomed them to a goal of absorption into the ultimate through self-discipline. The Sharia law of the Quran and Sunna was almost entirely ignored. Pork was shunned, which set the pork-eating Chinese apart from Malays and Indonesians almost as thoroughly as the use of beef set Muslims apart in Hindu India. (Pork-eating also separated the Chinese from the people of the mainland after the adoption of Theravada Buddhism led to widespread disapproval of the use of any flesh other than fish, which could be believed to have died naturally when taken from the water rather than deliberately killed for food.) However, Muslim Malay and Indonesian women continued to inherit equally with men, and they went about unhampered by most of the prohibitions which restricted Middle Eastern women. In at least one large Muslim Malay group, family relationships are still organized around the mother-child relationship despite the clear command of the Sharia to place the father-son tie first.

In adopting Islam, Malays and Indonesians ignored what did not harmonize with their established patttterns of belief and action as completely as the Chinese did when they adapted Buddhism to their preconceptions. The aspect of Islam that appealed to Malays and Indonesians was the spiritual exaltation of the individual whose mystical ecstasies enable him or her to escape from the mundane for a time, rather than the duty of the member of the community to obey unquestioningly the rules which have been divinely ordained for it. Only those most deeply involved with Indian and Arab Muslim merchants, like the small Javanese merchant community or the people of Acheh in northern Sumatra, became accustomed to the actual practice of such basic Islamic rituals as the five daily prayers. The pilgrimage to Mecca was popular among those who could afford it, but many who professed to be Muslims did not carry out the duties of prayer, alms, and fasting as devoutly as ordinary Muslims in India or the Middle East.

Even after the acceptance of Islam, Indian-inspired habits of thought persisted with respect to such matters as the role of the ruler. Most Malays and Indonesians continued to regard rulers as quasi-divinities concerned with spiritual matters, rather than as human beings enforcing God's commands on their fellows. This attitude probably contributed to the later failure of many rulers and their subjects to object vigorously to the establishment of indirect forms of European control, as long as the right to profess Islam was not seriously challenged.

The process of gradual (and partial) Islamicization did not start until the conversion of Acheh late in the thirteenth century. The Malays began to accept Islam shortly afterward. After the founding of Malacca in about 1401, the tempo of Islamicization speeded up noticeably. However, the first significant conversions to Islam in northern Java came less than a generation before the Portuguese seized Malacca in 1511. In the spice-growing islands of the Moluccas, only a few years separated the first adoptions of Islam from the sixteenth-century Portuguese missionary efforts. Thus the blending of Islam with Indian and local elements in the Malay peninsula and the islands took place side by side with European activity. This differed strongly from the blending of Theravada Buddhism with Indian, Mon-Khmer, and Burmese-Thai-Shan-Lao elements on the mainland, which not only began two centuries before the Europeans arrived in Southeast Asia but in addition was not much affected by them until the seventeenth and eighteenth centuries.

10

THE MODERN ERA: MAINLAND SOUTHEAST ASIA

Southeast Asians and Europeans (1500–1845)

The earliest Europeans in Southeast Asian waters were merchants and missionaries like the Polo family and the Franciscan friars, who used the sea route between China and the Middle East during the Mongol era. However, the first to reach the region under their own sail were the Portuguese. Once they reached India, the Portuguese decided to cut off the trade of their Arab and Indian Muslim rivals by making the Indian Ocean a Portuguese lake. Using Goa in western India as their headquarters, the Portuguese quickly captured the entrances to the Atlantic, the Red Sea, the Persian Gulf, the Bay of Bengal, and the Malacca strait.

By 1511, thirteen years after their first arrival in India, the Portuguese held Mozambique, Socotra, Hormuz, and Malacca, as well as Goa, and in 1517 they stationed a garrison at Colombo in Ceylon. To retain Malacca they had to fight its exiled sultan and the Achinese, but they weathered all attacks and were soon sending ships from Malacca to Burma, Ayuthia (the Thai capital on the Menam), Java, and the spice islands of the Moluccas. When Magellan's expedition reached the Moluccas in 1521, Spanish and Portuguese interests clashed. Soon fighting broke out, but Spanish reinforcements came too late, for they had to cross the Pacific from newly seized Mexico. By 1530 the Portuguese forced the Spaniards to agree to stay away from the Moluccas. Thereafter, Spanish efforts were concentrated on the Philippines, which they brought under their control after 1565.

The Portuguese soon saw that Muslim missionary successes were blocking peaceful expansion of Portuguese trade in Java. Religious as well as commercial considerations motivated both Javanese and Portuguese merchants. The Javanese favored the Arabs and Indians; the Portuguese wanted to seize the trade of the island from Muslim hands. Therefore, the Portuguese, who had already introduced Christianity to the few ports they controlled, supported missionary work on Java. They had little success. Instead of Christian converts, Muslim rulers like those of Bantam in the west and Mataram in the center took the lead in Javanese affairs. The Portuguese also supported Jesuit missionaries in the eastern islands, but many of their converts turned to Islam later in the century when Portuguese rapacity led the islanders to rebel against Portuguese rule.

The Portuguese won power in the Moluccas by aiding rival claimants to the thrones of the petty principalities of the islands. They then negotiated binding commercial and military treaties with those of their protégés who succeeded. Often they also proceeded to take whatever they wanted from the ordinary people, who feared to refuse these powerful allies of their rulers.

By the end of the sixteenth century, Portuguese traders from Malacca traded in Ayuthia, Cambodia, the Moluccas, Sulawesi (Celebes), and Kalimantan (Borneo), but Java and Sumatra were still largely closed to them. Along the Burma coast from Arakan to Tenasserim below the mouth of the Salween, the Portuguese name was more renowned for piracy than for trade. As one Portuguese observer ruefully commented, his countrymen might have been masters of the world if they could have been masters of themselves. Instead they tended to seek their individual fortunes regardless of the effect of their acts on future relations between Portuguese and Asians. The Portuguese soon became so generally hated that only their continued control of Malacca, Colombo, Goa, Hormuz, Socotra, and Mozambique enabled them to continue to trade in Southeast Asia. When the more capable seamen of the Netherlands and England entered the Indian Ocean in the seventeenth century, the Portuguese were quickly expelled from every outpost they had held between Goa, the remote eastern half of Timor near Australia, and Macao.

Despite the efforts of the Portuguese, most of mainland Southeast Asia remained almost unconscious of the arrival of Europeans, except as rulers in Burma, Ayuthia, and Vietnam purchased arms and hired mercenaries from them to use in their wars. Portuguese soldiers helped the Burmese unify the Irrawaddy valley between 1535 and 1555, conquer the Shan states, and attack Ayuthia in the lower Menam valley. Other Portuguese mercenaries manned the artillery of Ayuthia as it sought hegemony along the upper Menam, which had customarily paid homage either to Burma or to the Lao ruler at Luang Prabang. The Burmese held the capital of Ayuthia from 1570 to 1585, but ten years later the

Thai devastated the Irrawaddy delta in retaliation. Before entering Burma the Thai secured their flanks by attacking Cambodia in 1594 and carrying off Cambodian villagers to be settled in the Menam basin, just as the Burmese had transplanted villagers from the Menam to the Irrawaddy to replace those killed in the bloody fighting of 1535 to 1555.

The unity of Burma collapsed after 1595. Not only the Thai but also the Arakanese and the Portuguese raided the Irrawaddy delta, while warring chieftains vied for control elsewhere until the interior was reunited in 1610. Portuguese in the service of Ayuthia defended Tenasserim from the resurgent Burmese in 1614, but in 1615 Burma reasserted its overlordship of the upper Menam valley. Then many of the Mon left the lower Irrawaddy for the Menam after an unsuccessful rebellion. Rather than try to recapture them by a war on Ayuthia, the Burmese in 1635 withdrew to Ava four hundred miles upstream. The once fertile and populous delta became a land of weeds and swamps, and Burmese-Western intercourse slowed almost to a halt.

When the Manchu came to power in China, they sent an expedition into Burma in 1662 to seize the last Ming claimant to the imperial throne. While the Burmese were distracted, Ayuthia retook the upper Menam, but only for two years. Ayuthia did not regain the upper Menam again until 1727, after the Burmese dynasty had been weakened by strife over the succession to the throne.

By the late seventeenth century, Ayuthia had resident merchant communities from China, the Malay peninsula, Burma, Cambodia, Laos, Vietnam, Portugal, France, England, and the Dutch Republic. There were also a few Japanese, left stranded by the seclusion edicts of the Tokugawa shogunate. During the 1680s Ayuthia flirted with France, but after 1707 it renewed an old interest in Laotian affairs in the hope of forestalling Vietnamese interest in the central Mekong. (In 1707, after several generations of unity and independence, the Lao split into two kingdoms, one ruled from Luang Prabang in the north and the other from Vientiane farther south.) Ayuthia also interested itself in Cambodia, which still controlled much of the lower Mekong although it had lost most of the delta to the expanding Vietnamese.

Vietnamese had been settling in the fertile Mekong delta since the generation after the conquest of Champa in 1471. Late in the sixteenth century the Vietnamese in the south split off from the government in the north. At first the southern leaders claimed that they merely sought to restore authority to the Vietnamese emperor, who was under the control of a powerful northern family, but in 1600 the southern regime repudiated the powerless emperor and sought Chinese recognition, in vain. The Vietnamese of the south used Portuguese weapons against the northerners, who attacked them constantly from 1620 to 1674. The northerners promptly began trading with the Dutch. When the northerners finally gave up, the southerners turned on the Cambodians and in the next fifty years pushed the eastern border of Cambodia inland almost to its present location. Then the balance of forces underwent another rapid series of changes.

In 1740 the remaining Mon in the Irrawaddy delta freed themselves from Ava, and in 1752 used French weapons to capture Ava; but in 1754 the founder of a new Burmese dynasty drove them from Ava, won promises of allegiance from the Shan chiefs, and captured the delta. Many Mon leaders fled to Ayuthia, which led the Burmese to capture and destroy its capital in 1767 and to fight all the way to Luang Prabang. The unrest which these events caused among the tribes along the borders of southern China roused the Ch'ing to invade Burma in 1766. The Burmese fought them to a standstill. In 1770 the Ch'ing agreed to withdraw and to reopen trade if the Burmese would send tribute missions to Peking every ten years.

The struggle with Peking exhausted Burma's resources, enabling the Thai to expel the Burmese from the lower Menam valley and the Korat plateau in 1768. During the next decade the Thai placed a friendly ruler on the Cambodian throne in place of a pro-Vietnamese candidate, retook the upper Menam, conquered Vientiane, and won the homage of Luang Prabang. They also founded a new capital, Bangkok, where a new dynasty ascended the throne of the kingdom, then called Siam, in 1782.

Another new ruler came to power in Burma in 1782. His conquest of Arakan in 1784 brought his forces to the border of British-controlled Bengal. In 1785 he tried to take Siam, beginning with the Thai holdings in the northern Malay peninsula. The Thai defeated his men, recovered their Malay provinces, and forced the sultans of Kedah and three other Muslim Malay states to acknowledge their overlordship. The Burmese also tried unsuccessfully to take the upper Menam valley. They made no more territorial gains until 1822, when their seizure of Assam north of Bengal precipitated the British East India Company's decision to attack the kingdom of Ava.

While Burma was overextending itself in this way, Vietnam was being reunified. A rebellion in the south in 1773 forced the southern ruler to flee. He sought French aid and received some volunteer military and naval advisers. The southern rebels conquered the north by 1788, but lost the Mekong delta to the former southern ruler with his French advisers. The southern ruler then conquered the north in 1802, dethroned the long-powerless emperor, and (after two centuries) won Chinese recognition in 1803.

During the Vietnamese reunification, Bangkok annexed two western Cambodian provinces. Once Vietnam was united, Cambodia prudently began sending tribute to both its powerful neighbors, Siam and Vietnam. In 1812 Cambodia accepted a large Vietnamese garrison in place of the small Siamese force in the capital of Phnom Penh. Siam did not regain influence in Cambodia until 1841, after the Vietnamese won hatred by trying to annex the whole state. After four years of fighting each other, Siam and Vietnam agreed to protect Cambodia jointly. This arrangement later became an entering wedge for the French as they sought control of the Mekong basin.

The Siamese did not confine their attention to Cambodia. In 1828 the tributary state of Vientiane was made a province in retaliation for its ruler's attempt to reject allegiance to Bangkok. The Vientiane ruler fled to Hue, the Vietnamese capital, to seek aid, but when he tried to return to Vientiane, he was betrayed by a Lao prince and seized by the Siamese. The Vietnamese promptly captured the betrayer, executed him at Hue, and annexed his lands. However, Vietnam refused to accept tribute from Luang Prabang when it was offered in 1831 and 1833 in an attempt to win support against Siam. Since Vietnam and Siam were then at war over Cambodia, the Hue government apparently felt one fighting front was enough.

By the 1840s, Vietnamese influence on the central and upper Mekong was slight, while Siamese power there was great. Yet neither Vietnam nor Siam realized that the British attack on Burma in the 1820s had opened a period in which the power of the West would force sweeping changes on their traditional institutions. Even the Burmese were scarcely aware of the new era as yet.

Burma

BRITISH CONQUEST (1824–1885)

British interest in Burma stemmed from the British East India Company's position in Bengal. When the Burmese took Arakan in 1784, many Arakanese fled to eastern Bengal, which was nominally ruled by the Company, and used it as a base from which to attack the Burmese. From 1785 to 1824 Burmese military expeditions periodically crossed the border to retaliate against the Arakanese, sometimes with British permission and sometimes without it. In addition, between 1817 and 1822 the Burmese conquered Assam to the northeast of Bengal. Since the Burmese seemed to be preparing to invade Bengal next, the British decided to act.

In 1824 the British seized Rangoon in the delta and slowly fought their way up the Irrawaddy. In 1826 the Burmese ruler at Ava, four hundred miles inland, found the British Indian army almost at his gates.

To obtain their withdrawal, he agreed to give the British Arakan, Assam, and Tenasserim, to negotiate a commercial treaty, and to accept a British representative at Ava. The first agreement was swifty carried out, but not the second and third. He also paid an indemnity in return for British evacuation of Rangoon.

Soon after the British left Rangoon in 1826, the Burmese court at Ava decided to break the independent spirit of the Karen in southeastern Burma, who had aided the British against their Burmese overlords, and the few remaining Mon. The court also decided to deal with the British as little as possible and not to accept any humiliations in such intercourse as took place. Considerations of prestige on the part of both British and Burmese helped bring on a new war in 1852 over a Burmese official's attempt to extort money from two British ship captains. Between 1852 and 1855 the British seized the entire delta and annexed it to their Indian empire. However, Ava never recognized the annexation, even after it accepted a British representative in 1862.

As the 1860s progressed and the Suez Canal neared completion, the British grew interested in the possibility of entering the Chinese market by way of Burma. The British also promoted the commercial growing of rice in the delta. After 1870 the profits of rice-growing attracted many Burmese from the interior to the British-held areas.

The Mon and Karen made few objections to British rule in the delta, but former officials of the Ava government raised armed resistance to the British and those who served them until 1870. Baiting the local police became such a favorite pastime of the young that banditry (locally known as *dacoity*) remained a serious problem in the delta even after 1870. Old restraints on behavior gave way as commercial rice-growing and a money economy replaced the former patterns of self-sufficient village life. Commercialization soon went so far that even Buddhist monks began to accept and use money, to the alarm of the puritanical.

The profits of rice-growing for the market induced Burmese to move around freely, seeking high crop yields, instead of remaining in their home villages. In later years this mobility let Indian moneylenders acquire large agricultural holdings, as Burmese borrowed money to move to new localities and then defaulted on their loans. Sometimes they defaulted because of overestimating their prospective profits, but sometimes they simply absconded, an eventuality against which the moneylenders sought to protect themselves by charging uniformly high interest rates.

While rice production in the delta was commercializing, a capable new ruler, Mindon, came to the throne at Ava and in 1857 moved the capital to Mandalay. Salaries for government officials were substituted by Mindon for the former system by which each official was assigned the revenue of a certain area as income. The salaries were to come from a tax to be assessed on households and paid to the local officials regardless of the place of origin of the household head. Formerly each household had been under the jurisdiction of the officials of the area from which the household head came, no matter how far away that might be.

Cut off from the sea, the Burmese court under Mindon sought to counteract British influence in Burma by making overtures to France, which was becoming involved in the affairs of the region east of Burma. Mindon's death in 1878 was followed by dissension and rebellions. British merchants in Rangoon called for action to protect their interests in trade and teakwood. Using a dispute over payment for extracting teak logs in upper Burma as an excuse, the British attacked in 1885, while the French were occupied by a war with China over Vietnam. The new king was deposed, and the British annexed all his territories from the Chindwin basin to the Shan hills.

BRITISH RULE (1886–1906)

The Burmese of the interior rebelled immediately against British annexation. Fighting soon spread into the delta, where some monks joined the rebels. There the Karen, most of whom were either animists or converts of the American Baptist missionaries who had arrived in 1813, aided the British in hopes of winning future freedom from Burmese Buddhist control.

The British treated Burma as if it were part of India, applying the British Indian penal code and introducing the British Indian system of all-powerful district officers. To help put down the Burmese insurrections, in 1887 the British abolished the Burmese system of grouping villages into circles, and made each village head separately and directly responsible to the district officer for maintaining order and collecting revenue. This step increased the government's control of village affairs, but it also destroyed the old system of maintaining the local peace by referring disputes between people of different villages to the circle head for settlement. These measures did not apply to the tribal states in the Shan and western hills, which were separately administered from the lowlands and the coasts.

By 1890 some degree of order was restored, but lovers of tradition continued to deplore the disappearance of the monarchy and the loss of authority in the monasteries. In Ceylon, the British administration had agreed in 1845 to register officially the elections of abbots in the Buddhist monasteries, which gave the abbots enough official standing to maintain effective discipline among the monks, but in Burma the British made no such concession to the traditionally close relation between the monasteries and the state. As a result, monastic discipline in Burma declined sharply. Monks took their disputes to civil courts or simply disregarded the abbots' attempts to expel individuals for misconduct.

As monastic discipline declined, so did the monastic schools. The ideas of Burma's new rulers were not embodied in the Burmese language or the Buddhist scriptures taught by the monks. Burmese soon began to study English speech and Western ways in the hope of being hired by British officials and business firms.

The British set up municipal councils in the larger towns of lower Burma after 1874, but only Rangoon's functioned effectively. Elsewhere, the people did not support the councils, which were regarded as just another way to raise taxes. The rural district councils of 1884 were scarcely more successful in actually making and implementing policy. However, the British did include Burmese in the lower ranks of the civil service and made opportunities for Western education available to them. Soon an intermediary group appeared, comparable to those which developed in India and Ceylon. In 1897 an Anglo-vernacular high school was established at Moulmein, in an attempt to bring together the old education and the new. In 1904 a College Buddhist Association was founded in Rangoon, and in 1906 the Young Men's Buddhist Association was formed to promote the fusion of Buddhist and Western principles.

BURMA'S STRUGGLES FOR INDEPENDENCE
AND SEPARATION FROM INDIA (1906–1937)

As the years passed, Western-educated Burmese grew increasingly eager to capture power not only from the British but also from the descendants of the powerful families of the former kingdom of Burma. The Western-educated first made themselves heard during World War I. In 1916 the fifty branches of the Young Men's Buddhist Association led a protest against foreign visitors who refused to remove their shoes within the sacred precincts of Buddhist shrines. This movement gave young Burmese valuable experience in organizing campaigns and demonstrations. When Britain proposed to treat Burma differently from India after World War I, on the ground that it was not yet ready for the degree of self-government promised in the India Act of 1919, the Western-educated led a strong protest movement in 1920. In 1921 the British decided to revise their original plans and model the new provincial government of Burma on the pattern of divided powers provided for in the 1919 India Act. However, the powers of the provincial government over education, health, forestry, and excise taxes only extended to what the British called "Burma proper," the Chindwin-Irrawaddy basin and the coastal districts. The Shan states, the Karen territories, and the tribal areas of the western hills were still separately governed.

In the heat of the 1920–1921 struggle against the British, the Young Men's Buddhist Association objected to the high standards of the new University of Rangoon, claiming that the number of graduates was deliberately being kept low so that there would be a shortage of the educated leaders needed for self-rule. A general student strike swept through the government schools and many mission schools in 1921. Thereafter, the university and the schools were hotbeds of political agitation against whatever government was in power, at least until the military government of Ne Win fired on and killed some student demonstrators in 1962.

As part of the effort to turn the schools to nationalist ends, some Buddhist monks opened "national schools" to compete with the government schools. The older, stricter monks repudiated the leader of the national school movement, but his ideas appealed to many younger monks and the movement brought monks to the fore politically. A General Council of Buddhist Associations was formed and soon began to promote the athin movement. An *athin* was a village group which in theory was dedicated to upholding Buddhist virtues, but in practice concentrated on agitating against modernization and British rule.

The British tried to weaken opposition by expanding the area of self-government in the 1920s. Local councils were made elective, and the village headmen were given additional authority. Nevertheless, the athin movement grew, and agitation continued.

Most Burmese nationalists of the early 1920s believed that Burma should remain linked with India for some time, fearing that separation would enable the British to retard the progress of self-government in Burma, but some insisted on immediate separation for fear that otherwise Burma would be taken over by the Indian immigrants who were already active in its economy. In 1928 Burmese representatives asked the Simon Commission for separation from India, but by 1930 and the first London roundtable conference, Burmese leaders were again wondering whether separation would delay independence. They did not finally accept separation until it was made clear that if Burma did not choose separation then, it could not expect to be given separation later.

Neither separationists nor anti-separationists, with their talk of constitutional government, economic progress, and social reform, inspired much enthusiasm outside the cities. Most Burmese villagers and townspeople did not begin planning seriously for independence until after 1930, when village athin groups in the central delta rebelled in an effort to restore the traditional Burmese kingdom. The rebels, some of whom were monks, were put down by British troops and Karen volunteers.

ACHIEVEMENT OF INDEPENDENCE FROM BRITAIN
(1937–1948)

In the late 1930s, student demonstrations drew many Burmese to support the politically active students at the University of Rangoon. The students' open opposition to the British made them seem more nationalistic than the politicians and civil servants, whom many thought of as semi-traitors because they were cooperating with the British to some extent. The politicians and civil servants became especially unpopular after Burma was separated from India in 1937 under the provisions of the Government of India and Government of Burma Acts of 1935.

The Government of Burma Act gave the British governor responsibility for defense, foreign affairs, the stability of the currency, and the government of the Shan, Karen, and tribal areas. The rest of the affairs of the province were under the control of a two-house legislature. Seven-tenths of the lower house members were elected from territorial constituencies. The rest represented special interests ranging from Chambers of Commerce to the University of Rangoon. Half the upper house was chosen by the governor and half by the lower house. The franchise qualifications allowed about a third of the men and a tenth of the women of the province of Burma to vote in the general elections for the lower house.

Most Burmese expected separation from India to be followed by a large-scale exodus of the Indian moneylenders and laborers who had flocked to the rice-growing delta since 1870. When the Indians did not leave, ordinary Burmese tended to blame the British and those Burmese who worked with them. Many anti-Indian riots took place between 1932 and the Japanese invasion of 1942. The most serious one, in 1938, was not quelled for several months. It was partly instigated by politically minded monks incensed at an Indian printer for publishing a book critical of Buddhism.

The government established by the Government of Burma Act had only four years to function before the Japanese occupied the country, but that was long enough to convince the Burmese that they could govern themselves. When the Japanese arrived in 1942 they deprived both British and Indians of political and economic power. The Burmese tended to welcome this at first. Both monks and Thakins aided the Japanese. (The university students used the term *thakin*, which is roughly equivalent to "sir" in English, to indicate that the people of Burma were as entitled to respect as the British.) The Thakins set up a Burma Independence Army, later renamed the Burma Defense Army and finally called the Burma National Army. Most of the Burma Independence Army units were a mixture of socialist-inspired Thakin officers, eager for a modern state in which the government should ensure the welfare of all; anti-foreign peasants, anxious only to be left alone by outsiders; and dacoits or members of bandit gangs, who gladly seized the chance to make their looting quasi-respectable.

The good will of the Burmese toward their fellow Buddhists and fellow Asians from Japan was quickly dissipated by Japanese lack of respect for Burmese shrines and for Burmese aspirations toward dignified independence. Even after the Japanese granted Burma nominal independence in 1943, the public and private remarks of many Japanese showed their belief that Japan knew Burma's needs better than Burma's leaders did. By mid-1944 the leaders of the Burma National Army were ready to join the year-old Anti-Fascist People's Freedom League in conspiring against the Japanese. During the next year the AFPFL became the representative voice of Burma. It was backed by Thakins, socialists, Communists, the Burma National Army, youth organizations, monks, and some Karen; and it had promised self-determination to minority peoples like the Shan. However, when the British returned in the spring of 1945 they refused to accept the claims of the AFPFL.

The British government asserted in May, 1945, that three years of governor's rule would be needed to reestablish order and rehabilitate the war-damaged economy of Burma, and that it would not restore the prewar degree of autonomy or discuss independence during those three years. The AFPFL promptly led the people of Burma in a wave of protests. At first London ignored the protests, believing that the AFPFL leaders would soon begin to attack each other rather than the British. This obstinacy merely stirred up more protests. Finally, late in the summer of 1946, a new governor was appointed and authorized to negotiate with the AFPFL leaders, the most prominent of whom were U Aung San, U Nu, and Ne Win. In January, 1947, a satisfactory agreement was reached, and in April the people of the province of Burma elected members for a constituent assembly. Delegates to the assembly were also selected from the Shan, Karen, and tribal areas, which were to be included in the new state. The assembly was to draw up a constitution and serve as a legislature until the constitution went into effect.

Shortly after the constituent assembly met in June, 1947, it voted to sever all ties with Britain. In September it enacted a federal constitution providing for a two-house legislature, the lower house elected from territorial districts of roughly equal population and the upper chosen from the constituent states. The assembly hoped this arrangement would overcome the objections of Karen, Shan, and others to living with the large Burmese majority. In October the final arrangements for British withdrawal were made, and on January 4, 1948, Burma became an independent republic.

INTERNAL STRUGGLES AND EXTERNAL POLICIES
(1948–1974)

A few months before independence came in January, 1948, the assassination of U Aung San by a political foe deprived the AFPFL of its most widely accepted leader. Soon part of the small Communist party took up arms against the government of the new state, and most of the Karen pulled away from the AFPFL, complaining that the Karen state in the new Union of Burma was not being given an outlet to the sea. In March, 1948, shortly after a meeting in Calcutta of Southeast Asian Communist leaders, the entire Communist party of Burma declared war on the government. In July many former Burma National Army men joined the Communists, and in January, 1949, most of the Karen rebelled. The Karen hoped for British aid, but they did not get it. The largely Buddhist government in Rangoon termed the Karen the "Baptist rebels" and blamed Karen separatism on American missionary work. The situation became even more complicated late in 1949 when Chinese Nationalist troops fleeing the Chinese Communists linked forces with rebellious elements in the Shan states. However, most of the rebels were tamed by the time Burma held its second nationwide election in 1956. The government used a threefold approach: sharp military action against the insurgents, to restore order in the countryside; continued use of non-Burmese in the government and the army, to establish confidence in the intentions of the Burmese majority toward the minorities; and amnesty for all who renounced opposition to the government, to deprive fanatics of the ability to use fear of government punishment to retain their followers.

After 1953 the government took most of the Chinese Nationalist troops into custody and sent them to Taiwan. However, Communist China was not satisfied. Chinese pressure along the Burma border continued until the conclusion of a border treaty in January, 1960. The treaty recognized almost all the claims presented by Britain for Burma in the unratified treaty which the British had negotiated with China in 1914, for by then Communist China wished to counteract the unfavorable impression made in largely Buddhist Burma by the harsh repression of the Tibetan uprising of 1959.

Restoration of Buddhism to a central place in the life of Burma was a cardinal principle of U Nu, prime minister during most of Burma's first fourteen years of independence. U Nu was largely responsible for calling the sixth general council in Buddhist history to meet at Rangoon in 1955 to correct any errors which had crept into the scriptures, in preparation for the 2500th anniversary of the entry of the Buddha into nirvana in 544 B.C. (Preparations for that anniversary contributed to the upsurge of Buddhist feeling evidenced in the 1956 Ceylon elections, too.) U Nu also advocated replacing the neutral secular state of the 1947 constitution with an avowedly Buddhist state, although he added that all other religions should be freely tolerated.

These pro-Buddhist policies won U Nu support from many monks. However, others began to wonder whether politically minded monks might use their influence with the ordinary people to make them wish to return to the days of self-sufficient rural communities tied to the capital only by shared attitudes and a minimum of levies. Such thoughts were especially distasteful to army leaders like Ne Win, the commander in chief. In an age when insurgents could receive supplies by airplane, military leaders knew that internal stability and external independence required a tightly knit economy, society, and polity. When personal rivalries began to split the AFPFL, political stability was threatened. In 1958 U Nu invited Ne Win to replace him as prime minister so he could rebuild the AFPFL. Elections restored U Nu to office in 1960, but early in 1962 Ne Win replaced U Nu without invitation and abrogated the constitution. Bands of insurgents, some Communist-led, were reappearing, and economic development was slow. In 1964 the Karen finally agreed to lay down their arms in return for a promise that their state would be enlarged, but other insurgent groups continued to be active. An attempt to require Buddhist organizations to forswear political activity was given up after a monk burned himself to death in protest.

The military government continued its predecessor's policy of state support and control in all areas of economic activity—industrial, commercial, and agricultural—in line with Burmese Buddhist traditions of disdain for the profit motive of the private merchant. Mindful of the agitational role of the students in the past and the need for technicians in the present, it limited the size of liberal arts enrollments and encouraged vocational programs. It quickly nationalized most businesses, thereby ending the dominance of much of Burma's trade by Indians and Chinese, and rejected all nongovernmental investment and assistance from abroad. Not until 1972 was a private foreign firm allowed to aid in surveying Burma's nationalized petroleum resources.

In its relations with other governments, the Ne Win government sought primarily to avoid giving offense. Despite Burma's efforts to forestall Chinese intervention in its affairs, in 1967 the People's Republic of China recognized the small Communist insurgency as a liberation movement. This in turn encouraged insurgents among the minority hill peoples, particularly among those who still lived by shifting cultivation rather than sedentary agriculture. However, the schools, dams, roads, factories, and agricultural extension services which the military government was establishing in the hills proved to be effective competitors for minority loyalties, in conjunction with an unswerving central government policy of recognizing all minority cultures as contributors to Burma's national culture. When the Communists began desecrating shrines and killing leaders who were genuinely admired rather than feared, they antagonized many of the villagers whose support they sought. The villagers responded by joining the government militia rather than the Communists, and helped to hunt down the Communist leaders. Only in the northern Shan hills, near the Chinese and Laotian borders, was the Rangoon government's authority still effectively challenged by insurgents at the end of 1972.

Between 1966 and 1969 the Ne Win government moved to give all the people of Burma a sense of having a voice in their own affairs. Nationwide networks of elected peasants' councils and workers' councils were successfully established in the countryside and the towns, under the guidance of the military-sponsored Burma Socialist Program Party. The organization of these councils helped to weaken the appeal of the Communists and other insurgents. However, U Nu's proclamation from exile in 1970 that he would not hesitate to take up arms to overthrow the men who had ousted him in 1962 foreshadowed an insurgency potentially far more dangerous than either the dwindling Communists or the remaining hill country insurgents. Ne Win sought to counter U Nu's appeals by resigning his military posts in 1972 and preparing a new, secular, unitary constitution. The new constitution was adopted by popular vote in 1973, after Ne Win again forced U Nu to leave the country. The new unicameral legislature was elected in 1974. When it opened, Ne Win dissolved the Revolutionary Council that had ruled since 1962 and became the chairman of the Council of State, leaving the post of prime minister to the former minister for construction.

Thailand

VOLUNTARY AND GRADUAL WESTERNIZATION
(1851–1932)

Buddhist disdain for private profit also influenced the Thai, who avoided commercial pursuits so persistently that by the sixteenth century almost all internal and external trade was carried on by Chinese or other foreigners. However, after the Thai ruler decided in 1688 that French influence was becoming too strong in his domains, the Ayuthia government took care to prevent any foreign power from dominating its external relations. When Bangkok replaced Ayuthia, the same policy was continued. In 1826 and 1833, British and United States representatives obtained treaties at Bangkok granting limited commercial privileges, but the first consuls were not allowed to reside there until 1855, after the accession to the throne of Mongkut (formally, Rama IV), one of the most remarkable leaders of nineteenth-century Asia.

Mongkut spent his early manhood in a Buddhist monastery far from the intrigues of the court where his elder brother was king. In the monastery Mongkut studied not only Buddhist scriptures but Latin, mathematics, astronomy, and English. By 1851, when he ascended the throne, his omnivorous reading had awakened him to Siam's danger. If Siam failed to adjust to the Western sovereign state system, as it had formerly adjusted to the Chinese tributary system, it would probably be conquered piecemeal like Burma. To ward off this danger, Mongkut voluntarily signed treaties with Britain, France, the United States, Denmark, Portugal, the Netherlands, Prussia, and a number of other states between 1855 and his death in 1868. In line with the practice of the time, these treaties provided for tariff control and extraterritoriality as well as the establishment of consulates.

Mongkut also used a variety of European advisers, but their advice was rarely followed in its entirety by Siamese officials, who were anxious to forestall the possibility that their suggestions were part of some overall plan to take over the country. He used British economic advisers, but he balanced them with a general adviser from Belgium and military experts from Denmark and Italy; and he assiduously avoided using French experts because French interest in Vietnam and Cambodia alarmed him.

Mongkut and his advisers improved the transport network by constructing roads, canals, and modern ships. They also introduced the study of foreign languages and foreign ways. However, they made few fundamental alterations in Siam's internal life. It was Mongkut's son Chulalongkorn (Rama V) who attacked age-old practices in earnest. During his reign (1868–1910) Chulalongkorn abolished slavery and compulsory service. He established a centralized fiscal organization that could collect, apportion, and expend the revenues in accord with Western canons of efficiency. He encouraged railroads, and laid the foundations for a universal system of public education which expanded gradually until it finally reached almost all Thai children after 1960.

Chulalongkorn did not remain free to concentrate on internal affairs. During his reign Siam faced British pressures in the Malay peninsula and French demands on behalf of Vietnamese, Cambodian, and Laotian interests. However, diplomatic skill and British support enabled Siam to maintain itself as a buffer state between British Burma and the French in the Mekong valley. The diplomatic skill was epitomized in 1893, when a French naval commander delivering an ultimatum to Bangkok was congratulated on the skill and daring with which his ships forced their way past the Siamese coastal defenses. The British support was illustrated by an Anglo-French agreement in 1896, the result of British pressures on France, to respect the independence of the Menam valley. Through diplomacy and graceful yielding, Bangkok won the time required to consolidate its hold on the upper Menam, the Korat plateau, and the Malay peninsula north of Kedah, so that these regions would not fall to France or Britain like Cambodia, Laos, and four of the Malay sultanates.

Chulalongkorn's successor Vajiravudh (Rama VI) recodified Siamese law in line with Western models so that Western states would become willing to forgo extraterritoriality. He also joined the Allied side in World War I. Before he died in 1925 Vajiravudh persuaded the United States to abandon extraterritoriality, and gradually the other powers also relinquished it. By the time the United States acceded to Vajiravudh's request, extraterritoriality had already been given up by the Western powers in Japan and Turkey, was soon to be ended in Persia and a bit later in Egypt, and was partially gone in China.

Like his father and grandfather, Vajiravudh gave the highest offices to a small group of relatives and close acquaintances. However, many subordinate offices went to others who had studied abroad. Seven years after Vajiravudh's youngest brother succeeded to the throne, these foreign-educated officials led a coup d'état which forced the king to give Siam its first constitution, a far from radical document establishing a parliamentary monarchy. The 1932 coup was the first real sign that the changes introduced from the top during the preceding eighty years were arousing some enthusiasm farther down the social and political scale.

CONSTITUTIONAL MONARCHY (1932–1974)

The 1932 coup d'état was carried out by a handful of men in the army, the civil service, and the university at Bangkok. It did not result from outpourings of popular sentiment like the Burmese protest movements of the 1920s. Moreover, it looked exclusively forward, seeking the introduction of more elements of modernity into Thailand, as Siam was renamed a few years later. It did not try to face both future and past like most anti-colonial movements, looking backward to a lost independence and forward to a new freedom, for Thai independence had never been lost.

Phibun Songgram and Pridi Banomyong, the recognized leaders of the military men and the professors, soon ceased to agree on policy. During the 1930s when the militarists rose to power in Japan, their counterparts in Thailand displaced Pridi in favor of Phibun. In 1939 he began a "Thailand for the Thai" campaign, cutting off Chinese immigration, closing down the Chinese-language newspapers and schools used by the Chinese minority, and excluding non-Thai from a number of occupations. Attempts were also made to foster Buddhism as a binding force in Thai life. Reconversions from Christianity were encouraged, and non-Buddhists in government employ were not promoted.

As the Japanese advanced into Southeast Asia by way of the French possessions in Vietnam, Bangkok took advantage of French weakness and Japanese professions of friendship. In 1941 lands lost to French-protected Laos and Cambodia in 1904 and 1907 were recovered. When Japan went to war with the West in December of 1941, the Thai government bowed gracefully to Japanese strength, declaring war on Britain and the United States and letting Japan use Thailand as a base from which to seize Burma and Malaya from Britain. Thai citizens abroad counterbalanced this by starting an anti-Japanese Free Thai movement. The Free Thai helped to prepare the way for acceptance of a new Thai government as a peace-loving member of the United Nations in 1947. The new government, which replaced that of Phibun, was established under Pridi's guidance in 1944, near the end of the war. Shortly after the war it repudiated the 1941 treaty with France and restored the lands taken from Laos and Cambodia. It also annulled the anti-Communist law of 1933, which the Soviet Union strongly condemned. However, the unsolved shooting of the king in 1946 brought the Pridi government no support in a country where royalty was still revered by many. In 1948 the military returned Phibun to power. Pridi fled the country and in 1954 appeared in Communist China as leader of a new Free Thai movement—ready to take control once more, if the pro-Western military government should prove as unable to protect Thai independence as the wartime government of Phibun.

The military men who ran Thailand after 1948 interested themselves in economic development, which could provide their armed forces with supplies and give potential dissidents a stake in preventing rather than supporting revolts. They sought to maintain and even extend the prestige of the monarchy, which could provide a focus for national loyalty and justify their assumption of the role of promoters of national unity. They promoted universal education, which could develop not only feelings of nationalism but capacities needed for new economic activities. Many used their political power to acquire interests in both private and public concerns. They then used their increased income to attract more political followers, thereby gaining new political power and new economic leverage. This circular process brought most of Thailand's larger enterprises under the control of the military. Thailand did not commit itself officially to state supervision of economic life after World War II, as Burma did. However, private business people in Thailand, who were often at least partly of Chinese ancestry, were almost as deeply involved with government officials as were business people in more socialist-oriented states.

In the regime of the generals in post-1948 Bangkok, Phibun gradually lost power to Sarit Thanarat, who took command in 1957 by riding on the crest of a wave of public dissatisfaction with the fraud and intimidation evident in the 1956 parliamentary elections. The constitution was abolished and a constituent assembly appointed, but not until over a year after Sarit's quiet death and replacement by his deputy Thanom Kittikachorn at the end of 1963 did the outline of the new constitution begin to emerge.

Sarit and Thanom continued to apply the anti-Communist laws which Phibun reinstated in 1952, and to support the South-East Asia Treaty Organization which Thailand helped form in 1954. At first they feared that the People's Republic of China might use the large and wealthy Chinese minority to overthrow the monarchy and make Thailand subservient to Peking. By 1966 the threat posed by Communist support for minority insurgencies in the northern and eastern hill districts appeared even greater. As the insurgencies spread, the Thanom government sought even closer ties with the United States, though it began to have second thoughts after the People's Republic of China entered the United Nations in 1971 and United States President Nixon visited Peking in 1972. It also sought ties with other Southeast Asian nations, through the Association of Southeast Asia formed by Thailand, Malaysia, and the Philippines in 1961 and through the Association of South-East Asian Nations formed by Thailand, Malaysia, the Philippines, Singapore, and Indonesia in 1967. Within its borders, the Thanom government promoted rural improvement programs in the hill regions as a means of attracting minority loyalty, but by 1972 it had virtually lost its control of several hill districts near the Laotian border in the north, and was experiencing difficulties in some districts in the south, near the border with Malaysia. Most of these, like the areas which the government of Burma had the greatest difficulty in controlling, were populated largely by tribes which were still practicing shifting cultivation rather than settled agriculture.

Local elections were held throughout most of Thailand at the end of 1967, for the first time in a decade. In 1968 the long-awaited constitution was finally promulgated, and in 1969 the elections to the new national assembly gave the military leaders' United Thai People's Party thirty-five percent of the seats, the chief opposition party twenty-five percent, and independents thirty-three percent. The United Thai People's Party induced enough independents to join it so that it would have a majority; but factionalism within the party, and the resulting possibility that the now-legal opposition might gain power, persuaded Thanom to abrogate the new constitution and return to military rule late in 1971. A new interim constitution providing for an all-appointive legislative assembly was promulgated at the end of 1972, but martial law remained in effect. Thanom's son began maneuvering to succeed his father upon his retirement. After the experience of 1969–1971, the Thanom government appeared unwilling to risk a return to elective institutions until its political opponents became more manageable.

Then, in October of 1973, a series of Bangkok university student protests triggered by military interference in university affairs led to the resignation and departure from the country of Thanom and his associates, in the interest of restoring order in the capital. University rector Sanya Thammasak was made prime minister, martial law was ended, public expression of opinion was encouraged, and another new constitution was drafted. A national assembly was popularly elected at the end of the year. In 1974 it began debate on ratifying the new constitution, which called for an elected lower house for which government employees (civilian or military) were not eligible to run, an upper house elected by the lower house, and the use of a popular referendum to resolve the deadlock which would otherwise exist if the monarch refused to accept a statute enacted by the legislature.

The Mekong States: Vietnam, Cambodia, Laos

FRENCH INFLUENCE AND CONTROL OF INDOCHINA
(1660–1907)

Thailand was spared outright foreign conquest, but its rulers' choice of the path of diplomacy also spared it the stimulus of a nation-wide struggle against foreign rule. In Vietnam, where the French eventually took control after two centuries of deepening involvement, the story was different.

Under the aegis of Portugal, Jesuit missionaries converted some Vietnamese to Christianity. When Portugal's empire collapsed, the Jesuits appealed to France for aid and reinforcements, but by then Vietnamese leaders were taking alarm at this apparent danger to the Confucian system. The two French bishops who went out to Vietnam in 1660 found its rulers hostile to missionary work, now that the nonproselytizing Dutch afforded a source of European weapons. Therefore the bishops prudently withdrew to Ayuthia.

The French bishops were closely followed by the merchants of the government's French East India Company of 1664. In 1680 the Company opened a permanent trading post at Ayuthia and in the next few years persuaded the Thai ruler to send two embassies to France. In 1685 Ayuthia granted the French extraterritorial rights and a monopoly of the tin trade of one of its dependencies in the northern Malay peninsula. This growth of French influence alarmed the English, who tried to seize part of Ayuthia's southwestern territories in 1687. Many leading Thai also became alarmed, and in 1688 the French were expelled from Ayuthia lest their influence become too strong.

In the next few decades the growth of Dutch power in the Malacca strait kept France out of most of Southeast Asia. Between 1688 and 1714 the Dutch and the French were at peace for only four years. The French had opened a trading post in Vietnam after 1664, but they closed it in 1697, partly because of Dutch interference and partly because of Vietnamese indifference and even hostility to foreign trade. In 1761 the Dutch also closed their trading post in Vietnam. After 1700 the French decided to concentrate on Burma, befriending the Mon against the Burmese, but when the Burmese defeated the Mon in 1754 the French lost all influence in Burma.

Although European trade with Vietnam diminished, French-sponsored missionary work there continued. As the eighteenth century closed, the French bishop for southern Vietnam grasped what he saw as a golden opportunity. For almost two hundred years Vietnam had been divided into two principalities. In 1775 the ruler of the southern one was driven from his throne by rebels from the mountainous coastal region between north and south. The French bishop befriended the exiled ruler and in 1784 persuaded him to seek French help. In 1787 the bishop finally persuaded Paris to promise aid, but only a few hundred volunteers actually went to Vietnam, and the outbreak of the French Revolution in 1789 cut off hopes of further assistance. However, the volunteers taught the ruler's men to carry out combined infantry, artillery, and naval operations well enough to unite all of Vietnam in 1801–1802.

The bishop's fond hope was that the victorious ruler's favored son, whom he entrusted to the bishop for several years, would become Christian; but the young prince died before his father, and the man who ascended the throne in 1820 proved strongly anti-Christian. In 1833 he prohibited Christianity; in 1836, after a French priest was found in a band of rebels, he promised to execute any foreign priests caught in future. He also closed all Vietnamese ports except Da Nang, near the capital of Hue, to European vessels.

Despite the decrees, missionaries continued to come. The next ruler, who came to the throne in 1842, hesitated to kill them for fear that Vietnam would be attacked and humiliated as China was between 1839 and 1842. For several years he merely turned them over to the French naval officers who frequented Da Nang in search of a way to make it a French naval base. However, he promulgated a new set of anti-Christian ordinances in 1847, after an incident involving a missionary which culminated in a French naval attack on five Vietnamese naval vessels. Anxious missionaries urged Paris to act to protect Vietnamese Christians, but nothing was done until after the close of the Crimean War in Europe.

In 1856 the new and fervently Roman Catholic Second Empire of Louis Napoleon ordered Da Nang bombarded. In 1857 Paris decided to occupy three Vietnamese ports, but to leave the emperor on his throne at Hue; and in 1858 a combined French and Spanish fleet seized Da Nang. French forces took Saigon in the Mekong delta in 1859. Da Nang was evacuated in 1860, for it seemed less important than Saigon. In 1862 the emperor signed a treaty which ceded the coastal provinces of the Mekong delta to France, allowed the French to sail freely up the Mekong to Cambodia, authorized missionary work throughout Vietnam, paid France an indemnity, and opened two more ports to trade. In 1867 the French occupied the remaining delta provinces in an effort to end fierce resistance in the ceded areas. The emperor was required to accede to this new loss. The French forced the reluctant Cambodian king to accept their protection. (He had promised to do so in 1863, but in 1864 he had returned to his former Siamese allegiance.) Siam was induced to accept the situation by French recognition of its claims on western Cambodia.

Having brought the entire lower Mekong under their control, French officials in Saigon set out to learn whether the Mekong could serve as a highway into China. When their explorers found falls and rapids blocking the way farther upstream, they decided to turn their attention to the Red river in the north. In 1873 an enterprising naval commander seized Hanoi. The new republican government in France repudiated his act, but the Vietnamese emperor was alarmed enough to accept a French resident adviser at his court in Hue in 1874. A few years later the emperor invited the Ch'ing to send troops against some former T'ai-p'ing supporters who were terrorizing parts of northern Vietnam. The French feared the Ch'ing might also oppose their activity in the north, and therefore seized Hanoi again in 1882. In 1884 Hue put the Red river valley under the control of French officials who nominally represented the emperor. Now Hue only administered the narrow coastal plain between the Mekong and Red river deltas—assisted by the French resident adviser. The Ch'ing protested, but in 1885 were forced to agree that Vietnam was no longer a tributary of China.

In 1883 the French began to show interest in Laos along the central Mekong. Siam then controlled Vientiane directly and received homage from Luang Prabang. The French persuaded Luang Prabang to change its allegiance by offering timely help against a rebellion, and in 1888 Siam recognized the alteration. In 1893, under the pressure of a French ultimatum, Siam relinquished Vientiane and recognized the Mekong as the boundary between itself and the French sphere of interest. Since this arrangement let Siam annex some formerly Laotian lands west of the Mekong, it satisfied Siam as well as France. In 1904 renewed French pressure deprived the Siamese of these districts, but in 1907 France exchanged some of them for the Siamese-held western provinces of Cambodia, and also gave up French claims to jurisdiction over Laotians, Cambodians, and Vietnamese residing in Siam.

FRENCH POLICY IN INDOCHINA (1887–1930)

The conclusion of the 1907 Franco-Siamese treaty rounded out the domains the French referred to as Indochina. In 1887 France had formally inaugurated an Indochinese Union of the colony of Cochinchina in the Mekong delta and the protectorates of Cambodia, Annam (the narrow coastal plain), and Tongking (the Red river valley). In 1893 the new protectorate of Laos had been added to the Union. The Vietnamese resisted these arrangements fiercely, but by 1897 all but one of the guerrilla bands was dispersed. The last one operated until 1913. For a few years the Vietnamese were fairly quiet, but the Japanese defeat of Russia in 1905 emboldened some to propose that the Vietnamese take up Western learning so that they might expel the French.

Not long after acquiring power in Vietnam, the French opened schools in which instruction was given in French as well as in Vietnamese. The schools were designed to train subordinate officials like interpreters and to inject as much French culture into Vietnamese life as possible. They even used the Latin alphabet for the Vietnamese language, adopting a system developed by Jesuit missionaries. When a number of young Vietnamese chose to study in Japan, the French set up a university in Hanoi as a counterattraction. However, the students at the new university were so virulently anti-French that the authorities closed it within a year.

In addition to establishing new schools in Vietnam, the French built railroads and telegraph lines there and roads in Vietnam, Laos, and Cambodia. They opened new rice lands by dredging and draining in the Mekong delta, and started coal mines, rice and cotton mills, and coffee, tea, and rubber plantations. Most of these enterprises were launched in French-administered Cochinchina and Tongking, rather than in the indirectly controlled protectorates of Laos, Cambodia, and Annam. Vietnamese, Laotians, and Cambodians made little profit from them. The French discouraged the local people from entering commerce, banking, and industry, for they wished to exploit the region's resources themselves. Economic activity was left to the French and the growing Chinese communities of Saigon, Phnom Penh, and the major towns of Laos. Vietnamese found more outlets for business enterprise in Laos and Cambodia than in their own country.

The Vietnamese, having been forced rather than persuaded into association with France, reacted more sharply against French rule than Laotians and Cambodians. To meet local protests, the French introduced consultative assemblies elected by carefully limited segments of the populations of Tongking, Annam, Laos, and Cambodia before World War I. However, there was no real check on French authority anywhere in the regions they controlled. In 1915 the French abolished the traditional Confucian civil service examinations in Tongking, and in 1916 an uprising attempted to force their restoration, but to no avail.

The failure of the 1916 uprising cleared the way for new leaders, many of whom served in France as labor conscripts in World War I and returned with ideas gleaned from French acquaintances of liberal and even radical views. The French expected the prewar elective consultative assemblies to meet Vietnamese demands, but the stringent voting requirements and the assemblies' lack of power made them unsatisfactory. Vietnamese complained bitterly, but they were too far from Paris to be heard above the cries of French plantation owners, merchants, and officials, who insisted that Vietnamese could not run their own affairs. In 1927 a secret nationalist party was founded with the advice and support of the Kuomintang in China. Three years later the small group of Vietnamese Communists within the nationalist party betrayed its more moderate leaders to the French authorities, leaving the Communists as the sole active leaders of the nationalist cause. The Communists were prepared for an underground struggle for independence, for they had already formed their own clandestine organization under Nguyen Ai Quoc, who as Ho Chi Minh eventually became the first head of the Democratic Republic of Vietnam at Hanoi.

VIETNAM

INDEPENDENCE AND DIVISION (1930–1954). After 1930 only the puppet imperial court remained as a public symbol of Vietnamese unity. When a new emperor, Bao Dai, came to the throne in 1933, he called known young patriots like Ngo Dinh Diem into his cabinet and tried to loosen French control, but with no success. When Bao Dai yielded to French pressure, Diem resigned and retired from public life in protest. Then a socialist-minded Popular Front government in Paris in the late 1930s encouraged greater freedom of expression in the colonies. Some Communists began to agitate and propagandize publicly, only to be arrested when World War II began in 1939. Other Communists who had not disclosed themselves remained at liberty, but most of them were wiped out when they attempted an uprising in the Mekong delta late in 1940, after the French government at Vichy permitted the Japanese to occupy Tongking. Thereafter, the only Communists who could carry on the fight against France were the few who had left for China in the 1930s, like Nguyen Ai Quoc, who took the name of Ho Chi Minh in China to escape Nationalist detection.

The Kuomintang believed the Vietnamese refugees could be useful against the Japanese in Vietnam. The Japanese occupied the rest of Vietnam in 1941 and stayed there even after the Vichy government in France fell in 1944. The Kuomintang aided Ho Chi Minh and his followers against the French and Japanese, for they kept their Communist affiliations hidden. While in China they formed and led the League for the Independence of Vietnam, the Viet Minh. Between late 1943 and early 1945 the Viet Minh wrested much of the Red river basin from the French and Japanese. When the Japanese encouraged Bao Dai to proclaim the unity and independence of Vietnam in March, 1945, the Viet Minh refused to recognize him. Instead they administered the Red river valley independently, with Kuomintang approval. The Japanese also had the rulers of Cambodia and Laos proclaim independence in March, 1945.

After the close of the war in the Pacific, the Kuomintang accepted the surrender of Japanese troops as far south as the sixteenth parallel, refusing to allow French troops to return to northern Vietnam for six months. Ho Chi Minh used that time to establish a provisional republican government in the north and organize a network of Viet Minh followers throughout Vietnam. In March, 1946, the French recognized the republican government at Hanoi and promised to hold a referendum in Cochinchina on the question of uniting with the republic. In return they were allowed to send troops to help keep order in the Red river valley. The French also proposed an Indochinese Federation as part of a worldwide French Union. Although the proposal met little opposition, it also won little acceptance in Cochinchina, Annam, and Tongking. Recognizing this, the French decided to form their own republic in Cochinchina instead of holding the referendum. The Vietnamese therefore concluded they could only win independence by fighting. Both northern and southern Vietnamese forces began attacking French garrisons late in 1946.

Unfortunately for Viet Minh hopes of ending the war soon, France was able to call on the United States for aid against the Communist-led Viet Minh. After the Communist victory in China in 1949 made Communist Chinese aid to the Viet Minh a possibility, the French discarded the puppet republic in the south and appealed to American sympathy for Vietnamese unity and independence by recognizing Bao Dai as the ruler of a united Vietnam. The fighting lasted more than four years longer, but in July, 1954, the French and their supporters joined the Sino-Soviet bloc in agreeing at Geneva to recognize the independence of Vietnam, and also of Cambodia and Laos. An International Control Commission with representatives from India, Canada, and Poland was established to report on any military buildup which might contravene the agreements under which France was to withdraw from its former colonies. Since the Viet Minh controlled most of the north and the French held most of the south at the time of the agreement, the Viet Minh accepted a temporary partition of Vietnam at the seventeenth parallel. However, nationwide elections were promised within two years to establish a united government and determine its composition. The representatives of the Hanoi government signed the 1954 truce with France, confidently expecting that the network of Viet Minh supporters in the south would enable the Viet Minh to win easily in the anticipated 1956 elections. The foreign minister of the Bao Dai government resigned in protest against the French acceptance of the truce with Hanoi. Britain, the Soviet Union, and the People's Republic of China recognized the French agreements with Cambodia, Laos, and the Viet Minh, under which no additional arms or troops were to be introduced into any part of what had been French Indochina and the elections promised for Vietnam were to be supervised by representatives of the three states in the International Control Commission. The United States, however, issued a separate declaration pledging to work for nationwide elections supervised by the United Nations (like the nationwide elections the United Nations had earlier agreed to hold in divided Korea), and to view any repeated Communist attacks in Vietnam, Cambodia, or Laos as a serious threat to peace.

THE REPUBLIC OF VIETNAM (1955–1974). After the Geneva conference, some Viet Minh supporters left the south for the north and nearly a million refugees—mostly Christians—poured into southern Vietnam from the north. The government of Bao Dai accepted the task of settling the refugees, for it expected loyal support from them, and it needed support. Underground Viet Minh activity was continuing, there was disaffection in the army, and the leaders of two half-religious, half-political sects were gaining power. These two sects were eclectic, drawing elements from animism, Buddhism, and Christianity. Since their formation before World War II they had established their own villages and their own armed militia, which by 1954 were, in effect, private armies.

To cope with the situation, Bao Dai asked Ngo Dinh Diem to come out of retirement in 1954 and be his chief minister. As prime minister, Diem negotiated French withdrawal, put down the army dissidents and the sects, and resisted pressure from Hanoi to set a date for the unification elections. These policies won him increasing approval from the United States as well as from those Vietnamese in the south who opposed a Marxist solution to Vietnam's problems, or who wanted (like their ancestors of the sixteenth to the eighteenth century A.D.) to see southern Vietnam free from northern control. In October, 1955, a popular referendum declared him head of state in place of Bao Dai.

Three days later Diem proclaimed the replacement of the Vietnamese empire by the Republic of Vietnam and a year later put its first presidential constitution into effect.

When the Republic of Vietnam was established, the people of the south hoped for rapid economic development and social reform. Laws to improve the legal status of women were enacted at the insistence of Diem's influential sister-in-law, but in most fields the government moved more slowly than its supporters had expected. Viet Minh guerrillas continued to be active, obtaining arms and ammunition and even reinforcements from the north along what came to be known as the Ho Chi Minh trail, and receiving food and information from the villagers in whose areas they operated. They promised the villagers redistribution of the land, which appealed to the numerous tenant cultivators who were paying high rents to absentee landlords, and local control of local affairs, which appealed to all who resented the 1955 constitution's establishment of government-appointed village heads in place of locally-chosen ones. Local self-rule appealed especially to a number of the minority hill tribes who still lived by shifting cultivation and feared encroachment on their lands by the Vietnamese majority. However, like the Kuomintang in pre-1949 China, the Diem government felt it must wipe out all overt opposition before turning to rural improvement programs such as land reform. Nor was it willing to consider giving much autonomy to local leaders. Even the majority religious group, the Mahayana Buddhists, became suspect early in 1963 when some of its leaders began to protest that Roman Catholics received favored treatment from the government of Diem, whose oldest brother was the Roman Catholic archbishop of Hue. In November, 1963, the Diem government was swept away by a Buddhist-supported military coup d'état, whose leaders promised fair treatment for all and wholehearted prosecution of the war against the National Liberation Front, as the Communists and their supporters in the south called themselves after 1960. A series of military coups followed, as Roman Catholics and Buddhists alternately protested that their interests were being slighted. When the military leaders finally proposed a schedule for returning to constitutional government during 1966 and 1967, many did not believe them. Yet a constitutional assembly was elected in 1966, a new presidential constitution was put into effect, and southern-born military leader Nguyen Van Thieu was elected president in 1967. Buddhist leaders, who were likely to dominate any elected civilian government, protested out of dislike for continued military rule, but not as vigorously as they had protested the continuance of the Diem government.

The military rulers in Saigon were aware that the post-1945 experiences of Burma, the Philippines, and the Federation of Malaya showed that the simple reestablishment of order was the first prerequisite in convincing a peasant population that it had more to hope for from the government than it had to fear from the guerrillas. Unless the peasants felt the government could protect them, they would tend to succumb to the guerrillas' combination of force and propaganda. However, a comparison of Burma, the Philippines, and the Federation of Malaya with China also showed that military action had to be accompanied by two other policies to be successful: the use of positive inducements such as amnesty and land to attract waverers from the guerrilla cause, and the extension of benefits to the peasants among whom the guerrillas had to live. By the time Diem fell, these aspects of the struggle had been neglected for so long that the guerrillas were capable of sabotaging most of the new rulers' efforts to attract peasant support in guerrilla-infested areas. The guerrillas did not hesitate to use force or the threat of force to convince peasants that it was unsafe to oppose them.

In an effort to strengthen the Saigon government's hand, the United States increased its already sizable commitments to give military and economic aid, and in 1965 began bombing potential sources of guerrilla supplies in northern Vietnam. By 1968 United States forces were heavily engaged in fighting in the south, and many southerners had fled to the cities to escape either the National Liberation Front or the bombs and shells directed against National Liberation Front forces. Between 1968 and 1972, United States forces gradually withdrew from ground fighting, though they continued to take part in naval and air operations. However, heavy fighting continued between the Vietnamese contenders, and many of the refugees remained in the urban areas. Thieu sought to remedy the government's difficulties in the rural areas by restoring the selection of village heads to the villages, giving the heads more authority, and pushing a comprehensive land-reform program through the landlord-dominated legislature in 1970. During the next two years the attractiveness of the National Liberation Front to the people of the countryside began to wane somewhat, as the new village governments took hold and former tenants became government-registered owners of the land they tilled. In 1971, in an election in which neither of the other two leading potential candidates actually ran, Thieu was reelected president of the Republic of Vietnam.

During 1972 Thieu proceeded to consolidate his power by declaring martial law, curbing the press and the political parties, and making village heads once again appointive. By the opening of 1973 he felt strong enough to contain the National Liberation Front without supportive military action from the United States. He agreed to a cease-fire with the National Liberation Front, which was also signed by the United States and the Democratic Republic of Vietnam, and to the appointment of representatives to discuss the holding of elections in southern Vietnam with representatives from the National Liberation Front.

The last United States forces withdrew from the south as discussions on the nature of the elections began in Paris in March, 1973. Both Thieu and the National Liberation Front retained an effective veto in those discussions, since the terms of the cease-fire agreement provided that the decisions of the representatives of the Republic of Vietnam and the National Liberation Front on all matters having to do with the promised elections—timing, scope, organization, and supervision—must be unanimous in order to be binding. The governments of Canada, Hungary, Indonesia, and Poland agreed to provide members for a new International Commission of Control and Supervision, who would join with representatives of the contending parties to oversee the carrying out of the cease-fire. However, they realized that unless a decision was reached concerning the holding of elections, it would be difficult to prevent new military incidents between the forces of the Republic of Vietnam and those of the National Liberation Front. Canada withdrew from the commission three months after it was formed, as hopes receded for an early agreement on the holding of elections in the south. Iran took the place vacated by Canada. By the end of 1973 all prospect of agreement between the Republic of Vietnam and the National Liberation Front seemed gone, and in 1974 Thieu authorized his forces to undertake military action inside areas claimed by the National Liberation Front. He also occupied two small groups of islands in the South China Sea—also claimed by the People's Republic of China, the Republic of China, and the Philippines—which suddenly appeared important because of the possibility that oil might be found under the sea around them. The People's Republic of China quickly forced the Vietnamese off the uninhabited northern group, which lay as close to China as to any part of Vietnam, but did not challenge the Saigon government's occupation of the southern islands.

THE DEMOCRATIC REPUBLIC OF VIETNAM (1954–1974). The government of Ho Chi Minh in Hanoi unquestionably hoped that the Saigon government would not succeed in suppressing its guerrilla opponents, who were closely linked with the leaders of the Democratic Republic of Vietnam. In the years following the Geneva accords, the war-shattered economy of northern Vietnam was rebuilt with Soviet and Chinese aid. The Lao Dang, or Workers' Party, tightened its already strong control over every aspect of Vietnamese life in the north. Autonomous districts were established for the minority hill peoples, much like those across the border in the People's Republic of China. Schools were established to train the youth of the country in the skills and concepts thought most useful by the leaders. Agricultural land was redistributed to the peasants and then (despite peasant uprisings in 1956) regrouped into collective farms whose produce would be divided according to contributions in land and labor. Industrial, commercial, and transport facilities were taken over by the state.

Industrial output in northern Vietnam increased steadily from 1954 to 1964, but food production did not. In fact, food production during that period actually declined in some years. Vietnamese economist Hoang Van Chi has suggested that rice output may have declined because rice paddies need constant individual attention, and the collective system offers the individual little incentive to give any crop that kind of care.[1] Still, the Democratic Republic of Vietnam remained strong and united enough to continue supplying guerrillas operating in the territories of its neighbors in what had once been the French-controlled Indochinese Union, even after United States bombing raids began in 1965. As a supporter of such struggles, it was drawn increasingly into the orbit of its Chinese neighbor and away from the less guerrilla-minded Soviet Union. Nevertheless, its leaders continued to demonstrate their desire to remain on good terms with the Soviet Union. The Soviets reciprocated by providing the Hanoi government with anti-aircraft missiles and other military equipment.

Although the Democratic Republic of Vietnam did not acknowledge that its soldiers were supporting the National Liberation Front in the south, its representatives did agree in 1968 to initiate peace negotiations in Paris with representatives of the United States in public talks in which both the National Liberation Front and the Republic of Vietnam were represented. Ho Chi Minh hoped to see the talks concluded, but they remained as inconclusive after his death in 1969 as they had been until that time. His successors continued to strive, both on the battlefields in southern Vietnam and at the peace talks in Paris, for the replacement of the Thieu government with a friendlier regime. By the time Ho died, the Democratic Republic appeared to be willing to work with a separate state in the south, rather than continuing to attempt to incorporate north and south under a single government in the near future. Even the open use of northern troops in border regions of the south in 1972 had the declared aim of aiding the provisional government set up for the south by the National Liberation Front, rather than of reuniting north and south under the rule of Hanoi. The continued activity of northern Vietnamese, not only in southern Vietnam but in Cambodia and Laos, reminded many that the first formal Communist organization in Vietnam in 1929 had been named the Indochinese rather than the Vietnamese Communist party. When a cease-fire was finally

[1] "Collectivization and Rice Production," *The China Quarterly*, no. 9 (Jan.–Mar. 1962), 94–104.

agreed on at the beginning of 1973 through private negotiations between the Democratic Republic of Vietnam and the United States, and concurred in by the National Liberation Front and the Republic of Vietnam, it was recognized by all that the contest for supremacy in the Republic of Vietnam, Cambodia, and Laos was by no means over.

CAMBODIA

The period of French control had repercussions in Laos and Cambodia, but they were fewer and shallower than those observable in Vietnam. The protectorate governments continued support of the monastic schools, rather than establishing any sizable network of government schools comparable to those set up in Vietnam. Furthermore, most French officials and entrepreneurs in Laos and Cambodia used Vietnamese assistants rather than Laotians or Cambodians. Cambodians could even be grateful for French protection, for France preserved their lands from Siamese encroachment more successfully than they had been able to do.

In the early years of the protectorate, the loyalty of the Cambodian people to their monarch was strained enough by hatred of the French to produce two small Siamese-supported rebellions in 1866–1867 and 1885–1887, but as time passed, the French carefully and rather successfully fostered the belief that French administrators really did defer to the ruler's wishes. Slavery was abolished, a trans-Cambodian railway and a road network were built, and rubber plantations were established in previously uncultivated areas.

The French discouraged Cambodians from studying abroad. Since they had almost no schools other than the monastic ones, they learned little of the theories underlying the ways of modern economic, political, and social life. Consequently, the Vietnamese and the resident Chinese merchants were able to take over more and more of the country's economic life.

Most Cambodians accepted these changes placidly. No serious anti-French movement was undertaken until 1936, when Son Ngoc Thanh founded an anti-protectorate Cambodian-language newspaper. During World War II he cooperated with the Japanese and in 1945 made himself prime minister of Cambodia. Soon after the French returned, they arrested him. Some of his followers fled to Thailand and formed a Khmer Issarak (Free Cambodian) movement. With the backing of Pridi's government, the Khmer Issarak joined Viet Minh forces in eastern Cambodia against the French, but the overtly Communist sympathies of the Viet Minh eventually antagonized many of the Khmer Issarak.

The young king of Cambodia, Norodom Sihanouk, persuaded a

number of the Khmer Issarak to lay down their arms because they were only exasperating the French. However, the French would not be persuaded to leave Cambodia simply because they were exasperating the Khmer Issarak. The French even refused to deal with Sihanouk's cabinet because its members were associated with Son Ngoc Thanh. In 1952, in a last desperate gamble, Sihanouk abdicated as king, dismissed his cabinet, and founded the Sangkum political party so that he could compete at the polls with the party of Son Ngoc Thanh. He hoped to maneuver the French out of the country and thereby win his people's lasting allegiance. The daring gamble succeeded. In the fifteen years after 1954 his ability to maneuver his way unscathed through international rivalries, procuring diplomatic support and economic assistance from all sides, marked him as one of the shrewdest diplomats on the Asian scene. He maintained popularity at home as well, getting rid of most of the remaining leaders of Son Ngoc Thanh's party in 1962 as traitors conspiring with Hanoi to overthrow the monarcy. He used the monarchy as a symbol of unity and undertook some economic nationalization as a means of upholding Cambodia's economic independence. Although many Western leaders deplored his flirtation with the People's Republic of China, the realities of his country's position as he saw it—lodged between Thailand and the Republic of Vietnam, two United States-supported states whose earlier rulers had nibbled at Cambodian lands since the fifteenth century—made his desire for a counterbalancing power as understandable as his apparent anxiety to be on good terms with China, the traditional Colossus of the North to Southeast Asians.

As the tempo of hostilities in neighboring Vietnam increased in the mid-1960s, Sihanouk's balancing act became increasingly difficult. By 1969 his military officers were alarmed enough over the possible future implications of Vietnamese Communist use of Cambodian territory as a sanctuary that he felt obliged to make his chief general, Lon Nol, his prime minister. In March, 1970, while Sihanouk was out of the country, Lon Nol took over in a coup which led to Cambodia's becoming a republic, with Lon Nol as prime minister. Official Cambodian complaints about the presence of Vietnamese Communists led to a two-month sweep through much of eastern Cambodia by United States and Republic of Vietnam forces. The United States troops withdrew, but the Vietnamese stayed, a result which did not please all Cambodians. Cambodia became in effect partitioned between those who preferred the new republican government of Lon Nol and the presence of anti-Communist Vietnamese in Cambodia, and those who preferred the government-in-exile maintained by Sihanouk in Peking and the presence of Communist Vietnamese. Early in 1972, Lon Nol took over full power and proclaimed himself president. He appointed Sihanouk's long-time political opponent Son Ngoc Thanh as his prime minister. However,

Thanh stepped down later in the year, after elections to the upper house of the republic's national assembly gave an overwhelming victory to a political party led by another man. Shortly after the Vietnam cease-fire was signed in January, 1973, both Lon Nol and Sihanouk called on their supporters to refrain from offensive military operations so that all Vietnamese could leave Cambodia. Sihanouk hinted he might resign from his post as head of the government-in-exile in Peking; but in view of his record for political adroitness, few observers were prepared to believe he was ready to eliminate himself entirely from Cambodia's future. It remained possible—as Yemen had shown in 1970 and as Laos had tried to show since 1962—that royalists and republicans might agree to merge. After Sihanouk's well-publicized visit in the spring of 1973 to parts of Cambodia not held by Lon Nol's forces, some even speculated that Sihanouk would eventually become the head of whatever merger might take place.

LAOS

The former French protectorate of Laos became partitioned between Communist sympathizers and their opponents sooner than did Cambodia. It lay in a more exposed position than Cambodia, being next to both China and northern Vietnam, and had even less experience with nationalist movements. The first Laotian nationalist movement was the Lao Issara, or Free Lao, which was formed in 1945 by various princes including half-brothers Souvanna Phouma and Souphannouvong to protest the king's willingness to allow his friends and supporters the French to return to Luang Prabang. The Lao Issara formed a rival government in Vientiane which was driven out in 1947 by the French and sought refuge in Thailand. Souphannouvong opted for cooperation with the Viet Minh and went to northeast Laos to form the Pathet Lao (Country of Lao) movement with Viet Minh support, but most of the rest maneuvered their way into the royal government, which accepted them as temporarily misguided patriots. A constitution was established in 1947 which provided for elected national, provincial, and municipal councils, but which recognized the limits of the royal government's effectiveness by not attempting to prescribe any uniform pattern for village or district governance.

By the time of the 1954 Geneva agreement, the Pathet Lao had used the longstanding aversion of the hill tribes toward Luang Prabang to bring northeastern Laos under its control. In 1958 Souphannouvong used his position to force Souvanna Phouma (then prime minister) to give the Pathet Lao two cabinet seats, but after elections in which the Pathet Lao showed a strength alarming to many in the royal government, a strongly anti-Pathet Lao cabinet dominated by Phoumi Nosavan replaced Souvanna Phouma's coalition. Souphannouvong promptly began to reequip his forces, with Communist aid. In a series of campaigns beginning in 1960 the Pathet Lao captured most of the hill country, which incidentally made it easier for Hanoi to send supplies along the Ho Chi Minh trail through Laos to the National Liberation Front in southern Vietnam. The Pathet Lao even challenged the royal government's control in parts of the lowlands, though it was somewhat less successful in winning local support there. To valley Lao, the Pathet Lao appeared to represent primarily the hill tribes, with whom they had been at odds for centuries over matters such as the lowlanders' desire to establish permanent settled agriculture in some of the areas where the tribes continued to practice shifting cultivation. Finally in 1962 another international gathering at Geneva reaffirmed Laotian neutrality, called for withdrawal of all foreign troops, and recognized an uneasy coalition government which put both Phoumi Nosavan and Souphannouvong in a cabinet headed by Souvanna Phouma. After Souphannouvong retired in 1963 to the hill country, which the Pathet Lao controlled with little effective interference from Vientiane, Phoumi Nosavan crossed the Mekong to Thailand, leaving Souvanna Phouma in charge. A meeting between Souvanna Phouma and Souphannouvong in 1964 produced no agreement. The Pathet Lao boycotted the national assembly elections held between 1965 and 1972, on the ground that they contravened the terms of the 1962 agreement, but the royal government in Vientiane survived both its verbal and its continuing military attacks. A month after the Vietnam cease-fire agreement of January, 1973, renewed talks between representatives of Souvanna Phouma and Souphannouvong finally resulted in a cease-fire and an agreement for the formation of a new bipartite coalition government in which the Pathet Lao would play a larger role than they had in the tripartite coalition established in 1962. The agreement was not implemented fully until 1974, after the Pathet Lao had disclaimed any formal connection with the Democratic Republic of Vietnam, the National Liberation Front in southern Vietnam, or the Communists of Cambodia.

Both the Pathet Lao and the royal government sought to improve educational, health, and transport facilities in the regions they administered. Still, most Laotians remained tied to subsistence agriculture, whether of the sedentary or the shifting variety, and the persisting strife hampered the development programs of both sets of leaders throughout the 1960s. The continued use of the Ho Chi Minh trail through the Pathet Lao regions by the forces of the Democratic Republic of Vietnam made Souvanna Phouma lean somewhat more to the West than to the East as long as the conflict in southern Vietnam continued. He accepted the efforts of the United States to block traffic on the Ho Chi Minh trail by massive bombing raids, whch ended when the February, 1973, cease-fire agreement for Laos was signed. However, it was hard to see how landlocked Laos could afford or be allowed to be anything but neutral, surrounded as it was by two Communist states, two states fighting relatively small Communist-supported insurgencies, and two states in which Communist-supported insurgents controlled larger areas.

Japanese, Chinese, and Communists in Southeast Asia

THE JAPANESE IN SOUTHEAST ASIA

The first faint stirrings of open opposition to French rule did not come in Laos until the period of the Japanese withdrawal. The Japanese occupation of Southeast Asia between 1940 and 1945 was indeed a dividing line in Southeast Asian history, although not in the way the Japanese had intended. The Japanese meant to bring Southeast Asia into their own Greater East Asia Co-Prosperity Sphere when they occupied part of Vietnam with French permission in 1940. In 1941 they entered Thailand as a friendly ally, and in 1942 they entered the Philippines, Burma, the Malay peninsula, and Indonesia as victorious liberators from Western rule. However, the Japanese soon found that the more they appealed to Southeast Asians to unite against the West under Japan, the more the Southeast Asians displayed an embarrassing desire to run their own affairs. As the war went on and defeat loomed ever nearer, the Japanese tried to avert uprisings by acceding to these demands, at least outwardly. The last Southeast Asian state to proclaim its independence was the Republic of Indonesia, which did not formally claim full sovereignty until shortly after Japan's decision to surrender in August, 1945.

The brief period of Japanese rule was important because the Japanese eventually recognized the colonies of Southeast Asia as independent states, but it was also important because it led to new waves of anti-foreign fervor. Except for the Malays of the Malay peninsula, almost all groups and classes united against the Japanese and thereby prepared themselves to fight returning Europeans after the war. Somewhat unintentionally, the Japanese occupation even promoted national unification in Indonesia through insisting on the use of a standard Indonesian dialect throughout the islands and expanding the centrally-controlled radio network until its partly Indonesian-language and partly local-language programs reached even the most isolated regions.

The Japanese occupation also emphasized the existence of the sizable Chinese minorities in almost every part of Southeast Asia. At first the Japanese tried to integrate the Chinese into the local population or, if Chinese loyalty to the homeland was too strong, to turn their allegiance from the Kuomintang regime in Chungking to the Japanese-sponsored puppet government at Nanking. However, the Japanese soon found that Chinese sympathies lay overwhelmingly with those who were struggling against Japanese domination of China. Therefore, the Japanese turned to harsh repression of the Southeast Asian Chinese. This repression reemphasized the already noticeable distinctions between the Chinese of the Nanyang, the "southern seas" of Southeast Asia, and the peoples among whom they lived. That emphasis was almost as crucial a factor in postwar developments in some Southeast Asian countries as the experience of seeing Asians conquer Westerners and the achievement of at least a nominal independence in the last months of World War II.

THE CHINESE IN SOUTHEAST ASIA

From the time the Chinese entered the commercial life of Southeast Asia, they behaved as a separate people. They spread out from the ports into the countryside as shopkeepers, as moneylenders, as tin miners in the Malay peninsula, and after the early nineteenth century as cash-crop agricultural workers (although Indians also went to Burma and the Malay peninsula as agricultural laborers); but they always maintained their loyalty to China. They sent as much money home to their relatives as they could; they returned home themselves whenever possible. They also reared their children to be proud heirs of China's civilized traditions, whether the children's mothers were women of the local population, as they usually were before 1900, or women brought from China, as they often were after the advent of steamships and cheap transportation.

Until the twentieth century, the external allegiance of Southeast Asian Chinese to China bothered most Southeast Asians no more than Jewish sympathy for the state of Israel has disturbed most non-Jews in countries like Britain and the United States. Southeast Asians were not used to thinking of outsiders as posing a threat which could force them to choose between uniting in self-defense and succumbing to external rule. By 1900 China had not sent military forces to most Southeast Asian states for almost five hundred years, and even its neighbors in Burma, Vietnam, and Laos had felt its power only a few times since the 1420s. It was traditional for Southeast Asian states to accept stronger states as nominal overlords, as all but the Spanish Philippines did with China, and as Cambodia and Laos did with Vietnam and Siam. This tradition even enabled European states to be regarded in somewhat the same light as China, at least where Europeans infiltrated familiar local governments as in Cambodia, Laos, the Malay peninsula, and much of Indonesia, rather than attempting to replace the customary governmental system as in Burma and much of Vietnam. However, Southeast Asians gradually began to fear the loss of their identity as more and more new ways were introduced into their midst. By 1945 they were aware as never before that they were under a double handicap in their struggle for independence. In order to control their own affairs, they had to overthrow not only the political and economic power of the Westerners at the top, but the economic power of the Chinese who carried Southeast Asia's products to the Westerners' markets.

Southeast Asians began to realize the economic strength of the Chinese in their lands at approximately the same time that Chinese overseas began to realize their motherland needed their assistance. Sun Yat-sen and others of his generation campaigned vigorously and successfully for funds and volunteers among the Chinese of the Nanyang. Once the Chinese republic came into being, it began sending teachers to the Nanyang to set up schools in which the children of Chinese would learn not only pride in Chinese civilization but allegiance to the new Chinese nation-state.

Southeast Asians learned organizational techniques from the Chinese in their midst, but their dreams of independence received little sympathy from their Chinese co-residents. The Chinese were too engrossed in China's politics, and too concerned about their relations with Westerners in Southeast Asia, to pay much attention to Southeast Asian nationalism. As the twentieth century progressed, the Chinese in Southeast Asia divided into two hostile camps, the larger group favoring the Kuomintang and the smaller one favoring the Communists. Japan's invasion of China temporarily reunited them, but renewed civil war in China in the 1940s meant renewed divisions among Chinese overseas.

Chinese preoccupation with affairs in China eventually led many Southeast Asians to regard all Chinese as subversive elements. In Thailand, where there was no Western government to attack, the Chinese bore the brunt of dawning nationalist sentiment. Stringent anti-Chinese regulations were put into effect in the 1930s. (A Western government in Thailand might have protected Chinese traders from local attacks, as Western governments did in other parts of Southeast Asia.) The adamant opposition of the Chinese of every Southeast Asian country to the Japanese conquest of Southeast Asia, in contrast to the welcome which many Southeast Asians gave the Japanese at first, only heightened the feeling that the Chinese were a law unto themselves.

As Southeast Asians won independence after the war, and as the Colossus of Southeast Asia's North turned from the Kuomintang to the more sweeping and radical program of the Communists, most of the new states decided to make a strong effort to free their economies from

Chinese control. They also decided to promote rapid assimilation of the Chinese into the local populace, and to discourage the separate Chinese school systems that were still teaching loyalty to one or the other of the two governments that claimed to rule China.

The Southeast Asians set themselves a difficult task when they decided to convince their Chinese co-residents that they were part of the state in which they lived rather than part of China. At first the task was made still more difficult by the fact that both the Kuomintang and Communist governments openly continued to regard all Chinese overseas as Chinese citizens. However, in the late 1950s both the Kuomintang and the Communists began to tell the Chinese of the Nanyang that they could best serve China's interests by being loyal to the governments under which they lived. By then most Southeast Asian states had taken steps to encourage residents of Chinese ancestry to renounce all formal ties with either the Republic or the People's Republic of China. Still, it was 1960 before Communist China and Indonesia agreed on the means by which individuals could renounce their Chinese citizenship in favor of Indonesian citizenship.

The problem of assimilation did not seem alarmingly great in states where the Chinese community was small, as in the Philippines (1–2 percent), in Burma (1–2 percent), or in the region of Laos, Cambodia, and Vietnam (3–5 percent). The Chinese population in the former French empire was concentrated in the lower Mekong valley, with most of the Chinese in southern Vietnam and a smaller number in Cambodia. Even in populous Indonesia, where the small percentage of Chinese (2–4 percent) meant two to four million people, the difficulties were not as great as in Thailand. There the magnitude of the assimilation problem was much larger. Depending on whether "Chinese" was taken to mean "born in China," "one parent born in China," or "one parent whose self-identification was Chinese regardless of birthplace," Chinese might form as much as 15–20 percent of the population of Thailand. Thai resentment of Chinese economic power and of continued Chinese interest in China was correspondingly strong. As late as 1972, the Thai government was still promulgating legislation designed to force aliens (mainly non-nationalized Chinese residents) out of various kinds of businesses such as the local rice trade. In the Malay peninsula and Singapore the situation was so different quantitatively from the situation in any other part of Southeast Asia that for all practical purposes it also differed qualitatively. The 1947 census showed 1,884,534 Chinese, 2,427,834 Malays, and 530,638 Indians in British Malaya, and 730,133 Chinese out of 940,824 inhabitants in Singapore. The situation in Singapore was almost the exact reverse of that in the British-influenced areas of northern Borneo, where 1947 and 1951 censuses showed 227,832 Chinese out of 921,183 inhabitants. By the post-1945 era the influx of Chinese into the

Malay peninsula meant the Malays had no alternative to working with rather than against the Chinese. Malay leaders could not afford to use harshness in attempting to force the Chinese to unite with the Malays or they would be in real danger of being thrust aside in favor of an overtly Chinese state.

COMMUNIST MOVEMENTS IN SOUTHEAST ASIA

Some of the Chinese in Malaya became so discontented with their position that for a time after 1945 they supported a Communist campaign to take over the peninsula. Although the campaign was not successful, the ability of the Communists to win backing pointed up the potential strength of Communist appeals to dissatisfied groups in Southeast Asia. These appeals had begun even before the Russian revolutions of 1917, as Dutch Marxists brought Marxist ideas to Indonesia. By 1920 the small Indonesian trade unions were strongly Marxist-influenced, and so were many of the rising nationalist leaders. As soon as the Indonesian Communist Party was formed in 1921, some Indonesian nationalists joined it. Vietnamese learned of Marxism in France during World War I, although no formal Communist party was organized for Indochina until 1929. In 1930, four Filipinos who had recently returned to the Philippines from Moscow inaugurated the Communist party there. Burma's Communists were not numerous enough to organize a party until 1939.

In all of these colonially ruled areas, the fervor of those who embraced Marxism-Leninism in the pre-independence years was the fervor of Indonesians, Vietnamese, Filipinos, and Burmese opposing the political and economic dominance of Dutch, French, Americans, British, Chinese, and Indians. In most of them the Communists attempted to set up a Communist government in the transition era between colonial rule and independence after World War II. They only succeeded in northern Vietnam, although they won a wide following among Indonesian voters; but from their northern Vietnamese base they soon began running feelers into neighboring Laos, and strengthening their ties with sympathizers in southern Vietnam and Cambodia.

In the Malay peninsula, Singapore, and Thailand the situation was somewhat different. There the large Chinese communities were the first to receive Communist attention, as the Kuomintang propagandized among them during the 1923–1927 Kuomintang-Communist alliance. After that alliance broke down, Communists in the Malay peninsula, Singapore, and Thailand continued to work on Chinese sympathies for China's plight, and they established themselves firmly in the influential Chinese segment of the population. The Malayan Communist Party, which worked in Singapore also, was founded in 1931. It included scarcely any Malays, though a few Indians were scattered among the dominant Chinese, and when it tried to expel the British after 1948 it failed to win any appreciable support outside some sections of the Chinese community.

The Communist movement in Thailand was cast into obscurity by the anti-subversion laws of 1933. It did not reemerge until the brief postwar period of accommodation to the wishes of the victorious and veto-holding Soviet Union, between 1945 and Thailand's admission to the United Nations in 1947. When the Soviet Union established its first embassy in Bangkok in 1948, the embassy staff immediately began to encourage the formation of a Thai Communist party. However, the separately run Chinese party remained much stronger. The Thai took harsh measures against subversives and against Chinese after the generals returned to power in 1948. In fact, they tended to confuse anti-subversive and anti-Chinese measures. Not only were almost all of Thailand's Communists Chinese, but the government of the People's Republic of China was sponsoring the exiled Free Thai opposition movement headed by former prime minister Pridi.

Both in mainland Southeast Asia and in the islands, the Communists ran into some of the same kinds of difficulties they experienced in the Middle East, as well as situations unique to Southeast Asia. They could win support among minority hill peoples in every part of Southeast Asia for a "class conflict" consisting of attacks on the majority peoples' attempts to control them, but they could scarcely win majority support with such appeals. They could raise support among majority peoples for a "class conflict" consisting of attacks on the domination of the economy by those of Chinese ancestry, but they had to play down such appeals when they approached members of the Chinese communities. They found almost as much resistance as in most of the Middle East to the acceptance of a general doctrine of class conflict that would only exacerbate existing social divisions, in the face of the desire of the dominant nationalists to minimize the existence and the effects of those divisions. In addition, they found a similar lack of comprehension of the meaning of class conflict because of the continuance of household-centered life and the relative lack of experience with more impersonal forms of social and economic organization, at least where Western-introduced plantations, mines, and mills were not part of everyday life. There were exceptions, most notably among Vietnamese who shared the disillusionment of the Chinese with Confucianism's ineffectiveness in maintaining their independence from foreign rule, and also in poverty-ridden sections of eastern and central Java. However, for the most part the Communists won sympathizers for their attacks upon outsiders (whether these were seen as Westerners, Chinese, or majority peoples) and absentee landlords, rather than converts to full-scale class conflict in the original Marxist sense.

11

THE MODERN ERA:
THE MALAY PENINSULA
AND THE ISLANDS

The Philippines

SPANISH RULE (16TH TO 19TH CENTURY)

While the early Portuguese adventurers were seeking, and eventually failing, to win the Indies for themselves and for Christendom in the sixteenth century, the Spaniards whom they jealously drove from the Moluccas succeeded in establishing political, economic, and religious supremacy in the Philippines. In 1571, six years after their first conquests in the islands, the Spaniards founded Manila, on the island of Luzon, to serve as their capital. Within a generation they had taken over all of the coastal and lowland regions except the already Muslim portions of Mindanao and the Sulu islands to the southeast, which they never completely subdued; within a century they had penetrated all but the most remote of the hill districts.

The people in the districts the Spaniards controlled were quickly but superficially converted from animism to Roman Catholicism. At first the Spaniards governed by farming out districts to individual Spaniards who promised to keep the people quiet, see that they were instructed in Christianity, and pay the royal treasury a fifth of whatever tribute they might collect. However, by 1700 the governor-general at Manila appointed, paid, and removed his own administrators in the provinces. Since Manila was far from both Spain and its New World viceroyalties, the governor-general's freedom of action was limited only by the power of the archbishop of the Philippines who, in fact, was instructed by the crown to act as governor-general whenever the governor-general was absent or incapacitated. The Spanish clergy wielded power not only in

Manila but also in the provinces. Although the wealthier Filipino residents of the townships into which the provinces were divided had some voice in local decisions, they tended to rely on the priests to present their grievances to the government.

During the seventeenth and eighteenth centuries, the clergy greatly extended the agricultural lands which the kings of Spain granted to them to support the work of the church. In the late nineteenth century, when the Spanish administration in a rare fit of rationalism decided to sweep away the existing tangle of land rights, cultivation rights, communal holdings, and other forms of land tenure in favor of a unified system of hereditary transferable individual ownership, the church was the major beneficiary. Many wealthy Spaniards and Filipinos also benefited, usually at the expense of poorer Filipinos, somewhat as French settlers and wealthy Egyptians benefited at the expense of Algerians and poorer Egyptians, respectively, when land laws were altered in Algeria and Egypt in the mid-nineteenth century. Traditional rights of cultivation were replaced by a landlord-and-tenant system which gave almost no protection to the tenants, as when the British East India Company introduced the Permanent Settlement in Bengal in Cornwallis's time. Most Filipinos became caught between rising rents and the high interest rates of the moneylenders, the majority of whom were Chinese. The Filipinos remained devoted to the Christian faith and the Spanish culture which had become part of their lives in the three centuries of Spanish rule, but they were more than ready for changes in the roles of government and clergy when the newly rising power of the United States expelled the Spaniards from the Philippines in 1898.

FILIPINO UNREST (19TH CENTURY)

The Spaniards converted the Filipinos to Christianity. They introduced Spanish education, founding the first European-style university in Southeast Asia in 1645, and instilled aspects of the Spanish branch of European civilization from guitars to great landed estates raising commercial crops like sugar, tobacco, and hemp. However, they were slow to open the Philippines to trade with the rest of the world. For two hundred years Manila was almost as secluded as Tokugawa Edo. Some Chinese traders came to it to exchange silks, porcelains, and other goods for silver dollars from Mexico. A few ships sailed between Manila and the Spanish New World, but only one ship a year went to Spain.

Spanish educational efforts brought into being a Filipino intermediary group of priests, civil servants, and schoolteachers, but at first neither educated nor uneducated Filipinos questioned Spanish rule. Then, at the close of the eighteenth century, the opening of Manila to traders other than Chinese, Spaniards, and Latin Americans exposed the islands to outside influences. Rapid increases in trade enriched many Filipino merchants. They began sending their sons and occasionally their daughters to Europe to study, particularly after 1869 when the opening of the Suez Canal shortened the trip between Europe and the Philippines. As these students returned, they found that the new land laws were being used to deprive the poorer peasants of their land rights. Immediately, the ideas of liberalism and nationalism of which they had heard in Europe took on new meaning. They began to request reforms of the government officials in both Manila and Madrid.

Most of the returning Filipino students requested only a widening of civil liberties, elevation of the islands to the status of a province of Spain, and the lessening of the grip of the Spanish friars on the affairs of the church. However, their writings inspired others to seek full independence. In 1896 armed revolts began. When the United States fleet occupied Manila, as part of a war over the way Spain was handling Cuban demands for freedom, the rebels used the situation to proclaim Philippine independence in June, 1898. With support from tenants on church estates, the rebels established a provisional republican government which promptly decreed the confiscation of church lands and the expulsion of the Spanish friars.

To the republicans' disappointment, the United States decided in 1899 that the Filipinos were not yet ready to maintain the sovereignty they claimed. It took two years of hard fighting to convince Emilio Aguinaldo, president and military commander of the provisional government, that the United States was right. By 1901, when he capitulated and swore allegiance to the United States, independence had been promised as soon as Filipinos could manage a representative democratic government. United States military power also brought Mindanao and the Sulus under the effective control of Manila for the first time.

UNITED STATES RULE AND PHILIPPINE INDEPENDENCE (20TH CENTURY)

In 1907 the United States established a national legislature for the Philippines, with a small appointed upper house—most of whose members were United States citizens serving in the islands—and a lower house of eighty members elected from territorial constituencies by those men who could read and write Spanish or English. In 1913 the Filipino minority in the upper house became a majority. In 1916 all but two of its seats were made elective and the franchise was extended to men literate in any language, but the governor-general and the United States President and Congress retained the power to annul legislative acts. Popular elections for township heads and provincial governors were introduced before the end of 1917. The civil service was rapidly made Filipino, with 49 percent Filipino in 1903, 81 percent in 1913, and 94 percent in 1923. Rapid expansion of schools provided Filipinos with educational opportunities. In 1934 the United States government at last set a date for Philippine independence, and in November, 1935, an almost autonomous commonwealth government was formally inaugurated, with a Filipino executive led by a president and vice-president elected by universal suffrage.

The new commonwealth inherited some difficult problems from the past. One of these was land ownership. The United States had ended the first Philippine republic, but it accepted some of the republic's basic policies in modified form. For example, steps were taken to purchase church lands and enable tenants to buy the land they worked. However, land office personnel were predominantly underpaid Filipinos. A few wealthy individuals easily acquired large tracts of church lands and of new lands just being opened for cultivation, in another parallel to the disposition of state lands in mid-nineteenth-century Egypt. As a result, the percentage of tenant cultivators in the Philippines actually doubled from 1900 to 1935. Numerous local rural rebellions took place in central Luzon in the 1920s and 1930s. These rebellions boded ill for the new commonwealth unless its leaders gave high priority to land reform, but nothing was done, for many elected officials were from the wealthy landlord families, who were among the few that could afford the time and expense of political campaigning.

The United States promised the commonwealth independence in 1945, ten years after its inauguration. During the latter part of the decade of transition, the Philippine economy would be required to adjust to competing with other independent states in the United States market. Step by step, regular United States tariffs would be imposed on sugar, coconut oils, hemp, and other products which were then entering the United States duty-free. However, the tariff provisions of the Philippine Independence Act of 1934 were not put into effect because of the Japanese occupation of the islands between 1941 and 1945. After World War II the tariff provisions of 1934 were replaced by measures which postponed the eventual imposition of full tariffs to 1974.

Since the United States had set a date for Philippine independence, few Filipinos heeded Japan's claim to be freeing them from Western imperialism in 1941. Even those who accepted posts in the Japanese-sponsored republic formed in 1943 were not particularly pro-Japanese. Instead it was the returning Americans who were hailed in 1944 as liberators. New elections were held in April, 1946. In July the Philippines became the first Southeast Asian land to be recognized as free by its former rulers, to the great satisfaction of Aguinaldo, who had lived to see the independence promised his people forty-five years before. The

United States retained a residual presence by leasing several military and naval bases, but in 1966 the termination of the lease was changed from 2045 to 1991, and in the next few years some of the bases were turned back to the Philippine government.

The Japanese occupation offered the peasants a new chance to acquire land, this time by undertaking ostensibly anti-Japanese guerrilla attacks on landlords who acquiesced in Japanese rule to save themselves. In March, 1942, the Hukbalahap (People's Army Against the Japanese) was formed in central Luzon. Some of its leaders belonged to the small Filipino Communist party. When United States forces returned in 1944 the landlords procured their aid in trying to disarm the Hukbalahap, but in vain. The peasant supporters of the movement were determined to obtain land redistribution; the increasingly Communist leadership was determined to use peasant support to overthrow the Manila government. Alarmed at continued Hukbalahap strength, the government dismissed the most corrupt and incompetent of its army officers. It also took advantage of increasing United States interest in Philippine affairs after the Korean conflict opened in 1950 to obtain economic assistance. Most important of all, the government appointed a new secretary of national defense, Ramon Magsaysay. Magsaysay realized that military measures alone could not end the movement, for the peasants wanted land and would fight until they got it. Therefore, he set aside lands to distribute to those who renounced the Hukbalahap. By 1953 the Hukbalahap had almost disappeared, land redistribution was under way, and Magsaysay had been elected president.

In 1954, the Magsaysay government balanced its moves against landlords with the Philippine Retail Trade Nationalization Act—a move against wealthy Chinese business people who then held two-fifths of the islands' commercial investments. It also sought closer ties with the United States, with which the Philippines had signed a mutual defense pact in 1951, by calling a conference of states interested in Southeast Asian affairs. Australia, Britain, France, New Zealand, Pakistan, Thailand, and the United States responded and formed the South-East Asia Treaty Organization to oppose aggression against the member states or against newly formed Laos, Cambodia, and the Republic of Vietnam.

Magsaysay's death in an airplane crash in 1957 deprived the Philippines of the one political leader who had done much to improve the peasant's lot. The measures protecting tenants which he introduced were continued, but land redistribution slacked off so much that a new land reform bill had to be enacted in 1963. Even then, it was implemented so slowly that the Hukbalahap started reappearing in 1965. During 1970, a portion of the Hukbalahap forces surrendered, for the introduction of new strains of high-yield rice and of government-built roads and schools was depriving them of some of their supporters. However, by that time conflicts between the Muslim and animist inhabitants of Mindanao and new Christian settlers there from Luzon and other islands were confronting the government with a new set of problems. In 1970, the year in which Ferdinand Marcos began an unprecedented second four-year term as president, a constituent assembly was elected to review the constitution and make recommendations on which the people were expected to vote in 1974; but more than purely constitutional changes were needed to meet the crises of rural and urban unemployment in a state whose population growth rate was among the highest in the world.

The presidents who succeeded Magsaysay sought to use public funds to promote the growth of industry, which could eventually benefit the peasants by providing new markets for their cash crops, new goods for themselves, and new employment opportunities. They turned increasingly to Asia for trade, so that by 1971 Japan had replaced the United States as the Philippines' chief trading partner. However, progress was slow. Spanish rule had given the Filipinos Christianity and an acquaintance with European styles of life which made them far more like Latin Americans than Asians in many ways. United States rule had given them expanded educational opportunities and a period of supervised experience with representative self-government which introduced them to free elections (and the uninhibited practice of a pork-barrel, log-rolling politics in which blood was often shed over candidates and issues at election time). Nevertheless, a quarter century after independence, the predominantly agricultural character of the Philippine economy, the dominance of the landlords in the countryside, and the ascendancy of the wealthy merchants over the few small industrialists in the cities were only slightly altered. In the autumn of 1972, President Marcos decided to take drastic steps. He declared martial law, nationalized steel mills and public utilities, proclaimed a comprehensive land-reform measure by which rural tenants would become the owners of the lands they worked, and accepted a draft constitution from the constituent assembly which gave him virtually dictatorial powers. Early in 1973 the draft constitution was approved by public assemblies in the towns and villages, rather than by secret ballot. The Supreme Court rejected petitions challenging the procedures by which the new constitution had been presented and ratified, and formally declared the new constitution to be legally in effect. Amnesty was offered to both the Muslims and the remaining Hukbalahap insurgents, but only a few surrendered to the government forces at first. A popular vote approved Marcos' decision to remain president indefinitely after the expiration of the term he had begun in 1970. The Muslim areas were promised aid, fighting died down somewhat, and late in 1973 Marcos met with Muslim leaders; but sporadic outbursts of violence between local Muslims and Christian newcomers continued to occur in Mindanao.

The Malay Peninsula and Neighboring Regions

DUTCH ACQUISITION OF POWER IN MALAYA AND INDONESIA (1615–1743)

In contrast to the Philippines, the sultanates of the Malay peninsula managed to remain independent until the late nineteenth century. Until then the Europeans in the region—Portuguese, Dutch, and British—contented themselves with the port of Malacca, to which the British added the islands of Penang and Singapore. The Europeans also tried to put down Malay attacks on European shipping, which the Europeans regarded as piracy but which to the Malays were in part a protest against losing their freedom to use the straits without restraint.

The Portuguese held Malacca from 1511 to 1641, when the Dutch took it. The first Dutch ship reached Indonesia in 1596, seventeen years after the first English vessel to sail those waters. By 1615 the Dutch drove the Portuguese from the Spice Islands of the Moluccas, obtaining trade agreements and even oaths of loyalty from local rulers who welcomed the Portuguese departure. Meanwhile the English cultivated friendship with Acheh in northern Sumatra and opened new trading depots in Javanese ports to entice Moluccan rulers to trade with the English East India Company. However, the strong naval forces of the Dutch East India Company expelled the English from the Moluccas in 1628.

The Dutch seizure of Malacca from the Portuguese in 1641 effectively excluded the English from the South China Sea. It also persuaded the rulers of Acheh (always the rivals of Malacca) to work with the English against the Dutch in northern Sumatra. By 1683 the English East India Company no longer competed effectively with the Dutch east of Sumatra, but Achinese-English cooperation prevented the Dutch from doing much business in Sumatran ports. Dutch patrols forced all ships passing Malacca to put into the port, pay dues, and receive permits to continue. This procedure gave the Dutch control of the South China Sea trade, particularly after the region north of Malacca fell into the hands of adventurers from Sulawesi, or Celebes, who failed to pursue any consistent commercial policy.

From the 1680s to the 1780s the Dutch East India Company had scarcely a rival in the Malay peninsula and Indonesia, except for Acheh. The trade of the Indies from Malacca to the Moluccas was commanded by the Dutch from a fortified town in western Java, originally known as Djakarta and proudly renamed Batavia by the Dutch in 1619 after a combined English-Javanese attack failed to take it. The Dutch also ruled the Moluccas firmly through the petty sultans and princes.

The evident military and naval strength of the Dutch East India Company encouraged occupants and would-be occupants of royal thrones throughout Indonesia to seek Company aid, much as the military power of the French and British East India Companies led eighteenth-century Indian rulers to seek alliances with them. The interest was reciprocated, for the Dutch were as willing as the French or the English to win commercial advantages by military means. By 1705 the Dutch won control of most of the seaports of northern Java, in return for assisting the ruler of Mataram in central Java. Between 1740 and 1743 Mataram joined forces with the Chinese residents of Java, who feared that the harsh treatment the Dutch were meting out to Chinese vagabonds would be extended to all Chinese; but the combined Chinese-Mataram assault on the Dutch failed, and thereafter the Dutch controlled the rulers of Mataram even more thoroughly than before.

BRITISH REPLACEMENT OF DUTCH INFLUENCE IN MALAYA (1786–1824)

By the end of the eighteenth century the Dutch governed almost all of Java through their influence over local rulers. They used their power to insist on the planting, cultivation, and delivery of products like pepper, coffee, indigo, cotton, and sugar, which could be sold in Europe. In effect, the Dutch forced the Javanese to tailor their production to the price fluctuations of the world market without allowing them to advance from a subsistence to an exchange economy, much as both Dutch and Portuguese had done in the spice-growing Moluccas.

The Dutch control of trade through the Malacca strait ended in 1784, when the British required the Dutch to allow the British East India Company to trade in every part of Indonesia, as part of the treaty which ensured British withdrawal from Ceylon after the American Revolutionary War. The British had never lost interest in Southeast Asian trade. They had continued to trade with Burma even after they and the Dutch gave up permanent residence there as unprofitable in the mid-seventeenth century. In 1687, English East India Company forces from Madras tried to seize a port in Ayuthia's Malay territories, to counter French influence at the capital of Ayuthia. The English also frequented the ports of Kedah and Johore, on either side of Malacca, and in 1685 they established a foothold in the isolated harbor of Bencoolen in southwest Sumatra. They continued to use Bencoolen as a base for trade with the largely Dutch-controlled Indies throughout the eighteenth century. They bought the tin mined by Chinese residents on the island of Banka off eastern Sumatra and tried with little success to promote trade with Borneo. However, none of this amounted to much, and the British East India Company welcomed the privileges won in 1784.

After 1784 the British East India Company in Calcutta finally heeded the urgings of its traders in Malay waters, who wanted to follow up the new opening in Indonesia and feared that the French East India Company might repeat its attempts of a few decades earlier to establish outposts on the southern coast of Burma. In 1786 the British East India Company accepted the island of Penang from the sultan of Kedah, who ceded it in the hope of receiving British support against Bangkok's pressure to acknowledge the overlordship of a resurgent Siam. When he was not given the expected help, he allied with other Malay sultans to expel both the Dutch and the British, but the Dutch dispersed the naval forces of his allies and left him without hope of success. In 1791 he accepted a yearly payment from the British in lieu of an alliance. The British used Penang as a base from which to seize Dutch outposts in Malacca, Sumatra, and the Moluccas in 1795, as part of the series of campaigns in which they took Ceylon. However, the British did not decide until 1811 that they would have to take Java to prevent it from falling into the hands of a pro-French government. By that time they were using Malacca rather than Penang, which was too far north to be useful for patrolling the Malacca strait or trading with the East Indies.

When the British arrived in Java, the Netherlands government was in direct control of Javanese affairs, for the Dutch East India Company had been liquidated. During the eighteenth century, changes in European agriculture made fresh meat obtainable throughout the year. Therefore, Europeans ceased to need spices to mask the flavor of rancid meat, and Dutch East India Company profits dwindled rapidly. The costs of enforcing the forced-delivery system, whereby the Javanese raised certain crops and turned them over to the Company's agents, outstripped the profits. The company went bankrupt not only financially but morally as well, as its ill-paid staff used illicit means of gaining income; finally, the Dutch government abolished the Company in 1798. After a decade of discussion, the Dutch government decided to experiment with making local Javanese rulers officials in the Dutch administration instead of staying in the background as the Company had done and pretending the local rulers were the real sovereigns. The new policy was only applied in the rice-growing northeast. The Dutch government also set up the first Dutch-administered courts for Javanese, since the claim to rule directly in the region involved a responsibility to maintain law and order. However, unlike Dutch courts in Ceylon, the Dutch courts in Java applied local customary law, which in most districts blended large amounts of longstanding local practice with a few elements of the Sharia that were not directly opposed to local tradition.

It was this newly revised administration which the British under Thomas Stamford Raffles took over from the Dutch on Java in 1811. Raffles dispensed with the forced-delivery system in favor of letting the cultivators produce for a free market. He annexed outright some of the remaining sultanates. He then appointed officials to collect the land taxes assessed against each village, not only in the directly ruled parts of Java but in the sultanates on the rest of the island. He also collected the land taxes in money instead of produce, as a means of prodding cultivators into growing for the market as well as for their own needs.

Raffles protested loudly when Britain returned Java and Malacca to the Dutch in 1816 and 1818 after the close of the Napoleonic wars. The British retained Ceylon and the Cape of Good Hope in the interests of their expanding Indian empire, and Raffles believed they should also keep Java and Malacca, as a means of gaining Indonesia and the Malay peninsula. In 1819 he obtained the island of Singapore at the tip of the Malay peninsula from the sultan of Johore. There he inaugurated a free-trade policy which quickly brought the island wealth and a growing population of enterprising Chinese.

The rise of Singapore effectively ruined Dutch hopes of rebuilding a near-monopoly of trade through the Malacca strait. In 1824 the Dutch resignedly recognized the situation in an Anglo-Dutch treaty which effectively confined them to Indonesia. The Dutch exchanged Malacca for Bencoolen, and the British agreed not to interfere actively in the affairs of Sumatra or of any island south of Singapore. Thereafter, the Dutch devoted themselves to extending and intensifying their control in Sumatra, Java, and the islands to the east.

BRITISH POLICIES TOWARD THE MALAYS (1824–1941)

The arrival of the British in Penang, Malacca, and Singapore did little to disrupt the lives of the Malays at first. The Portuguese and Dutch had found the fiercely independent Malay sultans almost impossible to subdue, and had therefore contented themselves with requiring ships passing through the strait of Malacca to put in at the port of Malacca. Portuguese aid to a few petty rulers on Sumatra led some of them to move their people across the strait and organize the states of Negri Sembilan just north of Malacca, but this was the closest either Portuguese or Dutch came to influencing Malay internal affairs. Of the products of the Malay peninsula, only tin interested the Portuguese and Dutch enough to induce them to try to monopolize its sale. However, they failed to do so, for they could not control the ships which went from northern Sumatra, Ceylon, and India to tin-producing areas north of the entrance to the Malacca strait.

For some time the British followed the Portuguese-Dutch pattern. British East India Company administrators in Penang, Malacca, and Singapore avoided playing an active role in the Malay peninsula because military campaigns and the establishment of civil administrations in the Malay sultanates would be costly. In 1867, nine years after the abolition of the British East India Company, Penang, Malacca, and Singapore were combined into the single crown colony of the Straits Settlements. Yet as late as 1872 the British at Singapore declared that they did not intend to intervene in Malay affairs. By then a number of British subjects were active in the tin mines and other commercial enterprises of the peninsula. Many of these entrepreneurs were Chinese living in one of the Straits Settlements. Their safety was being menaced by periodic fighting not only among Malays, but also between the Malays and the Chinese who were coming from China in growing numbers to work as tin miners.

In 1873 the continued complaints of the Chinese and British merchants of Singapore led the British government to reverse its stand and seek to establish resident advisers in the Malay states. The British hoped to use the residents to lessen strife by persuading the sultans to introduce measures which would allay both Malay and non-Malay discontent. Since four of the nine major principalities were protectorates of Siam, the British concentrated on the five in the center and south. Within a year, rulers in three central regions accepted British advisers.

The states with British advisers remained separate from one another; but under the guidance of Singapore, each adviser tended to offer the same advice. Each state that accepted an adviser soon set up a state council which included not only the Malay nobles but also a few of the leading resident foreign business people. (Almost all the resident foreign business people were of Chinese ancestry, and many of them were under British protection because they came from Hongkong or the Straits Settlements.) The council deliberated under the presidency of the sultan and the watchful eye of the resident. Each state also set up a new semi-European penal code modeled on that established in India in 1861, and a court system using both European and Malay judges. To the greatest possible extent, local nobles were appointed as government-paid officials. Little effort was made to draw officials from outside the ranks of the nobles. In 1888 the British introduced these innovations into the fourth central region, bringing it forcibly into the residency system in response to complaints from Singapore merchants about the capricious way in which its ruler was administering the revenue, the courts, and the government monopolies.

In 1896 the British persuaded the rulers of the four central regions to unite in the Federated Malay States. Each state retained financial autonomy, but agreed to accept the decisions of the federal council, which included the sultans and their advisers. The federal council was presided over by a new British official, the Resident-General, whose headquarters were at Kuala Lumpur in Negri Sembilan in the heart of the federated region. In 1909 the powers of the federal council were expanded and five new members (four British, one Chinese) were included.

The sultan of Johore in the south, who granted his people a constitution in 1895, was alarmed at the prospects opened up by the 1909 arrangements. He not only refused to join the federation; he even managed to postpone accepting a resident adviser until 1914. The four Malay states north of the federation were equally concerned for their independence of action. Until 1909 they had acknowledged a purely nominal Siamese overlordship, but in that year Siam signed a treaty with Britain in which Britain promised that it would eventually relinquish the extraterritorial privileges acquired in 1855, while Siam declared that the four northernmost Malay states were no longer its protectorates. Despite all British efforts at persuasion, the four northern sultanates refused to do more than accept individual British resident advisers. Consequently, Johore and the four northern Malay states were called the Unfederated Malay States. In 1927 the federal council was again enlarged, but none of the unfederated states cared to join the federation then or later. No move was made to include the sultan of Brunei in northern Borneo in the federation. Since 1841 Brunei had given up several portions of its territory, first to the private British adventurer James Brooke and then to the British North Borneo Company. The only real link between Brunei and the Malay peninsula was the fact that the British resident adviser whom the sultan of Brunei accepted in 1906 belonged to the branch of the British civil service that worked in the Straits Settlements and the Malay states.

To the British, the opening of World War I enhanced the economic and military importance of the Malay peninsula with its tin, its productive new rubber plantations, and its strategic location. After the war they concentrated largely on further economic development, expanding the railway network begun earlier and encouraging still more Chinese and Indians (mostly Tamils) to come to the mines and plantations of the peninsula. The Chinese needed little encouragement. The laws of the Malay states did not let them hold agricultural land, for the Malays feared the more frugal and industrious Chinese would squeeze them out of their own rice-lands. However, to those who could save enough from their wages to make a start, the booming economy of the peninsula offered tempting opportunities to become a shopkeeper, moneylender, tin-mine owner, or wholesale dealer in rubber.

CHINESE-MALAY RELATIONS AND COMMUNIST
GUERRILLA ACTIVITY (1941–1960)

By the time World War II broke out in the Pacific in 1941, the Malays were, in effect, confined to the rice-lands to which they had clung so tenaciously, unwilling to exchange familiar ways for the world of plantations, mines, shops, banks, and factories. In the commercial sectors of the Malayan economy, Indians and Chinese furnished the labor, and Chinese and Europeans provided the leadership. The Malays were contented with what they had, and the British largely succeeded in reassuring them that Britain did not intend to interfere with Malay religion or custom. Therefore, the Malays felt little incentive to break with the past and work in rubber plantations, tin mines, or trading enterprises. The British resident advisers gradually introduced a civil service system into the Malay states, but only enough Malays to staff the governmental offices sought a Western education in the schools opened by the British. Thus the Malay peninsula entered the period of Japanese occupation with a government staffed by British and Malays and an economy managed by British and Chinese. This was a potentially explosive situation. Consequently, the Malays were not dismayed to see their Japanese conquerors treat the Chinese harshly.

The Japanese feared that unless the Chinese could be forced to cooperate, they would use their near-monopoly of the skills needed in the Malayan economy to sabotage the Japanese war effort. The Japanese therefore tried to frighten them into submission, but without success. The Chinese responded with slowdowns and work stoppages. They also formed the Malayan Peoples' Anti-Japanese Army which, despite its name, was basically Chinese. The MPAJA rarely did any fighting, but its propaganda convinced the Japanese, the other Chinese, the Malays, and the British that Chinese resistance was considerable. By contrast, the conduct of the Malays was admirable—or reprehensible—for few Malays made much show of resistance. As a result, many of the British felt more kindly toward the Chinese when they returned in 1945 than they had before the war.

When Japan surrendered, the MPAJA swaggered out of the jungle, proclaiming its intent to punish all collaborators. MPAJA members proceeded to liquidate as many as possible of those Chinese who opposed the Communists among MPAJA leaders, and they also attacked some Malays and Indians. (The Japanese had created an Indian National Army in the Malay peninsula for the purpose of attacking the British in India.) Alarmed Malays reacted by attacking Chinese indiscriminately. The returning British did not succeed in restoring order for months.

During the last months of World War II the British finally became convinced that their former policy of leaving government and rice-growing to Malays while non-Malays ran everything else was bound to lead to open clashes betwen the various peoples in the peninsula. They therefore decided to promote a common Malayan citizenship among Malays, Chinese, and Indians, in the hope of preparing the way for a united Malayan state. To that end, the sultans were induced to surrender the last remnants of their sovereignty to the British crown; all persons born in any Malay state or the Straits Settlements, or resident in the peninsula for ten of the past fifteen years, were promised full citizenship and freedom from the legal restrictions on non-Malays. The British also proposed to make the peninsula into one federal state, the Malayan Union, with a strong central government and weak state governments. Overwhelmingly Chinese Singapore would remain under British control as a separate entity.

A Malay leader from Johore hastily established the United Malay National Organization to oppose the British plan. Many British administrators, respected by both Malays and British, also opposed it. Meanwhile, most of the Chinese and Indian leaders openly continued to pay more attention to affairs in China and India than to their own situation. They indicated little interest in the British proposal, which gave added point to Malay charges that the projected Malayan Union sought to include people who did not wish to be included because their strongest political loyalties lay elsewhere. The British therefore dropped the proposal. They reinstated the sultans, and in 1948 they established the Federation of Malaya, in which the sultans delegated a limited number of powers to the federal government.

The rules for citizenship in the Federation of Malaya, which included Penang and Malacca but not the crown colony of Singapore, were less liberal than those proposed for the Malayan Union. Fewer than a fifth of the Chinese residents of the Federation became citizens in its first year. The Chinese now awoke to action. Some joined the short-lived multiracial Malayan Democratic Union; others joined the Communist party, which had used the Malayan Peoples' Anti-Japanese Army to entrench itself in the Chinese community.

After the collapse of the Malayan Union, Communist MPAJA leaders returned to their prewar activities of fomenting strikes, spreading propaganda, and infiltrating the Chinese schools, while they awaited the chance to use their wartime experience. Under the stimulus of the 1948 meeting of Asian Communist leaders at Calcutta, they decided to form the Malayan Peoples' Liberation Army, return to the jungle, and use guerrilla tactics to force the British out so the Communists could take over. The MPLA attacked British, Malays, and any Chinese who refused to give food, money, or other assistance. The resulting situation, which the British and Malays called the "Emergency," lasted from 1948 to 1960.

The MPLA never succeeded in establishing a "liberated area" in which it could set up a rival government. It could extort supplies and information from Chinese squatters who had illegally taken up cultivable land in isolated regions during the war years, by preying on their fears of being dispossessed by government soldiers under the laws which limited the ownership of rice-lands to Malays. However, it could not hold its ground against the relentless attacks of British and Malay forces. Gradually the MPLA became divided into scattered and uncoordinated units. One by one these units were forced to surrender as the British set up fortified villages, brought the Chinese squatters into them, assured the Chinese that they could retain the land they cultivated, and thereby gradually deprived the guerrillas of their chief sources of food and information. By 1960 the MPLA was reduced to a few hundred persons operating in the difficult terrain of the border between the Federation of Malaya and Thailand.

PROBLEMS OF ACHIEVING AND MAINTAINING INDEPENDENCE (1949–1974)

The spur of the Emergency helped to induce worried Malay and Chinese leaders to reach the compromises that made possible the inauguration of the independent Federation of Malaya in 1957. In 1949 non-Communist Chinese business people and others formed the Malayan Chinese Association. As the British and the Federation government put down guerrilla activities, the MCA won Chinese support for its program of cooperation with the Malays in the United Malay National Organization and with the Indians, who were forming a Malayan Indian Congress. By 1952 UMNO and MCA leaders were working closely together. (The UMNO and the MCA were later joined by the MIC to form the Malay-Chinese-Indian Alliance, which won most of the seats in the federal parliament in the elections of 1955, 1959, 1964, and 1969.) During 1952, Malayan citizenship rules were liberalized enough to allow more than half the Chinese to become citizens. The success of the elections for the municipal and village councils set up in 1951–1952 encouraged the British to establish elective state assemblies and in 1955 to hold the first nationwide elections for the federal legislature. At midnight on August 31, 1957, the Federation joined the free members of the Commonwealth, although Singapore continued to be ruled as a crown colony.

Requirements for citizenship in the Federation of Malaya were less stringent than the Malays wanted, but more stringent than the Chinese had hoped. Specified percentages of civil service posts and educational opportunities were reserved for Malays, to protect them from Chinese domination. Malay-Chinese cooperation survived the general elections of 1955, 1959, and 1964. One of its chief accomplishments was the replacement of the various Chinese, Malay, and other schools with one government-controlled school system, in which the leaders of the new state could hope to persuade Malay, Chinese, and Indian children that they were all Malayans, contributing to and benefiting from Malayan political and economic well-being.

Communal feeling ran highest in those states which had the largest proportion of non-Malay residents. However, there were other problems as well. In one province, with an almost entirely Malay population, the Malay peasants in the increasingly crowded rural areas came to associate the UMNO wing of the MCI Alliance with their also-Malay landlords. As a result, from 1959 onward they consistently voted for the candidates of the Pan-Malayan Islamic Party, whose platform was the implementation of Islamic social justice, rather than for UMNO candidates.

The period of the Emergency in the Federation of Malaya was also a period of emergency in Singapore. The growing strength of the People's Republic of China inspired pride in both Communist and non-Communist Chinese in Singapore. Singapore Communists persuaded, tricked, and intimidated many Chinese schoolchildren, dock workers, shopkeepers, wholesalers, industrialists, and bankers into staging strikes and giving funds for the intertwined causes of China and Communism. The British became thoroughly alarmed for the safety of their naval base on the island. When independence was demanded, they refused to grant it until order was restored. In 1946 they had given Singapore a largely appointed legislative council, but they retained the right to veto its acts when it became elective in 1955. They did not become willing to discuss self-government until late 1956, when the Chinese leader in the legislative council gathered the courage and the forces to expel the hundreds of overage students who were making the Chinese-language schools centers of Communist subversion. In 1959 the Singapore government was granted internal autonomy, but not control of defense or foreign affairs. Shortly thereafter, the leaders of Singapore and the Federation of Malaya began to seek a basis for union. This was done under pressure from Britain, which wished to give all its Southeast Asian holdings self-government, but did not believe Singapore could be self-sufficient. (Britain did not move in a corresponding way to give full independence to Hongkong because independence—as contrasted with internal self-government, which the British did begin to extend—would displease Peking unless it came in the form of absorption into the People's Republic of China. That in turn would have displeased many Hongkong Chinese, particularly the thousands who came to Hongkong as refugees from Kwangtung province and elsewhere. The Hongkong situation was further complicated by the fact that much of the colony's territory was held by Britain only on a lease which would expire in 1997. Not until 1974 did the British even recognize Chinese as an official language in the colony.)

Close economic ties between Singapore and the members of the Federation of Malaya made many in both areas wish for union. However, the Malays of the peninsula were reluctant to include Singapore alone in the Federation, for its large Chinese population would give the Chinese a numerical majority. Therefore the prime minister of the Federation proposed in 1961 that the three separately administered districts of Malay-inhabited British Borneo—Sarawak, Brunei, and British North Borneo (Sabah)—be included in an expanded federal state to be known as Malaysia. This proposal was agreeable to Singapore and Federation leaders, eager for union; it was agreeable to the British, eager to liquidate their empire; it was even agreeable to a number of Borneo Malays and to some Borneo Chinese. However, Brunei, reluctant to give up control of its oil revenues, finally declined to join Malaysia and remained a British protectorate. The Malays insisted on giving Singapore only 15 representatives in the central legislature, as opposed to 16 for Sabah, 24 for Sarawak, and 104 for the original eleven Federation members. In return, Singapore was allowed to run its own schools and its own labor affairs. (The British had already served notice on Sarawak Chinese in 1960 that their schools must replace Chinese with English as the medium of instruction by 1972 or lose state aid.) Malaysia Day was set for August 31, 1963, in spite of an abortive effort by a Brunei politician to proclaim the independence of all of northern Borneo at the end of 1962. However, Malaysia Day had to be postponed because of external objections to the new state.

When Britain accepted the idea of including northern Borneo in Malaysia, it did not reckon with Philippine claims to Sabah, based on the arrangements by which that region had passed from the Sultan of Sulu to one Baron Overbeck in 1878 and thence to the British North Borneo Company. Nor did Britain reckon with the strength of Indonesian desire to see northern Borneo come within Indonesia's sphere of influence by becoming independent from Britain separately from the Federation of Malaya. Both the Philippines and Indonesia insisted that the United Nations investigate Sabah and Sarawak attitudes toward the Malaysia proposal. The Secretary-General of the United Nations, U Thant of Burma, declared after a brief fact-finding mission that he was satisfied that the Malaysian federation was acceptable to its Borneo members, but the Philippine and Indonesian protests delayed Malaysia Day to September 16, 1963. Malaysia promptly severed relations with both states in a protest of its own. The Philippines and Malaysia restored consular relations within a year, but Indonesia did not sign a peace agreement with Malaysia until August, 1966. By that time, Indonesian fears that Chinese-dominated Singapore might in turn dominate Malaysia had been allayed, for the continuing rise in communal tensions between Malays and Chinese in the Malay peninsula had led the Malaysia government to request that Singapore withdraw from the federation in August, 1965.

Communal tensions remained high even after 1965 in Singapore and Malaysia. In Singapore, the ruling People's Action Party found it increasingly difficult to persuade the large Chinese majority to continue accepting the use of English as one of the state languages. However, the Party continued to dominate the legislative assembly, winning every seat in the 1972 elections. Singapore voters appeared to appreciate the role of Party leaders in promoting rapid industrialization. By 1971 the island city-state had the enviable distinction of achieving full employment, although the British withdrew from their naval bases there that year.

In West Malaysia, as the Malay peninsula came to be called, communal riots followed the passage of the 1967 law that made Malay the sole national language and relegated English to a secondary position. Many Malays felt that English should have been eliminated altogether. Many non-Malays wanted English to continue to have equal standing with Malay. The MCA began to lose the support of the Chinese community to anti-Alliance parties, while the MIC became plagued by factionalism. The elections of 1969 demonstrated both Malay and non-Malay disaffection, as the Alliance dropped from a parliamentary majority of 86 percent to one of 63 percent, and lost its majority in three state assemblies to various combinations of pro-Malay and pro-non-Malay opponents. A few days after the election, large-scale communal riots broke out in the capital. Government leaders responded by suspending the parliament and proclaiming a state of emergency. In 1970 they declared it illegal to attack the constitutional provisions regarding citizenship for Chinese and Indians, the position of the Malay rulers, the use of Malay as the national language, and the reservation of an appropriate percentage of scholarships, business licenses, and other opportunities for Malays and other indigenous groups (primarily Dyaks and others in Sabah and Sarawak, or East Malaysia). When the parliament was reconvened in 1971, its first order of business was to turn this decree into law, in hopes of preserving the public order required for the continuance of Malaysia's generally high rate of economic growth. In 1973 the cabinet was reorganized so as to include members of the Pan-Malayan Islamic Party as well as members of the Alliance. The move may have reassured Malays, but it seemed scarcely likely to reassure Chinese and Indian Malaysians. Nevertheless, the 1974 elections went smoothly, and the new National Front (the old Alliance plus the Pan-Malayan Islamic Party and a few other minor groups) took four-fifths of the seats in the national assembly.

Indonesia

THE CULTURE SYSTEM, THE PLANTATION SYSTEM, AND EXPANSION (1824–1908)

After the Anglo-Dutch agreement of 1824, the Dutch concentrated on protecting and developing their interests in Java, for the free-trade port of Singapore was cutting into their share of general Southeast Asian trade, and the rise of factory industry in the Netherlands was leading to a search for steady markets for Dutch manufactures. At first the Dutch retained the revenue system installed and made profitable by Raffles. However, the system also proved profitable to Chinese and Arab moneylenders, for most of the peasants preferred growing rice and borrowing money to growing other crops and selling them. In the 1820s the Dutch found that Raffles' revenue system was not profitable enough to pay for quelling uprisings. Therefore, they returned in effect to the forced-delivery system, under the new name of "culture system."

Under the culture system, each village was required to supply the government with a fixed amount of the crops the Dutch thought could best be grown in the region, and all villagers were required to give a fifth of either their time or their crops to fulfill the village quotas. The Dutch also ceased to treat the nobles as officials. Their old titles were restored, and they were allowed to keep whatever they could collect above the amount they had to turn over to the Dutch.

The culture system lent itself to the exploitation of the peasant. As the Dutch at home began to realize its results, they were horrified. Between 1862 and 1870 the Netherlands government reduced the list of items which the Javanese were required to produce to the two most profitable crops—sugar and coffee. Yet in 1870 the Netherlands government also let private Dutch citizens lease land from Indonesians or from the Dutch administration in the islands. This measure led to private plantations which exploited Indonesians as much as the culture system did; low pay was given for long hours, and initiative was not encouraged.

Privately held Dutch plantations were established not only in Java but in other islands. British interest in northern Borneo revived in the 1840s as a private Englishman, James Brooke, won the confidence of the sultan of Brunei. Consequently, the Dutch decided to acquire fuller authority in the rest of the Indonesian archipelago. In a series of campaigns from 1846 to 1870 they took control over principalities from southern and eastern Kalimantan or Borneo, Bali, and Sulawesi or Celebes to southern and central Sumatra. However, the subduing of Acheh lasted from 1873 to 1908, and during that time the Dutch also had to quiet Balinese revolts.

The Achinese had been attacking European shipping in northern Sumatran waters for generations. Once the steamship and the Suez Canal increased European traffic in the Indian Ocean, neither the British nor the Dutch were willing to let these raids continue. Furthermore, neither the British nor the Dutch—aware of possible danger from any extension of the new pan-Islamic movement to Muslim Malays and Indonesians—cared for Acheh's approaches to the Ottomans at Istanbul. In 1871 Britain agreed to forgo that part of the 1824 treaty which restricted Dutch activity in Sumatra to the area south of Singapore.

The thirty-five-year struggle between Dutch and Achinese began in 1873. Muslims all around the Indian Ocean watched its progress anxiously, and they communicated their anxiety to the thousands of Indonesian pilgrims who annually flocked to Mecca. The Dutch sought to counteract fears that their attack on Acheh was anti-Muslim by encouraging the pilgrimage, but their efforts were only partly successful. Indonesians still remembered how the Dutch had helped the half-Hindu local rulers of central Sumatra to subdue rebellious Islamic-purification movements among Muslims influenced by Wahhabi doctrines, brought from Mecca by returning pilgrims from the 1820s to the 1840s.

INTRODUCTION OF MODERN SERVICES, AND
INDONESIAN RESPONSES (1856–1941)

By the time Acheh fell in 1908, Dutch authority was grudgingly recognized everywhere in Indonesia. Thereafter, the Dutch concentrated on increasing production in agriculture, forestry, and mining, and on improving the railway, telegraph, and telephone networks which speeded up the movement of people, messages, and goods. The telegraph was introduced in 1856, the railroad in 1873, and the telephone in 1882. Without the railroads built into Achinese territory as it was captured, Achinese resistance might have lasted even longer than it did.

Dutch rule was largely confined to requiring traditional rulers to obtain from their people the goods and services the Dutch wanted. Even so, the Dutch in Indonesia exacted far more than the British in the Malay peninsula, who only required the Malays to maintain order well enough so that British and Chinese could exploit the peninsula's resources. Therefore, Indonesians resented the Dutch more than Malays resented the British, especially since the British carefully protected Malay religion and custom while the Dutch incurred strong suspicion from Muslim jurists, or ulama, by actively encouraging Christian missions. The maintenance of customary Indonesian law in Dutch courts also displeased the more orthodox Muslims, for customary law conflicted with orthodox schools of interpretation of the Sharia at many points, even when the principle of consensus was liberally applied.

The Dutch use of indirect methods of rule left the social and political life of most Indonesians almost intact. Sultans continued to maintain their courts not only in the outer islands but also in thickly settled Java. However, many Dutch officials felt that their power entailed an obligation to use that power beneficially. The result was an effort to increase the economic and social well-being of Indonesians, called the ethical policy.

In 1904 and 1905, as part of the ethical policy, autonomous councils of Indonesians, Europeans, and Chinese began to be established in rural areas and towns. In 1906 an elaborate system of village self-government was promulgated, which in practice became a means by which Dutch officials could supervise every aspect of Indonesian life. The Dutch worked to introduce modern health measures, agricultural methods, and schooling into Javanese villages, but the outer islands remained the preserve of European estate owners, tribes practicing shifting cultivation, and the numerous small settled coastal communities with their separate rulers. The officiousness with which the Dutch supervised the villagers aroused such hostility that the ethical policy accomplished little in terms of improved welfare. Moreover, the forcible subduing of Acheh had awakened anti-Dutch feeling among earnest Javanese Muslims before the ethical policy was begun.

Devout Muslims were not the only ones to distrust the Dutch. The Dutch were slow to expand the government-supported secular schools in which aspiring Indonesians could acquire Western learning, for they feared to stimulate Indonesian objections to their rule. Instruction in Dutch, and public secondary and higher education, were almost monopolized by the potential administrators: the Dutch, the partly-Dutch, and the Javanese aristocracy. The Chinese and most of the Indonesians were left to educate themselves. The Chinese made more progress than the Indonesians in this endeavor, supporting private Chinese-language schools which stressed Chinese learning.

Only a few Indonesian men and women learned enough about Western ideas and techniques to become convinced that their compatriots needed a rapid extension of Western ideas of nationhood and civic duty and a greater knowledge of Western science and technology. These few were dismayed at the lack of opportunity for Western education. In 1908, on Java, they formed the Budi Utomo or High Endeavor society to promote Western education and the idea of an Indonesia united by a common past, present, and future. However, they soon lost control of the nationalist movement to the Javanese and Sumatran merchants.

In 1911 the merchants of Java and Sumatra formed Sarekat Islam (Islamic Union) to promote commercial enterprise and Muslim allegiance among Indonesians, in response to a recent intensification of

Christian mission work and to the increasingly obvious attachment of Chinese merchants to the interests of China. In 1916 Sarekat Islam requested self-government for Indonesia. Two years later the Dutch formed the first Indonesia-wide advisory council, but its European majority and its selection procedures (half the members were appointed by the Dutch governor-general and half were elected by the local councils) ensured that its advice would rarely oppose Dutch interests. In 1925 this council was given an indirectly elected majority and an Indonesian plurality. In 1929 Java's twenty-two districts were combined into three provinces with partly indirectly elected councils in which Europeans were in a minority, but none of the councils had much power.

Dutch influence on the selection of Javanese representatives to the central and provincial councils kept out Sarekat Islam members. Under Marxist influence, Sarekat Islam declared itself opposed to capitalism in 1917, but in 1921 it expelled its few Communist members. The Communists then formed their own party and continued to organize strikes among newly unionized urban workers. The leaders of Sarekat Islam were deeply impressed by the principles of Gandhi. They established friendly ties with the Indian National Congress and embarked on a policy of protest through nonviolent noncooperation.

The Dutch tolerated neither strikes nor nonviolent noncooperation. When Communists led premature rebellions in 1926 they were either interned or exiled to Singapore. When Sarekat Islam leaders continued to refuse to have anything to do with the Dutch-run government, they too were interned, mainly in western New Guinea.

In the 1920s and 1930s, Sarekat Islam and the new National Party of Indonesia emulated the Chinese by opening nongovernment schools. The National Party was led by a young engineer named Sukarno, who admired both the secular modernization program of the Indian National Congress and the nonviolent noncooperation policy of Gandhi. Sarekat Islam and the National Party also founded banks, cooperatives, youth movements, women's organizations, cultivators' unions, and a literary movement for the use of a standardized dialect, Bahasa Indonesia, throughout the islands. The competition of the private schools forced the Dutch to extend the public schools, enabling more Indonesians to prepare for entrance into the colleges of agriculture, forestry, engineering, law, and medicine which the Dutch opened by the end of the 1920s. (The University of Batavia was not founded until 1941, twenty years after the University of Rangoon—and three hundred years after the first university in the Philippines.) Nevertheless, out of a Philippine population one-fourth the size of that of Indonesia, more Filipinos than Indonesians were taking college-level courses in 1941. The Dutch also restricted private Indonesian schools more than they did private Chinese schools. The Dutch moved far too slowly in the educational field to satisfy the Javanese-led nationalist movement, in which merchants, teachers, engineers, and lawyers far outweighed sultans and nobles.

JAPANESE OCCUPATION AND THE ACHIEVEMENT OF INDEPENDENCE (1942–1950)

By the time World War II opened, the Indonesian nationalist movement had supporters in almost every important center in the islands. Even though the nationalists were divided between the older Sarekat Islam and the newer, more vigorous, and somewhat more radical National Party, they were numerous and united enough to alarm the Dutch. Consequently, the Dutch refused to arm Indonesians as the threat of Japanese attack increased after 1940, even though Indonesians offered to fight.

The Japanese quickly defeated the small Dutch force in 1942. At first the Japanese ignored Indonesian aspirations for unity. They placed Sumatra under the military commander at Singapore and the eastern islands under the navy, and administered Java, Madura, and Bali separately. However, they soon released Sukarno and other nationalist leaders from internment, hoping to use anti-Dutch sentiment to promote enthusiasm for Greater East Asia. Some nationalists, including Sukarno, willingly used the opportunities the Japanese provided to promote Indonesian unity, such as the expanded radio network. Others worked underground against the Japanese, but with little success. By the closing months of the war, the Japanese felt sure enough of Indonesian friendship to arm Indonesians against the expected invasion of the Dutch and their allies. However, they did not let Sukarno proclaim the independence of the Republic of Indonesia until three days after Japan decided to surrender. The provisional constitution promulgated shortly afterward concentrated power in the hands of the president, who was Sukarno.

During the Japanese occupation, Indonesians were thrust into high administrative positions for the first time since the Dutch took over. As late as 1940 Indonesians held less than 8 percent of the higher civil service posts, a strong contrast to India where Indians formed 45 percent of the elite Indian Civil Service at that period. Indonesians realized that final authority lay with the Japanese, but their slight taste of freedom made it impossible for them to accept the return of the Dutch.

The Dutch flatly refused to take any notice of the new republic as long as the collaborator Sukarno led it, and they asked the British to help them accept the surrender of Japanese troops. Sukarno stepped down, enabling the Republic to negotiate with the returning Dutch late in 1945, but the Dutch only offered a continued association with the Netherlands. Meanwhile Republican, British, and Dutch armies were accepting the surrender of Japanese units. Republican and Dutch troops clashed more than once in this process. Dutch-Indonesian negotiations continued throughout 1946, while the Dutch brought the eastern islands and a few Javanese ports under their control. The rest of Java and Sumatra were left to the Republic.

Early in 1947 the Dutch and Indonesians agreed to form a federal Republic of the United States of Indonesia which would include the Republic of Indonesia in the west and the Dutch-controlled areas in the east. The Dutch then expected to be invited to reoccupy the western islands. When they were not, they accused the Republic—once more led by Sukarno—of breaking its word, and they attacked it in what they called a "police action to restore order." At the request of India and Australia, the United Nations Security Council issued a cease-fire order. In January, 1948, the Security Council obtained a truce and a reopening of negotiations between the Dutch and the Republic. Then a brief Communist-led uprising took place in eastern Java in March, 1948. Although it was quelled before it could spread, it became the excuse for another Dutch police action when talks broke down again at the end of 1948.

At the end of 1949, Indonesian and world opposition finally forced the Dutch to recognize the federal Republic of the United States of Indonesia as an equal partner with the Netherlands under the monarch. The arrangement did not last long. By August, 1950, the release of imprisoned nationalists in the east resulted in the toppling of the Dutch-managed puppet governments there, and the provisional federal constitution of 1949 was replaced by a new provisional constitution establishing a unitary government.

The Dutch had recommended the federal system as a means of providing for the disparity of interests between densely populated Java and the thinly populated outer islands, but they thoroughly discredited federalism in the nationalists' eyes by using it to cling to power in the eastern islands. The new provisional constitution of 1950 centered control of all Indonesian affairs in Djakarta (once Batavia). It was a parliamentary government in which the cabinet was controlled by the legislature, which in turn was dominated by its Javanese majority. The outer islanders therefore feared that the central government might ignore their interests, and leaders in Sumatra and Sulawesi rebelled in protest before the decade was out. The new Republic of Indonesia did not sever its last formal ties with the Netherlands until 1956, but after the promulgation of the 1950 constitution it paid so little attention to the Netherlands government that full Indonesian sovereignty was in effect achieved at that time.

PROBLEMS OF INDEPENDENCE (1950–1974)

The sovereign Republic of Indonesia faced a multitude of problems, political, economic, and social. Politically, it had to contend with the fact that the magnetic Sukarno could hardly be expected to play the colorless role of the usual president in a parliamentary government. President Sukarno was not inclined to confine his actions to those suggested by his prime ministers and cabinets. Conflicts between the president and a succession of cabinets led to such confusion that in 1960 Sukarno unilaterally proclaimed a return to the presidential constitution of 1945. This step was technically illegal, since it was not sanctioned by the constituent assembly, whose members were sent home in 1959 for failing to agree on a permanent constitution to replace the provisional one of 1950. However, it was in harmony with the political reality of Sukarno's extraordinary hold on the ordinary people of Indonesia. Even when the military finally decided in the fall of 1965 that his policies must be repudiated, they did not remove him from the presidency as the Algerian military under Boumedienne had done earlier in the year with the Algerian president. Instead they began by removing Sukarno's subordinates, and did not strip him of the title of president until 1968.

The form of the executive branch of government was not the only political issue. The legislative branch had its own problems. When the unitary republic of 1950 came into being, it had a parliament which did represent the major parties, but which also included many representatives of other interest groups like trade unions and women's organizations. Its members were not elected; they had been appointed by Sukarno and other leaders of the first republic of 1945 to 1949 on the basis of the service they and their groups had given to the nationalist cause. Nationwide elections were not held until 1955. When they were held, they made the deep cleavages within the body politic even clearer than before. Within two years of the election, and shortly after a visit to Mao's China, Sukarno concluded that parliamentary democracy with its accompanying practice of majority rule was not for Indonesia. Five divergent parties—the Communists, the Socialists, the secular-minded Nationalists, and the two anti-Communist heirs of Sarekat Islam, the reformist Masjumi and the more traditionalist but also less activist Nahdatul Ulama (Muslim Teachers' Party)—garnered a sizable number of legislative seats in 1955, although only the Masjumi won more than 15 percent of its votes from the outer islanders. Masjumi voters were almost evenly divided between Javanese and non-Javanese. With such great diversity among the legislators, agreement was exceedingly hard to reach even on the basis of a simple majority, let alone by the customary Indonesian method of talking a matter out until everyone agrees on what to do about it. Party leaders intrigued constantly in the hope of forming coalitions. Legislators crossed party lines in voting on the measures discussed, and few major problems were attacked for fear of losing votes. Moreover, the anti-Communists were unwilling to come to any kind of terms with the Communists even though the Communists had a large following in eastern and central Java. The

Darul Islam, a fanatical Muslim group which closely resembled the Muslim Brotherhood of Egypt, the Fedayin-i-Islam of Iran, and the Jamaat-i-Islami of Pakistan in its call for a return to traditional Islamic principles of state organization, had begun a rebellion against the central government in 1949 in western Java and later in parts of Sulawesi. The Darul Islam rebellion was in large part simply a protest against Sukarno's willingness to allow Communist political activity. It continued until 1965, when a coup led to the outlawing of the Communist party. Much of the money which paid for the successful organization of the Communist party on Java in the 1950s was wrested from Indonesian Chinese, after Indonesia's recognition of the People's Republic of China brought to Indonesia Chinese Communist representatives who could put direct pressure on Indonesian Chinese merchants and others.

By 1957 Sukarno was tired of party wrangling. Therefore, when he sent the constituent assembly home in 1959, disbanded the legislature in 1960, and proclaimed the restoration of the 1945 constitution, he appointed the new parliament himself instead of calling for elections. The Masjumi and Socialist parties were banned, but ten political parties ranging from the Communists to the Nahdatul Ulama continued to exist. Sukarno called for cooperation among the nationalist, religious, and Communist groups. He wove his way with care between the demonstrable strengths of religious traditionalists suspicious of almost all change, army leaders (many of them outer islanders) suspicious of Javanese domination and the growing Communist movement, and Communists eager to gain popularity by unwavering support of Sukarno. Apparent Communist friendship drew him toward Communist-favored positions. Although he refrained from making anti-Communist forces too weak to prevent Communist takeover, army leaders grew tired of his balancing act. In the fall of 1965 they used the apparently Communist-inspired assassination of a number of leading generals as the springboard for an open drive against the Communist party, which quickly won sympathy among Indonesian students and supporters of Darul Islam. By the spring of 1966, army and student leaders were clearly in control. Sukarno still held the presidency, but his tendency to emphasize Indonesia's international relations at the expense of domestic needs was being replaced by insistence on dealing with internal problems first, external affairs later. He was forced to yield power to General Suharto, and in 1967 was replaced by Suharto as acting president and forbidden to leave his residence. In 1968 he was formally dismissed as president, and he died quietly at home in 1970.

The political problems of Indonesia went hand in hand with its social and economic problems. The lack of unity in the body politic— the lack of general agreement on the goals of the state—reflected a lack of unity in the body social. Puritanical Muslims of what might be loosely termed the middle classes, who tended to support the more orthodox-minded reformists in the Masjumi party, battled against the very unpuritanical forms of Islam practiced by average villagers and workers, who tended to prefer the tradition-minded (rather than orthodox-minded) Nahdatul Ulama. The puritanical Muslims also attacked the secular orientation of many members of the new governing group, and were not satisfied with Sukarno's inclusion of "belief in one God" as the fifth and culminating point in the list of five principles (nationalism, humanitarianism, government by consent, social justice, and monotheism) which he enunciated as guiding ideas for the new Indonesia in the last year of Japanese occupation. The outer islanders' dislike of seeing most of the income from the government's collection and sale of their products go into economic development on overcrowded Java changed from a social and economic question to a political one in 1956. From 1956 to 1958 military insurrectionists in Sumatra and Sulawesi, who were protesting against Sukarno's willingness to work with the Communists, also sought to ensure that more of the outer islands' income would be used in the outer islands.

Lack of unity was not the only factor in the economic situation in Indonesia, the one Southeast Asian country in which annual production of goods per person apparently declined after independence. Economic growth was also hindered by the persistence of the idea that every enterprise should support all the people it could afford to hire. This may have been in part a carryover from the conditions of wet-rice agriculture, in which the need for many hands at certain times justified the division of the harvest among as many people as it could feed. All Dutch-owned enterprises were nationalized after 1956, although the government lacked trained personnel to run them, and other Western enterprises began to be taken over after 1960. The government also insisted that Indonesian citizens replace Chinese nationals in running many types of industrial and commercial firms. The usual result of this was that Indonesians were paid to become titular heads of Chinese firms while Chinese continued to manage them, as in Thailand.

As the Sukarno era ended, the Indonesian economy was one of the most stagnant in Southeast Asia. Part of the reason was corruption and inefficiency among the civil servants who issued licenses and supervised nationalized enterprises, but part seemed to be that Indonesians were simply unaccustomed to managing their own economic affairs after generations of being told by others what to raise, how to raise it, and where and when to deliver it, rather than making these decisions for themselves. Yet most rural Indonesians were not gravely concerned. They still had rice to eat, and their ruler provided them with festivals and demonstrations of prestige in the form of international sports gatherings and diplomatic conferences which involved the developing Asian and African states which Sukarno termed the New Emerging Forces of the world. However, he loudly refused to invite Israel (as a remnant of colonialism in the Middle East), the Republic of China (in deference to his deepening friendship with the People's Republic of China), or Malaysia after its formation. Though the students began to call for greater attention to economic problems in the fall of 1965, it was opposition to the godlessness of Sukarno's Communist supporters rather than opposition to Sukarno's economic policies that led the majority of Indonesians to accept the transfer of power from Sukarno to Suharto.

Sukarno's Indonesianization and nationalization programs, and his international gatherings, were probably inspired as much by political as by economic considerations. Official opposition to Chinese economic power was linked to disapproval of the unofficial assistance the Kuomintang gave the Sumatra and Sulawesi rebels of 1956–1958. It also helped prod Indonesian Chinese into choosing Indonesian rather than Chinese citizenship under the nationality treaty signed by Indonesia and the People's Republic of China in 1955 and finally ratified in 1960, and probably played a role in the decision of Indonesian Chinese students to demonstrate their loyalty to Indonesia by attacking the Chinese embassy in the spring of 1966. Nevertheless, resentment at the continued concentration of much of Indonesia's enterprise in the hands of those of Chinese descent continued to break out from time to time in attacks on Indonesian Chinese. Confiscation of Dutch enterprises was connected with official disapproval of the Netherlands' refusal to turn over western New Guinea to Indonesia, which claimed to be the proper heir to all Dutch possessions in the region. From 1956 onward Indonesia openly built up its military forces with Soviet aid, in preparation for an all-out move on western New Guinea, or West Irian as Djakarta called it. In 1961 the Dutch offered to place the area under United Nations supervision preparatory to a plebiscite in which the people of the area would choose their own future. In 1962 the Dutch agreed to relinquish the area to the United Nations, which in 1963 permitted Indonesia to administer it until a plebiscite could be held at some time within the next ten years. West Irian became a province of Indonesia in 1969, with the acquiescence of the leaders and councils of its tribes and settlements.

Indonesian demands for western New Guinea left the Portuguese on Timor unmoved. However, Indonesia's apparently increasing reliance on hatred of some external foe as a means of maintaining internal unity undoubtedly helped persuade Britain to hasten the inclusion of British Borneo in a federation with Singapore and the Federation of Malaya, before the settlement of the New Guinea question freed Indonesians to help northern Borneo on the path to independence. The British wished to take no risk of having an Indonesian liberation movement ruin the slender chance that strategic, Chinese-populated Singapore could be made both safe and self-governing by being brought into an independent state with a Malay majority. The abortive 1962 uprising in Brunei, which was approved if not sponsored by the Indonesian government, showed how close they came to missing that chance. Still, the new state of Malaysia became and remained the target of Indonesian opposition, expressed in speeches, rallies, periodical articles, diplomatic conferences, small-scale military landings which Malaysian and Commonwealth forces crushed, and temporary withdrawal from the United Nations when Malaysia took a seat on the Security Council in 1965. The Federation of Malaya had opposed Sukarno's aims too many times—giving asylum to some of the 1956–1958 rebels, acting as a market for rubber and copra smuggled out of Indonesia, protesting Indonesia's exclusion of Israel and the Republic of China from the Fourth Asian Games in 1962—and its crushing of its Communist movement offered too glaring a contrast to the situation in Indonesia for Sukarno and his Communist supporters to accept its expansion into Malaysia. Besides, opposition to Malaysia served the army's interest by providing an excuse for continued military preparedness. It also served Sukarno's interest by providing an external foe against which to rally Indonesia's diverse political groupings. After Chinese-dominated Singapore left the Malaysian Federation and after the army ousted the Communists from their previously influential position in the latter part of 1965, confrontation with Malaysia began to be replaced by opposition to Communism and concentration on economic growth as binding forces in Indonesia's internal political life. Indonesia returned to the United Nations in 1966. By the beginning of 1973 its international standing was high enough for its foreign minister to be asked to help mediate between Pakistan and Bangladesh, and for its troops to be invited to participate in the International Commission of Control and Supervision for the Vietnam cease-fire agreement.

The government of Suharto made visible economic progress. It renegotiated Indonesia's foreign debts on favorable terms, which made repayment look possible again after a period of some anxiety on the part of both Indonesians and their creditors. It brought down inflation from over 600 percent in 1966 to less than 10 percent in 1969, introduced new high-yield strains of rice, expanded the public utilities needed for industrial growth, and in 1973 began to redirect the school system toward vocational rather than literary subjects. It recognized the need to encourage family limitation so as to avert a doubling of the population before the end of the century. By 1969 it felt secure enough to begin releasing the hundred thousand or more Communists imprisoned in 1965 and 1966, although it found that there was still open hatred and fear of them in the areas where a quarter million or more Communists had been killed a few years before. Therefore it sent many of those it released to unpopulated islands, to found new settlements.

The Suharto government did not permit the Masjumi party to re-organize. The Masjumi leaders were tainted in the eyes of the military by their refusal to repudiate formally the fundamentalist Darul Islam during the period of the Darul Islam rebellion, a refusal which had also been a factor in Sukarno's original banning of the Masjumi. Consequently the military were unwilling to see the Masjumi name revived, and insisted that those who wished to support reformist Muslim candidates must organize a totally new party.

When the first parliamentary elections since 1955 were finally held in 1971 for a parliament of 360 elected and 100 appointed members, it was no surprise that the traditionalist Nahdatul Ulama again won slightly less than 20 percent of the elective seats. What was surprising was that the Nationalists fell from 22 to 6 percent and the Masjumi's successor, Partai Muslimin Indonesia (Parmusi), fell from 22 to 7 percent of the elective seats. The government-sponsored Sekber Golkar (Joint Secretariat of Functional Groups) evidently inherited most of the former Masjumi, Nationalist, Socialist, and even Communist vote, for it won 65 percent of the elective seats. In addition, most of the appointed members came from groups which were linked with Sekber Golkar. After the election, the Suharto government encouraged the Muslim parties and the non-Muslim parties other than Sekber Golkar to form two federated parties, one Muslim and one non-Muslim. Reluctantly, the parties agreed. Suharto's continued power was confirmed in 1973 by his election to a new five-year term as president. Later in the year he quietly negotiated border agreements with Thailand and Malaysia, and in 1974 with Singapore, Australia, and the emerging government of Papua in New Guinea. However, it proved less easy to resolve Indonesian territorial disputes with the Philippines. Suharto also announced in 1974 that Indonesians must be immediately enabled to obtain majority ownership in all firms in which there was foreign investment. Since most of the oil industry had been nationalized at the time when Dutch properties were taken over, this move affected primarily those businesses still held by residents of Chinese ancestry who had not accepted Indonesian citizenship.

INDONESIA AND THE AFRO-ASIAN WORLD: BANDUNG, 1955 AND 1965

In April, 1955, independent Indonesia staged its first dramatic diplomatic display by holding the first full-dress Afro-Asian conference at Bandung in western Java. Twenty-nine Asian and African countries sent representatives. Few of the friendly speeches made at Bandung were translated into lasting cooperation, despite the holding of later conferences and the establishment of a secretariat at Cairo. In fact, when the Sukarno government staged a lavish celebration of the tenth anniversary of the Bandung conference, in April, 1965, of the sixty independent (and mostly rather newly independent) Asian and African states invited, only thirty-five attended; and the head of the Thai delegation left before the celebrations closed, in protest against the strongly anti-Western and pro-Peking tone of the proceedings. It was hardly an auspicious prelude to the second full-dress Afro-Asian conference, which was scheduled to meet in Algiers two months later. The second conference had to be postponed until November because of the disturbances that followed the dismissal of Algeria's president by the Algerian military—perhaps to the relief of governments which were reluctant either to oppose the inclusion of the Soviet Union in the conference, as the People's Republic of China clearly wished, or to annoy Peking by favoring Soviet participation. By November, Indonesia itself was beginning to reverse direction, and the conference was quietly forgotten. Nevertheless, the Bandung conference of 1955 forced the West to recognize that Bandungia, as Vera Micheles Dean called the group of countries represented at Bandung in her book *The Nature of the Non-Western World* (New York: New American Library, 1957), had come of age. Its peoples would no longer accept Western control of their foreign relations any more than they would accept Western control of their internal political and economic life. They would accept assistance on a basis of mutual agreement among equal sovereign states, but not domination.

Of all the countries in which the first Afro-Asian conference could have been held, Indonesia was perhaps the most appropriate. The rich fabric of its heritage included Chinese, Indian, and Islamic strands. Indonesians were among the first Asians to fall under European control and among the last to win freedom from it. The Portuguese, the Dutch, the British, and the modernizing Japanese had left their imprints on its life. (After ten years of negotiation, Japan was finally beginning to reach satisfactory agreements with regard to reparations for wartime damages in Southeast Asian states. Its first pact, with Burma, went into effect during the month of the conference.)

Indonesia also shared almost every problem of every state represented at Bandung in 1955 and again in 1965. Conflicts among puritanical Muslims, nonpuritanical Muslims, and the secular-minded over the nature of the Indonesian state recalled the Middle East, although Indonesia's nonpuritans were more affected by their heritage from the pre-Muslim past than by new currents from the West. The overcrowding of rural Java, the rush to the cities in search of more jobs than were available, the glacial slowness of social changes, the creeping pace of economic development, and the availability of great natural resources were reminiscent of India. However, much of Indonesia was less crowded than most of India, Indonesia's resources were less suitable than India's for heavy industry, and India's economy was growing more rapidly than Indonesia's by almost any possible measure during the 1950s and early

1960s. The apparently growing importance of Communism in Indonesia brought to mind the attraction of Communism in post-World-War-I China for leaders uncertain of their course. Yet before the end of 1965 the values of the traditional order appeared to have overwhelmed Communist teachings, at least for the time being. The Indonesian tradition held that action should only be undertaken on the basis of mutual agreement, a view that was foreign to Chinese traditions of leadership by the elite. The dual nature of the Indonesian economy, divided between the subsistence agriculture practiced by the majority and the commercial enterprises such as plantation agriculture which outsiders had introduced, resembled the economies of other Southeast Asian states and also of many parts of Africa south of the Sahara. In almost all of Southeast Asia and in much of Africa, dual economies presented a multitude of problems to governments eager to unify their people economically, socially, and politically. Finally, there was the minorities problem.

Minorities in the outer islands of Indonesia feared the Javanese majority. In this they were like Kurds and Berbers in the Middle East; Muslims, Dravidians, and hill tribes in India; Tamils in Ceylon (and Sinhalese conscious of the Tamils of India); Karen, Shan, and others in Burma; Chinese and Malays in Thailand; hill tribes in Laos, Cambodia, the two Vietnams, and the Philippines; and Chinese and Indians in the Malay peninsula. In their grievances against those who made the economic policy of the state, they also resembled the Bengalis who were to break away from Pakistan in 1971 to form Bangladesh. Isolated tribes in Kalimantan faced Indonesians with problems like those of African leaders in trying to bring their people into the mainstream of twentieth-century life. There were many parallels between postindependence African states and Indonesia. Resentment against nonindigenous merchants who dominated local trade remained high, whether they were Chinese in Indonesia, Syrians and Lebanese in West Africa, or Indians and Pakistanis in East Africa. Both African and Indonesian leaders were striving to lessen the tensions between modernly educated secularists and those still accustomed to living under the rule of traditional leaders left in position by Western overlords. They were also working to reconcile differences and mutual fears between a variety of linguistic and cultural groups.

The spread of modern communication networks enabled minority groups everywhere to become more conscious of themselves. In the region of Bandungia, minorities could perceive not only the differences between themselves and the Western outsiders which made them willing to help the majority expel Western rulers, but also the differnces between themselves and others within the nation-state they helped to form. In addition, modern communications made it easier for minorities to organize effective movements for autonomy, especially if they were given outside assistance. Nationalist leaders in every Southeast Asian country, as in the remainder of Bandungia, therefore exerted themselves continuously to ensure the survival of their new nation-states. On the positive side, some stressed educational and linguistic unification, while others promoted plans for rapid economic progress which would need unity to succeed. On the negative side, some relied on military force to repress troublemakers, while others called up the specter of an external foe. Most used more than one of these methods of maintaining and increasing national unity, and all were acutely conscious that the same growth in self-awareness which enabled them to lead their compatriots to independence might foster divisive tendencies that would have to be overcome if their states were to survive.

Suggested Readings

Books available in paperback are marked with an asterisk.

Southeast Asia

GENERAL

DOBBY, E.H.G. *Southeast Asia*, 10th ed. London: University of London Press, 1967.

DU BOIS, CORA A. *Social Forces in Southeast Asia*. Cambridge: Harvard University Press, 1959.

FISHER, C.A. *Southeast Asia: A Social, Economic and Political Geography*, 2nd ed. New York: Dutton, 1966.

KUNSTADTER, PETER, ed. *Southeast Asian Tribes, Minorities and Nations*. Princeton, N.J.: Princeton University Press, 1967.

*RAWSON, PHILIP. *The Art of Southeast Asia*. New York: Praeger, 1967.

TO MODERN PERIOD

CADY, JOHN F. *Southeast Asia: Its Historical Development*. New York: McGraw-Hill, 1964.

*COEDES, GEORGES. *The Making of Southeast Asia*, trans. H.M. Wright. Berkeley: University of California Press, 1966.

*HALL, D.G.E. *A History of Southeast Asia*, 3rd ed. New York: St. Martin's Press, 1968.

HARRISON, BRIAN. *South-East Asia: A Short History*, 3rd ed. New York: St. Martin's Press, 1966.

MODERN PERIOD

*BASTIN, JOHN, and HARRY BENDA. *A History of Modern Southeast Asia*. Englewood Cliffs, N.J.: Prentice-Hall, 1968.

*BUTWELL, RICHARD. *Southeast Asia: A Political Introduction*. New York: Praeger, 1974.

ELSBREE, WILLARD H. *Japan's Role in Southeast Asian Nationalist Movements, 1940–1945*. Cambridge: Harvard University Press, 1953.

FIFIELD, RUSSELL H. *The Diplomacy of Southeast Asia, 1945–1958*. New York: Archon, 1958.

FURNIVALL, JOHN S. *Colonial Policy and Practice: A Comparative Study of Burma and Netherlands India.* New York: New York University Press, 1956.

GOLAY, FRANK H., et al. *Underdevelopment and Economic Nationalism in Southeast Asia.* Ithaca, N.Y.: Cornell University Press, 1969.

HANNA, WILLARD A. *Eight Nation-Makers: Southeast Asia's Charismatic Statesmen.* New York: St. Martin's, 1964.

KAHIN, GEORGE McT., ed. *Governments and Politics of Southeast Asia*, 2nd ed. Ithaca, N.Y.: Cornell University Press, 1964.

LEIFER, MICHAEL. *Dilemmas of Statehood in Southeast Asia.* Vancouver: University of British Columbia, 1972.

PURCELL, VICTOR W.W. *South and East Asia Since 1800.* London: Cambridge University Press, 1965.

*PYE, LUCIAN W. *Southeast Asia's Political Systems*, 2nd ed. Englewood Cliffs, N.J.: Prentice-Hall, 1974.

*SHAPLEN, ROBERT. *Time Out of Hand: Revolution and Reaction in Southeast Asia.* New York: Harper and Row, 1969.

*STEINBERG, DAVID JOEL, et al. *In Search of Southeast Asia: A Modern History.* New York: Praeger, 1971.

TATE, D.J.M. *The Making of Modern Southeast Asia*, vol. I (of three projected). New York: Oxford University Press, 1971.

THOMPSON, VIRGINIA, and RICHARD ADLOFF. *Minority Problems in Southeast Asia.* New York: Praeger, 1955.

* TILMAN, ROBERT O. *Man, State and Society in Contemporary Southeast Asia.* New York: Praeger, 1966.

TRAGER, FRANK N., ed. *Marxism in Southeast Asia.* Stanford, Cal.: Stanford University Press, 1959.

*VON DER MEHDEN, FRED R. *Religion and Nationalism in Southeast Asia: Burma, Indonesia, The Philippines.* Madison: University of Wisconsin Press, 1963.

CHINESE IN SOUTHEAST ASIA

ELEGANT, ROBERT S. *The Dragon's Seed: Peking and the Overseas Chinese.* New York: St. Martin's, 1959.

FITZGERALD, C.P. *The Southern Expansion of the Chinese People.* New York: Praeger, 1972.

HINTON, HAROLD C. *China's Relation with Burma and Vietnam: A Brief Survey.* New York: Institute of Pacific Relations, 1958.

NEVADOMSKY, JOSEPH-JOHN, and ALICE LI. *The Chinese in Southeast Asia: A Bibliography.* Berkeley: University of California Press, 1970.

PURCELL, VICTOR W.W. *The Chinese in Southeast Asia*, 2nd ed. London: Oxford University Press, 1965.

SKINNER, G. WILLIAM. *Chinese Society in Thailand: An Analytical History.* Ithaca, N.Y.: Cornell University Press, 1957.

WIENS, HEROLD J. *China's March Toward the Tropics.* Hamden, Conn.: Shoe String Press, 1954.

WILLIAMS, LEE A. *Overseas Chinese Nationalism: The Genesis of the Pan-Chinese Movement in Indonesia, 1900–1916.* Glencoe, Ill.: Free Press, 1960.

Mainland Southeast Asia

BURMA

BUTWELL, RICHARD. *U Nu of Burma*, rev. ed. Stanford, Cal.: Stanford University Press, 1963.

CADY, JOHN F. *A History of Modern Burma.* Ithaca, N.Y.: Cornell University Press, 1958.

DONNISON, F.S.V. *Burma.* London: Benn, 1970.

FURNIVALL, JOHN S. *The Governance of Modern Burma*, 2nd ed. enl. New York: Institute of Pacific Relations, 1960.

HAGEN, EVERETT E. *The Economic Development of Burma.* Washington, D.C.: National Planning Association, 1956.

HALL, D.G.E. *Burma.* London: Hutchinson, 1950.

*NASH, MANNING. *The Golden Road to Modernity.* Chicago: University of Chicago Press, 1972.

*PYE, LUCIAN W. *Politics, Personality and Nation-Building: Burma's Search for Identity.* New Haven, Conn.: Yale University Press, 1962.

SMITH, DONALD E. *Religion and Politics in Burma.* Princeton, N.J.: Princeton University Press, 1965.

*SPIRO, MELFORD E. *Buddhism and Society: A Great Tradition and Its Burmese Vicissitudes.* New York: Harper and Row, 1970.

TINKER, HUGH. *The Union of Burma.* London: Oxford University Press, 1967.

TRAGER, FRANK N. *Burma: From Kingdom to Republic.* New York: Praeger, 1966.

THAILAND

DEYOUNG, JOHN E. *Village Life in Modern Thailand.* Berkeley: University of California Press, 1955.

INGRAM, JAMES C. *Economic Change in Thailand, 1850–1970.* Stanford, Cal.: Stanford University Press, 1971.

INSOR, D. *Thailand: A Political, Social and Economic Analysis.* London: G. Allen and Unwin, 1963.

*MOFFAT, A.L. *Mongkut, the King of Siam.* Ithaca, N.Y.: Cornell University Press, 1961.

RIGGS, FRED W. *Thailand: The Modernization of a Bureaucratic Policy.* Honolulu: East-West Center, 1966.

VELLA, WALTER F. *The Impact of the West on Government in Thailand.* Berkeley: University of California Press, 1955.

*WILSON, DAVID A. *Politics in Thailand.* Ithaca, N.Y.: Cornell University Press, 1962.

MEKONG VALLEY

CADY, JOHN F. *The Roots of French Imperialism in Eastern Asia.* Ithaca, N.Y.: Cornell University Press, 1967.

*———. *Thailand, Burma, Laos, and Cambodia.* Englewood Cliffs, N.J.: Prentice-Hall, 1966.

KIRK, DONALD. *Wider War: The Struggle for Cambodia, Thailand and Laos.* New York: Praeger, 1971.

ZASLOFF, JOSEPH J., and ALLAN E. GOODMAN, eds. *Indochina in Conflict: A Political Assessment.* Lexington: Lexington Books, 1972.

VIETNAM

BUTTINGER, JOSEPH. *The Smaller Dragon: A Political History of Vietnam.* New York: Praeger, 1970.

*———. *Vietnam: A Political History.* New York: Praeger,, 1968.

FALL, BERNARD B. *The Two Viet-Nams,* 2nd rev. ed. New York: Praeger, 1967.

*———, ed. *Ho Chi Minh on Revolution: Selected Writings, 1920–1966.* New York: Praeger, 1967. (Paperback. New York: New American Library.)

*FITZGERALD, FRANCES. *Fire in the Lake.* Boston: Little, Brown, 1972.

*HALBERSTAM, DAVID. *Ho.* London: Barrie and Jenkins, 1971. (Paperback. New York: Random House.)

HOANG, VAN CHI. *From Colonialism to Communism: A Case History of North Vietnam.* London: Pall Mall, 1964.

*MARR, DAVID G. *Vietnamese Anti-Colonialism, 1885–1925.* Berkeley: University of California Press, 1971.

*McALISTER, JOHN T., and PAUL MUS. *The Vietnamese and Their Revolution.* New York: Harper and Row, 1970.

*PIKE, DOUGLAS. *Viet-Cong: Organization and Techniques of the National Liberation Front.* Cambridge: M.I.T. Press, 1966.

*SCIGLIANO, ROBERT. *South Vietnam: Nation under Stress.* Boston: Houghton Mifflin, 1963.

*VAN DYKE, JON M. *North Vietnam's Strategy for Survival.* Palo Alto, Calif.: Pacific Books, 1971.

WOODSIDE, ALEXANDER B. *Vietnam and the Chinese Model.* Cambridge: Harvard University Press, 1971.

*ZAGORIA, DONALD S. *Vietnam Triangle: Moscow, Peking, Hanoi.* New York: Pegasus, 1967.

CAMBODIA

HERZ, MARTIN F. *A Short History of Cambodia.* New York: Praeger, 1958.

LEIFER, MICHAEL. *Cambodia: The Search for Security.* New York: Praeger, 1967.

LAOS

DOMMEN, ARTHUR J. *Conflict in Laos: The Politics of Neutralization*, rev. ed. New York: Praeger, 1971.

LANGER, P.F., and J.J. ZASLOFF. *North Vietnam and the Pathet Lao*. Cambridge: Harvard University Press, 1970.

TOYE, HUGH. *Laos: Buffer State or Battleground*. New York: Oxford University Press, 1968.

The Malay Peninsula and the Islands

THE PHILIPPINES

ANDERSON, GERALD H., ed. *Studies in Philippine Church History*. Ithaca, N.Y.: Cornell University Press, 1969.

BARROWS, DAVID P. *History of the Philippines*, rev. ed. Yonkers, N.Y.: World, 1926.

COATES, AUSTIN. *Rizal: Philippine Nationalist and Martyr*. New York: Oxford University Press, 1968.

*CORPUZ, ONOFRE D. *The Philippines*. Englewood Cliffs, N.J.: Prentice-Hall, 1965.

GOLAY, FRANK, ed. *The United States and the Philippines*. Englewood Cliffs, N.J.: Prentice-Hall, 1966.

HAYDEN, JOSEPH R. *The Philippines: A Study in National Development*. New York: Macmillan, 1942.

KIM, SUNG HONG. *United States–Philippine Relations, 1946–1956*. Washington, D.C.: Public Affairs Press, 1968.

LACHICA, EDUARDO. *Huk: Philippine Agrarian Society in Revolt*. Manila: Solidaridad Publishing House, 1971.

QUIRINO, CARLOS. *Magsaysay of the Philippines*. Manila: Advocate Book Supply, 1964.

RAVENHOLT, ALBERT. *The Philippines*. Princeton, N.J.: Van Nostrand, 1962.

RIZAL, JOSÉ. *The Social Cancer*, trans. Charles Derbyshire. Manila: Philippine Education Company, 1912; 2nd ed. 1926.

SMITH, ROBERT AURA. *Philippine Freedom, 1946–1958*. New York: Columbia University Press, 1958.

TAYLOR, GEORGE E. *The Philippines and the United States*. New York: Praeger, 1964.

MALAYA, MALAYSIA, AND SINGAPORE

BELLOWS, THOMAS J. *The People's Action Party of Singapore*. New Haven, Conn.: Yale University Press, 1970.

*FLETCHER, NANCY MCHENRY. *The Separation of Singapore from Malaysia*. Ithaca, N.Y.: Cornell University Press, 1969.

GINSBERG, NORTON, and CHESTER F. ROBERTS, JR. *Malaya.* Seattle: University of Washington Press, 1958.

GULLICK, J.M. *Malaysia.* London: Benn, 1969.

HANNA, WILLARD A. *The Formation of Malaysia.* New York: American Universities Field Staff, 1964.

KENNEDY, JOSEPH. *A History of Malaya, A.D. 1400–1959.* New York: Macmillan, 1970.

MEANS, GORDON P. *Malaysian Politics.* London: University of London Press, 1970.

PYE, LUCIAN W. *Guerrilla Communism in Malaya.* Princeton, N.J.: Princeton University Press, 1956.

ROFF, WILLIAM R. *The Origins of Malay Nationalism.* New Haven, Conn.: Yale University Press, 1967.

TARLING, NICHOLAS. *Piracy and Politics in the Malay World.* Victoria, Australia: F.W. Cheshire, 1963.

TIEK, GOH CHENG. *The May Thirteenth Incident and Democracy in Malaysia.* Kuala Lumpur: Oxford University Press, 1971.

WANG, GUNG-WU, ed. *Malaysia: A Survey.* New York: Praeger, 1964.

WINSTEDT, SIR RICHARD O. *The Malays: A Cultural History,* 6th ed. London: Routledge, 1961.

INDONESIA

BENDA, HARRY J. *The Crescent and the Rising Sun: Indonesian Islam under the Japanese Occupation, 1942–1945.* The Hague: W. van Hoeve, 1958.

DAHM, BERNARD. *History of Indonesia in the Twentieth Century,* trans. P.S. Falla. London: Pall Mall Press, 1971.

FEITH, HERBERT, and LANCE CASTLES, eds. *Indonesian Political Thinking, 1945–1965.* Ithaca, N.Y.: Cornell University Press, 1970.

*GEERTZ, CLIFFORD. *Agricultural Involution: The Processes of Ecological Change in Indonesia.* Berkeley: University of California Press, 1971.

*————. *Peddlers and Princes: Social Development and Economic Change in Two Indonesian Towns.* Chicago: University of Chicago Press, 1970.

————. *The Religion of Java.* Glencoe, Ill.: Free Press, 1960.

HOLT, CLAIRE, ed. *Culture and Politics in Indonesia.* Ithaca, N.Y.: Cornell University Press, 1972.

*KAHIN, GEORGE McT. *Nationalism and Revolution in Indonesia.* Ithaca, N.Y.: Cornell University Press, 1952.

*LEGGE, JOHN D. *Indonesia.* Englewood Cliffs, N.J.: Prentice-Hall, 1964.

————. *Sukarno: A Political Biography.* New York: Praeger, 1972.

McVEY, RUTH T. *The Rise of Indonesian Communism.* Ithaca, N.Y.: Cornell University Press, 1965.

MINTZ, JEANNE S. *Mohammed, Marx, and Marhaen: Roots of Indonesian Socialism.* New York: Praeger, 1965.

NIEUWENHUIJZE, C.A.O. VAN. *Aspects of Islam in Post-Colonial Indonesia.* The Hague: W. van Hoeve, 1958.

PALMIER, L.H. *Indonesia and the Dutch.* London: Oxford University Press, 1962.

SIMON, SHELDON. W. *The Broken Triangle: Peking, Djakarta, and the PKI.* Baltimore: Johns Hopkins Press, 1969.

*SLOAN, STEPHEN. *A Study in Political Violence: The Indonesian Experience.* Chicago: Rand McNally, 1971.

VAN NIEL, ROBERT. *The Emergence of the Modern Indonesian Elite.* Chicago: Quadrangle Books, 1960.

VLEKKE, B.H.M. *Nusantara: A History of the East Indian Archipelago,* 2nd ed. The Hague: W. van Hoeve, 1965.

WERTHEIM, W.F. *Indonesian Society in Transition.* The Hague: W. van Hoeve, 1959.

Additional suggestions may be found in the following works and in the bibliographies listed therein:

American Universities Field Staff. *A Select Bibliography: Asia, Africa, Eastern Europe, Latin America.* New York: American Universities Field Staff, 1960, with supplements 1961, 1963, 1965.

HAY, STEPHEN N., and MARGARET H. CASE, eds. *Southeast Asian History: A Bibliographic Guide.* New York: Praeger, 1962.

JOHNSON, DONALD CLAY, et al. *Southeast Asia: A Bibliography for Undergraduate Libraries.* New Haven, Conn.: Yale University Press, 1970.

*TREGONNING, K. G. *Southeast Asia: A Critical Bibliography.* Tucson: University of Arizona Press, 1969.

PART FIVE

CONCLUSION

12

COMMON PROBLEMS

The Western Impact

THE EXTENSION OF WESTERN LAWS TO ASIA AND AFRICA

Of the major groupings in the arc of countries from Morocco to Japan, the Middle East was most closely related to Europe during the centuries when Western civilization was being formed from Greek, Roman, Christian, and Germanic elements. From the eighth to the tenth century A.D. Middle Eastern Muslims not only controlled much of Europe's trade but occupied large parts of its Mediterranean coast. Yet not until Spaniards and Normans began to make headway against Muslims in Spain and Sicily in the eleventh century did western Europeans study their foes' ideas and techniques seriously. When they did, however, they regained elements of Greek thought which proved invaluable in the scientific development of later years. The historical parallels between Christian-Muslim relations then and Western relations now with South, East, and Southeast Asia, the Middle East, and Africa south of the Sahara are far from perfect. Still, there are resemblances between the zeal of those who have taken up the cause of nationalism against Western technological, economic, and political power and the zeal of those who took the cross to fight the Saracens. Many recent nationalist movements have expressly upheld Islam, Hinduism, Buddhism, or some other religious system against Christian missionary activity.

During the period when Latin Christiandom was assimilating Middle Eastern learning, Mongol control of the lands from the Black Sea to the Yellow Sea enabled the Polos and others to travel the full length of

Asia. The travelers' accounts of what they found, together with a desire to weaken the Muslims of the Middle East by lessening their commerce, helped to induce later generations of Europeans to seek new routes to India and China when the collapse of the Mongols made the trans-Asiatic land route unsafe. By 1498 the Portuguese had reached India. By 1520 they had seized the entrances to the Indian Ocean, wrested control of it from its Muslim masters, and diverted most of Europe's trade with Asia for the next three hundred years from the Mediterranean-Middle Eastern route to the route around Africa. Not until the powerful Ottoman empire began to decline did western Europeans begin to seek shortcuts across the Middle East or to become involved in the Middle East as they were in South and Southeast Asia; and not until the late nineteenth century did they do much more than establish trading posts along the coasts of most of Africa south of the Sahara.

The first wave of European influence was felt primarily along the southern coasts of India, on Ceylon, and in the region from the Malay peninsula to the Philippines, where there were many small and warring states. Sixteenth- and seventeenth-century Europeans made relatively little impression on China, then ruled by the xenophobic Ming, on China's neighbors and tributary peoples the Koreans, Burmese, Thai, and Vietnamese, or even on inescapably maritime Japan, once the struggle for power among the daimyo was settled. Yet long before the eighteenth-century industrial revolution heralded nineteenth-century imperial expansion, Europeans won some political and economic control where they could play one principality against another and where foreign merchants and even foreign rulers were nothing new. However, European missionaries had little success except among those who, like Filipinos and many Africans, had not previously been converted to Islam by Muslim traders. The rapacity of many European traders did not impress the superiority of Christianity on Indians and Southeast Asians, and their own traditions ran counter to Christianity also. Muslims from West and East Africa to Indonesia were naturally disinclined to accept a faith which their religious instructors regarded as the partially erroneous predecessor of Islam. As Wilfrid Cantwell Smith describes the Muslim attitude toward Christianity:

The Jews committed one major blunder: they came to believe that the divine command applied only to themselves—instead of understanding that the prescribed pattern was a universal message, for all mankind.

In due course, to correct this desperate error, God sent another messenger, Jesus. His followers, as well as having certain other qualities and God-given favours, understood the universalist nature of the faith well; and have been zealous in extending the community to the ends of the earth. But they too made a fundamental, indeed a heinous, mistake: they took to worshipping the messenger, instead of heeding the message.[1]

Hindus and Buddhists rejected as ridiculous any belief in a permanent individual soul, preferring to believe that the selves they knew were impermanent bundles of consequences doomed to pass through a series of rebirths until extinction was achieved by absorption into the unknowable reality that sportively manifests itself in the phenomenal world.

Rebuffs to Christian missionaries did not deter other western Europeans from seeking trade in lands from India to Japan, but the actions of local rulers did affect them. Western European merchants were accustomed to taking active part in the councils of their rulers and feeling certain that their profits would not be capriciously confiscated, unlike merchants in the Middle East where slaves were often used as administrators or in South, East, and Southeast Asia where merchants were ordinarily segregated from the rest of society in some way. Western European merchants were also accustomed to working within reasonably stable political boundaries. They originally seized Indian Ocean ports to control Indian Ocean trade, but they soon began establishing forts and intriguing with local rulers so as to protect themselves from local warfare in a never-ending process which, for example, brought vast regions of India under British rule before the nineteenth century had more than began.

As Europeans extended control from Goa to Luzon, they either ran the administration themselves or watched the local ruler's management closely, but neither of these two methods of direct and indirect rule could be easily applied to the strong Ottoman empire of the sixteenth century. Only in the eighteenth century did Europeans begin to acquire full extraterritoriality, tariff control, and other special privileges in the Middle East. In the nineteenth century these commercial concessions led to political concessions such as the acceptance of European protectorates and debt control commissions as well. Similar tariff controls and extraterritorial privileges were imposed on China, Japan, Korea, and Siam; and Britain's acquisition of control over Burma and the Malay peninsula, like France's in Vietnam, was largely inspired by their rulers' unwillingness to extend comparable privileges to Western merchants. The movement of Britain, France, and other European states into Africa south of the Sahara was also largely motivated by the desire to ensure favorable conditions for European trade, in the face of local rulers' continued efforts to control all foreign merchants, whether from Europe, the

---

[1] Wilfrid Cantwell Smith, *Islam in Modern History* (Princeton: Princeton University Press, 1957), p. 13.

Middle East, or other African regions. Thus Western laws were extended to Asian and African shores by a combination of conquests, establishment of resident advisers, and tariff and extraterritorial concessions enforced by military and naval demonstrations.

PATTERNS OF ORGANIZATION IN EUROPE, ASIA, AND AFRICA

It was Western unity that enabled Western states to enforce their laws outside their boundaries for the benefit of their nationals. At the time of the fifteenth- and sixteenth-century explorations, western Europe had traveled farther than any other region along the road from a subsistence economy made up of nearly self-sufficient peasant households to an exchange economy in which the farmer as well as the worker produced for the maket. This commercialization was not only unifying economic life but making people think in terms of their region rather than their village. At the same time, industrial output was expanding as the energy of wind, water, and coal began to be harnessed in place of human and animal energy. However, political stability was also necessary for commercialization and industrialization. Without public order, farmers would not risk depending on others for their needs, and investors would not risk losing their mills or shops or shipments of goods to rioters and bandits. Although European rulers were seeking personal power when they brought every individual rather than only the heads of families, villages, and guilds under their personal jurisdiction, the result was greater public order, greater safety for commerce, and also a greater feeling of unity among their subjects. One ruler, one law, one faith, one language, one economy—these unities contrasted markedly with the disunities still apparent in most other parts of the world when western Europeans first began to travel to them.

During the period of European expansion most of the settled peoples of Asia and Africa were still dependent on subsistence agriculture and on human and animal energy. Most of them also still faced the problem of integrating unruly tribes into the framework of a sedentary society, either the pastoralists of the dry lands from Morocco to Mongolia or the shifting cultivators of the hillier and wetter lands from tropical Africa and the Himalayas to Laos and Luzon. Within each major region one religion—Islam, Hinduism, or Buddhism—was generally dominant, but in much of Africa local religions still prevailed over the missionary faiths of Islam and Christianity. In many parts of the Middle East and India there were sizable religious minorities, and east of India the observance of earlier animistic forms of religion persisted side by side with Buddhism and even to some extent with Islam. This confusion of religions, as it seemed to almost monolithically Christian Europe, was matched or even excelled by linguistic confusion. Those who spoke Turkish or Persian, Burmese or Thai, were usually separated by thinly peopled tribal districts whose inhabitants used a variety of tongues; those who spoke Sindhi or Bengali or Telugu were frequently ruled by conquerors who used a different language; those who spoke African tongues other than Hausa in the west or Swahili in the east could scarcely travel more than a few days without needing to use another language or find an interpreter. Only China, Korea, and Japan were as linguistically unified as western European states. Yet rulers cared little, for they were not attempting to supervise their individual subjects directly, except in the moral exhortations frequently posted in Chinese, Korean, and Japanese villages for the literate to read to the illiterate. They merely tried to oversee self-regulating groups: the neighborhood in East Asia; the guild or its equivalent in East Asia and the Middle East; the religious community in the Middle East; the caste group in India; the resident Arab, Indian, Chinese, and European merchants in the commercial centers; the village everywhere; and the roving tribe, wherever possible. They did not even try to enforce one law on all their subjects, but recognized different personal laws for different religious groups in the Middle East, different caste groups in India, and different classes in East Asia (with preferential treatment given to scholars in China and Korea and to scholars and warriors in Japan).

Of all these states, Tokugawa Japan was most like the states of western Europe, with its established linguistic unity and its growing economic unity. Tokugawa insistence on uniformity even gave it a single legal code, although that code still discriminated sharply between classes. Furthermore, Japan's rulers gave no allegiance to any outside authority, as Muslim rulers from time to time acknowledged caliphs, as Indian princes sporadically acknowledged paramount rulers, and as Koreans and Southeast Asians regularly acknowledged China's emperors through the tributary system. Finally, Tokugawa Japan approved displays of diligence and thrift—traits associated with the western European bourgeoisie—as means of improving others' opinion of oneself and one's associates. For all these reasons Japan was well prepared to adopt Western ways, once the Tokugawa grip was loosened.

EUROPEAN ENCOURAGEMENT OF COMMERCIALIZATION

Europeans used the strength they achieved through commercializing agriculture, using new energy sources, establishing direct contact between government and governed, unifying legal codes, and developing single national languages to introduce many of these changes into other parts of the world. Particularly in Southeast Asia and in parts of Africa, they indirectly commercialized agriculture by establishing plantations or by requiring peasants to furnish desired items in lieu of taxes, although in Southeast Asia and Egypt they also brought peasant cultivators of rice and cotton directly into the money economy. However, few Asians or Africans came to distinguish between borrowing for investment, to increase income, and borrowing for consumption, to spend on weddings or funerals or other observances. To both peasant and moneylender, wedding and funeral ceremonies seemed as productive as dikes and canals, for they promoted family solidarity, which ensured future labor supply. Yet they only prevented a drop in output, rather than increasing production per person. They thereby tended to put the peasant permanently in debt to the moneylender, especially where Europeans altered land laws (as in Algeria, much of India, or the Philippines) to admit only one set of permanent rights in land and to make this set of ownership rights transferable, not only voluntarily by sale but involuntarily by defaulting on a loan for which land was used as security. Such laws seemed villainous to cultivators, accustomed to mortgaging only their crops, but they were profitable to others like the zamindari of Bengal. European governments sometimes combined a redefinition of land ownership with laws allowing Europeans to acquire land not currently being cultivated by the local inhabitants. African peoples in Kenya and southern Africa, who practiced long-term shifting cultivation because of local soil and climate conditions, lost much of their fallow land to Europeans in this way.

Commercial agriculture and the exchange or money economy that accompanies it still involve relatively few Asians and Africans, although Japanese and Taiwanese farmers sell their produce to Japan's cities and much of the agricultural produce of Morocco, Algeria, Tunisia, and Egypt goes to European markets. However, a number of Africans south of the Sahara turned to working for monetary wages in foreign-established mines, factories, and farms after European governments began imposing a tax which had to be paid in money (rather than in crops or other products) in order to persuade Africans either to grow desired crops for foreign buyers or to work in foreign-established enterprises. Inanimate energy and the improvements it makes possible in transportation and communication are also far from plentiful in Asia and Africa. From Morocco to Taiwan, donkeys, camels, oxen, and water buffalo still share streets with bicycles and motor vehicles. Nevertheless, railways, motor vehicles, airplanes, the telegraph, the telephone, and the radio enable governments to extend control as never before into villages and tribal areas, and thereby to establish direct rather than indirect relationships with those they govern.

The Modernizers' Response

THE NEEDS OF MODERNIZING NATIONALISTS

Europeans rarely ruled directly in Asia and Africa. They preferred to use local leaders as much as possible, giving greatest authority to those who accepted the largest amounts of Western teaching. Since this Western teaching frequently included instruction in Christianity as well as in European languages and methods of doing things, many Asians and Africans came to associate Christian missions with European commercial, diplomatic, and imperial activities, and to instigate attacks on the foreign religion, its adherents, and the officials of foreign governments who encouraged its spread. The Tientsin incident of 1870 was only one of many such occurrences in many places.

Those who led such attacks sought to preserve the old order, not to establish a new one. The impulse to adopt new ways usually came from outside the accepted guardians of the old order. There were some exceptions, like Mongkut of Siam or the followers of the outside lords in Japan (whose outsideness did, however, leave them somewhat dissatisfied), but usually those who wished to adopt European economic and political techniques were those who knew both cultures—born into the local society, but familiar enough with the ways of Europeans to mediate between the Europeans and their own people. They were the ones who knew enough about European life to realize that European power in Asia and Africa did not stem from magic or divinity, as the less sophisticated assumed at first, but from the cohesiveness and solidarity of the nation-state. Compared to the French, English, Dutch, Germans, or Russians, as Sun Yat-sen said in twentieth-century China, his own people were like a rope made of separate particles of sand instead of interwoven hempen fibers.

Some of the would-be modernizers concentrated on social and economic reforms, others on political independence, but all agreed that as the persons best acquainted with the modern West they were the logical leaders of society. They also believed they would continue to be the logical leaders until the old ways were effectively displaced by the new. Sun Yat-sen's "period of political tutelage" was only one of many statements of this general belief which came to be shared by the graduates of Western-language schools everywhere from Morocco and Ghana to Indonesia and Korea. Even in Japan, where Westernization-modernization came first and most easily, Western-language education played its part. Of the three hundred highest officials of the early Meiji era, slightly more than a fifth had studied with Westerners or been closely associated with them for some time, which is remarkable in view of the small number of Rangaku (school of Dutch learning) adherents and the shortness of the period between the opening of Japan and the fall of the Tokugawa. Still more remarkable is the disproportionately large share of the thirty crucial decision-making positions held by men long acquainted with Westerners.

Thus the downfall of Western power in Asia and Africa after World War II was not brought about by its bitter tradition-loving opponents like the Sanusi, the Achinese, or the Boxers. The end of what the Indian historian K. M. Panikkar has called the "Vasco da Gama era" was brought about by those who met the Westerners halfway, at first to preserve their own footing and then to break the Westerners' hold on their lives and those of their compatriots. These men and women, the modernizers or modernizing nationalists, won the allegiance of most of their fellow nationals by continual repetition of the themes of linguistic, religious, and cultural unity which they saw in Western nation-states, although they often antagonized minority groups in the process. Using the new techniques of communication and transport, such as the printing press and the railway, they forced or persuaded their Western overlords to recognize the country they wished to make a nation-state—only to discover that many of their followers mistakenly interpreted their anti-Western speeches and articles as anti-Westernizing too.

Upon winning independence, the modernizers generally set up a constitutional government with an elective legislature to which the head of the executive branch was usually responsible. Like the European originators of representative parliamentary government, they assumed this would ensure the endorsement and acceptance of government actions and policies by the people as a whole. As a result, the almost universal discovery that modernizers and anti-Westernizers could agree only on anti-foreignism was often made in the legislature, as it was in Indonesia. The tendency in such a case, or in any case from the Persia of Reza Khan to the Burma of Ne Win and many newly independent states of Africa after 1960 where the parliament seemed not to be moving in the direction desired by whoever commanded the loyalty of the armed forces, was for the military to take over regardless of constitutional provisions.

Whether through parliamentary or through nonparliamentary rule, the modernizers concentrated on replacing the subsistence economy with an exchange economy and increasing their people's interaction with one another and with the outside world. The new means of transport and communication on which they relied for these purposes also enabled them to begin promoting the use of the same laws, the same language, and the same understanding of nationhood throughout the country. They believed that only in these ways could they make their people cease to be a "rope of sand," as the leaders of Japan had done. The Japanese inspired budding modernizing nationalists from Egypt and Nyasaland (now Malawi) to Ceylon and Vietnam by their victory over Russia in 1905.

In order to succeed, the modernizers and their peoples needed many things. They needed a national law, a national language, a national loyalty, and a national school system in which these three unifying forces could become part of every individual's thinking. They needed inanimate energy and the machines it could run. They needed commercial rather than subsistence agriculture. Above all, they needed an extensive nationwide transport and communications network, since only the free flow of people, ideas, and goods could unify the nation's economic, political, social, and intellectual life. Most of the modernizers regarded the state as responsible in greater or lesser degree for building and maintaining the transport and communications network, promoting agriculture and industrial growth, educating the young, and working toward unity in language, law, and loyalty. However, actual performance was conditioned by experience, resources, and the will to work more than by ideological fervency.

TRANSPORTATION AND ENERGY. The political divisions of the Middle East, South Asia, East Asia, Southeast Asia, and Africa south of the Sahara vary widely in their development of transport networks, as shown by the figures in Table I for ton-kilometers of railway traffic per person per year and for motor vehicles per thousand persons (both of which should be read in conjunction with the figure for persons per square kilometer). In general, East Asian countries make greater use of their railways while Southeast Asian and African states use theirs least, with the exceptions of thinly populated Mauritania and highly developed South Africa and Southern Rhodesia. Motor vehicles are commonest in the Middle East with its great open spaces, in the wealthier parts of East and Southeast Asia like Japan, Singapore, and Brunei, and in the European-settler-ruled state of South Africa. However, nothing approximating the volume of traffic in the United States or the Soviet Union is found even in Japan, which has more ton-kilometers of railway traffic per person per year than any other Asian or African country except Mauritania, South Africa, and Southern Rhodesia. Japan is also the only Asian or African state other than Hongkong, highly developed Israel, the oil-rich principalities of Brunei and the Persian Gulf, and South Africa to use more than the equivalent of a thousand kilograms of coal per person per year in inanimate energy.

The measure of inanimate energy consumed can be a sensitive indicator of the level of economic modernization, since the heaviest consumers of electricity, petroleum, coal, wood, and other fuels are the

Table I.

USE OF TRANSPORTATION FACILITIES AND INANIMATE ENERGY

(Figures are for 1970 except where date is given in parentheses)

Name of Country	Population in 1000s	Population Density per km.²	Railway Freight: Ton-km. per Person	Passenger and Commercial Motor Vehicles per 1000	Energy: kg. Coal per Person
MIDDLE EAST					
Afghanistan	17,087	26	—	3 (1969)	27
Algeria	14,330	6	91	17	462
Bahrain	215	360	—	62	9,623
Egypt	33,329	33	100	5	268
Iran	29,256	18	94	12	939
Iraq	9,440	22	155	12	597
Israel	2,910	141	161	76	2,278
Jordan	2,309	24	—	9	295
Kuwait	757	47	—	240	9,764
Lebanon	2,787	268	7	55	719
Libya	1,938	1	—	75	646
Morocco	15,525	35	171	20	194
Oman	657	3	—	—	46
Qatar	79	4	—	—	1,873
Saudi Arabia	7,740	4	4	15	965
South Yemen	1,436	5	—	9	449
Syria	6,247	34	16	8	483
Tunisia	5,137	31	259	20	247
Turkey	35,232 (1968)	45	159	9	487
United Arab Emirates	179 (1968)	2 (1968)	—	—	806
Yemen	5,733	29	—	—	13

Name of Country	Population in 1000s	Population Density per km.²	Railway Freight: Ton-km. per Person	Passenger and Commercial Motor Vehicles per 1000	Energy: kg, Coal per Person
SOUTH ASIA					
Bangladesh	61,823 (1971)[a]	427 (1971)[a]	80 (1969)[b]	2[b]	98[b]
Bhutan	836	18	—	—	—
Ceylon (Sri Lanka 1972)	12,514	191	29	11	156
India	537,047	164	239 (1969)	2	191
Nepal	10,850 (1969)	78 (1969)	—	0.7 (1968)	14
Pakistan	55,774 (1971)[a]	70 (1971)[a]	80 (1969)[b]	2[b]	98[b]
Sikkim	194	27	—	—	—
EAST ASIA					
China, People's Republic	787,176 (1971)[c]	82 (1971)[c]	396 (1971)[d]	1[e]	526[f]
China, Republic	14,035	390	187	7	925
Hongkong	3,959	3,829	8	32	1,021
Japan	103,386	280	605	168	3,210
Korea, Dem. Republic	13,892	115	580[e]	—	526[f]
Korea, Republic	31,793	323	242	4	796
Macao	314	19,265	—	12	255
Mongolia	1,248	1	—	—	526[f]
SOUTHEAST ASIA					
Brunei	121	21	—	104	2,769
Burma	27,584	41	27	2	65
Cambodia	6,701 (1969)	36 (1969)	11 (1969)	5 (1969)	66
Indonesia	121,198	81	5 (1968)	3	111
Laos	2,962	13	—	4	62
Malaysia	10,799	32	112	33	455
Philippines	36,849	123	3 (1969)	12	279
Singapore	2,075	3,571	—	89	818
Thailand	35,814	70	63	8 (1969)	245
Vietnam, Dem. Republic	21,154	133	—	—	526[f]
Vietnam, Republic	18,332	105	3	5 (1969)	302

Name of Country	Population in 1000s	Population Density per km.²	Railway Freight: Ton-km. per Person	Passenger and Commercial Motor Vehicles per 1000	Energy: kg. Coal per Person
AFRICA					
Botswana	648	1	—	8	—
Burundi	3,544	127	—	1 (1969)	9
Cameroun	5,836	12	46	11	92
Central African Republic	1,612	3	—	7 (1969)	61
Chad	3,706	3	—	2 (1969)	23
Congo	936	3	547	—	207
Dahomey	2,686	24	36	6 (1969)	32
Ethiopia	25,046	20	9 (1967)	2	32
Gabon	500	2	—	21	818
Gambia	364	32	—	12	52
Ghana	9,026	38	34	7	164
Guinea	3,921	16	—	5 (1969)	97
Ivory Coast	4,310	13	98	22	227
Kenya	11,247	19	115g	11	153
Lesotho	1,043	34	—	4	—
Liberia	1,171	11	35	20	295
Madagascar	6,750	11	43	13	67
Malawi	4,438	37	23 (1968)	4	46
Mali	5,022	4	—	2 (1969)	21
Mauritania	1,171	1	5,336	9 (1969)	93
Mauritius	836	409	—	22	182
Niger	4,016	3	—	2 (1969)	27
Nigeria	55,074	60	29	1	45
Rwanda	3,587	136	—	1 (1969)	10
Senegal	3,925	20	46	15	149

Name of Country	Population in 1000s	Population Density per km.²	Railway Freight: Ton-km. per Person	Passenger and Commercial Motor Vehicles per 1000	Energy: kg. Coal per Person
Sierra Leone	2,512 (1969)	35 (1969)	7 (1964)	12 (1969)	104
Somalia	2,789	4	–	7 (1968)	38
South Africa	20,113	16	2,843	103	2,769
S. Rhodesia	5,270	13	1,233	34	524
Sudan	15,695	6	171	3	115
Swaziland	408	24	–	19 (1969)	–
Tanzania	13,273	14	115[g]	5[h]	71[h]
Togo	1,862	33	11[g]	6 (1969)	65
Uganda	9,806	41	115[g]	4	72
Upper Volta	5,384	20	–	2	13
Zaire	21,568	9	89	6 (1969)	73
Zambia	4,295	6	–	18 (1968)	540
SOVIET UNION AND UNITED STATES					
Soviet Union	242,768	11	10,276	–	4,445
United States	204,800	22	5,436	522	11,144

[a] From *The Far East and Australasia, 1972* (London: Europa Publications, 1972).

[b] Figures for undivided Pakistan.

[c] Figures from United Nations Demographic Office.

[d] Based on *People's Republic of China: An Economic Assessment* (Washington, D.C.: Government Printing Office, 1972).

[e] From Norton Ginsburg, *Atlas of Economic Development* (Chicago: University of Chicago Press, 1961).

[f] *United Nations Statistical Yearbook, 1971* (New York: United Nations, 1972). Indicates 526 kg. coal energy equivalent for all of Communist Asia.

[g] *United Nations Statistical Yearbook, 1971* (New York: United Nations, 1972). Gives a combined railroad freight figure for Kenya, Tanzania, and Uganda; 115 ton-km. per person is the amount of freight per person for the combined population.

[h] Figures for Tanganyika only, not for Zanzibar and Pemba.

All figures taken from or based on *United Nations Statistical Yearbook, 1971* (New York: United Nations, 1972) except as noted above.

machines needed to replace a subsistence with an exchange economy. Allowance for the effect of the energy needs (and the profits) of the petroleum industry must be made in Libya, much of the Arabian peninsula, Iraq, and Iran, but the order of rank of other states of the Middle East—from Israel and Lebanon through Turkey, Syria, Algeria, Jordan, Egypt, Tunisia, and Morocco down to Oman, Afghanistan, and Yemen— corresponds fairly closely to their economic level, except in the case of Tunisia, whose high railway traffic figure indicates its higher development. East Asian countries in general use considerably more energy per person than Middle Easterners, who in turn use more than most South and Southeast Asians or most Africans. In part, this can be attributed to the need to use fuel for winter heat in much of East Asia and the Middle East, but it also reflects generally higher levels of economic development. Within areas, the differences between India and most of the rest of South Asia, between Malaysia and the rest of Southeast Asia (other than Brunei, Singapore, and possibly the Democratic Republic of Vietnam), and between South Africa and the rest of Africa south of the Sahara are particularly marked.

INVESTMENT AND ECONOMIC PLANNING. All the countries of Asia and Africa need more transport facilities and productive machines as they change from a subsistence to an exchange economy. They therefore need more investment; yet investment is hard to obtain. People in the West are accustomed to receiving personal dividends from paying taxes, buying stock, or putting unused income into savings or life insurance, all of which can be used to finance roads, factories, or hydroelectric plants. However, generations of experience conditioned most of the people from Morocco to Japan to see tax collectors, merchants, and moneylenders as greedy and self-seeking. The introduction of European governmental practices helped persuade many of them that tax collectors did not have to be rapacious, but European plantations, European land laws, and European loans and railway concessions did not convince them that business firms and banks could be trusted.

One reason many developing nations have tended to prefer government planning and direction of economic life to reliance on private initiative is that governments can collect revenue to be used for investment. Not only do they have force at their disposal, but their reputation has improved. However, there are other reasons. Few are prepared to undertake the tasks involved in economic modernization; most of these individuals have been active in nationalist movements; and modernizing nationalists feel that a concerted attack on economic problems is needed. Above all, a national economic development plan provides a whole new series of goals which can best be achieved through nationwide cooperation, now that the original nationalist goal of political independence has been achieved.

Table II.

EXTENT OF LINGUISTIC UNITY

Name of Country	Percent of Population Speaking Major Language
MIDDLE EAST	
Afghanistan	50 (Pushtu)
Algeria	80 (Arabic)
Iran	67 (Persian)
Iraq	79 (Arabic)
Israel	54 (Hebrew)
Libya	94 (Arabic)
Morocco	85 (Arabic)
Tunisia	30 (Arabic)[a]
Turkey	91 (Turkish)
SOUTH ASIA	
Ceylon (Sri Lanka 1972)	60 (Sinhalese)
India	42 (Hindi)
SOUTHEAST ASIA	
Burma	75 (Burmese)
Cambodia	85 (Khmer)
Indonesia	45 (Javanese)
Laos	95 (various Lao dialects)
Malaysia	49 (Malay)
Philippines	21 (Tagalog)
Singapore	78 (Chinese)
Thailand	91 (Thai)
Vietnam, Democratic Republic	84 (Vietnamese)
Vietnam, Republic	82 (Vietnamese)

[a] Does not include those who speak both Arabic and Berber.

Figure for Morocco based on Charles F. Gallagher, "North African Problems and Prospects, Part III: Language and Identity," American Universities Field Service North Africa Series, X, v (New York: American Universities Field Service Staff, 1964).

Figures for Democratic Republic of Vietnam and Republic of Vietnam based on Bernard B. Fall, *The Two Viet-Nams* (New York: Praeger, 1963).

Figures for Iraq, Philippines, and Thailand based on *United Nations Demographic Yearbook, 1963* (New York: United Nations, 1964).

Figures for Turkey based on *United Nations Demographic Yearbook, 1964* (New York: United Nations, 1965).

Figures for Algeria, Ceylon, and Tunisia based on *United Nations Demographic Yearbook, 1971* (New York: United Nations, 1972).

All other figures taken from Gabriel Almond and James Coleman, eds., *The Politics of the Developing Areas* (Princeton, N.J.: Princeton University Press, 1960).

LINGUISTIC UNITY. The motif of building national unity through economic development and unification is most explicitly illustrated by the exhortations of Communist leaders in mainland China, northern Vietnam, northern Korea, and Mongolia to advance the nation through co-operative effort in shops, offices, factories, mines, collectives, and communes. It is also visible in states like Egypt, Israel, India, and Burma, as it was in the Turkey of Ataturk or in Meiji Japan. Such promotion of economic unification requires not only facilities for transport and exchange, but demonstration projects in such things as raising poultry for city markets or making metal articles with electrically powered tools, and above all, means of making the results of these demonstration projects widely known so that others are encouraged to try them. In other words, there is a need both for face-to-face two-way conversations between student and teacher, peasant and agricultural extension worker, villager or towndweller and party cadre, and for impersonal one-way means of communication like the printed word, the radio, and the motion picture. All of these means of communication require the use of a common language.

In the countries of East Asia, language barriers are few. Even in the People's Republic of China, the most linguistically diverse of East Asia's political units, fewer than 7 percent of the people do not speak one of the major dialects of the Chinese language. In all the Arab lands but Algeria, Iraq, Libya, Morocco, and Tunisia almost everyone speaks Arabic. However, elsewhere in the Middle East and in South and Southeast Asia there are sizable linguistic minorities, as Table II shows; and in Africa south of the Sahara only four political units report that half or more of their people speak the same language.

Linguistic unity is not a guarantee of mutual understanding between leaders and led. Even where all use the same language, new terms and new meanings given to old terms can cause confusion. On the other hand, lack of linguistic unity need not be an insuperable obstacle to nation-building. The belief that people work together best when they are persuaded of the benefits of cooperation, rather than coerced, can be not only maintained but instilled in others as long as enough of the nation's leaders live by that belief. The faith of India's leaders in the power of persuasion, for example, has made it possible for them to remain committed to the principles of an untrammeled press, freedom for opposition politicians, and civilian control of the military long after many of their neighbors ceased to adhere to those principles.

COMMUNICATION AND FORMAL EDUCATION. The question of language is important to modernizing nationalists as they seek to spread the messages of "In union there is strength" and "Out of many, one." The question of how many receive the messages directly through press and radio is also important. Turkey, Lebanon, Egypt, India, China, and Japan have had vernacular newspapers since before 1900. Japan has more daily newspapers per thousand persons than the United States, but only five other Asian and African political units have more than one paper for every ten people—Israel, the three urban concentrations of Hongkong, Macao, and Singapore, and the thinly populated state of Mongolia, whose rulers would seem to be relying heavily on newspapers to reach their people. Though the figures do not show it, the other Communist states of Asia rely heavily on the radio, manufacturing most of their radio receivers to receive signals only on the wave-length of the state radio network. In the use of both newspapers and radios, as in the use of inanimate energy, motor vehicles, and railways, South and Southeast Asia rank lower on the average than East Asia and the Middle East, and most of Africa south of the Sahara ranks lower still.

There is rather less disparity in the number of motion pictures seen per year than in the radio and newspaper networks. Motion pictures are important as inculcators of new patterns of behavior because they demonstrate those patterns before the beholder's eyes (and ears, if the dialogue is in a familiar language), although their place is taken by television as a country like Japan (215 television sets per thousand people in 1970) moves toward the affluence of the United States (412 sets per thousand people at that time). It is therefore significant that Indians see more films than do Egyptians, although Egypt's sizable motion picture industry turns out motion pictures for the entire Arab world, and that the Chinese of the mainland and the Nanyang see many films produced under Communist Chinese auspices. Nevertheless, the effect of motion pictures, radio, and newspapers is limited unless their audience has opportunity to study and practice the techniques of the new way of living: reading, so as to understand printed directions; following schedules, so that tasks can be planned and performed in series; and looking at others in terms of their abilities rather than their family and friendship ties. Consequently, the modernizers almost invariably emphasize education as much as they can in the face of all the other tasks crowding in on them.

Very few Asian and African states have reached the levels of literacy of Japan or the developed European, North American, and Australasian states. Ten of the nineteen Middle Eastern states listed in Table IV, four of the then five South Asian states, not more than two of the eight East Asian political units, four of the eleven Southeast Asian states, and thirty of the thirty-seven African states had fewer than three-fifths of their young people in school toward the end of the 1960s. However, only three Middle Eastern, one Southeast Asian, and seventeen African states had fewer than three-tenths of the appropriate age group in school at that time. Three South Asian states were still in that category, while all of the East Asian political units were above that level. Only oil-rich Bahrain and Brunei, the Democratic Republic of Vietnam, and the Congo Republic had as high a percentage of their school-age population in school as Japan, the Soviet Union, or the United States.

INFORMAL EDUCATION. Formal schooling can enable people to learn a second language so that they can communicate with fellow nationals

Table III.

COMMUNICATIONS MEDIA

(Figures are for 1970 except where date is given in parentheses.)

Name of Country	Population in 1000s	Daily Papers per 1000	Radios per 1000	Motion Pictures Seen per Person per Year
MIDDLE EAST				
Afghanistan	17,087	6	16 (1968)	1.1
Algeria	14,330	14 (1968)	52 (1969)	2 (1967)
Bahrain	215	—	1,075 (1968)	6
Egypt	33,329	23 (1968)	132	1.8 (1969)
Iran	29,256	8[a]	93 (1968)	0.6 (1969)
Iraq	9,440	5 dailies (1968)	180	1.3 (1965)
Israel	2,910	208	229 (1968)	12
Jordan	2,309	24	65	0.9
Kuwait	757	35	148	5
Lebanon	2,787	52 dailies	215	172 cinemas
Libya	1,938	20 (1967)	44	—
Morocco	15,525	14 (1966)	60	1.3 (1967)
Qatar	79	—	—	3 (1969)
Saudi Arabia	7,740	10	11	—
South Yemen	1,436	—	52 (1960)	0.2 (1963)
Syria	6,247	5 dailies	224	112 cinemas (1967)
Tunisia	5,137	16 (1969)	77	1.6 (1968)
Turkey	35,232	41 (1969)	87	—
United Arab Emirates	179 (1968)	—	—	2 cinemas (1960)
Yemen	5,733	—	—	0.4 (1965)
SOUTH ASIA				
Bangladesh	61,823 (1971)[b]	6 (1968)[a,c]	14[c]	3 (1968)[c]
Bhutan	836	—	—	0.3
Ceylon (Sri Lanka 1972)	12,514	49	41 (1969)	8
India	537,047	14 (1969)[a]	22	4 (1969)
Nepal	10,850 (1969)	3[a]	5	—
Pakistan	55,774 (1971)[b]	6 (1968)[a,c]	14[c]	3 (1968)[c]
EAST ASIA				
China, People's Rep.	787,176 (1971)[d]	—	16 (1969)	6 (1960)
China, Republic	14,035	64 (1963)[e]	103 (1969)	66 (1967)
Hongkong	3,959	485 (1969)	170	19
Japan	103,386	511	255 (1968)	2.4
Korea, Dem. Rep.	13,892	—	60[f]	—
Korea, Republic	31,793	66 (1969)	126	5
Macao	314	114 (1967)	29	30 (1965)
Mongolia	1,248	103	129	1.5
SOUTHEAST ASIA				
Brunei	121	56 (1969)	107	20
Burma	27,584	9 (1969)[a]	15	8 (1968)
Cambodia	6,701 (1969)	22 (1968)	153 (1968)	3 (1967)
Indonesia	121,198	7 (1965)[a]	114	—
Laos	2,962	3 (1967)	17	0.3 (1969)
Malaysia	10,799	74 (1969)	41 (1968)	9 (1969)
Philippines	36,849	27 (1966)	45 (1968)	951 cinemas (1965)
Singapore	2,075	201	49	14
Thailand	35,814	21 (1969)[a]	78	565 cinemas

Table III. (Continued)

COMMUNICATIONS MEDIA

Name of Country	Population in 1000s	Daily Papers per 1000	Radios per 1000	Motion Pictures Seen per Person per Year
Vietnam, Rep.	18,332	67	73 (1969)	1.4 (1967)
AFRICA				
Botswana	648	20	13	9 cinemas (1964)
Burundi	3,544	—	18	0.04
Cameroun	5,836	3	37 (1969)	38 cinemas (1969)
Central African Rep.	1,612	0.6 (1967)	30	0.4 (1965)
Chad	3,706	0.2 (1969)	16	0.4 (1968)
Congo	936	0.7 (1969)	69	24 cinemas
Dahomey	2,686	1	32	0.4
Ethiopia	25,046	1[a]	6	—
Gabon	500	—	124	3 cinemas (1960)
Gambia	364	—	137	15 cinemas
Ghana	9,026	46[a]	78	2 (1969)
Guinea	3,921	1	23	16 cinemas (1959)
Ivory Coast	4,310	10	17	48 cinemas (1965)
Kenya	11,247	14	48 (1969)	0.8 (1963)
Lesotho	1,043	—	5	1 cinema (1965)
Liberia	1,171	6	132	0.8 (1966)
Madagascar	6,750	8	80	0.7 (1969)
Malawi	4,438	—	20	4 cinemas (1965)
Mali	5,022	0.6 (1968)	12	0.5 (1968)
Mauritania	1,171	—	47	0.07 (1963)
Mauritius	836	78 (1969)	124	10 (1969)
Niger	4,016	0.5 (1969)	25	0.2
Nigeria	55,074	7 (1966)[a]	23	67 cinemas (1960)
Rwanda	3,587	—	8	4 cinemas (1968)
Senegal	3,925	5	69	1.5 (1965)
Sierra Leone	2,512 (1969)	16 (1969)	56 (1969)	0.05 (1969)
Somalia	2,789	2	18	1.7
South Africa	20,113	40 (1967)	144 (1967)	—
S. Rhodesia	5,270	16	28	26 cinemas (1961)
Sudan	15,695	8[a]	12 (1969)	40 cinemas (1968)
Swaziland	408	—	32 (1969)	0.2 (1969)
Tanzania	13,273	5 (1969)	11	0.5 (1960)
Togo	1,862	7	22 (1969)	0.2 (1964)
Uganda	9,806	8	64 (1967)	0.3 (1965)
Upper Volta	5,384	—	16	0.2 (1969)
Zaire	21,568	1 (1969)[a]	4	0.1
Zambia	4,295	13	18	17 cinemas (1961)
SOVIET UNION AND UNITED STATES				
Soviet Union	242,768	336	390	19
United States	204,800	302	1,412	5

All figures taken from *United Nations Statistical Yearbook, 1971* (New York: United Nations, 1972) except as noted.

[a] Circulation figures do not include all daily newspapers in the country.
[b] From *The Far East and Australasia, 1972* (London: Europa Publications, 1972).
[c] Figure for undivided Pakistan.
[d] Figure from the United Nations Demographic Office.
[e] From *United Nations Statistical Yearbook, 1970* (New York: United Nations, 1971).
[f] From Philip Rudolf, *North Korea's Political and Economic Structure* (New York: Institute of Pacific Relations, 1959).

Table IV.

EDUCATION

Name of Country	Year	Age-group of which Percentage Is Taken	Percent in Primary and Secondary Schools	Rank by Category
MIDDLE EAST				
Afghanistan	1969	7–18	13	D
Algeria	1968	6–18	41	C
Bahrain	1969	5–19	91	A
Egypt	1969	6–17	52	C
Iran	1969	6–17	45	C
Iraq	1969	7–18	49	C
Israel	1969	6–17	81	B
Jordan	1969	6–17	52	C
Kuwait	1969	6–17	78	B
Lebanon	1969	6–17	74	B
Libya	1969	6–17	69	B
Morocco	1969	6–17	32	C
Qatar	1969	6–17	79	B
Saudi Arabia	1969	6–17	22	D
South Yemen	1969	7–17	33	C
Syria	1969	6–17	62	B
Tunisia	1968	6–18	66	B
Turkey	1969	7–17	68	B
Yemen	1969	7–18	5	D
SOUTH ASIA				
Bangladesh[a]	1968	6–17	29	D
Bhutan	1968	6–17	6	D
Ceylon (Sri Lanka 1972)	1969	5–16	72	B
India	1965	6–17	41	C
Nepal	1969	6–16	18	D
Pakistan[a]	1968	6–17	29	D
EAST ASIA				
China, People's Rep.[b]	1958	5–19	46	C
China, Republic[b]	1967	6–17	75	B
Hongkong	1969	6–17	84	B
Japan	1969	6–17	93	A
Korea, Dem. Rep.[c]	1965	all ages	16	B
Korea, Republic	1969	6–17	75	B
Macao	1968	5–19	50	C
Mongolia	1969	8–16	81	B
SOUTHEAST ASIA				
Brunei	1969	5–19	108	A
Burma	1969	5–15	56	C
Cambodia	1970	6–18	66	B
Indonesia	1965	7–18	42	C
Laos	1969	6–18	25	D
Malaysia:				
(Sabah)	(1969)	(6–18)	(69)	(B)
(Sarawak)	(1969)	(6–18)	(56)	(C)
(West Malaysia)	(1969)	(6–18)	(62)	(B)
Philippines	1965	7–16	84	B
Singapore	1969	6–17	80	B
Thailand	1968	7–18	56	C
Vietnam, Dem. Rep.[c]	1967	all ages	24	A
Vietnam, Republic	1969	6–17	64	B

Table IV. (Continued)
EDUCATION

Name of Country	Year	Age-group of which Percentage Is Taken	Percent in Primary and Secondary Schools	Rank by Category
AFRICA				
Botswana	1969	7–18	52	C
Burundi	1969	6–18	18	D
Cameroun	1969	6–18	57	C
Central African Rep.	1969	6–18	40	C
Chad	1969	6–18	15	D
Congo	1969	6–18	93	A
Dahomey	1968	6–18	21	D
Ethiopia	1969	7–18	11	D
Gabon	1969	6–18	83	B
Gambia	1969	6–18	21	D
Ghana	1970	6–21	39	C
Guinea	1968	7–18	20	D
Ivory Coast	1969	6–18	42	C
Kenya	1968	6–18	39	C
Lesotho	1969	6–18	64	B
Liberia	1969	6–17	39	C
Madagascar	1968	6–18	44	C
Malawi	1968	6–17	27	D
Mali	1969	6–18	15	D
Mauritania	1968	6–18	9	D
Mauritius	1969	6–18	67	B
Niger	1968	7–19	8	D
Nigeria	1966	6–19	17	D
Rwanda	1965	7–18	38	C
Senegal	1965	6–18	24	D
Sierra Leone	1969	5–18	21	D
Somalia	1969	8–19	7	D
South Africa	1965	6–17	68	B
S. Rhodesia	1968	7–17	60	B
Sudan	1969	7–18	18	D
Swaziland	1969	6–17	57	C
Tanzania	1968	7–19	24	D
Togo	1969	6–18	39	C
Uganda	1969	6–18	32	C
Upper Volta	1965	6–18	7	D
Zaire	1969	6–18	64	B
Zambia	1969	7–18	57	C
SOVIET UNION AND UNITED STATES				
Soviet Union	1969	7–17	95	A
United States	1969	6–17	107	A

All figures taken from *UNESCO Statistical Yearbook, 1971* (Louvain: UNESCO, 1972) except as noted.

Category A = 90% or more, of number of persons actually in appropriate age group, in primary or secondary schools.

Category B = 60% to 89%.

Category C = 30% to 59%.

Category D = 0% to 29%.

a Data for undivided Pakistan.

b From *UNESCO Statistical Yearbook, 1969* (Louvain: UNESCO, 1970).

c Based on *The Far East and Australasia, 1972* (London: Europa Publications, 1972).

who ordinarily use a different language or with persons from the outside world, but formal schooling is not enough to educate them to live in the modern world. Therefore, modernizing leaders have used radio, newspapers, motion pictures, and television (when they can), as well as older techniques like the slogans and news bulletins written or posted on walls in the People's Republic of China in continuation of the ancient tradition of exhortative placards. They have also used rural development programs to convey the ideas of cooperation within a national rather than a local framework, and they have leaned heavily on whatever nationwide political networks were built up before they came to power. Experience counts, however. Those Asian and African peoples among whom there were no cohesive popular movements or political parties before World War II only began to develop genuinely strong popular parties after ten to twenty years of determinedly modernizing rule.

Governments and parties use many methods of enlarging their peoples' horizons from the village or the town to the nation. First of all, they use meetings devoted to speeches and discussion. In the Communist states everyone is required to attend the meetings of his or her age, residence, and occupational groups or face the penalty of being declared counterrevolutionary. Elsewhere, attendance at political meetings is left more to individual choice. Since few care for a steady diet of speeches and discussions, entertainment media are also used—not only motion pictures and television, but older forms too. In the fifteen years between the Long March and the expulsion of the Kuomintang from the mainland, the Chinese Communists rewrote old tales and made up new ones for the traveling theatrical troupes which were a familiar part of Chinese life, trained companies to play them, and sent them out to edify as well as amuse the people in the areas they controlled. After 1949 the Communists greatly expanded this program. They also encouraged the composition and teaching of songs like "I Am a Collective Farmer," which could be sung by the people's choruses that sprang up throughout China under Communist inspiration, and they printed collections of songs to send abroad for use in youth groups and other potential recruiting grounds. During the Great Proletarian Cultural Revolution era that began in 1966, they even forbade theatrical troupes to perform all but a few specially prepared Chinese operas and dance-dramas.

The use of song, which has roused nationalist fervor at least since the time of the French Revolution and the "Marseillaise," is not confined to Communists. Since 1905 the Indian National Congress has used the Bengali folksong "Bande Mataram" (Hail to thee, my mother) to awaken loyalty to the Indian motherland. However, the People's Republic of China, in the million-poem movement of 1958, became the first state to expect the happy peasant or laborer to write patriotic poetry.[2] Story-tellers, puppeteers like the manipulators of the figures in the traditional shadow-plays of Java, and other familiar types of traveling entertainers have all been used by political leaders throughout Asia and Africa. Outside the Communist bloc, perhaps U Nu of Burma demonstrates most strikingly the role of entertainment in politics, although the writings of poet-president Leopold Sedar Senghor of Senegal are of far higher literary quality. U Nu began writing plays and novels, as well as more overtly political documents, in the 1930s. In the perilous autumn of 1950, when Burma's very survival was menaced by internal strife, he wrote a play called *The People Win Through*, using the experiences of villagers and insurgents to illustrate the evils of seizing political power by force. The number of political speeches given by its characters made it strongly reminiscent of the first novels written in the Ottoman empire and Japan in the late nineteenth century. Nevertheless, the lesson it taught helped make it part of the curriculum in every middle school in Burma until the rise of Ne Win.

CHANGES IN LEGAL AND SOCIAL STRUCTURES

The introduction of new legal codes based on Western principles of individual responsibility and equality before the law has made it easier for modernizing leaders to release their people from traditional family, clan, village, guild, caste, and other attachments so that they can form a new attachment to the nation-state. This alteration in judicial and legal systems has not been accomplished quickly, nor is it yet completed. Sharia courts are still in constant use in Morocco and the Arabian peninsula. Even in Japan, where European-influenced penal, civil, and commerical codes went into full effect before 1900, family law left little room for freedom of action in family matters to anyone but the family head until after 1945. The Meiji leaders expected to build a unified Japan on the basis of the family, not on the basis of the individual like most contemporary modernizers. They succeeded remarkably well, in part because Japan possessed one of the world's strongest traditions of giving unswerving support to one's superior even at the expense of self and family. That tradition is perhaps best illustrated by the forty-seven knightly retainers of the Tokugawa period who avenged their master's

[2] S. H. Chen, in "Multiplicity in Uniformity: Poetry and the Great Leap Forward," *The China Quarterly*, no. 3 (July–Sept. 1960), 1–15, translates this example on page 2:

> Each year our farm production grows,
> Grains and cotton pile up mountain high, Hurrah!
> Eat the grains, but don't forget the sower,
> The Communist Party's our dear Ma and Pa.

disgrace by killing the daimyo responsible and who were then deeply grateful to be allowed to commit suicide (in place of being executed) as a reward for the loyalty they had shown.

Defeat and occupation in 1945 brought changes in Japanese family law and family relationships much like those which were already taking place from Algeria and Senegal to China and Korea. Wives and young people have become less subservient to husbands and parents, as laws change and opportunities to earn a living outside the family household multiply. However, the Japanese tradition of national loyalty seems strong enough to survive almost any catastrophe, as it has already survived the crisis of recognizing defeat. One imperial decree sufficed to halt the professionals of the Japanese army in 1945, in contrast to those professionals in the French army in Algeria in 1962 who fought on against the Algerian nationalists for months after the government they claimed to serve commanded them to stop.

THE CONSTANT DILEMMA: TO COERCE OR TO PERSUADE?

Modernizers everywhere have realized the importance of adopting and implementing codes of law based on the individual rather than on groups, inculcating a national rather than a local or communal loyalty, teaching the skills and attitudes appropriate to an industrial rather than an agricultural society, and replacing the subsistence economy with one based on large-scale exchange. However, few have proven capable of bringing about these manifold changes without resorting in some degree to coercive measures resembling those used by Communist governments in Asia. When the Kuomintang failed to promote economic and social change rapidly enough to meet China's need for greater internal cohesion in the face of external pressures, many Chinese turned almost in despair to the Communists who claimed to meet all their needs at once. The Chinese Communists attacked the Western states which had been most active in China, while appropriating Western scientific and industrial technology as rightfully theirs. They attacked those Chinese who had failed to save their country by adopting these techniques, while praising the cultural heritage of the common people as a means of making the Chinese nation more cohesive than Sun Yat-sen's rope of sand. Above all they attacked the profit-motivated private enterprise system under which Westerners exploited China's resources, and proclaimed the need to substitute social profit for individual or family profit.

In their attack on private enterprise, the Chinese Communists have been joined to some extent by many other leaders. Most of these leaders have repudiated class warfare as divisive of the nations they are trying to unite, but they see untrammeled private profit-making as an invitation to social atomization. Desperately anxious to overcome whatever social, linguistic, ethnic, religious, and geographical barriers there are to unity, a number of them have placed social and political as well as economic life under firm government control, and some have come close to repressing those who do not share the language or the religion of the majority. The decline of the Spanish monarchy, which lost many of its most enterprising subjects through religious persecutions during the centuries when the more tolerant Swiss confederation was successfully overcoming linguistic, religious, and geographical barriers to unity, should have been instructive. Yet most modernizing nationalists tend to see only danger in the growing self-consciousness of minorities as expanding educational, transport, and communications networks enable them to become more aware of their differences from the majority. The modernizers want the members of all the communities which comprise the state to see themselves and the others as parts of a larger whole, but often their unifying policies seem repressive to minority groups.

The degree to which the modernizers achieve their goal of mutual acceptance will strongly affect the course of the modernization process. Yet prior to 1950 only the government of the new India was enough aware of this to commission a study of the attitudes held toward one another by different groups so that potentially dangerous hostilities could be counteracted. Since 1950 a number of leaders have begun to pay more attention to the problems involved in persuading men and women that they can realize their identity as selves even more fully if they see themselves as part of a large and diverse body of people than they can if their social horizons are more limited. Religious freedom has been given increasingly specific guarantees; those who use different languages have been reassured that their right to do so will continue to be recognized. Most of these efforts are not yet assured of success among the reluctant and the distrustful. Nevertheless, their outcome will ultimately determine the fate of the wide variety of attempts being made between the Atlantic and the Pacific to transplant the institutions of the nation-state from their original habitat to new and very different environments.

Suggested Readings

Books available in paperback are marked with an asterisk.

*ADELMAN, IRMA, and C. T. MORRIS. *Society, Politics and Economic Development.* Baltimore: Johns Hopkins, 1967.

ALDERFER, HAROLD F. *Local Government in Developing Countries.* New York: McGraw-Hill, 1967.

*ALMOND, GABRIEL, and JAMES COLEMAN, eds. *The Politics of Developing Areas.* Princeton, N.J.: Princeton University Press, 1960.

ANDERSON, J.N.D., ed. *Family Law in Asia and Africa.* London: G. Allen and Unwin, 1968.

*APTER, DAVID. *The Politics of Modernization.* Chicago: University of Chicago Press, 1965.

——, ed. *Ideology and Discontent.* New York: Free Press, 1964.

ASHFORD, D. E. *National Development and Local Reform in Morocco, Tunisia and Pakistan.* Princeton, N.J.: Princeton University Press, 1967.

BINGHAM, WOODBRIDGE, et al. *A History of Asia,* 2 vols., 2nd ed. Boston: Allyn and Bacon, 1974.

*BLACK, CYRIL E. *The Dynamics of Modernization.* New York: Harper and Row, 1966.

*——, and T.P. THORNTON, eds. *Communism and Revolution: The Strategic Uses of Political Violence.* Princeton, N.J.: Princeton University Press, 1964.

BOXER, C.R. *The Dutch Seaborne Empire: 1600–1800.* New York: Knopf, 1965.

——. *The Portuguese Seaborne Empire: 1415–1825.* New York: Knopf, 1960.

BRAIBANTI, RALPH, and J.J. SPENGLER, eds. *Tradition, Values and Socio-Economic Development.* Durham, N.C.: Duke University Press, 1967.

BUSS, CLAUDE A. *Asia in the Modern World.* New York: Macmillan, 1964.

CRESSEY, GEORGE B. *Asia's Lands and Peoples,* 3rd ed. New York: McGraw-Hill, 1963.

*DEAN, VERA MICHELES. *The Nature of the Non-Western World.* New York: New American Library, 1957.

*EAST, W.G., et al. *The Changing Map of Asia,* 3rd ed. rev. London: Methuen, 1958.

EASTON, STEWART C. *The Rise and Fall of Western Colonialism.* New York: Praeger, 1964.

*EMERSON, RUPERT. *From Empire to Nation.* Cambridge: Harvard University Press, 1960. (Paperback. Boston: Beacon Press.)

FIRTH, R.W., and B.S. YAMEY, eds. *Capital, Savings and Credit in Peasant Societies.* Chicago: Aldine, 1969.

*GEERTZ, CLIFFORD. *Islam Observed: Religious Development in Morocco and Indonesia.* New Haven, Conn.: Yale University Press, 1968. (Paperback. Chicago: University of Chicago Press.)

GINSBURG, NORTON. *Atlas of Economic Development.* Chicago: University of Chicago Press, 1961.

———, and JOHN E. BRUSH. *Pattern of Asia.* Englewood Cliffs, N.J.: Prentice-Hall, 1964.

HAY, STEPHEN N. *Asian Ideas of East and West: Tagore and His Critics in Japan, China and India.* Cambridge: Harvard University Press, 1970.

HIGGINS, BENJAMIN H. *Economic Development: Principles, Problems and Policies,* rev. ed. New York: Norton, 1968.

HOSELITZ, BERT F., and W.E. MOORE, eds. *Industrialization and Society.* The Hague: Mouton, UNESCO, 1963.

*HUNTINGTON, SAMUEL P. *Political Order in Changing Societies.* New Haven, Conn.: Yale University Press, 1968.

*JOHNSON, CHALMERS, ed. *Change in Communist Systems.* Stanford, Cal.: Stanford University Press, 1970.

*JOHNSON, JOHN J., ed. *The Role of the Military in Underdeveloped Countries.* Princeton, N.J.: Princeton University Press, 1962.

KAHIN, GEORGE McT., ed. *Major Governments of Asia.* Ithaca, N.Y.: Cornell University Press, 1963.

*KEBSCHULL, H.G., ed. *Politics in Transitional Societies.* New York: Appleton-Century-Crofts, 1968.

KENNEDY, MALCOLM D. *A History of Communism in East Asia.* New York: Praeger, 1957.

LACH, DONALD F. *Asia in the Making of Europe,* 2 vols. in print in 1973. Chicago: University of Chicago Press, 1965.

LAMB, ALASTAIR. *Asian Frontiers.* New York: Praeger, 1968.

*LASSWELL, H.D., and DANIEL LERNER, eds. *World Revolutionary Elites.* Cambridge: M.I.T. Press, 1965

*LITTLE, IAN, et al. *Industry and Trade in Some Developing Countries: A Comparative Study.* New York: Oxford University Press, 1971.

*MEAD, MARGARET, ed. *Cultural Patterns and Technical Change.* New York: New American Library; also Paris: UNESCO, 1953.

MIKDASHI, ZUHAYR. *The Community of Oil Exporting Countries: A Study in Governmental Cooperation.* Ithaca, N.Y.: Cornell University Press, 1972.

*MILTON, DANIEL, and WILLIAM CLIFFORD, eds. *A Treasury of Modern Asian Stories.* New York: New American Library, 1961.

MOORE, CHARLES A., ed. *The Status of the Individual in East and West.* Honolulu: University of Hawaii Press, 1968.

*MYRDAL, GUNNAR. *An Approach to Asian Drama.* New York: Random House, 1968.

*———. *Asian Drama,* 3 vols. New York: Twentieth Century Fund, 1968. (Paperback. New York: Random House, 1971.)

NAIR, KUSUM. *The Lonely Furrow: Farming in the United States, Japan and India.* Ann Arbor: University of Michigan Press, 1969.

*NAKAMURA, HAJIME. *Ways of Thinking of Eastern Peoples: India, China, Tibet, Japan,* rev. English trans. ed. Philip P. Wiener. Honolulu: East-

West Center, 1964. (Paperback. Honolulu: University of Hawaii Press.)

*NORTHROP, F.S.C. *The Meeting of East and West.* New York: Collier Books, 1968.

OLIVER, ROBERT T. *Communication and Culture in Ancient India and China.* Syracuse, N.Y.: Syracuse University Press, 1971.

*PANIKKAR, K.M. *Asia and Western Dominance.* New York: John Day, 1954. (Paperback. Riverside, N.J.: Macmillan.)

RIGGS, FRED W. *Administration in Developing Countries.* Boston: Houghton Mifflin, 1964.

*ROBINSON, HARRY. *Monsoon Asia, a Geographical Survey.* New York: Praeger, 1967.

*SCALAPINO, ROBERT A., ed. *The Communist Revolution in Asia,* 2nd ed. Englewood Cliffs, N.J.: Prentice-Hall, 1969.

*SCHRAMM, WILBUR. *Mass Media and National Development.* Stanford, Cal.: Stanford University Press, 1964.

*SMITH, DONALD E., ed. *Religion, Politics, and Social Change in the Third World.* New York: Free Press, 1971.

Social Science Research Council, Committee on Comparative Studies. *Studies in Political Development,* 7 vols. Princeton, N.J.: Princeton University Press, 1963–1971.

    1. *PYE, LUCIAN W., ed. *Communications and Political Development* (1963).

    2. *LA PALOMBARA, JOSEPH, ed. *Bureaucracy and Political Development* (1963).

    3. *WARD, ROBERT E., and DANKWART RUSTOW, eds. *Political Modernization in Japan and Turkey* (1964).

    4. COLEMAN, JAMES, ed. *Education and Political Development* (1965).

    5. PYE, LUCIAN W., and SIDNEY VERBA, eds. *Political Culture and Political Development* (1965).

    6. LA PALOMBARA, JOSEPH, and MYRON WEINER, eds. *Political Parties and Political Development* (1966).

    7. *BINDER, LEONARD, et al. *Crises and Sequences in Political Development* (1971).

*SPENCER, JOSEPH E. *Oriental Asia: Themes Toward a Geography.* Englewood Cliffs, N.J.: Prentice-Hall, 1973.

———. *Asia, East by South.* New York: Wiley, 1954.

SPENCER, R.F., ed. *Religion and Change in Contemporary Asia.* Minneapolis: University of Minnesota Press, 1971.

*STEWARD, JULIAN, ed. *Contemporary Change in Traditional Society,* 3 vols. Urbana: University of Illinois Press, 1967.

*SWAMY, SUBRAMANIAN. *Economic Growth in China and India, 1952–1970.* Chicago: University of Chicago Press, 1973.

SWEARINGEN, A. RODGER, ed. *Leaders of the Communist World.* New York: Free Press, 1971.

TAYLOR, CHARLES L., and MICHAEL C. HUDSON. *World Handbook of Political and Social Indicators,* 2nd ed. New Haven, Conn.: Yale University Press, 1972.

TINKER, HUGH. *Ballot Box and Bayonet.* London: Oxford University Press, 1964.

*VON DER MEHDEN, F.R. *Politics of the Developing Nations,* 2nd ed. Englewood Cliffs, N.J.: Prentice-Hall, 1969.

WARD, BARBARA E., ed. *Women in the New Asia.* Paris: UNESCO, 1963.

WARD, ROBERT E., and R. E. MACRIDIS, eds. *Modern Political Systems: Asia,* 3rd ed. Englewood Cliffs, N.J.: Prentice-Hall, 1972.

WARRINER, DOREEN. *Land Reform in Principle and Practice.* New York: Oxford University Press, 1969.

WITTFOGEL, KARL A. *Oriental Despotism.* New Haven, Conn.: Yale University Press, 1957.

WRIGGINS, W. HOWARD. *The Ruler's Imperative.* New York: Columbia University Press, 1969.

*YOHANNAN, JOHN D., ed. *A Treasury of Asian Literature.* New York: John Day, 1956. (Paperback. New York: New American Library.)

INDEX